HISTORICAL ATLAS OF THE RELIGIONS OF THE WORLD

HISTORICAL ATLAS OF THE RELIGIONS OF THE WORLD

Isma'īl Rāgī al Fārūqī
EDITOR

David E. Sopher
MAP EDITOR

Macmillan Publishing Co., Inc.
NEW YORK

Collier Macmillan Publishers
LONDON

Printed in the United States of America

Macmillan Publishing Co., Inc.
866 Third Avenue, New York, New York 10022

Collier-Macmillan Canada, Ltd.

Library of Congress Cataloging in Publication Data

al Faruqi, Isma'il Ragi A (date)
Historical atlas of the religions of the world.

Includes bibliographies.
1. Religions. 2. Religions—Maps. I. Sopher, David Edward, joint author. II. Title.
BL80.2.F28 912'.1'2 73-16583
ISBN 0-02-336400-9

Printing: 1 2 3 4 5 6 7 8 Year: 4 5 6 7 8 9 0

Preface

This book is a venture of a new kind. It is a historical atlas of the religions of the world. Besides old materials that have been mapped before, it contains new materials that have arisen out of fresh research. The geography of religion is a terrain of varying degrees of development. The terrain of Western Christianity leads all other religions in the amount and quality of research so far accomplished. The works of geography of religion dealing with Christianity are the result of inestimable efforts of more than two centuries of advanced study in Europe and America. This is not the case in the geography of any other religion except one, Biblical religion. Ancient Hebrew religion follows closely after Christianity. The research done in the geography of Biblical religion has been significant largely because of its overlapping Christian origins. The history and geography of Judaism in the Christian Era has commanded little scholarly interest by comparison, though the amount of work accomplished in the last one hundred years is phenomenal. On the other hand, all the research hitherto done by the world's scholars in the geography of Islām, Hinduism, Buddhism, and Chinese and Japanese religions is still elementary and in that of traditional religions—especially in Africa—still nonexistent. To present a "historical atlas of the religions of the world" is therefore a daring proposition. It can be but a modest beginning. In presenting to the reader the results of their research, the main purpose of the editors and authors is to draw attention to the large fields—yet unexplored—that lie ahead. It is only as the inception of a new task and a spur for further research that this venture has been undertaken.

All this notwithstanding, this book has unique advantages. The essays, by themselves, constitute an introduction to the history of the religions of the world, written in most cases by scholars of world reputation who are adherents of the faiths they interpret to the reader. By themselves, they make this publication worthwhile as a history of religions. Added to their wealth of ideas and ideational categories with which to order the infinite variety of religious data are two other constituents: illustrations and maps. The former include figures, tables, and various charts, as well as reproductions of great works of art. They are all designed to furnish insight into the nature of the relevance of a particular faith either to the aesthetic or the ritualistic or the politicosocial life of the adherents, or into the spatiotemporal expansion of that faith, the singularity or variety of styles and cultures that it enveloped, interacted with, and assimilated.

The two latter objectives are also the purposes of the maps. Maps are not only for the geographer. Certainly not the maps of this book! In furnishing as they do an immediate view of a religion as it has existed in space and time, as it has expanded or contracted, as it has interacted with other faiths, as it has associated itself with one or more races of mankind, with one or more cultures, with one or more topographies and ecologies, they provide an understanding of that religion's movement. They are an inestimable help to the student of religion, of history, of civilization to acquire through a few maps an intuitive grasp of the patterns that the history of a religion reflects in all fields of interaction. Indeed, his understanding of any religion, culture, or civilization will remain fragmentary until he has achieved a grasp of these patterns. For it is not an exaggeration to claim that patterns are not only important but essential. No amount of writing or talking could convey such an intuition of pattern as does its visual representation in a map.

THE EDITORS

Acknowledgments

The Editor acknowledges with deep gratitude the assistance of: The Department of Religion of Temple University throughout the period of manuscript preparation; Dr. Lois Lamyā' al Fārūqī in furnishing and preparing the illustrations of the Ancient Near East and Islām; Dr. Bibhuti S. Yadav in furnishing and preparing most of the illustrations of Hinduism, and in reviewing the article on Theravāda Buddhism following the passing of Dr. G. P. Malalasekera in 1972; Dr. Robert A. Kraft in furnishing and preparing illustrations 15-2, 15-3, 15-4; Dr. Samuel Laeuchli in furnishing and preparing illustrations 15-1, 19-2, 19-3, 19-4, 19-6, 19-7; M. Bayyūmī, M. Khalīfah, 'Aṭa Sīd-Aḥmad, Anīs Aḥmad, M. Ḥamdūn, Isma'īl Ḥamīd, and Braimah Awwal, doctoral candidates in Islamics at Temple University, in preparing the two chronologies of Islām; Ms. Hawāzin al Fārūqī in preparing the index; Mr. Dyno Lowenstein who drew the maps.

I. R. F.

A Word About the Maps

The collection of maps in this atlas is designed to present the geographic context of two kinds of histories. There is the geography of the religious myths themselves, and that of the communities of their believers. What can be mapped in either of these categories will vary greatly from one religion to another.

The fundamental myth of one religion may take place in the real world, involving persons, places, and events for whose existence the evidence can meet the strictest requirements of historical scholarship. Another may be set in a mythic world, or the real world mythologized. The maker of maps of religion must be aware that by his insistence on giving "a local habitation and a name" to what may be highly charged symbolic events he can severely distort their religious meaning. Such maps, if they can be provided at all, should be used, then, chiefly as guides to the geographical horizons of the receivers of the myth, to their perceptions of their world and of their place in it.

A religious community's history—its relations with other religious systems, its political and economic fortunes—will in varying degree shape the ways in which the myth is elaborated and reinterpreted in the lived religion of the community. These differences in historical experience as well as differences in the institutions maintaining communities of fellow believers and bridging the physical distances separating them mean that a different map content must be found to tell each religious society's history.

Finally, the problem of comparing ideas and phenomena of different religions has its effect on the categories of data that can be mapped. When this is taken together with the differences in the locational specificity of religious myths, in the organizing institutions of religious systems, and in the history of religious communities, explanation and justification are provided for what may at first glance seem to be the indulgence of idiosyncrasy in the choice of topics for the maps exhibited in this atlas.

Another factor contributes importantly to the diversity of map content: the very great difference in the availability of data and in the extent of previous thematic mapping of the different religions. For the purposes of this atlas there is an embarrassment of riches in the mapping of Old and New Testament events and of Christian ecclesiastical history, as well as many aspects of Christian social history. In contrast, surprising in view of the volume of scholarly work and of available historical resources, proportionally much less has been done in connection with Judaism and Islām, and very little attempt seems to have been made to deal cartographically with the Eastern religions. Our task has been to limit the number of maps dealing with Biblical geography and the history of Christianity, which might be compiled from easily accessible materials, while searching for and seeking to develop maps that would show how other religions have grown, not only in a territorial or demographic sense. The atlas contains several maps that treat cartographically for the first time, to our knowledge, particular topics in the history of religions, although it omits others that are staples of Biblical and general historical atlases and the textbooks of religion. Decisions to omit such cartographic staples (a map of Paul's journeys, for example) reflect both space limitations and the wish to maintain some degree of ecumenical balance in the allotment of maps among the religions.

One effect of space limitations has been to encourage innovation in the presentation of data mapped in other sources; a number of the maps combine material from other maps in novel ways and may therefore have some additional heuristic value. Where one might have found two maps, each showing the state of a religious community at different periods, here we will have one that puts emphasis on the changes occurring in the interval. This involves the sacrifice of some detail in order to enhance the presentation of dynamic processes using an economy of means; see, for example, Maps 22 and 53.

We have wanted to present in our maps, to the best of our ability, each religion's own view of the world. Authors of the text have assisted in varying degree, some contributing in an indispensable way to the creation of the product presented here. It has been the responsibility of the Map Editor to ensure the accuracy of the material presented and to decide the manner of its presentation, with all that that entails for the interpretation that the reader is led to. Conversely, the Map Editor assumes no responsibility for matter in the text. Although we are heavily indebted to several of our collaborators for their assistance, they are in no way responsible for any errors or misrepresentations that may be found in the completed map work.

* * * * * * * * *

A Supplementary Note on Names and Dates. In letting each religion speak for itself to some degree, one cannot use a fully consistent system of place naming, such as the one advocated by the U.S. Board on Geographic Names and followed in a number of contemporary world atlases. The policy followed here has been to transliterate, according to some current scholarly convention for the language concerned, those names that are part of the religious historical tradition of the religion being mapped. Not wishing to impede communication with the map reader, we have left other names either in their conventional English form or in the official form now followed in the country where the place is located. In a number of maps that cover a large time span, such as the two cited above, the set of places shown on the map never have existed together at any one time. In such cases, our inclination has been to use common English forms of the place names as providing convenient designations for points within a spatial and temporal continuum, the main purpose of such a map being to display a pattern of dynamic spatial relations.

Years are dated according to the internationally followed Christian calendar, but where appropriate the Christian forms B.C. and A.D. are replaced by B.C.E. (Before the Christian or Common Era) and C.E. (of the Christian or Common Era), respectively, or joined to the dating system proper to each tradition.

Syracuse University

DAVID E. SOPHER

Cartographic Sources

GENERAL

EMMERICH, HEINRICH, *Atlas Hierarchicus*. Mödling, Austria: St. Gabriel Verlag, 1968.

Encyclopaedia Judaica. Jerusalem: Macmillan, 1972. 16 vols.

HERMANN, ALBERT, *An Historical Atlas of China*. Rev. ed. Chicago: Aldine, 1966.

MCEVEDY, COLIN, *The Penguin Atlas of Medieval History*. Harmondsworth: Penguin Books, 1961.

New Catholic Encyclopaedia. New York: McGraw-Hill, 1967. 15 vols.

ROOLVINK, R., et al., *Historical Atlas of the Muslim Peoples*. Amsterdam: Djambatan, n.d.

SOPHER, DAVID E., *Geography of Religions*. Englewood Cliffs, N.J.: Prentice-Hall, 1967.

STIER, HANS-ERICH, et al., *Westermanns Atlas zur Weltgeschichte*. Braunschweig: Westermann, 1963.

DE VRIES, S., et al., *An Atlas of World History*. London: Nelson, 1965.

RELIGIONS OF THE PAST

BEEK, MARTIN A., *Atlas of Mesopotamia*. New York: Nelson, 1962.

VAN DER HEYDEN, A. A. M., and Scullard, H. H., *Atlas of the Classical World*. London: Nelson, 1959.

Religions of the American Indians:

DRIVER, HAROLD E., and WILLIAM C. MASSEY, "Comparative Studies of North American Indians." *Transactions of the American Philosophical Society,* Vol. 47, 1957.

MOONEY, JAMES, *The Ghost Dance Religion and the Sioux Outbreak of 1890.* Washington: U.S. Government Printing Office, 1896.

STEWARD, JULIAN H., *Handbook of South American Indians.* Washington: U.S. Government Printing Office, 1947–1963. 7 vols.

SWANTON, JOHN R., *The Indian Tribes of North America.* Washington: U.S. Government Printing Office, 1952.

ETHNIC RELIGIONS OF THE PRESENT

Shintō:

Japan. Ministry of Education, *Religions in Japan.* 2nd. ed. Tokyo: Government of Japan, 1963.

Ninth International Congress for the History of Religions, *Points of Religious Interest in Japan.* Tokyo: Science Council of Japan, 1958.

OKADA, Y., and S. UJITOKO, *Shintō Shrines and Festivals.* Tokyo: Kokugakuin University, 1964.

Judaism:

AHARONI, Y., and M. AVI-YONAH, *The Macmillan Bible Atlas.* New York: Macmillan, 1968.

GILBERT, MARTIN, *Jewish History Atlas.* New York: Macmillan, 1969.

Israel. Department of Surveys. *Atlas of Israel.* 2nd. ed. Jerusalem: Survey of Israel, 1970.

UNIVERSALIZING RELIGIONS OF THE PRESENT

Buddhism:

CH'ÊN, KENNETH, *Buddhism in China.* Princeton: Princeton U.P., 1964.

DUTT, SUKUMAR, *Buddhist Monks and Monasteries of India.* London: Allen & Unwin, 1962.

LAMOTTE, ETIENNE, *Histoire du Bouddhisme indien.* Louvain: Institut Orientaliste, Université de Louvain, 1958.

ZÜRCHER, E., *The Buddhist Conquest of China.* Leiden: E. J. Brill, 1959. 2 vols.

———, *Buddhism: Its Origin and Spread in Words, Maps and Pictures.* London: Routledge & Kegan Paul, 1962.

Christianity:

ENGELS, J., *Grosser Historischer Weltatlas.* II. *Mittelalter.* Munich: Bayerischer Schulbuch-Verlag, 1970.

FREITAG, A., *Twentieth Century Atlas of the Christian World.* New York: Hawthorn, 1963.

GAUSTAD, EDWIN S., *Historical Atlas of Religion in America.* New York: Harper & Row, 1962.

JEDIN, H., et al., *Atlas zur Kirchengeschichte.* Freiburg: Herder, 1970.

VAN DER MEER, F., and Mohrmann, C., *Atlas of the Early Christian World.* London: Nelson, 1958.

Islām:

BENNIGSEN, ALEXANDRE, and CHANTAL LEMERCIER-QUELQUEJAY, *Islam in the Soviet Union.* New York: Praeger, 1967.

FROELICH, J. C., *Les musulmans d'Afrique Noire.* Paris: Éditions de le'Orante, 1962.

GIBB, H. A. R., *The Travels of Ibn Baṭṭuṭa, A.D. 1325–1354.* Cambridge: Hakluyt Society, 1958; 1962. 2 vols.

LEWIS, I. M., *Islam in Tropical Africa.* London: Oxford U.P., 1966.

ROUX, JEAN-PAUL, *L'Islam en Asie.* Paris: Payot, 1958.

TRIMINGHAM, J. SPENCER, *Islam in East Africa.* London: Edinburgh House Press, 1962.

Contributors

Isma'īl R. Al Fārūqī

Dr. Isma'īl Rāgī al Fārūqī, born in Palestine, is Professor of Islamics at Temple University, Philadelphia. He studied at the American University of Beirut, Indiana, and Harvard and did postdoctoral work in Islam at al Azhar University in Cairo and in Christianity and Judaism at McGill University in Montreal as a Rockefeller Foundation Fellow.

Professor al Fārūqī has held teaching posts at the Institute of Islamic Studies at McGill University, Montreal; the Central Institute of Islamic Research, Karachi; the Institute of Higher Arabic Studies of the League of Arab States, Cairo; and Syracuse University. He has held visiting professorships at Cairo University, Azhar University, and Alexandria University.

His publications include a number of articles in *The Canadian Journal of Theology, The Journal of the American Academy of Religion, The Bulletin of the Faculty of Arts of Cairo University, The Muslim World, Numen, Zygon,* and other periodicals. Besides a number of English translations, of which the latest is Haykal's *The Life of Muhammad* (Philadelphia: Temple University Press, 1973), he is the author of *'Urubah and Religion* (Amsterdam: Djambatam, 1961), *Christian Ethics* (Montreal: McGill University Press, 1966), *Particularism in the Old Testament and Contemporary Sects in Judaism* (Cairo: League of Arab States, 1963, 68),and coauthor of *The Great Asian Religions* (New York: Macmillan, 1969).

David Edward Sopher

Dr. David Edward Sopher, Professor of Geography, Syracuse University, was born in Shanghai. He studied at the University of California and taught there as well as at the University of Minnesota and Sacramento State College. His specialty is religious and cultural geography, and he has done extensive and intensive research in the Indian subcontinent. He is the author of *The Sea Nomads* (1965), *Geography of Religions* (1967), and a large number of articles in many learned journals.

Jacob B. Agus

Dr. Jacob B. Agus was born in Poland and educated in Poland, Palestine, and America. He graduated from Yeshiva College in 1933 and was ordained by the same institution in 1935. He received the degrees of M.A. and Ph.D. from Harvard University, Department of History, Division of the History of Philosophy of Religion, in 1938 and 1939. His first book, *Modern Philosophies of Judaism* (New York: Behrman House, 1940), was listed among the one hundred "best" Jewish books in the 1942 Book Exhibit in Boston. He served for twelve years (1956–1968) as editorial consultant to the *Encyclopaedia Britannica* in regard to articles dealing with the history and philosophy of Judaism. He is the author of seven books on Jewish philosophy and history, representing the classical current in Jewish thought. He served as a visiting professor at Temple University and the Reconstructionist Rabbinical College. He is now Visiting Professor of Modern Philosophy at Dropsie University, Philadelphia.

Charles Wei-Hsun Fu

Dr. Charles Wei-hsun Fu, born in Taiwan, is Assistant Professor of Religion at Temple University. He studied at the National Taiwan University (B.A.), the University of Hawaii (M.A.), the University of California at Berkeley (on an East-West Center Fellowship), and the University of Illinois (Ph.D). He taught at the National Taiwan University and at Ohio University. His publications include *A Critical History of Western Philosophy* (3rd ed.) and *The Fundamental Problems of British Empirical Philosophers,* as well as a number of articles of which the following are especially significant: "Morality or Beyond: The Neo-Confucian Confrontation with Mahayana Buddhism" and "Lao Tzu's Conception of Tao," published in *Philosophy East and West* and *Inquiry,* respectively.

Stanley Gevirtz

Dr. Stanley Gevirtz, born in Brooklyn, New York, is Associate Professor of Palestinian History in the Department of Near Eastern Languages and Civilizations and in the Oriental Institute of the University of Chicago. He has been a member of the faculty since 1958 and is an authority on Biblical Hebrew literature and the cultures, languages, and literatures of ancient Syria and Palestine. His book, *Patterns in the Early Poetry of Israel,* was published in the series "Studies in the Ancient Oriental Civilizations" by the University of Chicago Press. He has also contributed to the *Journal of Religion, Judaism, Journal of Near Eastern Studies,* and other scholarly journals.

Lawrence Krader

Dr. Lawrence Krader was born in New York City and was educated at the City College of New York and Harvard University. He is Ordinarius at the Institute of Ethnology of the Free University of Berlin. Previously he held teaching positions at Harvard, Cornell, Columbia, Ohio State, Chicago, Waterloo, Syracuse, and other universities and has acted as Secretary General to the International Union of Anthropological and Ethnological Sciences. Among his major publications are *Peoples of Central Asia, Formation of the State, Primitive Reification and Mythology, Buryat Religion and Society,* and *Buryat Shamanism.*

Weston La Barre

Dr. Weston La Barre, James B. Duke Professor of Anthropology, Duke University, was born in the United States. He studied at Princeton University and Yale University. He taught at Rutgers University, New York University, the University of Wisconsin, Northwestern University, the University of North Carolina, and the University of Minnesota. He was Editor-in-Chief of *Landmarks in Anthropology* from 1965 to 1970. He was Sterling Fellow of Yale University, a Guggenheim Fellow, and a recipient of the Roheim Award. Among his major publications are *The Peyote Cult* in *Yale University Publications in Anthropology,* No. 19 (New Haven, Conn.: Yale University Press, 1938), *The Ghost Dance· Origins of Religion* (New York: Schocken Books, 1972), *They Shall Take Up Serpents: Psychology of the Southern Snake-Handling Cult* (Minneapolis: University of Minnesota Press, 1962), and a very large number of articles and more than fifty editions of works by others.

Samuel Laeuchli

Dr. Samuel Laeuchli, born in Basel, Switzerland, is Professor of Patristics at Temple University, Philadelphia. He studied at Basel, at the Sorbonne, Paris, and at Union Theological Seminary, New York. He has traveled all over the Mediterranean world and spent sabbatical and study leaves in Rome as well as in Greece. His major publications include a study on the Council of Elvira, *Power and Sexuality* (Philadelphia: Temple University Press, 1972); a book of essays on the ancient Church, *The Serpent and the Dove;* two books on methodology, *Searching in the Syntax of Things* (Philadelphia: Fortress Press, 1972) and *The Language of Faith;* and a book on archaeology, *Mithraism in Ostia.*

Gunapala Piyasena Malalasekera

Dr. Gunapala Piyasena Malalasekera was born in Panadura, Sri Lanka, on 9th November 1899 and passed away in Colombo on 23rd April 1973. He was educated at St. John's College, Panadura, and the University of London where he obtained the degrees of D.Litt., Ph.D. He taught at the University of Ceylon and served as Head of the Department of Pali and Buddhist Civilization. Following nine years of service in the diplomatic corps of his country, he reverted to the field of education as Chairman of the National Council of Higher Education. Dr. Malalasekera was the Editor-in-Chief of the Encyclopaedia of Buddhism. Among his many publications are the following: *The Pali Literature of Ceylon; Dictionary of Pali Proper Names; The Buddha and His Teachings; The Extended Mahavamsa and Commentary on the Mahavamsa.* At various times he was President of the World Fellowship of Buddhists, President of the All-Ceylon Buddhist Congress, and President of the Ceylon Society of Arts.

John Mbiti

Dr. John Mbiti was born in Kitui, Kenya, and was educated at Makarere College, Kampala, Uganda, at Barrington College in Rhode Island, and at the University of Cambridge. He was a visiting professor at Selly Oak College in Birmingham, England, and at the University of Hamburg. He joined the faculty of Makarere University in 1964 and rose to full professorship and chairmanship of its Department of Religion. Among his notable publications are *African Religions and Philosophy, Concepts of God in Africa, New Testament Eschatology in African Background, Love and Marriage in Africa,* and *Introduction to African Religion.*

Raj P. Nanavati

Dr. Raj P. Nanavati was born in Baroda, India, and is a graduate of the Massachusetts Institute of Technology and Syracuse University. He is currently Associate Professor of Electrical Engineering at Syracuse University.

Venkatarama Raghavan

Dr. Venkatarama Raghavan was born in Tiruvarur, Thanjavur District, Tamil Nadu State, India, and was educated at the University of Madras (Ph.D., 1935). He held successively the positions of Lecturer, Reader, Professor, and Head of the Department of Sanskrit at his *alma mater*. He was Fellow of the Jawaharlal Nehru Memorial Foundation (1969–1970), and since 1971 has been Chairman of the Academic Committee of the First International Sanskrit Conference. He is the author of a large number of works, including *The Religion of the Hindus, The Sources of the Indian Tradition, The Indian Heritage, The Mahabharata, The Bhagavata,* and *The Concept of Culture.*

Khushwant Singh

Mr. Khushwant Singh, born in the Punjab, India, is Professor in the Guru Gobind Singh Department of Religious Studies at Punjabi University, Patiala. Previously, he was an attorney-at-law at the High Court in Lahore, member of the Indian Foreign Service, and a visiting professor at Oxford University, the University of Rochester, and Princeton University. He has written fiction (for example, *Mark of Vishnu, Train to Pakistan, I Shall Not Hear the Nightingale*) as well as nonfiction. Besides a number of translations and editions of Sikh literature, he is the author of the authoritative *History of the Sikhs* in two volumes. Among his other publications are *The Heritage of the Sikhs, Guru Gobind Singh, Maharaja Ranjit Singh,* and *Aspects of Punjabi Literature.* Currently, Professor Singh is editor of *The Illustrated Weekly of India.*

Gerard S. Sloyan

Dr. Gerard S. Sloyan was born in New York City and studied at Seton Hall University, South Orange, New Jersey (A.B., 1940), the Seminary of the Immaculate Conception, Darlington, New Jersey (1938–1943), and The Catholic University of America, Washington, D.C. (S.T.L., 1944; Ph.D., 1948). He was ordained a priest in 1944 and taught from 1950 to 1967 in the Department of Religious Education, The Catholic University of America, serving as Chairman from 1957 to 1967. He has been a Professor of Religion (New Testament) at Temple University since 1967 and Chairman of the department since 1970.

His publications include *The Three Persons in One God,* (Englewood Cliffs, N.J.: Prentice-Hall, 1963), *Jesus on Trial* (Philadelphia: Fortress, 1973), and articles in *Concilium* and *The New Catholic Encyclopedia.* He was also the English editor of the New Testament for *The New American Bible,* which was widely published in 1970.

Table of Contents

Preface v

A Word About the Maps vii

The Contributors xi

List of Maps xxi

Part One Religions of the Past 1

1 The Ancient Near East: Mesopotamia 3

2 The Ancient Near East: Egypt 15

3 The Ancient Near East: Canaan-Phoenicia 29

4 The Religious Matrix of Greater Syria 33

5 Ancient Greece and Rome 35

6 Shamanism 45

7 Amerindian Religions 51

Part Two Ethnic Religions of the Present 59

Localized in the Lands of Their Birth 59

8 Traditional Religions in Africa 61

9 Hinduism 69

10 Jainism 97

11 Sikhism 105

12 Confucianism and Taoism 109

13 Shintō 127

Dispersed

14 Zoroastrianism 133
15 Judaism 139

Part Three Universal Religions of the Present 159

16 Theravāda Buddhism 161
17 Mahāyāna Buddhism (China) 185
18 Mahāyāna Buddhism (Japan) 195
19 Christianity 201
20 Islām 237

Appendix: Chronologies 283

Indexes 323

List of Maps

1 The Religions of the World
2 Distribution of Religions by Major Regions c. 1970
3 Ancient Mesopotamia 4
4 Ancient Egypt 19
5 Localization of Myth in the Ancient Greek World 36–37
6 Distribution of Some Religious Features in Pre-Christian and Early Christian Europe 38
7 Religious Traits of the American Indian: Culture Areas at the Time of European Contact 54
8 Religious Traits of the American Indian: Stimulants and Narcotics in Religious Use 55
9 India in the Vedic and Epic Literature 71
10 Indian Religions: Places of Pilgrimage (*Tirthas*) 72
11 Indigenous Religions of the Indian Subcontinent: Hinduism, Buddhism, Jainism, Sikhism 86
12 Indigenous Chinese Religions 111
13 Japan: Places of Religious Importance 129
14 Shintō Adherents in Japan 132
15 Shintō Adherents in the Japanese Population 132
16 Buddhist Adherents in the Japanese Population 132
17 Christian Adherents in the Japanese Population 132
18 The Israelite Kingdom under David and Solomon 143
19 The Hasmonean Kingdom in the First and Second Centuries B.C.E. 145
20 The Jewish Diaspora in Roman Times c. 100–400 C.E. 147
21 Expulsion and Migration of Jews from European Cities and Regions, Eleventh to Fifteenth Centuries C.E. 148–149
22 Places Associated with the Lives of Leading Jewish Rabbis, Theologians, and Writers on Judaism (Sixth Century C.E. to the Present) 150–151
23 Jewish Emigration from Eastern and Central Europe 1881–1939 153
24 Change in Jewish Population 1939–1969 153
25 Reduction of Jewish Communities in Eastern Europe 1933–1956 154
26 Jewish Migration to Israel 1881–1970 154
27 Distribution of Jews c. 1970 155
28 Jews in the United States 155
29 Jewish Urban Communities (1956) 156
30 World Jewish Population by Major Regions 156
31 The Hearth of Buddhism: Places and Events in the Life of the Buddha 163
32 Development of Buddhism in South Asia 174
33 The Buddhist World from the First to the Ninth Century C.E. 176–177
34 Buddhism in Asia from the Ninth Century 180–181
35 Buddhism in China 187
36 Early Growth of Christianity 202
37 The Church in the Fourth and Fifth Centuries 209

38 Monastic Institutions from the Fourth to the Eighth Century 213
39 Monophysite and Nestorian Churches from the Seventh to the Eleventh Century 214
40 The Ecclesiastical Organization of Europe c. 1050 216–217
41 The Nestorian and Roman Catholic Presence in Asia, c. 650–1550 223
42 The Church of Rome and the Protestant Reformation 225
43 Christianity in the New World to the Middle of the Eighteenth Century 228
44 Distribution of Protestant Denominations in the English Colonies c. 1750 228
45 Nineteenth Century Catholic and Protestant Missions in the Old World 232
46 Distribution of Christianity c. 1970 234
47 World Christian Population by Major Regions 234
48 Christian Denominations in the Conterminous United States 235
49 The Middle East During the Life of Muḥammad 239
50 Places in Central Arabia Associated with the Life of the Prophet 242
51 Plan of the Holy City of Makkah (Mecca) 245
52 The Muslim World in the Ninth Century C.E. 250–251
53 Muslim Rule and Influence from the Second Half of the Thirteenth Century C.E. 256–257
54 Travels of Ibn-Baṭuṭa (1325–1354 C.E.) 258
55 Duration of Muslim Rule in South Asia 259
56 Islamic Schools of Law, Sects, and Reform Movements 261
57 Spread of the Orthodox Law Schools 261
58 Crusader Attacks and Muslim Response in the Twelfth and Thirteenth Centuries C.E. 271
59 Distribution of Muslims c. 1970 276
60 World Population of Muslims by Major Regions 277
61 Muslims in South Asia 278
62 Muslims in Malaya and Singapore 278
63 Muslims in Nigeria 278
64 Islām, Culture, and the State 279
65 Pilgrim Traffic to Makkah (Mecca) 280

1 Religions of the World

RELIGION OF THE MAJORITY OF THE POPULATION

- Christianity
- Islām
- Buddhism
  - Buddhist, Confucianist, Taoist, and other elements mingled (China, Korea, Vietnam)
  - Buddhism and Shintō intermixed (Japan)
- Hinduism
- "Animism" (includes Shamanism)
- Judaism

Where followers of a religion form a substantial minority of the population, the following symbols are used:

A "Animism"
B Buddhism
C Christianity
H Hinduism
J Judaism
M Islām
O Chinese religious blend (see above)

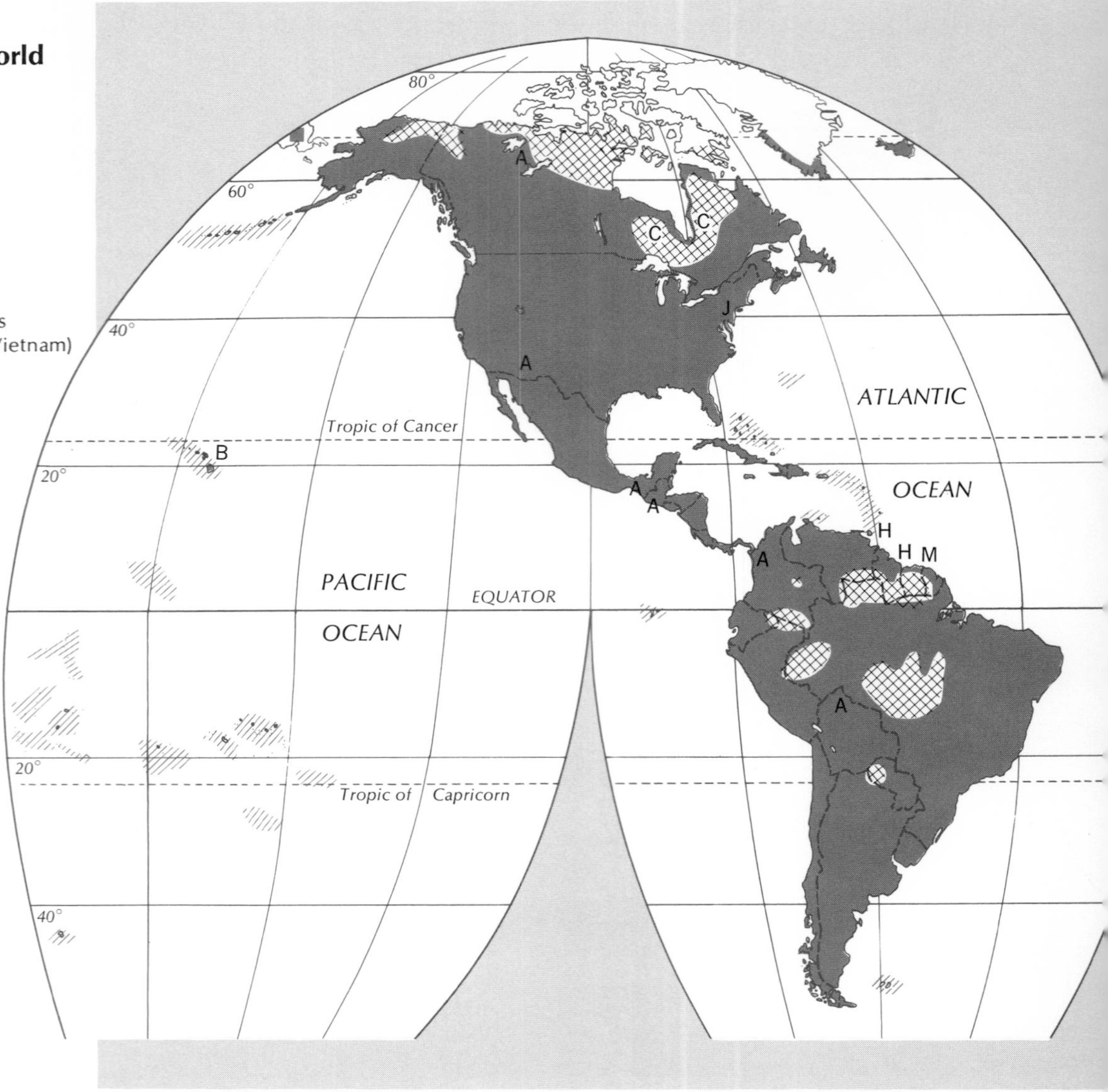

2 Distribution of Religions by Major Regions c. 1970

Christianity differentiated, thus

R Roman Catholic
P Protestant
OX Orthodox, Coptic, etc.

☐ Other religions or religion unspecified

☐ = 25 million persons

The area of a square is proportional to the total population and is divided into patterned areas that correspond to the proportion in that population of the religious groups

See Map 1 for key to symbols

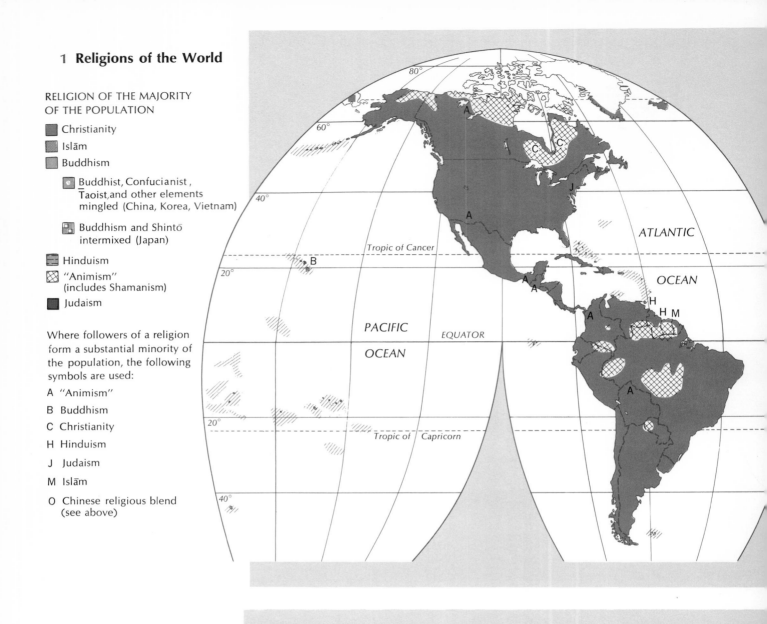

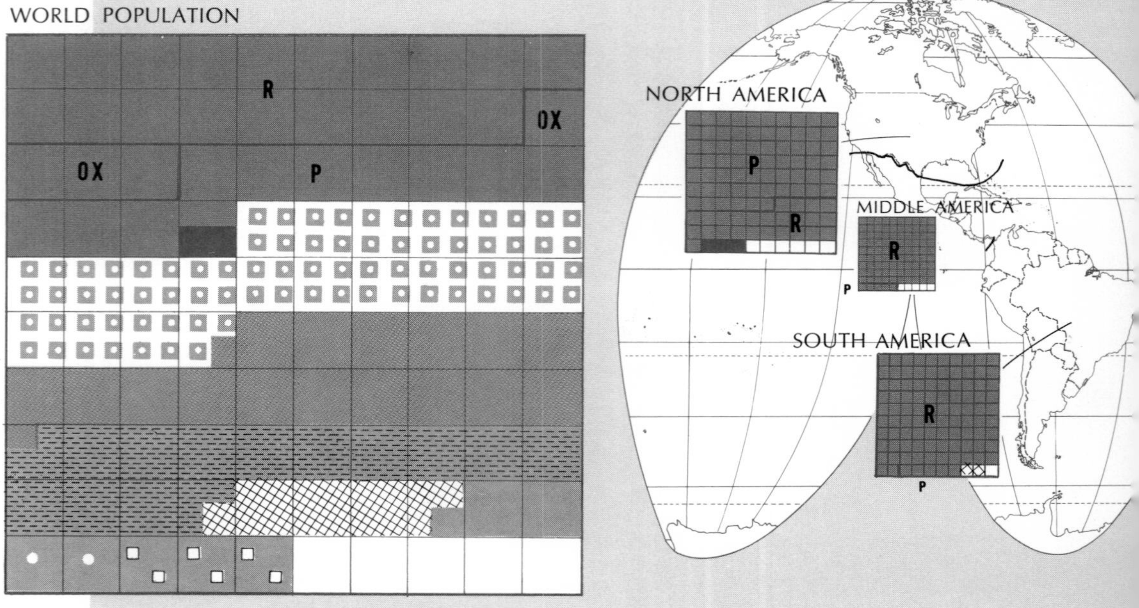

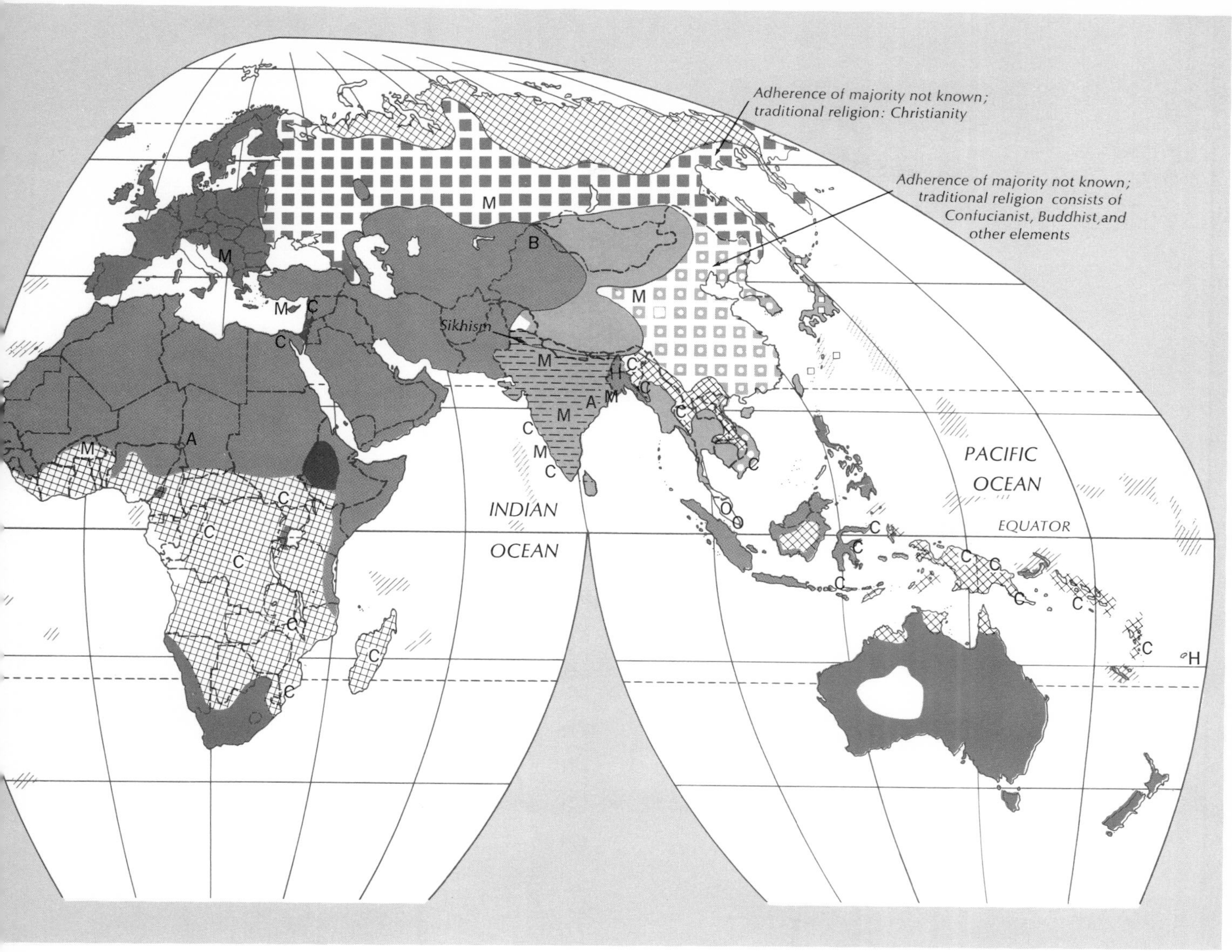
Adherence of majority not known; traditional religion: Christianity
Adherence of majority not known; traditional religion consists of Confucianist, Buddhist and other elements
Sikhism
PACIFIC OCEAN
INDIAN OCEAN
EQUATOR

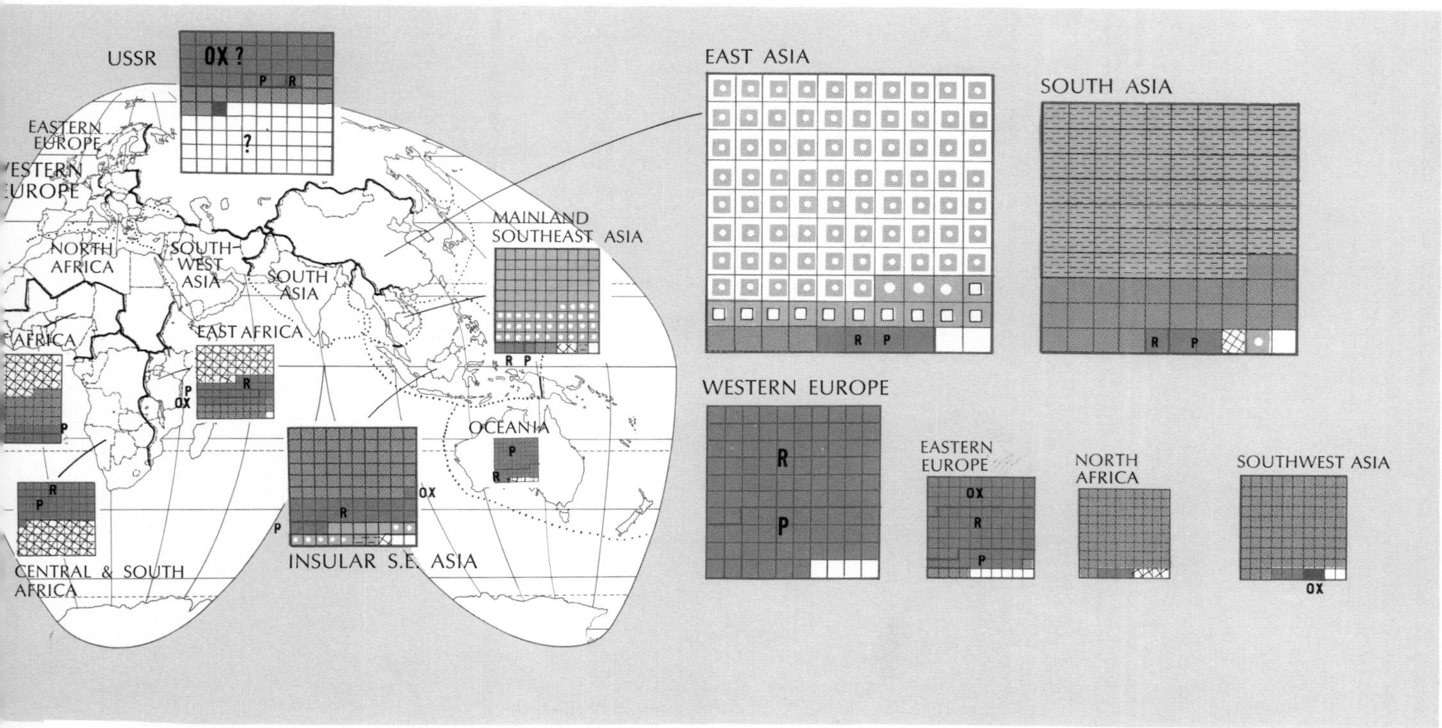
USSR
EASTERN EUROPE
WESTERN EUROPE
NORTH AFRICA
SOUTH-WEST ASIA
SOUTH ASIA
MAINLAND SOUTHEAST ASIA
EAST AFRICA
OCEANIA
INSULAR S.E. ASIA
CENTRAL & SOUTH AFRICA
EAST ASIA
SOUTH ASIA
WESTERN EUROPE
EASTERN EUROPE
NORTH AFRICA
SOUTHWEST ASIA

PART ONE RELIGIONS OF THE PAST

The Ancient Near East
Ancient Greece and Rome
Shamanism
Amerindian Religions

1

The Ancient Near East: Mesopotamia

Isma'īl R. al Fārūqī

It has been said that the ancient Near East was the cradle of civilization. Today, when the works of Egyptology, Sumerology, Assyriology, and related disciplines fill shelves in the neighborhood bookstore, this is a platitude. The explanation of the rise of civilization remains obscure, however. Whereas no historian will dispute the Near East's first building with stone, discovery of the wheel and of the arch, invention of the alphabet and writing, of irrigation and agriculture, of the political state and its social order, very few realize that at the base of all these achievements are questions of religious order that Near Eastern man raised and answered in a very special way.

Simultaneously, in the two fertile valleys flanking the Near East—Egypt and Mesopotamia—these questions were asked: What is ultimate reality? Who and what am I? Where did I come from and where am I going? What is my relation to myself? to others? to nature? to ultimate reality? What is good and how can I know it? What may I hope for? What is my destiny? The answers in each of the two areas were different; but each created a civilization that nursed and sustained man in body and spirit for thousands of years. Both crystallized around the middle of the fourth millenium B.C.E. Complex civilizations appear to have risen rapidly and almost simultaneously in the two areas. Even today, the dominant ideas of both civilizations are operative among us.

Genesis and Flowering

The territories of the Arabian Peninsula, the Tigris-Euphrates Valley, and Greater Syria have always constituted a unity that is not political but cultural. These lands constitute a single theater (Map 3). At its heart is Arabia, a sheltered region that has seen extremely little penetration by outsiders. Speculation about prehistorical origins abound. But history knows of only a Persian and an Abyssinian penetration in the sixth century C.E. that hardly survived that century. On the other hand, history records numerous waves of migration from Arabia to the adjacent lands. Being surrounded by sea boundaries on three sides, Arabia sent its migrant peoples northward. The northern region is known as the Fertile Crescent. It is indeed a crescent, whose extremities stand on the mouth of the Tigris-Euphrates and the mouth of the Nile and whose belly is a continuation of the Arabian desert itself. The Fertile Crescent is really no less an edge or surrounding of the desert than Hijaz or Yaman. The two river basins in the northeast and northwest constituted frontiers for the people of the Peninsula, beyond which they did not want to go. Beyond the Tigris-Euphrates basin and surrounding it to the north and the east stood what must have appeared to the people of the plains a forbidding high plateau and impenetrable snowy mountains; beyond

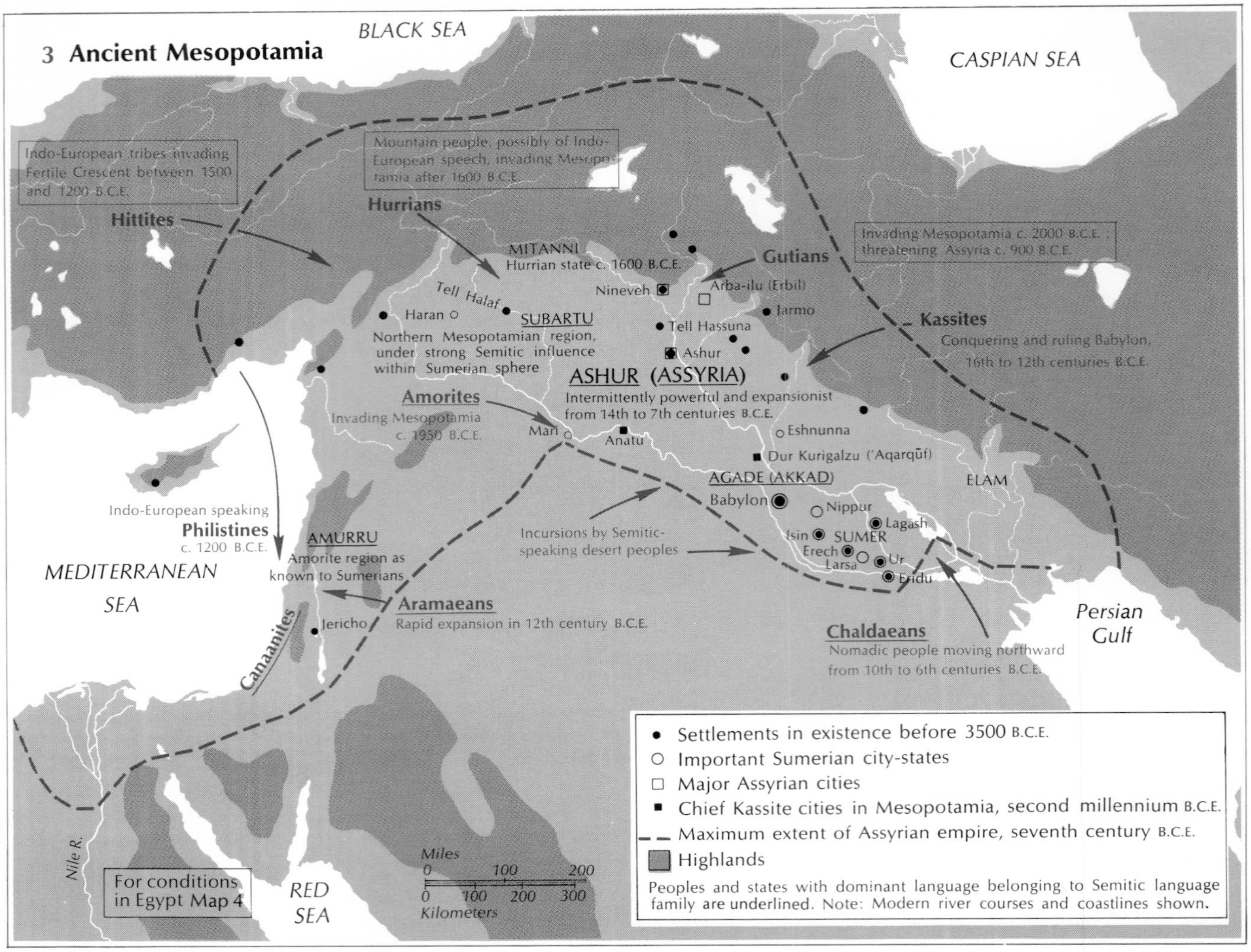

Syria, an impassable sea; and beyond the Nile delta, an impenetrable desert.

This region was regarded by its inhabitants as one undivided stage for players conscious of a common identity and possessed by a common mission. The people moved about a good deal, but the old natives and the newcomers in any one of these movements belonged to the same ethnic entity. Certainly, in the distant past strangers to the region (Indo-Europeans from the northeast, Hittites from Anatolia, and Nilotic peoples from Africa) entered the scene, as did the Persians, the Greeks, the Romans of later times, and the Turks, European Crusaders, the British, and the French still more recently. All these were temporary penetrations that ended either by being repulsed or by being absorbed, while the essential character of the region remained the same. Despite their political or military ascendancy, the newcomers to the region soon became assimilated in language, religion, culture, and custom. The movement of people native to the region has tended to follow a simple pattern: from the Peninsula to the Fertile Crescent, or from one part of the Crescent to another, because of the meager means of subsistence provided by the desert and the affluence of the river basins. From the earliest historical time, the record speaks of people moving out of the Arabian Peninsula in repeated waves. Pastoral people have always sought a living in irrigated land and have often done so through intermarriage with the farmers. The Sumerian poem of Dumuzi and Enkimdu[1] is expressive of this fact of the settling of desert people on the river banks through intermarriage. It may have always taken an argument to settle the issue arising out of the event: whether an argument of contest

[1] James B. Pritchard (ed.), *Ancient Near Eastern Texts* (Princeton: Princeton U. P., 1955), pp. 41–42.

in economic and cultural value between farmer and shepherd, such as the aforesaid poem indicates or, where communication breaks down, one of force expressed in the Cain and Abel legend. Whereas the latter are said to belong to the same household, which is a simple way of expressing common ancestry, the former assumes standards of valuational measurement and the common understanding and appreciation of them that only upbringing within one and the same culture can bring about.

The reverse movement, from river basin to desert, is unreasonable and less likely to occur. The known instances of it were products of natural or human catastrophes. History knows of southern Arabs (e.g., Ghassan, Lakhm, Tanūkh, Ṭayy', and Kindah tribes) emigrating to the desert from their fertile valley following the destruction of the Ma'rib dam (450–540 C.E.) and the resultant cessation of agriculture after the flood; and of Hebrew patriarchs emigrating into the Syrian Desert (their movement was along the periphery of the desert—Ur-Mari-Padan Aram-Damascus-Negeb-Egypt) because of religious conflict between monotheist Abraham and his polytheist people. The road the Hebrews took betrays their inability to traverse the desert in a straight east-west line, a fact that suggested to F. W. Albright that until that time the camel, the only vehicle capable of such crossing, had not yet been domesticated—which is probable though by no means certain. For it is not unreasonable to think that people who have been accustomed to riverland living are not, and that the people who have grown up in the desert are, capable of traversing the desert on camel back. At any rate, the riverland people would be bound by their sheep- or goat-based economy to stay close to pasture. So would the desert nomads if their means of transportation was the donkey, before the camel's domestication. The same consideration furnished Albright grounds for denying the Arabian Desert as the origin of the Akkadian, Amorite, and other major Near Eastern migrations. Even it it were certain that the camel had not by then been domesticated, there is nothing that would have prevented the desert people from reaching Mesopotamia on donkey back or on foot, moving slowly along the desert periphery in a clockwise arc from Yaman, through Hijaz and Moab, and along the very route Abraham took in reverse direction. Such movement would have brought the Akkadians into Sumer from the north, thus corresponding to a Sumerian myth about Akkadian origins.

The foregoing facts of Near Eastern history have contributed to the ethnological unity of the region. For a people who live over the millenia in a sheltered location, who are not subject to large-scale immigration from other lands, and who repulse or totally absorb the few newcomers that do emigrate into their midst will come to constitute an ethnic unity in the sense of sharing a common genetic pool and a common consciousness of that pool. This need not be taken to mean a claim to racial purity, but it does mean that it is safe to take the inhabitants of the impenetrable core of the sheltered theater, in this case the Arabian desert, as the purest archetype of the group.

Buttressing these claims for the unity of the Near East is another unity in the realm of language. When the languages of the Near East were discovered it was found that they bore great resemblance to one another. The European scholars concerned invented the name "Semitic Family" and applied it to these languages and the peoples that spoke them. The observed unity is a fact; the name was reached *faute de mieux*. It betrays the caller's concern with Old Testament genealogy. What concerns us here is the fact and not the name.

The unity of these languages consists in an identity of root words; of grammatical and syntactical forms; of idioms and figures of speech; of consonants, vowels, and vocalizations; and finally of literary forms. At the center of the Near Eastern family of languages stands Arabic. It is the only surviving language that has been spoken continuously and without change for two thousand years and probably for much longer. Biblical Hebrew and Ethiopic are not comparable. The former had ceased to be a spoken language for nearly two millennia and is far from being understood by the speaker of modern Hebrew on account of the profound and extensive vocabulary of modern times that modern Hebrew seems to have adopted. The latter case, Ethiopic, has been preserved in the Church liturgy but is hardly understood even by the clergy. Modern Ethiopians speak Amharic, a language based on, but widely different from, Ethiopic. Arabic, on the other hand, has remained the same and has been spoken and clearly understood by the literate and illiterate alike.

Though historical records do not go much beyond the first millennium B.C.E. (South Arabian archaeology being still in infancy and Hijaz archaeology yet unborn), philology and linguistics have indeed established that Arabic is the most archaic as well as the most comprehensive member of the "Near Eastern" family. Its forms have not changed through the ages and it includes more of the varieties of linguistic forms than any of the other members. Indeed, it stands to them all as a progenitor would to its progeny, including in itself all or most of the essential characteristics of its progeny. The process is due to separation from the mother-tongue, *Ur-Semitisch*, and either to the resultant acculturation in the region or simply to change through time as result of ever-new situations presented by life. Under these influences, the idioms suffer slight change without losing their original connotation. A synonym may come to denote all the referents of those terms of which it is a synonym because those other terms have lapsed from consciousness through nonuse. Sophisticated rules of a developed grammar may leave only a vestige of themselves, in the long absence of conservative elements of society in the new region where the emigrants had settled. Finally, a foreign term of the natives may be directly borrowed by the newcomers and incorporated into their language. Although all these changes are possible and indeed actual, the literary values, the genres and forms of *belles lettres* of all the Near Eastern languages have never changed. Every characteristic of Sumerian, Babylonian, Assyrian, Canaanite, and Hebrew literary art is at once true of all the other literatures and more so of Arabic literature than all the others. Samuel Noah Kramer's characterization of Sumerian literature might well have been used to describe Arabian literature; the same could be said of Sabatino Moscati's characterization of every other Semitic literature. Lengthy repetition, parallelism, elaborate metaphor and simile, chorus and refrain, recurrent formulae, long speeches, absence of close-knit plot structures, disconnected (nondevelopmental) narratives, no climax or conclusion, little or no intensification of emotion and suspense, no characterization or psychological delineation, stylized broad types rather than individual personalities—these were the literary forms, plots, motifs, stylistic devices, and aesthetic techniques common to all the Near Eastern peoples. They are true of Sumerian, Babylonian, and Assyrian literature as they are true of the Hebrew Bible and the Qur'an. The literary aesthetics of these peoples has remained the same throughout the five or six millennia of Near Eastern history, thus evidencing beyond the shadow of a doubt, a common origin and a continuing common sense of literary beauty. Because language is the mirror and reservoir of consciousness, linguistic and literary unity imply a common fund of experience and an interaction and communion long enough to imprint these forms on consciousness and intense enough to knead them into its fabric so that they become inseparable.

Linguistic analysis has helped reconstruct some facets of the history of the Near Eastern peoples. For com-

1-1 Winged bull of Khorsabad, Iraq. Winged bulls or lions with human heads often guarded entrance gateways in ancient Assyria. The statue shown was discovered at the palace of the Assyrian King Sargon at Khorsabad. It dates to the 8th century B.C.E. (Courtesy of the Arab Information Center.)

monalty of language implies some common experience; and common experience of two peoples is common living, common history. Thus we know that Arabs from the desert or its outskirts came to settle in Mesopotamia long before the Sumerian city-states blossomed around 2800 B.C.E. and that by then a large fund of common experience, living, and history must have been developed to support the common patterns of grammar, syntax, and phraseology and indeed to bring about and maintain through the millennia identical literary forms. The repetition of this fact in Near Eastern history and the comprehensiveness of Arabic warrant the conclusion that it was the Arabs who fanned out of their desert into the Fertile Crescent, whether slowly over generations or brusquely; that with every major migration they brought with them linguistic and cultural reforms that produced a new crystallization of culture and that stimulated and nourished a new growth of civilization. Otherwise the common elements between Arabic and Akkadian, the language of the non-Sumerian Near Easterners whose advent, settlement, and ascendancy produced the Sumerian crystallization, would remain inexplicable.

The geographical, ethnic, and linguistic community of the Near East, the last implying a long community of history, is further corroborated by a unity of religious culture. The most salient characteristic of the religious culture of Near Eastern man is his conception of his relation to God. Unlike his peers in all other civilizations, he saw himself as the servant of a transcendent deity. He did not hold himself under any illusion of grandeur, for his lot was that of an ephemeral servant. The crumbling of his works did not disturb him, and the meniality of his profession did not make him despondent. And yet, this very vocation in which he saw his destiny was to be his eternal glory. For he was truly only a servant—but to God, Who is the transcendent *summum bonum*. To serve such a Being meant therefore to make the will of God real, to embody it in creation. To become actual, to enter the realm of space-time, the transcendent good depended upon his effort. He was then a cosmic bridge through which the moral good or the higher will of divinity could enter space-time. He was indeed his Master's vicegerent on earth, bearer of a divine mission and fulfiller of a divine task.

Furthermore, to serve the deity meant to build irrigation canals and dikes; to cultivate the land, turning it into gardens; to produce food; to build temples; to maintain records, for which he had to invent writing; to organize men into society and order them to work as a team; to set up government to maintain the social order and defend it against its enemies—in short to create civilization and to "make" history. The least important character in cosmic history thus became the vortex and fulcrum of all history.

Theogony

The ancient Mesopotamian regarded reality as dual. There was nature—which is material, changing, ephemeral—including himself, a creature among countless creaturely beings; and there was God or Ultimate Reality, immaterial, immutable, eternal—Master and Creator of the world. The one is empirical, the other transcendent. Between them stands an infinite chasm. Surely there were many gods, everyone of whom was associated with some creaturely phenomenon or element. Conversely, everything in nature was regarded as alive, endowed with a character and personality all its own and somehow constituting a hierophanous occasion or theater for divinity. Salt was addressed as a god and so were flint, the reed, and the wind, not to speak of the astral bodies. What is remarkable, however, is that not a single phenomenon or element of nature was ever taken as circumscribing completely or including exhaustively the God with whom it was associated. Nothing in creation was taken as convertibly equivalent to the Godhead. The association was always functional—one would even say accidental—but never total. Thus, the charge of idolatry should not be leveled against the Mesopotamian. For he never subscribed to the total identification of the divine with the natural, which is the essence of idolatry. He did subscribe at times, however, to *association* of the divine with the natural. That is the work of the mythopoeic mind, of a mind incapable of rising to the level of abstraction required to see the divine as transcendent.

To this consideration of the divine belongs the problem of monotheism and polytheism. The Mesopotamian had many gods—a whole pantheon full! So far, however, the evidence does not show that these gods were gods *sui generis*, self-existent and autonomous in their own right. The suspicion that they were mere names, attributes, aspects, or functions of one and the same Supreme Deity never left them. The cosmic assembly of gods who voted Marduk all the power (The Tablet of Destinies) were essentially feudal barons called into session by the central ruler in order to meet a special emergency: the rage of Ti'amat, the flooding salt water of the sea, which brought destruction to agriculture. Thus it was that Anshar, the supreme ruler, called Kaka, his beloved vizier, to travel to the distant lands and summon their gods to the assembly.[2] Thus, also, the so-called gods

[2] Ibid., p. 30.

1-2 Tablet found at the Sumerian city of Nippur, Isin Period, second millenium B.C.E. The clay tablet's inscriptions tell the stories of the Creation, the Flood, and the Epic of Gilgamesh. (Courtesy of the University Museum, University of Pennsylvania.)

acknowledged the lordship of Marduk and gave him not only obeisance but worship. "By as many a name as we have called him" they shout in chorus, "he shall be our god" and they praise him by "proclaiming his fifty names."[3] He "verily is *the* God, the creator of everything. . . . The commands of his mouth we have exalted above the gods. . . . Verily he is the lord of all the gods of heaven and earth; the king at whose instruction the gods above and below shall be afraid . . . shall quake and tremble in their dwellings. . . . Verily he is the light of the gods, the mighty prince."[4] Moreover, the gods could die—indeed, they did die and Marduk resurrected them.

[3] Ibid., p. 51.
[4] Ibid., p. 52.

He could have even created them! It was he "who restored all the ruined gods, as though they were his own creation, restored the dead gods to life."[5] He is the one "whom no god whatever can equal."[6] Obviously "the god" and "gods" did not refer to the same kind of being. A god who owes this much to God, whose relationship to the Supreme Being is describable in such terms, cannot himself be God. The same tablet of *Enuma Elish* gives the same number of fifty to both the names of Marduk and to the "great gods who took their seats in the assembly." Moreover, the names leave hardly any of the divine functions to the gods, as Marduk according to the Babylonian version (Enlil, in the Assyrian and the Sumerian) assumes all. It is not therefore correct to describe Mesopotamian religion as simply polytheistic. For the many gods were either no gods at all but provincial human rulers or apotheoses of Marduk's attributes and functions. To say associationist, rather than polytheist, would therefore be truer of Mesopotamian religion as far as scholarship has yet been able to establish. The Mesopotamian shared the same *shirk* or "associationism" with the pre-Islamic Arab. Both recognized God as existent and one; but both associated with the Godhead beings that were not God.

Anthropogony

Man, the Mesopotamians held, was created by Marduk for the sole purpose of serving the gods. Because each god was at the same time lord of a manor, man was put on the land as a serf, to do God's bidding. His *raison d'être* or destiny is this service to deity. His works are not lasting and he knows it. He has no claim to eternity or to pursue his own good. It is the service of God that should be his constant objective. His distinction is his freedom to do or not to do the divine will. Reward and punishment, happiness, health, children, long life, prosperity, and their opposites are what the gods will mete out to him in this life depending on his option and his success. There is no doubt he was equipped at creation with all that it takes to succeed and to fail. His is the choice. He begins innocent; he may end up blessed or guilty. A necessary corollary to this anthropological principle is the malleability of nature, of creation, to receive the agency of man. The earth will yield corn and oil and fruit, and the cattle will multiply—if man does his duty. The Mesopotamian had no idea of a resisting or a recalcitrant nature. The *thou* in nature was not insurmountable provided man ful-

[5] Ibid., p. 58.
[6] Ibid.

1-3 Fragment of a stele set up by Ur-Nammu, the king of Sumer and Akkad and founder of the Third Dynasty of Ur, circa 2250 B.C.E., limestone. On the middle register the king is shown making offerings to the moon god Nannar (right) and to his consort goddess Nin-gal (left). (Courtesy of the University Museum, University of Pennsylvania.)

filled what was expected of him. Despite the fact that natural phenomena were often associated with one divine presence or another, one may venture to describe nature as profane, a creature created that man might do his duty and that, in consequence, both he and God might be happy. Every man had a personal god to help him achieve success where resistance was met. But the personal god was not whimsical: "When thou dost plan ahead, thy god is thine; when thou dost not plan ahead, thy god is not thine."[7]

It is in the communication of the divine will that any contact is made between God, the transcendent creator, and man, the creature. There is neither possibility of nor need for a disclosure of the divine self. All that is needed, and is possible, is the transmission of a command.

Revelation meant for him, therefore, making known the law. This took place by means that the mythopoeic mind can understand: portents of nature, omens in the internal organs of sacrificial animals, and dreams. The content of revelation was always the law, that is, the "how" of service.

The media of revelation had this primitive beginning, but they improved. Improvement was early at the center of government, where the national king had to make universally known the will of the supreme cosmic God of whom he was the vicegerent, whereas on the provin-

[7] Henri Frankfort (ed.), *Before Philosophy: The Intellectual Adventure of Ancient Man* (Baltimore: Penguin, 1967), p. 219.

1-4 A sketched reconstruction of the entrance to the Temple of Nin-Khursag at al 'Ubaid, built about 2600 B.C.E. by King A-anni-pad-da of the First Dynasty of Ur. Nin-Khursag was the goddess associated with fertility throughout Mesopotamia. (Courtesy of the University Museum, University of Pennsylvania.)

cial and personal levels improvement was tardy. At the time when Sumerians and Akkadians mingled and the former could no longer conceive for themselves a separate identity, the breakthrough came with King Lipit-Ishtar, the first Akkadian "shepherd" king to rule over both groups and to crystallize the heritage. "When the great Anu the father of the gods and Enlil the King of all the lands, the lord who determines destinies . . . had called Lipit-Ishtar . . . the wise shepherd . . . to the princeship of the land in order to establish justice . . . to banish complaint, to turn back enmity and rebellion . . . and to bring well-being to the Sumerians and Akkadians, then I, Lipit-Ishtar . . . established justice in Sumer and Akkad in accordance with the word of Enlil. . . . Verily in accordance with the true word of Utu. . . . Verily in accordance with the pronouncement of Enlil . . . I erected this stela."[8] The medium of revelation of divine will is a "word" and the content of the words of God is the law. The perfect example is, of course, Hammurabi, whose prologue and epilogue to the code[9] leave no doubt as to the divine dictation and origin of the law. In the famous stela, Hammurabi is shown receiving the law in a scroll directly from the god Shamash. Through the whole millennium that separates the two codes, the form and philosophy behind them did not change; only the panegyric of the king became longer. Later, the Hebrews were to understand revelation in terms of law and to regard the Sinai decalogue as the highest form of communication of divine will.

[8] Pritchard, pp. 159–161.
[9] Ibid., pp. 164–180.

Cosmogony

It is in relation to his fellowmen that the Mesopotamian achieved his greatest and noblest insight. His society was both earthly and heavenly or cosmic, the former being the concrete, the latter the ideal archetype. Both, however, were real and impinged upon him with force. He was a citizen of both at once.

The emergence of the social order was for the Mesopotamian the very act of creation. Before it, nothing was except chaos, where darkness mixed with light, and the sweet river water with sea water and the land was marshy, uninhabitable, and full of Ti'amat's beasts. Creation meant for him the investiture of Marduk, the slaying of Ti'amat or chaos, the establishment of law and order on earth and in heaven, the beginning of organized agriculture, of controlled irrigation, of centralized government, of raising zigurrats, of writing and of keeping records of men's affairs—in short, of culture and civilization.

Religion was life and life was religion. To worship God was to fulfill one's quota of production, to obey one's ruler, to maintain the system of irrigation that makes life possible for all. Because the state was cosmic and heavenly, its earthly counterpart could have no

1-5 Relief at the top of a stele from Babylon, eighteenth century B.C.E., diorite. Hammurabi stands before the enthroned sun god, Shamash, prepared to receive the Law. (Louvre, Paris, courtesy of Professor M. A. Beek, *Bildatlas der assyrisch-babylonischen Kultur.*)

necessary limits. It too must be universal and every man entitled to citizenship precisely by virtue of his humanity. God created mankind—not only the Mesopotamians—to serve. Man then everywhere, "all men in the four regions of the earth," were citizens and upon them fell the same duty of service to "the first being of all the lands,"[10] the "lord of the lands."[11] The Mesopotamian world did not extend beyond Akkad, Elam, Subartu, and Amurru—"the four regions." To extend this far, however, was to establish well its universality, for Subartu and Elam did not belong to the "Semitic" family of nations, nor did their languages belong to the "Semitic" family. Yet they were among the "four regions" of which Marduk was lord. As Hammurabi put it describing himself, "When lofty Anu, lord of heaven and earth . . . appointed Marduk . . . to execute the Enlil functions over the totality of the people. . . . Then did Anu and Enlil call me to afford well being to the people, to cause righteousness to appear in the land, to destroy the evil and the wicked, that the strong harm not the weak and that I rise like the sun over the black-headed people, lighting up the land."[12]

The supreme value by which the social order lived was discipline. This was the cardinal or mother virtue that gave rise to man's fulfillment of his labor and the production of his sustenance and comfort, to his harmonious relation with his fellowmen. All men were related in the same way to God. Everybody produced; God stored in His zigurrat and recorded; He distributed food to all according to need. The Mesopotamian manor-of-the-god was the first organized community where man gave to man by giving to God, for the common good. In Mesopotamia, large-scale agriculture could not be undertaken without the concerted cooperation of people all along the sides of the two rivers, in the maintenance of dikes, canals, drains, and reservoirs. This physical necessity the Mesopotamian transfigured into the Cosmos—the ordered world of heaven under Marduk—thus ennobling the cooperative and orderly social system and endearing it to men's hearts. The material realities and needs were spiritualized the better to be fulfilled, with a greater resultant contentment. The unordered human group was for the Mesopotamian an object of the deepest pity and fear. Humans without a state were sheep without a shepherd, savages from whom only evil could proceed, a dangerous threat to life and civilization, to goodness and decency.

This is the politicization of society *par excellence*, the reader might say. But it was a politicization made ethical by the value of obedience, the obedience of every Mesopotamian to the circles of authority in which he stood. Intelligence, he saw, was in the ear, not in the heart. For it is through the ear that one listens and hears the command or desideratum of one's brother, father, elder, superior, and of one's God—of the Almighty.

The earthly social order, like the heavenly, was based on justice. Marduk's cosmic government was just, and so was that of his vicar on earth, the central king. In the provinces, the local god and his human vicegerent,

[10] Ibid., p. 57.
[11] Ibid., pp. 57–58.

[12] Ibid., p. 208.

the *ensi,* applied the central government's jurisdiction. The law was proclaimed and known. The scale of justice was absolute: Good deeds must meet their due rewards and evil ones their punishments. At the beginning, the local or personal god obtained justice for his province or protégé, for the machinery of justice was not efficient and its reach was limited. The trend, however, was for extension of that reach, and justice, in consequence, was enjoyed by ever-growing numbers. The age of Hammurabi represents an apogee of this development. The Mesopotamian entertained no doubt that the way of discipline, of hard work, of obedience, of loyalty was itself the way to the protection, appreciation, and blessing of God, and hence to health, long life, sons, wealth, and honor among one's fellows—the gifts that only God could and did bestow.

Decay

For three millennia, this religion and ethic remained the same, despite the succession of empires and states. All subscribed to the same principles and recognized the same realities. The names of the Supreme Deity changed from Enlil to Marduk and Ashur, and those of the lesser deities were exchanged among themselves as their functions passed from one god to another, as fortune passed military, political, and economic favors from one group to another. The transfer of power may have been accompanied with some violence against the ruling dynasty or the people at large, though more often the former than the latter. But no transfer of political power was ever accompanied with violence to the reigning ideology. The language suffered some idiomatic and grammatical changes, for the political change was an index of the ascendancy of another group of people. The literary genres and forms, however, remained the same. Some of the *dramatis personae* of the myths changed, but the myths themselves continued undisturbed. From the early settlement of emigrants from Arabia and the rise of the Sumerian city-states around and before the end of the fourth millennium, the Fertile Crescent experienced the political ascendancy of Ur, Larsa, Isin, Mari, Assyria, and Babylon; of Akkadians, Amorites, Canaanites, and Aramaeans. From the sixteenth century B.C.E. it had fallen in whole or in part under the invasion and extensive occupation of armies of "nonSemitic" foreigners who never belonged to the Near Eastern family. These were the Hittites, the Kassites, and the Hurrians, coming from the lands adjoining Mesopotamia to the northwest, the northeast, and the north respectively; and the Philistines coming from the sea in the twelfth century. Some of these were speakers of Indo-European languages mixed with the native inhabitants of the lands to which they had migrated. They came with a radically different language, social and personal ethic, and mythology and world view and with different aesthetic expressions in the visual arts. And yet, after a generation or two, the invaders assumed the language, religion, art, and world view of the Near Easterners, forgot their origins, and became almost totally acculturated. The Hittites, Kassites, and Hurrians brought with them the horse and chariot and a social structure in which a noble class dominated the masses and a king was only one among his peers. Following their conquest, they divided the land into fiefs and bound these by treaty to the central power. Their acculturation, like that of the Mongols of the thirteenth century C.E., destroyed the difference between conqueror and vanquished. As one scholar has put it, "Like Rome in the Middle Ages, despite its political decadence, Mesopotamia in the age of the peoples of the mountains celebrates the triumph of its culture."[13]

Mesopotamia won the battle of religion, language, ethos, and culture against the "peoples of the mountains," even as it succumbed to them militarily. But the battle did not leave Mesopotamia without a scar. Indeed, something happened in the process that launched the land on its course to political and economic disaster. What the nature of the event was and how it produced the cultural change we do not as yet know. What is certain is that shortly after the period of ascendancy of these alien Indo-Europeans, Mesopotamia began to show signs of decay.

Whereas one may characterize the early period (3,000 years) as one in which men understood clearly what they wanted and knew what they should expect, this period began to witness a dislocation of standards, a clouding of ethical vision. The moral categories on which the life of the state stood and around which, consequently, the life of the individual revolved broke down. Man was supposed to make civilization and history in service to the deity. The meaning of his whole life derived from this link. His personal self-realization and satisfaction was itself the realization of the social goal of state and civilization. Now he began to differentiate between the two and ask that his personal life justify itself in itself. Thus the old legend of Gilgamesh[14] reinterpreted man's life as tragedy, as one full of self-

[13] Sabatino Moscati, *Face of the Ancient Orient* (Garden City, N.Y.: Doubleday, 1962), p. 64.

[14] Pritchard, pp. 72–93.

exertion without reward, of planning without future, of the frustration of all major hopes. In despair, it even counseled immersion in hedonistic pursuits. The whole base of Mesopotamian civilization centered around the notion that man was created mortal to serve the immortal gods for a brief span. Now he began to seek immortality for himself because he found no more satisfaction in his destiny as mortal servant. Self-centeredness came to replace his old centeredness around God, the cosmic state, and civilization.

The legend of Ludlul bel Nemeqi,[15] often referred to as "The Righteous Sufferer" or the Mesopotamian "Job," focused all attention on the personalist problem of the imbalance of virtue and happiness. This imbalance is an undeniable fact of all existence at all times. But under the old view, man's commitment to the service of God and the cosmic state overruled any consciousness of it, any preoccupation with its daily inequities. With that self-absorption in God's service shaken, every facet of the imbalance became fascinating and horrifying. Although the legend counseled man, in conclusion, to refrain from questioning God's justice and trust to His judgment, it hit its mark by reflecting the growing obsession with personal happiness. And when, as history always proved, this new ideal turned as elusive as immortality, the life bent upon its pursuit foundered and collapsed. The result was a thoroughgoing skepticism regarding all claims, a morbid cynicism toward all values. The "Pessimistic Dialogue Between Master and Servant" and the "Dialogue About Human Misery"[16] are expressive of this state of affairs, the last before actual collapse. In these poems, every ethical value is questioned and nothing is certain. The heart that beats with "the surge of the sea rushing forth" and contains a "spring of water which gathers all wisdom" is now empty. It has "rejected the truth, . . . despised the decree of the god," and roams aimlessly over the land.

[15] Ibid., pp. 434–437.
[16] Ibid., pp. 437–440.

Is it possible that this decay could have had its inception in the arrival of the Kassites, Hurrites, and Hittites on the scene? One cannot say for certain. It is a fact, though, that these peoples knew no dualism of being, no transcendent God, no subjection of man and creation to the will of a divine Beyond. They were earthbound and their gods earth-absorbed. Is it possible that while suffering Mesopotamianization, they injected their naturalism, their worldism, their personalism into Mesopotamia's soul? Despite these changes, however, the people and their languages continued to live. And they did until a resurgence by their descendants reasserted the old culture in new form.

Bibliography

DHORME, EDOUARD. *Les Religions de Babylonie et d'Assyrie.* Paris: Presses Universitaires de France, 1949.

HALLO, WILLIAM W., and J. J. A. VAN DIJK. *The Exaltation of Inanna.* New Haven: Yale U. P., 1968.

HEIDEL, ALEXANDER. *The Gilgamesh Epic and Old Testament Parallels.* Chicago: U. of Chicago, 1963.

———. *The Babylonian Genesis.* Chicago: U. of Chicago, 1967.

KRAMER, SAMUEL NOAH. *History Begins at Sumer.* London: Thames and Hudson, 1961.

———. *Sumerian Mythology.* New York: Harper, 1961.

LANGDON, S. *Babylonian Menologies and the Semitic Calendars.* London: British Academy, 1935.

OPPENHEIM, A. LEO. *Ancient Mesopotamia.* Chicago: U. of Chicago, 1972.

———. *Letters from Mesopotamia.* Chicago: U. of Chicago, 1967.

WOOLLEY, C. LEONARD. *The Sumerians.* New York: Norton, 1965.

———. *Ur of the Chaldees.* New York: Norton, 1965.

2

The Ancient Near East: Egypt

Isma'īl R. al Fārūqī

Genesis and Flowering

Contrast

In Mesopotamia, as we saw in Chapter 1, floods did take place. When they did, they were caused by storms in the northland, the mountain region. As the rains fell, the Tigris and Euphrates rose; the greater and more torrential the storm, the faster and stronger the onrush of the waters downstream. Heavy rain storms came to Mesopotamia in fall, winter, and spring, and they were never predictable. The distance between the highlands and the lowlands was relatively short; the cities were concentrated in the south and were built on the banks of the river. The supporting agriculture depended upon river water for irrigation and could not but keep close to the river banks. In consequence, every great storm brought sudden unpredictable devastation to southern Mesopotamia. The flood was irregular, the destruction immense and inescapable. Nearer the sea, the flood destroyed the dikes that held back the salt water, which then mixed with the fresh and brought utter ruin to every living thing. There was no good whatever in the flood; it brought nothing but destruction. Naturally, the Mesopotamian regarded it as an evil and dreaded it. Its suddenness and unpredictability made it look to him like the arbitrary whimsy of a personal will capable of the greatest anger. His mythopoeic mind represented the storm, the apparent cause of the flood, as Enlil, the almighty god himself, or the executive "prime minister" of a still higher and mightier god.

In reaction to these irrational vagaries of nature, the Mesopotamian turned to man and society. Man can be reasonable, and he can be trusted to cooperate with his fellowmen to make life possible. He can plan ahead and execute his plan. Besides, this human providence was thought to be the only trustworthy agency. Because nature could not be trusted, rational care, or human ordering, had to be the *conditio sine qua non* of existence. The first cause of human life appeared to the Mesopotamian to be in the social order. For only when men disciplined themselves into cooperation with one another under the planning eye of a supreme authority were chaos, untimely death, and destruction stopped and life and happiness made possible. The social order thus became the greatest and most primal fact in his consciousness. On its model and in its terms the Mesopotamian represented nature. Chaos was genuine, primitive nature; it became cosmos when the gods, in primeval assembly, resolved to yield their authority to the one supreme ruler whose first task was to subdue chaos, to assign the destinies, to institute irrigation and agriculture, to bring into being an organic social order—in short, to create civilization. No wonder that this beginning of civilization was seen as itself the beginning of life, of nature, as creation. Order, therefore, did not arise from or in nature; it was put there, imposed upon nature from the outside, from the realm of nonnature, the realm of reason, will, and planning personified as deity. The greatest achievement of the greatest god was the conquest of chaos, of nature. Hence, the Mesopotamians' cosmology was a projection of their sociopolitical order; their religious ethic, an extension of their civility. Intelligence was in the ear, i.e., in the capacity to hear the divine commandment, to cognize the ought-to-do; and felicity was the life of obedience, of fulfillment of the command. This polarity of nature and social order was the hallmark of Mesopotamian religion and civilization.

The exact opposite was the case in ancient Egypt. Instead of the natural being a function of social order, the social order was a function of the natural. The natural order was prior and final; the social was secondary and instrumental. The social derived its pattern as well as its norm from the natural; the natural found its norm in itself, in its own rhythm and inviolate pattern. We may ask: Why did nature possess the Egyptian's attention? What in nature possesses such power and appeal? How did nature come to lay its grip upon his consciousness?

Egypt has simple topography: it consists of a narrow flat bed, through which runs the Nile and at the end of which stands the Delta. The bed is irrigated and hence green. Beyond is highland, where the water does not reach; it is arid and desert. Beyond this immediate boundary is an uninhabitable land of death and darkness. The Nile is the central fact of Egypt, for the whole country is no more than a very long narrow strip of land made green by its proximity to the Nile water. If the land has any rhythm, temper, style, or momentum, it derives it from that of the Nile. For without the river, in the total absence of rain, the desert is be-all and end-all, and Egypt would be a continuation of the Sahara.

The dominant feature of all Egyptian agriculture is the annual river flood. Late summer is the season when the rains in highland Ethiopia and East Africa, having percolated through the soil and down the valleys, reach Egypt in a steadily rising surge. In August, the surge swells into a mighty stream that covers the whole of cultivable Egypt and transforms its villages into islands. It is destructive in its fury; animals run wild, houses are demolished, man's things are carried away, fruit trees are uprooted and washed away, and threats to man's life and his children abound. Indeed, as in Mesopotamia, the flood is chaos. It is a realm in which life, agriculture, and civilization are impossible.

And yet, the flooding of the Nile is regular. It happens once a year and always at the same season. Certainly the level of the flood varies and is rarely the same, but there is no year that does not have its flood. A low-level flood would be the exception, not the rule. Moreover, the flood never comes suddenly, because it is not the result of a sudden torrential rainstorm. The signs of any flood crest, whether small or devastatingly high, are always noticeable, and they were measured on the Nile water gauge. The Nile flood has never taken the Egyptians by surprise.

Still more important is the fact that because of the flatness of the land, the Nile flood is shallow, and its course, although powerful, is relatively slow. During the flood, the water is red with silt, which it gathers in the highlands and deposits on the flooded lands downstream. This alluvial silt fertilizes the land, as the flood soaks it with moisture. As soon as the flood waters recede, the land is ready for cultivation. Indeed, what was once desert has become so fertile with these annual deposits that vegetation starts sputtering out of the earth before the flood water disappears. The flood is then a source of some destruction, but more a source of life.

There is another fact central to Egyptian life: the sun. By itself, the sun is destructive in its fiery reach. It burns up and destroys every living thing. In the desert that is Egypt, the sun does indeed burn, and the hot, dusty air of the desert suffocates. And yet the advent of this heavenly destroyer is regular and predictable. Like the flood, one knows what to expect of it. During the summer, the sun blasts and comes near to destroying Egypt, and yet no sooner have the flood waters receded than it becomes the efficient cause of all vegetation growth. It is the land exposed to the sun that first bursts with green sheaths of grass. The annual flood and the daily rising and setting of the sun together constitute the fulcrum of existence. Through this fact the Egyptian saw the world as well as himself.

Cosmogony

Before God emerged as the regularly flooding Nile and the daily rising and setting sun, the world was chaos. *Nun,* or chaos, is the flood waters raging everywhere and the darkness enveloping all. It is full of danger and death. It is the whole world except the part ordered by the Nile and the sun. Indeed the Nile issues from Nun, the underworld water springing from the caverns, and ends in Nun, the ocean that surrounds the earth. Nun is not only the Mediterranean but, equally, the impassable marshland on both sides of the Delta and the lowland regions on both sides of the river where the flood waters never disappear. The sun also issues from Nun when it rises in the morning. Nocturnally, it returns to cross the realm of darkness, namely Nun. Death and resurrection, daily for the sun and annually for the earth—that is the eternal pattern of being and life! That is *cosmos* emerged out of *chaos!*

Two theories explaining this emergence presented themselves to the Egyptian mind: creation through generation (a theory associated with Heliopolis) and creation through thought and speech (associated with Memphis). The generation theory conceived of Chaos as consisting of four couples, Nun-Naunet, Hu-Hauhet, Kuk-Kauket, and Amun-Amaunet, representing respectively the primordial waters, primordial formlessness, darkness, and hiddenness, qualities that properly belong to chaos. Atum emerged from Chaos on a hill where vegetation is first to spring after the flood. Upon his emergence, Atum created one pair of gods: Shu-Tefnut (air-moisture), which in turn generated the divine pair of Geb-Nut (earth-sky). In turn, Geb-Nut generated two other divine pairs, Osiris-Isis and Seth-Nephtys, which brought about all the creatures as well as the orders (i.e., the levels or strata of being and the laws or patterns that govern existence on each level). The political, moral, and spiritual orders of men were equally the creation of the gods. This was the first ennead in theology. The generation in question is implied in the case of Atum, for nothing explicit can be said of chaos, *ex hypothesi.* Atum, however, as in a sneeze, spat Shu and sputtered Tefnut, who then began the process of male-female reproduction. The second theory equates Nun with Ptah and gives him priority as the creator of Atum and all the gods. The first god who emerged from the primeval hillock was Ptah, whose city was Memphis. The process by which Ptah created the whole ennead of gods was thinking (*sia,* or perception) and commanding what was thought to be (*hu,* or authoritative utterance). This is the first logos doctrine. Both theories are found crystallized around 3000 B.C.E.

What is breathtakingly creative in this system is, *first,* the realization that there are no two orders of reality, no duality of being, but one and the same order, one and the same reality. Being is a continuum: out of primordial chaos—which is neither conquered nor annihilated, for it continues under us whence the Nile comes and the sun rises, and around us whither the Nile ends, the sun sets, and where desert or marsh begins and extends *ad infinitum*—emerge the gods and from these men, plants, animals, and things. There is no ontological gap either at the beginning (for cosmos is only separated from chaos as night is separated from day, and each continues in his proper realm), nor between gods and men, for the gods are themselves the real Nile, the real sun, the real air, the real moisture, the real earth, the real sky, the real sheath of green grass springing on the primeval hillock. The world is "monophysite," as John Wilson has aptly said. It has one nature.

We must at this point qualify a statement we made previously, that is, that the Egyptian view is the exact opposite of the Mesopotamian. The exact opposite of the Egyptian view of reality is in fact the Upanishadic Hindu view (see Chapter 9). There, being or reality is also one. Both views are "monophysite." Reality, in the Hindu view, belongs solely to Brahman in that "everything is Brahman," *ta twam asi.* Trees, rivers, mountains, and men have no reality other than the spiritual, which is Brahman, their individuated, concrete existence in space-time being a necessary accident, an unreal *maya.* But whereas in Hindu thought the one reality is spiritual and divine in substance and "natural" or concrete only in unreal appearance, in Egypt the one reality is concrete and natural in substance and "divine" only in perception, i.e., when seen with the eye of reason or by the intuiting heart, in the religious sense. In India, substance as a prime metaphysical category belongs to the spiritual or divine, to Brahman. Everything else is accidental or derivative. In Egypt, it belongs to concrete nature in space-time, and everything else is accidental or derivative. The Mesopotamian view stands between these two poles in that it rejects monophysitism. Granting being and reality to the two realms of the transcendent and the empirical, the divine and the natural, it regards them both as being, as real, and as utterly disparate, the one as the *creator ex nihilo* of the other.

Second, the Egyptian system is creative in its conception of the human order in the manner and likeness of the natural, which is the necessary consequences of the monophysite nature and unity of all being. At some prehistoric time, the Nile Delta, or Lower Egypt, and Upper Egypt were two separate societies, the lower a vast marshland jungle and the upper a narrow river bed flanked by a narrow strip of the same jungle. To have large-scale agriculture, not only did the jungle have to be cleared and the marshland drained, but irrigation canals had to be cut into the dry land. Once this was done, such a system called for maintenance, which in turn required a strong, closely knit social organization, capable of long-term planning and execution with foresight. Eventually the two portions were united under one ruler, and large-scale agriculture, strong centralized government or planning, and maintenance of authority became possible. In the Egyptian mind, civilization, the political and social order, and creation were all one and coalesced. Hence the social order became identified with the natural, though we may continue to speak of two orders, bearing in mind that the natural is prior and ultimate.

2-1 Façade of the Temple of Ramses II (1299–1232 B.C.E.) at Abū Simbel. The temple is dedicated to Ramses II as Pharaoh-god in addition to the chief Egyptian gods Re-Harakhti, Ptah, and Amun. These four seated colossi hewn from the virgin rock are statues of Ramses himself. (Courtesy of UNESCO/Laurenza.)

The Cosmic State

If we may call Mesopotamia *transcendentalist,* i.e., holding to an utterly other, *a priori, sui generis* nature of God, we may not call the Egyptian view *immanentist.* For it does not hold that God, the one reality, is ontologically or perceptually present in the other but rather that it *is* the other. Hence, the gods of Egypt have no need for any hierophanous vehicles. The river Nile is not unto the God Nile as the reed is unto Innanna. The river with its water, mud, bed, and banks is itself all there is to the god "Nile"; the sun is not an appearance of Atum, a representative, symbol, individuation, or objectification of Atum, but the very Atum himself in all his glory. Likewise, the blade of green grass is itself Osiris, Atum, and Ptah. One of his viziers, Rekhmire, defined Pharaoh as "a god by whose dealings one lives, the father and the mother of all men."[1] He is god, *en chair et en os;* indeed, he is all there is to god. Obviously, he is that by which everything lives. He is not only the gods and goddesses who represent the functions of kingship but also those of the natural order. Thus, he is the Nile, the sun, the plant, the animal, the air, the moisture, and the source of all their energy, activity, movement, death, and resurrection. What he does as man, he does as god and *vice versa.* Though Pharaoh or god is absolute wisdom, he does occasionally act in jest or pettiness. For he is equally man and there is no line anywhere dividing the two.

Pharaoh was always "King of Upper and Lower Egypt," (Map 4) for the united kingdom came to be with creation. He administered the land through officers, levied taxes, and ordered the execution of vast public work projects. Of no ruler was Louis XIV's famous statement *"L'état c'est moi"* truer than of Pharaoh. Not only the whole of social, economic, political, and military activity was his initiative and jurisdiction, but also the geophysical, demographic, botanical, zoological, meteorological, and astronomical. For a government officer to be instructed to perform a function was no more and no less than a tree being caused to grow or bear fruit, for the Nile itself to rise. Pharaoh had only to command—and what he commanded would come to be. Our minds have been railroaded into the perspective of the Biblical redactors, where Pharaoh is regarded as a tyrant enslaving the Hebrews as well as his own people. The truth is that the Egyptians never saw the Phar-

[1]Henri Frankfort, *Ancient Egyptian Religion* (New York: Harper, Torchbooks, 1961), p. 43.

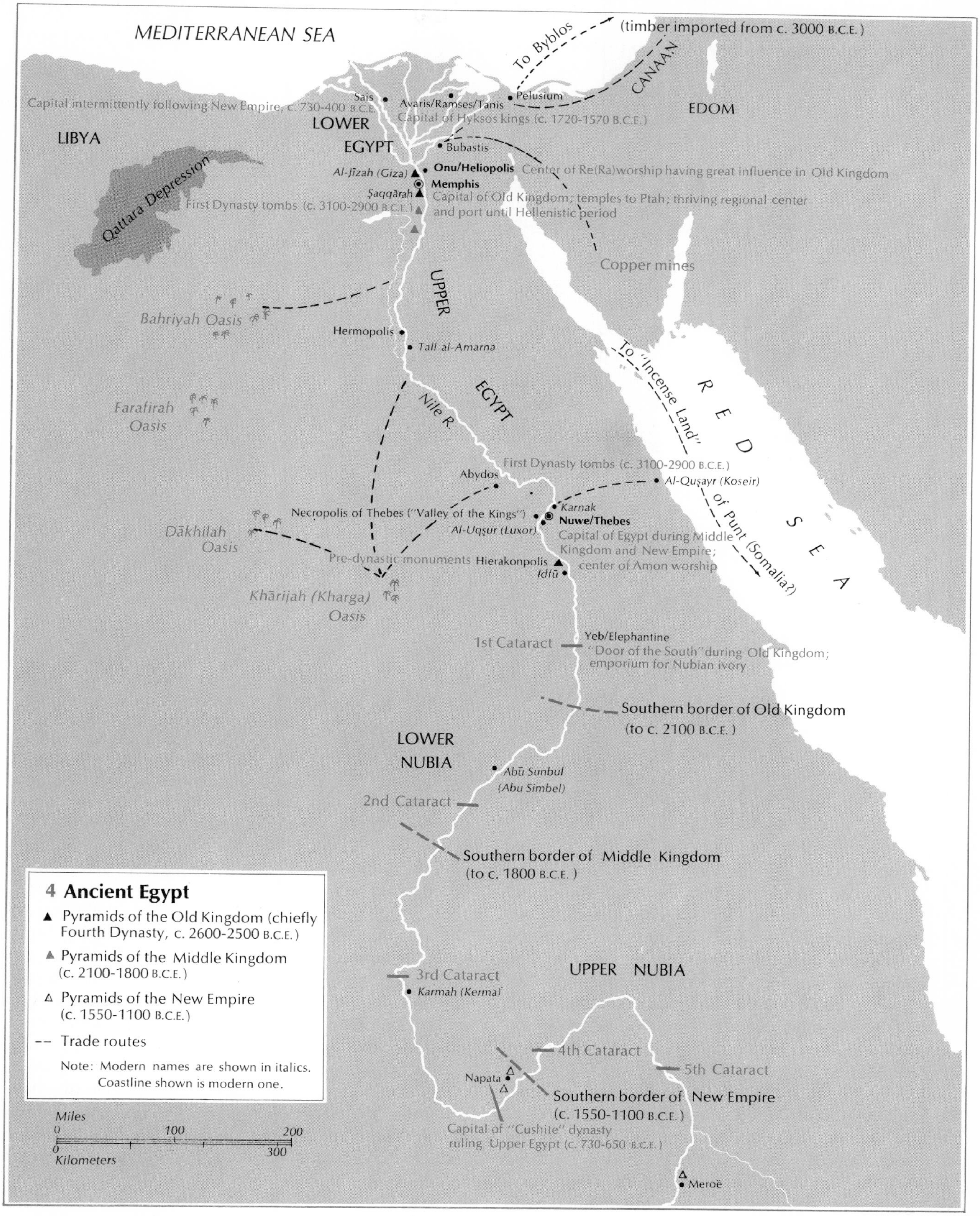

MEDITERRANEAN SEA
To Byblos
(timber imported from c. 3000 B.C.E.)
CANAAN
EDOM
Sais
Avaris/Ramses/Tanis
Pelusium
Capital intermittently following New Empire, c. 730-400 B.C.E.
Capital of Hyksos kings (c. 1720-1570 B.C.E.)
LOWER EGYPT
LIBYA
Bubastis
Qattara Depression
Al-Jīzah (Giza)
Onu/Heliopolis
Center of Re(Ra)worship having great influence in Old Kingdom
Memphis
Ṣaqqārah
Capital of Old Kingdom; temples to Ptah; thriving regional center and port until Hellenistic period
First Dynasty tombs (c. 3100-2900 B.C.E.)
Copper mines
UPPER EGYPT
Bahriyah Oasis
Hermopolis
Tall al-Amarna
To "Incense Land"
RED SEA
Nile R.
Farafirah Oasis
First Dynasty tombs (c. 3100-2900 B.C.E.)
Abydos
Al-Quṣayr (Koseir)
of Punt (Somalia?)
Karnak
Necropolis of Thebes ("Valley of the Kings")
Nuwe/Thebes
Al-Uqṣur (Luxor)
Dākhilah Oasis
Capital of Egypt during Middle Kingdom and New Empire; center of Amon worship
Pre-dynastic monuments
Hierakonpolis
Idfū
Khārijah (Kharga) Oasis
1st Cataract
Yeb/Elephantine
"Door of the South" during Old Kingdom; emporium for Nubian ivory
Southern border of Old Kingdom (to c. 2100 B.C.E.)
LOWER NUBIA
Abū Sunbul (Abu Simbel)
2nd Cataract
Southern border of Middle Kingdom (to c. 1800 B.C.E.)
4 Ancient Egypt
▲ Pyramids of the Old Kingdom (chiefly Fourth Dynasty, c. 2600-2500 B.C.E.)
▲ Pyramids of the Middle Kingdom (c. 2100-1800 B.C.E.)
△ Pyramids of the New Empire (c. 1550-1100 B.C.E.)
-- Trade routes
Note: Modern names are shown in italics. Coastline shown is modern one.
3rd Cataract
Karmah (Kerma)
UPPER NUBIA
4th Cataract
5th Cataract
Napata
Southern border of New Empire (c. 1550-1100 B.C.E.)
Capital of "Cushite" dynasty ruling Upper Egypt (c. 730-650 B.C.E.)
Miles
0
100
200
0
300
Kilometers
Meroë

2-2 Closeup of two of the colossal statues of Ramses II (Nineteenth Dynasty) to whom the rock temple at Abu Simbel is dedicated. At far lower left, incised symbols of the Sun, the river Nile, and the jackal-headed mortuary god Anubis can be seen. (Courtesy of UNESCO/United Nations.)

aoh as a tyrant. He was God, to whom all things belonged. When he commanded something to be done, the Egyptian happily complied, because to execute the divine command was for him an act of worship. The tremendous public works—the pyramids, the highways, the boats, the canals, the transportation of stone from distant quarries—all these were executed by *corvées* assembled *ad hoc* from among the villagers. A document from the Middle Kingdom (2050–1800 B.C.E.) describes how groups of one thousand, fifteen hundred, and two thousand men transported from the Red Sea eighty blocks of stone on rollers "without a single man getting exhausted, without a man thirsting on the way, without a moment of ill will. On the contrary, the whole army came home in good spirits, sated with bread, drunk with beer, as if it were the beautiful festival of a god."[2] Surely! For in their hard toil they were worshiping, and by accomplishing the project they were helping nature itself do what must necessarily be done. Three thousand years of continuous history witnessed no rebellion—a fact possible only under the assumption that the authority of the king was divine. For where one's stand is that of faith, rebellion against it is ruled out by definition.

Furthermore, an officer or judge of the state could be mistaken or unjust, but never Pharaoh, or the state. Actually, the name *Pharaoh* is the anglicized Hebrew rendering of the Egyptian *per-aa*, "the Great House," which stood for the king as divine presence. Pharaoh

[2] Ibid., p. 38.

ruled with *Maat* ("justice"), which replaced chaos in the act of creation of this world. *Maat* was hence inseparable from it, for it was the law by which the cosmos runs and nature conducts itself. Thus, the ethicopolitical notion of justice coalesced with that of natural law. Both were equally necessary, absolute, and universal. Nevertheless, obedience to Pharaoh or his officers was not a passive affair. Men did not resign themselves to their fates as to an inscrutable and inevitable decree. Where they felt injustice or error, they spoke out demanding that virtue be rewarded with happiness. For that was the law of nature, not the happenstance pronouncement of an overhasty officer.

In addition to *Maat,* the King ruled with love and compassion for his subjects. He was their shepherd, protector, and benefactor, "master of graciousness, rich in sweetness, and he conquers by love. His city loves him more than its own self . . . the herdsman of every one, without evil in his heart."[3] Some of his "natural" functions were also effects of his beneficence, such as the high level of the Nile and the abundance of fertilizing silt, of food and animals. Not by accident did the Egyptians use the shepherd's crook to signify their king. To him belonged both authority and power, as well as love and magnanimity. He was always equipped with the requisites of both: knowledge and self-effacement. "*Hu* (authoritative utterance) is indeed that which is in thy mouth, and perception is in thy heart."[4] The Pharaoh was omniscient. Nothing escaped him, whether past, present, or future, for he knew the laws of the cosmos. His personal identity was nothing, for the king was always willing to dissolve himself and all personal grandeur into the archetypal ideal of kingship—God. Thus, Egyptian archaeology hardly knows of any self-asserting Pharaoh. All Pharaohs, more or less, look alike, and the sculptors never sought to represent a person but always Pharaoh-ness, in other words, God. Even Queen Hatshepsut had herself represented in the usual style as male, complete with rolled beard and broad shoulders.

Anthropogony

There is no answer to the question, Why was man created? The same question, if asked concerning man, would have to be raised concerning nature as well as the gods themselves. Likewise with the question of when man was created. If asked, the Egyptian would surely have answered, with surprise at the question, that man has always existed, along with the gods with whom he constitutes one and the same continuum of reality. To the Egyptian, man is; and this reality was sufficient, as sufficient as it was in the case of trees, mountains, sky, and the gods. Indeed, the degree of otherness, of numinousness, of divinity normally predicated of men was even less than that belonging to the animals. Archaeologists have found so many mummified cats, dogs, birds, and even crocodiles that Frankfort "with painful embarrassment . . . [admits this is] polytheism with a vengeance."[5] Actually, it is not polytheism at all, but the very opposite. It is not monotheism, to be sure, for this is an idea that presupposes duality of being, as it asserts the unity of the membership of one of the two classes into which reality is divided. It is instead monophysitism, which is the view that one and only one substance exists in which all beings partake. Animals in this view are no less divine than men. Neither is it a leftover trait of earlier primitivism such as in traditional African religions. For Egyptians made no claim of descent from an animal as from a totem, none was ever the object of sacrifice or the ceremonial meal, and in most cases the religious significance of one or another species was universal. Nor did the Egyptian revere an animal for a peculiar quality of the species, such as strength. They perceived that animals as such conformed with the commands of nature with ease, immediacy, and innocence; they never seemed to err in knowing or fulfilling the purposes of nature; and whatever the impediments or obstructions in their way to fulfillment, they never failed to surmount them. Evidently then, they stood closer to the one pervasive reality of all beings than men, or had superior or more direct means of contact. Their animality or naturalness, contrasted with man's freedom of action and liability to error, gave them an edge over man. Their use in sculpture and painting or in masks used in cultic observances was meant to convey the presence of divinity normally present in those animals.

As for the gods, men were regarded as being of the same nature though, admittedly, with a lesser degree of divinity than either the gods or the animals. The monophysite nature of all reality precluded any differentiation of kind between one member in the continuum and any other. It was not, however, opposed to differentiation by degree. Thus, there are theogony stories but no creation stories whether of men, animals, or plants. Khnum, the rain-god, is mentioned once as the creator of men on a potter's wheel. But this is more a descrip-

[3] Henri Frankfort (ed.), *Before Philosophy: The Intellectual Adventure of Ancient Man* (Baltimore: Penguin, 1967), pp. 80, 88.

[4] Ibid., p. 93.

[5] Frankfort, *Ancient Egyptian Religion,* pp. 9–10.

2-3 First Gateway, Karnak, in the complex of temples at Karnak. This site was hallowed ground as early as the Third Dynasty (third millennium B.C.E.). (Courtesy of the American Museum of Natural History.)

tion of Khnum than an anthropogonic account. The creation of gods is important because it is the beginning of reality. Its accounts purport to tell us that, whether by fertilization and reproduction, or noetic conception and verbal commandment, reality created itself, that it is and will eternally continue to be. Man is an integral part of this reality. His existence needs no further explanation or justification than the existence of reality itself as a whole. Like any other constituent of reality, men partake of that one substance, and this consubstantiality with other beings endows men with the same capabilities. Differences are all matters of degree and they can be surmounted by magic. One of the Pyramid texts tells that by proper magic man can contend and threaten—nay, "devour"—the gods.[6] Surely, no more evidence of monophysitism may be required. In Mesopotamia, the very idea of "one nature" would be the height of arrogance—blasphemy.

[6] *Before Philosophy*, p. 77.

The Meaning of Life

Reality is. Man is. For the Egyptian, these two propositions are true as well as convertible. Their assertion needs no justification. If any law is to be laid for them, it would have to come from within. Because there is no *ratio essendi* to a man's life outside of that life itself, it cannot have for purpose anything but the discharge of its own latent energies and properties. This view is not far from the "ethics of being" propounded by the Scholastic philosophers, in which a norm was normative because it signified "more" or "higher" being than its opposite, nor from the ethics of the naturalists throughout the ages. The difference is that the Egyptians were far more consistent and throughgoing in their naturalism.

In Mesopotamia, the norms were in the mind of God, in His will, which we have found to be known mediately through portents and dreams or immediately through revelation of the law. The ought-to-be was radically different from the actual, and morality consisted in transforming the latter into the likeness of the former. Whether it was the land, the human person, or society, all had to suffer transformation and disciplining so as to fulfil the divine will, which was definitely not of this world. Indeed, it was there claimed that man's greatness consisted precisely in being the cosmic bridge, the instrument of actualization of a divine will that is not yet actualized. In Egypt, the so-called "divine will" is already actualized *in toto* throughout reality; indeed, it is the law of nature. What is required of man is not to violate it, to correspond and harmonize with the eternal laws. It is wrong to describe Mesopotamian ethics as dynamic and Egyptian ethics as static, for the amount of change man brings about in the actual world depends upon his culture's moral vision rather than on the metaphysical groundwork on which the vision is based. In fact, Mesopotamia transformed nature no more than did Egypt. But whereas the former justified its action as fulfillment of an ought that is not actual, the latter did so in correspondence and harmony with an ought that is already there in actual reality. Any ought coming from the one would differ from that of the other in its *ratio cognoscendi:* The Mesopotamian could be known through revelation; the Egyptian through inspection. It was this feature of the ought that made the content of morality in Mesopotamia a matter of disclosure or revelation and in Egypt a matter of study and analysis.

2-4 Granite statue of the lion-headed goddess of war, Sakhmet. (Courtesy of the Metropolitan Museum of Art, Theodore M. Davis Collection; bequest of Theodore M. Davis, 1915.)

Thus Egypt produced the first book of ethics. Moral counsel as such is as old as man, but that the content of morality is a fact to be sought in nature, a fact teachable precisely because it is actual in nature, was new. Late Upanishadic speculation and Socrates were the earliest after Egypt to hold that virtue is, in an epistemic sense, teachable. Ethical treatises were written by many in Egypt, by officers of the government and by elders whose long lives and experience entitled them to address their progeny or others with their "wisdom." Known as "The Teachings," the ethical treatises offer guidance on all matters, from the gravest to the least detail of good manners. They do not present themselves as advice but as signals or warnings on the road of life, that *Maat,* or justice, being what it is, this action is virtuous and will be rewarded with prosperity and happiness; that is evil and will be punished. Without the deeply religious overtone, the teachings are liable to be misunderstood as pragmatic counsels. Nothing could be farther from the truth. They were given as statements of the laws of reality and nature, indications of how the gods will operate the world, for they are the rulers, the judges, the guardians, and the whole realm of divinity itself in the person of Pharaoh, a living being, who does in fact command.

The literary as well as the artistic evidence point to an ethic of life affirmation. A great *joie de vivre* pervaded the life of the ancient Egyptian. His obligation was to live life to the full, to participate in the life of society, to execute Pharaoh's command and build up Egypt in the process, serenely to enjoy his own attunement to the cosmos around himself. Reality or life being a river, to flow with it at its pace is to attain felicity. The good life is the life of attunement. However hard it may be, the decree of Pharaoh or of his officer or judge is natural law. Morality demands compliance with it, but so does happiness. On the other hand, the pleasures of a well-provided home; of healthy, loyal children; of the hunt; of the activities of ploughing, irrigating, and harvesting; of learning; of recreation; and of a contented old age—all are man's to enjoy in pure innocence.

The virtuous and hence happy person was called the "silent man"; the vicious and hence unhappy, the "passionate man." The former is disciplined and patient; he is always calm and has a cool presence of mind; he is modest and never loses his temper; upright in his duties and conscientious about his fellows, he enjoys an established equilibrium and poise. The "passionate man" on the other hand is quarrelsome, irritable, angry, self-centered, and greedy: "He is like a tree growing in the open. Suddenly, comes its loss of foliage and its end is reached in the shipyards."[7] These definitions do not point to meekness but to a middle way between aggressiveness and resignation. "He who reckons all day," wrote Ptahhotep, "has never a happy moment; he who feasts all day cannot keep his family. One reaches one's goal according to one's steering; while (in turn) one steering oar is released and the other grasped."[8] In every case, life would be a happy affair, for there is no built-in contradiction, no necessary evil. If man is deaf to the experience and wisdom of his parents, elders and superiors, then it is his passion that is to blame. Passion cuts down self-restraint and destroys vision and insight; only then is tragedy not far behind.

Egyptian life knew no distinction of the religious from the secular. Religious duties or ceremonies were secular ones, as the service of Pharaoh was worship. The Egyptian found his devotion and piety in the actual business of living, of ruling or obeying. The temples were places of habitation for the gods and one went into them as if to communicate with a public official. Even the Egyptian's grave and cemetery were places where he continued to lead his blessed life, as we shall see.

[7]Frankfort, *Ancient Egyptian Religion,* p. 66.
[8]Ibid., p. 68.

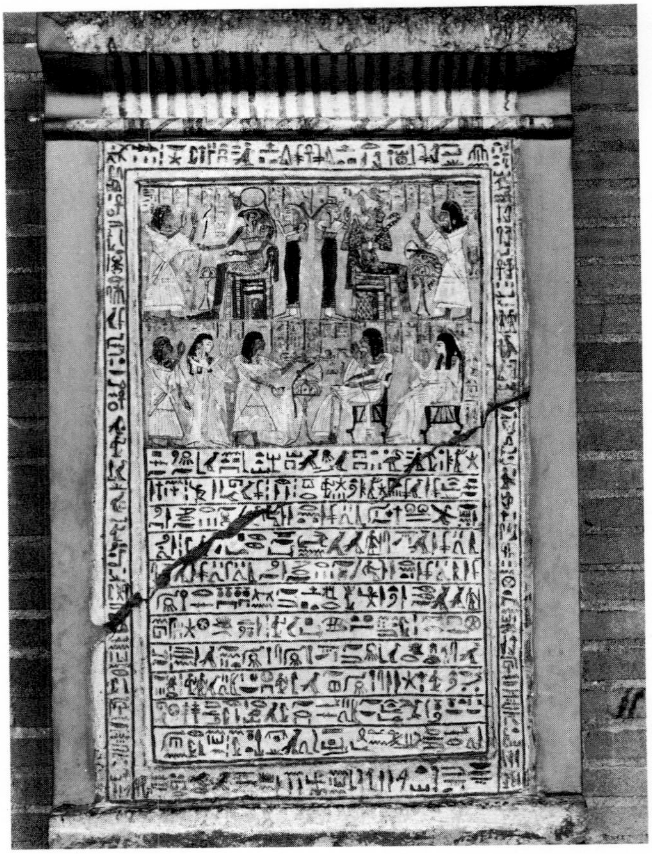

2-5 Stela from tomb of high official, Twentieth Dynasty, sandstone. The upper panel of sunken relief shows the entombed man worshipping Osiris and Isis (right) and the falcon-headed sun god Re-Harakhte and his companion Ma'at (left). The lower panel shows the entombed man and his wife (right) approached by three relatives. The main inscription begins with a hymn to the sun god, while the encircling inscriptions contain prayers for the deceased. (Courtesy of the University Museum, University of Pennsylvania.)

The Hope of Afterlife

The essence of religious experience in Egypt is the realization that this reality is the only one there is, that it is all one and the same, that it is ultimate, the source of all authority, of all truth and value. Once this monophysitism is grasped, it is easy to understand why the Egyptians regarded death not as an end of life but merely as a slight interruption, a shift in gears of operation, as it were. Life, like reality, is eternal. The death of the person is an occasion for transfer from one routine of actuality to another, not an exit from the cosmic flow. Theoretically, there is and can be no exit from that flow, but it is possible to join the eternal flow either as a sentient, wholesome individual or to be devoured by animals in the flow and thus lose one's individuality.

The animals are permanent and no death of a member of a species ever affects that permanence. The same is true of Pharaoh and Egypt as a whole. When one Pharaoh dies, Horus takes over. But Horus is himself the new king who is crowned in place of the departed. The departed linger on in the emotions and dreams of their survivors. All these realities convinced the Egyptians that death cannot be the end. If one were to "survive" death and join the cosmic flow, he would do so under one of three categories. He might join in the procession of Atum, the sun, and flow with the cosmos as Atum's procession circles the earth to rise out of Nun on every morning. Or he might join the chthonic Osiris and rise with him every spring as he rises in every vegetation and is crowned and recrowned in every Pharaoh. Or, finally, he might join the eternally immobile and restful circumpolar star, gazing at the cosmic flow without participation in any movement internal to it. The last alternative was regarded by Egyptians as the worthiest and most blessed. And yet, the person would join these divine dependencies only in one aspect of afterlife. In another, he continued to reside in his grave, if he was given one by his people. Consequently, the grave should be as beautiful and as fully equipped with the amenities of living as a real home. Moreover, where the real equipment could not for any reason be secured within the grave, the mythopoeic mind accepted a picture of it as a substitute. Hence, Egyptian graves were full of either real objects, animals, and foods or of pictures of them. Pharaoh's tomb had pictures of representative groups of his courtiers, officers, armies, workers, and farmers.

The body of the dead is the substrate of his afterlife. If it were destroyed, all future hope would be lost or

2-6 Fragment of a papyrus scroll from the beginning of the New Kingdom. The papyrus contains magic formulae for the use of the deceased in the hereafter and is adorned with painted scenes of the deceased in adoration of various deities. The text is taken from the "Book of the Dead," which from the beginning of the New Kingdom was considered as necessary funerary equipment. (Courtesy of the University Museum, University of Pennsylvania.)

jeopardized. Hence it was necessary that the body be mummified and preserved. This requirement led to the development of a most advanced science of embalmment and grave architecture. The process of mummification is, when properly administered, a religious sacrament (*Sakh*) whose effect is transfiguration of the deceased into an *akh,* or spirit. It is as *akh* that the person joins Atum, Osiris, or the North Star. His *Ka,* or vital force during his life, is not spent at death. It survives and can leave the grave through a carefully built-in opening transfigured into a bird, baboon, or other animal. The purpose of such sorties is to visit the dear relatives.

If the body, the substrate of all existence, has properly been given its final sacrament and enclosed in its grave, the person's afterlife journey begins. Aided by whatever attendants and equipment he was given in his grave, the deceased travels across the dangerous swamps of the West, the "Field of Rushes," towards the Hall of Judgment where Re, and later Osiris, will count up his deeds, weighing them in the scale against *Maat* ("justice"). Man's deeds, therefore, are crucial if he is to pass the judgment and be awarded his credentials of innocence to join the eternal company of the gods.

The hope of the Egyptian, we may say, was to endure with an eternally flowing cosmos. Such hope was clearly based on the absolute value Egyptians attached to life and to nature, the one and only reality. Not only did they see their kingdom and social order as nature, not only did they see their gods or ultimate reality as nature, but even death—the very antithesis of nature—their genius transfigured and understood as a continuation of nature capable of being as glorious as nature itself was in the life of every human person.

Decay

For three millennia, two of them within the full purview of history, this Egyptian religion's view was the unchallenged base of culture and ethics. The population of the Nile Valley between the Mediterranean Sea and Kerma, on the third cataract of the Nile, adhered to and practiced this religion. Kerma was the southern frontier, where Egypt maintained a large trading post and garrison. Beyond were lands where the Nile ran through a narrow valley and peoples of alien (primitive) religions and cultures with whom the Egyptian could trade but whom he felt he had to keep out of his kingdom. South of the Delta the eastern and western frontiers hugged the Nile, beyond which there was nothing but the impenetrable desert. Near the Delta, Libyans to the west and Asians to the east necessitated the maintenance of garrisons. Within Egypt the population was homogeneous. Despite the fact that they belonged to two different ethnic groups—the "Egyptian" in the north and the black "Abyssinian" in the south—enough intercourse had taken place between them in prehistorical time to produce the homogeneity requisite for union of the two lands. After unification, however, no racial change took place during the period under study. Consequently, Egypt presents us with the unique spectacle of a united land governed by a highly centralized government under one and the same religion, language, and culture for three thousand years.

This record of social stability and endurance of a religion and culture is the longest ever. Certainly it was assisted by the fact that Egypt was almost insulated by sea to the north and deserts on the east and west. The south was open but the people who lived there posed little threat to the mighty, unified Egyptian state. Toward the end of the eighteenth century B.C.E. this insulation broke down before waves of people crossing the Sinai from the Arabian desert and arriving in Egypt in sufficient numbers to overcome resistance and set themselves on the throne of Egypt. These were the Hyksos, a part of a much larger migration from the Arabian desert into the Fertile Crescent as well as from Mesopotamia to other points within the Fertile Crescent. The Hyksos brought the horse and chariot to Egypt as well as new metals and new technologies to extract and to use them. Toward Egyptian religion and culture the Hyksos were generally oblivious if not contemptuous, and they did not intermix with the natives. They were content to extract tribute and even allowed a local dynasty to rule autonomously in the southern regions from its capital, Thebes.

From Thebes the war of liberation began after about a hundred years of Hyksos dominion. Within one or two generations the alien "Asiatics" were driven out of Egypt and the Theban cult of Ammon was reestablished throughout Egypt. The Asiatics, however, continued their pressure even after being driven out, thus necessitating that Egypt give them hot pursuit. The persistence of this frontier pressure finally drove Egypt into entering a stage of wars and expansion on foreign soil. She was thus drawn into the drifting sands of Fertile Crescent politics and founded in the process the Egyptian Empire, which lasted until the Assyrian invasion (1570–663 B.C.E.). Thereafter began a period of great weakness and instability highlighted by a Chaldean invasion in 568 B.C.E., two Persian invasions in 525 and 342, a Greek invasion in 332, and a Roman invasion in 46 B.C.E.

2-7 Stela from a priest's tomb at Abydos in the district of Thinis, Nineteenth Dynasty, limestone. The upper adoration scene shows the tomb owner worshiping before Osiris, the god of the nether world. He is accompanied by his wife and son. Behind Osiris is the god's wife Isis and her son, the falcon-headed god Horus. The god Anubis is represented by the recumbent jackal. The lower half shows the priest and his wife offering a tray of food to his seated parents. On the left are various views of funeral preparations and rites. In the lower right corner the priest's soul is depicted as a bird with human head and hands. (Courtesy of the University Museum, University of Pennsylvania.)

The Hyksos hegemony in Egypt, which lasted 160 years, did not produce significant change in the religion and culture of Egypt. For the most part, the Hyksos kept themselves aloof and did not interfere in cultural affairs, despite the fact that they belonged to a wholly different religious system. But the imperial expansion that followed exposed Egypt to Mesopotamian religion in the provinces of the Fertile Crescent. Mesopotamian religion had by then developed into a variety of sects removed from the early Mesopotamian vision by varying degrees of corruption. A great cultural interchange between all the peoples of the eastern Mediterranean took place while political power was snatched by one giant from another. However, the resultant process of cross-fertilization did not benefit Egypt. Rather, it contributed to its decay by intensifying the erosive influence already at work on Egyptian religion.

The first sign of decline was the rise of petty states within Egypt and the corresponding weakening of the central government during the First Intermediate Period (2200–2050 B.C.E.). Although politically Egypt recovered from this "first illness," as Wilson called it, yet it constituted the first challenge to the identity of Pharaoh's command with natural law, and hence it must have suggested a discrepancy between the divine and natural orders. Two and a half centuries later, the Hyksos brought about great humiliation to Egypt and, undoubtedly, resurrected and intensified whatever doubts the first illness had produced and the Middle Kingdom (2050–1800 B.C.E.) had succeeded in abetting. It was from the Middle Kingdom, however, that evidence comes to us of a growing concern for the realization of justice for all. The previous debacles had injected doubt regarding the identity of the moral and the natural worlds, regarding their mutual convertibility. Because the two worlds are one and the same reality, the successful counteraction by the Theban dynasty might have been expected to bring back the old confidence. In fact, it did, but only at the cost of a shift in the moral consciousness of Egypt. The new emphasis on universal justice meted out by the gods without discrimination as to the relative strength of the citizen was already a compensatory notion, resorted to precisely in order to make up an existing discrepancy between nature, or actuality, and justice. Following A. C. Breasted, Wilson called this a growth in "social conscientiousness," which it undoubtedly would have been if the ideal were modern man's morality. From the standpoint of the self-confident Egyptian of older times, the so-called growth was real decline.

The experience of empire brought with it a commitment to national unity and to maintenance of a frontier that now ran through the northern reaches of the Fertile Crescent. The agents of this nationalism were the priests, for it was in the name of the Theban gods, temples, and priesthood that the call to oust the Asiatics was first made. Now, with one foreign enemy succeeding another, the temple priesthoods called for and obtained greater support from the masses of people for so long subject to xenophobic propaganda. The new rallying pulled away from the center, Pharaoh, and grouped the citizens into various temple-loyalists. The consequent reduction of Pharaoh's power could not but further help erode the essential core of Egyptian faith. Finally, as the temples grew in power, they took over

2-8 Sandstone block showing King Akhenaten (1370–1352 B.C.E.) and his family worshiping the sun disk. (Courtesy of the University Museum, University of Pennsylvania.)

the wealth of the region they dominated, and a fair percentage of the farmers found themselves dispossesed of the means of achieving well-being in this world by their own individual effort. Having moved themselves into the center of economic and political life, the religious notions shifted further in order to maintain that dominion. Hence, the old value of "the silent man," which originally meant the harmonization of personal life with the cosmic flow of nature, now came to mean passivity, submission, and meekness. Man's hopes were pinned on the redress of the imbalance of virtue and happiness in the afterlife, for the afterlife became a refuge, the ultimate refuge, from the unhappiness of this world. The old confidence in oneself that stood at the base of the identification of nature, of actuality, with all being and all reality had slowly slipped and given way to cynicism. This-worldly happiness became the arbitrary gift of whimsical fate, not the working of a necessary law of nature. Evidently, this was the death of the classical Egyptian religion.

Bibliography

Erman, Adolph. *Die Aegyptische Religion.* Berlin: Koeniglichen Museen, 1904.

———. *The Ancient Egyptians: A Sourcebook of Their Writings.* New York: Harper, 1966.

Frankfort, Henri. *Ancient Egyptian Religion.* New York: Harper, Torchbooks, 1961.

Steindorff, George, and Keith C. Seele. *When Egypt Ruled the East.* Chicago: U. of Chicago, 1963.

Van Seters, John. *The Hyksos: A New Investigation.* New Haven: Yale U. P., 1966.

Wilson, John A. *The Culture of Ancient Egypt.* Chicago: U. of Chicago, 1951.

3

The Ancient Near East: Canaan-Phoenicia

Stanley Gevirtz

By Canaanite-Phoenician religion, we mean the religious views and practices of the inhabitants of Syria, Lebanon, Palestine, and Trans-Jordan as evidenced in the coastal cities of Syria and in the inland cities of Palestine in the Bronze Age (*Canaanite:* ca. 2500 B.C.E. to 1200 B.C.E.), in the coastal cities of southern Syria (modern day Lebanon) in the Iron Age (*Phoenician:* ca. 1200 B.C.E. to 300 C.E.), and in the Phoenician colonial settlements in the islands of and the lands adjacent to the Mediterranean Sea (*Punic* and *Neo-Punic:* ca. 750 B.C.E. to 300 C.E.).

The Gods

The particularism that was characteristic of the political structure of Canaan (owing in part to its geographical configuration) was characteristic as well of its religious life. Although the Canaanites appear to have recognized a large pantheon, each of the city-states held its own patron deities in highest veneration.

The Canaanite Period

If the mythological literature from Bronze Age Ugarit (a city on the northern coast of Syria, destroyed ca. 1235 B.C.E.) may be taken as a reliable guide, the recipients of Canaanite worship were, in origin, those forces empowering the natural phenomena that most directly affected the economic life: principally, water and aridity. The chief god of the pantheon, El, has his home "at the source of the two rivers, in the midst of the headwaters of two deeps." El's consort, Asherah, bears the epithet "Mistress Asherah of the Sea." The protagonist, Baal, is frequently characterized as the "Rider of the Clouds" and is thus clearly identified as the lord of rain and storm. The opponents of Baal are Yamm ("Sea"), whose parallel appellation is "Judge River"; Ashtar (ʿṯtr), who appears to be the god of irrigation waters; and Mot ("Aridity," "Death"). Alone among the major deities the significance of Anat, Baal's virgin sister-consort who delights in battle, remains obscure. It is not impossible, however, that her name may mean "Fountain." All other figures in the myth are subsidiary.

Of the two neighboring temples excavated in the city of Ugarit one was dedicated to the worship of Baal, the other to Dagan. In the extant myths the latter is known only as the father of Baal and plays no role whatever.

The Phoenician Period

Inscriptions of the first millennium B.C.E. yield no mythological information, but particularism and abstraction are in evidence.

In Byblos the most frequently cited divinity is the

"Lady (*b'lt*) of Byblos," whose temple in that city may have been founded as early as the middle of the third millennium B.C.E. We read also of the "lord (*b'l*) of Heaven," the "Mighty (Splendid) Lord," and "all (*or* the assembly of) the holy gods of Byblos."

Sidonian inscriptions refer chiefly to "Ashtart, our Lady," but also to "Eshmun, the holy prince," to the "Lord of Sidon," to "Shulmanu," to "Ashtart-name (?)-of-Baal," and to the "holy gods."

Inscriptions from Tyre cite only "my Lady, Ashtart" and the "Lord of Heaven," but in a treaty between the Assyrian conqueror Esarhaddon and the Tyrian ruler Baalu, there are invoked in addition to these two Bethel, Anath-Bethel, the "Lord of Malagê," the "Lord of Saphon," Milqart ("king of the city"), and Eshmun. That Milqart may have enjoyed a dominant position in the pantheon of Tyre is suggested by the tribute presented yearly in his temple by representatives of that city's colony, Carthage.

The Punic Period

In the several thousand votive inscriptions found at Carthage those divinities cited most frequently are the god Baal Ḥammon and the goddess Tanit-face (?)-of-Baal. The latter, whose origin is obscure, assumed a dominant position at Carthage from the fifth century B.C.E. on. Milqart and Eshmun had temples dedicated to their worship there, and still other deities are represented only in onomastica.

The Cult

Cultic Installations

Worship was conducted in enclosed temples and in open-air shrines. The Canaanite-Phoenician temples, frequently tripartite in structure, consisted of an antechamber, an open-air pillared court, and a shrine before which was an altar. The officiant reached the latter and the shrine, set somewhat higher than the rest of the structure, by ascending a short flight of steps. Most conspicuous among the cultic furniture were the altar, the standing stone(s) and a grove(?) or wooden pole. The latter two are held by some authorities to represent male and female aspects of deity respectively. The standing stones (stelae or "sacred pillars"), varying in size from the miniature to the gigantic, are often found grouped together in formation. Among the more impressive groups are those in the Temple of the Obelisks at Byblos, the High Place at Gezer, and the Bronze Age sanctuary at Hazor. Incense stands and burners are also found.

Inside some temples or associated with them have been found figurines cast in bronze, occasionally overlaid with gold leaf. These often depict male and female deities (the males usually in warlike stance) and animals.

Cultic Personnel

The inscriptions refer to priests and priestesses and to votaries of both sexes. A hierarchy is intimated by the appearance of the title "chief of priests" (*rb khnm*) occurring in Bronze Age Ugarit, in Phoenician, and in Punic inscriptions. City-state rulers on occasion performed priestly functions and in the Persian and Hellenistic periods bore priestly as well as royal titles.

The Egyptian tale of Wen-Amon (twelfth century B.C.E.) and the Hebrew scriptures note the existence and activities of Byblian and Tyrian "prophets." These communicated with and attempted to influence the will of deity by the performance of ritual dances, by imploring the god to respond with a sign, and by the ritual act of drawing blood. Evidence for sacred prostitution, for sacred male and female prostitutes, is meager, late, and subject to other interpretation.

Cultic Offering

Central among the cultic acts throughout the long history of Canaanite-Phoenician religion was the presentation of gifts or sacrifices to deity. The purpose of these varied from simple expressions of gratitude, to payment for (or share of) favors received, to hope that the worshiper's request might gain favorable reception. Accompanied by burning incense, sacrifices consisted of libations, meal, bird and animal offerings, and, in the Phoenician-Punic period at least, human beings as well.

In the Bronze age legend of King Keret from Ugarit the hero is instructed by El to sacrifice to Baal a lamb/kid, bread (?), a *msrr*-bird, wine, and honey. In other Ugaritic religious texts large cattle, oxen, and rams are also cited as appropriate sacrificial animals. Prior to offering his sacrifice Keret is advised to undergo ritual ablution, to "wash from hand to elbow, from finger(-tip) to shoulder."

Biblical references and archaeological finds suggest that the sacrificial system in the temples of Phoenicia

3-1 "Altar of burnt offerings" at Megiddo, which may have been in use from c. 2500 B.C.E. to 1800 B.C.E. (Courtesy of the Oriental Institute, The University of Chicago.)

continued essentially unchanged. In the tariffs from Carthage and Marseilles (ca. third century B.C.E.) the designated items of sacrifice include domesticated cattle, wild game, fowl, meal, and milk. Priestly shares were strictly regulated according to the value of the offering and the means of the offerer. Misappropriation was severely condemned (cf. I Sam. 2:12–17) and at Carthage and Marseilles was subject to fine.

Human sacrifice, thus far unattested in the literary and religious texts from the Canaanite period, is known in the Phoenician and Punic periods to have persisted down into the third century C.E. In the course of Alexander's siege of Tyre, for example, human sacrifice, having been abandoned for some centuries, was reinstated in an attempt at appeasing divine anger. And Diodorus relates that during the war with Agathocles, the Carthaginians believed that their god was angry because they had been in the habit of substituting the children of slaves for those of noble family.

Concern for the Dead

Burial

Forms of burial varied through the centuries, but elaborate adornment, richly carved sarcophagi, funerary offerings, sacrifices to the dead, and curses upon the violator of the tomb suggest a belief in a life beyond. Miniature terra-cotta masks of uncertain significance, found occasionally in Phoenician tombs, are frequently encountered in Punic burials, where they assume a very characteristic grotesque appearance.

Mourning Rites

The ritual of tearing the flesh as an act of mourning is vividly described in a myth from Ugarit. Upon learning of the death of Baal, El sits upon the ground, pours dirt upon his head, and tears the flesh of his chest and back, his arms and face. The practice recorded in the Bible of rending the clothing appears to be a substitute for this.

Bibliography

Albright, W. F. *Archaeology and the Religion of Israel.* Baltimore: Johns Hopkins, 1942.

———. *Yahweh and the Gods of Canaan.* London: Athlone, 1968.

Bottéro, J., M. J. Dahood, and W. Caskel. *Le antiche divinità semitiche.* Ed., S. Moscati. Roma, 1958.

Buisson, R. du Mesnil du. "Origine et évolution du panthéon de Tyr," *RHR,* CLXIV (1963), 133–163.

CAQUOT, A. "Le dieu 'Athtar et les textes de Ras Shamra," *Syria,* XXXV (1958), 45–60.

COOK, S. A. *The Religion of Ancient Palestine in the Light of Archaeology,* "The Schweich Lectures, 1925." London: 1930.

DUSSAUD, R. *Les origines cananéennes du sacrifice israélite.*

EISSFELDT, O. *El im ugaritischen Pantheon.* "Berichte über die Verhandlungen der sächsischen Akademie der Wissenschaften zu Leipzig, Philologisch-historische Klasse," Band XCVIII, Heft 4. Berlin: 1951.

GASTER, T. H. *Thespis.* Garden City, New York: Doubleday, 1961 [first pub. 1950].

———. "The Religion of the Canaanites," *Ancient Religions.* Ed., Vergilius Ferm. New York: 1950, pp. 113–143.

GINSBURG, H. L. "Ugaritic Myths, Epics, and Legends," *Ancient Near Eastern Texts Relating to the Old Testament,* ed. J. B. Pritchard. Princeton: Princeton, 1955, 129–155.

GORDON, C. H. "Canaanite Mythology," *Mythologies of the Ancient World.* Ed., S. N. Kramer. Garden City, New York: Doubleday 1961, pp. 181–218.

GRAY, J. *The Legacy of Canaan,* "Supplements to Vetus Testamentum." V. Leiden: E. J. Brill, 1965 [first pub. 1957].

HARDEN, D. *The Phoenicians,* "Ancient Peoples and Places." 26. London: 1962.

KAPELRUD, A. S., *Baal in the Ras Shamra Texts.* Copenhagen: 1952.

LAGRANGE, M. J. *Études sur le religions sémitiques.* Paris: Gabalda, 1903.

LARGEMENT, R. "La religion cananéenne," *Histoire des religions,* ed. Maurice Brillant and René Aigrain, IV. Paris: Bloud et Gay, n. d., 177–199.

MOSCATI, S. *The World of the Phoenicians.* Tr., A. Hamilton. "History of Civilization". London: 1968.

OLDENBURG, U. *The Conflict Between El and Ba'al in Canaanite Religion.* Leiden: E. J. Brill, 1969.

POPE, M. H. *El in the Ugaritic Texts,* "Supplements to Vetus Testamentum," Vol. II. Leiden: E. J. Brill, 1955.

——— and W. Röllig. "Syrien. Die Mythologie der Ugariter und Phönizier," *Wörterbuch der Mythologie.* Ed. H. W. Haussig. 1. Abteilung: *Die alten Kulturvölker,* Teil I: *Vorderer Orient.* Stuttgart: 1961; pp. 217–312.

ROSENTHAL, F. "Canaanite and Aramaic Inscriptions," *Ancient Near Eastern Texts Relating to the Old Testament,* ed. J. B. Pritchard. Princeton: Princeton, 1955, 499–505.

SMITH, W. R. *Lectures on the Religion of the Semites.* London: 1914.

4

The Ancient Near East: The Religious Matrix of Greater Syria

Isma'īl R. al Fārūqī

Multiple Influences

Although some have conjectured as to the time and place of the first Semitic Arabian penetration into Syria (modern Syria, Lebanon, Palestine, and Trans-Jordan), there is as yet no definitive evidence. However, because most of the mountains, rivers, villages, and cities of the area have Semitic names, it is safe to hold that Semites from the Arabian desert (see Chapter 1) were in the area right when the area's history began in the fourth millennium B.C.E. Their presence in these territories, however, did not produce at any time a distinctively new civilization such as it produced in Mesopotamia. Neither did these territories produce a distinctive civilization that is non-Semitic. Why?

Syria (including all the territories between Egypt, Anatolia, and Mesopotamia) was from the dawn of history to Alexander under the influence of either Egypt or Mesopotamia. Politically, the area may be divided into a southern half, which, together with most of the coastline, was under Egyptian influence, and a northern half, which was under Mesopotamian influence. Local autonomous regimes became possible only during the weakness and crisis of the two big empires between 1200 and 900 B.C.E. Thereafter, the area fell piecemeal, first under Assyria and then under Babylon and became no more than an administrative province. Ethnically, Syria suffered constant infiltration by Semitic desert peoples, large-scale immigration of the Hittites in the sixteenth century, of Philistines around 1200, and finally transfer of large sections of the population under Assyria (from 900 onward) and Babylon (from 600). Culturally the Egyptians did not exert much influence because they were satisfied to rule and to extract taxes from a distance. The desert peoples exerted most of the cultural influence, whether directly as newcomers or indirectly as transmitters of the already crystallized civilization of Mesopotamia. The political and military vicissitudes to which the area was constantly subjected, being the crossroads of the empires, gave little chance for any influence to grow and bear fruit and imperiled any concerted effort at building a civilization. Syria has in fact been a fringe area, divided and redivided into petty states, buffer zones, and areas of political and cultural influence and subject to continuous bickering and warfare. Internal and foreign wars have indeed left very few remains of the past.

The first impression that the evidence furnishes of Canaanite-Phoenician deities is certain paganism, in which the deities are deifications of natural forces or elements, and certain polytheism, in which each city or locality has its own pantheon of gods.

A second look at the evidence reveals that these deities are fluid in that their names, attributes, and functions are often interchanged. Albright has argued that even their sex is not constant.[1] This fluidity is perhaps the result of reduced individuation of the deity, or it may be the cause of it. At any rate, it fits well with that attitude in which interest is more in the godhead as such than in the god's individual person. Further evidence of this generic interest is the fact that most of these deities' names are common nouns (El, Elohim, Baal, Balit, Yamm, Mot, Ashtar, Eshmun, Milkom, Milqart, Shalem, and so on), not proper names. Whoever used them must have thought of something generic rather than specific. Furthermore, in the greatest majority of instances, these gods had open sanctuaries marked with a tree, an uncut stone, or some other formless object, and some of them were associated with mountains, rivers, storm, thunder, rain, desert, or sea at large, as it were, without a specific statue, temple, or locality to particularize them. This fact betrays a definite disinterest in the god's person, a concentration on the sheer presence of the numinous power.

We may then move, though cautiously, to correct the image of Canaan we inherited from the Old Testament, an image distorted by doctrinal interest. There is no doubt that many of Syria's deities were Mesopotamian, but in Syria these deities were not systematized into an organic unity. All that was said of them in Mesopotamia is true here, with the exception that in Syria they stood unrelated to society-making because there were no people organically bonded together so as to produce civilization. Other deities, the Amoritic, which carried kin-title names such as *'Ammu, Khalu, Abu,* and *Akhu,* reflected the social bonds of the tribe, which remained the sole basic unity of Amorite society. Finally, there are the fertility gods and goddesses serving as projections of the feelings of peoples eking a bare subsistence out of an infertile soil and hence obsessed with the processes of agriculture: rain and fertilization, women and reproduction.

Hebrew Reform

Fertility gods apart, because agriculture in the desert is not significant, the religious situation in Syria was not different from that of pre-Islamic Makkah. Generally speaking, it represents a decadent stage of development. The old, civilization-making ideas are lost but not their receptacles, in which a distant echo of them continues to resound. Religiously speaking, God, as transcendent and ultimate reality, remains, but without His transcendence exercising the major role as maker of social and natural order. These functions are fragmented and taken over by a plurality of deities, though even they, being gods, must reveal some of the transcendence belonging to divinity by refusing to be wholly associated, or identified, with their specific function or element. This is decadence, properly speaking, for both the original and its decadent development must be in evidence if the change is not a mere supplantation of one thing by another. The reform, as and when it comes, would reassert the original and seek to purge it of its corruption. Such was to be the role of Abraham and of the prophetic tradition that he initiated. In the course of reforming Canaan, the Hebrew prophets reformed the whole Mesopotamian tradition as well. Moses had indeed reforged the bonds of unity with the ancient Mesopotamian-Semitic (Arabian) world view when he reasserted the unity, transcendence, and relevance of God in the revealed law of Sinai.

That the Mosaic breakthrough was indeed a revivification of something Semitic (Arabian) and some twenty-five centuries older is more than corroborated by the evidence at hand. Moses' personal awakening came at the hand of Jethro, an Arab chieftain at Midian. The breakthrough at Sinai was a recrystallization of the God-of-the-Mountain cult at Horeb. Moses' fury at association with God of anything in nature (the calf) is a reassertion of Abraham's stand against his father Terah's associationism. The Mosaic understanding of God's relation to the world as law is a reassertion of Hammurabi's understanding. Finally, the whole religious experience and call of Moses would have been in vain unless it was grasped, seized, and pursued with a sense of destiny by an amphictyony of Semitic (Arab) tribes, among whom those who exited from Egypt were a tiny minority. Surely these tribes and the peoples with whom they forged an alliance could not have been capable of it unless it was already known to them (linguistically, metaphysically, socially, and aesthetically), though not so clearly known and intensely felt as in the faith of a Moses.

[1] W. F. Albright, *Archaeology and the Religion of Israel* (Baltimore: Penguin Books, 1942), p. 71.

5

Ancient Greece and Rome

Samuel Laeuchli

The Records

The history of religion in classical antiquity is a significant chapter in the evolution and crisis of civilization. To trace the stages of that evolution, two kinds of evidence are available: the artistic-archaeological material—temples, altars, lararia, tumuli, sculptures, frescoes; and the textual material—myths, epics, inscriptions, decrees, dramas, theological writings. The documentation witnesses to ancient man's extraordinary artistic and intellectual acumen as well as to the manifold role of religion in the shaping of society. Not that "religion" was ever one thing, one definable phenomenon; it is in a plurality of functions, by a constant accruement of traditions, and with a growing tension between mythic and antimythic beliefs that the phenomena that are called in retrospect "classical religion" made their far-reaching impact on the formation of Western culture.

A rich heritage of architectural, archaeological, and artistic material is accessible and enlivens greatly the study of ancient religion. Everywhere in the museums of Europe artifacts, jewelry, figurines, vases are preserved and give us a vivid introduction into the world of classical religion. Few large monuments have survived from the early epochs, the Etruscan, Celtic, pre-Hellenic, and early Hellenic ages (Maps 5 and 6). We still can visit the caves of Crete and the Mycenean funeral monuments (beehive tombs discovered by Schliemann), the spectacular Etruscan necropoleis (Cerveteri, Orvieto, Tarquinia), pre-Roman traces in North Africa (Dougga), Celtic dolmens, and the astronomical clock of Stonehenge, which may or may not be related to Cretan or Mycenean culture.

It is the century of Pericles, however, from which have come down to us some of the greatest religious buildings of all ages: the Parthenon on the Acropolis and the temple to Hephaistos on the Agora of Athens; the temples of Bassae in the Peloponnesus and of Aegina on that island near Salamis; temples on the south coast of Sicily, in Segesta, Selinunte, and Agrigentum; and the Hera temples of Paestum south of Sorrento. The Doric temple is one of the most impressive introductions to ancient religion: elevated on the stereobate, with its columns hewn from the quarries, each column with its entasis, each columnade with its decreasing width of intercolumnation, it stands as a sacred symbol of tribe and polis, consisting of three parts: the pronaos in front, the cella in the center with the cult idol; and the opistodomos in back. But it must be pointed out that all these great classical temples, traditional and archaic in their conception, date from an age in which the cultic-mythic creativity was long past its peak and the crisis of religion was already in full flux.

A much larger number of temples has been preserved from Hellenistic and Roman periods. For almost a thousand years, architects and rulers wanted to build, restore, and rebuild Doric, Corinthian, and Ionic temples at often immense cost. In Didyma stands the temple to Apollo, in Sardes the temple to Artemis. Baalbek and Sabratha, Pergamon and Sunion have superb structures. Rome had its own traditions, as in the temple of Fortunatus near the Tiber; in the Maison Carrée of Nîmes and its sister building in Vienne; in the triadic temples to the Capitoline Trinity of Sbeitla. Besides the rectangular temple, a round temple was also part of the religious architecture, the tholos: Delphi and Tivoli, the Vestal Temple of the Forum and the Pantheon.

Imperial Rome also developed other forms of religious sanctuaries, many of which went back to models of earlier periods: sanctuaries to the Egyptian Isis (Sabratha, Pompei); caves and house churches to the Persian Mithra (Ostia, Capua, Rome, London); synagogues of diaspora Judaism (Delos, Ostia, Dura Europos); temples to the imperial cult (Antoninos Pius in the Forum); tombs of Caesars (Hadrian and Augustus, near the Tiber River); and finally the Christian house churches and basilicas in which the heritage of classical antiquity was both continued and modified by the new religious tradition that replaced paganism as a political and intellectual force. These are only a few names typical of a magnificent religious creativity, from the age of the Athenian democracy to the fall of Rome. What kind of a development can be detected behind this archaeological material?

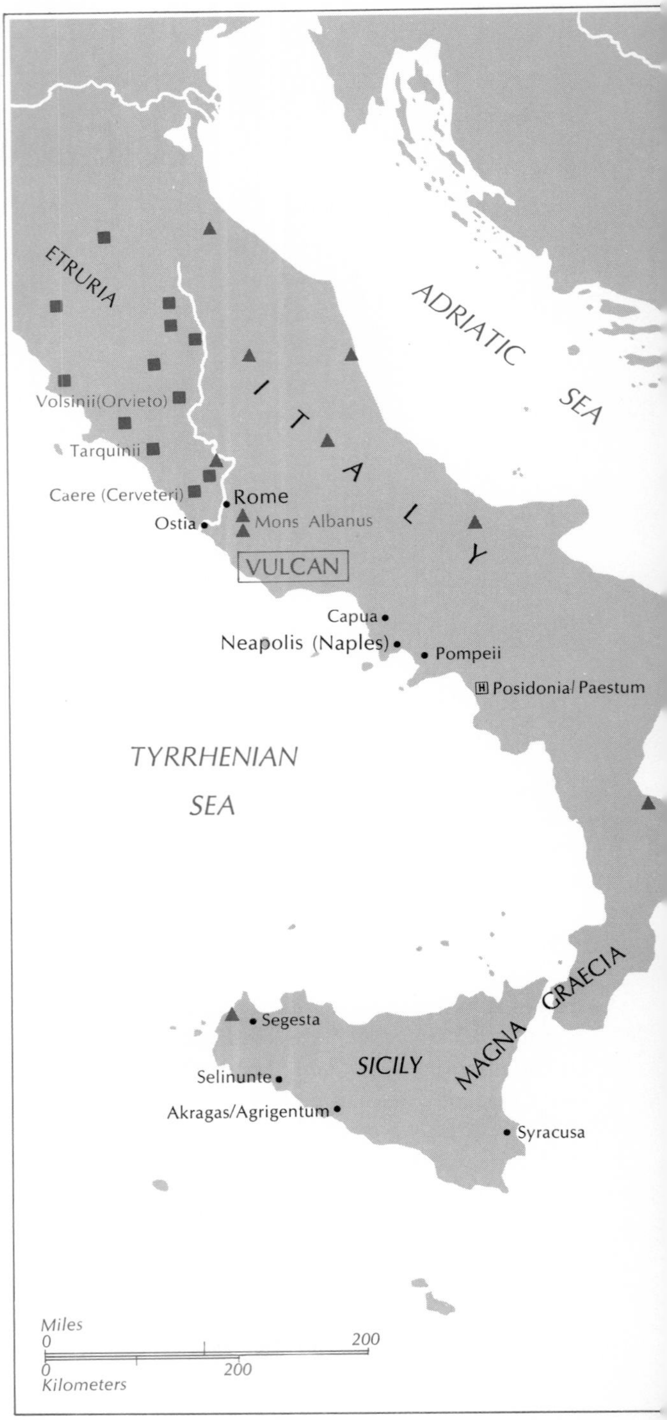

Origins: The Pre-Olympian Substrate

The religious texts allow us insights into the creation and crisis of mythic symbolization and cultic practices and reveal distinct stages in the emergence of scientific and historical consciousness in man. The first stage, reaching back into prehistoric times, precedes the creation of classical Greek and Latin religion. When the Greek tribes broke into the lands of the Aegean Sea, between 2000 and 1100 B.C.E. and when the Latin tribes reached the Appenine Peninsula, they brought along rites and beliefs from their old-Indo-European past, but they also found rites and beliefs that belonged to the natives, some of them Indo-European, others indigenous or reminiscent of and related to ancient Near Eastern religions. We can no longer identify these elements with certainty, but we must reckon with the possibility that

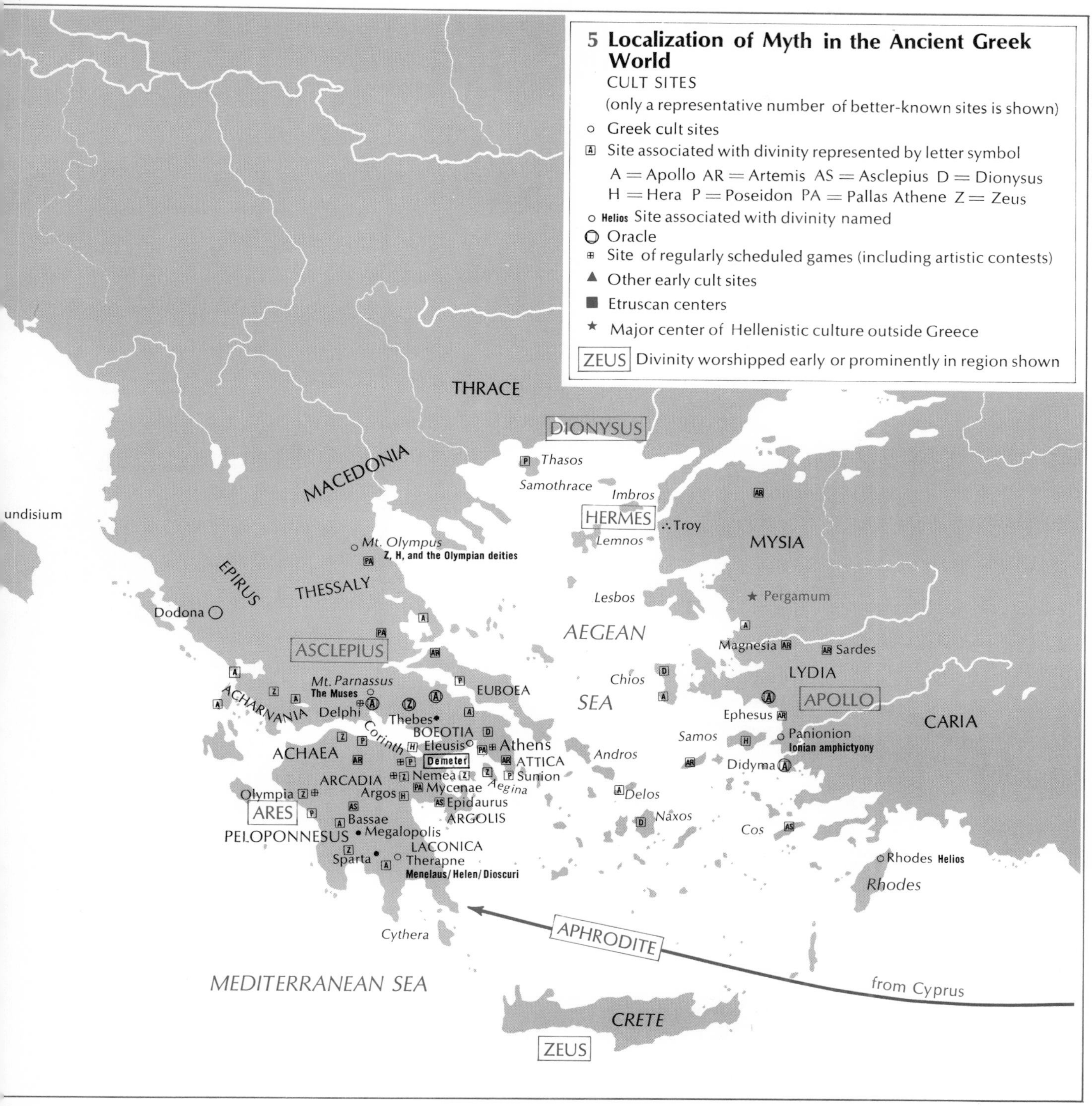

5 Localization of Myth in the Ancient Greek World

CULT SITES

(only a representative number of better-known sites is shown)

o Greek cult sites

Ⓐ Site associated with divinity represented by letter symbol

A = Apollo AR = Artemis AS = Asclepius D = Dionysus
H = Hera P = Poseidon PA = Pallas Athene Z = Zeus

o **Helios** Site associated with divinity named

Ⓞ Oracle

⊕ Site of regularly scheduled games (including artistic contests)

▲ Other early cult sites

■ Etruscan centers

★ Major center of Hellenistic culture outside Greece

ZEUS Divinity worshipped early or prominently in region shown

THRACE

DIONYSUS

P Thasos

Samothrace   Imbros   AR

MACEDONIA   HERMES ∴Troy

                ·Lemnos   MYSIA

·Mt. Olympus
PA Z, H, and the Olympian deities

EPIRUS THESSALY   Lesbos   ★ Pergamum

Dodona Ⓞ

                              AEGEAN   A
PA   Magnesia AR   AR Sardes
ASCLEPIUS
                    A   LYDIA
A   Mt. Parnassus   EUBOEA   Chios D   APOLLO
Z   The Muses   SEA   A
ACHARNANIA ⊕Ⓐ Delphi   A   Ephesus AR
A   Z   Samos   o Panionion
        Corinth BOEOTIA D   Ionian amphictyony   CARIA
ACHAEA   H Eleusis Ⓞ PA⊕Athens   Andros
            P Demeter AR ATTICA   Didyma Ⓐ
ARCADIA ⊕Z Nemea Z P Sunion
Olympia Z⊕ Argos H Mycenae Aegina   AⒶDelos
ARES   P AS Epidaurus
        ▲Bassae   ARGOLIS   D Naxos
PELOPONNESUS ·Megalopolis   Cos
            LACONICA   o Rhodes **Helios**
        Sparta· Ⓐ o Therapne
            Menelaus/Helen/Dioscuri   *Rhodes*

Cythera   APHRODITE

MEDITERRANEAN SEA   from Cyprus

                CRETE

            ZEUS

undisium

6 Distribution of Some Religious Features in Pre-Christian and Early Christian Europe

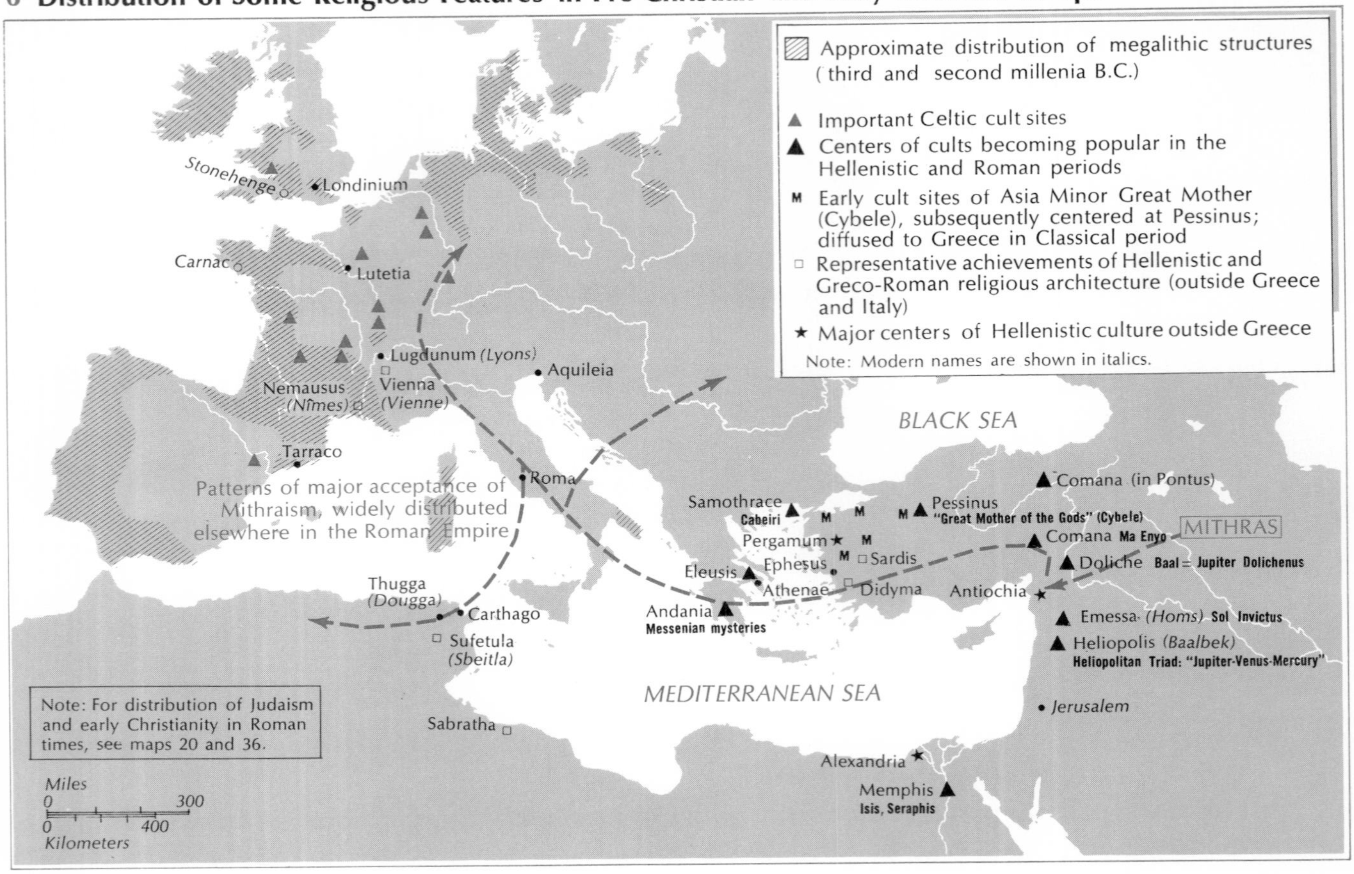

5-1 The Hephaisteios in Athens, formerly called "Theseion." (Courtesy of Samuel Laeuchli.)

5-2 The Greek temple at Segesta, in the Eastern part of Sicily. The well-preserved fifth-century B.C.E. hexastyle temple appears never to have been finished. (Courtesy of Samuel Laeuchli.)

5-4 Hera Temple, Paestum (Italy) 5th century B.C.E. (Courtesy of Samuel Laeuchli.)

5-3 Temple at Selinunte (Sicily). (Courtesy of Samuel Laeuchli.)

5-5 Ancient Roman Religion: *Fortuna Virilis* Temple near the Tiber. (Courtesy of Samuel Laeuchli.)

5-6 A Roman Tholos in Tivoli, north of Rome. (Courtesy of Samuel Laeuchli.)

5-7 A Mithra Sanctuary in Ostia Antica. (Courtesy of Samuel Laeuchli.)

Greek and Roman gods and rites go back to times before the Greeks established their cultures in Minoan Crete, Mycene, Achaea, and so on. Traces of archaic religious customs and symbols have often survived in the lowest strata of society, preserved in fairy tales and sagas, in folk customs, magic, and superstition, and perhaps in what are called the mystery cults, rituals in which man attempted to return to the roots of civilization.

Mythic Flowering

The second stage represents the creation of classical Greek religion proper. The Greeks, and in their wake, at times parallel and at times independently, the Roman tribes, created an immensely rich world of gods and half-gods, heroes, *kouroi*, *bacchae*, nymphs and satyrs, *kore*, and *chthonoi*. The religious world spanned both the

Olympian (heaven) and chthonic (earth) spheres. The famous gods of antiquity came into being or were taken over from previous or related sanctuaries and tribes: Poseidon, the symbol for the sea; Aphrodite, the symbol for love; Ares for war; Hephaistos for fire. Zeus was the god of thunder and became the father-god in the Greeks' first attempts to create a mythic-metaphysical order out of the complex experiences of life. We can still identify places where some of these gods were worshiped in early periods: Crete worshiped Zeus, who according to Minoan tradition was born and died on that island; Argos venerated Hera; Asia Minor, Apollo. Vulcan can be traced to early Latin times. These gods began to function for an increasingly larger audience and took on characteristics of other deities. In North Africa, for instance, Baal and Tannit became Saturn and Dea Caelestis; Apollo "went" from Asia Minor (Didyma) to Greece (Delphi), Rome, and the various provinces of the Empire.

The emerging Greek religion began to form an ideological structure. Mount Olympus became the assembly of gods, a projected circle of aristocratic rule, governed by Zeus and his jealous wife, Hera. Kronos became the father of Zeus, Uranus the father of Kronos, and by such symbolic coordination, "power," "time," and "heaven" were coordinated into a cosmic framework. Trinities arose, Syriac, Egyptian, the old Roman trinity (Jupiter, Mars, Quirinus) and the Capitoline one (Jupiter, Juno, Minerva). The Pantheon of Agrippa and Hadrian, built to the twelve planetary gods, was the magnificent expression of cosmic order. The religions also dealt with the problematic of man, with fate (the *Parci*), with death (*Hades*, the place where continuation of life was imagined, without reward or punishment), and with the human problems of good and evil (Prometheus, Kronos, Sisyphus, Daedalus). And some of the great mythic tales, to this day major achievements of Western man's ingenuity, came into being: Medea, Antigone, Oedipus, Theseus.

The locus of religion was the holy ceremony, such as the ritual performed in the tribe or polis by the priest, the sacrifice of a holy animal or the offering of nonbloody gifts, the holy wedding, and the ritual dance. The person who performed the sacrifice was the priest, the place was the altar, the architectural symbol the temple, and the center of religious urban life became the *temenos*, the holy realm within a city. The religious customs played a key role in the realms of urbanization, politics, and war as well as in the peoples' individual lives.

The mythic models and rituals served many functions. They allowed man to deal with scientific and moral problems, with death and tragedy, astronomy, physics, and history. They served medical purposes and offered, as in the Asclepias cult (Pergamon, Epidaurus), important psychiatric and physical therapy. They became symbols of historical perspective (Thebes, Troy, Mycene, Rome) and helped to undergird the social order by supplying it with justification (Pallas Athene, Castor and Pollux, Dido). One cannot treat classical religion as anything like a historical unity. Greek religion, for instance, appears much more personal, individualistic, and pluralistic than the religion of the Romans, who emphasized the public, contractual aspects (*do ut des*). There does not seem to have been a priest class in Greece as compared with the *pontifices* in Rome. However, it is a mistake to posit a clear dichotomy between Greek and Roman religion as if two separate religious types could be held against each other. Each of them was in itself a complex phenomenon. The notion of imperial worship, to give one example, goes back not only to Hellenistic and Oriental but also to pre-Roman Western models of deified kingship. It is frequently said that the crisis of Roman religion came when Latin man, shortchanged by the lack of personal satisfaction in his tradition, turned east for psychological fulfillment; but Olympian religion had had its crisis, as serious as the Roman one, centuries before the first worshipers of Magna Mater reached the Palatine Hill.

5-8 The Temple to the Olympian Zeus in Athens from the time of Hadrian but going back to an early Greek Sanctuary. (Courtesy of Samuel Laeuchli.)

Decay of Mythic Religion

The third stage through which the bulk of mythic material has actually come down to us was poetic and philosophical. When ancient man began to become conscious of myth as mimesis, of dealing with myth as poetry, the religious naïveté was gone. In his use of religious imagery, conceiving his gods in the image of man—capricious, quarrelsome, petty, and often limited in understanding—Homer was no longer an authentic believer. After him, the great playwrights of Greece shaped in mythic types the drama of mankind: Prometheus, Orestes, Medea, Oedipus. To be sure, some of the dramatists appear intellectually and politically conservative (Aristophanes), whereas others reveal a highly developed critical awareness (Euripides), yet they all display the same artistic sovereignty. Man had become the master of his icons, knowing all too well that he was a mere mortal in the face of crushing cosmic forces. The philosophical enterprises arose together with and from the same roots as the poetic consciousness. When philosophers like Thales and his followers postulated certain elements—water, fire, air—as primal reality, they did not *eo ipso* envisage a threat to religion. But it turned out to be one. The language of religion was opened to rational cynicism, the gods were replaced by abstractions, ideas, and hypostases, and although many philosophers for centuries tried to harmonize mythic models with the new Hellenistic rational categories of thinking, the conflict between myth and reason could not be eliminated anymore. Both Plato and Euripides recognized in that conflict the dawn of a religious and social crisis, tragically symbolized in the death of Socrates, a crisis on which modern civilization is built.

What created such poetic and critical consciousness was the same dynamic that had led to the creation of the gods: the desire to explain and justify, to master the world by an intellectual vision, within the social and technological context. An extensive urbanization, the creation of polis and urbs, had created the locus for sophistication and intellectual creativity; a wide interchange of cultures, commercial as well as military, made

5-9 Eleusis, with the island of Salamis in the background. (Courtesy of Samuel Laeuchli.)

people recognize the relativity of religious traditions. Scientific and technological discoveries were made, schools were founded, libraries were built, all of which contributed to transforming the mythical age of antiquity into a metaphysical one, a process, to be sure, that reached its climax long after the barbarians crushed the Roman lines.

The mythic crisis led to a number of reactions, the first being the desire to romanticize the religious past—the cultural past!—by revival and artificial restoration. As the Jews tried to return to the world of the Torah, Augustus tried to revive extinct religious customs; as Herod rebuilt the Yahweh temple of Jerusalem, Hadrian rebuilt the Zeus temple in Athens. As late as 361 C.E., Julian the Apostate attempted to revive moribund pagan rites.

In another reaction, ancient man not only romanticized the past but by returning to archaic myths created a new kind of religious experience: the arcane initiation into a mystery cult. When in the seventh or sixth century B.C.E. the Athenians began to walk to Eleusis in order to worship Demeter, they entered a hidden temenos and meant to become participants of the goddess's mysterious reach. In the course of antiquity, one mystery cult after another came into being, each with its own contribution of archaic particles (wine and bread, water and blood, killing and rising), creating the arcane temple, the house church with its own secret liturgy, and promising its initiates eternal life (the *Basilica Sotterranea* in Rome). From Asia Minor came the cult of Magna Mater with its blood baptism (taurobolium), a cult that reached Rome as early as 200 B.C.E.; from Egypt came Isis and Serapis, for which Hadrian longingly reconstructed the Canopus in his villa outside Tivoli; from Persia and Asia Minor came Mithra, a male cult exceedingly popular in the urban and military circles of the empire (Map 6). And everywhere we find traces of Dionysus (Bacchus, Liber Pater).

There was also a philosophical reaction to the crisis of myth. Ancient scholars tried to save religious traditions by allegorizing them, transforming the meaning of texts in order to adapt them to new social experiences and ideas. By means of *exegesis* and *eisegesis,* Jewish scholars reinterpreted the Pentateuch (Philo), pagan scholars Homer. But other thinkers wanted to replace religious beliefs by humanistic value systems. For centuries, bitter conflicts took place between competing proreligious and antireligious philosophic groups.

One of the results of the critical development was the politicizing of religion. The priests of Didyma appeared on the threshold of the temple's cella and made their pronouncements; the priests of Delphi used the mumblings of an intoxicated woman to advise, as the political

5-10 The Apollo Temple in Delphi. (Courtesy of Samuel Laeuchli.)

scientists of antiquity, the city-states of Greece. In order to strengthen their rule, kings of the Hellenistic lands as elsewhere pretended to be of divine character. Caesar claimed to be the offspring of Venus Genetrix and his follower established the cult of the emperor (inscriptions of Priene and Tarragona). The Roman Empire was based on shrewd religious-political device, the worship of the emperors (*divi, invicti*).

The crisis of myth and society also brought forth dualistic theological schemata about cosmos and redemption. Ever since Job and Plato, a growing number of ancient men no longer accepted the mythic projections of nature and history as sufficient explanations for a life experienced in its tragic predicament. For them, different from the widespread Hellenistic mysticism and different from all natural philosophy or theology, the problem of life was not solved by looking to a cosmic order; the problem *was* the cosmic order. A new kind of speculative mythology and philosophy, in dualistic modes of theological constructs (pseudomythological in fact, because mythic images were artificially rearranged and intermingled with abstract ideas) reaching its full development in Christian, Gnostic, Mandaean, Manichaean, and Cabbalistic thought structures, expressed the lostness and alienation of man and offered as an alternative to the cosmic tragedy a utopian eschatological, apocalyptic, or transcendental redemption.

Bibliography

BAILEY, CYRIL. *Roman Religion and the Advent of Philosophy,* Vol. VIII of *The Cambridge Ancient History.* Cambridge: Cambridge U. P., 1930.

———. *Phases in the Religion of Ancient Rome.* Berkeley: U. California, 1932.

CUMONT, FRANZ. *Les Religions orientales dans le paganisme romain.* Paris: Paul Geuthner, 1963.

DES PLACES, E. *Les Religions de la Grèce antique,* Vol. III of *Histoire des religions.* Paris: Bloud et Gay, 1955.

FABRE, P. *La Religion romaine,* Vol. IV of *Histoire des religions.* Paris: Bloud et Gay, 1955.

FESTUGIÈRE, A. J. *Personal Religion Among the Greeks.* Berkeley: U. of California, 1954.

GRANT, FREDERICK C. (Ed.). *Ancient Roman Religion.* New York: Liberal Arts Press, 1957.

———. *Hellenistic Religions: The Age of Syncretism.* New York: Liberal Arts Press, 1953.

GRANT, M. *Myths of the Greeks and Romans.* Cleveland: World, 1962.

GRESSMANN, H., *Die orientalischen Religionen im hellenistisch-römischen Zeitalter.* Berlin-Leipzig: 1930.

GUTHRIE, W. K. C. *Orpheus and Greek Religion.* New York: Norton, 1967 [first pub. 1935].

———. *The Greeks and Their Gods.* London: Methuen, 1950.

HARRISON, JANE ELLEN. *Prolegomena to the Study of Greek Religion.* New York: Meridian, 1960 [first pub. 1922].

———. *The Religion of Ancient Greece.* London: A. Constable, 1921.

KERENYI, K. *The Gods of the Greeks* (tr. from German). London: Thames and Hudson, 1951.

———. *The Religion of the Greeks and Romans.* London: Thames and Hudson, 1962.

MURRAY, G. *Five Stages of Greek Religion.* Oxford: Oxford U. P., 1925.

NILSSON, M. P. *Greek Folk Religion.* Gloucester, Mass.: Peter Smith, 1971 [first pub. 1940].

———. *Greek Piety,* tr., H. J. Rose. Oxford: Clarendon, 1951 [first pub. 1948].

———. *History of Greek Religion,* tr., F. J. Fielden. Oxford: Clarendon, 1949 [first pub. 1925].

6

Shamanism

Lawrence Krader

Nature of Shamanism

Shamanism is the name given to the beliefs, rites, practices, science, art, and world view of the *shaman*, who is a religious leader, a primitive healer, a visionary, and a soothsayer, as well as of his followers or the people among whom or for whom he functions as a shaman. The shaman is first reported in the European world by seventeenth-century travelers to eastern Siberia; the concept and the human figure were reported by the Chinese who came into contact with those peoples in earlier millennia. The term is originally derived from the Tungus, a group of languages spoken in northeast Siberia; it is further derived (by some) from the Sanskrit term for Buddhist monk, *śramaṇā*, whence Prakrit *samana* and so on. The view that we will develop here is, first, that shamanism is found in eastern Siberia and is characteristic of the life of the peoples there; it is closely related to the practices of central and inner Asia and neighboring parts of the Arctic, both in Eurasia and in America. Second, like phenomena have been reported in the Near East, in south Asia, in Oceania, in all the Americas, in ancient Greece, in the Upper Paleolithic hunting cultures of Western Europe, which have recorded their cults on the walls of caves, and in Africa south of the Sahara (Maps 1 and 2). Plainly, two meanings of the terms *shaman* and *shamanism* are at work here: that which is directly shared by different peoples, where contact is proved; and that which refers to the analogies and comparabilities that anthropologists have discovered. We will seek out the core meaning of shamanism in the first sense, leaving the discovery of analogies and comparisons elsewhere to others who hold that it is a universal aspect of religion, responding to comparable cultural conditions and corresponding to like workings of the human mind.

Restricting the reference to Siberia and the neighboring parts of the Arctic and inner Asia, we find that shamanism is not only a religious phenomenon but also a matter of the general culture of these peoples, for the shaman is the bearer of the practical nature lore, the mythology, the philosophy, and moral judgments in those cultural conditions in which such matters are not divided up into the concerns of specialists.

The shaman among the Tungus peoples and the neighboring Yakuts and Buryats comes unwillingly to his calling. He suffers spiritual anxiety and the relentless quest finally drives him to become a shaman. Having experienced the religious answers, he becomes the spiritual healer of his people. The people need him, for they suffer from the same religious anxieties. Associated with these anxieties, and thereby magnified into fantastic compulsions and obsessions, are typically the fears that they will be infertile or childless or that food for themselves and their families will run short. They wander

6-1 Shaman's coat. Gold tribe, Siberia. Front view. (Courtesy of the American Museum of Natural History.)

about in nervous chanting groups, dancing a swaying, tottering dance called *naygur* (in Buryat), going from village to village under the lead of a shaman. One such group was dedicated to a certain figure of old who died childless. The Tungus peoples have a widespread practice of ascetic withdrawal from the world, in which the more sensitive loses his own will entirely and imitates some sound or movement until he drops from exhaustion; this is called *olonism,* from a Tungus word meaning "fright." The Chukchis, who live on the Asian side of the Bering Strait, consider that their shamans are "soft to die"; they readily give up life by losing the will to live and allowing themselves to die from exposure. Frequently the shaman is a transvestite and a homosexual.

The shaman in all these cases is a marginal man or woman who does not usually participate in the daily chores of securing a living. He is a social radical for whose talents his people find special use. He is not only the healer of his people, he is also charged with the cults of prevention of disease among the herds of cattle, horses, and reindeer. He is the master of the spirits of the animals they hunt. In ancient times the shaman was the leader of his tribe in their collective enterprises, the most important of which was the great annual hunt in which the game was driven into a common pound whence food for the entire group was taken for the ensuing year.

The shaman-to-be regards himself and is regarded by his people as one elected by the supernatural agency. He is usually the descendant of a line of shamans, seeking a personal vision in a state of trance, in which he gains the aid of a spirit-familiar. His quest is in the

6-2 Tofa Shamaness in full costume (front), Southern Siberia. (From V. Dioszegi, *Glaubenswelt und Folklore der Sibirischen Völker.* Budapest: 1963.)

Arctic wild, in which he suffers greatly, a young person, starving, frightened, alone for weeks on end. As a shaman he masters and is mastered by this spirit, who divines the future for the shaman's patient or his group. The shaman in his state of transport receives and interprets "messages" from his spirit, which come to him alone. Shamans are male or female. Among the Chukchis, the male were to the female as 2:1, being considered generally the more powerful of their kind. Yet among the most powerful of all the Chukchi shamans at the turn of the century was a woman.

The Eskimo shamans are not unlike those of the Chukchis, Tungus, and Buryats. One Eskimo shaman asked the ethnographer the eternal religious questions: Why are we here? Why do we suffer? He knew that the lot of his people was hard. Such questions are also posed by the Chukchis, for the shamans are precisely the kind of persons who probe and question on behalf of the tribe.

The shaman is a specialist among peoples who have few other specialties of function of any sort, for all families live alike and perform the same chores to get their living. He is both honored and detested by his social group. Just as he comes unwillingly to his calling, his group comes unwillingly to him. The Buryats, more evolved than their neighbors to the north, consider the shaman to be the worst kind of person, yet they need him. He is the "wild," "bad" man who performs a necessary function for the group. The world is dangerous, uncontrolled. Pestilence descends upon the herd or on the people without cause or reason; the shaman is the center of the cult whereby it is warded off as we ward off the devil. The shaman likewise is the repository of the rationalizations whereby the catastrophe is accounted for, and he is the focus of the practices whereby its worst effects are brought under control. He stands between the group and the harsh surrounding elements, a kind of human lightning rod.

The shaman is polarized into two types, often combined in the same person: the good, "white" shaman and the evil, "black" shaman. The white shaman practices his arts, in which there is a good deal of prestidigitation and hypnosis of his audience as well as himself, of curing people or discovering herds that have disappeared in the Arctic blizzards by acts of divination. The black shaman is an unloved person, a curse to his people, bringing them harm, a kind of witch, making compacts with evil spirits, for which he must be killed by the group in a fearsome ceremony and buried face down with a stake of unclean wood driven through his body.

There is no general doctrine of shamanism, for its practitioners never gathered in an ecumenical congress to iron out their differences. The shamanism of each group varies from the next, but there is enough commonalty amongst them to warrant the use of the term for them all.

Historical Retrospect

Shamanism in inner and northern Asia has been reported in the historical records of the Chinese and Iranians since medieval times; it has been reported in regard to themselves in the ancient Greek, Chinese, and Iranian records. The dimension of shamanism that emerges from the ancient and medieval accounts differs from

6-3 Ikon of Manchu Shaman, Manchuria. (From S. V. Ivanov, *Materialy po izobrazitel'nomu iskusstvu narodov Sibiri, XIX - nachala XX v.*, Moscow Leningrad: 1954.)

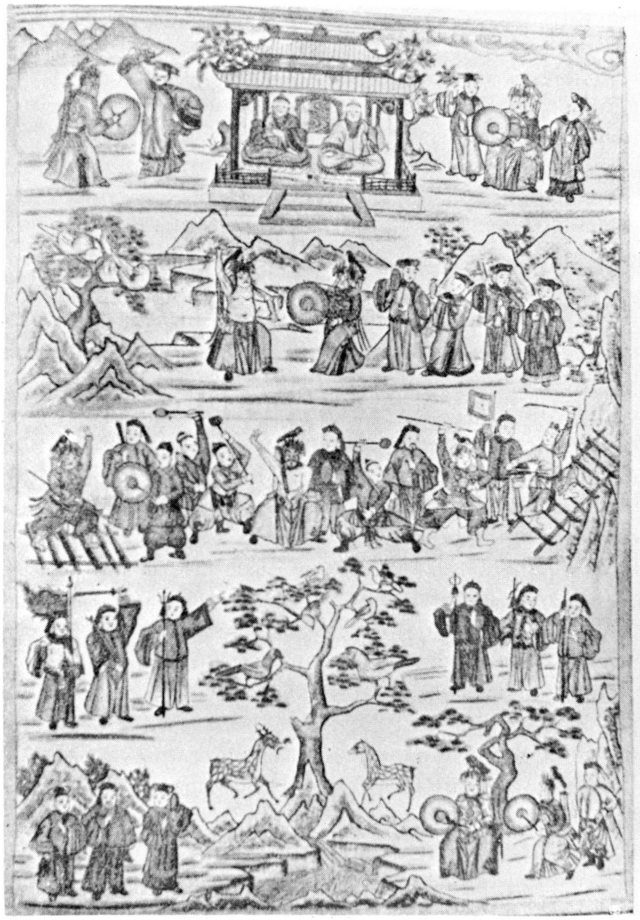

contemporary ethnographies in content; whereas the latter treats primarily of shamanism of the small communities, occupied with local concerns and localized fears and anxieties, without deep historical records, the ancient and medieval reports indicate that shamanism was bound up with complex political and social enterprises of vast extension. Shamans played a significant part in the Mongol empire of Genghis Khan. They presided over rituals at his court, divining the outcome of battles, curing disease as courtiers, and intriguing with rival religionists—Buddhist, Christian, and Islamic.

The Tungusic, Eskimo, Chukchi, and other shamans of the twentieth century are undoubtedly the outcome of deep historical development, but we do not know what it is. They represent their own fate as unhappy, their cultural and psychological atmosphere as a sorry one. It is doubly so because they know they are weak relative to the forces of nature and to the social, economic, political, military, and religious forces around them. Their collective misery is reinforced by their consideration that their own fate was at one time happier because it was freer and more productive. The present-day accounts of these peoples point to a distant past when the figure of the shaman was quite different. The Buryats are a case in point. According to their myths, the shaman in olden times (about four hundred years ago) was a figure of veneration, spiritual beauty and love, the dispenser of justice, the leader of the tribe, a true, good, and decisive man. The form that we know their shamanism to take today reflects the collapse of the traditional social and cultural conditions of the people; it therefore cannot be taken as the original form of their religion, just as the entire body of what we know about shamanism cannot provide the form of the original religion of mankind. The insight that it provides into the prehistoric and ancient religions is partial, to be used with caution. It is to be mistrusted if taken as a whole, because modern-day shamanism expands one part of shamanism, the local, miserable, ecstatic, or trance form, the individual or family concerns, and it contracts or even loses all the other sides that we normally expect from religion: the rationalization of the cosmic forces and our place therein, the support by myth of the social unity, and the ritual expression of the resultant force of social cohesion. We are therefore dealing, in the contemporary ethnographic accounts of shamanism, with the outcome of religion, or its eschatology, and not the origin of a religious state, or its etiology.

There are hints that formerly the shamanism of the Buryats was connected with the hunting ritual of a pastoral people who had formerly been a hunting people. Writing in the nineteenth century, W. Radloff had expressed a theory of shamanism in regard to the pastoral peoples of Asia generally, holding that it had been widespread among them and had originally been a religion of hunting peoples, which they had formerly been and from which they had emerged into pastoral life. Since Radloff's time H. Findeisen, M. Eliade, A. Lommel, and W. La Barre have sought the origin of shamanism in the religious and artistic life of the hunters of the Paleolithic period, based upon interpretation of the paintings and engravings on the cave walls of France and Spain. Shamanism emerged in a period when the human species was coming forth in the cultural forms as we know them; the Paleolithic form of hunting ritual, with men cloaked in animal skins and headdresses, has a general relation to the hunting ritual of the shamans.

Coming forward in time to the ancient period of Iran (Zoroastrianism), Greece (the cult of Orpheus), and China, we find certain colorful but quite general depictions of something like present-day shamans reported in the poetic-allusive language of those times: we are frustrated in our search because it is not the language of the shamans themselves. Shamanism is a widely held set of religious beliefs and practices, world view, magical rites, and primitive science of the highest antiquity. It is found in the Americas, where it is reported both with and without the state of trance or ecstasy among its practitioners; it is found in Oceania and in Africa, where, in the form of witchcraft, it corresponds to the black shamanism of Asia. It is at once a form of religion and more than a religion. It burgeoned forth in its most classic and fullest form in inner and northern Asia in historical times.

Bibliography

GENERAL

Eliade, Mircea. *Shamanism, Archaic Techniques of Ecstasy*, tr. Willard R. Trask. New York: Bollingen Foundation (Pantheon), 1964.

La Barre, Weston. *The Ghost Dance: Origins of Religion.* Garden City, N.Y.: Doubleday, 1970.

Lewis, I. M. *Ecstatic Religion: An Anthropological Study of Spirit Possession and Shamanism.* Harmondsworth, Eng.: Penguin, 1971.

SIBERIA

Bogoraz, Waldemar. *The Chukchee* (*American Museum of Natural History*), Leiden: E. J. Brill Vol. XI. 1904–1909.

Krader, Lawrence. "Buryat Religion and Society," *Southwestern Journal of Anthropology,* X, (1954).

———. "Primary Reification and Primitive Myth (Chukchi)," *Diogenes,* No. 56 (1966).

Shirokogoroff, S. M. *Psychomental Complex of the Tungus.* 1935.

ESKIMOS

Boas, Franz. *The Central Eskimo.* Lincoln: U. of Nebraska, 1964 [first pub. 1888].

Rasmussen, Knud. *The Intellectual Culture of the Iglulik Eskimos.* 1929.

———. *The Intellectural Culture of the Copper Eskimos.* 1932.

ANCIENT GREECE

Dodds, E. R. *The Greeks and the Irrational.* Berkeley: U. of California, 1951.

Rhode, Erwin. *Psyche,* 2 vols. (1893). 1966.

PALAEOLITHIC EUROPE

Lommel, Andreas. *Shamanism, the Beginnings of Art.* New York: McGraw-Hill, 1967 [first pub. 1961].

7

Amerindian Religions

Weston La Barre

The first American Indians were paleo-Asiatic hunters immigrant over Beringia, the wide land that connected Siberia and Alaska during and after the fourth Pleistocene glaciation. As demonstrated by culture traits universal or nearly universal in both Americas (the dog, the bow and arrow, basket types, shamanism), Indians were hunters and fishermen of late Paleolithic and early Mesolithic material culture corresponding to a very old *Urkultur* of Eurasiatic Stone Age hunters.[1]

Shamanism and Spirit Power

Because sacred systems are projections into the unknown of secular social structures (Durkheim), Indians supposed that wild animal species, like themselves, each had a powerful progenitor-protector, much like the hunting-band chief. This "Owner"—in the sense that the mysterious male spirit-principle or life-soul owns the material body—or "Owner of the Animals" (the "Spirit of the Wild" of Old World hunters) was further structured to meet the wishful fantasies and economic needs of hunters, because no amount of bravery or skill can guarantee success in the hunt. As Boas early noted, shamanism is the base of Amerindian religion. Earliest, perhaps, the shaman, dressed in their skins, claimed special magic power over animals or ritual identity with them. He himself was Master of the Animals; or, alternatively, as their totem kinsman or protégé, he had as "guardian spirits" the supernatural masters of animal species.

With pretended competence to meet specific needs, the shaman ministered to all uncontrolled elements of luck or accident in the hunting band, the sacred counterpart of the secular chief—although, especially in Middle and South America these functions were often combined in one man (Montezuma, the Inca, Amazonian shaman-chiefs, even the Pueblo priestly-political hierarchy). To meet each life anxiety the shaman had a requisite power: control over hunters' luck and the fertility and availability of game, control over the weather, ability to cure injury and disease, supernatural protection in warfare, prognostication of the future, clairvoyance regarding lost objects and distant events, and the like.

"Medicine power" for these purposes—Algonkan *manitou,* Iroquoian *orenda,* Siouan *wakan,* Jivaro *kakarma*[2]—as a vast supernatural reservoir in nature that

[1] Amerindian "culture areas" at the time of European contact are shown on Map 7.

[2] Amerindian peoples mentioned in the text are located on Map 7.

7-1 Hopi Kachina dancer, painting by Louis Aiken. (Courtesy of the American Museum of Natural History.)

the individual might tap or acquire, is misleadingly translated as "Great Spirit," for Amerindians were not monotheistic and had no proper Creator God. Moreover, medicine power is impersonal, though variously possessable by persons, much like impersonal Melanesian *mana*. Indians sought impersonal *power* but did not "worship" personified *gods*, at least not until the late specialized agricultural religions had been built locally on a pan-American shamanistic base. In male-centered Amerindian societies, medicine power was directly sought in order to fill male roles in sexual conquest, war prowess, and hunting skill.

To get medicine power, usually about puberty, the youth made a vision quest. The shaman was only *primus inter pares* in this: in North America nearly all males, in South America primarily only shamans, sought supernatural power, and shamans sought additional symbolic powers of the same magic order. By fasting, attempting to remain sleepless for a ritual number of days and nights in some lonely place, lacerating himself, beseeching, and proclaiming his weakness and helplessness, the youth might succeed in arousing the pity of powers who would vouchsafe him "medicine," usually to be embodied in some physical form such as a medicine bundle. Such revelations in paranormal psychic states would probably be best interpreted as REM-dream states induced by sleeplessness in conditions of sensory deprivation.

Scalp taking in North America and head taking in South America were other ways of accumulating the male spirit-power thought of as resident in the head or hairy parts; in some areas of America, other body parts were taken. Sporadically in Texas and Mesoamerica, but most notably in South America and the Caribbean, cannibalism was another way to incorporate the spirit power of victims. In a sense, human sacrifice in classic Mexico was merely feeding such spirit power to more individuated "gods," as when Huitzilopochtli was impersonated by the bravest captive enemy, and then through sacrifice his spirit was incorporated into the war god's accumulated *mana*. Amerindian "gods" are thus in turn only reconcentrated medicine power, and gods were still cannibals when men had long left off any but part cannibalism of hearts or the like. For the rest, hunters ate animal flesh for physical life, so why not get scalps, head, and hearts for spirit power?

The transition from medicine power to gods is evident in another fashion. Medicine bundles were individually acquired, but they could be inherited, like dream power or medicine songs. Blackfoot entrepreneurs accumulated medicine bundles as a form of spiritual power and even traded them like commodities. When Plains winter-hunting bands assembled for seasonal tribal rites, certain paramount fetishes—the Cheyenne sacred arrows, the Kiowa Ten Medicine Bundles—became tribal power-laden palladia toward which the tribal Sundance was directed. With agriculture, the accumulation of priestly rite, and increased political coherence, tribal palladia passed easily into cult "gods" and war medicine became Huitzilopochtli when nourished with spirit power over time.

In the same sense, and in the same politicoeconomic progression, the Sundance became the assembled power quest of a tribe, after which, commonly, parties of men went off on the warpath (Map 7). Under the sociocultural conditions of acculturational stress from white

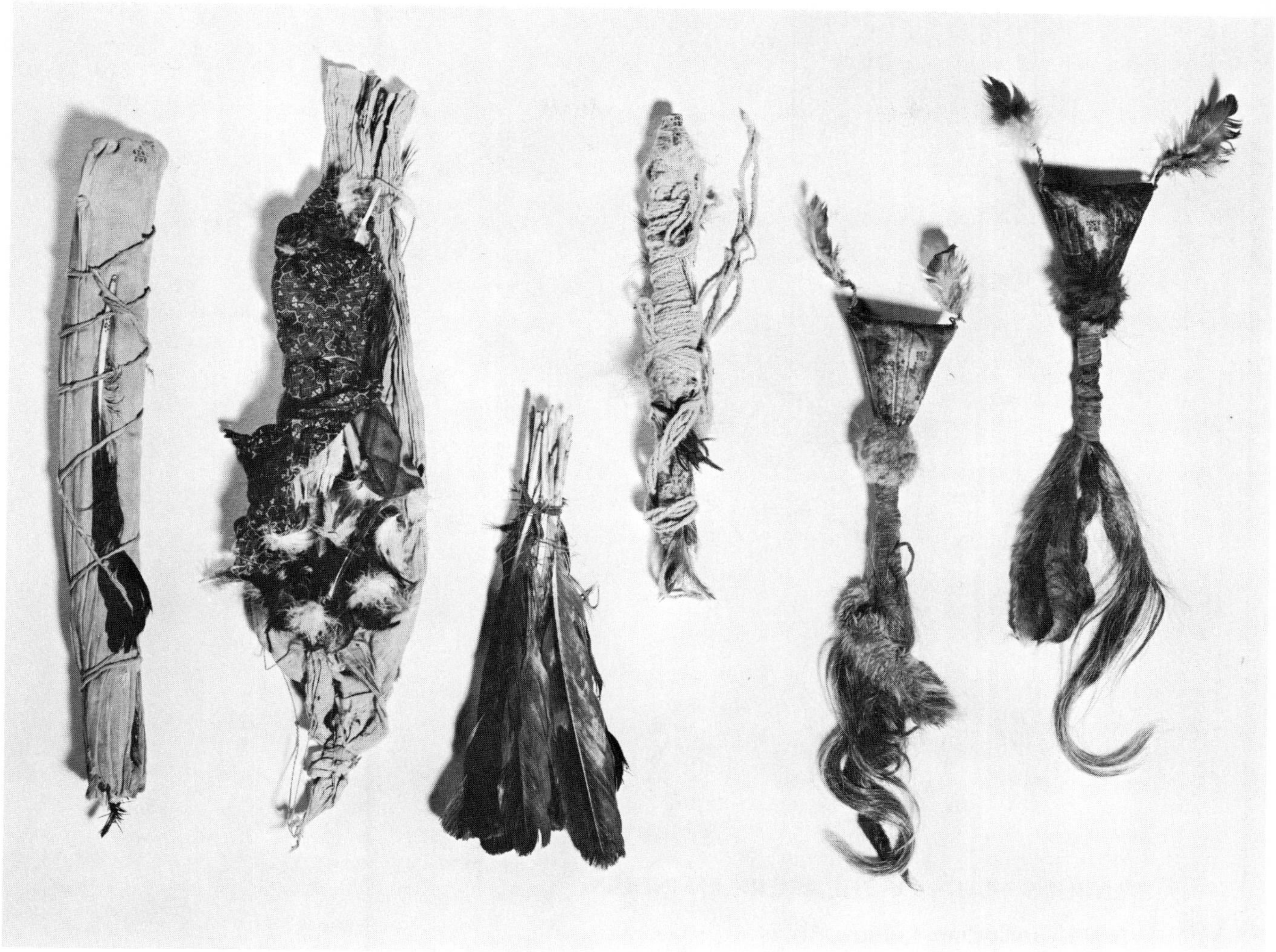

7-2 Navajo ceremonial bundle. (Courtesy of the American Museum of Natural History.)

pioneers, the Ghost Dance was in turn an intertribal crisis cult magically seeking the return of the past. And, finally, the Peyote Cult was an assembled vision quest, often of individuals from many diverse tribes and calling on the pharmacologic power of the hallucinogen mescaline (Map 8).

Besides vision quest, trophy-taking, and cannibalistic incorporation, American Indians had therefore still another way of getting supernatural "power," through the use of psychotropic plants (Map 8). Any mind-altering effect of an incorporated plant was interpreted by them as *prima facie* evidence of its containment of sacred medicine power. As though they were culturally programmed to seek such substances, pre-Columbian Indians had the astonishing number of merely a hundred psychotropic drug plants, whereas the whole of the Old World had only a half-dozen major narcotics and hallucinogens. Even tobacco, with mild enough immediate effects, was everywhere in the New World used only in sacred contexts, from solemnizing a truce with the peacepipe in North America to the supernatural sanctioning of a tribal compact as when the Amazonian youth dipped his spatula into boiled tobacco syrup and licked it off.

The violent *Datura* species were much used in puberty rites ("jimson weed" *huskinawing* ordeal in Virginia) in southern California and the Southwest, as well as in Amazonia. *Ilex* infusions were used as the "Black Drink" in the Carolinas, and again as *maté* or "Paraguayan tea." Coca, source of the complex group of alkaloids in cocaine, was pan-Andean and beyond in pre-Columbian South America. The Mazatec and other groups of north-

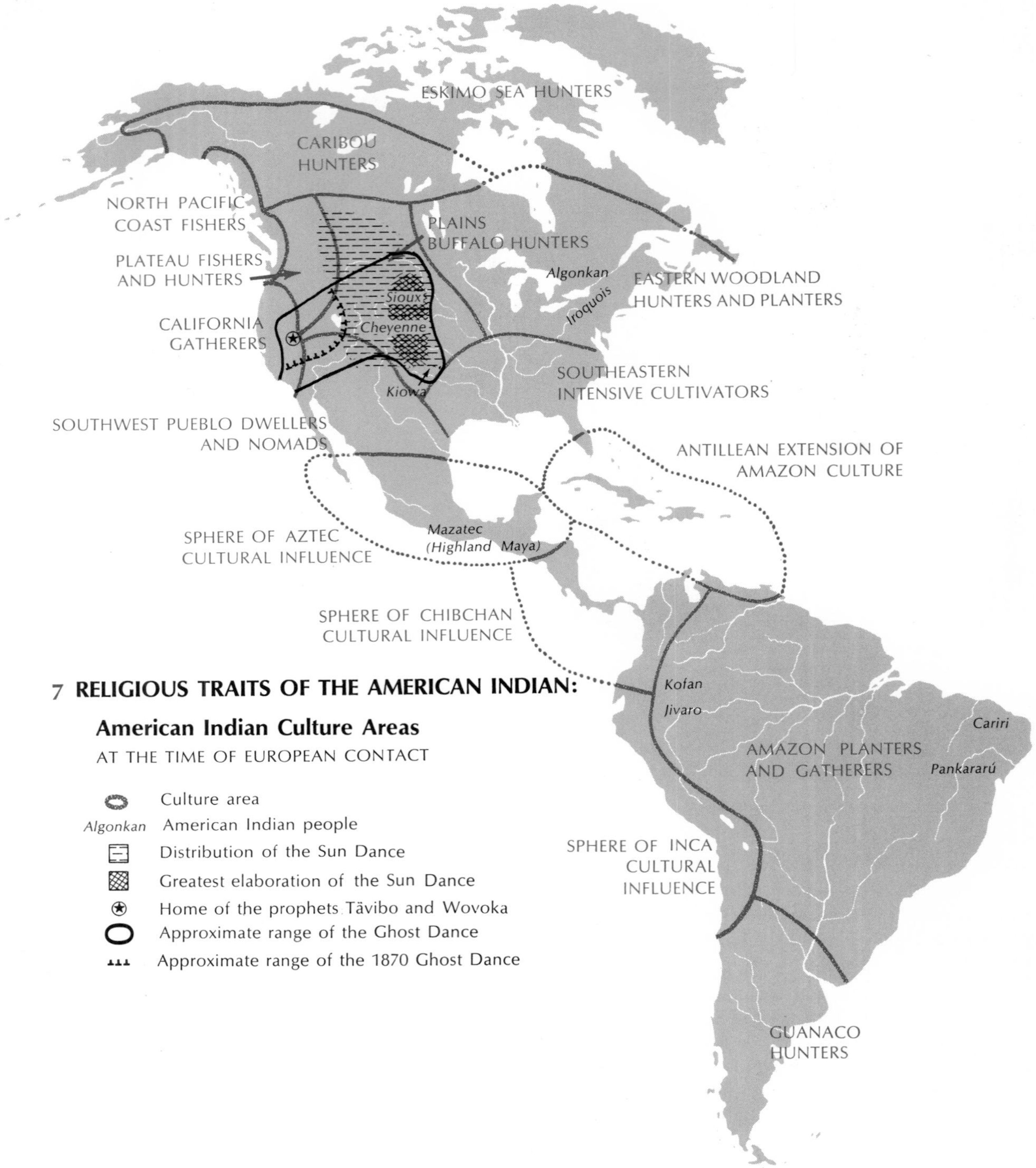

7 RELIGIOUS TRAITS OF THE AMERICAN INDIAN:

American Indian Culture Areas

AT THE TIME OF EUROPEAN CONTACT

- Culture area
- *Algonkan* American Indian people
- Distribution of the Sun Dance
- Greatest elaboration of the Sun Dance
- Home of the prophets Tävibo and Wovoka
- Approximate range of the Ghost Dance
- Approximate range of the 1870 Ghost Dance

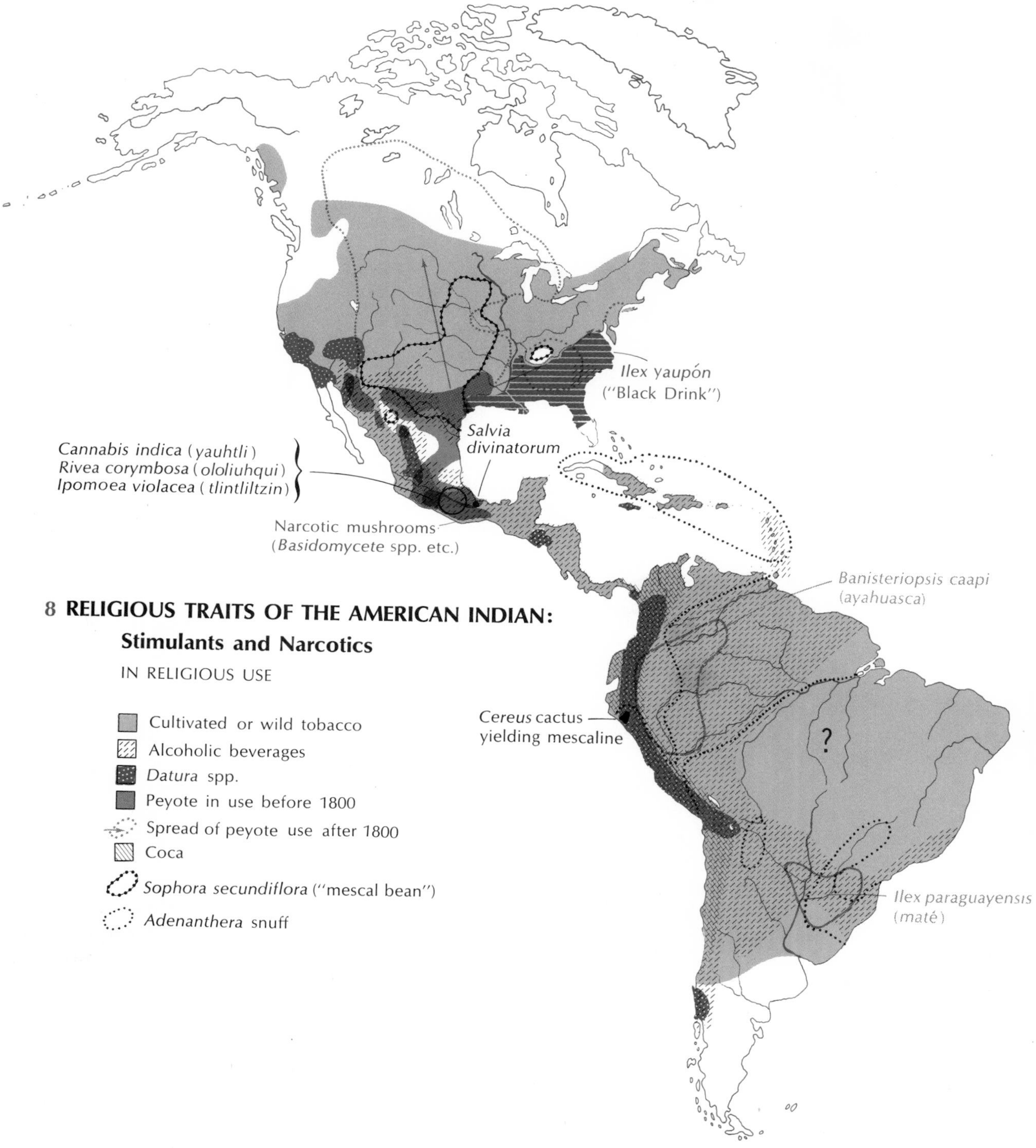

8 RELIGIOUS TRAITS OF THE AMERICAN INDIAN: Stimulants and Narcotics

IN RELIGIOUS USE

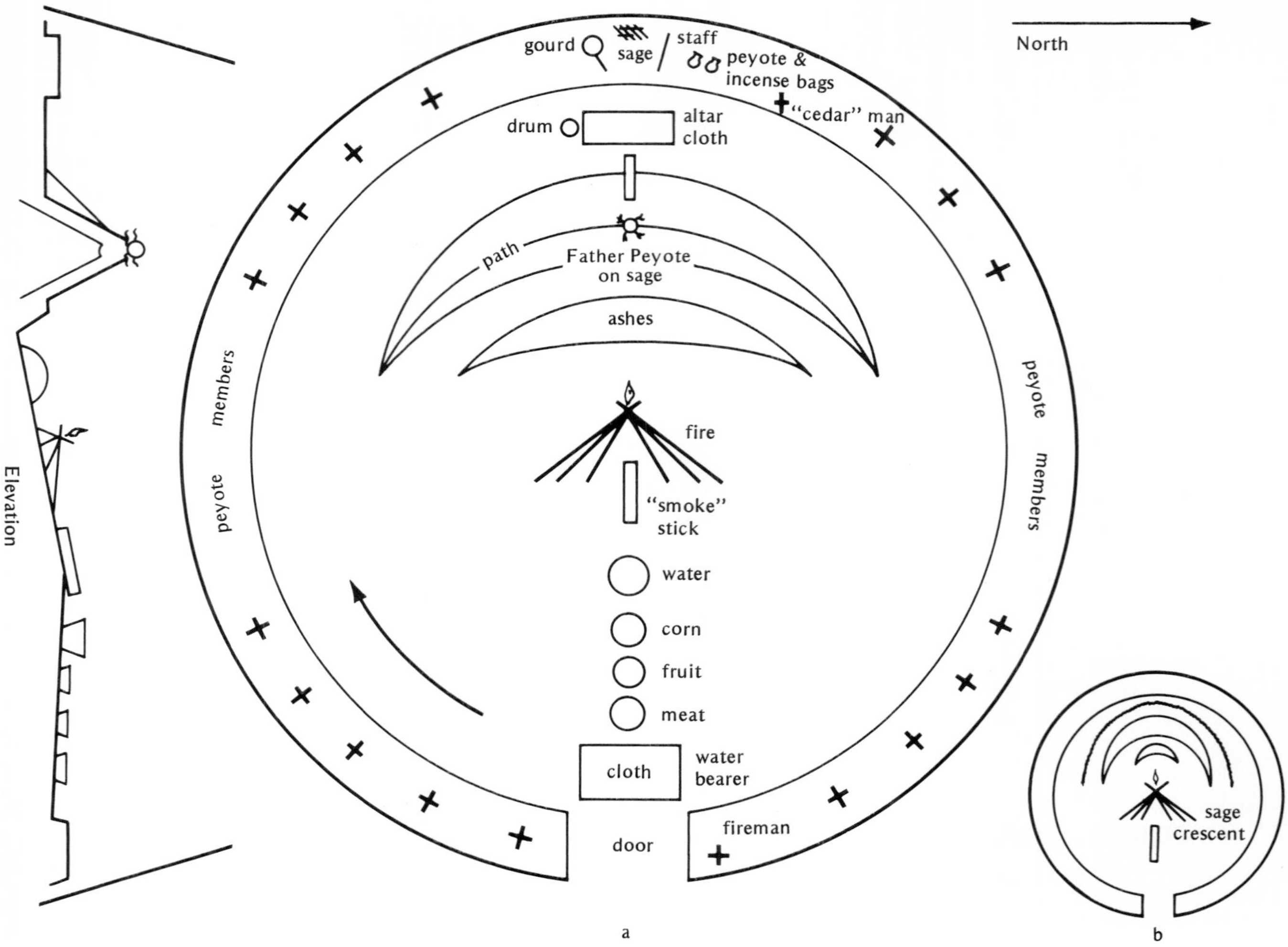

7-3 Arrangement of interior of tipi for peyote meeting. *a,* Kiowa standard peyote meeting; *b,* Comanche horseshoe moon variant.

west Mexico were rediscovered in recent times to be still using the ancient Aztec *teonanacatl,* narcotic mushrooms of various *Basidiomycete* species, paralleling a similar shamanistic antique use of fly agaric (*Amanita muscaria*) among Paleosiberians and early Indo-Europeans. The highland Maya of Guatemala, according to archaeological discoveries, had a narcotic mushroom also. In the southern Plains, in Texas and northeastern Mexico, a prepeyote "Red Bean" cult using *Sophora secundiflora* was known from pre-Columbian to protohistoric times. Among their dozen vision-producing drugs the Aztec had *peyotl* (*Lophophora williamsii,* source of the predominant contemporary cult of Indians of the United States and Canada), *yauhtli* (marihuana or *Cannabis indica*), *ololiuhqui* (*Rivea corymbosa* morning-glory seeds), *tlitliltzin* (*Ipomoea violacea*)—both of which last contain the amides of lysergic and d-lysergic acids, chanoclavine, and clymoclavine, hitherto known only in the ergot fungus *Claviceps purpurea. Salvia divinatorum* is a "diviners' mint" from the Mazatec. Ritual drunkenness on native beers and wines was widespread from the non-Pueblo Southwest southward to Andean and Amazonian South America. *Yopo* snuff (*Adenanthera peregrina*) was a hallucinogenic snuff of Amazonia and the Caribbean; *parica* snuffs of the Orinoco basin are quite different (*Virola* species). *Ayahuasca, caapi,* and *yaje* are names for the violent hallucinogen *Banisteriopsis caapi,* widely used by Amazonian shamans. Recently a mescaline-containing *Trichocereus* has been discovered in cult use in northern Peru. *Yurema* is a little-known hallucinogen of the Kariri and Pankaruru of eastern Brazil; the Kofan use *Brunfelsia* narcotics. There are many poorly known Amazonian narcotics; there is even a narcotic species of bamboo grub.

Cosmology

In cosmology, Amerindians take the physical universe for granted. Supernaturals, properly speaking, are not creators but only "transformers" (the Californian Earth Diver, for example, makes land of mud dredged from the bottom of the sea). Shamans, also, merely control the *changing* aspects of eternity, such as the weather, animal and human life, earth cataclysms, and the sun and the moon. Species representatives, such as Coyote, Raven (also found in eastern Siberia), and Manabus the supernatural Hare, do nothing a human shaman or culture hero could not do. At most, charismatic leaders of crisis cults in both North and South America are mere earth renewers or transformer shamans.

Conspicuous in American Indian religion is the Trickster, in whom we may see the animal-familiar of the shaman (who *is* the shaman) writ large. A being supernatural in magic power, in a sense the Trickster is the anti-Establishment *manipulator* of Things As They Are, the promethean hero like the West African Legba. Coyote does all the culture forbids, like speaking to a daughter-in-law and worse; grandiose Raven often comes a cropper, having bitten off too much by far; Manabus teaches man new arts, especially sexual ones. The Trickster is a world-transformer, culture hero, a fertility figure, and a figure of fun all in one. He is both the power source and the mocker of the shaman, who similarly unites dreamer, bard, teacher, envoy, historian, doctor, divine, entertainer, magician, and clown. Though these attributes have long since been separated into diverse offices and functions, there is no doubt that originally he was a unitary figure, the shaman and his power-animal. Thus among staid, masked rain priests in the Pueblos he is the mud clown, doing everything obscenely and backwards; he charges around an Iroquoian long-house rite like a slapstick comedian. In Sibero-America he is his own medicine show, impresario and actor alike. American Indians know that behind their masks the gods are only shamans dancing.

Bibliography

Benedict, Ruth. *The Concept of the Guardian Spirit in North America.* Menasha, Wis.: The American Anthropological Association, (Memoirs, No. 29), 1923.

Boas, Franz. *The Mind of Primitive Man.* New York: Macmillan, 1916.

———. *The Religion of the Kwakiutl Indians.* New York: Columbia U. P., 1930.

Durkheim, Emile. *The Elementary Forms of the Religious Life,* tr. Joseph Ward Swain. New York: Free Press, 1965 [first pub. 1915].

Hultkrantz, Ake. *Conceptions of the Soul Among North American Indians.* Stockholm: Ethnographical Museum of Sweden, 1953.

La Barre, Weston. *The Ghost Dance: Origins of Religion.* Garden City, N.Y.: Doubleday, 1970.

Lowie, Robert H. *The Religion of the Crow Indians,* New York: The Trustees. Anthropological Papers of the American Museum of Natural History, Vol. XXV, Part 2, 1922.

Park, Willard Z. *Shamanism in Western North America.* Evanston: Northwestern U. P., Ill.: 1938.

Parsons, E. C. *Pueblo Indian Religion,* 2 vols. Chicago: U. of Chicago, 1939.

Radin, Paul. *The Trickster: A Study in American Indian Mythology.* New York: Philosophical Library, 1956.

Reichard, Gladys A. *Navaho Religion,* 2 vols. New York: Bollingen Foundation, 1963 [first pub. 1950].

Slotkin, J. S. *The Peyote Religion.* Glencoe, Ill.: Free Press, 1956.

Spier, Leslie. *The Sun Dance of the Plains Indians: Its Development and Diffusion,* New York: The Trustees. Anthropological Papers of the American Museum of Natural History, Vol. XVI, Part 7, 1921.

Tax, Sol (Ed.). *Indian Tribes of Aboriginal America.* Chicago: U. of Chicago, 1952.

Teicher, Morton I. *Windigo Psychosis.* Seattle: American Ethnological Society, 1960.

Thompson, Stith. *Tales of the North American Indians.* Cambridge, Mass.: Harvard U. P., 1929.

Wissler, Clark. *Ceremonial Bundles of the Blackfoot Indians,* New York: The Trustees. Anthropological Papers of the American Musuem of Natural History, Vol. VII, Part 2, 1912.

PART TWO
ETHNIC RELIGIONS OF THE PRESENT

Localized in the Lands of Their Birth

Traditional Religions in Africa

Hinduism

Jainism

Sikhism

Confucianism and Taoism

Shintō

Dispersed

Zoroastrianism

Judaism

8

Traditional Religions in Africa

John S. Mbiti

The Sources

African Traditional Religion is intricately bound to the social and cultural life of African peoples. Therefore it has no founder, and its history is also the history of African peoples in their tribal or other ethnic distribution. Scholars are just beginning to wrestle with the problem of the history of Traditional Religion, which is in part the oral history of each African people. Myths, stories, narratives, biographies, religious names of individuals and places, religious concepts and practices, social institutions, ethics and proverbs, all reveal a history of Traditional Religion that goes back to ancient times.

The main difficulty about studying the history of traditional religion is that it has no sacred writings. Furthermore written records are rare, apart from those of the societies that came into contact with Islamic culture and European traders, explorers, and missionaries, and even most of these written records date largely from the nineteenth century onward. It is to be noted also that religious objects like shrines, altars, magical and medical objects, sacred stools, masks, and religious dress, from which a certain amount of historical study can also be scrutinized, do not last many generations on account of climatic conditions in tropical Africa. There are, therefore, few religious objects available today that go back more than one and a half centuries.

We are left, therefore, with primarily oral sources in the form of language, concepts, myths, stories, proverbs, prayers, ritual words, secrets of religious personages, songs, and music, from which we may gather something about the history of Traditional Religion. Though Africa is a vast continent, there are remarkable similarities in these areas of Traditional Religion from the east to the west and southward.

Geographical Distribution

Today, African Traditional Religion spreads over an area of about two thirds of Africa, including Madagascar (Maps 1 and 2). Its distribution lies south and west of a line that could be drawn eastward from Senegal, through southern Mali, Upper Volta, Nigeria, central Chad, and central Sudan to northern Ethiopia, and then southward across eastern Ethiopia and along its border with Somalia to the coast of Kenya. North of that line, covering one third of Africa, Islam is predominant, but closer studies of local religious practices and ideas would show certain traits of Traditional Religion. In the area occupied by Traditional Religion we find also Christianity, both in its ancient form in Ethiopia and in its modern form through missionary activities assisted by African converts of the nineteenth and twentieth centuries. There is an island of ancient Christianity in Egypt, which otherwise is largely Muslim.

Christianity predominates over precisely the same geographical area as Traditional Religion. There is, therefore, a religious overlapping today between Traditional Religion and Christianity, so that the majority of African Christians have scarcely abandoned their Traditional Religious beliefs. It is clear also that Traditional Religion has prepared the ground for the rapid expansion of Christianity in Africa in the twentieth century, currently at the rate of about 6 per cent per annum, a rate almost unparalleled and unknown throughout the history of Christianity. African Traditional Religion and Christianity are largely compatible, and for that reason Traditional Religion has readily accommodated Christianity even though the latter in its Western form has tried to exterminate the former. The traits of Christianity, Islam, and African Traditional Religion present in the religious life of contemporary Africans cannot be measured; nor can the adherents of these religions. True religious statistics in Africa tend to show a total figure greater than the population of the continent. As a working guide, however, in 1971 there were about 75 million Christians, 140 million Muslims, and 120 million adherents of Traditional Religion. (Note should be taken of other religions of Africa, namely, Judaism, Baha'ism, Hinduism, Sikhism, Zoroastrianism, Jainism, and Buddhism, but the numbers of their adherents are comparatively few even if some are on the increase.)

African Traditional Religion is confined more or less to each of the peoples of Africa: it is not a world religion; it has no missionary expansion or intention. Therefore there are no conversions to Traditional Religion, even if ideas, concepts, rituals, ceremonies, and beliefs may spread from one tribal area to another through migrations, tribal conquests, intermarriages, travel, and other contact.

Contact with World Religions

The greatest impact upon Traditional Religion has come from its contact with both Islam and Christianity, a contact that has precipitated mutual influence. It must be emphasized that the conversion of African peoples to either Islam or Christianity has not meant a complete abandoning of Traditional Religion. Whereas Islam and Christianity have brought new cultures, their cultural interchange with African cultures is greater than actual religious change. Obviously there are degrees to these changes, and the areas that are predominantly Islamic show only a few traits of Traditional Religion, whereas those that are predominantly Christian have tended to incorporate more of the Traditional Religious and cultural background. The reason is that Islam crossed into Africa immediately after its inception in the seventh century C.E. and, within a few centuries, conquered and occupied nearly the whole area where it is predominant today, expanding thereafter only on the fringes. Christianity on the other hand, even though it reached Egypt, Ethiopia, the Sudan, and northern Africa within the first five centuries of its history, suffered setbacks when Islam conquered Egypt and North Africa in the seventh and eight centuries and later the Nubian kingdoms of the Sudan, which harbored many Christians until the end of the thirteenth century. It was not until the nineteenth and twentieth centuries that Christianity spread to its present reach in Africa. Therefore the presence and activities of Traditional Religion are still evident in Christian Africa. Indeed, in some areas of Africa today there is a resurgence of Traditional Religion in terms of activities like sacrifices, festivals, medical practices, and so on, which are being done more openly now than they were during the colonial period. Conversions to Christianity come almost exclusively from followers of Traditional Religion, currently at the rate of about 3–3.5 per cent per annum of the population, whereas on the average conversion to Islam is virtually nil. In proportion to the population of Africa, adherence to African Traditional Religion has been rapidly declining since the beginning of the twentieth century.

Note should be taken of the fact that the spread of African peoples through slavery to North America, Latin America, and the West Indies meant that Traditional Religion was carried there as well. In these lands Traditional Religion has been retained by peoples of African descent, but with modifications under mainly Christian environment and languages other than African.

Main Religious Beliefs in African Traditional Religion

God

It is held by all of the African societies under consideration that there is one God, the creator, preserver, and sustainer of all things. He is invisible, and no African peoples are known to have drawn or carved representations of God. A word for God exists in each of the African languages, some of the words being used commonly among dozens of languages, indicating that the belief is ancient and was already there before these languages evolved. God is believed to be kind, just, and good. In some societies He is regarded as father and friend. People make sacrifices, offerings, and prayers to Him, and His name is sometimes used in making blessings or taking solemn agreement (covenants) or oaths.

Divinities

In some African societies it is believed that there are divinities that are next to God in the spiritual hierarchy. The divinities either are personifications of natural phenomena (like rain, wind, thunder, lightning, and death) and/or natural objects, (like rivers, lakes, outstanding rocks, forests, and so on) or are assistants, messengers, and agents of God. The belief in the existence and activities of divinities is commonly found in African societies that traditionally have had central rulers (kings or chiefs) assisted by minor chiefs and subchiefs. Thus the concept of divinities headed by God himself can be interpreted as the spiritual counterpart of the earthly political structure. In many African societies where traditional kings and chiefs exist, they are regarded as sacral or divine even if a clear distinction is drawn between the human rulers and God.

Spirits

The belief in the existence of spirits is widespread throughout Africa, though some societies attach more significance to the spirits than do others. Spirits may be classified into several categories: those created in the form of spirits, the disembodied spirits of human being long dead, spirits of people recently dead (now generally referred to as the living dead), malicious spirits, divination spirits, nature spirits (which occupy trees, ponds, rivers, and so on), clan spirits, and family spirits. People claim to see spirits; others to be possessed by them (for good purposes like divination or as tormentors often asking for something such as meat to be presented to them); others claim to hear spirit voices or see spirit lights. On the whole African peoples endeavor to keep in touch with family spirits (the living dead) through the use of libation and prayers and sometimes sacrifices and offerings. This method of contact has wrongly been called ancestor worship, but African peoples distinguish between what they do to God and what they do to their family or clan spirits. Often the living dead act as intermediaries between men and God, so that prayers, sacrifices, and offerings may be addressed through them to God. In some societies, especially in West Africa, there

8-1 Masquerade costume of the Egungun masquerade, Yoruba people of Nigeria. This is a symbol of the continuation of life in the hereafter, since the spirit lives on. (Photograph taken in June 1971 by permission of the Institute of African Studies, University of Ibadan.

are masquerades performed annually or otherwise during which the spirit world enters the human world and special people dress up in masked form to represent the visit of the spirits (see Figure 8-1). These festivals also renew human contact with the spirits, in a friendly relationship between the two worlds.

Man

In African beliefs, man was created by God and there are many myths that depict this origin of man. According to some myths, man as husband and wife was lowered from the sky to the earth; in other myths God used clay to mold man; other myths tell that God pulled man out of the marshes or waters; and there are still other myths that say that man came out of a tree like fruits or out of the knee of another creature of God. Many African societies depict the original state of man as one of happiness, immortality, resurrection in case of death, childlike ignorance, and one where God was as father to his children. But the original state of bliss was lost to man, and many myths tell how this happened. According to some, man disobeyed one or another of God's laws; in others, a creature of God interfered; in some, people pestered God until he withdrew from them; and in other myths the direct link between man and God was broken when an animal ate the ladder between earth and heaven.

The life of the individual among many African societies is marked with various rites, particularly at birth, the initiation period (often but not always during puberty and adolescence), marriage, and burial. Some of these rites are elaborate and may last from a few days to several years.

Birth ceremonies are observed more or less in all African societies. They are an occasion for rejoicing, naming the child, thanking God or the living dead for the arrival of the child, introducing the child to relatives and neighbors, cleansing both the mother and the child from birth impurities, and ensuring that the mother and child are protected against harm of both a physical and a mystical nature. Initiation rites generally take on the form of circumcision for boys and clitoridectomy for girls, but not all African peoples observe them that way. In some societies the initiated boys and girls spend in seclusion periods lasting from a few days to two or more years, during which time they are introduced to tribal wisdom, history, and responsibilities of adulthood; undergo hardships to discipline and train them for life; and are prepared for marriage, which generally follows sooner or later thereafter.

Marriage is a religious undertaking according to African Traditional Religion. There is a vast variety of customs and ceremonies connected with marriage. It is primarily a family-to-family undertaking, whether the marriage partners choose each other or are chosen by parents or other relatives. Marriage ensures the physical continuity of the individual and the human race. Therefore it is a duty for everyone to get married, except in extremely few cases, because failure to do so is an offense against society and the person concerned has nobody to remember him upon dying. With marriage goes procreation, and the main purpose of marriage is to bear children. The more children a family has, the stronger is its life. Where no child is born in a marriage, the husband marries another wife (if the wife is barren), or the wife produces children with the "brother" of her husband (if he is barren or impotent). There are customs in some African societies in which a person who dies before marriage is married in absentia by his parents or close relatives, and children are born on his behalf. Thus plural marriage (or polygamy, as it is often called) is accepted and respected according to Traditional Religion and in African societies.

Funeral rites are observed very carefully and meticulously to ensure that the departed is not offended. The rites serve to send off the spirit to the spirit world, to give comfort to the bereaved, to counteract the effect of death and in a sense reclaim something of the lost immortality, and to remind the living of the thin barrier there is between those who are alive and those who have departed. At funeral ceremonies, people both weep and rejoice; sometimes they fast, ending the fast with a big feast. In some societies funeral rites last over several months or years. There are societies that bury foodstuffs, weapons, money, personal belongings, and former servants or wives with the dead, to ensure that he has some property or someone with him in the next world or that he has the means to defend himself on the journey or food to eat along the way.

Kinship through blood and betrothal is a central concept in African relationships within the traditional setup. The clan system, duties and responsibilities, marriage, and various taboos are all structured according to this deep sense of kinship that African peoples hold. It is within this that one says, "I am because we are, and since we are therefore I am."

Death and the Hereafter

Originally man was free from death or had the gift of resurrection according to some African myths. Later death came into the world, but according to Traditional Religion, death is not the end of man. Life continues hereafter. This belief is held all over Africa. There are, however, differences as to the nature of the next world and where it is. On the whole, it is pictured as almost a carbon copy of the present life, and the physical environment is similar to that of the living. The "people" of the next world are, however, spirits and not human beings. As long as the dead are remembered personally by someone in the family who is still alive, they may be regarded as the living dead, but once they pass beyond that point, they simply enter the state of collective immortality in which they often lose their human names and are not recalled in the memory of anyone although they might be mentioned in genealogies.

Characteristics of the departed may be observed in a newly born child, in which case it is believed that the departed has been reincarnated. But this is only relative and partial reincarnation because not the entire departed person is reborn—he continues to exist separately as a spirit and only traits of his character and physical features are reproduced. Many African peoples remember their departed relatives through acts of libation, leaving bits of food for them, and through seeing them in dreams or hearing their voices and responding to any demands they might make. Through divination the departed may also be contacted, especially if there is a crisis in the family, like illness or misfortune, or a major undertaking.

On precisely what the ultimate end of man in the next world is African Traditional Religion is apparently silent. But there is neither heaven nor hell, and in most societies there is neither punishment for evil deeds in the present life nor rewards for good life. In some societies leading personalities of the nation are elevated informally to be major spirits (like clan spirits) or divinities (but the latter is rare). Tribal and clan founders are often regarded more highly than other spirits and there are cults in their memory in some societies.

Magic, Sorcery, Witchcraft, and Mystical Power

All over Africa where Traditional Religion is found, there exists also the belief in a kind of mystical power that manifests itself, or is applied, in the form of magic, medical practice, divination, sorcery, and witchcraft. There is no precise English word for it, though African languages have their own exact terms to distinguish its different usages and manifestations. Ultimately the power comes from God, but only a certain number of people know how to harness and use it for the good of society or its injury. It is feared as bad magic, witchcraft, and sorcery; but it is used in traditional medicine, to protect people and property, to give success and fortune, to find out offenders, and even to do things that would sound scientifically incredible (such as changing people into animals, causing injury from a distance, and so on).

The Religious Life

In Traditional Religion there is a variety of personages responsible for the religious activities symbolizing religious concepts. These include kings, chiefs, priests and priestesses, rainmakers, medicine men, diviners, ritual elders, musicians and drummers, poets, and keepers of sacred places and traditions. Some undergo long training at the end of which there is often a formal commissioning thus declaring them publicly to have qualified. In some societies, these offices are hereditary, whereas in others there has to be a concrete calling (usually through the living dead or the divinities). Religious personages are respected in their communities, and there are taboos governing their person and life.

The ethics and morals of African Traditional Religion are embedded in the customs, traditional laws, taboos, and traditions of each African people. God is regarded as the ultimate sanctioner and upholder of morality. Human relationship through kinship and neighborliness is extremely important, and traditional ethics and morality are built largely around human relationships. Custom regulates what ought not to be done and what ought to be done. Stealing, the beating of people, showing disrespect to elders, telling lies, practicing witchcraft and bad magic, sleeping with someone else's wife, murder, deliberate injury to persons and other people's property, and so on are considered great offenses severely punishable by society through ostracism, compensation, payment of fines, shame, beating, stoning, and even death. On the other hand, kindness, politeness, generosity, hospitality, respect, industriousness, thriftiness, and hard work are good morals that children are taught in many African communities.

Society rewards the good and punishes the evil. If an offending person is not detected by his community, it is often held that either the departed or God himself will punish him, and when a misfortune befalls him, then people reason backwards that he must have done something wrong. Because of the closeness of people with one another through kinship and neighborliness, tensions arise regularly, and there are many accusations laying blame on one another. At the same time the sense of kinship generates a wide range of expectations of help

8-2 Kasubi tombs, Kampala, Uganda, in which four Baganda kings are buried. It is one of the central places associated with the religion of the Baganda people. (Courtesy of John S. Mbiti.)

8-3 A hunting trophy (or object to insure successful hunting) of the Bayaka people, Zaire. (From the collection of African museum of Professor Father P. Frank de Graeve, Louvain-Haverlee, Belgium.)

from relatives, so that within the traditional setup the needs of shelter, food, and security are met by relatives.

Africans celebrate life, and this is clearly reflected in Traditional Religion. Festivals cover all areas of life: birth, initiation, marriage, and the funeral on the individual level; the beginning of the rain season, planting time, harvesting time, hunting time, fishing time, a successful raid or war campaign, the coronation of a ruler, the sight of a new moon, and in form of masquerades on the community level. There are rarely set days for these festivals; instead they are marked whenever it seems to be most suitable and convenient. Eating, dancing, singing, drumming, and rejoicing are the main characteristics of traditional festivals, whereas in others the making of sacrifices and offerings as well as praying may accompany the festivals. People turn up in great numbers for communal celebrations and festivals. Such gatherings strengthen social cohesion, as well as renewing community values and reviving community customs and traditions.

Sacred Places and Objects

Sacred places and objects vary from people to people, and within this century many have been abandoned or lost. Sacred places include temples, shrines, groves, waterfalls, mountains, rivers, ponds, springs, altars, sacrificial spots, trees, rocks, hills, graves of leading personalities or family members, and places of some historical importance. In some homesteads there are shrines where the living dead are remembered (through libation and setting before them bits of food, grain, or beans). Each region has or has had its sacred places, some of which are used for making sacrifices, offerings, prayers, or ceremonial gatherings. Burial places for kings are often regarded as sacred.

Sacred objects are of different kinds, including hunting trophies, masks, drums, amulets, divination objects, rainmaking stones and objects, carvings, certain animals, colors and numbers, and so on. As with sacred places, there are many taboos that protect these objects, the breaking of which may entail misfortune or even death, served by the community.

On the Future of African Traditional Religion

The strength of African Traditional Religion lies in the fact that it has influenced if not determined the African cultural, social, ethical, and philosophical heritage. We find its mark everywhere in African traditional life. It has given African peoples their past and largely their present. The question is whether in the changing scene of life Traditional Religion will cope with it and survive through it. In the traditional concept of time, African peoples did not concern themselves with a distant future beyond two or so years, other than in matters of natural rhythm like physical growth from birth through marriage to death and the rhythm of the seasons. Now they are facing changes, many of which are out of the traditional concepts of time and normality. The environment is changing rapidly: children attend school, people migrate to live and work in cities, and for many the yearly seasons no longer directly affect their life. A new orientation of life is underway both for individuals and communities.

Traditional Religion is being stretched into new areas of life, such as the problems of urban communities (like unemployment, ambition for promotion, money economy, impersonal relationships, and so on), encounter with other religious systems (mainly Christianity and Islam), secularization, mass media, mixing of ethnic groups in schools and cities, and wide and rapid travel. We see Traditional Religion making its appearance through a proliferation of traditional medical consultants in and around major cities; through a growing recognition of its importance in churches, schools, and institutions of higher learning; and through research being carried into Traditional Religion in universities and studies of it being undertaken on a high academic level. We see it also reaffirming itself in various religious movements, particularly those of the African Independent Churches as well as some Muslim communities. African nations speak more and more about African heritage, and some encourage it through dance groups, collection of oral history and literature, preservation of traditional monuments, and even incorporation of traditional rites on important occasions such as funerals of national figures.

In these ways, Traditional Religion is gaining some recognition, even if it lacks educated adherents and spokesmen other than those who are interested in it only academically. No doubt as more of African heritage is salvaged and revived, Traditional Religion, which has been largely responsible for it, will thereby be brought to the foreground. But whether it will be able to wrestle with and give effective guidance in problems of national development and technological progress is a different issue. Like other religions, Traditional Religion will no doubt contribute something in the area of human values, morals, and ethics, but it will also have to let itself be changed and pruned by new ideas. It will continue to prepare the religious ground for the expansion of Christianity, and it is possible that through this contact Christianity will give a stage for the universalization of some of its values. Its festivals will diminish in most cities, partly because the ever-growing urban environment is radically different from the village environment and partly because of the modern trend to supplant traditional festivals with national ones. Some of the beliefs in Traditional Religion will no doubt change as a result of its confrontation with Christianity, Islam, and secularization. Others may be universalized in the process.

Bibliography

Abrahams, W. *The Mind of Africa.* London/New York: 1963.

Ashton, E. H. *Medicine, Magic and Sorcery Among the Southern Sotho.* Cape Town; 1943.

———. *The Basuto.* London: 1955.

Baeta, C. G. *Prophetism in Ghana.* London: 1962.

Bernardi, B. *The Mugwe: A Falling Prophet.* Oxford: 1959.

Bleek, D. F. *The Naron: A Bushmen Tribe of the Central Kalahari.* Oxford: 1928.

BOHANNAN, L. and P. *The Tiv of Central Nigeria.* London: 1953.

BULLOCK, C. *The Mashona.* Cape Town: 1927.

CAGNOLO, C. *The Akikuyu.* Nyeri: 1933.

CAROTHERS, J. C. *The African Mind in Health and Disease.* Geneva: 1953.

DAMMANN, E. *Die Religionen Afrikas.* Stuttgart: 1963.

DANQUAH, J. B. *The Akan Doctrine of God.* London: 1944.

DESCHAMPS, H. *Les religions de l'Afrique noire.* Paris: 1960.

ELIADE, M. *Patterns in Comparative Religion.* New York/London: 1958.

EVANS-PRITCHARD, E. E. I. *Witchcraft, Oracles and Magic Among the Azande,* Oxford: 1937; II. *Nuer Religion.* Oxford: 1956; III. *Theories of Primitive Religion.* Oxford: 1965.

FIELD, M. J. *Religion and Medicine of the Ga People.* Oxford: 1937.

———. *Search for Security.* London/New York: 1960.

GRAY, R. F. *The Sonjo of Tanganyika.* Oxford: 1963.

HADFIELD, P. *Traits of Divine Kingship in Africa.* London: 1949.

HAYLEY, T. T. S. *The Anatomy of Lango Religion.* Cambridge: 1947.

IDOWU, E. B. *Olodumare: God in Yoruba Belief.* London/New York: 1962.

KENYATTA, J. *Facing Mount Kenya.* London: 1938.

LIENHARDT, G. *Divinity and Experience: The Religion of the Dinka.* Oxford: 1961.

LOW, D. A. *Religion and Society in Buganda 1875–1900.* Kampala: n.d.

MBITI, J. S. *Concepts of God in Africa.* London/New York: 1970.

MEYEROWITZ, E. L. R. *The Akan of Ghana: Their Ancient Beliefs.* London: 1958.

NADEL, S. F. *Nupe Religion.* London: 1954.

PARRINDER, E. G. I. *African Traditional Religion.* London: 1962; II. *West African Religion.* London: 1961; III. *Religion in an African City.* London; 1953; IV. *Witchcraft.* London: 1958; V. *Comparative Religion.* London: 1962; *African Religion.* Harmondsworth, N.Y.: 1969.

SMITH, E. W. (Ed.). *African Ideas of God.* London: 1961.

9

Hinduism

Venkatarama Raghavan

On Hindu Religious Knowledge and Its Sources

Hinduism, a modern name, is the main and oldest religion of the great subcontinent of India, based on and authenticated by abundant literary records. It has had no specific name such as many other religions have, not owing its origin to any individual founder. Its anonymity is otherwise stated in one of its traditional designations, *Sanātana dharma,* a term that could be rendered as *philosophia perennis.* The eternal truth or truths and the laws or the paths to realizing them were "revealed" through a body of "seers," who are said to have "seen" the sacred hymns or articulations embodying those truths and teachings. These seers are hence called *Ṛṣis,* because of their "seeing" or having had the "vision" of the truths; as having been "heard" by them, this body of knowledge is also called *Śruti,* the emphasis in both descriptions being on the nonhuman, ahistorical origin or basis of this religion. These primal texts or articulations are called *Mantras,* i.e., products of meditation, also explained as "capable of saving the mind." The *Ṛṣi* is also, on this ground, known as *Muni,* "the silent contemplative one." Silence, contemplation, vision, these are phases of the process by which the *Muni* or *Ṛṣi* saw the truth; this process is called *Tapas,* signifying at once austerity, the turning inward of the faculties, and immersion in contemplation (*ālocana*). If a further source for these truths and visions of the *Ṛṣis* and *Munis* is to be sought, such would be the Supreme Being (*Mahat Bhūtam*) from whom these issued forth as its life-breaths. The simile of *life-breaths* conveys on one hand the spontaneity of their emanation from the Supreme Being. On the other, the wisdom that they embody conveys the very essence of the Supreme Being. As such, these visions and articulations constitute the supreme truth. As knowledge, this is caled *Veda;* as coming down in authentic tradition from the Supreme Being through the seers and sages, it is called *Āgama;* as the Lord's command that guides and is binding on us, it is *Śāstra.* Such then is the founder or founders of Hinduism. For over five thousand years, the *Ṛṣi*-seer or *Muni*-meditator has been the charismatic medium, maintainer, inspirer, and disseminator of this religion. The Vedic seers like Vasiṣṭha and Viśvāmitra, who, with others of their class, dominate the epic stage; the Buddha and the Jina of the reformative movements; the interpreters and stabilizers of the intellectual phases that saw the formulations and expositions of the different approaches or schools of philosophy known as *Darśanas,* namely the *Ācāryas* (teachers) like Śaṅkara, the medieval men of God (*Sādhus*) who put across all these teachings to the masses in songs in the local languages (e.g., Ālvārs, Nāyanārs, Kabīr, Nānak, and so on; nay, the modern leaders of

9-1 The Chammund Bull, 12th century C.E. Vehicle of Lord Śiva, symbolizing Śiva's asceticism and rigid religious discipline. (Courtesy of the Philadelphia Museum of Art, photograph by A. J. Wyatt, staff photographer.)

thought, e.g., Rāmakrishna, Vivekānanda, Gāndhi, Aurobindo, and several traditional teachers like Ramana—all are images of this persistent prototype of Hinduism, the *Maha-ṛṣi.* The very gods have their chief aspect in their role as *Ṛṣi: Nārāyaṇa* in penance at the hermitage in Badarī and Śiva in penance on Mt. Kailāśa thus representing the embodiment of knowledge and the communication of it as teacher.

In continuation of the revelations of what the seer saw or heard, he "remembered" and "recollected" and, in further explication of the primal truths, elaborated these revelations in a complementary body of teachings called *Smṛti* (recollection). The codes of conduct, like those of Manu; the epics, in one of which occurs the *Bhagavad Gītā;* and the aphoristic formulations of the different approaches of philosophy like the *Vedānta* or *Brahma Sūtras*—all come under *Smṛti.*

The language of these basic and most ancient sacred books of Hinduism, which came to be called *Saṁskṛta,* is the eastern-most branch of the Indo-European or Indo-Germanic family. It is in fact the discovery in modern times by Western scholars of *Saṁskṛta* in India that led to the discovery of the kinship of most of the languages of Europe, Greek, Latin, Teutonic, Slavonic, and so on and to the formulation of the theory of the "family of Indo-European languages." The nearest neighbor or sister language to the west, from which the Indian branched off, is the Old Persian. Persian and Indian texts have thus a common and most intimate relation.

It would be clear from the above that the northwest of India was the first home of this religion (Map 9). From the hymns of the *Ṛgveda,* the oldest of this literature of *Veda,* different chronological stages and geographical areas are known to be the periods and places of their composition. The rivers referred to, particularly, point to the land of the seven rivers (the Kabul, the Indus, and the five rivers of the Punjab)—a region stretching from Afghanistan and Kashmir to Sarayū in the east—as the oldest habitat of the *Ṛṣis,* their *Mantras* and religion. The next big stretch of this religion was over the Gangetic doab. The region between the Sutlej and the Jumnā was the principal area in which this religion first spread and from which it moved to the rest of the Indian subcontinent. For this reason it was called Brahmāvarta (Manu, II:17). The rest of the Indian subcontinent followed.

The *Ṛṣis* and their followers came to be known as *Ārya* ("noble"). The Ārya was also called the *Śiṣṭa* ("the disciplined one"), having undergone a purification through sacraments, whose conduct, as well as speech, showed a distinct refinement. In this respect, an Ārya was contrasted with *Mleccha,* ("the mixed"), not brought under a systematic scheme of life and conduct nor a codified norm of speech. This brings us to the question of the earlier inhabitants of the country, the Muṇḍas

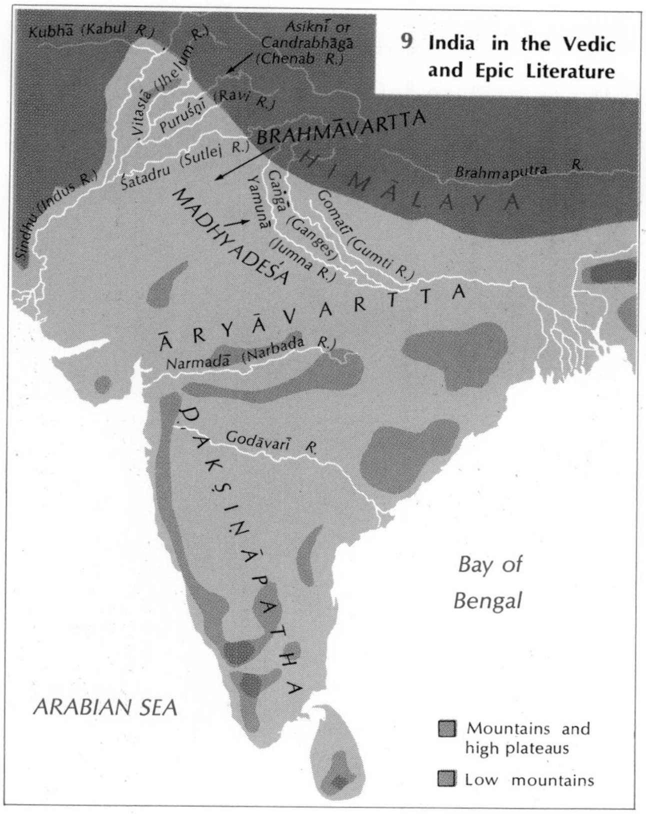

9 India in the Vedic and Epic Literature

and the Draviḍians, whose languages and descendants, about one fifth of the whole population, continue to this day, the latter particularly in a highly developed form. But on them, Sanskrit, its religion, and culture have, through the centuries of coexistence, exerted their far-reaching influence.

The *Ṛgveda,* the earliest record of Āryan religion and culture, refers to several conflicts and battles, some of which are with peoples not of their way of life, speech, and worship and called generally *Dāsas* and *Dasyus.* These were evidently the older inhabitants of the area over which the Ṛgvedic people were spreading. With their expansion over further and further regions, the older inhabitants were subdued or, as it was the more general case, assimilated by acculturation.

Linguistically, of the four language families of India, the Austro-Asiatic groups of the *Khāsis* of Assam and the *Muṇḍas* (Kols) of central and east India and the Draviḍian groups of the south and certain parts of central India form the most important outside the Indo-European or Āryan. The Austric substratum was overlaid by the Dravidian in some areas. Although both these had come under the powerful synthesizing influence of the Āryan-Sanskrit speech and culture, the contact, the coexistence, and the process of synthesis through the centuries have also been characterized by the assimilation by the Sanskrit tradition of elements of the Muṇḍa and Draviḍian in speech, religion, and customs. On behalf of the Draviḍian, it has been contended that the artifacts excavated at the Indus Valley sites of Harappā and Mohenjo-Daro show a developed civilization that was pre-Vedic and whose cities were destroyed by the Āryans. This civilization has generally been taken as Draviḍian. None of these interpretations of the finds has been completely proved or accepted, as the very script of these finds remains to be deciphered. The theory of invasion and killing as responsible for the disappearance of the civilization has been disproved,[1] and further excavations have shown in areas other than the sites mentioned above, layers disclosing artifacts of this culture. Among the finds of the Indus Valley is a cross-legged seated figure, apparently in austerity, and taken as representing Śiva as a *Yogin,* and from this it has been further surmised that the worship of Śiva and Yoga practices were non-Āryan and pre-Vedic. Some go to the extent of suggesting that some of undesirable features of later Hinduism, such as caste, priesthood, phallic worship, and pollution practices, which are not borne out by the *Ṛgveda,* were heritages of the Harappan civilization. Interpretations of this script and cultural material have also been not wanting that consider all this as part and parcel of the composite post-Vedic culture that had already begun to evolve all over the country.

The leading Draviḍian group, Tamil, which, next to Sanskrit has the oldest literature, shows already in its earliest poems and grammar the influence of Sanskrit on language, literature, and religious practices, notably the Tamil kings performing Vedic sacrifices. Even its earliest inscriptions, which are in the pan-Indian Brāhmī script and have been dated from about the second century B.C.E., show admixture of Prākṛt words. Another phenomenon of this historical-*cum*-geographical process may also be noted. As this culture and its bearers moved ahead, eastward and southward for one reason or another, the areas they left behind became sometimes culturally poorer; in the earlier phases, this was true of the extreme northwest, which even came to be abused as having relapsed into *Mleccha*-land; in later historical times, when North India was invaded often and overlaid by cultural patterns from outside, South India became a haven of the indigenous, orthodox or pristine culture that took shelter there. Hence the renaissance in religion and philosophy and arts from the south in Pallava (sixth

[1]See, for example, G. F. Dales, "The Mythical Massacre at Mohenjo-daro," *Expedition,* Vol. 6, No. 3 (1964), 36–43.

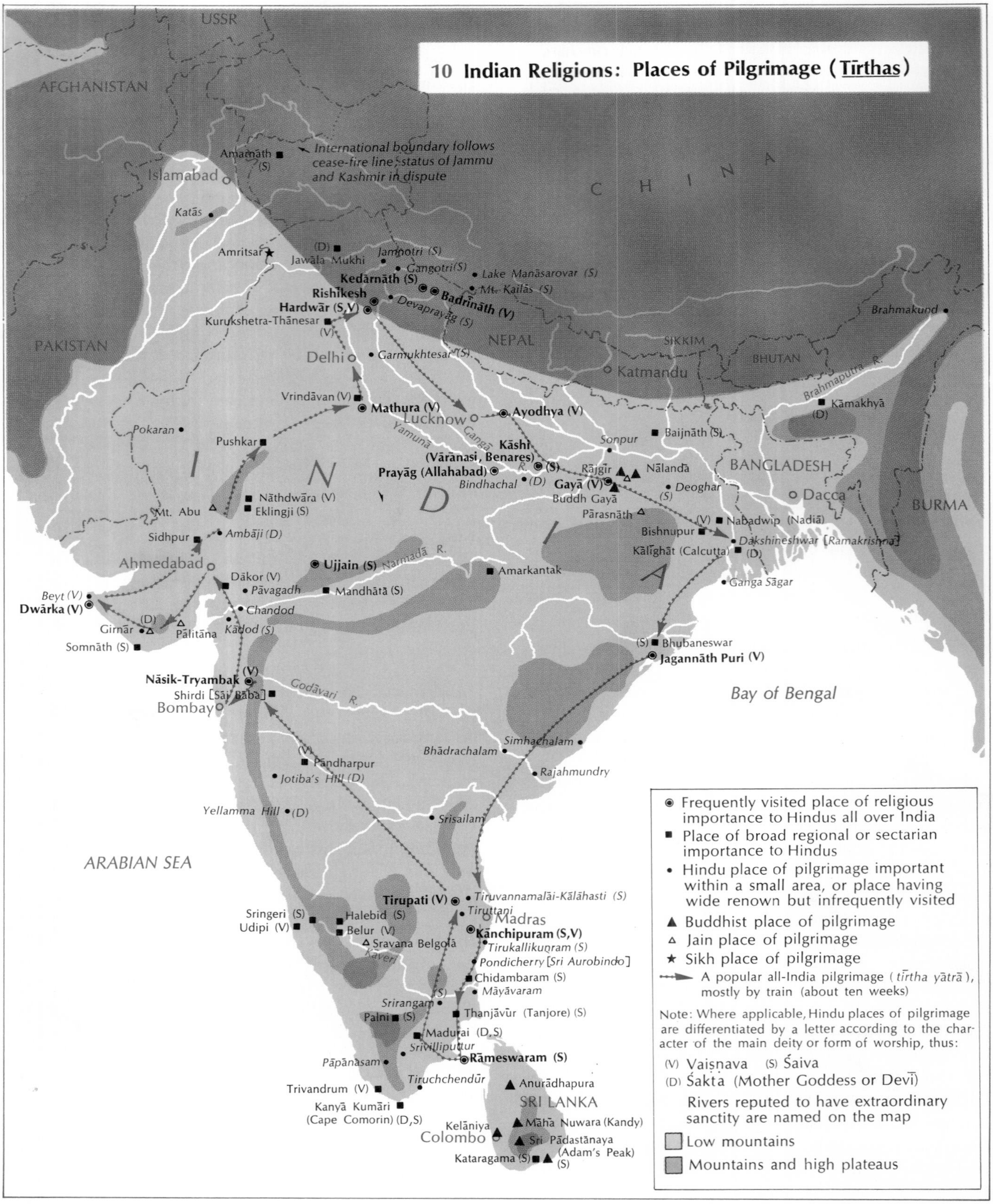

10 Indian Religions: Places of Pilgrimage (Tīrthas)

USSR

AFGHANISTAN

Islamabad ○

CHINA

International boundary follows cease-fire line; status of Jammu and Kashmir in dispute

Amarnāth ■ (S)

Katās •

Amritsar ★

(D) ■
Jawāla Mukhī ●

Jamnotri (S)
● Gangotri (S)

• Lake Manāsarovar (S)
● Mt. Kailās (S)

Kedārnāth (S) ⊙⊙

Rishīkesh
Hardwār (S,V) ⊙⊙
Kurukshetra-Thānesar •

● ● **Badrīnāth (V)**

Devaprayāg (S)

Brahmakund •

PAKISTAN

Delhi ○

(V)

Garmukhtesar (S)

NEPAL

Katmandu ○

SIKKIM

BHUTAN

Brahmaputra R.

Pokaran •

Vrindāvan (V) •

I
N
D

Mathura (V) ⊙
Lucknow ○

● **Ayodhya (V)**

Kāmākhyā (D)

Pushkar ■

Yamuna

● **Kāshī**
(Vāranasi, Benares) ⊙
Prayāg (Allahabad) ⊙
Bindhachal •

Sonpur ○

● Baijnāth (S)

BANGLADESH

Dacca ○

BURMA

Mt. Abu △

Nāthdwāra (V) ■
Eklingji (S) •

Sidhpur ■
• Ambāji (D)

Ahmedabad ○

Dākor (V) ■
• Pāvagadh
Mandhātā (S) ■

Beyt (V) •
Dwārka (V) ⊙

(D) •
Girnār • △ △
Somnāth (S) ■

• Chandod
Kāvod (S) •
Pālitāna △

● (S) ▲ ▲ Nālandā
Gayā (V) ▲ △
Buddh Gayā
Pārasnāth △
• Deoghar (S)

Ujjain (S) ⊙
Narmadā R.

• Amarkantak

Bishnupur •
Kālīghāt (Calcutta) •
(V) ▲ • Nabadwip (Nadiā)
Dakshineshwar [Ramakrishna]
(D) •

• Ganga Sāgar

Nāsik-Tryambak (V) ⊙
Shirdi [Sāi Bābā] ■
Bombay ○

Godāvari R.

(S) ■ Bhubaneswar
Jagannāth Puri (V) ⊙

Bay of Bengal

(V) •
Pandharpur •
• Jotiba's Hill (D)

• Bhādrachalam

Simhachalam •

Yellamma Hill • (D)

• Srisailam

• Rajahmundry

ARABIAN SEA

Sringeri (S) •
Udipi (V) ■

Halebid (S) ■
Belur (V) ■
Sravana Belgola △
Kāveri

Tirupati (V) ⊙ ● *Tiruvannamalai-Kālāhasti (S)*
• Tiruttani
Madras ○
Kānchipuram (S,V) ⊙
• Tirukallikuṇram (S)
• Pondicherry [Sri Aurobindo]

Chidambaram (S) •
• Māyāvaram

Srirangam •
(S)

Palni ■ (S)
Madurai (D,S) •

• Thanjāvūr (Tanjore) (S)

Pāpānasam •
• Srivilliputtur

● **Rāmeswaram (S)**

Trivandrum (V) •
Tiruchchendūr •

Kanyā Kumāri
(Cape Comorin) (D,S)

▲ Anurādhapura

SRI LANKA

Kelāniya ▲
Colombo ○

▲ Maha Nuwara (Kandy)

▲ Sri Pādastānaya
(Adam's Peak)

Kataragama (S) ■ ▲ (S)

Legend:

⊙ Frequently visited place of religious importance to Hindus all over India

■ Place of broad regional or sectarian importance to Hindus

• Hindu place of pilgrimage important within a small area, or place having wide renown but infrequently visited

▲ Buddhist place of pilgrimage

△ Jain place of pilgrimage

★ Sikh place of pilgrimage

→ A popular all-India pilgrimage (*tīrtha yātrā*), mostly by train (about ten weeks)

Note: Where applicable, Hindu places of pilgrimage are differentiated by a letter according to the character of the main deity or form of worship, thus:

(V) Vaiṣṇava   (S) Śaiva

(D) Śākta (Mother Goddess or Devī)

Rivers reputed to have extraordinary sanctity are named on the map

▢ Low mountains

▢ Mountains and high plateaus

century–850 C.E.), Cola (850–1200 C.E.), and Vijayanagara (1336 C.E. onwards) and in modern times.

The assimilation of gods, goddesses, and religious practices of the local people, referred to above, continued and is best reflected in the religious books called the *Purāṇas.* Local deities got attracted to major deities of like characteristics in the Āryan pantheon and this assimilation is best illustrated by the numerous forms and names of female deities that coalesced into one Great Mother Goddess.[2] Already the epics, particularly the *Mahābhārata,* described holy places spread all over the country to which pilgrimages were undertaken by the people. The spread of this culture is also seen in the increasing recognition and incorporation of these sacred places, sanctified by association of the epic characters and gods and demigods, hills, rivers, forests, and particular spots, which became the sites of temples all over the country. Thus the whole country, from Kailāśa and Badarināth in the Himalayas to Rāmeśvaram and Kanyākumārī at the southern tip of the peninsula and from Kāmakhyā in Assam in the east to Somanāth in Kathiaw̄ar in the west, became the blessed land, *Puṇyabhūmi* (Map 10).

The religion and philosophy, and the sociology and way of life included in them, are referred to today by the modern word *Hinduism,* derived from the word *Hindu,* referring to the people. Hindu, which is the basis of the name India, is not an indigenous name but one by which the foreigners to the west and northwest of the country referred to it, based on the nearest great physical feature that they came to know, namely the river Indus (Sanskrit: *Sindhu,* pronounced by Persians as *Hindu*). A larger geographical name of this territorial stretch is Jambūdvīpa, and a more precise historical name still valid is Bhārata-varṣa or Bhārata after a prominent clan of the Vedic times, the Bharatas, or one of its rulers named Bharata.

Sometimes historians in their periodization schemes assign a separate stage for Vedic religion—wrongly called Brahmanism—and give the name Hinduism to the post-Vedic form of the religion as it evolved in the course of the expansion and consolidation of this culture over the subcontinent. But such a distinction should be made rather cautiously. What constitutes and still continues to be the core religious or philosophical belief goes to Vedic thought; the forms or details that flowed into it adjusted themselves to the basic thought pattern and did not distort or destroy it, although by shifts of emphasis or outward expression they sometimes obscured the unchanging inner truth. It is in this way that the most prominent characteristic of Hinduism, in its space-time aspect, has been till today a luminous example of unity in diversity, of variety and synthesis, of a harmony of the one Truth and its manifold forms and diverse approaches. All schools of thought claimed Vedic basis and justified thereby their claim to unbroken tradition and orthodoxy, as against Buddhism and Jainism.

Genesis

Vedas[3]

The *Ṛgveda,* the oldest sacred writing of Hinduism, represents also the oldest and most extensive surviving Indo-European literature we have. Its age is still being discussed. On astronomical grounds, some parts of it have been shown to come from about 4500 B.C.E. Critical textual evidence would assign it to 1500 B.C.E. Other internal evidence would point to 2000–2500 B.C.E. Archaeological evidence of the 14th to the 16th centuries B.C.E. has been found at *Boghazkoi* in Asia Minor, showing that Hittites and Mitannis had invoked the Ṛgvedic deities Indra, Mitra, Varuṇa, and Nāsatyau in a treaty between them and that a couple of centuries earlier the Kassites knew the Ṛgvedic solar deity Sūrya, thus betraying a religious heritage common to all these people and the Āryans of India. Pre-Zoroaster Persian gods and religion and Ṛgvedic gods and religion are almost identical. The institution of sacrifice, *Yajña* (*Yasna*); the sacred drink, *Soma* (*Homa*); the priests *Hotar* (*Zoatar*) and *Atharvan;* the deities Indra, Varuṇa, Mitra, and so on; the moral order *Ṛta,* the total number of gods being thirty three; and the institution of initiation (*Upanayana*)—all these are common to old Persian and Vedic religion. In fact, the greatest Vedic sacrifice, that of the horse (*Aśvamedha*); the setting up of sacrificial posts (*Yūpas*); and the threefold grouping of society into the learned priest, the fighting warrior, and the people at large (*Brahma, Kṣatra,* and *Viś*)—all were prevalent among Indo-European peoples, Romans, Celts, and so on. The prevalence of many schools (*Śākhās*) is a prominent characteristic of Vedic literature, with reference both to the texts and to the ritual practices. A good many of

[2]See Venkatarama Raghavan, "Variety and Integration in the Pattern of Indian Culture," *Far Eastern Quarterly,* Vol. 15, No. 5 (1955–56), 497–505.

[3]For representative selections and translations of the texts forming the basis of hinduism, see Venkatarama Raghavan, *The Indian Heritage,* The Indian Institute of World Culture, Bangalore, 2nd. Ed., 1958.

these must have been lost. What survived was put together as the *Ṛgveda Saṁhitā* ("collection"), now preserved in only one school, the *Śākala.* This collection comprises 1,028 hymns classified in ten books. The oldest, Books II–VII, are collections of specific families of Seers; one whole book (IX) brings together the hymns on *Soma.* The tenth book, although miscellaneous and later, has a character of its own, having more hymns of philosophical, social, and popular interest. All these are in verses, in poetic style, its authors being called *Kavis,* a name by which, later, Sanskrit poets came to be known. Although these hymns show clearly a sacrificial setting, they had probably a parallel literary tradition also as pure prayers adoring the different gods.

THE GODS. THEIR IDENTITIES. The gods whom the Ṛgvedic seers praised and prayed to are thirty three and are personifications of powers or phenomena of nature. They fall in three classes: those of the earth, like Agni ("fire"); of the atmosphere like Indra, Maruts ("winds"), and Rudra; and of the sky, like Sūrya ("sun"). Light, power, and benevolence are their most prominent qualities, apart from their natural features. Agni in the home is the nearest and friendliest god. He receives all the oblations and conveys them to the other gods. Fire worship was therefore primary and it continues to be so for the Hindu. From birth to death, all his rites are done in and before Fire. Next to the Fire rite came other offerings to gods and the partaking by the devotee of the invigorating drink of the juice of the vine called *Soma,* and this *Soma* is praised in a large number of hymns and is said to bestow immortality and raise the gods to their godhood. *Soma* did not continue in Hindu worship but the offering of different kinds of food and drink, which the worshiper then partakes of as the divine blessing, is an essential part of Hindu worship, whether at home or in the temple.

By far the most-invoked and the greatest god of the *Ṛgveda* is Indra, who dominates the scene with his ubiquitous manifestations and striking powers. He is the personification of thunder and rain, he who smites the demon of dark clouds and releases the nourishing waters. With his brilliant personality and victorious exploits, he exemplifies the Āryan hero with his glittering, speeding chariot. Closely associated with Indra are the Maruts, the high winds and thunderstorm. Of these Maruts, Rudra is the Lord or parent, endowed with the powers of bringing disease as well as healing and fertilizing. Increasing importance is seen for Rudra as Śiva in the *Yajurveda,* where a whole section is devoted to his praise as the god embodying everything. Rudra-Śiva remains dominant as one of the three major forms of god worshiped by Hindus all over India.

The next prominent group of gods are the solar deities. Of these, Mitra brought people together and was god of faithfulness and pacts; Pūṣan was lord of paths; Vivasvat, the rising sun; a group called Ādityas, later counted as twelve with distinct names, presided over the twelve months of the year; Aśvins, the two twilights and also the youthful heavenly doctors; Uṣas, or Dawn, claims some of the most beautiful poems; and Sūrya, Savitar, and Viṣṇu, the three most prominent sun gods. Sun worship is one of the essential ingredients of Hinduism. The most sacred and efficacious prayer (*Mantra*), which Brahmans repeat thrice everyday at dawn, noon, and sunset and which is the prototype of *Mantras* of all deities, is the one addressed to the solar deity, Savitar. Viṣṇu, the sun that pervades the sky, coalesced with other deities like Nārāyaṇa and later with Kṛṣṇa and others to become, like Rudra-Śiva, the object of worship of the second largest section of the people of different schools of Vaiṣṇavism all over India. Of waters, Parjanya ("rain"), Nadis ("rivers") and Āpas ("actual waters") were worshiped. Bathing in sacred rivers is an essential part of Hindu pilgrimage. The Hindus regard water as purifier and rejuvenator, as there is no Hindu religious act without bath or cleaning by sprinkling or sipping of water. Earth and heaven, jointly Dyāvā-Pṛthivī, were adored as mother and father. Bṛhaspati or Brahmaṇaspati was the Lord of prayers; Tvaṣṭṛ was the heavenly architect; Viśvakarman or Prajāpati, the father of all; and Hiraṇyagarbha, the seed and creator. Aditi, the goddess, is everything, sky and earth, father and son, the people and all that is or will be (I:89). Many goddesses of intellectual nature were adored; Vāk ("speech") leads this class. Śraddhā ("faith") is important and persisted as a necessary adjunct of all worship and rites. The guardian deity of the house was worshiped as Vāstoṣpati and so also was that of the field, Kṣetrasya Pati. In a later supplemental hymn in the *Ṛgveda,* Agni ("fire") is prayed to for bestowing plenty, prosperity, and beauty (*Śrī*). This hymn *Śrīsūkta* later attained great importance, which it still enjoys, and the goddess Śrī (Lakṣmī) became the consort of Viṣṇu. Some ancient priests and sages are also adored; the ancestors (*Pitaras*) are spoken of in some groups; worship of ancestors became part of Hinduism and every Hindu is expected to offer libations (*tarpaṇa*) to his own ancestors on the days of the new moon and the new year, the solstices, eclipses, and so on. He is also expected to offer food on the dates of their death (*Śrāddha*). Of animals the horse symbolized the sun. The cow (*Go*), goddess of plenty, which is venerated all through the history of Hinduism, figures very much in Vedic descriptions and imagery. So also the bull, which later became the vehicle of the major deity, Śiva. Even birds formed part of divine symbolism.

The demon world of the *Ṛgveda* is not so full as in the later times; Vṛtra (from the root "to cover"), who is darkness and the witholder of the waters and whom Indra slays, is the leading evil force. The Rākṣasas were enemies of sacrifice and were a class of people. Asura, originally the great God, became in course of time degraded because of the post-Zoroaster enmity between Persian and Indian, and in later Vedic and all through the epics and *Purāṇas,* Asura and Deva figure as opposing forces, demonic and divine.

THEIR FUNCTION. The Ṛgvedic conception of God receives its full statement in X:121: His being the primary being and source, support and master of everything; the immanent being and life and strength of all; the sovereign God whom other gods obey and He that promulgated the sacrifice and all the true laws for the sustenance of mankind.

In their prayers to their deities, the seers displayed every aspect and variety of the feeling that drew the one to the other, so that all moods of devotion and conceptions of God as father, mother, brother, friend, lord, and even lover are already seen in these hymns.

Although each deity had a nuclear, distinctive characteristic, the seers described their deities in a body of divine attributes common to all. Every deity that the seer praised was supreme for him, an attitude that has been called henotheism or kathenotheism and that developed in the later ages of *Bhakti* ("devotion") as the doctrine of the favorite deity (*Iṣṭadevatā*). The seers also often combined two deities like Indra-Agni, Indra-Viṣṇu, Mitra-Varuṇa, and so on. God Prajāpati (Lord of Beings) and the Goddess Aditi (I:89) were invoked in universal terms (X:121), and the hymn to the former attributes to him all those traits that one would associate with the universal God, but without giving the deity any name. This trend reaches its completion in an emphatic declaration of the poet in two verses (I:164, 46, and X:114, 5): "The one Truth, the wise speak of in diverse ways, calling it Indra, Mitra, Varuṇa, Agni, Suparṇa, Mātariṣvan"—which is very close to the unity that was later taught by the *Upaniṣads.* Thus, in the *Ṛgveda,* there is a progress seen clearly from polytheism toward monotheism and pantheism.

A further advance in thought should be noted. In X:90, the universe is described as born by the dismemberment of the one cosmic transcendent being (Puruṣa), who is said to undergo a sacrifice. From him are born time and the seasons, animals and birds, the very scriptures (Vedas), the four classes of human beings, the sky and earth, and so on. Several parallels to this conception of creation have been found among the Indo-Europeans of Europe. Besides the above-mentioned form, it is also said that God first creates a female principle and then the creation appears. In both these forms the idea occurs in the *Upaniṣads* and persists in later schools of religion and philosophy. In X:72, 2–6, Brahmaṇaspati, like a smith, forged the universe; from the nonexistent the existent came, and then the quarters, earth, the gods, and so on. Far more profound is X:129, where the poet sings of the mystery of creation: "In the beginning there was neither non-being nor being, nor worlds, sky nor anything beyond; neither death nor immortality; neither night nor day: there was that One which breathed without air, by its own strength, and became creative by its own power of contemplation. Desire, the first seed of the mind, the nexus of the existent in the non-existent, came upon the Being. . . . Where did this creation come from, He who was supervising it from above knows or knows not!"

Thus through the performance of acts of sacrifice and other rites for propitiating the gods, through prayers to them and through the awareness of a cosmic or Supreme Being in which everything found its origin and unity, the *Ṛgveda* provided the seeds of all three paths of classical Hinduism, Action (*Karman*), Devotion (*Bhakti*), and Knowledge (*Jñāna*).

MAN. MORALITY. Punishment of sins and deceit is the prerogative of the gods, according to the *Ṛgveda.* The greatest guardian of morality is Varuṇa, who watched the conduct of persons even in their secrecy and bound sinners and punished them. The seer prayed to Varuṇa to save himself from the sin of failure to observe divine laws (I:25, 1–3; VII:89, 12). Nonpayment of debts was deemed a great sin. Three important words that the *Ṛgveda* contributed to Hindu moral thought are *Ṛta, Satya,* and *Dharma.* From the orderly manner in which nature moved, *Ṛta,* from the root meaning "to go," rose to mean "moral order," the observance of which made nature beneficent to man (I:90). The opposite of *Ṛta* is *Anṛta,* that which is false. *Satya* is Truth in all its aspects, and *Dharma* is the laws and religious observances, which sustain humanity. Of these, *Ṛta* was absorbed into *Satya,* and *Satya* and *Dharma* became two key words of Hinduism. *Dharma* comprehended, besides one's duty, whatever was right and proper or beneficent to oneself and others, in fact everything coming under religion, so that one can call Hinduism Hindu *Dharma.* It is to resurrect the reign of *Dharma* ("good") and to put down *A-dharma* ("evil") that God incarnates himself from time to time, embodying and exemplifying *Dharma* in his own life on earth, as in His Rāma-incarnation.

The last book of the Ṛgveda (X:14, 18) speaks of the disposal of the dead by burning and of burial. Life was identified as *Āsu,* on whose departure the spirit or soul (*Manas,* later *Ātman*) passed to heaven and, as we shall see, was born again. Heaven was above in the high skies, an abode of light and happiness, and this was promised to those who practiced penance (*Tapas*) and liberality and also to heroes who died fighting. In heaven, the spirits (ancestors) stayed with their lord, Yama.

SOCIETY AND THE ARTS. Social glimpses are also to be had from the *Ṛgveda*. The last book has a hymn on the marriage of Sūrya (sun maiden) with Soma (X:85), and the *Mantras* of this are still used in the central sacrament of the Hindu family, marriage. Gifts, liberality, and offers of food are praised in a few hymns. Chariot racing was a prominent pastime. Gambling was a common game and its evils are pointed out in a hymn (X:34). Dice was an obsession of the Āryans, and as to how it can lead to fratricidal war and national ruin is illustrated by the great epic *Mahābhārata.* Professions like those of carpenters and doctors and occupations like agriculture and cattle tending are mentioned. Chariot building is a highly praised art, to which the seer compares his own fashioning of the hymn; so also hymn-weaving is compared to the weaving of drapery. The *Yajurveda* affords glimpses of kingship, of political institutions, different kinds of state officers, organized vocational groups, and, generally, of the instruments of social integration into the framework of the Āryan community. Besides the importance of the *Atharva Veda* for the history of Indian medicine, the highlights of the hymns of this *Veda* are the long hymn on Mother Earth (XII:11), who is wide and rich enough for mankind to live therein together in amity and who is sustained by great Truth, stern moral order, dedication, penance, and spiritual wisdom; and the hymns on the Supreme (abstract) Being designated diversely as *Brahman* (the Great, X:8), *Ucchiṣṭa* (that which is left over, XI:7), and *Stambha* (the Great Pillar, X:7). Apart from officiating in different capacities, the seers and poets indulged in literary exercises like propounding riddles and discussions of religious questions (*Brahmodyas*). Love of the arts of music, of voice and flute, lute, and drum, and of dance was widespread. The religious sacrifice included vocal and instrumental music. For singing in the sacrifices by a special class of priests called *Udgātṛs* ("singers"), the prayers of the *Ṛgveda* were set to music. This musical version of the *Ṛks* forms the second *Veda,* called *Sāman,* meaning "music." The art of Indian music is derived from this *Sāma Veda,* as is also the philosophy of the art that it is an aid to religious worship, contemplation, and spiritual attunement.

THE CULT. The third *Veda* is *Yajus,* meaning "sacrifice," of which a few recensions survive to this day. The best known are the *Kṛṣṇa* and *Śukla Yajus* ("black" and "white"), the former being mixed with sacrificial formulae and the latter comparatively free from them. The verse portions of the *Yajus* are from the *Ṛgveda.* Already the *Ṛgveda* is full of references to sacrifice (*Yajña*), its various elements, and a variety of major and minor priests performing its various acts. But it is in the *Yajur Veda* that the picture of the sacrifice emerges clearly with their number, nature, purpose, and symbolism. The *Vedas* know no images of gods nor temples; sacrifices were performed in special halls or sheds, and there were altars and sacrificial posts, specific places with sacred grass strewn over where gods were invoked to present themselves. Fire is the most important and offerings were made in it; animals to be sacrificed were tied to the posts. Sacrifices were undertaken by the priests for the benefit of an individual (*Yajamāna*), almost always a king but possibly an affluent Brahman. They were obligatory or for specific desires, and they were performed daily, periodically, or for a long duration. Each home maintained three fires: the daily fire-rite or *Agnihotra,* which is even now kept up in several orthodox Pandit families; the fortnightly rites related to the new moon and the full moon; rites in honor of ancestors. Corresponding to these were three four-monthly rites. An elaborate ritual, *Agnicayana,* is the raising of the fire altar with a huge pile of brick in the form of a bird. Two symbolically significant sacrifices are the one in which Man (Puruṣa) is symbolically sacrificed, recalling the Ṛgvedic cosmogonic hymn of the Supreme Being undergoing sacrifice for creation, and the *Sarvamedha,* in which the deity is the Supreme Being and the performer, one who realized God's universal presence and gave away all his possessions. The consecration of the king was done with the *Rājasūya* sacrifice, and his sovereignty was celebrated with the horse sacrifice, *Aśvamedha,* the greatest of sacrifices. The sacrifices were very impressive performances, with the *Ṛgvedic* prayers, the *Saman*-singing, lute music, literary and philosophical debates, extensive feeding, and gifts. At the end of the sacrifice there were prayers for social, national, and universal prosperity and welfare.

The Brāhmaṇas

The next stage of Vedic thought is the prose exegesis that commented upon, elaborated, and commended the hymns, sacrifice, and rituals mentioned in them; they are called *Brāhmaṇas,* meaning "related to Brahman." The method of exegesis comprises the principles of injunction for doing a thing ordained or good and prohibition of an undesirable thing; the above are supported by

Arthavada, which takes the form of praise of the good (*Stuti*) and censure of the bad (Nindā). In further support of this, precedents in the form of ancient myths and legends called *Purākalpa, Parakṛti,* and *Itihāsa* are used. Each of the four *Vedas* has more than one such *Brāhmaṇa.* This large literature shows the development of the stories and myths of the gods and the cosmogony figuring in the hymns and has other narratives of kings and sages and legends, such as that of the flood found among other ancient peoples as well. Apart from the details of rituals, the *Brāhmaṇas* register also an advance in the symbolic and esoteric interpretation, each deity and rite being dealt with on three planes: the natural (*adhibhūa*), the sacrificial (*adhiyajña*), and the personal, mystical, or philosophical (*adhyātman*). The latter part of the *Brāhmaṇas* are called *Āraṇyakas* ("to be cultivated in forests"), and there the high spiritual approach becomes more marked. Although in the former part the sacrifice is prominent, ethics and morality are also stressed—the virtues of truth, pleasant speech, faith, righteousness, penance, scriptural learning, charity, and so on. Other intellectual and moral concepts also are deified and prayed to: shame at doing wrong, fortitude, intellect, desire, and anger. The worship of the sun gets strengthened, and as in the case of Śiva and the long hymn on Him in the *Yajus,* its *Āraṇyaka* (*Kṛṣṇa* Yu., I, i, ff.) carries a long litany on the Sun (*Sūryanamaskāra*) that is to this day recited along with prostrations at every step, on Sundays and other occasions like birthday and illness, for longevity and health.

The Upaniṣads

The peak of Vedic thought was reached in what has been appropriately described as the conclusive part of the *Vedas,* the Vedānta, or the *Upaniṣad.* The *Upaniṣad,* forming the last section of the *Brāhmaṇas,* is called so because it embodies knowledge to be imparted by the teacher to the pupil sitting near in seclusion (*Upa-ni-sad*). The *Upaniṣads* are the most widely known of Indian texts, having been translated into Latin in 1801–1802 from the Persian version of the seventeenth century and then into other European languages; they have exercised much influence on some Western thinkers. From what has been stated already of the growth of philosophical thought, pantheism, and the conception of unity in the *Ṛgveda* and the *Brāhmaṇas,* it may be seen that the monism, pantheism, and monotheism of the *Upaniṣads* was a natural development of Brāhmaṇical thought in which, as contrasted with the sacrificial, the *Kṣatriyas* (" kings") who were the patrons took active interest. The prose and dialogue form of the *Upaniṣads* is interesting from the literary point of view, the narratives adding to its liveliness and the similes and parables to its beauty.

The Upaniṣadic texts are of two kinds: one postulating an impersonal absolute, devoid of duality (*Advaita*) and attributes (*Nirguṇa*), and the other speaking of a personal being, endowed with quality (*Saguṇa*). The former defines the ultimate and only reality as the one universal substratum called *Brahman* of the form of *Sat, Cit,* and *Ānanda* ("existence," "consciousness," and "bliss"), unbound by time or space, impartite, and unchanging, of which the phenomenal, finite, and changing world of names and forms is a modification or appearance. This Brahman, the Supreme Self or Overself (*Parama-Ātman*), being only one, is identical with the individual embodied self of everyone (*Pratyagātman*). In four *Upaniṣads* of the four *Vedas,* this identity is thus affirmed by quintessential statements: "Knowledge is *Brahman*"; "That thou art," the best known; "I am *Brahman*"; and "This Self is *Brahman.*" Above all there is the greatest of symbols, the nearest to the Supreme Being, the mystic syllable *OM,* which is not analyzed and is to be understood and contemplated. Among the well-known metaphors and similes are that of the body as the chariot and the self as the rider in it and that of the rivers from different directions falling into the one sea and losing their identities and even so the lump of salt being put into water and disappearing. Important are the analysis of the real nature of life, greatness, knowledge or light, love, and bliss. The teacher asks the pupil to probe beyond the sense and life breaths and see what constitutes real being; beyond all properties and possessions that are external and involve duality and dependence on something external and see that (the Self) which is established in itself and therefore constitutes real and intrinsic greatness (*Chāndogya,* VII, xxiv, v). The pupil is further expected to see beyond the lights of sun, moon, stars, and fire in order to find the inner light with which not only in utter darkness but in deep sleep one "sees" things (*Bṛhadāraṇyaka,* IV, iii, 2–7), as well as to attain real love and the most precious object of one's love, for the sake of which all else is dear, *viz.* one's Self (*Bṛhadāraṇyaka,* II, iv, 1–5). Finally, the student is urged to move through the five sheaths or levels of being, namely, the food-fed body, life breaths, mind, knowledge, and bliss (*Taittirīya,* III, 2–6); and last but not least, through the states of waking and dreaming if he is to reach that deep sleep where nothing outside is known, the Self is immersed in its own bliss, and on waking up one remembers only that he has slept well (*Māṇḍūkya* et al.). Of this Self, the supreme one beyond everything, the two most frequent descriptions are in terms of light (*Jyotis*, the light of lights) and the infinite Ether (*Ākāśa*). Another memorable description of the Self is that it is the sole restful and auspicious thing (*Śāntam Śivam Advaitam*). In addition to the glowing and elevated diction, there are also cascades of uplifting descriptions of the Great Brahman and sublime abstract prayers, an oft-quoted one among them being "Lead me from the false to the true, from darkness to light, from death to immortality."

This Self alone being real, all the phenomenal world is real only as long as it is not realized. It is realized only by knowledge, not by any acts or rituals. The latter are limited and lead to endless regress and bondage in life cycles in which the results have to be worked out. *Brahman* transcends good and bad, but the discipline necessary to realize it includes ethical and moral conduct, refraining from vice, and developing quietude, composure, and renunciation. After knowing about it from the scripture and the teacher, it has to be thought out and confirmed for oneself through reasoning and then continuously meditated upon (*Nididhyāsana*) till it is realized and made part of oneself; actual experience of it is the fruition of the process, and it is to be realized here and now.

The doctrine of transmigration, of after-life and the soul passing from life to death and to birth again, together with the connected doctrine of *Karman* or acts and their consequent results to be experienced in body, is well established in the *Upaniṣads*. In fact, the Upaniṣadic philosophy of liberation, Self-realization, and attainment of immortality is an answer to the specific problem of the soul being caught in embodied existence in the cycle of birth and death. Already, the doctrine is presupposed in the references to previous births by sage *Vāmadeva* and others and to the stay of the soul after death in plants and so on. It is also involved in the very theory of sacrifice and acts of charity and the enjoyment of their fruits in heaven, after death.

In the same major *Upaniṣads* there are also texts that speak of a personal Supreme Being, the immanent controller, which however does not contradict the impersonal aspect of the Being, according to monists. The *Upaniṣad* texts are not exhausted with the above; there are numerous texts bearing this name that speak of a personal God, designated Śiva, Viṣṇu, Devī, Sūrya, and all the members of the Hindu pantheon. In these, in addition to knowledge (*Jñāna*), devotion (*Bhakti*) is inculcated. Some *Upaniṣads* deal with the details of *Yoga* (the process of sense control and concentration), some with the act of renunciation and the practice of the life of a mendicant, and still others with the modes and materials of devotion.

First Flowering: The Smṛti Writings

Vedāṅgas, Upavedas, and Sūtras

For the correct preservation of the Vedic texts and for their understanding and utilization in the performance of the sacrifices described in them, a set of six scientific disciplines grew: phonetics, grammar, etymology, prosody, ritual codes, and astronomy for the determination of the correct timings of sacrifices. The last include the *Śulba sūtras* on the measurements and construction of sacrifical altars, which disclose advanced geometrical knowledge including a Pythagorean theorem. These six accessories of the *Veda* are called *Vedāṅgas.* Further scientific and artistic developments were codified in a set of four ancillaries of the *Vedas* called *Upavedas,* dealing with medicine, archery and military science, music and dance, architecture, and polity.

Finally, a need was felt to remember the *Vedas'* injunctions and teachings and to codify the latter and prepare brief texts for guidance. This called for a new literary form, brief statements, aphorisms (*Sūtras*), which called for still more explicative, elaborative, and commentary literature. Of the six Vedic accessories mentioned above, *Kalpa,* relating to the performance of rites, developed in this style a number of texts for the different *Vedas* and their several schools that differed from each other in procedure and details of the rites. In fact more Vedic schools have survived in the ritual handbooks than in hymnal collections. In one set of these ritual texts is presented the Vedic sacrifices and offerings and in another set, the domestic rites. The former rites have been mentioned under *Yajur Veda.* The latter governing domestic life must be noted, for they have had more universal vogue and longer survival, some of the major ones among these still forming part of a Hindu's life. The married man sets up a domestic fire in his house that he maintains all through his life and at which he makes all his rites and offerings. He performs some fire offerings to Sūrya, Prajā-pati, and others seasonally. There are five *Yajñas* or offerings that he makes daily, which because of their social and humane significance are called "the great sacrifices" or *Mahāyajñas.* They are reciting the *Veda* (*Brahma Yajña*), making offerings to gods (*Devayajña*), making offerings to all kinds of beings including animals, which had European parallels, and attending to and feeding guests. The householder has been the pivot of the society and the support of the student, the wayfarer, and the mendicant; hospitality has been a prominent and persisting characteristic—nay, a national weakness—of Hinduism. A Hindu's life is to undergo a process of refinement and ennoblement for which a scheme of sacraments (*Saṁskāras*) has been formulated from inception in the mother's womb to death. *Puṁsavana* is the sacrament that is done for the pregnant wife to induce the birth of a male child. The rite at birth is *Jāta-karman,* naming is *Nāma-karaṇa,* first feeding *Annaprāśana,* first tonsure *Caula,* and so on. Two most important sacraments are *Upanayana* ("initiation") and *Vivāha* ("marriage"), which are still performed in a festive manner and at much expense; with the former, which has its Persian parallel, the *Brāhmana,* the *Kṣatriya,* and the *Vaiśya* are born again, as it were, in the life of the spirit and are hence called *Dvija,* the twice-born; the twice-born is initiated into the *Gāyatrī mantra,* which he has to worship and recite at the three junctures of the day (*Sandhyā*), dawn, noon, and sunset; and after this initiation, he seeks a teacher and starts his life of studentship. At the end of his studies, after certain rites connected with the completion and his return, he finds a wife for himself and undergoes the sacrament of marriage. The last important sacrament is cremation on one's death and the funeral ceremonies. The annual ceremony to be done by one in honor of the departed parents, the *Sraddhā,* has already been mentioned.

Forming part of this corpus of texts of the different schools are the aphorisms and metrical texts on *Dharma* referred to as *Dharma Sūtras* and *Smṛtis.* They have coverage common with the *Gṛhya Sūtras.* The most prominent feature of the *Dharma* texts is the codified social pattern, the frame that is to transmit and safeguard for centuries Hinduism and its culture. This pattern has three interrelated fourfold schemes. The first is the four classes (*Varṇas*): *Brāhmaṇas,* the men of religion and learning; *Kṣatriyas,* the rulers; *Vaiśyas,* the commercial and agricultural communities; and *Śūdras,* the remaining workers and untouchables. The second is the four stages of life: the student (*Brahmacārin*); the householder (*Gṛhastha*); the retired (*Vānaprastha*); and the mendicant who has renounced everything (*Sannyāsin*). The third is that of values: *Dharma,* comprehending prescribed duties and virtues and righteous conduct appropriate to each class and stage; *Artha,* acquisition of possessions; *Kāma,* emotional gratification; and *Mokṣa,* spiritual salvation. The second scheme is called *Āśrama,* a state of life conducive to the disciplining of man, and the third *Puruṣārtha,* meaning the basic aspirations of man or the mainsprings of human activity. The ideology of the four aims of human pursuit as envisaged in the *Smṛtis* is that the *summum bonum* is the last, spiritual salvation; the other three are to serve that goal. The second and third, material gains and pleasures, form the actual impulses of man, which, though legitimate, take aggressive unsocial and self-corrupting forms and hence have to be chastened by the two other more ideal urges, righteousness and spirituality, the first and last. To be solely secular and hedonistic is reprehensible. This fourfold plan of life is called *Caturvarga;* in older texts, the last (*Mokṣa*) is included in the first (*Dharma*) and the scheme is called *Trivarga* ("three aims"): in that arrangement, *Dharma* is classified into two kinds, the positive right activity (*Pravṛtti*) and the passive negative one or retirement (*Nivṛtti*). Although these four aspirations apply to all men, the second and third classes (kings and merchants) and the second and third aims (gain and pleasure) go together. The *Brāhmana* upholds the first and last, *par excellence.* Although there is a hierarchy in these three schemes, no inferiority or superiority is involved; each in his class and station and at his duty and each contributing to the common good and self-perfection by dedication to his appointed work—this is the philosophy of this unique aspect of Hindu organization as set forth in the *Smṛtis.* The *Smṛtis* are the total text of life and comprehend every department, including cosmogony and world view, man and his nature, education, family life, sacraments, social obligations, kingship, government, law and justice, productive avocations, and philosophy. Of the large body of texts in this class, the earlier ones in prose aphorisms and the later ones in verse, some are comprehensive and some devoted to particular topics. The most important of the prose texts are those of the sages Āpastamba and Gautama and of those in verse, Manu and Yājñavalkya. *Smṛti* means "recollection" and emphasizes the fact that it is ultimately based on the authority of *Śruti,* the Revelation of Veda. All *Smṛtis* are therefore linked to the different Vedic schools. Of all the *Smṛti* authors, the foremost charismatic personality is Manu. This patriarch figures already in the Vedic flood legend and the Veda says of his teachings, "Whatever Manu said is medicine." Manu's influence extends to Southeast Asia.

Epics

The *Smṛti* includes also the two epics the *Rāmāyana* of Sage Vālmīki and the *Mahābhārata* of sage Vyāsa. Already in the *Ṛgveda,* there were poems praising royal patrons and donors and in the *Yajus* and the *Brāhmaṇas* narratives about ancient kings. The latter mentioned also among members of the State the *Sūta,* the minstrel-custodian of the heroic annals. Of the many ruling clans figuring in the *Vedas,* by merger and interrelation, two great royal dynasties began to loom large, tracing their origins to the sun and the moon. Lays and rhapsodies recited and sung on the lives of specific heroes called

Itihāsa and *Ākhyāna* are referred to in the *Upaniṣads* also. These were even called the fifth *Veda.* In the wake of these lays rose the two *Itihāsas* or epics of Vālmīki and Vyāsa. The first is in 24,000 couplets and the second in 100,000 couplets. The ideology of the epic is to present the story and through it reinforce the Vedic teachings. The *Vedas* and their ancillary lore being prevalent only among the learned strata of the society, the *Itihāsas* adopted the popular and appealing medium of narratives that were recited in public. In later historical times, kings made endowments for such public recitals of the epics and their exposition to gatherings at temples and festivals, an institution that is largely responsible for the wide dissemination among the masses of the moral cultural values of Hinduism and that is still in force. The two epics have also had a large role in Indian art, music, drama, dance, painting, and sculpture, through all of which their characters held their sway over the people. The virtues that they exemplified inspired and sustained the people: Rāma and Yudhiṣṭhira maintained *Dharma* and *Satya* (righteousness and truth) at all costs; Rāma showed his obedience to his father and helped him to keep his plighted word; Bharata and Lakṣmaṇa displayed brotherly love, loyalty, and service; Karṇa displayed liberality; and Sitā upheld chastity and devotion to the husband. *Dharma* in a comprehensive sense is the central message of both epics, the steadfast pursuit of which itself gave man the opportunity to enjoy the material welfare (*Artha*) and the emotional satisfaction (*kāma*) consistent with morality.

The *Rāmāyaṇa,* which is a more finished poetic creation, made of its hero Rāma a national ideal and idol. Rāma, one of the most popular deities, is worshiped by Hindus in innumerable temples and is the center of a cult of devotion (*Bhakti*) and of adoring his name; his birthday (*Rāma Navami*) and his victory (*Rāma līlā*) are national festivals and a considerable number of Hindus are named after Rāma and his synonyms. In each regional language the earliest works to be written are translations or versions of the *Rāmāyaṇa* and the other epic, and in each area the local-language *Rāmāyaṇa* is also the greatest poem, e.g., Kamban's in Tamil (twelfth century C.E.) and Tulasi's in Awadhī (Hindi) (1532–1623 C.E.). It is through Tulasi's version, the *Rāma-carita-mānasa,* that Gandhi learned his *Rāma* and realized the potency of the god's name, which he considered in illness more effective than medicine. It was Rāma's exemplary rule of righteousness, called *Rāmarājya,* that Gandhi held up as the ideal government for India.

While the leading characters in the other great epic, the *Mahābhārata,* remained through the centuries the beacon lights of conduct for the nation, that epic of Vyāsa excelled the epic of Vālmīki by growing into an encyclopedia of national wisdom on principles of right conduct, polity, and philosophy, and the moving spirit behind its whole drama of the fratricidal feud and the resultant war, Kṛṣṇa, the kinsman, friend, philosopher, and guide of the heroes, became, by the side of Rāma, the center of worship, with diverse schools of devotion based on him and claiming as many, if not more, temples and literary and artistic activities celebrating him. As large a number of Hindus bear his name or its variations as that of Rāma, and his birthday (*Janmāṣṭamī*) is also a national holy day. But the greatest role in which Kṛṣṇa is immortal is as the teacher of the philosophy enshrined in the discourse that he gave to his kinsman Arjuna, whose chariot he elected to drive on the field of the great battle. This discourse, called the *Bhagavad-gītā* ("song of the lord"), is, next to the *Upaniṣads,* the most widely known Sanskrit philosophical classic, available today in almost all the languages of the world.

Purāṇas

Another class of Sanskrit literature and religious books of Hinduism, perhaps the largest, is represented by the *Purāṇas,* which deal with the following topics: primary creation, secondary creation after dissolutions, the hierarchy of the sages and patriarchs, the periods of these, and the dynasties of kings who ruled the earth. Purāṇic cosmogony and geography envisage the whole world, and even in their recast forms they preserve the race memory and the places and peoples outside India and the visits of ancient Indian kings for warlike and other expeditions to foreign realms. The great wars of *Devas* and *Asuras* ("gods" and "demons") that form the recurrent theme of the *Purāṇas* are historically reminiscent of the great schism and opposition of post-Zoroaster Persian culture and the Vedic culture but it underwent the ethical orientation of the eternal conflict of the forces of *Dharma* and *Adharma,* of righteousness and good, against their opposites. Cosmogony and history and the rise and fall of kingdoms have been used here to draw out this message of *Dharma* and how it eventually triumphs over evil. This reestablishment of the reign of *Dharma* is the work of the great teachers, sages, and patriarchs who appear from time to time and of the Lord who incarnates Himself with different names and forms among men and by example, precept, charismatic personality, and selfless work for humanity restores the balance in the scales of values. The *Purāṇas,* which, like the two *Itihāsas,* were expounded in public, furnished themes for literature in Sanskrit and the regional languages and for artistic expressions in music, dance, drama, painting, and sculpture; they form the

9-2 Parvati, South India, 16th century C.E. Consort of Lord Śiva, symbolizing motion, divinity of females, and perfect womanhood. (Courtesy of the Philadelphia Museum of Art, photograph by A. J. Wyatt, staff photographer.)

basis of popular Hinduism. The various forms in which God manifested Himself for the resurrection of *Dharma* and for blessing humanity with His grace (these forms being worshiped at home and in the temples) are all described here.

These numerous deities are based on the three primary forms, the trinity of popular Hinduism: Visṇu, Śiva, and the mother goddess Devī or Śakti. Accordingly the *Purāṇas* fall into three major classes celebrating the triumph and grace of these three major inspirers of devotion: *Vaiṣṇava, Śaiva,* and *Śākta.* There are eighteen major *Purāṇas,* which, among them, carry about 400,000 verses. Then there are eighteen minor ones (*Upapurāṇas*) and several Purāṇic texts called *Saṁhitās* and texts called *Māhātmyas* om the legends, sanctity, and importance of particular holy places, temples, sacred cities, forests, rivers, and lakes. Even the major *Purāṇas* deal with these sacred places and pilgrimages (Tīrtha) to them. Another important subject of the *Purāṇas* is the year-round *Vratas* and *Pūjās,* periodical observances involving baths, austerities, worship, and so on, which punctuate the Hindu religious calendar. The *Purāṇas* are important for historical data on the ruling dynasties of India of the historical period roughly up to the sixth and seventh centuries C.E. and

9-3 Maithuna, Bhuvaneshwars, 11th century C.E. Signifies erotic mysticism and the cosmos as expressions of the Urge (Kāma) to enjoy. (Courtesy of the Philadelphia Museum of Art, photograph by A. J. Wyatt, staff photographer.)

for the history of religious sects relating not only to the forms of the three main deities (Viṣṇu, Śiva, and Devī), but also to the lesser divinities like Sūrya and the sons of Śiva, Gaṇeśa, and Kumāra. They are valuable also for the history of diverse branches of knowledge, the arts, and byways of Sanskrit learning and popular lores, music, dance, painting, architecture, iconography, poetics, astronomy, medicine, precious stones, physiognomy, polity, archery, military science, and so on.[4]

Second Flowering: Schools of Speculative Thought

The next stage of development of Hindu thought is one of intellectual ferment, philosophical speculation, searches, and formulations of schools of thought, orthodox and heterodox. The latter were reformist movements. There was continuous growth within Hinduism, and new ideas were not stifled but incorporated or adjusted and assimilated and a harmonious system worked out within its framework. Hinduism was thus a growing organism and at the same time one that did not throw out the earlier phases but conserved the old and that by reinterpretations, synthesized the new with the old. The *Upaniṣads*, the latter part of the *Vedas*, were against the sacrifices enjoined in the former part. Upanishadic thought was accepted as the higher philosophy, and the performance of action (ritual) was adjusted thereto by being reconceived as aid to the necessary mental purification leading to it, no longer as an end in itself.

Śāstras

There are six schools that are called *Śāstra*, meaning "that which commands, directs, and controls." Their basic texts are in the form of words, phrases, and cryptic statements or *Sūtras*, the *Sūtra* being the *sine qua non* form of any system of organized thought. All six *Śāstras* relate to the fourth and final aim of man, spiritual salvation (*Mokṣa*). *Dharma Śāstra* of the first aim has already been explained. Before we turn to *Mokṣa*, let us take a quick look at the second and third aims of human life, namely, material welfare (*Artha*) and pleasure (*Kāma*). It is not correct to say that the Hindu attitude to life was negative. The *Śāstras* on *Artha* (polity and economic welfare) and *Kāma* (enjoyment) disprove such a characterization of Hinduism. The most important *Artha Śāstra* is the comprehensive treatise on government and affairs of the world composed by Kautilya-Cāṇakya, who was prime minister of the emperor Chandragupta Maurya of Pāṭaliputra (4th century B.C.E.). The *Kāma Śāstra* has its primary text in the *Kāma Sūtras* by Vātsyāyana, which deal with promotion of love. Both the *Artha Śāstra* and the *Kāma Śāstra* come within the general scheme of the four aims of man, and both the texts emphasize at the outset the balanced pursuit of all the four aims and the need to see that neither *Artha* nor *Kāma* endanger *Dharma*. Even poetry and drama, such as the poet Kālidāsa wrote, were considered a sweet and persuasive form of *Śāstra* in so far as they too inculcated the higher value of *Dharma* (as exemplified by the hero) as against *Adharma* (as embodied in the villain).

SĀṀKHYA. Outside of the Upaniṣadic philosophy, the first system of thought to be propounded was the *Sāṁkhya* associated with Sage Kapila, a reformist said to have added the fourth stage to the scheme of life of the *Smṛtis*, namely, that of absolute renunciation, but his attitude was quite in keeping with the trend of the *Upaniṣads*, a few of which already show signs of the growth of his system of *Sāṁkhya*. Later, sage Kapila is established as a manifestation of Lord Viṣṇu Himself. This school accepted the duality of being or soul or spirit (*Puruṣa*) and matter (*Prakṛti* or *Pradhāna*), the former being infinite in number and the latter one; the former sentient, the latter inert. The proximity of the spirit induces activity in matter, which evolves into the universe. Matter is made of three strands: the sublime, the active, and the inert, accounting respectively for knowledge and happiness, passion and sorrow, and stupor and ignorance. The categories into which matter evolves are twenty-three: the great intellect *Mahat* (*Buddhi*); ego (*Ahaṁkāra*); the five subtle elements (*Tanmātras*), which produce the five gross ones of earth, water, fire, air, and ether (*Mahābhūtas*); and the five senses of knowledge (*Jñāna-Indriyas*) or smell, taste, sight, touch, and hearing; and the mind (*Manas*), which coordinates perception through the five senses and the five organs of action (*Karma-Indriyas*). The spirit or soul being sentient, its intelligence is reflected in objectifications of matter, and worldly experience goes on as long as the connection of soul and matter continues, through the cycle of births. Knowledge is essentially discrimination (*Viveka*) that the self or spirit is uninvolved and untainted intelligence and all experience belongs to matter; the cultivation of this knowledge and seeing through the evolutionary

[4]Editor's Note: Jainism (see Chapter 10) and Buddhism (see Chapter 16) arose as reforming movements.

and experiential drama of matter ends in the self's isolating itself, whereupon matter ceases to evolve and present its experiences to the spirit. The earliest surviving text of this school is the *Sāṁkhya Kārikās of Īśvarakṛṣṇa* in seventy verses (ca. 300 C.E.), translated into Chinese 557–569 and commented upon by many. It is the *Sāṁkhya* that forms the philosophical background of the epics and *Purāṇas.* The *Sāṃkhya* is considered by some scholars to have influenced Greek thought.

The doctrine of the three *Guṇas* (*Sattva, Rajas,* and *Tamas*), first formulated by the *Sāṁkhya,* also became a common heritage of all the schools—nay, it became in all fields a tool of analysis for a threefold evaluation of things into good, middle, and low. Other ideas in *Sāṁkhya* common to *Vedānta* are the *Puruṣa,* which is Intelligence and its essential noninvolvement in phenomenal experience, and the accountability of all phenomenal creation and experience to matter, *Prakṛti,* which is thus almost the same as Vedāntic *Māyā* and the *Śakti* of theistic schools. An important part of *Sāṁkhya* thought is its theory of causation and the consequent nature of reality. Its theory is one of evolution of a result that is already in existence in a latent manner in the cause, e.g., a pot in the clay.

YOGA. With the same system of thought as its basis, the sister school of *Yoga* developed with Sage Patañjali as its promulgator. It is the practical side of the *Sāṁkhya,* giving an elaborate process of physical, mental, and ethical discipline and means of control of senses and aids to achieve mental concentration and contemplation, the ultimate goal being to extricate the spirit from the involvement in matter and to achieve for the former isolation or existence in itself. The only difference between the *Sāṁkhya* and the *Yoga* is that whereas the former is agnostic, the latter accepts God, holds Him as the First Teacher and holds the mystic syllable *OM* as His Name. The *Yoga* of Hinduism, which is now known all over the world, is the systematization of the earlier Vedic concept of *Tapas* ("penance"), a common heritage of the Indian schools including Buddhism and Jainism, and the basis of all asceticism.

VAIŚEṢIKA AND NYĀYA. The theory that the effect is newly created was propounded by the logicians in two closely related schools that later merged into one, *Vaiśeṣika* and *Nyāya,* promulgated respectively by Kāśyapa-Kaṇāda and Gautama-Akṣapāda. They were realists and pluralists who analyzed the universe into a set of conceptual and material categories whose correct knowledge led to welfare here and in the hereafter. These categories are substance, quality, action, generality, particularity, inherent relation, and negation or nonexistence. Substance was analyzed into the five elements earth, space, time, soul, and mind. Soul was of two classes, the individual soul of beings and the supersoul, which was God. God they held only as the efficient cause of the world, the material cause of which was analyzed to the substances mentioned above. At the basis of these causal elements was the final molecule or atom (*Parama-aṇu*); each atom had its own ultimate distinctive characteristic (*Viśeṣa*), from which the school was called *Vaiśeṣika.* The individual soul possessed qualities like pleasure, pain, effort, knowledge, and so on. Final salvation, called *Apavarga,* is the cessation of all qualities of pain and pleasure; the whole chain of experience of pain (in which all worldly pleasure is also included) is defined as wrong knowledge, which led to attachment and aversion and consequent activity and to birth-death cycles. This analysis of pain and liberation runs parallel to that of the Buddha, but the great difference is the acceptance here of God as the Creator. The *Nyāya* developed an elaborate system of logic to prove the existence of God as Creator and was, for some centuries, a powerful critic of Buddhism. Although the basic categories of reality were the same in these two schools of logic, *Nyāya* added a number of topics relating to logic and debate. The contributions of *Nyāya* to the field of logic comprise the precise definition of categories, theories of perception, and the methodology of inference, which were of enduring nature. Even schools that were beyond *Nyāya's* theistic view accepted its methodology and it became a basic discipline, along with grammar, for all systematic study. A galaxy of logicians—Vātsyāyana (400 C.E.), Uddyotakara (ca. 600 C.E.), and Udayana (tenth century C.E.)—gave ceaseless battle to an equally capable succession of Buddhist and Jain logicians and held the fort of theism and contributed considerably to the waning of Buddhism. The followers of *Vaiśeṣika* and *Nyāya* were confirmed monotheists and worshipers of Śiva-Paśupati, and they practiced *Yoga* and a type of initiation and mendicancy. All of them were devoted to the arts of music and dance as aids to their devotion. They were widely patronized by kings all over the country, as inscriptions show, and had organized monastic establishments and lineages of teachers. In its later school, known as the *Navya-Nyāya,* and developed in Bihar and Bengal in the thirteenth century, formal and semantic logic and definition were perfected by a long line of logicians from Gaṅgeśa (1200 C.E.) to Gadādhara (1700 C.E.).

PŪRVA AND UTTARA MĪMĀMSĀS. Of the six orthodox systems of philosophy the two remaining ones are directly based on the two parts of the *Veda* and are hence called the *Pūrva* ("former") and the *Uttara* ("latter") *Mīmāṁsās* ("enquiries"), the promulgators of which were the sages Jaimini and Vyāsa-Bādarāyaṇa. The enquiries (*Mīmāṁsā:* from root for "man," "to think") are of the purport of the two respective parts of the *Veda:* teaching action and ritual (*Karma, Dharma*) and knowledge and Supreme Self (*Jñāna, Brahma*). The former expounds *Dharma* as revealed by the *Veda,* its source, and establishes the revealed character and authority of *Veda* against other critics, notably the Buddhists. It discusses several other related questions like the nature of words, their constituents and the fixity of the relation between word and meaning. It elaborates the methodology of interpretation and the analysis of meaning and is hence called *Vākya* ("science of sentence"). The *Mīmāṁsā* is a realistic school and holds the interesting doctrine that the world is not created but eternal. The most outstanding later commentator and philosopher of the school was Kumārila (seventh century C.E.), whose refutations of the Buddhistic theories contributed not a little to the decline of that school.

The latter *Mīmāṁsā* is the systematic exposition of the knowledge part of the *Veda,* the *Vedānta* or *Upaniṣads,* and this was promulgated in the *Vedānta* or *Brahma Sūtras* by Vyāsa (Bādarāyaṇa). This is the school of greatest prestige, which threw into the background all other schools and made them mere academic disciplines. The *Brahma Sūtras* selected crucial passages from the *Upaniṣads* and presented in an organized manner in four chapters the philosophy of *Brahman* as the ultimate truth and source of the creation, sustenance, and dissolution of the universe; all passages were shown to be in harmony with this doctrine; the interpretations in favor of *Sāṁkhya, Vaiśeṣika,* and so on were refuted; and the means to the attainment of this knowledge and its eventual realization were set forth.

The Bhagavad Gitā

The quintessence of the *Upaniṣads* is also to be found in the great book the *Bhagavad Gītā,* in eighteen chapters and seven hundred verses. It forms an unrivaled epitome of Hinduism in all its phases and highlights. Owing to its masterly summary and synthesis and its brilliant form and style, it has deservedly become famous in modern times as the single complete and compact scripture of Hinduism. Hinduism, in its final and full form, comprises three paths: action, devotion, and knowledge (*Karman, Bhakti,* and *Jñāna*); all three are dealt with here. The absolutist and theist alike find here a harmonious approach: how the one truth, transcendent and immanent, takes from time to time personal forms and incarnations (*Avatāras*) to put down unrighteousness and restore righteousness, to give the example of selfless service. A new definition is given to the term *Yajña,* originally "sacrifice," enlarging it to mean all dedicated acts intended for self-purification and propitiation of the Almighty. Disinterested performance of one's duty, referred to as *Karma-yoga,* helps to take the evil out of action, that is, its fruits: births and deaths. The God, who gives this discourse to Arjuna, also reveals his cosmic form, assures protection, and calls upon man to renounce the sense of ego, that is, of oneself being the doer, and to take refuge (*Śaraṇa*) under him. Knowledge of the one equal truth in all (*Sama*) is taught as that which purifies and sterilizes action and exalts devotion. From metaphysical doctrines to ethics, from practical steps like the performance of Yogic, exercise to the choice of proper food and control of daily habits—the work packs within its short extent everything.

Ācāryas

ŚAṄKARA. The formulation of the *Śāstras* in aphoristic style brought into being a galaxy of *Ācāryas* ("teachers") who gave the interpretations traditionally handed down in their schools through commentaries on these aphorisms. Of these *Ācāryas,* the greatest charismatic figure, whose personality continues as a living force and but for whose mission in the eighth century Hinduism would not perhaps have survived, is *Śaṅkara.* He was born in Kālaḍi in Kerala, in the southwest corner of India. As a brilliant young saint-philosopher, he walked all over India debating with rival schools, establishing his philosophy, visiting shrines, singing hymns, and consolidating the whole country into a lasting cultural unity. This unity is an intellectual and emotional integration, for according to his philosophy the worship of God in any name and form and by any kind of approach led to the same goal, and under the large umbrella of his philosophy all sects and kinds of worship found a place. He is therefore hailed traditionally as the establisher not only of the monistic philosophy but also of the six modes of worship (*Ṣaṇ-mata*) of the gods Śiva, Viṣṇu, Devī, Sūrya, Ganeśa, and Kumāra.

Before Śaṇkara, there were several commentators on *Vedānta,* but they had all adopted a composite approach to both *Mīmāṁsās,* on both of which they commented; they coordinated the doctrine of *Karma* and *Jñāna,* considering the relation between Supreme Self and the individual self as both a difference and an identity and the relation of the universe to the *Brahman* as an evolution or transformation. The earliest monist philosopher that we now know to have departed from the above interpretation is the grammarian Bhartṛhari (600 C.E.); he spoke of the theory of causation as a transfiguration, according to which the effect was an appearance and had, comparatively speaking, an ephemeral reality. The absolutist philosophy of the *Upaniṣads* and its emphatic affirmation of the *Brahman* as the sole reality, the individual souls being identical with it and the phenomenal world being only empirically real, was effectively expounded by Gauḍapāda (seventh century C.E.) in his verses attached to the *Māṇḍukya Upaniṣad.* In his wake came his grand-pupil, the great Śaṅkara, who once for all enthroned the nondualist thought (*Advaita*) as the leading philosophy of Hinduism. According to Śaṅkara, and the Upaniṣadic philosophy, knowledge alone leads to liberation and there is no need for performance of ordained acts or any acts; on the other hand, discrimination of things into the enduring and the evanescent and cultivation of detachment, quietude, and earnest desire to be released are the necessary requisites for embarking on the enquiry into *Brahman* knowledge.

The primary works of Śaṅkara are his commentaries (*Bhāṣyas*) on the three basic texts of *Vedānta,* namely, the ten major *Upaniṣads,* the *Brahma Sūtras,* and the *Bhagavad Gītā;* some minor works presenting his teachings in a simple manner, of which the most important are *Viveka Cūḍāmaṇi* ("crest-jewel of discrimination") and *Upadeśasāhasrī* ("a thousand teachings"); and a large number of still more popular works of the form of hymns to the absolute (*Niguṇa Brahman*), as well as to different forms of God in the shrines that he visited (*Saguṇa Brahman*). He also reorganized the monastic order, which led to opposition from those following the prevailing order. In his line came a chain of monastic centers (*Maṭhas*) in different parts of the country having successions of *Śaṅkarācāryas* to this day; all of these men are held in great veneration and one of them today at the center at *Kāñcī* in Tamil Nad is the most charismatic personality and has recently been responsible for a fresh religious upsurge in the south.

Phenomenal existence, in Śaṅkara's interpretation, is comparatively unreal, being a superimposition (*Adhyāsa*) on reality, even as, out of one's delusion, a snake appears as a rope or water appears in a mirage. There are thus two orders of reality, the fundamental and the empirical (*Vidyā* and *Avidyā, Brahman* and *Māyā*), even as in the case of waking experience and dream experience. The world is not unreal, but it is empirically real and is sublated only when one has realized the *Brahman.* Nor does Śaṅkara's position render the concept of a personal God ineffective; Śaṅkara was an ardent devotee and but for his work all religious worship and temples would have been lost. From the point of society and the world, the most significant contribution of *Advaita* as stabilized by Śaṅkara is the doctrine of *Jīvanmukti,* liberation while yet in this body and continuing to work for the uplift of humanity. This liberation is possible because on the rise of knowledge and realization, man becomes immediately a free agent, equal to God, and so long as his body lasts he can, like an incarnation of God, work for the welfare of humanity.

Among ideas that Śaṅkara reinforced is the sense of unity in diversity that, as noted at the beginning of this chapter, came from the *Ṛgveda* and led to the doctrine of diverse paths to the same goal and many names and forms of the one Truth and the tolerance and freedom of worship. Not only did several elements of mythology bring together the deities in interrelation, but they produced composite forms of deities such as Ardhanārī (Śiva and Devī), Harihara (Śiva and Viṣṇu), and Dattātreya (Brahmā, Viṣṇu, and Śiva in one). All these cut across sectarianism. But a true philosophical basis to this religious pluralism, open-mindedness, and tolerance, which forms the precious heritage of the *Smārta* (following the *Smṛtis*) tradition, was provided by Śaṅkara's philosophy.

PRĀKṚT ĀCĀRYAS.[5] Now at the end of the classical *Śāstra* period we have the second great upsurge toward the popular movement. The ancient colloquial languages (*Prākṛts*) born out of Sanskrit had at this time begun to bring into being the local languages of the various regions of the country, and these popular languages now came to be employed for religious propagation. This was necessitated in a way by the two heterodox schools' (Buddhism and Jainism) developing a missionary spirit and using the peoples' languages for their writings. The earliest of the movements for religious renaissance through the popular languages came from the Tamil country in south India, where Buddhism and Jainism had gained strongholds. It was the age of the great Pallava rulers of Kāñcīpura, one of whom, Mahendravikrama, was converted from Jainism to Śaivism by a Śaiva saint, Appar (seventh century C.E.), who was himself reclaimed from the Jain fold by his Śaivite sister. Appar's young contemporary was Jñānasambanda, who vanquished the Jains at Madurai and reclaimed the Pandyan King. Of the ninth century are two other important Śaiva saints, Sundaramūrti and Māṇikkavācakar of the northern and southern parts of the Tamil country. These four and three other Śaiva saints were the great singers and composers of Śaiva hymns in Tamil called *Devāram,* meaning "worship of God."

[5] See Venkatarama Raghavan, *The Great Integrators: The Saint Singers of India.* New Delhi: Publications Division, Government of India. 2nd Ed., 1969.

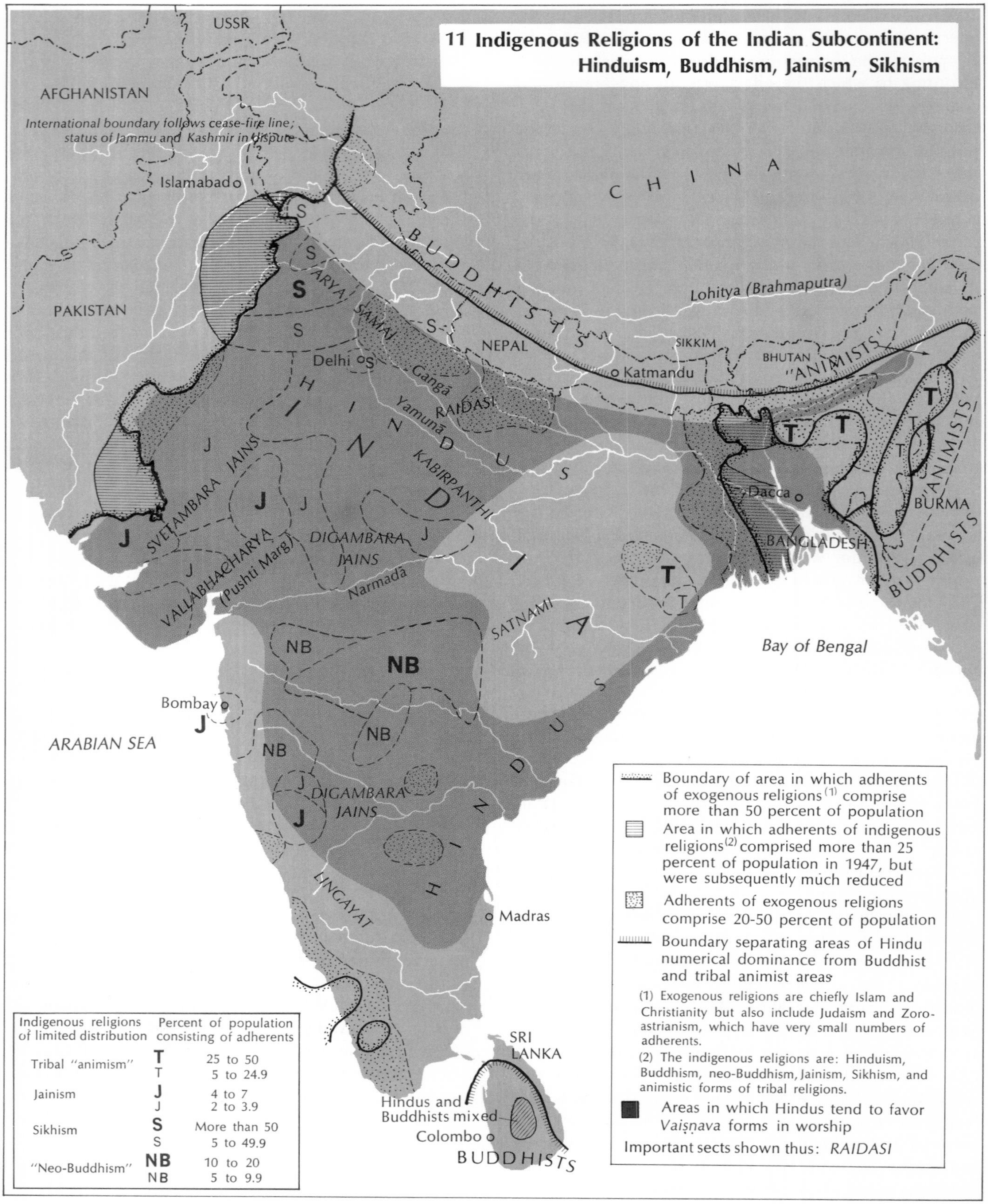

**11 Indigenous Religions of the Indian Subcontinent:
Hinduism, Buddhism, Jainism, Sikhism**

USSR

AFGHANISTAN

*International boundary follows cease-fire line;
status of Jammu and Kashmir in dispute*

Islamabad

PAKISTAN

CHINA

BUDDHISTS

Lohitya (Brahmaputra)

Delhi

Ganga

NEPAL

Katmandu

SIKKIM

BHUTAN

"ANIMISTS"

S

SARYA

SAMAJ

RAIDASI

Yamuna

H I N D U S

KABIRPANTHI

"ANIMISTS"

BURMA

SVETAMBARA JAINS

VALLABHACHARYA
(Pushti Marg)

DIGAMBARA
JAINS

Narmada

T

Dacca

BANGLADESH

BUDDHISTS

SATNAMI

I N D I A

Bay of Bengal

NB

NB

Bombay

J

ARABIAN SEA

NB

J

DIGAMBARA
JAINS

H I N D U S

LINGAYAT

Madras

SRI
LANKA

Hindus and
Buddhists mixed

Colombo

BUDDHISTS

	Boundary of area in which adherents of exogenous religions [1] comprise more than 50 percent of population
	Area in which adherents of indigenous religions [2] comprised more than 25 percent of population in 1947, but were subsequently much reduced
	Adherents of exogenous religions comprise 20-50 percent of population
	Boundary separating areas of Hindu numerical dominance from Buddhist and tribal animist areas

[1] Exogenous religions are chiefly Islam and Christianity but also include Judaism and Zoroastrianism, which have very small numbers of adherents.

[2] The indigenous religions are: Hinduism, Buddhism, neo-Buddhism, Jainism, Sikhism, and animistic forms of tribal religions.

Areas in which Hindus tend to favor *Vaiṣṇava* forms in worship

Important sects shown thus: *RAIDASI*

Indigenous religions of limited distribution		Percent of population consisting of adherents
Tribal "animism"	**T**	25 to 50
	T	5 to 24.9
Jainism	**J**	4 to 7
	J	2 to 3.9
Sikhism	**S**	More than 50
	S	5 to 49.9
"Neo-Buddhism"	**NB**	10 to 20
	NB	5 to 9.9

9-4 Dancing Śiva, southern India, 16th century C.E. The cosmic dance symbolizes the kinetic aspect, the pulsing force through the power of which the whole world is created, sustained, and destroyed. Under the right foot is the demon of Ignorance. (Courtesy of the Philadelphia Museum of Art, photograph by A. J. Wyatt, staff photographer.)

The movement that started in the Tamil area spread to the adjacent Karṇāṭaka region, from there to Mahārāṣṭra and Gujarat and Rajasthan, then to all the Hindi-speaking areas of the north, to Mithilā, Bengal, and Assam in the east, and then back to the Andhra and Tamil, thus completing the cycle (Map 11). In Karṇāṭaka also, as in Tamil, there were the twin movements of devotees of Śiva and Viṣṇu, the former called *Śiva-śaraṇas* ("those who had taken refuge with Śiva") and the latter, *Haridāsas* ("servants of Hari-Viṣṇu"). The former led to the school of *Śaiva* philosophy of this area called *Vīra-Śaivism* or *Lingāyata,* whose founder was minister Basava of Kalyāṇ in the twelfth century C.E., this movement also put forth a line of saints, including women and members from all classes. The *Haridāsas,* drawn similarly from all classes, became affiliated with the dualistic school of *Madhvācarya,* and the greatest saint of this line is Purandaradās (1480–1564), who holds a place of distinction in music also.

The saints who sang in Mahārāṣṭrī medium the *Gītā* and other Sanskrit scriptures and also several didactic and devotional songs are a group of about fifty drawn from all classes. The greatest of them are Jñānadeva (d. 1290), Nāmadeva (1269–1344); Tukhārām (1608–1649); and Rāmadās (1608–1681), the guru of Śivājī. The foremost saint-singer of Gujarat is Narasiṁha Mehta, and

Princess Mīrā Bai of Rajasthan, like the Tamil Āṇḍāl, sang as the Lord's Bride. Kashmir, the meeting place of many schools, including the Islāmic Ṣūfī, produced the woman mystic Lallā (fourteenth century). Punjab is the home of Nāṇak and his successors, whose songs are preserved in the *Granth Sahib,* the basis of Sikhism. In the present Hindi-speaking areas arose Kabīr (1380–1460), a Muslim mystic teacher of Nanak, who sought to reconcile Islām with Hinduism and thus to open a common way to God through the mystical experience. Among the other prominent saints were Sūradāsa (ca. 1550), and the blind Kṛṣṇa-singer of Agra, Tulasidas (1532–1625) author of the Bible of the Hindi world, viz the *Rāma-cvita-mānasa.* Kṛṣṇa-Love also produced Vidyāpati in Mithilā and Caṇḍīdās (both ca. 1350) as well as Caitanya (1485–1513) in Bengal. Śaṅkaradeva of Assam (1449–1588) consolidated both society and religion in Assam with his *Sattras* or centers of devotion and propagation of the same through song and drama based on *Bhāgavata* and other *Purāṇas* and the epics. The saint-singers of the Hindi area were many and were in several schools. Rāmadās of Bhadrācalam (seventeenth century) sang in Andhra, and Tyāgarāja (1767–1847), a Telugu, sang in the heart of the Tamil land. Between the *Nāyanārs* and *Ālvārs* and *Tyāgarāja,* Tamilnadu had a galaxy of saint-singers who sang in Tamil; a class of mystics, known as *Siddhas* who sang symbolic songs. Kamban, the author of the Tamil *Rāmāyaṇa;* Aruṇagirināthar (fifteenth century), the rapturous hymnist of the Deity Kumāra; the Vedantist Tāyumānavar (seventeenth to eighteenth centuries); and last but not least the universalist Rāmalingasvāmi (1823–1874).

Bhakti: Popular Religion

Historians have described this period as the age of *Bhakti* ("devotion"). The mystic singers and their songs in the local languages reenergized religious thought and produced new philosophical schools. Thus after Śaṅkara produced his famous monistic exposition of the *Vedānta,* in Tamil country a line of philosopher-worshipers of Viṣṇu built up the second important interpretation of *Vedānta* based on *Bhakti* ("devotion") to the Supreme Being, conceived as one but endowed with personality and infinite auspicious qualities and having the universe of inert and conscious entities as His Body. The pioneers of this school, which came to be called *Viśiṣṭādvaita,* were Nāthamuni and his grandson Yāmuna (eleventh century C.E.). The actual commentator on the Vedāntic texts and primary teacher of the school is Rāmānuja (1017–1137), born at Śrīperumbudūr near Madras. Along with devotion, the school stressed surrender to God as essential. The Lord's spouse, Lakṣmī, acted as a mediator of the Lord's grace. The followers of this school, who were called *Śrī Vaiṣṇavas,* fell into two schools: the older *Ten-Kalai* (the southern school) and the later *Vaḍakalai* (the northern school), differing from each other on the doctrine of the Lord's grace. The former adopts the analogy of the cat carrying her kitten in her mouth, with

9-5 Śiva-Ling, Mathura, North India, 1st century C.E. Symbol of cosmic creation and fertility, prevedic, pre-Aryan in its antiquity. (Courtesy of the Philadelphia Museum of Art, photograph by A. J. Wyatt, staff photographer.)

the little one not exerting itself, and the latter adopts the analogy of the monkey carrying its little one, which, by its own effort, clings to the mother. In the former view man has only to receive the Lord's grace, and in the latter, it is still given to him but he has to work for it. The former school particularly spread considerably among classes outside the Brahman community. *Śrīvaiṣṇavism* consolidated itself also through some big temples of South India (e.g., Tirupati and Śrīraṅgam) and from Tamil Nad spread to Mysore, where Rāmañuja had a sojourn, to Āndhra, and then to North India (Map 11).

Three other later schools based on devotion to Viṣṇu (Kṛṣṇa), prevalent in the North, whose teachers produced theistic interpretations of *Vedānta* are Viṣṇusvāmin (13th century C.E.), Vattabhācārya (1479–1531), Nimbāska (12th century C.E.), and the followers of Caitanya in Bengal.

All *Vaiṣṇava* schools practiced ecstatic devotion or love to Kṛṣṇa and His Consort Rādhā (symbol of the devotee), and among the texts forming their basic inspiration are the *Bhāgavata Purāṇa* and the musical lyric poem on Rādhā-Kṛṣṇa-love, the *Gītagovinda* of Jayadeva (twelfth century). The *Gitagovinda* stands at the head of the *Bhakti* age, playing a unique role in all India in devotion, music, and dance. Rāma also had a prominent part in the North Indian devotional movement. The pioneer in the Rāma cult was Rāmānanda (ca. 1400) of Banaras, teacher of Kabīr. Tulasi came in this tradition, and a number of other saints arose in the wake of Kabīr, Dādu, and so on.

9-6 Rāmachandra Avatāra, Punjab, 11th century C.E. Incarnation of Viṣṇu as Rāma, god of popular Hinduism; Rāmāyana, the most popular Hindu texts depicting the story of Rāma. (Courtesy of the Philadelphia Museum of Art, photograph by A. J. Wyatt, staff photographer.)

Of the schools that developed around Śiva, Kashmirian *Śaivism,* monistic and dualistic, developed its own basic *Sūtras* (ninth century) and produced a large literature in Sanskrit. To the monistic branch of Kashmir *Śaivism,* Śiva is the Supreme Being, regarded as absolutely unique and endowed with personality. On realizing Him, one is enabled to "recognize" the true nature of the world, which is not absolutely unreal but is an appearance of the Supreme Being (*Ābhāsa*). With the admixture of *Tantras* and the mysticism of speech, Kashmirian *Śaivism* became an amalgam.

To the dualist *Śaiva,* the three main categories are the Lord (Pati, Śiva) the soul (*Paśu,* meaning "the animal under the Lord's protection," "the flock"), and the bond (*Pāśa*). This is a realistic and pluralistic school. God is only the efficient cause of the universe and not its material cause too, as in *Vedānta;* the material cause is matter (*Prakṛti, Māyā*), as in *Sāṁkhya.* Individual souls become bound because of three impurities (*Malas*): *Āṇava,* which reduces its all-pervasive nature to the atomic; *Karman,* acts done by man; and *Māyā,* by which the soul becomes embodied, experiences, and transmigrates. Liberation is from these three impurities and is gained by personal effort and God's grace. The liberated soul is Śiva-like and enjoys Śiva-bliss through Śiva but does not become one with Śiva; it is again both identity and difference. The prevailing *Śaivism* in the Tamil area is of this form.

The *Vīra Śaivism* (exclusive *Śaivism*) of Karnāṭaka is also called *Liṅgāyata* because its followers wear permanently the replica of a Śiva-*liṅga* on their bodies.

After Viṣṇu and Śiva, the third great deity of the Hindu pantheon is Śakti or Devī, Mother Goddess, whose worship attained large proportions as an integral part of the concept of Supreme Being, as its dynamic and mediating aspect, called variously, Śakti, Vimarśa, Śrī, and so on. Śakti worship is called *Śākta* and it has its own Sūtras, commentaries, and independent treatises. A vast and bewildering mass of literature known as *Tantras* dealt with her numerous forms as prevalent in popular worship in different parts of the country. The one Śakti takes the three primary forms of Devī, Durgā, Lakṣmī, and Sarasvatī, presiding respectively over power, prosperity, and knowledge. The form in which Devī destroyed some demons (Mahiṣāsivamardanī), particularly one in the form of a buffalo, is the most adored form. She is celebrated in the text of seven hundred verses called *Devīmahātmya,* which is read, sometimes with repeated oblations in fire.

In her aspects of beauty and benevolence, she is adored as Lalitā and celebrated in the *Lalitopakhyāna* and in the hymn of thousand names called *Lalitāsahasranāmastotra.*

Of the other forms of divinity in popular worship, first comes Gaṇeśa, god of impediments and their removal, who is celebrated in his own *Pūrāṇas, Upaniṣads, Gītā,* hymns, and esoteric tāntric texts. Esoterically Gaṇapati is identified with Śakti and regarded as an embodiment of the mystic syllable *OM.* There is hardly a street, especially in Tamil country, which has not a temple to Him. His younger brother Kumāra, once worshiped widely in the north too, has his stronghold in Tamil Nad, where he is considered to be sporting on all hills and has five special hill shrines to his credit. He and Gaṇeśa are also worshiped in all Śiva temples.

9-7 Viṣṇu, Chedi School, 12th century C.E. Viṣṇu in Yoga-slumber, reclining on sesa (sandstone). (Courtesy of the Philadelphia Museum of Art, photograph by A. J. Wyatt, staff photographer.)

9-8 Sūrya Deva, Bengal and Bihar style, 12th century C.E. The sun-god, symbol of motion. His charioteer is Aruṇa; seven horses are harnessed to his chariot. (Courtesy of the Philadelphia Museum of Art, photograph by A. J. Wyatt, staff photographer.)

With Śiva and Pārvatī (Śakti), the divine parents, child Kumāra forms a trinity; the image Somāskanda represents this symbolism of the trinity, the transcendent lord, his creative energy, and the universe, conveyed by the three constituent syllables of *OM* (*A*, *U*, and *M*). Kumāra is also an image of beauty and valor and is the hero of much devotional and lyrical song and poetry.

Worship of the sun (*Sūrya*) and its continuity has been mentioned under the *Vedas*. During historical times, Mithra worshipers from the Middle East and East Europe migrated to India and augmented the ranks of sun worshipers. Several Purāṇic texts glorify the sun, and sun temples are found all over India. The sun is also worshiped as the center of the planetary system for health, success, and so on.

Associates and missiles of major deities are also separately worshiped: e.g., Hanuman, the monkey-devotee whose exploits are described in the *Rāmāyaṇa* and who is the symbol of power and success and whose popularity ranks next to that of Gaṇeśa; and the discus, Sudarśana, the destroyer of demons, in the hand of Viṣṇu. The chief missile of a deity (Astra-Deva), the discus of Viṣṇu, and the trident (Triśūla) of Śiva are part of the round of worship of the respective deities in their temples. Hindu worship includes the planets (*Grahas*), snakes (*Nāgās*), trees, and plants, all of which come down from ancient times. On waysides, on banks of rivers or tanks, and near temples, the holy *peepul* tree (*Aśvattha*) with snake stones around it is a common sight; people circumambulate and pour water and milk at the foot of the tree and on snakes and snake pits. Bilva (*Aegle Marmelos*) is the sacred tree of Śiva and the abode of Lakṣmī. *Tulasī* (the balsam) is a plant sacred to Kṛṣṇa. There is no crudity or contradiction in this spectrum of worship from the planet and the slender plant to the supreme Brahman, for this varied spectrum is but the reflection of the one great light and this truth is never forgotten even by the most common worshiper.

The *Veda* describes physical features of gods, but there were no images or temples in the Vedic age. There were of course elaborate sacrificial altars, which certainly supplied the nucleus of a sacred edifice. The *Rāmāyaṇa* refers to such sacred edifices for worship and also to some spots where a deity is invoked. In the Mauryan age (fourth century B.C.E.) images of gods were referred to. The origin of a temple was to be seen not only in the altar but also in hut dwellings and chariots and on backs of elephants on which royalty rode. The important parts of a temple, which also show the stages of its historical growth, are the sacred tree, the flag, the platform for offering, the tank, and the inner *sanctum sanctorum*, in which the main deity is enshrined. The last is the symbol of the recess of the heart where the Lord dwells, which is brought out also by the early temples, which were caves. The sanctity of temples is due to the association of saints, to manifestations of special forms of the deities and their exploits or grace toward particu-

9-9 Durgā, Mamallapuram, 16th century C.E. The goddess Durgā, equipped with the weapons of all the gods, and riding on a lion, kills the Buffalo demon called Mahiṣā and consequently vanquishes the demon (Asura). (Courtesy of the Philadelphia Museum of Art, photograph by A. J. Wyatt, staff photographer.)

9-10 Gaṇeśa, 8th century C.E. God of Ganas, son of Śiva and Parvati, symbol of Wisdom, in dancing pose. (Courtesy of the Philadelphia Museum of Art, photograph by A. J. Wyatt, staff photographer.)

lar devotees, or to the esoteric power of certain *yantras* or mystic charts laid in the inner shrine. Pilgrimages to shrines for special festivals or as expiation or for special merit or mental solace are part of a devout Hindu's program. Each family has its hereditary shrine and deity. With sculptures and paintings of gods and their various forms and deeds, with music, dance, and drama, and with festivals the temple has indeed exercised the greatest effect and attraction to the people. With historical events in its inscriptions, literary manuscripts in its archives, halls for meetings of elected bodies for local administration and religious discourses, the temple, through the ages, has also been the center of all local community life. The major temples have high philosophical significance, as in Cidambaram, and profound symbolism in the images. As one stands in the Cidambaram temple, for example, on the left one sees one kind of symbolic representation of the cosmic process and in front another kind of representation of the same. The first is of Viṣṇu lying in mystic slumber on the primeval waters on the coils of endless time (the serpent couch) with the creator on the lotus emerging from His navel. The second is of Śiva in his mystic dance in the ether of the inner heart (*Dahara ākāśa*) signifying the five acts of creation, sustenance, destruction, obscuration, and blessing. The image of Siva as *Dakṣiṇāmurti,* at the foot of the *Vaṭa* tree is a grand conception of teacher and knowledge, the students being aged, the teacher young, and the teaching, silence. So also is the conception of the image of *Ardha-nāri,* half-Śiva (male) and half-Śakti (female), the static and dynamic aspects in one. The basic form of Śiva, set up in the *sanctum sanctorum* of temples, is called *Liṅga,* meaning "symbol"; it is just a column of stone, the most abstract of images possible. The *Atharva Veda* describes the Supreme Being as a pillar (*Skambha,* X:7); Śiva manifested himself as a pillar, a column of flame, whose top or bottom could not be found. Some historians have confused themselves and others by mixing this concept with phallic worship.

Each home has also its miniature shrine, and one does not cease to be a Hindu if one does not go to a temple and prefers to do all his worship at home. *Sālagrāmas* (sacred ammonite pebbles found in the rivers Gaṇḍakī and Narmadā and representing Viṣṇu and Śiva) or mystic charts (*Cakras*) or metal images or pictures are worshiped at home. The *Cakras* are concentrations of divine power, inlaid with mystic syllables and laid at the base of the images in the temples. The most famous is the *Śrīcakra* of Devī. At home and in private, the religious practices include the reading of scriptures; the repetition of *Mantras,* names of gods, and prayers; meditation; observance of periodical worships, austerities, and propitiations with fasts or feasts; and the celebration of select holy days sacred to particular deities.

9-11 Mandapa, Madura, 16th century C.E. Pillared Temple, one of the most important and richest temples in India. (Courtesy of the Philadelphia Museum of Art, photograph by A. J. Wyatt, staff photographer.)

9-12 One of the Hindu temples at Kahjurāho, India, erected between 954 and 1002 C.E. by the kings Dhanga and Ganda. These temples are famous for the perfection of their architecture and sculpture. The obvious eroticism in their reliefs symbolizes the union between the soul and the Brahman-Ātman. (Courtesy of the Government of India Tourist Office.)

In religious reading, repetition, and recitation, there is first the repetition of the Lord's Name (*Nāma*)[6] or a short formula (in which one has been initiated duly by a teacher), embodying some mystic syllables along with *OM*, expressing obeisance to the particular deity, and called *Mantra*. The Sanskrit prayers, praises, and psalms form a prodigious literature,[7] taken from the *Purāṇas* and also composed by great teachers, poets, and devotees; they range from strings of 108, 300, or 1000 names to literary compositions embodying doctrines, devotion, and poetry.

From the second century C.E. onward Hinduism, its great epics, the Sanskrit language and certain poems and religious texts in Sanskrit, the Hindu arts of music, dance, and drama and sculpture and temple building spread all over southeast Asia, Indonesia, Malaysia, Thailand, Cambodia, Laos, Vietnam, and, nearer home, Burma and Ceylon. Some forms of Hindu culture are still to be found there, even in parts of these areas where people were later converted to Islām. Nepal on the Indian border and Bali in Indonesia are Hindu countries outside India. Hindu arts put forth fresh forms, a free synthesis of cults, and a new bloom in these areas. The largest Hindu temple complex is in Cambodia, not in India.

Modern Reform Movements

The advent of European traders and rulers and Christian missionaries brought a new force. While on one side large-scale conversions to Christianity went on, like the earlier conversions to Islām, on the other, Sanskrit and Hinduism and its culture were discovered by the Orientalists of the West, and in their wake, Indians who had received modern Western education rediscovered for themselves their historical and cultural image. The result was a reinterpretation and a renaissance of Hinduism. Several reforms of old practices that were not to the modern taste and were obsolete were given up; social changes came, with greater mobility and equality among the classes. In religion and philosophy greater

[6]On the doctrine of the Lord's Name, see Venkatarama Raghavan, Introductory Thesis, *The Spiritual Heritage of Tyagaraja*. Madras: R. K. Martin, 1965.

[7]See Venkatarama Raghavan, *Prayers, Praises and Psalms*. Madras: G. A. Natescu & Co., 1938.

attention came to be bestowed on their more pristine form, on intellectual aspects as against the ritualistic. The need to reply to the ill-informed or prejudiced Orientalist or missionary critic led to a deeper study of Hinduism. The sacred writings, thanks to printing, became available both in the original and in translation to all people. Adopting Western methods, new religious groups like the *Brahmo Samāj* grew among the Western educated classes. This *Samāj,* founded by Rāja Rām Mohan Roy in 1828, is confined to Bengal. Concurrently, the new spirit for reform and search into the original teachings brought into being two lines of activity. One was the rise of the organization called *Ārya Samāj,* with its call of "Back to the Vedic Hymns," started by Svāmi Dayānanda Sarasvatī in 1875; one of its aims is to reclaim Hindus converted to other faiths. The Ārya Samājists are concentrated in the Punjab although they have branches and followers all over India (Map 11). The other line of activity is the crying halt to the rapid Westernization of life and neglect of the indigenous spiritual culture that has bestowed a unique character on Indian civilization. The new upsurge of patriotism and struggle for freedom from British rule were also imbued with this cultural recovery, and Bālagangādhara Tilak, Mahātmā Gāndhi, and Aurobindo, all of them modern commentators on the *Gītā,* had had a religious and spiritual mission in the midst of their political and public activity. Tilak emphasized *Karma-Yoga;* Gāndhi emphasized *Ahiṁsā* ("noninjury"), truth, and unattached discharge of duty (*Anāsakti Yoga*); Aurobindo leaned more to *Tantra* and *Yoga* and the earliest mysticism of the Vedic seers. Gāndhi owed his charisma to his traditional religious roots, like practice of *Bhajan,* faith in Rāma's name, and so on, and was a complete philosopher with his economic program of cottage industry and village uplift and the social mission of uplift of the lowest classes and eradication of untouchability. The most charismatic of modern Hindu leaders who put new life into Hinduism is Svāmi Vivekānanda; his teacher was Rāmakrishna, a traditional god-realized soul. Vivekānanda (1863–1902), who visited the Chicago Parliament of Religions (1893), founded in 1897 the Mission in the name of his teacher that now has a worldwide network of missions. Although cosmopolitan and in India devoted to a great deal of social and educational work, Vivekānanda and the Rāmakrishna Mission are exponents of the *Advaita Vedānta* of Śaṅkara.

Poet Rabindranath Tagore, who was responsible for a literary and artistic awakening, was also a Vedāntist and advocated on that basis the universal religion of man. Among those who had expounded Hinduism and *Advaita* to the West with rare eloquence and distinction, the name of S. Radhakrishnan stands foremost; his approach is that of Śaṅkara but modifies the degree of the unreality of phenomenal existence.

The success of Vivekānanda spurred many Hindu religious leaders to spread abroad Hinduism in one form or other; several of them did their work quietly and some succeeded in founding missions, all of which have contributed to the reflowering of Hinduism and the strengthening of some tradition or other of it, devotion or Vedāntic knowledge or *Yoga.* Among foreigners who gave a helping hand to this emergence of Hinduism with a new strength are those who founded (1882) the International Theosophical Society, Madam Blavatsky, Colonel Olcott, and Mrs. Annie Besant.

Alongside of this awakening and these modes of work with modern orientation, there has been a considerable amount of revival and awareness and increase in the tempo of ministry of the orthodox Vedāntic, *Śaiva,* and *Vaiṣṇava Maṭhs* and *Maṭh-heads* and other traditional scholars and those of spiritual realization, saints who performed miraculous acts of blessing and who were not themselves attached to any *Maṭh* but whose influence led to the founding of new religious and spiritual centers and movements after their names. Among the former may be mentioned the present *Śaṅkarācārya* of Kāñchī, the most active and best known among those of this class; and among the latter, Sai Baba of Shirdi in Mahārāṣtra (d. 1918), a Brahman child brought up by Muslim parents and Ramaṇa Maharṣi of Tiruvannāmalai, who was with us till recently.

Bibliography

AVALON, ARTHUR. *Principles of Tantra.* Madras: Ganesh and Co., 4th edition, 1969–1970.

BARY, WILLIAM W. *Sources of Indian Tradition.* New York: Columbia University, 1964.

BHANDARKAR, R. G. *Vaiṣnavism, Śaivism and Minor Religious Systems.* Strassburg: 1913, Reprinted in India.

BHASKARA, LAUGAKSI. *Arthasamgraha,* tr., G. Thibaut. Banaras: Benares Sanskrit Series, No. 4, 1882.

DASGUPTA, SURENDRANATH. *A History of Indian Philosophy,* 5 vols. Cambridge: Cambridge U. P., 1922–1955.

DEUSSEN, PAUL. *The Philosophy of the Upaniṣads,* English translation. Edinburg: T. & T. Clark, 1919.

DUTT, MANMATHA NATH. *A Prose English Translation of the Mahabharata,* 3 vols. Calcutta: M. N. Dutt, 1895–1905. *The Ramayana, Translated into English Prose.* Calcutta: 1891–1894.

ELIADE, MIRCEA. *Yoga: Immortality and Freedom.* New York: Pantheon, 1958.

FARQUHAR, J. N. *An Outline of the Religious Literature of India.* London: Oxford University Press, 1920.

HIRIYANNA, M. *Outlines of Indian Philosophy.* London: George Allen and Unwin, 1949.

MACDONELL, A. A. *Hymns from the Rigveda.* London: Association Press, 1922.

———. *Vedic Mythology.* Strassburg: 1897, reprinted in India recently.

MORGAN, KENNETH (ed.). *The Religion of the Hindus.* New York: Ronald, 1953.

Poddar, H. P., tr. *The Bhāgavata.* Gorakhpur: Gitā Press, 1952.

RADHAKRISHNAN, S. *Indian Philosophy,* 2 vols. New York: Macmillan, 1923, 1927.

———. *The Hindu View of Life.* London: Allen and Unwin, 1927.

———. *The Principal Upaniṣads.* London: Allen and Unwin, 1953.

———. *The Bhāgavad Gita.* London: Allen and Unwin, 1953.

——— and Charles A. Moore (Eds.). *Source Book in Indian Philosophy.* Princeton: Princeton U.P., 1957.

RAU, T. A. GOPINATHA. *Elements of Hindu Iconography,* 2 vols. Madras: Law Printing House, 1914–1916.

SARMA, D. S. *The Renaissance of Hinduism.* Banaras: Benares Hindu U.P., 1944.

———. *What Is Hinduism?* Mylapore, Madras: Madras Law Journal Press, 1945.

VIVEKANANDA, SWAMI. *Raja-Yoga.* London: Longmans, Green, 1896; 8th ed., Almora: Advaita Ashrama, 1947.

WHITNEY, W. D. *Atharvaveda Samhitā,* English translation, 2 vols. Cambridge, Massachusetts: Harvard Oriental Series, 1905.

WILSON, H. H. *Rigveda Samhitā,* English translation, 6 vols. London: 1850–1888, reprinted in Poona.

10

Jainism

Rajendra P. Nanavati

Genesis

Jainism[1] is the religion of the person who aspires to become *Jina,* or conqueror of worldly passions. The adherents of this religion are called Jains. Believing that their religion has existed throughout all time they hold that it will continue to exist for all time, though its acceptance by men will wax and wane.

In most of the non-Jain writings, Mahāvīra, who lived from 599 to 527 B.C.E. (or, according to another estimate, from 549 to 477 B.C.E.), is identified as the founder of the religion. The Jains claim that he was not the first but the last, the twenty-fourth *Tirthankara,* or saving pathfinder, of the present half of the time cycle. Each half of the time cycle is supposed to have twenty-four Tirthankaras, twelve great lords or emperors, twenty-seven great wise men or teachers, and seven, fourteen, or fifteen lawgivers. The appearance of a *Tirthankara* is bound with the moral and religious decay of the people and hence their need for reawakening and religious revivification. There is historical proof for the existence of the twenty-third *Tirthankara,* who lived from 872 to 722 B.C.E., but none for the earlier ones, who are supposed to have existed considerably before recorded history. The twenty-second *Tirthankara,* Aristanemi (or Neminath), is linked only through legendary accounts with the heroes mentioned in the Indian epic *Mahabharata* and the legend of Krishna, whose first cousin Aristanemi is supposed to be.

Mahāvīra, "the great victor," was born the son of the Kshatriya chief Siddhartha and his queen Trisala in Vaisali (in Basarh, Bihar). He married Yasoda, a fellow Kshatriya, who bore him a daughter, Anavadya, whom he gave in marriage to a member of the same caste, Jamali. Mahāvīra's parents were the followers of Parsvanatha, and he was brought up in the Jain tradition. As worldly pleasures were of little interest to Mahāvīra,

[1] Jainism and Buddhism gave notice of their rejection of the caste system, which on the practical level of this-world realities confirmed the sufferers of social inequities in their sufferings while promising them eschatological, after-death deliverance only. Both rejected the Hindu system of ritual and sacrifice, which, by their time, had rigidified into an *ex opera operata* machinery devoid of spiritual power or moral sincerity. Both movements repudiated the Hindu proliferation of gods and godlets and, in their enthusiasm, developed an agnostic attitude toward God.

Undoubtedly, Mahāvīra and Gautama, the Buddha, founders of the two movements, were justified in their rebellion. The *Smṛti* literature had embellished and crystallized Hinduism, but it had codified it among the masses into spiritless, frozen institutions. Hinduism was far from dead. It rose to the occasion and, at the Jain and Buddhist challenge, it launched another recasting of itself, this time with more discursive sophistication, for rather than give in to the reformist criticism by rejecting the criticized institutions, Hindu thinkers reinterpreted the whole tradition and did so with a view to rejuvenating and revivifying their spiritual inheritance. Thus another flowering of doctrine took place; another glorious stage of development was reached.

he became, with the consent of his elders, an ascetic at the age of thirty. He gave up everything he owned, including even his clothes. For twelve years he practiced self-discipline and meditated in search of truth. He became an ill-treated, wandering mendicant, moving on foot and exposed to the bites of insects, reptiles, and dogs, but always meditating. Where he was welcome, he never tarried for fear of developing any attachment. He stopped wandering only during the rainy season, for fear of treading on some unobservable living creatures. During this period, he converted some princes and rulers, who were members of his own caste and to whom he was also related. Mahāvīra was a contemporary of the Buddha, and although they knew of each other they never met. The Buddhist tradition reports that Gautama disagreed with Mahāvīra's teachings and vehemently opposed asceticism, the central theme of Jainism, as not leading to salvation. At forty-two, he finally attained *Kevalajnana,* or omniscience. This is that state in which the human being has all the attributes of perfection but one, namely, that which confinement in his own body denies. In this state he has infinite joy, compassion, knowledge, and peace. A person who has reached this state is certain to reach *Moksha,* or the state of ultimate perfection, upon death. Mahāvīra reached *Moksha* at the age of seventy-two in Pavapuri in Bihar.

After he reached omniscience, Mahāvīra continued his wanderings throughout the modern states of Bihar, northwestern Bengal, and parts of Uttar Pradesh. For thirty years he preached his message in Ardhamagadhi, the language spoken by commoners of the region. The Jain scriptures were written in this language rather than Sanskrit, the language of Hindu scriptures, so that the common people could have direct access to it without the mediation of priests, elders, or scribes.

A fair number of Mahāvīra's immediate disciples were women. Among his male disciples, three achieved fame: Gautama Indrabhūti, who posed questions to Mahāvīra and elicited the answers that comprise Jain metaphysics and ethics; Sudharman, who elaborated the master's aphoristic answers into a system and was the latter's companion and disciple; and Jambūsvāmin, who edited Sudharman's works and presented them to posterity in their present shape.

It has been noted that Mahāvīra was brought up in the Jain tradition. Evidently, the tradition is older than its so-called founder. Before Mahāvīra, it was known as the sect of Pārśva, who preceded Mahāvīra by some 250 years. Pārśva was a historical figure, though reports about his life are all legendary. Born in Banaras, he was the princely son of King Aśvasena. One of the Jain cults is associated with him. In Jain temples, he is represented flanked by a seven-headed cobra. Mahāvīra never repudiated anything associated with Pārśva, be it view or practice.

Flowering

There are a number of Jain scriptures called *Sūtras,* of which the most important is the *Kalpasūtra* containing the life and teachings of Mahāvīra. It is in the *Tattvārthādhigama-sūtra* that we find Jain doctrine elaborated systematically. Like any Brahmin *Sūtra,* this work is written in laconic style. Umāsvāti, the author, composed the text with metrical *bhasyas* consisting of thousands of verses.

Cosmology

Motion, rest, space, *Atma* (the Real Self) or soul, and matter are the basic elements of which all the world and the nonworld are made. All are eternal; all but the soul are lifeless; and all but matter are spiritual. Soul and matter are plural, whereas motion, rest, and space are all singular. Motion and rest have no self-existence but are always predicates of souls and matter. Space is an attribute of both the world (*loka*) and the nonworld (*aloka*), of which the world is but a very small part. Any body is made of a number of *paramanu* or atoms ordered alongside one another without fusion or amalgamation. Such groups form *skandhas* enjoying other attributes than those of their constitutive atoms.

There are two kinds of bodies: the Karmic and the fiery. The former is the outcome of previous thoughts, words, and/or actions following the Hindu Law of Karma. The latter is a vehicle of potential energy. Beings come to be either through *manifestation,* as of a god or another spiritual existent; through *coagulation,* as in the case of the lowest forms of life; or through *procreation,* as in the case of higher animals and man.

There are three worlds: the underworld or hell, the world we live in, and the upperworld or heaven. The underworld is made of seven superposed regions, each constituting a kind of torture and terror. The upperworld is a region far above the stars, an inverted replica of the underworld, and contains the illustrious and glorious abodes of the gods. At the top is the pure white region where the "perfected" souls of men dwell in *Moksha.* In between the two stands our world, a flat horizontal region called *Jambudvipa,* centered around Mount Mandara or Meru, and a small fraction of it is

Bharatavarsa or India. The inhabitants of both higher and lower worlds, which popular religion represents as gods and demons respectively, do make appearances —some lengthy—in this world.

Anthropology

Besides gods and demons, this world is inhabited by men and animals. "Animals" include not only what zoology studies but all plants and atoms of earth, fire, water, and wind, each of which has a soul, a *jiva,* perceptible or subtle, developed or undeveloped. In parts of this world, time does not flow and life is constant, eternal bliss, for *Karman* here does not apply, is neither acquired nor gotten rid of. It is only in Bharatavarsa that the Law of Karma obtains. Here, time runs in six periods of growing deterioration or lessening bliss, and in reverse direction in each complete time cycle.

The number of souls (i.e., of all animated beings) is eternally the same. Men constitute a small fraction, and their souls witness the mental functions they discharge, or *upayayoga;* their causal efficacy or *labdhi;* and reason, or *samjnana.* Human souls, however, can never know the truth of anything with absolute certainty. Every proposition they make is valid only under a set of several presuppositions (*aneka*), and its contrary is just as valid provided it is made successively to rather than simultaneously with it. Jainism hence developed a totally relativistic theory of knowledge (*nayavada*). Ethically, this extreme skepticism sobered the Jains and protected them from making any claims about an "absolute truth" of their teachings. It also projected ideal being as *Kevalajnana,* or omniscience.

Man's soul being associated through the Law of Karma to matter, the ethical life is a pursuit of release of the soul from its bondage. The bondage is brought about by the attachment to desires for all that is not *Atman,* the Real Self, and it can be broken through the disengagement exercises of the ascetic life. True liberation comes to him who is truly detached and has transcended both likes and dislikes and who has conquered all passions.

Ethics and the Religious Life

The central themes of Mahāvīra's teachings were truth, *ahimsa* ("nonviolence"), and *aparigraha* ("nonattachment"). He taught that every living thing has a soul inherently equal to every other in the possibility of its attaining *Moksha.* Thus one must be respectful of all that lives. The Jains hold nonviolence to be the greatest religion. One must be nonviolent in thought, word, and deed.

The concept of the creator of the world is totally rejected. What Jains call "gods" are simply mortals who because of many good deeds done in their previous lives earned a right to be in the upperworld. Such "gods" have no function such as creation, government, or judgment. They simply are. They can indeed fall into the lower regions in case of temptation, like any man. Jains believe that the world has always existed and will always continue to exist. The same belief also applies to the soul, which is inherently perfect. The presence of Karma, acquired by an unkind thought, word, or deed, eclipses the inherent brilliance of the individual soul. When a Karma is acquired it results in a future circumstance during which certain consequences follow. For example, if you are unkind to another person, in the future you will find yourself in a situation where the other person can be unkind to you. The only way of getting rid of the Karma is to suffer its consequence with complete control over oneself so that a new Karma is not acquired in the process. Liberation is then seen as being free of Karmas, thus allowing the soul to be its true self, which is perfection, or *Moksha.*

So long as Karmas are intertwined with the soul, it is caught in the cycle of birth and death, to be reborn again and again, sometimes as an animal, a plant, an insect, or a human being. The Jains hence feel a kinship with *all* life and observe a strictly vegetarian diet. Ideally they should eat no more than absolutely necessary. On certain days of the month they eat no fresh vegetables. They also may not eat anything that grows underground, e.g., potatoes and onions. It is advisable that they not eat before sunrise or after sunset to prevent any unnecessary death of insects that abound especially at those times in India. The Jains are also supposed to drink only water out of which all living things have been filtered and which has been preboiled.

Souls that have reached *Moksha* are beyond the reach of those souls that have not yet attained it. These latter may be helped only by their own effort. They can be helped by the belief that those before them who reached *Moksha* were human beings too, special in no way other than that they had made the supreme effort to perfect themselves.

There are many more than *Tirthankaras* who have reached *Moksha.* In the state of *Moksha* they are all equally perfect. The distinguishing feature of the *Tirthankaras* is that during the process of reaching *Moksha* they helped a very large number of beings toward self-realization.

The Jain is expected to develop mental discipline and purity of thought. Simplicity of life and fasting are considered essential. Each is encouraged to find his own endurance level. Any level of participation, from giving up but one meal on a single day to a fast of eight days, is appropriate. Each day an ideal Jain is expected to examine his past night and the past day for things he did that he should not have done or things he avoided doing that he should have done. Such introspection is called *Pratikramana.* In addition, a Jain may do one or more daily *Kshamāyaks,* periods each of forty-eight minutes duration, of meditation and study of religious literature. A typical contemplation goes as follows: "Let there be friendship with all living beings, delight at the sight of the virtuous, compassion for the afflicted, and tolerance towards those who are ill behaved." The main function of a Jain *Sadhu,* or pious man, is the search for truth. He does *not* head the Jain temple, nor does he perform any ceremony at births, deaths, or marriages. He may not own anything and may not hold jobs. He goes to Jain homes (each day that he is not fasting) *after* normal mealtimes and may accept only leftover food that is offered him without his asking for it.

Saṃgha is the collective name of the adherents. It is composed of monks and nuns (*nirgranthas,* "free from civil ties"; *bhikṣu,* "mendicant"; and *sadhu,* "pious man") and the laity (*upāsaka,* "servant"; and *śrāvaka,* "listener"). Anybody is entitled to join the order of monks or nuns from the age of seven and a half years. He must give up all possessions, shaving his head and taking the five unconditional vows of noninjury to life, truthfulness, not using anything not given in alms, continence, and nonpossession of property. The first, *ahiṃsā,* overshadows everything else and turns the monk's life into a constant watch against injury to the smallest insect. Further, the monk's time is occupied with study and teaching, or with meditation, except that part of it spent on visiting Jains and traveling. So far, however, he is only a novice, an apprentice. As he grows older and becomes mature, he has to take seven more vows detailing and circumscribing the first "great five." The twelve vows are not the exclusive obligation of monks but fall equally on all Jains as the desiderata of morality and piety. Jainism is indeed a religion in which distinctions between lay and cleric completely break down. The cult, which consists of hymns, visits to holy places, and fruit, rice, and milk offerings to the statues of the twenty-four *Tirthankaras,* is an affair of the laity. The monks do not officiate though they can participate. The monk's business is merely to lead the model life and, to a much lesser extent, to teach. He who has rejected the experience of the fruits of any passions, of any Karman, has shed that Karman forever and launched himself on the path of liberation. He must go through fourteen stages in the ascent, beginning from that of false belief (*mithya-drasti*) to that of omniscience (*Kevala jnana*), and finally to *Moksha,* which is attained only upon death.

There is primarily individual worship or meditation in the temple as frequently and at a time on any day that the individual desires it. The function of the temples is hence to provide a place where the Jain may go for peaceful and quiet meditation; that of the intricate carvings is to provide pleasant surroundings and reminders of the exemplary lives the great *Tirthankaras* lived. Despite this purely personal use of the temple, the Jains have raised religious buildings of exquisite beauty and workmanship on hilltops or in secluded valleys (Map 10). The marble Delwara Jain temples on top of Mount Abu contain intricate carvings and richness of design and are known throughout the world. The Parshvanatha temple at Khajuraho is largest and best among the Jain temples in the state of Madhya Pradesh. A beautiful Jal Mandir (lake temple) is erected surrounded by water having thousands of lotus plants at Pavapuri (in Bihar state), where Mahāvīra attained *Moksha.* One of the most frequently visited places of pilgrimage for the Jains is the city of more than five hundred temples built on the Shatrunjaya Hills at Palitana in Gujarat.

10-1 Inside one of the many marble Jain temples on top of Mount Abu, the idol of a Tirthankara—one of the predecessors of Mahavira who led an exemplary Jain life and hence became a god—sits in meditative repose surrounded by exquisite figurative carvings in marble (10th century). (Courtesy of Dr. R. Nanavati.)

10-2 Mount Abu, with its several Jain temples, which were built around 1032 C.E., commands a magnificent view of the surrounding countryside in Rajasthan. Here Jains who have dedicated their lives to asceticism and meditation find the isolation and freedom to pursue and realize their religious ideals. (Courtesy of Dr. R. Nanavati.)

The best-known Jain festival is *Pajjusana* in August. It is celebrated for eight or ten days, according to one's sect. Fasting and meditation are practiced as much as possible. On the last day of the festival the Jain asks forgiveness of all living beings for any offense he may have committed in thought, word, or deed. It is customary for the oldest members of the family to ask pardon from the youngest member and for employers to ask forgiveness of the employees.

Schisms, Decay, and Revival

The tradition relates that nine of Mahāvīra's disciples founded communities (*gana*). Second-century B.C.E. inscriptions confirmed Jain divisions extant in the region of Mathura. One of their leaders, Bhadrabahu (of the sixth generation, who died 170 years after Mahāvīra), preserved texts and community by enjoining upon them to migrate southward. The same leader supposedly taught Asoka's grandfather, Chandragupta, who fasted unto death. Another leader, Suhastin, converted Aśoka's grandson, Samprati, who carried the faith to Ạndhra and Drāviḍa regions. Evidence of Jainism is also found in second-century B.C.E. Orissa and Mysore.

A schism took place at that time between Digambara ("sky-clad" or "nude") adherents, who, as their name indicates, regarded as binding Mahāvīra's practice of shedding all clothes, and Śvetāmbara ("white-robed") adherents. Later on, other elements combined with this issue to make the schism permanent and unbridgeable. Digambaras hold women incapable of achieving liberation because they cannot go about sky-clad without disrupting the normal course of life. They can be liberated only through reincarnation as men. Digambaras also tolerate no idols or statues whatever and their temples are empty. They reject the Śvetāmbara view that Mahāvīra was transplanted as embryo from the womb of Devānandā to that of the Kshatriya lady Triśalā. Digambaras further divided into Kāṣṭha, Mūla, Māthura, and Yāpanīya Saṃghas in the third and fourth centuries B.C.E., but the differences separating them are superficial and insignificant. Vaṭṭakera and Kuṇ ḍakunda, earliest systematizers of Jain teachings (seventh to eighth centuries C.E.), were Digambara. Umasvati (eighth to ninth centuries), author of the *Tattvārthādhigamasūtra*, is claimed by them as well as by the Śvetāmbara. The latter invoke as canonical source a composite text (*gaṇi-piḍaga, āgama, siddhānta*) that was the result of an early council held in Patna, some of whose members were taught by Bhadrabahu, and a later council held in Valabhī in Gujarat, 980 years after Mahāvīra. Apparently, between the two councils, Jain strength shifted from east to west India. It was in the ninth century C.E., under King Amoghavarṣa I (815–877), that Jain thought and activity reached its highest peak. Great thinkers like Samantabhadra, Akalaṅka, Vidyānanda,

10-3 Jain temple in Calcutta, another masterpiece of architectural decoration. Jainism did spread to Bengal and eastern India, though its adherents there remain few. (Courtesy of Government of India Tourist Office.)

Patrakesarin, and Prabhacandra engaged their counterparts in Brahminism and Buddhism and argued with and refuted them with their exacting logic and epistemological skepticism. Toward the end of the tenth century according to the Tamil sources, and the twelfth according to the Kanarese, Jain intellectualism declined and began a general retreat before Śaiva, Vaiṣṇava, and Vīra-Śaiva Hindu teachers. To aid in the decline, Hindu kings imposed suppression and persecutions.

Hīravijaya, leader of the Tapā gaccha, a Śvetāmbara Saṃgha dating from the thirteenth century, was invited by the Muslim emperor Akbar to live with him in the royal court at Fatehpur Sikri until 1584. This led to the Jain claim that Akbar was a convert.

The Jains rejected the Hindu caste system along with the excessive ceremonies in Hindu temples. However, they do not mind having a Hindu officiate at a wedding or other ceremony because, in a sense, they have officially no clergy. Surely, there may be and are intercaste marriages, whether with Hindu or Jain spouses. But this does not constitute Jain intercaste marriage because Jains do not believe in caste at all. It could only be viewed as such from the outside, i.e., from the Hindu view. Jains might see themselves or others as belonging to castes, and others might even worship at Hindu shrines. But such practice, though real, runs against the norms held by the canonical scriptures and religious leaders.

Hinduism, with its flexibility, began to accept from the ninth and tenth centuries most of the Jain principles. This is the primary reason for Jain decline. Another reason was the laxity of the monks in their ascetic observance. The latter weakness was met as early as the eleventh century when a *gaccha samvat* separated and gave itself the new name of *Kharatra,* meaning "energetic." It was led by Jineśvara, who indignantly chastised the monks for their laxity and indulgence. The former weakness was alleviated by publication and circulation of Jain scriptures and holy writings, which are enormous by any standard. More recently, in 1946, a world missionary organization was founded in Aliganj in Uttar Pradesh.

Begun in the east, the Jain movement spread to the south and west and is now strongest in Gujarat (Map 11). The Śvetāmbara center is Kathiawar and the Digambara, Mysore. Jains number about 4 million, but their influence on the life and thought of India far surpasses their number. Because they are forbidden to engage in agriculture—such profession would necessarily involve fighting insects and thus do violence to their faith—the Jains have recourse to business, trade, and other urban professions. Many have amassed great wealth, created generous charities, built educational institutions, taken on government posts, and achieved great social, political, and economic influence.

Bibliography

BASHAM, A. L. *History and Doctrine of the Ajivikas, A Vanished Indian Religion.* London: Luzac, 1951.

HANDIQUI, K. K. *Yaśastilaka and Indian Culture.* Sholapur: 1949.

JAIN, CHAMPAT RAI. *What is Jainism?* Allahabad: n.d.

Jaina Sutras, Parts I–II, translated from Prākrit by Hermann Jacoby. New York: Dover Publications, Inc., 1968.

JAINĪ, JAGMANDAR LĀL. *Outlines of Jainism.* Cambridge: The University Press, 1940.

SCHUBRING, WALTHER. *The Religion of the Jainas,* tr., Amulyachandra Sen and T. C. Burke. Calcutta: Sanskrit College, 1966.

Suttāgama, 2 vols. Bombay: Nirnaya Sagar Press, 1952–1954.

WILLIAMS, R. *Jaina Yoga: A Survey of the Medieval Śrāvakācāras.* London: 1963.

11

Sikhism

Khushwant Singh

The great majority of India's 9 million Sikhs live in the region between Delhi and the country's border with West Pakistan (Map 11). They speak one language, Punjabi, which they write in the Gurmukhi script. Scattered communities of Sikhs are also found in different parts of the globe, notably in East Africa, England, and the Pacific Coast of Canada and the United States.

Genesis and Nature of Sikhism

The word *Sikh* is derived from the Sanskrit *shishya,* meaning "disciple"—the Sikhs being disciples of their ten gurus or teachers, beginning with Nanak (b. 1469) and ending with Gobind Singh (d. 1708).

Sikhism was a branch of the Hindu Bhakti movement. It also drew considerable inspiration from Islāmic Sufism. Nanak, though born a Hindu, worshiped at Muslim holy places and is also said to have gone on pilgrimages to Makkah and Madīnah. His followers were both Hindus and Muslims. His teaching was an eclectic mixture of Vedantic Hinduism and Sufism. He accepted the Hindu cycle theory of birth, death, and rebirth, and *karma,* whereby man's life on earth is determined by actions in previous lives. Nanak preached strict monotheism and forbade the worship of idols. He believed that the best way to approach God was through repetition of his name (*nām*) and singing hymns of praise (*kīrtan*). This was best done under the guidance of a teacher-guru. He was severely critical of the Hindu caste system and made it obligatory for all his followers to eat together in the guru's kitchen. Sikhism emphasizes the unity of the godhead using the Vedantic concept of *Aum* (or *Ôm*), the mystic syllable as a symbol of God. To this he added the qualifications of singleness and creativity and thus made *ik* ("one") *Aum Kar* ("creator"), which was later given figurative representation as ੴ. The opening lines of the celebrated morning prayer *Japji,* which are known as the *mool mantra* ("root belief") of Sikhism define God as the One, the Truth, Creator, Immortal, and Omnipresent. He is also *Nirankar*—formless and beyond human comprehension. Sikh scriptures use many names, both Hindu and Muslim, for God. Nanak's favorites were *Sat Kartar* ("True Creator") and *Sat Nām* ("The True Name"). At a later stage the word *Wah Guru* ("Hail Guru") was added and is today the Sikh synonym for God. Sikhism is often described as *Nām Marga* ("the way of *Nama*") because it emphasizes the constant repetition (*Jap*) of the name of God and the *gurbani* (the divine hymn of the gurus). *Nama* cleanses the soul of sin and conquers the source of evil,

11-1 Founder of Sikhism, Guru Nanak, by Sobha Singh (1965).

haumain ("I am") or the ego. Thus tamed the ego becomes a weapon to overcome lust, anger, greed, attachment, and pride. *Nama* stills the wandering mind and induces a superconscious stillness (*divya dritst*), opens the "tenth gate" (the body having only nine natural orifices) through which enters divine light and a person attains the state of absolute bliss.

Sikh History

Nanak passed on succession to a disciple, Angad (1534–1542), who on his death promoted another disciple, Amar Das (1552–1574) to be the third guru. Amar Das nominated his son-in-law Ram Das (1574–1581). Thereafter all the gurus were of one family. Sikhism soon broke away from its parent communities, the Hindus and the Muslims. Ram Das's son, the fifth guru, Arjun Mal (d. 1606), compiled the *Ādi Granth*, the Scripture of the Sikhs. This is an anthology of verse containing writings of the Sikh gurus as well as Hindu and Muslim saints of Northern India. He built the *Harimandir* ("temple of God") at Amritsar, which became the Sikhs' chief city and place of pilgrimage. He was persecuted by the Moghul government and was tortured to death. On his martyrdom, his son Hargobind (1606–1644) persuaded the Sikhs to take up arms. Hargobind's grandson Har Rai (1647–1661)and Har Rai's son Har Krishan (1661–1664) remained passive. But the ninth guru, Tegh Bahadur, who was Hargobind's son, took up the cause of the Hindus, for which he was persecuted by the Moghuls and executed in Delhi in 1675. Tegh Bahadur's son Gobind Rai finally converted the Sikhs into a fighting fraternity in 1699, which he called the *Khālsā*—from the Arabic/Persian *Khāliṣ* meaning "pure." He made it obligatory for the *Khālsā* to wear their hair and beards unshorn and always carry a saber (*kirpan*) on their person. The *Khālsā* were forbidden to drink or smoke and put under oath never to molest women. The *Khālsā* used the common surname *Singh* ("lion").

Gobind Singh's *Khālsā* were hounded out of the Punjab. All his four sons were killed: two died fighting, two were executed. He declared the succession of gurus at an end and was assassinated in 1708. Thereafter the Sikhs have looked upon the *Ādi Granth* as the "living" representation of their ten gurus. The *Khālsā* led by Banda Singh Bahadur rose against the Moghuls and for eight years ransacked northern India. The *Khālsā*-Moghul conflict continued after Banda's execution (1716). The invasions of the Persian Nādir Shāh (1738–1739) and the Afghān Aḥmad Shāh Durrānī (1747–1769) created a power vacuum in northern India that was filled by the Sikh chieftains. Ranjit Singh (1780–1839), a minor Sikh chief, consolidated his hold on the Punjab and with a modernized army extended his frontiers beyond Kashmir into Tibet, across the Indus to the lands of the Pathans and southward to Sind. He was checkmated by the English, who did not let him expand eastward.

Crisis and Reform

After Ranjit Singh's death the Sikh kingdom disintergrated rapidly. The turbulent *Khālsā* army was provoked into conflict with the English and was defeated in a series of sanguinary battles. In 1849 Ranjit Singh's son Dalip Singh was deposed and the Sikh kingdom was

11-2 The Holiest Sikh site: The Golden Temple, Amritsar, Kashmir. Amritsar was declared holy to the Sikhs by Arjun, their leader, in 1581. The Temple was begun then and received numerous renovations and additions down to 1948–50 when its present outside appearance took final shape. It is the Sikhs' only pilgrimage site.

annexed to the British Empire. The English recognized the martial qualities of the *Khālsā* and recruited them into their own army. The *Khālsā* stood by the British in the Sepoy Mutiny of 1857 and thereafter fought in British campaigns in different parts of the world. Though less than 2 per cent of the population of India, they formed more than 20 per cent of the British Indian Army in the two world wars.

The *Khālsā* have often been threatened with extinction because of the reluctance of the younger generation to conform to the tradition of keeping their hair and beards unshorn. Because they have always intermarried with Hindus, have observed Hindu festivals and customs, and are governed by Hindu law, the dividing line between Hindus and Sikhs was always very thin. A clean-shaven *Khālsā* became in effect a Sikh or a Hindu believing in Sikhism. The British helped to preserve the separate identity of *Khālsā* by making the wearing of long hair and beard obligatory for those who joined the armed services. Thereafter the tradition was kept alive by reform movements, the *Singh Sabha* of the 1890's and the *Akālī* of the 1920's. The *Singh Sabha* carried out a vigorous program of education and social reform. Many hundred Sikh schools and a college were opened where Sikh religion and *Khālsā* traditions were included in the curriculum. A spate of religious literature was produced in Gurmukhi.

The *Akālīs* ("immortals") began as a body of volunteers to take possession of Sikh temples (*Gurdwārās*), which had come under the control of hereditary priests

11-3 Ranjit Singh (1780–1839). Founder of Sikh militarism and political ascendency in northwest India, he collaborated with the British against the Muslim Moghuls and Afghans.

who were more Hindu than Sikh. It became a mass movement and after five years of bitter struggle, the government agreed to hand over the management of shrines to an elected body of Sikhs. By the Sikh Gurdwārās Act of 1925 was established the Shiromoni Gurdwārā Prabandhak Committee, which controls the fortunes of Sikh temples and disburses funds to maintain schools, colleges, and hospitals. Since its inception the SGPC has been controlled by the *Akālī* party.

The government of independent India abolished privileges attaching to religious communities; thereafter, *Khālsā* members who had conformed for the sake of privilege began to give up external symbols in increasing numbers. The lapse back into Hinduism assumed serious proportion. It was one of the reasons for the *Akālī* party's demand for a Sikh majority state. In 1965 this demand was conceded. In the recently created state of Punjab, the Sikhs form 60 per cent of the population. It has a Sikh chief minister and the ruling party, the *Akālīs*, are committed to maintaining the separate Sikh identity through a persuasive continuation of the *Khālsā* traditions.

Bibliography

ARCHER, JOHN CLARK. *The Sikhs: In Relation to Hindus, Moslems, Christians and Ahmadiyyas: A Study in Comparative Religion.* Princeton: Princeton U. P., 1946.

BANERJEE, INDUBHUSAN. *Evolution of the Khalsa,* Vols. I and II. Calcutta: 1936.

CUNNINGHAM, J. D. *A History of the Sikhs from the Origin of the Nation to the Battles of the Sutlej.* London: John Murray, 1849.

FIELD, DOROTHY. *The Religion of the Sikhs.* London: John Murray, 1914.

KOHLI, SURINDER SINGH. *A Critical Study of the Ādi Granth.* New Delhi: 1961.

LATIF, SYED MUHAMMAD. *History of the Punjab from the Remotest Antiquity to the Present Time.* Calcutta: Calcutta Central Press Company, 1891.

MACAULIFFE, M. *The Sikh Religion,* 6 vols. Oxford: Oxford U. Press, 1909.

MCLEOD, W. H. *Guru Nanak and the Sikh Religion.* Oxford: Clarendon, 1968.

NARANG, GOKUL CHAND. *Transformation of the Sikhs or How the Sikhs Became a Political Power.* Lahore: Tribune Press, 1912.

SINGH, KHUSHWANT. *A History of the Sikhs,* Vols. I and II. Princeton: Princeton U. P., 1964.

SINGH, SHER. *Philosophy of Sikhism.* Delhi: Sterling, 1966 [first pub. 1934].

SINGH, TRILOCHAN, et al (eds.). *Selection from the Sacred Writings of the Sikhs.* London: Allen & Unwin, 1960.

12

Confucianism and Taoism

C. Wei-hsun Fu

The Great Tradition and the Little Tradition

The Chinese people have a very unique way of approaching religion. Unlike most of the great world religions, the Chinese tradition lacks from the beginning any monotheistic concept of personal creator-deity, as well as a highly organized religious institution. The religious problem of creation by an omnipotent God or any supernatural power has never occurred to the Chinese, and no great religious establishment has ever made an effective bid for superiority over the state throughout Chinese history. To the Chinese, who are basically this-worldly and practical minded, religion means for the most part a teaching or doctrine full of human wisdom, philosophically designed to orient or guide men toward the fulfilment of the best possible way of life. This helps explain why there is no equivalent in Chinese for the word *religion* as understood by Western man. In Mandarin the term for religion is *tsung chiao.* The former word means "clan," "sect," "devotion," or "origin," and the latter, "teaching" or "doctrine." Confucianism is primarily an ethical philosophy of life created by the great moral sages; Taoism teaches that eternal happiness lies in man's total identification with Nature; and finally, Buddhism through Sinicization, lost its Indian other-worldly transcendentalism and pragmatically prescribed a *Nirvāṇa* for here and now in this very life. These three teachings are to the Chinese but different roads toward the same destination and are mutually interpenetrated and partially identified with one another. The Chinese tradition has such a syncretic and harmonizing tendency that in everyday religious practice the average Chinese makes no distinction between, for example, a Taoist shrine, a Buddhist monastery, and a Confucian temple. And the religious ideal of the Chinese tradition is typically reflected in the expression *san-chiao ho-i,* meaning the grand, harmonious unity of the three teachings of Confucianism, Taoism, and Buddhism. In general, the majority of the Chinese people do not have a particular religion of their own, and their nondiscriminating attitude toward religious belief often leads them to the conclusion that because all religions are somehow beneficial to man in one way or another, they are equally good and welcome.

However, the predominant this-worldliness of Chinese religion does not mean that it is completely free from the supernatural. The latter is evidenced in the worship of ancestors and heaven, constitutive of Chinese religiosocial organization. To understand fully this supernatural element, it is necessary to distinguish two levels of religion. On one level, there is the religion of the intellectuals, who are rationalistic, self-conscious, critical. They formulate the patterns and guide the masses in matters of metaphysics, religion, ethics, political philosophy, and culture. This creative minority is the author of "the Great Tradition," in which religion and philosophy are inseparable. On the other level, there is the religion of the masses devoted to the worship of a diffused pantheon of gods, spirits, and deified heroes. Theirs is an extremely eclectic religion that combines and overshadows animism, shamanism, Buddhism, Taoism, Confucian ethics, and the cult of the ancestors. The masses mostly follow the creative minority, standing eager to take advantage of every religious belief and practice. Thus, whether the three strands of the Chinese tradition are basically philosophy or religion depends on the perspective taken: to the creative minority of the Great Tradition, Confucianism is called *Ju-chia* (the philosophy of the learned), Taoism *Tao-chia* (Taoist philosophy), and Buddhism *Fo-hsüeh* (Buddhist philosophy); to the masses of the Little Tradition, these are called *K'ung-chiao* (Confucian religion), *Tao-chiao* (Taoist religion), and *Fo-chiao* (Buddhist religion), respectively.

Confucianism

Genesis of the Confucian Tradition

Confucius (551–479 B.C.E.), founder of the Confucian tradition, is universally acclaimed the first philosopher and educator in Chinese history. Despite his modest self-evaluation that he was merely a transmitter and not a creator, he molded the basic pattern of the Chinese mind in almost every aspect of Chinese civilization, such as philosophy, religion, social decorum, government, and education, as well as the traditional way of life—the humanist, moral way—as understood and upheld by the

12-1 Portrait of Confucius, stone rubbing, Ming Dynasty. (Courtesy of the Carl Zigrosser collection.)

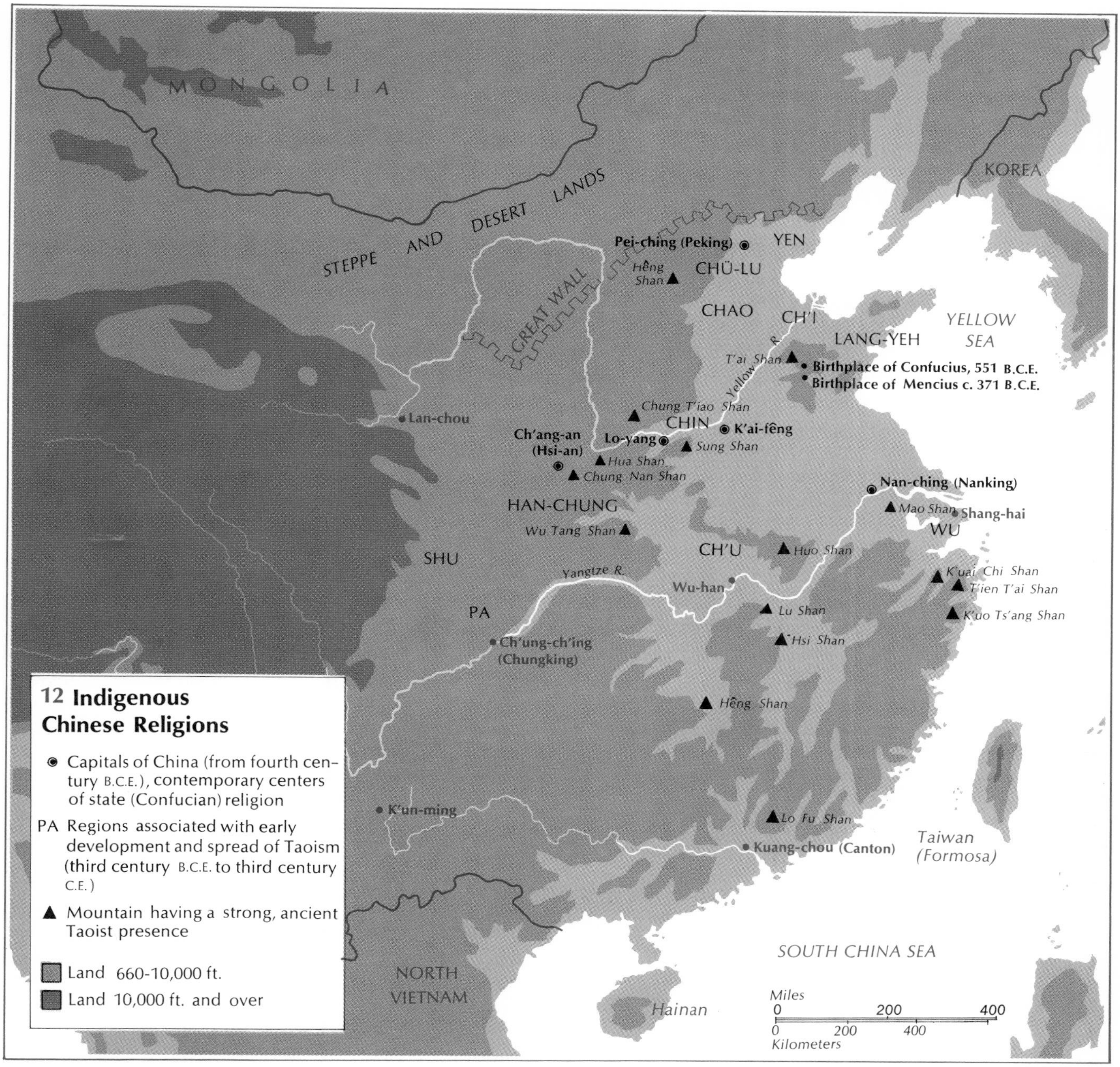

Chinese people. He is attributed with compiling and contributing to the Six Classics, i.e., the *Classics of Changes, Odes, History, Ceremonies,* and *Music,* and the *Spring and Autumn Annals,* all of which represent the most important literary and philosophical heritage of China.

Born into a noble but poor family in the state of Lu, somewhere near the present town of Ch'üfu in Shantung (Map 12), he lost his father in childhood and was forced to secure his education and make his way in the world by himself. When young he served in minor governmental posts in Lu, but his political career was unsuccessful and short-lived. He began, in his fifties, to travel with his disciples around several feudal states in search of a ruler who would put his teaching into practice, but he finally returned, after total disappointment, to Lu and devoted the rest of his life to moral education without class distinction. He was said to have had three thousand pupils, seventy-two of whom were known to master the Six Classics or the "six arts" of ceremonies, music, archery, charioteering, writing, and mathematics. His great success in private education left such a tremendous impact on the subsequent institution of the literati that the Confucian elite have ever since become the key bearers of the Chinese cultural tradition.

In the early religious history of China Confucius was the central figure in the ethicosocial reform of the ancient cult, which consisted of five religious elements: (1) ancestor worship; (2) worship of *Shang-ti* (the Lord-on-High) or *T'ien* (Heaven) and its subordinate systems of nature gods; (3) belief in the existence of the soul; (4) sacrificial rites; and (5) shamanistic divination. Ancestor worship was based on the belief that the (departed) soul has the dual nature of *p'o* (the earthly or *yin* component) and *hun* (the heavenly or *yang* component) and that *hun* would send down blessings to the survivors, whereas *p'o* would turn into a harmful *kuei* (demon) if not placated by proper burials and sacrifices. Without explicitly denying the existence of spiritual beings, Confucius attempted a complete reform of the magical and utilitarian cult of ancestor worship into a system of ethicosocial efficacy. He transformed the sacrificial rites for the dead by purging them of superstitious fear and infusing them with moral significance. This he achieved through the ideas of filial piety and deep respect and remembrance. As to the supernatural, he was always silent about extraordinary forces and disturbing spirits. As an agnostic humanist, he insisted that one should seek the meaning of this very life rather than engage in fruitless inquiry into life after death. In his view, one is unqualified to speak of serving the spirits without being first able to serve men. The ancient belief in the immortality of the soul was later mixed up with the idea of Immortals (*hsien*) in Taoist religion as well as with the Buddhist belief in the Pure Land and has been kept alive by the conservative masses. Through Confucian influence, however, Chinese intellectuals came to maintain a rationalistic belief in the "threefold immortality" of virtue, of worthy service, and of good words. Social immortality came to replace individual immortality.

12-2 The Supreme Ultimate (T'ai Chi), with its two symbolic modes *Yin* and *Yang* surrounded by the *Eight Trigrams* (Pa Kua). A black dot appears within the light-colored *Yang*, symbolic of the embryonic *Yin*, and a light dot within the dark-colored *Yin*, symbolic of the embryonic *Yang*.

In pre-Confucian China people also believed in the existence of an anthropomorphic supreme being, who had an intelligence and will to reign in heaven and who directed the operations of the universe. The Shang people worshiped their tribal god, *Shang-ti*, as the spiritual patron of their dynasty. But the Chou's conquest of the Shang inaugurated a transition from tribal to feudal society, and the idea of *Shang-ti* was gradually superseded by the more universal *T'ien* or Heaven. By the time of Confucius, Heaven had become a kind of supreme *moral* reality or order, as is shown in the expression *T'ien-ming* (the Mandate or Decree of Heaven). In connection with this, the Chou gave a new interpretation of moral retribution, declaring that the appointment of kings and officials were justified only by their moral deeds approved by Heaven and that the Chou's overthrowing of the corrupted Shang Dynasty was perfectly in accord with the Decree of Heaven. Confucius as a man of religious sentiment never questioned the idea of Heaven but seemed to have a less anthropomorphic understanding of Heaven when he said that it did not speak. What is religiously significant here is that, in following the Chou's moral interpretation, Confucius advised that one should joyfully accept, through moral cultivation, one's own destiny (*ming*) as decreed by Heaven. Religiously speaking, to know the Mandate of Heaven is to realize one's destiny, and to realize one's destiny is to become a man of moral excellence or *jên* (humanity or human-heartedness). And, finally, to be a perfectly moral being is to be a man of supreme happiness. Only through the moral perfecting of man as exemplified by the sage, Confucius held, does the way of man become identical with the Way of Heaven.

The moral way of Confucian humanism presupposes the moral perfectibility of man: "It is man that can make the Way great, and not the Way that can make man great." We thus find in the Confucian teaching a new connotation of *chün-tzu* ("son of the ruler") as a (morally) superior man. The superior man regards his distinction as lying in *yi* ("righteousness") rather than profit and strives hard toward the goal of sagehood, where *jên*, the unifying principle of Confucian teaching, will be realized to the utmost. Actually, *jên* refers to what is morally perfect in humanity. It can be realized through the practice of *chung* and *shu; chung* means loyalty to oneself or conscientiousness or refers to the positive aspect of the golden rule ("Do to others what you wish yourself"), and *shu* means moral reciprocity or altruism, reflected in the negative aspect of the same rule ("Do not do to others what you do not wish yourself"). Both *chung* and *shu* complement each other in the process of realizing *jên*. In seeking prominence and prosperity, Confucius said, one has to help others to achieve the same.

In his moral teachings Confucius also mentioned other important virtues. Filial piety (*hsiao*) and brotherly respect (*t'i*) are the starting point for the practice of *jên; li* (decorum, ceremonies, or rules of propriety) constitutes a necessary social norm for harmonious order. There are other important virtues, such as wisdom (*chih*) and courage (*yung*). All of these Confucian virtues are but a concrete specification of the moral contents of *jên*.

Confucius's conception of humane government grounded in his moral theory also exerted a great influence on government and social structure. His own words, "Let the ruler *be* a ruler, the minister *be* a minister, the father *be* a father, and the son *be* a son," clearly illustrate the doctrine of the Rectification of Names, according to which there should be perfect agreement between one's actual status or position and the corresponding Name to which is attached the relevant ideal moral essence. Only humane government can promote the best possible harmonious relations between men, and the rulers have a moral obligation to govern the state by virtue and moral example rather than by mere enforcement of laws or application of brutal force. It follows from this that only the sage-king is qualified to rule. Hence Confucius's emphasis on the moral education of those aspirants for political leadership.

Flowering and Crystallization

MENCIUS. The most important figure in the Confucian tradition after Confucius was Mencius (371?–289? B.C.E.), "the Second Sage," as he is called by the Chinese people. He was a native of Tsou, near Confucius's old home of Lu, and was said to study with a disciple of Tzu Ssu, Confucius's grandson. Like Confucius he lived in a period of political chaos and moral decay and tried all his life in vain to get a hearing for his teaching among the feudal lords of his time. Finally he retired and wrote with his disciples the *Book of Mencius*.

As the first molder of the Confucian tradition, Mencius developed an intuitional ethical theory grounded in his famous theory of human nature. Confucius seldom spoke of human nature, but Mencius spoke to the subject explicitly. He taught that human nature is originally good, that man is distinguishable from the beast by the moral sense inherent in his mind and evidenced by instinctive behavior. Anyone who happens to notice a child about to fall into a well will *naturally* feel a sense of alarm and compassion, without thinking of utility or consequences. As a person, he simply cannot bear to see the suffering of the child. According to Mencius's doctrine of Four Beginnings, all men are born with a sense of (1) commiseration, (2) shame and dislike, (3) modesty and yielding, and (4) (moral) right and wrong, each of which is respectively the beginning of *jên*, *yi* ("moral oughtness"), *li* ("propriety"), and *chih* ("wisdom"). Because man is born with an innate knowledge of the good and an innate ability to do the good, he is entitled to become a sage if he constantly develops what is potentially there. In particular, Mencius emphasized *yi* as a *natural extension* of the *jên* in oneself to other men. In his refutation of two extreme views, i.e., Mo Tzu's doctrine of universal love without distinctions and Yang Chu's hedonistic egoism, Mencius advocated the principle of gradational love starting with filial piety and ending with love for all men. In accordance with this principle, he formulated the Five Constant Relations in human society, i.e., (1) parents and children, (2) ruler and minister, (3) husband and wife, (4) old and young, and (5) friend and friend, each of which is respectively defined in the moral terms of affection, righteousness, distinction (in work), proper order, and trustworthiness. These five relations have since then functioned as the general pattern of the traditional social structure in China, and Mencius's influence here cannot be overemphasized.

In holding the theory that man's nature is originally good, Mencius was quite aware of the difficulty involved, namely, the origin of moral evil. His solution lies in that evil is not inborn but the outcome of man's failure to resist environmental influences (external temptations). Moral education consists in teaching man to restore the original mind he has lost. However, if man has not lost his moral mind and continues to cultivate and refine it, he may attain sagehood, the humanistic means to supreme happiness in this life.

Like Confucius, Mencius considered humane government the political ideal. He vindicated a kind of Confucian democracy: "In the constitution of a state . . . the people rank the highest, the spirits of land and grain come next, and the ruler counts the least." The appointment of a ruler is made by Heaven, whose Decree can be detected through the expressed will of the people. If a king is so wicked as to violate the Mandate of Heaven, then there is moral justification for the people to revolt and dethrone him. Like his master, Mencius was also a man of strong religious spirit and believed that man's full development of his moral potentials is the way to know nature, that to know nature is the way to know (the Mandate of) Heaven, and that to cultivate one's moral mind and await one's destiny is the way to fulfill one's destiny. If one is able to nourish the "magnanimous, moral energy" in oneself, one can attain to sagehood and therefore identify oneself with the universe (Heaven) as a whole. This is the ethicoreligious goal of Mencius.

THE LI-CHI. Together with the *Analects of Confucius* and the *Book of Mencius,* the two short essays in the *Li-chi* (Book of Rites), namely the *Great Learning* and the *Doctrine of the Mean,* make up the basic teachings of early Confucianism. These four works were later carefully selected, with philosophical commentaries, by Chu Hsi in the twelfth century to form the "Four Books" used as the required textual assignments for civil-service examination from 1313 to 1905. The *Great Learning* gives a systematic account of the moral, educational, and politicosocial teachings of the Confucian tradition. The Way of the Great Learning (for adult education) consists in the "three fundamentals" of (A) exemplifying (man's inherent) illustrious virtue, (B) loving (or reforming) the people, and (C) resting in the supreme good. This can be accomplished by following the eight steps of (1) investigation of things, (2) acquisition (extension) of knowledge, (3) sincerity of the will, (4) rectification of the mind, (5) cultivation of personal character, (6) regulation of the family, (7) governance of the state, and (8) pacification of the world. The first five steps complete the required discipline of self-cultivation (A), and the next three steps describe the way to serve society (B). Finally, the highest goal (C) can be reached by the complete realization of *jên* as the *summum bonum* in the "world of grand unity." The *Great Learning* provides a clear and gradational method of moral education for all Confucian aspirants determined to become men of "sageliness within and kingliness without," and therefore a method of qualifying themselves as elite under the stringent demands of traditional China.

The *Doctrine of the Mean,* possibly written by Tzu Ssu (492–431 B.C.E.), sets up a metaphysical foundation for the Confucian ethics and psychology of "preserving the mind and nourishing man's nature." The Mandate of Heaven, as metaphysical reality, is now understood in terms of an eternal, "soundless and odorless," transforming and sustaining power, operative within the nature of men and all things. The famous line, "The hawk flies up to heaven and the fishes leap in the deep," is quoted from the *Classic of Odes* to illustrate the Way of Heaven "clearly seen above and below." Together with the "Appended Remarks" of the *Classic of the Changes,* which describes the Way of Heaven in terms of "the creative process of production and reproduction," the *Doctrine of the Mean* later became an important metaphysical bridge between Taoism, Buddhism, and Confucianism and thus prepared an overture to the philosophical synthesis of these teachings in Neo-Confucian thought.

The metaphysical quality of (the Way of) Heaven that brings man and things together is called *ch'êng* (sincerity). Macrocosmically *ch'êng* is an active force transforming and completing all things; microcosmically it constitutes the real principle of man, revealed through the state of centrality or equilibrium (before feelings and emotions are aroused) and harmony (of feelings and emotions after they are aroused). To embody the reality of *ch'êng* in oneself, one should "search within oneself" (*shên-tu*) in everyday moral practice, testing it against the ideal of the Mean ("centrality and normality"), i.e., freedom from onesideness and extraordinariness. For the superior men who seek to attain sublime transcendence right in the Mean of everyday practice, two complementary approaches are recommended, namely, "following the path of inquiry and study" (search for knowledge) and "honoring the moral nature" (supremacy of virtue). These two approaches subsequently represented two opposing tendencies in the Neo-Confucian movement, i.e., Ch'êng-Chu rationalism and Lu-Wang intuitionism.

HSÜN TZU. The last great molder of early Confucianism was Hsün Tzu (fl. 298–238 B.C.E.), a naturalist and realist who was a native of the state of Chao. He established himself as the most eminent scholar at the academy of Chi-hsia in the state of Ch'i. He was diametrically opposed to Mencius in the doctrines of human nature and moral education, as well as in the concept of Heaven. According to his naturalistic explanation, man is born with inherent desires for profit and sensual pleasure and is therefore originally "evil." But he differs from the beast in that he has the intelligence to become good and attain to sagehood. Knowing that man's uncontrolled, natural desires and emotions would lead to strife and disorder, the sage-king created *li* ("social norm") and *yi* ("morality") and instituted laws and systems, so that they could become well disciplined and conform with the Way (*Tao*). Man's goodness is therefore the result of social restraints and cultural refinement. Against Mencius's thesis that man can naturally develop his original, moral mind, Hsün Tzu emphasized acquired learning, man-made rules of conduct, and the rectification of names based on social convention. As to the idea of Heaven, he regarded it as simply Nature itself, which operates with constant regularity. Nature cannot send down blessings, and man should devote himself to his own work without reliance upon the impossible Mandate of Heaven. And against Mencius's view that one's knowing Nature through the full nourishment of the mind leads to one's knowing Heaven, he insisted that the sage would not seek to know Heaven. Thus, in his naturalistic explanation of Heaven, Hsün Tzu came closer to the Taoists than any other Confucianist. And because of his emphasis on conventional institution and external control of man's nature, he contributed to the authoritarianism that resulted in the dictatorship of the Ch'in (221–206 B.C.E.). As a matter of fact, Han Fei and Li Ssu, both of whom were leading legalists who served as the Ch'in ministers, were his own pupils. In the Han dynasty he also had an extensive influence on the naturalists like Wang Ch'ung (27–100? C.E.). Since then he had been long neglected until the nineteenth century, whereas Mencius was considered the real successor to Confucius. Interestingly, he is today regarded by Fung Yu-lan and other top scholars in the People's Republic of China as the greatest materialist in ancient China.

The Ascendency of Eclectic Confucianism as the State Cult

In the year 221 B.C.E., the king of Ch'in, one of the seven states in the Warring States Period, finally conquered all his rivals and unified China. With the assistance of Li Ssu, he abolished ancient feudalism and built up for the first time in Chinese history a centralized empire under strict dictatorship. And for the sake of complete ideological control, he buried alive hundreds of scholars and burned all books except those in the imperial archives and works on medicine, divination, and agriculture. Because of their ideological conflict with the Ch'in emperor and his legalist advisers, the Confucianists became the first target of the unprecedented massacre of the intellectuals. After the Han overthrew the Ch'in dynasty, legalism and Taoism first won the favor of the early emperors, but Confucianism gradually ascended to the leading role and was finally established as the state cult. Among others, some reasons for its new prestige are the following: (1) Being the only experts on the classics, the Confucian scholars were not only authorized but asked to compile and interpret those books rediscovered after the proscription; (2) the Han needed to institute rites and ceremonies, and the Confucian specialists were naturally assigned to such a task; (3) in order to justify their ruling position, the Han emperors were eager to use the Confucian scholars to invent a new Han ideology. Tung Chung-shu (ca. 179–ca. 104 B.C.E.) was a great theorizer in such an attempt. He was chiefly instrumental in the Han's proclamation of Confucianism as the state religion in 136 B.C.E., as well as in the establishment of a national academy in 124 B.C.E. with departments corresponding to the Five Classics. (Among the Six Classics, the *Classic of Music* was lost.) To his credit was also the initiation of the examination system for the selection of government officials based on their knowledge of the Confucian classics. As to his theoretical contribution, he eclectically developed, in his *Luxuriant Gems of the "Spring and Autumn Annals,"* a metaphysic of the reciprocal responsiveness of man and Heaven and combined it with the *yin-yang* cosmology. He further combined the theory of Five Agents (wood, fire, earth, metal, and water) with the Confucian politicosocial teaching. The change of four seasons and other natural phenomena he cleverly explained in terms of the *yin-yang* interaction and the mutual production of Five Agents in proper order. And in his grand metaphysical scheme of Heaven-man interconnection, the ruler corresponds to Heaven; and the "three bonds" of sovereign, father, and husband, all being *yang* (the positive, male principle), become the standards of subject, son, and wife, all being *yin* (the negative, female principle). However, through Tung's eclectic molding of the Confucian doctrine adopted by the Han rulers as the state ideology, Confucianism achieved its supremacy in both theory and practice.

Confucian Dormancy

Tung's eclecticism did not add any new creative thought to Confucianism despite his remarkable success in achieving the Confucian monopoly. For several centuries after Tung, Confucian scholars lost their philosophical vitality because their talents and efforts were exhausted on textual criticism and commentary. In contrast, Taoism entered a new phase through the Neo-Taoist movement, and Buddhism also began to develop Chinese *Mādhyamika* metaphysics and other philosophical doctrines by way of its interaction with Taoist philosophy. Meanwhile, both Taoist religion and Pure Land Buddhism gradually attracted masses who desperately waited for a new gospel of salvation during the long period of political struggle, social instability, and war. From the declining era of the latter Han to the middle of the T'ang, the whole philosophicoreligious scene was dominated by either Taoism or Buddhism or both. The struggling Confucianists were unable to battle against the flowering of the other two traditions until the eighth century T'ang, when two outstanding Confucianists, Han Yü (768–824) and Li Ao (fl. 798), opened a vehement attack upon the Taoist nonaction and the Buddhist "silence and annihilation" and endeavored to restore the humanist tradition of Confucianism deeply concerned with government, education, and other worldly affairs. However, Han and Li, both of whom were basically literary-minded, could not create a new Confucian philosophy to cope with the profound metaphysical systems of Taoism and Buddhism. The Neo-Confucian movement they planted had to await nearly three centuries for its own harvest.

The Rise of Neo-Confucianism

The development of Neo-Confucian thought began in the eleventh-century Sung dynasty. The man who opened its philosophical vista was Chou Tun-yi (1017–1073), who laid the foundation of Neo-Confucian metaphysics and ethics in *T'ai-chi-t'u-shuo* (An Explanation of the Diagram of the Supreme Ultimate) and *T'ung-shu* (Comprehensive Understanding of the *Classic of the Changes*). He borrowed and revised the *Diagram* drawn by the Taoist school and incorporated it into Confucian thought in such a way that he was able to construct a fresh Confucian metaphysical system, the embryonic form of which already existed in the *Doctrine of the Mean* and the *Classic of the Changes.* Ultimate reality in Chou's system is called the Ultimateless (because of its incorporeality, formlessness, and infinity) and also the Supreme Ultimate. It generates *yang* through movement and *yin* through tranquillity after its activity has reached its limit. The two primordial forces of *yin* and *yang* are established through their mutual interaction. Out of this interaction emerge the Five Agents or five material forces, each with its own specific nature. Consolidation then follows because of the integration of the reality of the Ultimateless with the essences of *yin* and *yang* and the Five Agents. Here, the *ch'ien* ("creative") principle becomes the male element and the *k'un* ("receptive") principle becomes the female element. The interaction of *yin* and *yang* engenders and transforms all things, and these in turn produce and reproduce, resulting in unceasing transformation and reproduction. This whole process is to be understood as metaphysical and symbolic and not spatiotemporal. The "Appended Remarks" to *The Classic of the Changes* states that "what is metaphysical is called the *Tao,* and what is phenomenal is called concrete things." The general understanding of the Neo-Confucianists, especially Ch'êng-Chu rationalists, about the relation of this statement to Chou's system is that the Supreme Ultimate refers to the *Tao* or the (Heavenly) principle, whereas *yin-yang,* Five Agents, and all things refer to the phenomenal. The metaphysical principle (*li*) and the material force (*ch'i*) are the two inseparable aspects of the same reality. As to human nature and morality, Chou regarded man as the most intelligent because he receives the greatest natural endowments and because, when he attains sagehood, he "regulates himself according to the mean, to correctness, love, and righteousness, and takes quiescence as the essential, thus establishing the highest standard for mankind."

Taking a somewhat different approach, Chou's contemporary, Shao Yung (1011–1077), developed a numerical and objective metaphysical system, and another Neo-Confucianist, Chang Tsai (1020–1077), worked out a monistic philosophy of *ch'i* (material force) by identifying *ch'i* with the Supreme Ultimate and discarding *yin-yang* and the Five Agents as generative forces. In spite of the Confucian tone of his discussion of personal cultivation and sagehood, Chang is today considered by the Communist scholars as one of the greatest materialists in Chinese thought.

The most significant movement in Neo-Confucian thought concerns the controversy between two opposing schools, i.e., Ch'êng-Chu rationalism and Lu-Wang intuitionism. This division was already existent in the different views of the Ch'êng brothers, Ch'êng Hao (1032–1085) and Ch'êng Yi (1033–1107), though they did not themselves fully recognize their divergent views in their philosophical thinking. Chu Hsi (1130–1200), the greatest Neo-Confucian synthesizer, completed Ch'êng Yi's dualistic metaphysics of *li* ("principle") and *ch'i* ("material force") and developed a corresponding theory of human nature by way of adapting Chang Tsai's view of "the mind unifying nature and feelings." According to Chu, man has a twofold nature, the heavenly and the material; the principles of humanity, righteousness, propriety, and wisdom are inherent in the mind because of heavenly nature, but man may lose his moral mind because of his uncontrolled desires and emotions, which come from material nature, which is moral nature mixed up with *ch'i.* The proper way to the attainment of sagehood is, in addition to serious introspection within the mind, to examine things exhaustively with a view to realize the (moral) principles.

As against the "Nature is Principle" view of the Ch'êng-Chu School, Lu Hsiang-shan (1139–1193) followed strictly the Mencian line of thinking and held that "Mind is Principle." He rejected the dualistic thesis that mind is the "possessor" of the (moral) principles that constitute Heavenly nature, and interpreted "the investigation of things" to mean "the investigation of mind," for to him all principles are inherent and complete in the mind. In other words, (moral) principles and the mind are one and the same thing. Hence Lu's emphasis on "honoring the moral nature" (supremacy of virtue) rather than "following the path of inquiry and study" (search for knowledge). He criticized Chu's philosophy as that of the divided, aimless, and drifting mind searching for isolated, trivial details; whereas Chu deplored Lu's deviation from the Confucian path by a dangerous association with *Ch'an* (Zen).

Under the Ming dynasty, Lu's idealism culminated in the philosophy of Wang Yang-ming (1472–1528). His main thesis consists in (1) mind itself as principle, (2) the extension of intuitive knowledge within, and (3) the unity of knowing and doing. He also gave an idealistic interpretation of *ko-wu* ("investigation of things") to mean "to eliminate what is incorrect in the mind so as to preserve the correctness of its original substance," as opposed to Chu's objective and rationalistic investigation. Despite the flat denial by both Lu and Wang of their affiliation with *Ch'an* Buddhism, many Confucian idealists in the later period of the Ming did create a kind of *"mad Ch'an"* to cause the decline of Lu-Wang idealism.

From the last period of the Ming to the Ch'ing dynasty a new positivistic and pragmatic reaction against the orthodoxy of Sung-Ming Neo-Confucianism gradually evolved. First, Wang Fu-chih (1619–1692) developed a philosophy of concrete materialism, based on which he rejected the abstract notions like the Supreme Ultimate or Heavenly Principle as senseless and stressed the material concreteness of all things as well as the exhaustive study of political institutions and history rather than fruitless metaphysical speculation. Yen Yüan (1635–1704) went a further step in advocating practical Confucianism and urged learning through actual experience and practice. Tai Chên (1723–1777), another Ch'ing Confucianist, maintained a philosophy of principle as order, according to which principle is nothing but the order of concrete things in terms of "daily affairs such as drinking and eating." Near the end of the Ch'ing dynasty, most Confucian scholars began to engage themselves, because of the technological challenge from the West, in the discussion of the problem of "Chinese learning as substance and Western learning as function," but failed to find out a workable solution, as in the case of K'ang Yu-wei's philosophy of the grand unity as well as of T'an Ssu-t'ung's philosophy of humanity.

The Ideological Struggle of Confucianism in Modern China

Since the birth of the Republic of China in 1912, the life and death of the Confucian tradition has been, in connection with the problem of modernization (science and democracy), one of the biggest issues among the intellectual leaders. On the one hand, there were a number of conservative campaigns attempting a nostalgic restoration of Confucianism as a state cult, but they all turned out to be abortive. On the other, a modern movement led by Hu Shih (1891–1962) and Ch'ên Tu-hsiu, (1879–1942), the twin leaders of the Cultural Renaissance that began in 1917, signaled an anti-Confucian *coup de grace* with the radical slogan "Down with the Confucian House!" This campaign was carried through the early 1930's before the Sino-Japanese War. The transient China also witnessed some serious philosophical enterprises of Fung Yu-lan (b. 1895), Hsiung Shih-li (1885–1968), et al. to create a new synthesis of Confucian philosophy and other traditions, Buddhist or Western. But after the Communist revolution in 1949, Confucianism again suffered another setback and was reinterpreted in the strict light of dialectical materialism. The total change of Fung Yu-lan's philosophical view expressed in his confession is a very striking example. It remains to be seen whether the humanist way of Confucianism, which has been for more than two thousand years the main tradition of China, can survive and even rejuvenate itself in the People's Republic of China.

Taoism

Taoist Philosophy (*Tao-chia*)

ORIGIN. The origin of Taoism as a philosophy is not certain even today. According to the orthodox account of Ssu-ma Ch'ien, the author of the *Historical Records,* an older contemporary of Confucius called Lao Tzu composed the book of *Tao-te-ching* and was therefore the real founder of the Taoist tradition. However, this traditional view has been challenged by quite a number of Chinese scholars and Western Sinologists in the past sixty years. Some scholars even suspected that the book itself did not appear before the book of *Chuang Tzu.* Whether or not this is the case, it seems safe to say that the basic ideas and passages of *Lao Tzu* probably existed before *Chuang Tzu.* According to the legend Ssu-ma noted, Lao Tzu was the keeper of the archives of the court of Chou in the sixth century B.C.E. and instructed Confucius once on the rules of propriety. At the age of 160, he grew disgusted with the decay of the Chou Dynasty and decided to pursue the "Way and Its Virtue," which is itself the meaning of *Tao-te-ching*, in a more congenial atmosphere. Before he departed from the scene, he wrote the *Tao-te-ching* of about five thousand characters at the request of Yin-hsi, the keeper of the Hanku pass. Because of its profound philosophical thought expressed cryptically in a very short treatise, the book *Lao Tzu* attracted more commentaries than any other Chinese classic in the past two thousand years. Not only Taoists but also eminent Confucian and Buddhist philosophers indulged in this kind of writing.

LAO TZU. Lao Tzu's philosophy can be characterized as a nondualistic naturalism. In the opening passage of *Tao-te-ching*, he announced, "The *Tao* that can be expressed in words is not the eternal *Tao*; the name that can be named is not the eternal Name." In other words, *Tao* as metaphysical reality is ineffable and nameless, because the absolute *Tao* is, as Lao Tzu said, totally invisible, inaudible, formless, infinite, boundless, vague, and elusive—in short, transcendent. Thus, our conceptual, dualistic grasping of the undifferentiated *Tao* by any human means would simply lead to failure. From *our* point of view, however, we can somehow detect—but only in a *relative* sense—the nature of *Tao* through its manifestation. Hence, we give to it various provisional names such as "Nonbeing," "the One," "the Great," "the Subtle and Profound Female," "the Uncarved Block," "the Ravine of the World," "the Mother of All Things," or the word "*Tao*" itself. The *Tao* manifested to us is Nature, which is no more than the ontological totality of the myriad things in the world. Lao Tzu also gave a symbolic, cosmological account of natural causation and evolution, but he did not attempt a teleological explanation of the myriad things of the world. He said; "From *Tao* comes One, from One comes Two, from Two comes Three, and from Three comes all things." *Tao* is not merely the "mother" of all things but is also regarded by Lao Tzu as the invariable law of nature underlying the perpetual change and transformation of all things. The eternal flux of being is manifested by *Tao* itself, which contains within it the principle that anything that reaches an extreme would immediately revert to the opposite. The practical implication of this notion for human life is the principle,

12-3 Translation of inscription: This is Lao Tzu worshiped by ironsmiths. (Courtesy of the Philadelphia Museum of Art, photograph by A. J. Wyatt, staff photographer.)

"calamity is that upon which happiness depends, and happiness is that in which calamity is latent." Therefore the wise man of *Tao* should follow the natural way by cultivating the Taoist virtues (*tê*) such as *wu-wei* ("non-action"), spontaneous naturalness, simplicity, tranquillity, impartiality, selflessness, humility, tenderness, nondesire, noncompetition, nonpossession, and nonknowledge. In short, the wise Taoist should lead a spontaneous and simple life by identifying himself with the great *Tao* or Nature, which "never makes any ado and yet nothing is left undone."

Lao Tzu's naturalism led him to the conclusion that all unnatural things such as war, taxation, punishment, (secular) knowledge, ceremonies, social conventions, and human morality should be condemned or discarded. He advised kings and rulers to manage their affairs without much ado (*wu-wei*) and accomplish their tasks without laying any claim. To Lao Tzu, the best government policy is that of *laissez-faire*. He even drew a utopian picture of a small country with few people, whose primitive but spontaneous way of living makes them self-sufficient and happy without bothering themselves to know anything outside their society.

CHUANG TZU. The next important Taoist philosopher was Chuang Tzu (369–ca. 286 B.C.E.), in whose book all the basic ideas of Lao Tzu are fastidiously embellished and enlarged. His life is little known to us; he was said to be a native of the state of Sung, to have served as a petty official at the Lacquer Garden, and declined to have once an offer to become prime minister in order to lead a life of complete freedom. The philosophies of Lao Tzu and Chuang Tzu are virtually the same, but there are some slight differences in personal style and doctrinal emphasis, as well as in the method of expression. Lao Tzu was very much interested in the application of Taoist philosophy to political and social affairs, whereas Chuang Tzu showed utter indifference to any earthly matter. The latter spoke mainly of individual spiritual emancipation from the dusty world, as well as of the mystical vision of *Tao* in its infinite dimensions. Lao Tzu used a simple, rhythmic but cryptic language to express his natural way, whereas Chuang Tzu composed his philosophical essays skillfully in various literary forms, such as witty allegory, paradox, parable, fanciful imagery, humor, irony, satire, and so on. His philosophical profundity aside, Chuang was one of the best literary men in Chinese history, and his creative insight and versatility in style have been a great stimulus to the artistic imagination of many poets and landscape painters.

On the conception of *Tao* as nature or the spontaneous totality of all things, Chuang Tzu elaborated three metaphysical points. First, he described *Tao* as belonging neither to being nor to nonbeing. This new dimension of *Tao* was later taken by Huai Nan Tzu and then the Neo-Taoists, for whom it functioned as a Taoist metaphysical equivalent to the *śūnyatā* ("emptiness") of Mahayana Buddhism. Second, he stressed the ubiquity of *Tao* by saying that it exists in everything, no matter how banal or hateful. For insofar as anything is, it is *Tao*. Third, he understood the manifestation of *Tao* in terms of the endless process of change and transformation of things into their opposites. What is metaphysically implied here is that all things in the universe are absolutely equal from the point of view of *Tao*.

Chuang Tzu's transcendental Taoism led him to a total disregard of mundane affairs and to a vindication of personal emancipation through equalization of all things and opinions. From the standpoint of a vulgar man *sub specie temporis*, he declared, there is always a duality of things and opinions, such as utility/disutility, beauty/ugliness, noble/mean, true/false, right/wrong, self/other, awakening/dreaming, full/empty, being/nonbeing, and so on. From the standpoint of a *Tao*-man *sub specie aeternitatis*, however, all dualities are relative, the result of human folly and attachment. The *Tao*-man equalizes all dualities and transcends them. Once all distinctions, human and relative, are completely forgotten, the Taoist sage "harmonizes things according to the order of nature" and "pursues the middle course."

The highest goal of life to Chuang Tzu consists therefore in the complete identification of oneself with nature. Such a man will find eternal happiness in his metaphysical realization that "the universe and I exist together, and all things and I are one," and that "The perfect man has no self; the spiritual man has no achievement; the true sage has no name."

It is very interesting to note the mystic tone in Chuang Tzu's philosophy when he talks about the methods of "fasting of the mind," of "sitting in forgetfulness," and so on. His idea of "sitting down and forgetting everything" has been a main source of inspiration to Zen masters ("sitting in meditation") as well as to the Neo-Confucianists ("quiet sitting"). When Ch'êng Hao admitted, for instance, that "there is nothing better than to become broad and extremely impartial and to respond spontaneously to all things as they come," his expression sounds very like Chuang Tzu's rather than a Neo-Confucianist's.

LIU AN. The most prominent Taoist after Lao Tzu and Chuang Tzu was Liu An (d. 122 B.C.E.), grandson of the first Han emperor. As the prince of Huai-nan, he patronized thousands of learned scholars who assisted him to compose *Huai Nan Tzu*, a collection of twenty-one essays. The main thesis of its metaphysical thinking comes from Lao Tzu and Chuang Tzu. Lacking originality, Liu occasionally engaged in word play. He described *Tao* as universal and absolute nothingness transcending both space and time. "There was a time before the time which was before the beginning," he wrote, and "There was a time before the time which was before nothingness." Much of his cosmological thinking is also borrowed from the *Classic of the Changes.* Like *Lao Tzu* and the *Classic of the Changes, Huai Nan Tzu* helped contribute to the formation of orthodox cosmological theory generally accepted by both Taoist philosophers and Neo-Confucianists.

In spite of its Taoist approach, *Huai Nan Tzu* showed a strong eclectic tendency. For example, it adapted much of the Confucian method of self-cultivation and the authoritarian views and methods of law enforcement followed by the legalist school. In it are also found myth, legend, astrology, calendar, and folk religion, as well as the ideas of (earthly) immortality and breathing techniques. It stimulated the subsequent amalgamation of Taoist philosophy with Taoist popular religion. *Huai Nan Tzu* can be regarded as a book combining various ancient thoughts with Taoism as foundation.

Rise of Neo-Taoism

In the early period of the Former Han, the emperors leaned toward Taoism instead of Confucianism. Emperor Wên (179–157 B.C.E.) successfully adopted Lao Tzu's political doctrine of *laissez-faire.* He abolished mutilating punishments, reduced the land tax, pursued an appeasement policy toward the northern invaders, practiced economy, and interfered in his people's affairs as little as possible. His son Ching Ti (156–140 B.C.E.) was the first emperor to recognize *Lao Tzu* as a classic. But after Emperor Wu established a Confucian bureaucracy on the pattern of Tung Chung-shu, Taoism did not develop any new thought. The decay lasted until the Wei-Chin period (220–420 C.E.), when the intellectual movement of Neo-Taoism arose under the leadership of Wang Pi (226–249), Ho Yen (d. 249), and Kuo Hsiang (d. 312), and others. This movement is often described sociologically as a negativist escape from reality. Its rise is explained as strong reaction against protracted political warfare among ambitious politicians and generals, miserable social conditions, and the unprecedented great loss of population by repeated floods and droughts. Philosophically speaking, however, Taoism was rejuvenated and flourished in this period of social instability. Many outstanding works were produced by Neo-Taoists who were able to put fresh metaphysical wine into old Taoist bottles. These were sometimes syncretic in adopting the politicosocial philosophy of Confucianism. Wang Pi even considered Confucius a greater sage than Lao Tzu and Chung Tzu. For, he reasoned, Confucius did not (have to) speak of forgetfulness as he had already forgotten that he had learned to forget. Nor did he, according to Wang Pi, speak of nondesire as he had already reached the stage of lacking any desire to be without desire. Lao Tzu and Chuang Tzu, on the other hand, could not help talking and talking about their forgetfulness and nondesire.

Wang Pi had started a new movement before he died at the age of twenty-four. His two philosophical commentaries on *Lao Tzu* and the *Classic of the Changes* are themselves original works and inspired both Buddhists and Neo-Confucianists toward a new way of metaphysical thinking. He went beyond Lao Tzu in calling *Tao* "original nonbeing" (*pên-wu*), which is the original substance transcending all distinctions and descriptions. He also gave a new interpretation of the cosmology of Lao Tzu (in Chapter 40): "All things in the world come from being, and the origin of being is nonbeing. In order to have being in total, it is necessary to return to nonbeing." Most important of all, in Wang's conception of "original nonbeing" both substance and function are mutually penetrating: "Although it is valuable to have nonbeing as the function (of all things), nevertheless there cannot be substance without nonbeing." The idea of the nonseparability and interpenetration of substance (reality) and function (manifestation) is attributed to Wang Pi and was later adopted and developed first by the Chinese Buddhists, then by the Neo-Confucianists.

Another great work in the history of Neo-Taoism is the *Philosophical Commentary on Chuang Tzu* attributed to Kuo Hsiang, who, in all probability, appropriated his ideas from another Neo-Taoist, Hsiang Hsiu (fl. 250). The Hsiang-Kuo interpretation of Lao-Chuang philosophy made some significant revisions of Taoist metaphysics. First, they conceived *Tao* as *literally* nothing: "*Tao* is everywhere; and everywhere it is nothing." Thus Lao Tzu's symbolic statement that all things come into being from *Tao* or being comes into being from nonbeing was reinterpreted to mean that all things come to be *by themselves,* or that being comes into being *by itself.* This is a new theory of self-transformation, according to which all things exist and transform themselves spontaneously, each according to its own principle. Being simply the grand totality of these self-transforming concrete things in the universe, *Tao,* as such, does not really exist. Whereas Wang Pi emphasized nonbeing as reality, the Hsiang-Kuo thesis emphasized the self-existing being of the myriad things; whereas the former spoke of *one*-in-many (original nonbeing transcending all things), the latter preferred *many*-in-one.

Hsiang-Kuo's new interpretation of *wu-wei* ("non-action") and *yu-wei* ("having activity") in early Taoism illustrates the two teachers' philosophical efforts to purify Taoist naturalism. Because new institutions and morals spontaneously replace the outdated and therefore unnatural ones, to let the former go ahead without intervention means to be *wu-wei,* whereas to oppose the former by holding to the latter would mean (artificial) *yu-wei.* In the case of the individual's life, if he fully exercised his ability and discharged his capacity, then he is practicing the Taoist virtue of *wu-wei.* Otherwise, he is *yu-wei.* Hsiang-Kuo particularly emphasized the self-sufficiency of spontaneous living without imitating the sages, for imitation is unnatural, useless, and even harmful. Chuang Tzu's distinction between "greater knowledge" and "small knowledge" was not only removed but simply forgotten. And his high-minded spiritual emancipation by "traveling in the transcendental world" was replaced by Hsiang-Kuo's immanent happiness in terms of a simple, natural man's self-sufficient and spontaneous living according to himself. The Hsiang-Kuo interpretation of Chuang Tzu paved a new path toward a synthesis of Neo-Taoism and Mahayana Buddhism, especially *Ch'an* (Zen) in which we find many naturalistic expressions, such as "Everyday-mindedness is *Tao*" or "Wood-chopping or water-carrying: herein is found the wondrous *Tao,*" all showing a profound influence of Chuang Tzu by way of the Hsiang-Kuo interpretation.

Apart from the metaphysical movement of Neo-Taoism, there was a correlated movement of "pure conversation" (*ch'ing-t'an*), led by the literary men of the Neo-Taoist school like the Seven Worthies of the Bamboo Grove. These romantic Taoists totally discarded secular ambitions and worldly values and advocated an unconventional way of life according to feelings or sentiments, expressed in refined and elegant phraseology. This romantic movement lasted from the middle of the second century through the sixth.

Taoist philosophy gradually declined after the fourth century, by which time it began to interact with Mahayana Buddhism, Chinese *Mādhyamika* in particular. Its influence on Buddhist thought and linguistic expression was tremendous during this period, when the Buddhists engaged in the extremely difficult task of translating the Sanskrit and Pali texts into Chinese. Buddhist adoption of Taoist terms, such as *Tao, nameless, nonbeing, vacuous, substance, function,* and so on, partly enabled the imported tradition to take root in Chinese soil. But the greatest influence of philosophical Taoism upon Buddhist thought is to be found in the development of *Ch'an* Buddhism, probably the most interesting instance of Sinicization of Buddhism. One can never comprehend the original meaning of *Ch'an* without reference to the Taoist notions of *wu-wei, tsu-jan* ("spontaneous naturalness"), *wu-hsin* ("no-mind"), the Way (*Tao*), and so on.

Despite their attack upon the Taoist *wu-wei,* the Neo-Confucianists in general also learned a great deal from the Taoists with respect to the practice of tranquillity and simplicity (of the mind), not to mention their borrowing and adapting of the Taoist cosmological ideas. Thus, through its philosophical influence on both Buddhism and Confucianism, Taoism as a way of life has never lost its strong hold on the Chinese people, as is evidenced by the Chinese saying, "In office a Confucianist, in retirement a Taoist, and on deathbed a Buddhist." In many aspects of cultural activities in China, such as landscape painting, poetry, tea drinking, calligraphy, and sometimes politics, there has been a very strong Taoist molding of the Chinese mind in terms of the spirit of harmony, simplicity, spontaneity, naturalistic individualism, and enlightened freedom.

Taoist Religion (*Tao-chiao*)

EARLY DEVELOPMENT. Although the philosophical teachings of Lao Tzu and Chuang Tzu were carried over into the Neo-Taoist movement, magicoreligious Taoism not only twisted the original philosophical stock into a superstitious cult of longevity and (actual physical) immortality but deified Lao Tzu as *T'ai-shang Lao-chün* (the Supreme Lord *Lao*) and honored *Tao-te-ching* as a divine book revealed to the human mortals. Taoist religion is indeed a very confusing conglomeration of the philosophy of Lao Tzu (and other early Taoists), the *yin-yang* doctrine of Tsou Yen, a pleasing legend of the Isles of the Blessed such as Mt. P'êng Lai and of the Taoist Immortals (*hsien*), alchemy, magical talismans, an indigenous Chinese form of *yoga,* collective sexual orgies, revolutionary secret societies, ununified sects and temple armies defending an unsuccessful theocratic state, folk religion, the continuously growing pantheon of gods including the Taoist immortals, Buddhist Bodhisattvas, and national heroes, as well as of the Confucian moral doctrine and the Buddhist belief in karmic retribution and the existence of hell. No less confusing is the huge Taoist canon (*Tao-tsang*), a bible of no less than 1,464 titles drawn up on the lines of *San-tsang* (the Chinese Buddhist Tripitaka) and including many non-Taoist texts as well. This canon has been compiled and expanded over a period of fifteen centuries.

One conspicuous feature of the ecclesiastical organization of Taoist religion is that there has never been,

12-4 Lao Tzu, Sung Dynasty (960–1297). (Courtesy of the Metropolitan Museum of Art, gift of Mrs. Abby Aldrich Rockefeller, 1942.)

throughout its history, a permanent central authority governing all Taoist sects and monasteries. Like the Buddhist community in China, the Taoist has been always atomistic in nature. According to the orthodox account, the origin of Taoist religion can be traced back to 143 C.E., in which year Chang Ling (or Chang Tao-ling), a popular religious man noted for healing the sick, organized the movement and required all the converts to contribute five pecks of rice as payment for their cure or as dues of the cult. This earned him the nickname "rice-thief" and his cult the name "the way of the Five Pecks of Rice." It was also called the Way of Heavenly Masters because he won the honorific title "Heavenly Master" (*t'ien-shih*), which his direct descendants have retained ever since. His movement spread rapidly in the declining era of the Later Han, and his son Chang Hêng, then his grandson Chang Lu, built a theocratic state in Hanchung. Believing that his patients became sick because of their sins, Chang Lu imprisoned them, as a method of treatment, to think over their sins. Final expiation was done by writing their sins on three pieces of paper, one of which was exposed on a mountain top for Heaven, one buried for Earth, and one cast in a river for Water. He also required his sinners-converts to repair roads and forbade animal killing in spring and summer and the use of fermented liquor. He constructed wayside inns for travelers without charge. The Buddhist belief in karmic retribution and/or the Confucian moral teaching probably had some impact on these practices. He ruled his state for thirty years but finally surrendered in 215 C.E. to Ts'ao Ts'ao, the father of the first king of the Wei, and was rewarded with high honors and a princely fief.

Meanwhile in eastern China a certain Chang Chüeh formed another movement called *T'ai-p'ing-tao* (the Way of Grand Peace), became the leader of the Yellow Turbans revolting against the Han, and almost overthrew the dynasty. He announced an immediate advent of a new era, promised to found a utopian order, and healed the sick by confession of sins in dramatic public ceremonies, in addition to the use of talismans and lustral water. Like Chang Lu, he organized a clerical hierarchy and took himself the title of "Heavenly General." Despite the fact that these two movements were geographically apart and had no connection with each other, they shared many common features in both theory and practice. The rebellion of the Yellow Turbans was later suppressed by the Han, but the sect of Heavenly Masters continued its existence and organized a hereditary patriarchate.

TAOIST SEARCH FOR EARTHLY IMMORTALITY. Aside from the above two collective Taoist movements during the last period of the Later Han, there were a few specialists on long-life practices who formed all the small Taoist sects of an individual, esoteric nature. These specialists all aimed at earthly immortality, regardless of the different methods used, such as grain avoidance, breathing techniques, elixirs (cinnabar and gold), and so on. Among them, the most important was Wei Po-yang (fl. 147–167), the author of *Ts'an-t'ung-ch'i* (The Three Ways Unified and Harmonized), which is perhaps the oldest surviving source on alchemy in the world. In cryptic phraseology echoing *Tao-te-ching,* it attempted a synthesis of Taoist philosophy, the doctrine of *yin-yang* and of the Five Agents, alchemy, and hygiene. It recommended, among other things, trance meditation and embryonic respiration and particularly emphasized the efficacy of swallowing the elixir called returned cinnabar, by means of which, he promised, one could become an immortal and possess magical powers. He believed that cinnabar or gold could transform the human body and make it "immune to fire and water." Wei's book is the first systematic treatise on both internal alchemy and external alchemy, and many subsequent Taoist works such as *Huang-t'ing-ching* and *Lung-hu-ching* followed its basic ideas.

The greatest theoretician of Taoist alchemy after Wei was Ko Hung (253–337?), who wrote a book entitled *Pao-p'u-tzu*, a Taoist encyclopedia on the art of long-life practice and immortality. In this book he absorbed all the ideas he knew of through his extensive reading of the Taoist (and the Confucian) texts, with no regard for incoherence or contradiction. He laid a metaphysical foundation adapted from Lao Tzu for his art of immortality. He also provided specific formulas for embryonic respiration, "bedroom technique," and preparation of elixirs like the "cinnabar of ninefold transformation." He denounced magic, shamanism, and prayers and recommended avoidance of garlic, mustard, and so on for one hundred days before an alchemical experiment. He also divided immortals into three classes, depending on which elixir they took. In addition to these specifications, he stressed the importance of good deeds and urged the practice of the Confucian virtues of filial piety, loyalty, humanity, and the like. To him Taoism was the root and Confucianism the branch. His moral consideration seems to have been influenced by the Buddhist belief in karmic retribution. He was thus one of the forerunners in religious Taoism who maintained the grand unity of Taoism, Confucianism, and Buddhism. Because of its systematic and detailed theorization of Taoist alchemy, *Pao-p'u-tzu* became the blueprint for the two most popular tracts, *T'ai-shang Kan-ying P'ien* (Tractate on Actions and Retributions) and *Yin-chih-wên* (The Silent Way of Recompense).

TAOIST CONFRONTATION WITH BUDDHISM. In 444 Taoism was proclaimed the official religion of the Northern Wei through the campaign of K'ou Ch'ien-chih (365–448), who conspired with Ts'ui Hao, the Confucian prime minister, to turn the emperor against the Buddhists. K'ou's purpose was to eliminate Buddhist gods and ceremonies, whereas Ts'ui aimed at the restoration of a Confucian ideal state to Sinicize the uncivilized Northern Wei people. K'ou assumed Chang Ling's old title "Heavenly Master" and won the favor of Emperor Wu. Under their influence the emperor issued decrees destroying all Buddhist temples, *sutras*, *stupas*, and works of art and executed all the monks in the realm. This first persecution of Buddhism in China was not simply a matter of Buddhist-Taoist confrontation but was also an episode in the Sinicization of a non-Chinese race.

One important point in the Taoist-Buddhist debate during the period of Six Dynasties concerns the problem of priority. The Taoists contended, on the basis of the forged account made in Wang Fu's *Hua-hu-ching* (*Sutra* on Lao Tzu's Conversion of the Barbarians), that Lao Tzu had gone to India after his westward departure from China and had converted the Buddha. The Buddhists, of course, denied it as sheer nonsense. The biggest debate on this issue first took place in 568 and was attended by both Taoists and Buddhists, as well as by some Confucian scholars. Through the machinations of the Taoist priests Chang Pin and Wei Yüan-sung, Emperor Wu of the Northern Chou decided to rank Confucianism first, Taoism next, and Buddhism last. Being dissatisfied with this decision, the Buddhists criticized both the Taoists and the emperor. He was infuriated and finally proscribed Buddhism in 574. In this second religious persecution, over 3 million monks and nuns were forced to return to the laity, and forty thousand temples were demolished. Much to the surprise of Wei and Chang, the decrees also proscribed Taoism, for the emperor concluded that Taoism was just as bad as Buddhism, in practicing magic and deceiving the people, for example.

But Taoism regained its prestige in the early period of the T'ang. Emperor Kao Tsung, for example, worshiped at Lao Tzu's temple and gave him the title "Supreme Emperor of the Mystic Origin." Emperor Hsüan Tsung decreed that a Taoist temple be built in every city of China and that every noble family should keep a copy of *Tao-te-ching*. Later he even allowed the use of the Taoist texts instead of the Confucian classics for the civil-service examination. He was perhaps one of the strongest imperial patrons of Taoism in Chinese history. The Taoist influence on the T'ang politics reached its peak when Wu Tsung reigned, for he followed the Taoist proposals and began to issue in 842 a series of anti-Buddhist decrees, which resulted in the third persecution of Buddhism in China. The year 845 marked the end of the apogee and the beginning of the decline of Buddhism. The fourth and last religious persecution occurred in the year 955 of the Later Chou dynasty after the T'ang.

SECTARIAN DIVISION AND DECLINE. Devoid of any centralized organization, Taoism split into nearly ninety sects during its tumultuous history. Special attention deserves to be paid to the three leading sects that emerged in the twelfth century as a result of the Taoist attempt at mobilizing the people against the alien invaders from the north. First, there was the *Ch'üan-chên* (Preservation of Purity) sect, divided into the northern and the southern schools. The former was founded by Wang Chê (1112–1170), who incorporated *Ch'an* meditation and the Confucian moral teaching of meritorious deeds into the Taoist system so as to harmonize the Three Teachings. He preached ascetic withdrawal from worldly affairs and tried to purify Taoist teaching by urging the restoration of man's nature to its original purity as the highest goal. His successor Ch'iu Ch'ang-ch'un (1148–1227) was invited by the Yüan Emperor Genghiz Khan in 1219 to reside in the White Cloud Temple in Peking. The founder of the southern school was Liu Hai-ch'an, who aimed at the cultivation and prolongation of life through both internal alchemy and the external means of charms, incantations, and the like.

The second sect, *Ta-tao* or Great Way, was organized by Liu Tê-jên, who promoted the practice of asceticism. The *T'ai-yi* (Great Unity) sect was formed by another Taoist priest, Hsiao Pao-chên, who recommended the practices of magic and charms in order to realize the Great One (*Tao*) and the Three Origins of Existence (Heaven, Earth, and Man).

Under the Yüan dynasty the Preservation of Purity sect continued to enjoy the imperial patronage and flourished in North China. At the same time, there emerged in South China the *Chêng-yi* (True Unity) sect, which traced its origin back to Chang Ling. Chang Tsung-yen, the founder, claimed to be the thirty-sixth in the apostolic succession from Chang Ling and was the Heavenly Master in the office at Mt. Lunghu (the Dragon and Tiger mountain). After that the title and ecclesiastical jurisdiction of the Changs became hereditary. In 1383, after the first Ming emperor conquered the Mongols, Chang Chêng-ch'ang of this orthodox sect was assigned to head the new Taoist Control Office and supervised all the Taoist activities throughout the Empire. Later in the long reign of Ming Shih Tsung, Shao Yüan-chien, another priest from the Dragon and Tiger mountain, was given high honors and made general head of the Taoist religion. He was probably the last Taoist priest who won high imperial favor. Afterwards Taoist religion began to decline and lose its prestige, and was finally rejected by the intellectuals as mere superstition. The rise and development of Neo-Confucianism was certainly an important contributing factor to the decline of Taoist religion. After centuries of decay, the orthodox church of the Changs has reached the end of the road. The sixty-third Heavenly Master, who fled to Taiwan for refuge, will probably be the last successor. Today in Taiwan most officials and intellectuals are very reluctant to support Taoist religion, and very few people follow it. Its fate in the People's Republic of China is even worse, for the Communists are particularly hostile toward it, accusing it of promoting superstition and suspecting that it houses subversive secret societies. Their suppression in 1950 of the *Yi-kuan-tao* (Way of Pervading Unity) and other secret societies associated with this religion is a typical example. Although there is a National Taoist Association in China, it is too powerless to do anything for the survival of Taoist religion. Although philosophical Taoism still arouses great interest in China as well as in the West, Taoism as a religion of the masses seems to have been fading away.

Bibliography

CHAN, WING-TSIT. *Religious Trends in Modern China.* New York: Columbia U. P., 1953.

——— (ed. and tr.). *A Source Book in Chinese Philosophy.* Princeton: Princeton U. P., 1963. Also Princeton Paperbacks.

——— (tr.). *The Way of Lao Tzu.* Indianapolis: The Library of Liberal Arts, 1963.

——— (tr.). *Reflections on Things at Hand.: The Neo-Confucian Anthology.* New York: Columbia U. P., 1967.

CHANG, CARSUN. *The Development of Neo-Confucian Thought.* New York: Bookman Associates, Vol. I, 1957; Vol. II, 1962.

CHANG, CHUNG-YUAN. *Creativity and Taoism: A Study of Chinese Philosophy, Art, and Poetry.* New York: Julian Press, 1963.

FUNG, YU-LAN. *The Spirit of Chinese Philosophy,* tr., E. R. Hughes. London: Kegan Paul, 1947. Also Beacon Press Paperbacks.

———. *A Short History of Chinese Philosophy,* Ed., Derk Bodde. New York: Macmillan, 1948. Also Free Press Paperbacks.

———. *A History of Chinese Philosophy,* tr., Derk Bodde. Princeton: Princeton U. P., Vol. I, 1952; Vol. II, 1953.

———. *Chuang Tzu.* Shanghai: Commercial Press, 1933. Reprinted, New York: Paragon, 1964.

GILES, H. A. (tr.). *Chuang Tzu, Mystic, Moralist, and Social Reformer.* London: Allen & Unwin, 1961.

GRAHAM, A. C. (tr.). *The Book of Lieh Tzu.* London: John Murray, 1960.

KALTENMARK, MAX. *Lao Tzu and Taoism,* tr., R. Greaves. Stanford: Stanford U. P., 1969.

LAU, D. C. (tr.). *Tao Te Ching.* Baltimore: Penguin, 1963.

LEGGE, JAMES (tr.). *The Texts of Taoism,* 2 vols. New York: Dover, 1962.

LEVENSON, J. R. *Confucian China and Its Modern Fate: A Trilogy.* Berkeley: U. California, 1968.

LIN, YU-TANG. *The Wisdom of Lao Tzu.* New York: Modern Library, 1948.

Moore, C. A. (Ed.). *The Chinese Mind.* Honolulu: East-West Center Press, 1967.

Needham, J. *Science and Civilization in China, Vol II: History of Scientific Thought.* Cambridge: Cambridge U. P., 1956.

Thomson, L. G. *Chinese Religion: An Introduction.* Belmont, Calif.: Dickenson, 1969.

Veith, Ilza (tr.). *The Yellow Emperor's Classic of Internal Medicine.* Berkeley: U. of California, 1966.

Waley, Arthur (tr.). *The Way and Its Power.* London: Allen & Unwin, 1935. Also Evergreen Paperbacks.

Watson, Burton (tr.). *The Complete Works of Chuang Tzu.* New York: Columbia U. P., 1968.

Welch, Holmes. *Taoism: The Parting of the Way.* Boston: Beacon, 1957.

Wilhelm, Hellmut. *Change: Eight Lectures on the I Ching,* tr. from German by C. F. Baynes. New York: Pantheon, 1960. Also Harper Torchbooks.

Wilhelm, Richard. *The Secret of the Golden Flower: A Chinese Book of Life,* tr. from German by C. F. Baynes. New York: Harcourt, 1962.

———. *The I Ching or Book of Changes,* tr. from German by C. F. Baynes. Princeton: Princeton U. P., 1967.

Wright, Arthur (Ed.). *Studies in Chinese Thought.* Chicago: U. of Chicago, 1953. Also Phoenix Paperbacks.

Wu, John (tr.). *Tao Teh Ching.* New York: St. John's U. P., 1961.

Yang, C. K. *Religion in Chinese Society.* Berkeley: U. of California, 1961. Also CAL Paperbacks.

13

Shintō

Joseph M. Kitagawa

Early History

While the word *Shintō* ("The Way of the Gods") was coined in the sixth century C.E., we shall use the term *early Shintō* to refer to the loosely organized religious traditions of the prehistoric and early historic Japanese people. Most scholars agree that the earliest phase of the prehistory of Japan, with its sub-Neolithic culture, can be traced to the fourth millenium B.C.E. Around the third century B.C.E., the cultivation of rice, spinning, and weaving, together with the use of iron, were introduced to Japan. Only in the third or fourth century C.E. did Japan enter the historic period. Throughout the long prehistoric period a number of ethnic groups infiltrated the Japanese islands. This migration of various peoples continued well into the early historic period. Already by the end of the prehistoric period, however, the inhabitants of the Japanese archipelago seemed to have reached some degree of self-awareness as one people having a common language and culture. Contrary to popular belief, the Japanese have not merely adopted the culture and technology of other civilizations. What has characterized the Japanese way of cultural borrowing is their remarkable ability to remember what is indigenous and what is not. Yet even the Japanese, like Europeans and Americans, often tend to overlook the true provenance of cultural imports after centuries of domestication. The earliest collections of myth, the *Kojiki* (712 C.E.) and *Nihongi* or *Nihonshoki* (720 C.E.), are by no means examples of "pure" indigenous belief. Even at this early time, the influence of China and other cultures can be discerned. Not only were both of these documents written with Chinese characters, the *Nihongi* was actually written in Chinese. Chinese ideas also made their way into these documents, for example notions about *yinyang.* Even the mythological material that is not Chinese probably had its origin far from the Japanese islands. According to Oka Masao,[1] there were at least five major ethnic groups that went into the making of the Japanese people. Each of these made its unique contribution to the emerging social and religious life of Japan. The Austro-Asians, coming from somewhere south of the Yangtse River, brought with them the dry-field method of rice cultivation and a matrilinear society. Japanese religion was to inherit its shamanesses from these people, as well as some of its more important female deities, such as Amaterasu (the "sun goddess"), Izanami, and Ukemochi. The Austro-Asians were finally assimilated by a group of immigrants from Melanesia, peoples who lived by cultivating yams and taro and by hunting. The Melanesian social organization was matriarchal. Their mythology and cosmology was of a "horizontal" sort in which the deities came to man not from

[1] *Kulturschichten in Alt-Japan,* an unpublished dissertation.

13-1 Mount Fuji, the sacred mountain. (Courtesy of the Japan National Tourist Organization.)

heaven but from across the sea or from some faraway land. Another immigrant group in prehistoric times were the Micronesians who practiced water-field rice cultivation. Their villages were arranged patrilinearly and according to age groups. There is reason to believe that peoples coming to Japan from the north came to dominate the various peoples originating in Southeast Asia, China, and the South Pacific. These northern peoples were, first, the Tungusic folk, cultivators of rice and millet. Their religious life was characterized by a Siberian type of shamanism. Their mythology and cosmology was of a "vertical" type (in contrast to those of the Melanesians), stressing the descent of gods from the sky and the ecstatic ascent of shamans from earth to heaven. The group that finally gained control over all others were the Altaic peoples, also from northern Asia. Their cosmology and shamanism closely resembled that of the Tungusic folk. Some believe that their chief deity, Takamimusubi, was later transformed into the so-called sun goddess Amaterasu. (Because Amaterasu did such "earthly" things as hide in a cave and cultivate rice fields, some scholars have speculated that she was originally an earth goddess.) During the so-called Tumulus (*Kofun*) Period (250–600 C.E.), these Altaic peoples replaced the exogamous patrilineal clans of the Yayoi Period (250 B.C.E.–250 C.E.) with their own clan (*uji*) system. The basis of clan solidarity was not blood relationship but the worship of a common clan deity (*ujigami*). The leader of the clan (*uji no kami*) was patriarch, priest, and ruler at the same time. The leading clan, worshipers of Amaterasu, became the imperial house of Japan. The story of their conquest of the land, from Kyushu to the central region called Yamato, came to be told mythologically as the campaign of the first legendary emperor, Jimmu. This so-called Yamato kingdom, which was established around the fourth century

13 Japan: Places of Religious Importance

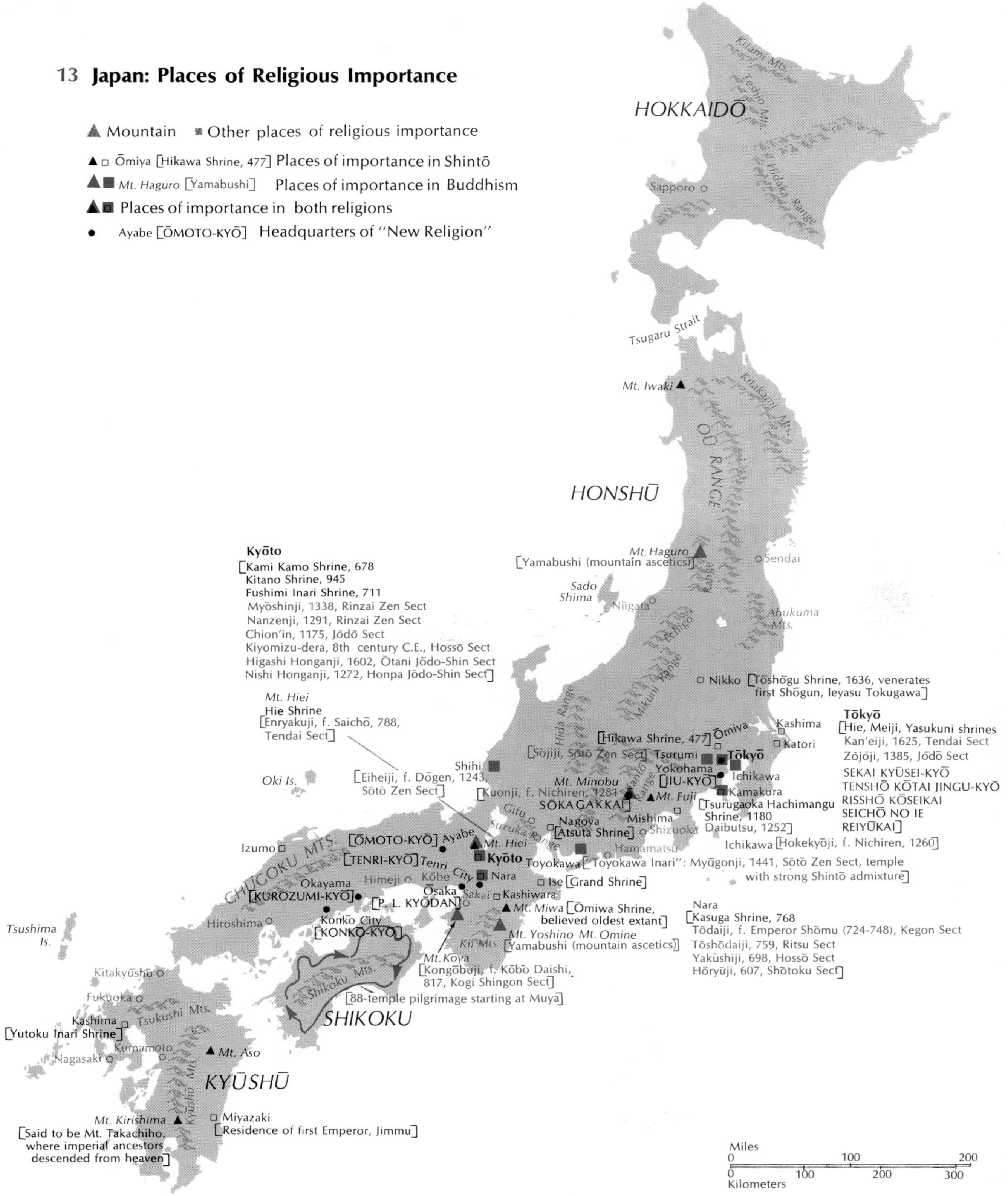

▲ Mountain ■ Other places of religious importance
▲ □ Ōmiya [Hikawa Shrine, 477] Places of importance in Shintō
▲■ Mt. Haguro [Yamabushi] Places of importance in Buddhism
▲■ Places of importance in both religions
● Ayabe [ŌMOTO-KYŌ] Headquarters of "New Religion"
HOKKAIDŌ
Kitami Mts.
Teshio Mts.
Hidaka Range
Sapporo
Tsugaru Strait
Mt. Iwaki
Kitakami Mts.
OU RANGE
HONSHŪ
Mt. Haguro
[Yamabushi (mountain ascetics)]
Sendai
Sado Shima
Niigata
Abukuma Mts.
Echigo Range
Mikuni Range
Hida Range
Kantō Range
Nikko [Tōshōgu Shrine, 1636, venerates first Shōgun, Ieyasu Tokugawa]
Kyōto
[Kami Kamo Shrine, 678
Kitano Shrine, 945
Fushimi Inari Shrine, 711
Myōshinji, 1338, Rinzai Zen Sect
Nanzenji, 1291, Rinzai Zen Sect
Chion'in, 1175, Jōdō Sect
Kiyomizu-dera, 8th century C.E., Hossō Sect
Higashi Honganji, 1602, Ōtani Jōdo-Shin Sect
Nishi Honganji, 1272, Honpa Jōdo-Shin Sect]
Mt. Hiei
Hie Shrine
[Enryakuji, f. Saichō, 788, Tendai Sect]
Tōkyō
[Hie, Meiji, Yasukuni shrines
Kan'eiji, 1625, Tendai Sect
Zōjōji, 1385, Jōdō Sect
SEKAI KYŪSEI-KYŌ
TENSHŌ KŌTAI JINGU-KYŌ
RISSHŌ KŌSEIKAI
SEICHŌ NO IE
REIYŪKAI]
Kashima
Katori
[Hikawa Shrine, 477] Ōmiya
[Sōjiji, Sōtō Zen Sect] Tsurumi
Tōkyō
Yokohama
[JIU-KYŌ]
Ichikawa
Kamakura
[Tsurugaoka Hachimangu Shrine, 1180
Daibutsu, 1252]
Ichikawa [Hokekyōji, f. Nichiren, 1260]
Shihi
Oki Is.
[Eiheiji, f. Dōgen, 1243, Sōtō Zen Sect]
Mt. Minobu
[Kuonji, f. Nichiren, 1281]
SŌKA GAKKAI
Mt. Fuji
Mishima
Gifu
Suzuka Range
Nagoya
[Atsuta Shrine]
Shizuoka
Hamamatsu
Izumo
CHŪGOKU MTS.
[ŌMOTO-KYŌ] Ayabe
Mt. Hiei
[TENRI-KYŌ] Tenri City
Kyōto
Toyokawa ["Toyokawa Inari": Myōgonji, 1441, Sōtō Zen Sect, temple with strong Shintō admixture]
Nara
Himeji
Kōbe
Okayama
[KUROZUMI-KYŌ]
Ōsaka
Sakai
Kashiwara
Ise [Grand Shrine]
[P. L. KYŌDAN]
Mt. Miwa [Ōmiwa Shrine, believed oldest extant]
Nara
[Kasuga Shrine, 768
Tōdaiji, f. Emperor Shōmu (724-748), Kegon Sect
Tōshōdaiji, 759, Ritsu Sect
Yakushiji, 698, Hossō Sect
Hōryūji, 607, Shōtoku Sect]
Hiroshima
Konko City
[KONKŌ-KYŌ]
Mt. Yoshino Mt. Omine
Kii Mts.
[Yamabushi (mountain ascetics)]
Mt. Koya
[Kongōbuji, f. Kōbō Daishi, 817, Kogi Shingon Sect]
Tsushima Is.
Shikoku Mts.
[88-temple pilgrimage starting at Muya]
SHIKOKU
Kitakyūshū
Fukuoka
Tsukushi Mts.
Kashima
[Yutoku Inari Shrine]
Kumamoto
Nagasaki
Mt. Aso
KYŪSHŪ
Kyūshū Mts.
Mt. Kirishima
[Said to be Mt. Takachiho, where imperial ancestors descended from heaven]
Miyazaki
[Residence of first Emperor, Jimmu]
Miles
0 100 200
0 100 200 300
Kilometers

C.E., was, in effect, a confederation of autonomous clans, united by the religious prestige of the imperial clan, which based its claim to authority on its solar ancestry. Although in the course of history, the imperial family often lost its political power, its religious authority was rarely questioned. In this way, early Shintō provided a basic framework for the political structure of Japan, even though its ideal of the "unity of religion and government" (*saisei-ichi*) was not actualized in later history. Although most of the imperial rituals were naturally performed at the court—which was located in various places until it took up a settled residence in Nara (710) and later Heian (Kyoto, 794)—the shrine at Ise has long been associated with the imperial family (Map 13). The lofty status of this shrine, dedicated to Amaterasu, was acknowledged for the first time in 673–674. The status of this and other Shintō shrines came under minute supervision of the government with the compilation of the *Engi Shiki* (Institutes of the Engi Period, compiled in 927). In the eleventh century, the government designated Ise and twenty-one other shrines (including Iwashimizu, Kamo, Matsuo, Hirano, Inari, Kasuga, Gion, and Kitano) as "specially privileged," i.e., due to receive offerings from the court at their regular festivals. Ise has symbolized the faith in the supremacy of the imperial line throughout Japanese history. In the fourteenth century, this shrine became the focal point of the so-called Ise Shintō, a movement to rid Shintō of its Buddhist accretions and reassert the rule of the emperor over the military dictators. This movement had a strong impact on Kitabatake Chikafusa (1293–1354), who was one of the architects of the imperial-rule movement under Emperor Go-Daigo. His book, *Records of the Legitimate Succession of the Divine Sovereigns* (*Jinnō-shōtō-ki*), written in 1339, differed from pure Ise Shintō by recognizing the part played by Buddhism and Confucianism in the national life of Japan.

The "Shintō of the Imperial Household" is, however, only one aspect of the "Way of the Gods." Another is the religion of the common folk. Here we find "indigenous" beliefs and customs inextricably interwoven with Taoist and Buddhist elements. The syncretism of Shintō

13-2 The grand shrine at Isé. Dedicated to the worship of the sun-goddess Amaterasu, its sacred precincts secluded behind one outer and two inner fences, the shrine at Isé and its accompanying buildings conform to the ancient architecture of Japan. It is rebuilt of unpainted wood every twenty years, and we see it here after it has been renewed. (Courtesy of the Japan National Tourist Organization.)

and Buddhism practiced by Shingon Buddhism was known as *Ryōbu Shintō* (Two-Sided), whereas in the Tendai tradition it was styled *Sannō Ichijitsu Shintō* (Mountain-King One-Truth). This relationship persisted through the nineteenth century.

There has never been an absolute distinction made between the traditions of the folk and those of the elite classes. Since the time of Gyōgi Bosatsu—a shamanistic Buddhist made "archbishop" by the court in order to raise funds to complete the great statue of Lochana Buddha (749)—these two aspects of Shintō have lived in symbiosis. The folk aspect of Shintō can be clearly traced back to the prehistoric shamanism and agricultural religion described above. From earliest times, we find female diviners (*miko*) in Japan, some of them being virgins, others having hereditary offices. Some of the early empresses and imperial concubines were likewise shamanesses. There were also traveling diviners (*ichiko*) and charismatics who were permanently possessed by the spirits of foxes, snakes, badgers, and so on (*monomochi*). Where the folk had been influenced by Buddhism, the leadership of popular religious movements often fell into the hands of unordained "clergy" (*ubasoku*). These and other holy men (*hijiri*) often degenerated, as time went on, into outcast entertainers. The entertainment they provided was a secularized version of folk and shamanistic dance and music. Through this process of secularization, myth and religion deeply penetrated the performing arts of Japan.

Religion in Modern Times

In modern times, Shintō became the backbone of the ideology of the Japanese state. In 1868, the first year of Emperor Meiji's rule, a Department of Shintō was set up. At the same time, the government began to take steps to separate Shintō from Buddhism. This led to the persecution and destruction of Buddhism in many provinces (the *haibutsu kishaku* movement of 1868–1871). In 1869, the Department of Shintō was elevated to a position above the Grand Council of State, and an Office of Information was established within the Department of Shintō. The government now appointed professional storytellers, actors, and fortune-tellers as missionaries for the national religion. The Buddhist system was transformed into a Shintō parish system. In 1871, Shintō shrines and priests were brought under the direct control of the government. Buddhist temple lands were confiscated and statues of the Buddha were removed from the Imperial Palace.

By 1872 a turning point had been reached. The missionary system had proved to be a failure. With the establishment of the Shintō Ministry in 1871 and then the Department of Religion and Education in 1872, the idea of a syncretistic state cult began to dominate the thinking of the Meiji oligarchs. In 1872 a system of national priests (*kyōdō shoku*) was established. In 1873 the government established the *Daikyōin* (Great Institute of Instruction) and related institutions for the training of the new national priests. The *Daikyōin*, however, was dominated by Shintōists from the beginning and failed, probably for this reason. After the *Daikyōin* was dissolved in 1875, the Department of Religion and Education had little to do and was itself discontinued in 1877.

Gradually the artificial synthesis of Shintō and Buddhism represented by *Daikyōin* faded from sight. In 1884 the national priesthood was discontinued. From this time on, the government was content to rely solely on State Shintō (*Kokka Shintō*) for its support. In 1899 the Department of Education, in its well-known Order Number 12, forbade the teaching of religion in Japanese schools, at the same time insisting that State Shintō was not a real religion. The result was a mute state cult whose significance was made known only by Imperial Rescripts and by the orders of the Department of Education. With its priests forbidden to preach, the schools now became the catechetical institutions of the state religion. This made it possible for the government to give the appearance of allowing complete freedom of religion while, in fact, supporting a state religion in both its schools and its shrines. Now the government could support a Shintō cult without seeming to detract from Buddhism, Confucianism, and Christianity. By 1900, the creation of the Office of Shrines and the Office of Religions guaranteed the complete separation of the state cult from other religions. These offices continued to control the religious life of the nation until 1945. During the 1930's the government began to exert even tighter control, but by then the basic framework for the newly concocted religion of ethnocentric nationalism had been laid down. In 1939 the Religious Bodies Law gave the Department of Education complete authority over all sects both in matters of doctrine and in organization. After Japan's surrender in 1945, State Shintō was abolished and in the following year religious groups were given the right to become "legal persons," encouraging the rapid growth of many "New Religions." Even in its disestablished condition, Shintō, together with Sect Shintō, continued to be a viable force in the religious life of Japan (Maps 14 to 17).[2]

[2] For bibliography, see works listed at end of Chapter 18, "Mahāyāna Buddhism (Japan)", p. 199.

Shintō, Buddhism, and Christianity in Contemporary Japan

14
Shintō Adherents in Japan
(c. 1968)

■ 1 million adherents

15
Shintō Adherents in the Japanese Population

Location index 1.00 represents approximately 67 percent of the population

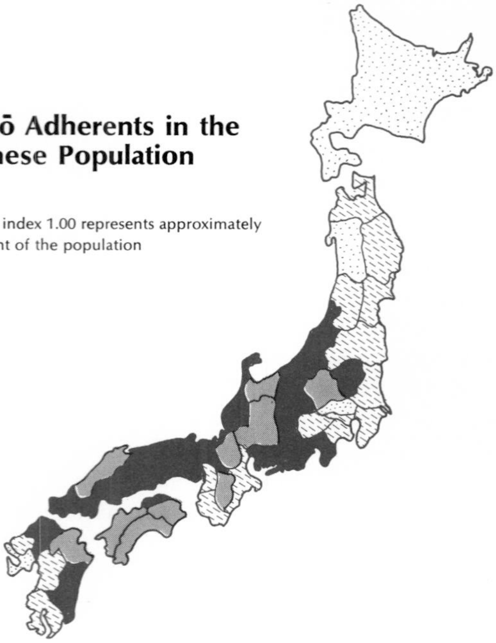

16
Buddhists in the Japanese Population

Location index 1.00 represents approximately 68 percent of the population

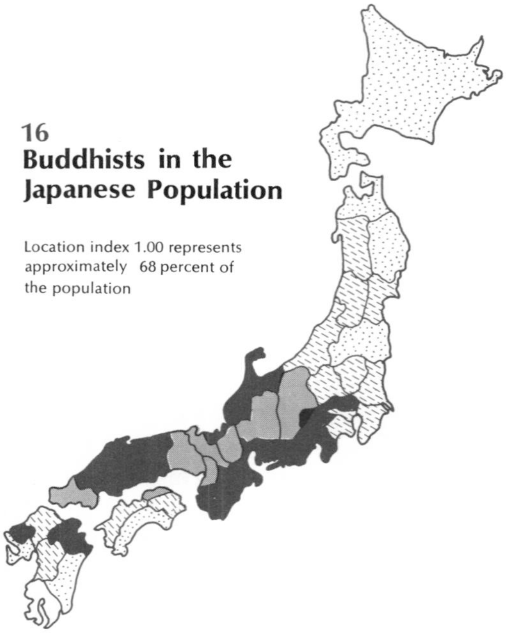

17
Christians in the Japanese Population

Location index 1.00 represents approximately 0.7 percent of the population

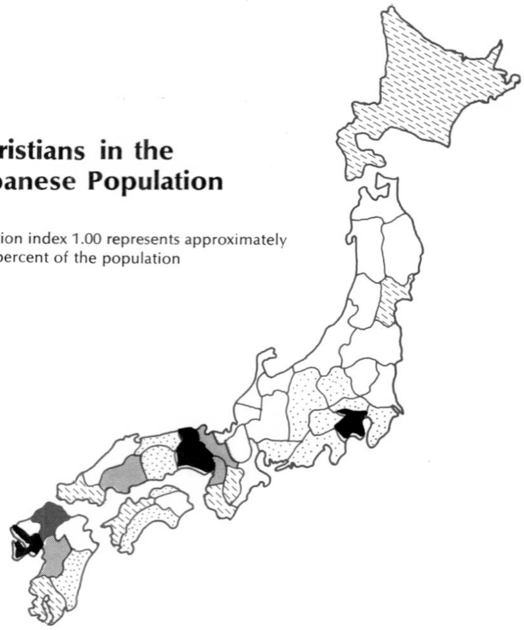

LOCATION INDEX

- Less than .5
- .5 to .749
- .75 to .99
- 1.00 to 1.249
- 1.25 to 1.49
- 1.5 and over

The location index is the ratio of the value of areas (prefectures) to the mean value of the whole area (i.e., Japan).
Use of the index permits ready comparison of the range and pattern of variation on the three maps.
The location indexes were derived from 1960 population data and 1968 data on religious adherence.

Note: The total of adherents in Japan and in many prefectures is more than 100 percent because individual adherence to both Shintoism and Buddhism is common.

14

Zoroastrianism

Isma'īl R. al Fārūqī

Genesis and Flowering

Historical Setting

Zoroastrianism is the name of the religion founded by Zoroaster or Zarathustra (Zaradusht) (628–551 B.C.E.). He claimed to be a prophet to whom God had spoken in person. Born in Chorasmia (modern Khwarizm, in northeastern Iran), an area constantly subject to the ravaging raids of nomads, Zoroaster became sensitive to the need of protecting the peaceful farmers against the recurring predatory invaders. Both nomads and farmers were remnants of an older Aryan migration that had brought men as well as novel religious ideas to Greece and that finally reached and settled down in India. Farmers and nomads, however, represented different strata in time and mixture with the natives. The farmers were a mixture of earlier generations of Aryans and natives who had abandoned some of the older ways for those of settled life. The nomads, on the other hand, were later generations of a pastoral people who continued the ancestral life of raiding, sacrificing bulls, drinking the fermented *Haoma* (Sanskrit *Soma*) juice and worshiped a multitude of deities called *daevas.* Their life and religion were one with those who produced the *Vedas* of Hinduism (see Chapter 9), members of the same stratum of Aryan migration. The religion of Zoroaster was, essentially, a critique of nomadic religion and a crystallizing reform of the farmer's religion. The nomads' buccaneerish life of raiding and robbing, of killing useful cattle, and of drunkenness was evidently evil, a lie or *Druj;* their gods, who commanded and blessed such actions, demonic; their priests, deluders of the people; and their rulers, wicked (*Yasna,* 48:8–12). The contrast of the two opposites and the thought of their persistence dominated Zoroaster's mind and gave form to his new religion. The problem of life and destiny was for him a question of wickedness or righteousness, falsehood or truth, chaos or cosmos, darkness or light. Despite the polarity of their views, the two peoples belonged to the same stock. The superiority felt by the nomad toward the farmer was equally felt by the Aryan (Iranian = "noble") farmer toward the native. Both farmer and nomad belonged to a society organized along tribal lines.

The "settled" Iranians divided into ten tribes, according to Herodotus, six of whom lived in cities and villages and four in deserts. Each was ruled by an elected elder who also functioned as a judge. Three of these tribes kept themselves aloof from the natives and monopolized political and military power. In time, they combined to form a monarchy. Cyrus was of the Pasargad tribe, who defeated the Medes (the less aristocratic and mixed tribes) with the help of the other two aristocratic ones. Even within the tribe, society divided into three classes: the men of religion, the warriors, and the peasants and workers. Each class had its own uniform and dwelling quarter in the cities. Members of equal rank greeted one another by kissing and worshiped in their own temple, which had a name connoting the rank and profession of the adherents. The religious class's temple was called *Khorbad* or "the source of inspiration, intelligence, and wisdom"; that of the warriors *Goshnasp*, or "source of energy and courage"; that of the farmers and workers *Borzin-Mihr*, or "source of perfection of work and love for agriculture." Zoroaster himself had three sons, who, on the success of their father, became chiefs of the three classes. Following the Greek invasion and the establishment of the Sāsānī dynasty, a fourth class of government clerks and officials, called *dabīrān*, appeared, whose status was like that of the farmers. In time, the *dabīrān* class dislodged the farmers from their third place in the hierarchy. The farmers became the fourth or lowest class and were treated like slaves. The people were commanded to observe the classes and were counseled that they would remain in peace as long as the class remained intact. The king was the head of all classes and was venerated as a god. There was no legal process by which a person could transfer from one class to another. Only in an extremely rare case could the king change a person's class, but even that could come only after passing near-impossible examinations and tests by priests.

Theology

At the center of Zoroaster's religion stands God, called Ahura Mazda, or simply Ahura, who is a God of goodness. He chose the good, or holy spirit, and made it the determinant of all his deeds. Ahriman, on the other hand, chose the evil spirit and thereby became the god of evil. Before Zoroaster's reform, Ahura Mazda and Ahriman were both Aryan deities (*daevas*) to whom the choice of good and evil as the twin spirits presented itself. By this choice Ahura Mazda separated himself from the rest. According to one source the twin spirits were generated by Ahura; according to another they were the sons of Zurwan-i-Akinarak, or Eternal Time (Chronos?); according to the third, only the good spirit was the son of Ahura and later identified with him. Thus, at source Persian dualism was vague and undecided and became more defined and rigidly established as time passed. Though dualistic, Zoroaster's reform brought about a monotheism of the God of goodness, demoting the *daevas* from the status of the divine to that of demons who do Ahriman's bidding. It was, however, their own choice of the evil spirit that brought about their and Ahriman's downfall. Heaven thus was cleft into two opposing forces struggling against each other for dominion and supremacy.

Ahura Mazda, having chosen the good or holy spirit, generated the Good Mind, Righteousness or Truth, Right-mindedness, Kingdom, Wholeness, and Immortality. These were regarded as attributes of Ahura Mazda, as well as apotheosized autonomous spirits, and later became archangels utterly separate from Ahura and created by him. As qualities of the divine, they were not exclusive. Men who have made the right choice would enjoy these attributes. Unlike the Mesopotamian, the ancient Persian did not regard the sacred as a totally other reality but as a genus of which one species is God

14-1 Carved stone relief and inscriptions from Behistun, along ancient caravan route, end of the 6th century C.E., reign of Darius the Great. Surmounting the scene is this stylized symbol of Ahura-Mazda, with its radiating rays of the sun. (From M. A. Beek, *Bildatlas der assyrisch-babylonischen Kultur.*)

in heaven; another is worldly such as Zoroaster himself; and a third is neither celestial nor terrestrial, such as the angels. In his providence, Ahura is assisted by six holy immortal beings, each of whom protects one of the following realms: Good Thought, Fire, Metals, Country, Health, and Agriculture. After these come thirty gods, each of whom looks after one day of the month. Ahura is then the chief of a celestial host, as Zoroaster is chief of a worldly host.

Anthropology and Ethics

The separation of Ahura from Ahriman as a result of their choices of the good spirit and the evil spirit, respectively, pitted them against each other in struggle for dominion, but not until after Ahura enjoyed three thousand years of unchallenged rule in full glory and light. Then, out of darkness, emerged Ahriman and gave battle to Ahura. Ahura could not vanquish the new power. Hence, he created the world and man as a means to bring about Ahriman's defeat. The *Gathas* use the simile of the farmer devising a trap into which the predator animal would fall and exhaust himself struggling to get out. So the world was created as an attractive snare for Ahriman. The Gods and angels assist in "setting up" and "keeping up" the snare, and so does the righteous man. For his *raison d'être* is to lend his hand in this cosmic battle by cultivating the earth and, indeed, making it the most attractive garden, to the end that the devil may be ensnared thereby, enter, and be trapped into it.

Man is created by God of soul and body. The soul is divine and immortal. At death, every soul is given a three-day taste of what is to come, whether suffering in the Fire or bliss in Paradise. The wind then carries it to the Path, where it is questioned and judged by three judges, the angels Mithra, Thraosh, and Rashnu. The soul is then commanded to walk on the Path, which becomes vast, smooth, and leading to Paradise if its life was one of good thought, good word, and good action, and narrow and impassable otherwise with the result that the soul will fall into hell below. If the soul's debits and credits balance, it will be placed in an in-between place called *Hamishtagan.* Finally, twelve thousand years after creation, the Saoshyant, a divine-human savior born of Zoroaster's seed, will come to bring about the *Frashkart,* or the final vindication of Ahura. On this day, the Saoshyant will resurrect all bodies and unite them to their souls. He will then plunge the whole of mankind into molten metal and thus purify them of all their sins and misdeeds. After purgation, all men will enter Paradise for ever and ever, where all will praise the Wise Lord and the Immortal host with one voice.

The souls of men, being immortal beings, were consulted by Ahura before creation of their bodies, to which they were assigned. They chose their destiny in order to help in the cosmic struggle. They are hence free and responsible beings. Some things of the world are by fate, such as life, wife and children, and wealth; others by action, such as virtue and vice; a third variety by nature, such as sexual prowess, eating, and sleeping; a fourth by character, such as friendship, respect, generosity, and righteousness; and finally a fifth by heredity, such as body, understanding, and intelligence.

In order to fulfil his destiny, man ought to populate the earth and cultivate it by settled farming. The *Avesta* reports Ahura Mazda as commanding his prophet: "I tell you, Zoroaster, that a married man is better than a bachelor; that a man with a family and children is better than without." Zoroastrianism went far indeed toward guaranteeing progeny to everyone. It permitted and blessed unrestricted polygamy, concubinage, and incest. Ahura held many rewards for those men who marry their daughters, sisters, and mothers. If a married man died without children, his wife was given in marriage to a relative and half of the issue of the new marriage—called *abdāl* in the Arabic sources—were attributed to the deceased husband. Then and only then would his wife follow him into heaven. Without male offspring, no man will enter heaven. In order to procure salvation for a deceased childless relative whose widow for any reason does not remarry and reproduce, the religion prescribed remarriage for the deceased by proxy. The new husband marries his new bride in the name of the departed and attributes half of his offspring to him.

Two classes of wives were recognized: the "privileged," who inherited along with their children, and the "servant" wives, who did not, nor did their children. Both classes of wives could be legitimately remarried to another husband with the same legal consequences. A woman's religion was of no significance in marriage, but her class was. For if she married above her class, she became a "servant" wife. She was a "privileged" wife only within her class. Still more complexity was added to the social system by the institution of divorce. A woman was divorced by repudiation, with or without authority to remarry, as divorce did not terminate her husband's mastery over her. In case she remarried, her offspring remained his. Depending on the status of his wife and the widow or divorcee, he added to his harem, and finally, depending on the status of the mother as slave or concubine, a man could have eight classes of children in his household.

Decay and Reform

Zoroaster sought the protection of Vishtaspa, or Goshtasp, king of his native Khwarizm, for his religion, which was not granted. Accused of heresy and disloyalty, Zoroaster had to flee. After a while, his religion gained ground and he returned to convert the ruler and to help him establish the new religion. Cyrus, a prince of the Pasargad tribe, defeated the Medes and built the first monarchy over the whole of Iran with the help of the other two tribes, which, like the Pasargad, preserved their racial purity. Unification under Cyrus spread Zoroastrianism across the length and width of Persia. But it was not until Ardashir I (226–241 C.E.) that the *Avesta,* the scripture, was collected and Zoroastrianism as it was then understood became Persia's official religion. At all other times, including the period of Sāsānī rule after Ardashir, several religions and varieties of the Zoroastrian tradition coexisted.

Manichaeanism

Manichaeanism is the name of the religious movement launched by Mani, who claimed for himself the status of prophet on a par with Zoroaster. Born in 205 C.E. at Ecbatana, modern Hamadan, to a Parthian royal family that ruled the province in the interval between the Greeks and the rise of the Sāsānī Empire, he began to teach his religion under Sabur (241–272) and succeeded in converting the king. Sabur declared Manichaeanism the official state religion in 242. A few years later, while the new religion was gaining popularity, Sabur reconverted to Zoroastrianism. Mani ran away into an exile that lasted for twenty years and during which he traveled to and preached in distant lands. In Khorasan and Tibet he was met with welcome, but the greater honor was accorded to him in India. After Sabur's death in 273, Mani returned home under Hormuz's short-lived reign of one year. Bahram I succeeded Hormuz to the throne and, like Sabur, was first attracted sufficiently by Mani's reform to convert and then repulsed by it to relapse back to Zoroastrianism. This time, however, Mani was not to escape. He was executed by the king and his body hung on the portal of Gundaysabur as a warning to all subversives. His religion spread far and wide, into China on the east and into the Roman Empire in the West, where it claimed a decade of Augustine's adult life.

After his death, Mani's followers gathered his thoughts in a book called *Ki falaya* containing epistles to his disciples. His religion was a syncretic combination of Zoroastrianism, Christianity, and Buddhism. He interpreted the *Avesta* of Zoroaster in a commentary (Zand; hence the term *Zandiq* or interpreter of the *Avesta,* which Mani and all Zoroastrians regarded as inviolate).

From Buddhism Mani took asceticism and made it a pillar of his religion, and from Christianity he took celibacy for the religious order and the idea of a "savior," attributing it to himself as the "Paraclete." The universe, in his view, was created of a mixture of Light and Darkness. When Light gave battle to Darkness, a parcel of itself went out and mingled with Darkness, which prevented its return to the source. Another parcel went in the opposite direction and suffered the same fate. Out of one (Arabic, *humamah*) was created man; out of the other, the world. In creation, therefore, is built the tension between the higher (Light) and the lower (Darkness), each struggling for release and return to its primordial source. Both are eternal, and so are air and earth. Only the devil, created out of pure Darkness, is not eternal. There are eight heavens and eight earths, all destined for a clash at end of time, when Light will triumph.

In the meantime, man's duty is to purge himself of Darkness by resisting desire, stinginess, wine and meat, sex, magic, and hypocrisy, and he should not join the faith until he can do so effectively. Knowing human weakness and possible relapse after conversion, Manichaeanism divided its followers into the Perfect or Righteous Ones, the pious and virtuous, and the Listeners or those incapable of strict observance. The latter, however, must realize their incapacity, prepare the food for the Perfect or Righteous Ones, and present it kneeling. They should "seal" their mouths, hearts, and hands against evil words, intentions, and deeds. The Perfect or Righteous Ones should have no more than one day's food and one year's clothing. Their concern should be ever to preach and above all to practice asceticism, especially by abstaining from eating meat.

Mazdakism

Towards the end of the fifth century C.E., another religious reform movement was launched by Mazdak. It came in 497, a time of national defeat and humiliation, as Persia was battling the Huns to the north, the Romans to the west, and dissident factions within. Exploitation by the master class of the lower classes and social corruption had by then assumed extraordinary proportions, and the time was ripe for radical revolution. Mazdak asked King Kobad (488–531) the question, "How do you judge a man who has the antidote but does not help his scorpion-bitten neighbor?" The king answered, "He shall be put to death." Immediately, Mazdak left the royal court for the streets, announcing to the masses, "The King has permitted you to get food from the rich and kill them too." Ready for revolt, the masses took this as signal for a popular uprising against royalty, the priesthood, and all the aristocrats. The ladies in the palaces were raped and the masters' honor torn down, and Zoroastrianism, the official state religion, lost all respect among the people. Realizing the desperateness of the situation, Kobad sided with the people against his own class, the nobles, and the clergy. But he was nonetheless dethroned and Jamasp crowned in his place. He returned four years later (502) to cooperate with the classes he had permitted Mazdak to attack and to rebuild the exhausted, vanquished country with the help of both nobles and clergy. Under his successor, Anū Shirwān (531–579), Mazdak was executed and the ancient religious institutions reestablished.

Certainly, Mazdakism expressed the Persians' yearning for freedom, egalitarianism, and classlessness—in short, for a new social order in the name of religion. But Mazdakism was unable to achieve this goal. The return to the old religious institutions was a return to the old ways, and the country awaited reforming winds from an unexpected source: Islamic Arabia.

Effect of Zoroastrianism on Other Religions

Zoroastrianism rubbed shoulders on its own soil first with Judaism and then with Christianity. It taught the latter through the former. It is safe to say that the whole of Jewish eschatology, angelogy, Day of Judgment and Paradise and Hell, resurrection of the flesh, and Messianism, both exilic and postexilic, came from Persia. In turn, these ideas, having become Jewish, exercised enormous influence on Christianity.

Persia also supplied Christianity with a number of categories used in the mass. The *Haoma* plant was called the "Son of God." It was pulverized and a fermented juice produced from it that, through the performance of ritual, underwent transubstantiation and was called the "blood of the Son of God." The act was referred to as "the sacrifice of the Son" to the Father. The participant drank the juice and thereby partook of the deity.

Later, the ascetic life of the men of religion stood to gain from the ascetic practices of Mani, predominantly abstinence from meat, alcohol, and sex, which Mani learned from the Buddhists during his twenty-year exile.

Today, Zoroastrianism and its offshoots, Manichaeanism and Mazdakism, have completely disappeared from Persia. Manichaeanism achieved some popularity in the Roman Empire, but it remained an underground religion and was fought by both Western and Eastern churches. At the time of the Islamic conquest of Persia (635–651), a few Zoroastrians managed to flee to China and to India. The former were absorbed in the following century. The latter have survived to the present day, and they live mostly in the area around Bombay (Map 10). They number about 150,000 and are, in the majority, urbanized industrialists, tradesmen, and government officers.

Bibliography

Avesta, in *The Sacred Books of the East,* Vols. IV, XXXI, XXXIII. Mystic, Conn.: Lawrence Verry, Inc. 1965–1966 (Reprinted Edition).

Duchesne-Guillemin, Jacques. *The Hymns of Zarathustra.* Boston: Beacon, 1963; *La religion de l'Iran ancien.* Paris: Presses Universitaires, 1962.

Girshman, R. *Iran.* Baltimore: Penguin, 1961.

Huart, Clement. *Ancient Persia and Iranian Civilization.* New York: Knopf, 1927.

Jackson, Abraham Valentine W. *Zoroaster, The Prophet of Ancient Iran.* New York: Columbia U. P., 1919.

——— and L. H. Gray. *Foundations of the Iranian Religions.* Bombay: 1925.

———. *Zoroastrian Studies.* New York: AMS Press, 1928.

Moulton, J. H. *Early Zoroastrianism.* London: Williams and Norgate, 1913.

Olmstead, A. T. *History of the Persian Empire.* Chicago: U. of Chicago, 1963.

Shahristani, 'Abdul Karim (d. 1153 c.e.). *Al Milal wa al Nihal.* Cairo: Al Azhar Press, 1947.

Zaehner, R. C. *Zurvan, A Zoroastrian Dilemma.* Oxford: Oxford U. P., 1955.

———. *The Teachings of the Magi.* London: Allen & Unwin, 1956.

15

Judaism

Jacob A. Agus

Genesis

Judaism emerged on the stage of history slowly and gradually, like a tree; its roots were nourished by the cultures and faiths of prehistoric peoples and by the great civilizations of the ancient Near Eastern world. Yet from its inception it was marked by a deep sense of uniqueness. From the Babylonian world, where Abraham was born, the Hebrews derived a body of traditions centering around the concept of law. The human order must be regulated by just laws, even as the cosmic order is governed by fixed laws. In the Biblical faith, this law derives from God, Who transcends the world, overcomes the stars, or blind fate, and mingles compassion with justice. From Egypt, where the Hebrews first prospered and were later enslaved, they came forth with a fierce dedication to freedom, a passion reflected in the first of the Ten Commandments. From their revulsion at the "abomination" of Egypt, they derived an aversion to the priestly caste system that is echoed in the Mosaic declaration, "Ye shall be unto Me, a kingdom of priests and a holy nation" (Exodus 19:6). Psalmists and prophets were concerned with the inner life of man, but the Hebrew Bible shows hardly a trace of the Egyptian preoccupation with the post-mortem career of the soul, though eternal life in the company of God is frequently assumed to be the lot of the righteous.[1] And although the Canaanites were bitterly scorned and degraded by the conquering Hebrews, the Canaanite-Phoenician emphasis on the gods of life and fertility left its impress on the religion of the Bible. The rites of fertility were an abomination, but the Lord loves this earthly life of men and women, and He desires to be served in joy and with a good heart (Deuteronomy 28:47).

The roots of Hebrew religious culture in the civilization of the ancient world are acknowledged indirectly in Scripture, and modern archaeology furnishes thousands of illustrations of this development. In Scripture and in ancient Jewish tradition, monotheism was the first faith of mankind, as it emerged fresh from the hand of the Creator; the various pagan cults were due to degradation of the pristine faith. Abraham began to reverse the process by identifying God as the One Judge of all men. Isaac and Jacob continued this course of development. With Moses, God was revealed at once as the Governor of history, the Source of freedom and of compassion.

In rabbinic Judaism, the Name, *Elohim,* stands for His Policy of Law, *middath ha-din,* and the Name that must not be pronounced, *YHVH,* stands for the Policy of Compassion. Philo describes the two phases of the Divine Being as Sovereignty and Creativity ("De Migra-

[1]M. Dahood, Psalms 101–150, *Anchor Bible,* pp. XLVI–LII.

15-1 The earliest known Jewish synagogue, 245 C.E., at the ancient city of Dura Europos in the Syrian desert.

tione Abrahami," 32). In later Judaism, the formula "The God of Abraham, the God of Isaac, and the God of Jacob" is interpreted as the God Who is revealed in steadfast love (*hesed*), in awe and fear (*pahad*), and in the quest for truth (*emeth*).

In Scripture, attention is focused on the radical difference between the religion of the Hebrews and the diverse cults of the pagans. Indeed, the gulf between mature Biblical monotheism and paganism is vast and unbridgeable. When many gods are worshiped, the real object of worship is man himself, with the diverse gods holding out conditional promises for the satisfaction of his many needs—rain and healing, wisdom, courage, or victory. In monotheism, God becomes the center of man's universe. In Him all ideals have their source and culmination. Man is worthy only if "he walks before the Lord, seeking to be perfect" (Genesis 17:1). The various gods of paganism reflect the varied forces of life—hence, their sexuality, their specialization, their bursts of passion, their susceptibility to rites of magic, and their ultimate subjection to the furies of fate in a "cosmic twilight of the gods." In the Biblical faith, God is seen in the perspective of the human spirit: "He brings into being" (etymology of *Yahweh*) and "He is a Living Presence, when a man calls upon him in distress" (interpretation of "I am that I am" in Jewish tradition). On the one hand, He is the Creator, source of all power; on the other, He is the Compassionate Source of all love and all ideals. Our humanity derives from Him the diverse human quests—for truth, for goodness, for inner purity, for perfection of personality in holiness, and for the perfection of human society in the messianic future.

Monotheism cannot but transform the entire life of a people, even if this process should require centuries for its progressive unfolding. So in the millenium covered by the Hebrew Scriptures, we note occasional backsliding, the residual holdout of pagan attitudes, the slow permeation of a people's psyche by the implication of being covenanted unto the One God. The creative atmosphere is guarded from sterile complacency by tensions between the priest and the prophet, between the psalmist and the sage, and between the exponents of religion and those of military power. The literary

15-2 Hebrew amulet for protecting a woman in childbirth, written with various colored inks (black, red, green, yellow, blue) on fine vellum. The focus is on the divine name YHVH (tetragrammaton or four-lettered name), supported by other divine names, titles, attributes, as well as biblical and associated religious symbols, words, phrases, and passages. Found in a *geniza* (storeroom) of an old synagogue in Cairo. (Courtesy of the University Museum, University of Pennsylvania, Philadelphia.)

prophets constitute a unique and magnificent phenomenon, providing an inspiring example for future ages.

Amos bursts upon the horizon like a fresh breeze ending a hot and humid spell. He challenges the people to concern themselves with justice rather than with rituals, and he reminds the people that to be a "chosen people" is to be committed to the highest demands of God, Who will not forgive horrendous moral transgressions on the part of His people.

Hosea stresses the notion of divine love and His forgiveness. To be covenanted unto Him is to make a total commitment, in "righteousness and judgment, in steadfast love and compassion" (Hosea 2:18–22). Isaiah explicates the notion of holiness as a cosmic goal and as the special destiny of Israel. He projects the belief in the ultimate establishment of the Kingdom of God (Isaiah 2:1–4). Micah adds that each nation may reach the ultimate goal in its own way, through the reorientation of its own tradition (Micah 4:1–5). Jeremiah adds the personal pathos of his own experience as a prophetic teacher in a time of great historical changes, enabling his people to meet disaster with unbowed heads. Ezekiel, the prophet of the exile, stresses the responsibility of the individual as well as the rebirth of the religious community. In the Babylonian exile, the great unknown Deutero-Isaiah phrased in imperishable verse Israel's vision of the messianic future and its conception of its own destiny—to be "a light to the nations," even if they might have to endure the tragic fate of a "Suffering Servant" (Isaiah 49:1–6; 52:13–15; 53:1–2).

The "Torah of Moses," in behalf of which the last canonical prophet preaches, gave shape and form to the monotheistic faith. The holidays were now reinterpreted to stand for events in history rather than for the rhythms of nature. Passover, the spring festival, was now the remembrance of the Exodus; Shabu-oth, the festival of first fruits, became the remembrance of the Covenant at Sinai; Sukkoth, the harvest festival, came to mark the wandering of the Israelites in the wilderness. And the Sabbath was observed both as an occasion for dramatizing the ideal of *imitatio dei,* resting as did God after creation, and as a reminder of liberation from bondage in Egypt. The Sabbath was observed as a "delight," symbolizing man's glory in belonging to the company of God.

Historical Crystallization

The Second Commonwealth

The Holy Temple, built by King Solomon (d. 928 B.C.E.) and rededicated by King Josiah (d. 609 B.C.E.), was destroyed in the year 586 B.C.E. By that time, the northern kingdom of Israel, comprising the so-called Ten Tribes, had already been dispersed and resettled in the northern provinces of Assyria for four generations. When Cyrus, founder of the Persian Empire, had issued his famous edict permitting the Judean exiles to return to Jerusalem and rebuild the Temple (538 B.C.E.), there was already a widespread Jewish Diaspora. In the Book of Esther, the archetypal anti-Semite, Haman, speaks of

15-3 Page from a medieval parchment Hebrew codex containing Exodus 21:35–22:20, in three columns of writing. Notice the tear at the lower part of the page, which has been sewn. The use of spacing and indentation corresponds roughly to the traditional masoretic division of the biblical text into open and closed paragraphs. Found in a *geniza* (storeroom) of an old synagogue in Cairo. (Courtesy of the University Museum, University of Pennsylvania, Philadelphia.)

Jewish people "scattered and dispersed" in all the provinces of the vast Persian Empire, extending from India to Ethiopia.

This great Jewish Diaspora was made possible primarily by the refusal of Jewish refugees and immigrants to give up their unique faith and adopt the ways of their pagan neighbors. Although all peoples in that area were uprooted by the ebb and flow of conquering armies, the Jews were alone in resisting the natural solvents of syncretism and assimilation. They could not join their neighbors in a good-natured exchange or combination of various deities and forms of worship. For theirs was a "jealous God," different from all other gods; to worship Him was to stand alone, condemning other cults. As Jeremiah wrote in his letter to the exiles in Babylonia, "The gods that have not created heaven and earth will disappear from under the heavens" (Jeremiah 10:11). "Ours is the one true God," the prophets proclaimed; in effect, "all other gods are vanity."

This *Kerygma* of the Jewish teachers appealed powerfully to many Gentiles, launching a vast tide of conversion to the Jewish faith (Isaiah 56:6; Esther 9:27; Malachi 1:11). At the same time, Jewish propaganda was inevitably offensive to the unconvinced pagans. The Jews appeared to be intolerant and unfraternal, refusing to join their neighbors at the communal feasts, circuses, and carnivals, for in ancient times all activities were associated with religious rites.

The vast Jewish Diaspora was so constituted that it could function under local guidance and with maximum adaptation to local circumstances. This network of communities was held together by a deep loyalty to the living heart of world Jewry—the Holy Land and its capital, Jerusalem, with its Holy Temple and its schools of thought clustered around the Sanhedrin, the High Priests, and other officials. This loyalty was wider and more varied than that of a religious community. It included the sharing of Biblical memories and the pathos of the messianic hope, as well as the pride of being of "the seed of Abraham" and the fellow-feeling of partici-

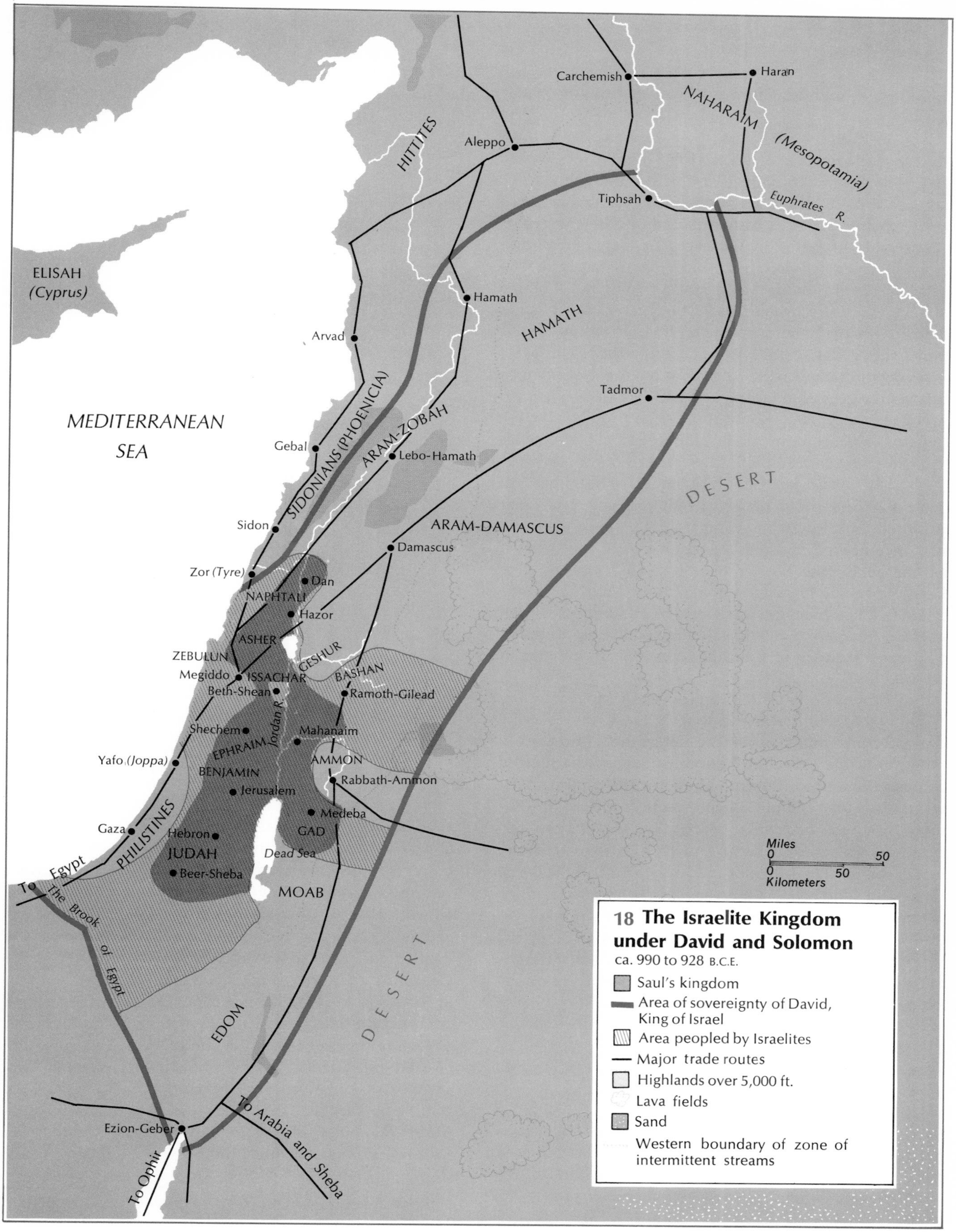
Carchemish
Haran
NAHARAIM
(Mesopotamia)
HITTITES
Aleppo
Tiphsah
Euphrates R.
ELISAH
(Cyprus)
Hamath
HAMATH
Arvad
Tadmor
MEDITERRANEAN
SEA
SIDONIANS (PHOENICIA)
ARAM-ZOBAH
Gebal
Lebo-Hamath
DESERT
Sidon
ARAM-DAMASCUS
Damascus
Zor (Tyre)
Dan
NAPHTALI
Hazor
ASHER
GESHUR
ZEBULUN
Megiddo
ISSACHAR
BASHAN
Beth-Shean
Ramoth-Gilead
Jordan R.
Shechem
Mahanaim
EPHRAIM
AMMON
Yafo (Joppa)
BENJAMIN
Rabbath-Ammon
Jerusalem
Medeba
PHILISTINES
Gaza
Hebron
GAD
JUDAH
Dead Sea
To Egypt
Beer-Sheba
MOAB
The Brook of Egypt
EDOM
DESERT
Ezion-Geber
To Arabia and Sheba
To Ophir
Miles
0 50
0 50
Kilometers
Saul's kingdom
Area of sovereignty of David, King of Israel
Area peopled by Israelites
Major trade routes
Highlands over 5,000 ft.
Lava fields
Sand
Western boundary of zone of intermittent streams

18 The Israelite Kingdom under David and Solomon
ca. 990 to 928 B.C.E.

pation in a holding action for God against the pagan world.

The institutions that nourished this peculiar loyalty were the synagogues and the Holy Temple. The synagogues may have originated among the Babylonian exiles out of the conventicles of the prophets, or they may have resulted from the attempt to associate the entire countryside of Judea in the sacrificial regimen of the Holy Temple (*maamad*). In any case, the synagogue was a unique institution in the ancient world. It was a house of reverent study, prayer, and the organization of philanthropies. It functioned without a priesthood or a bureaucracy of any kind. It was open to the uninitiated, indeed to unbelievers, so that a large crowd of sympathizers, the so-called "fearers of the Lord" attended the synagogues regularly. Some of these "spiritual converts" joined the community of the faithful in the course of time and became complete converts or "righteous proselytes." In particular, Gentile women found it easy to enter the household of Israel. All full converts were regarded as children of Abraham. The synagogue was not encumbered by laws of ritual purity, nor was it hampered by the barrier of a foreign language. The Greek-speaking Jews prayed and studied in their native tongue. The synagogue appealed to the minds as well as to the hearts of the people. It allowed the proliferation of diverse schools of interpretation and, in general, it favored local initiative.

And when the Second Temple was destroyed by the Romans (70 C.E.), the synagogues were ready to carry on, with only minor modifications in their liturgy.

At the same time, the various synagogues collected contributions from their members for the central treasury of the Holy Temple. Their members looked to Jerusalem as their metropolis or "mother city." Their talented and pious sons were sent to Jerusalem to study in its schools. The heads of the Sanhedrin and the Temple would send scholar-messengers to the various cities in order to apprise them of the latest developments in the Jewish faith. With some exaggeration, Josephus asserts that the one Law of Judaism prevailed throughout the vast Diaspora, though its sanctions were exclusively moral.[2]

Sects and Movements

SAMARITANS. The Samaritans were the first separatist sect. It would be more true to say that they were not fully accepted by the Jewish community that was

15-4 Portion of a parchment *palimpsest* page from a medieval codex, with a rabbinic Hebrew text (*Bereshith Rabba*) written over the lines of a text of Ezekiel in Palestinian Aramaic (see especially the top margin of the page). Found in a *geniza* (storeroom) of an old synagogue in Cairo. (Courtesy of the University Museum, University of Pennsylvania, Philadelphia.)

reconstituted in Jerusalem during the Persian period. Deriving from the mixture of Ephraimite remnants and ethnic groups imported by the Assyrians, they were scorned on religious as well as on ethnic grounds (II Kings 17:24–41). In addition, the procedure for the acceptance of proselytes was not yet developed in the Persian period. Also, the ancient bans against the seven Canaanite and other neighboring nations were then still in force (Ezra 9:1; Nehemiah 13:23–31). The Samaritans accepted the Hexateuch, the Pentateuch plus the book of Joshua, and following the conquest of Alexander the Great built a Holy Temple on Mount Gerizim.[3] This Temple was destroyed by John Hyrkanos (ca. 130 B.C.E.), but the Samaritans continued to offer their Paschal sacrifices on their "Mountain of Blessing." Their status within Judaism remained ambiguous. At times they

[2]Flavius Josephus, *Contra Apionem,* Book II, Chap. 20.

[3]Flavius Josephus, *Antiquities of the Jews,* Book XI, Chap. 4 (3); Book XI, Chap. 8 (6).

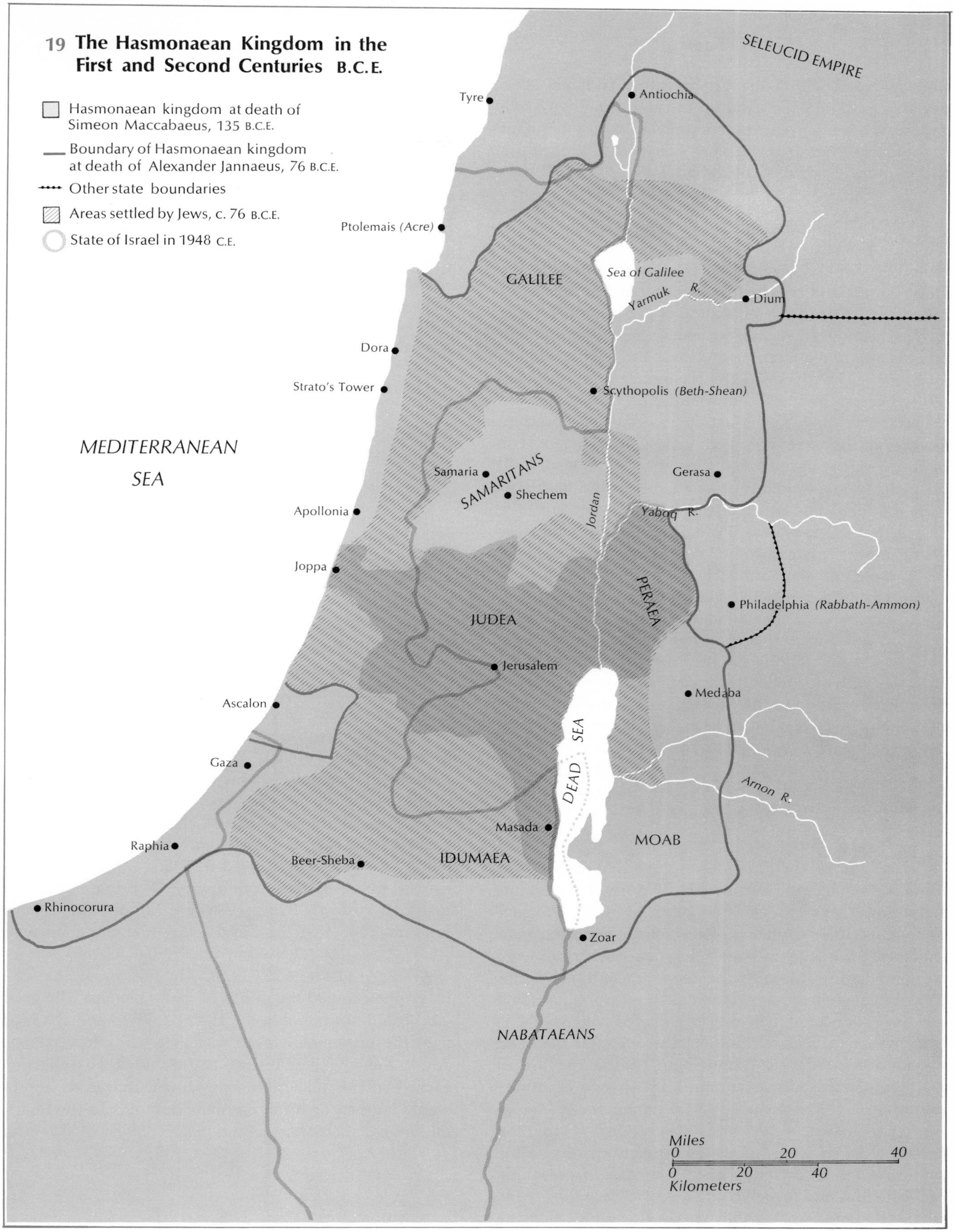
19 The Hasmonaean Kingdom in the First and Second Centuries B.C.E.
Hasmonaean kingdom at death of Simeon Maccabaeus, 135 B.C.E.
Boundary of Hasmonaean kingdom at death of Alexander Jannaeus, 76 B.C.E.
Other state boundaries
Areas settled by Jews, c. 76 B.C.E.
State of Israel in 1948 C.E.
SELEUCID EMPIRE
Tyre
Antiochia
Ptolemais (Acre)
GALILEE
Sea of Galilee
Yarmuk R.
Dium
Dora
Strato's Tower
Scythopolis (Beth-Shean)
MEDITERRANEAN SEA
Samaria
SAMARITANS
Shechem
Gerasa
Apollonia
Jordan
Yaboq R.
Joppa
PERAEA
Philadelphia (Rabbath-Ammon)
JUDEA
Jerusalem
Medaba
Ascalon
DEAD SEA
Gaza
Arnon R.
Masada
MOAB
Raphia
Beer-Sheba
IDUMAEA
Rhinocorura
Zoar
NABATAEANS
Miles
0 20 40
0 20 40
Kilometers

were included within the Congregation of Israel, as a deviant sect, like the Sadducees; at times they were treated as a semi-idolatrous community. A tiny remnant of some three hundred souls has survived and continues to live amidst their Arab neighbors in the city of Nāblus.

SADDUCEES. The Sadducees were the followers of the high-priestly family "the sons of Zaddok," mentioned by Ezekiel (Ezekiel 44:15). They controlled the Holy Temple and the cluster of central institutions associated with it from the rebuilding of the Second Temple to the Hasmonean Revolt against Antiochus Epiphanes and his abortive attempt to suppress the Jewish religion (167 B.C.E.). The success of the Hasmonean princes (Map 19) led to the institution of Hanukkah (165 B.C.E.) and the election of Judah Maccabee's youngest brother, Simon, as ethnarch and high priest (140 B.C.E.). The Sadducees were out of office, for a generation or so, until the latter years of John Hyrkanos, when the Pharisees were deposed. The two groups vied for power until the destruction of Jerusalem (70 C.E.), with the Sadducees losing influence steadily but continuing their hold on the Temple and the Sanhedrin.

The Sadducees rejected the Oral Law, the belief in the resurrection of the body, and the general spirit of religious democracy that matured gradually among the Pharisees. As manipulators of power, they maintained close ties with the Hellenists and the Romans, restricting the role of religion to the sacrificial system of the Temple. Their condemnation of Jesus and, later, their persecution of the Apostolic community were motivated by the fear that any messianic movement might ignite the revolutionary mood of the people and trigger cruel blows of retribution by the Romans.

PHARISEES. The Pharisees emerged out of the proliferating synagogues and houses of study. Their name, signifying "separatists," was given to them by their opponents, the Sadducees. They referred to their own leaders as "the sages of Israel." Because the Scribes were concerned with unfolding the deeper meaning of Scripture, they developed new methods of interpretation and new basic concepts that were designated collectively as the Oral Law. Their central doctrines were (1) that God is both transcendent and immanent; (2) that every man is an "image of God" in a unique way—hence, of infinite importance; (3) that man was designed to be "a co-worker with God in the works of creation"; (4) that the people of Israel were the vanguard of humanity in the service of the One God—hence, the need of preaching to the nations and proselytizing them; (5) that the Divine Law is designed to "purify mankind"; and (6) that the "Kingdom of God" or "the kingdom of heaven" will be established on earth through the leadership of a Messiah and that, howsoever it begins, the *eschaton* will include the vindication of the Israelites in the Holy Land, the ingathering of the exiles, the downfall of all wicked governments, the Day of Judgment for all nations, and the conversion of all men to "the true faith." This Kingdom of God will embrace the righteous of the past, who will be resurrected, and it will usher in "the World to Come" (*'olam ha-ba*), a state of purified, ethereal life, marking the end of our earthly form of existence (*'olam hazeh*). Generally lenient, they insisted that even the wicked are not punished in hell more than twelve months.[4] Hillel, founder of the dominant school, asserted that the essence of Torah was the Golden Rule: "What is hateful unto you do not do unto others; the rest is commentary, go and learn."[5]

The Pharisees were in one sense an order of pietists; in another, the pietistic masses of the people. Members of this lay order undertook to observe the rituals with extreme rigor, to tax themselves for the maintenance of the Temple, and to study Torah and teach it in the synagogues. Their emphasis on Torah learning and reflection led them to tolerate wide disagreements in theoretical matters. They aimed at disciplining and standardizing the conduct of the people, but they allowed considerable latitude for intellectual speculation. Following the destruction of the Temple, the Pharisaic sages took over the leadership of the Jewish community. Their Oral Law was edited and formulated in the *Mishna* (ca. 210 C.E.), the *Jerusalem Talmud* (350 C.E.), and the *Babylonian Talmud* (500 C.E.).

In the first century C.E. the Pharisees did not take part in the persecution of the Apostolic community by the High Priest. Rabban Gamaliel, their leader, put it succinctly: "If it is from God, it will succeed; if not, it will fail" (Acts 5:34). He allowed that God might well make use of the Christian community to bring masses of mankind closer to Him, even if it is not His will that Jews abandon their Law and follow the Christian way.

APOCALYPTIC CIRCLES. The vision of the Last Days preoccupied the minds of many pietists. The good God could not possibly forsake His world and abandon it to the power of wicked men. He *will* intervene one day in the course of history and establish His reign on earth—on this all visionaries agreed. But as to how it would happen or when opinions differed. To the Pharisaic sages, such speculations were at best of doubtful

[4]Mishnah, Aidayot II, Chap. 10.
[5]B. T. Shabbat, 31a.

Jewish population c. 300 C.E. variously estimated at three to six million. Within the Roman Empire, Jews comprised at least 5 percent of the total population.

By the end of the fourth century C.E., many Jews in the eastern part of the Empire, themselves recent proselytes, had become Christian.

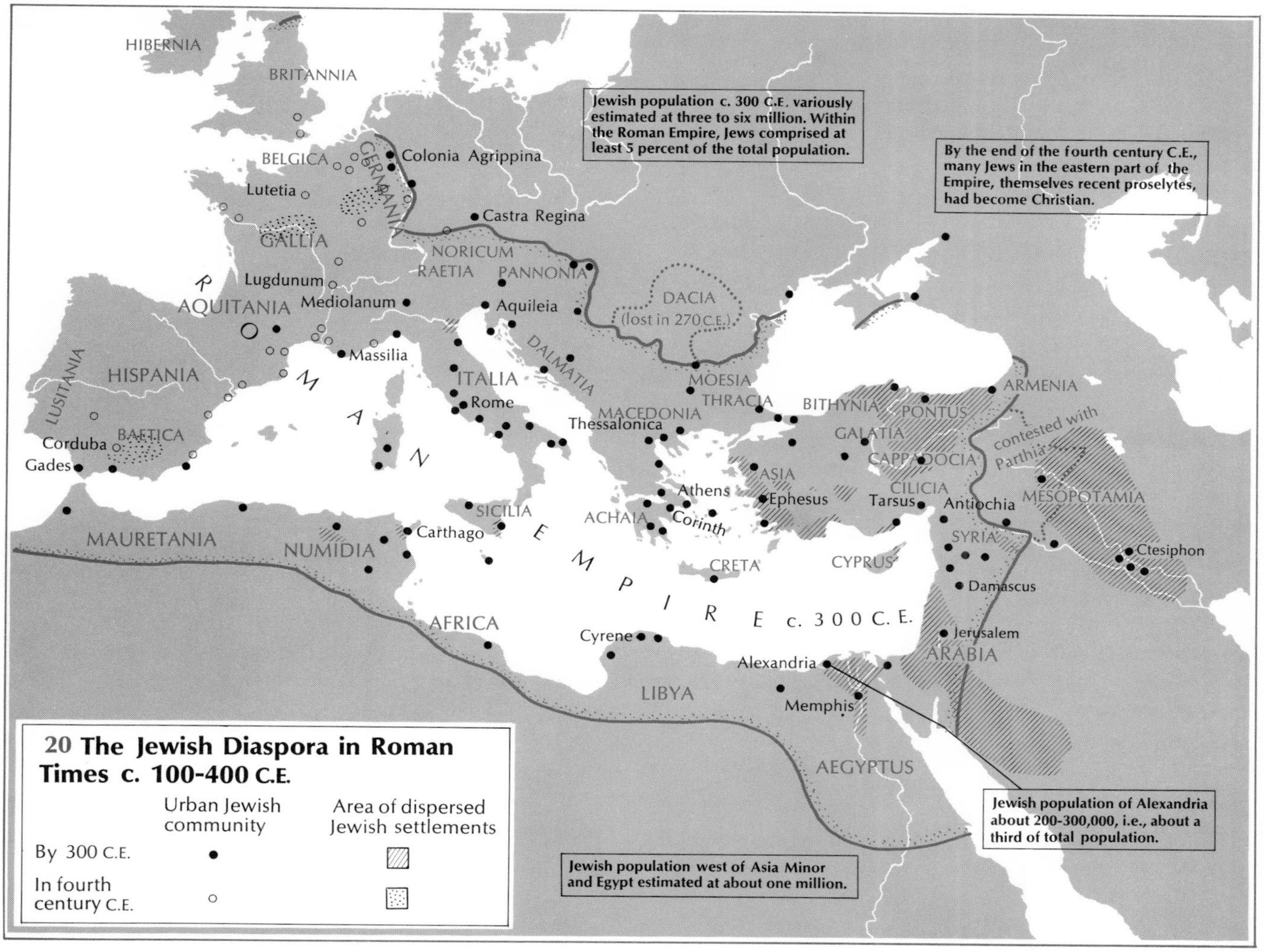

20 The Jewish Diaspora in Roman Times c. 100–400 C.E.

	Urban Jewish community	Area of dispersed Jewish settlements
By 300 C.E.	●	▨
In fourth century C.E.	○	▒

Jewish population of Alexandria about 200–300,000, i.e., about a third of total population.

Jewish population west of Asia Minor and Egypt estimated at about one million.

value—valid in the hope they sustained, dubious in the details of their vision, dangerous in the frenzied enthusiasms that they might arouse.[6] Nor can we speak of the Pharisaic sages as being of one mind in regard to such books as IV Ezra, sections of Enoch, the Book of Baruch, and the Psalms of Solomon. Some of the visionaries were probably Essenes.[7]

ESSENES. The order of the Essenes was more monolithic than the other sects of the Second Commonwealth. Yet they too allowed some variations because some of their branches consisted of married people.[8] Generally they lived in monastic communities, sharing all posses-

sions, regulating their dinners with scrupulous care, as if they were eating sacrificial offerings in the Temple.[9] They refused to offer animal sacrifices in the Temple; they believed in immortality of the soul, not in resurrection of the body; they labored under the somber mood of predetermination; and they devoted themselves with extreme zeal to a life of ascetic purity and holiness. We know more about them today because of the discovery of the Dead Sea Scrolls (1949). They drew a deep line of demarcation between themselves, "The Children of Light," and all others, "The Children of Darkness."[10]

ZEALOTS. The Zealots were a militant offshoot from the Pharisaic community. They believed that it was

---

[6]B. T. Sanhedrin, 97b.
[7]R. H. Charles, *Apocrypha and Pseudoepygrapha*, 2 vols. Oxford: Oxford U. Press, p. 19.
[8]Flavius Josephus, *Wars of the Jews*, Book II, Chap. 8, §13.

[9]Ibid., Book II, Chap. 8, §2–13.
[10]Millar Burrows, "*The Dead Sea Scrolls*" (New York: Viking, 1955), p. 371.

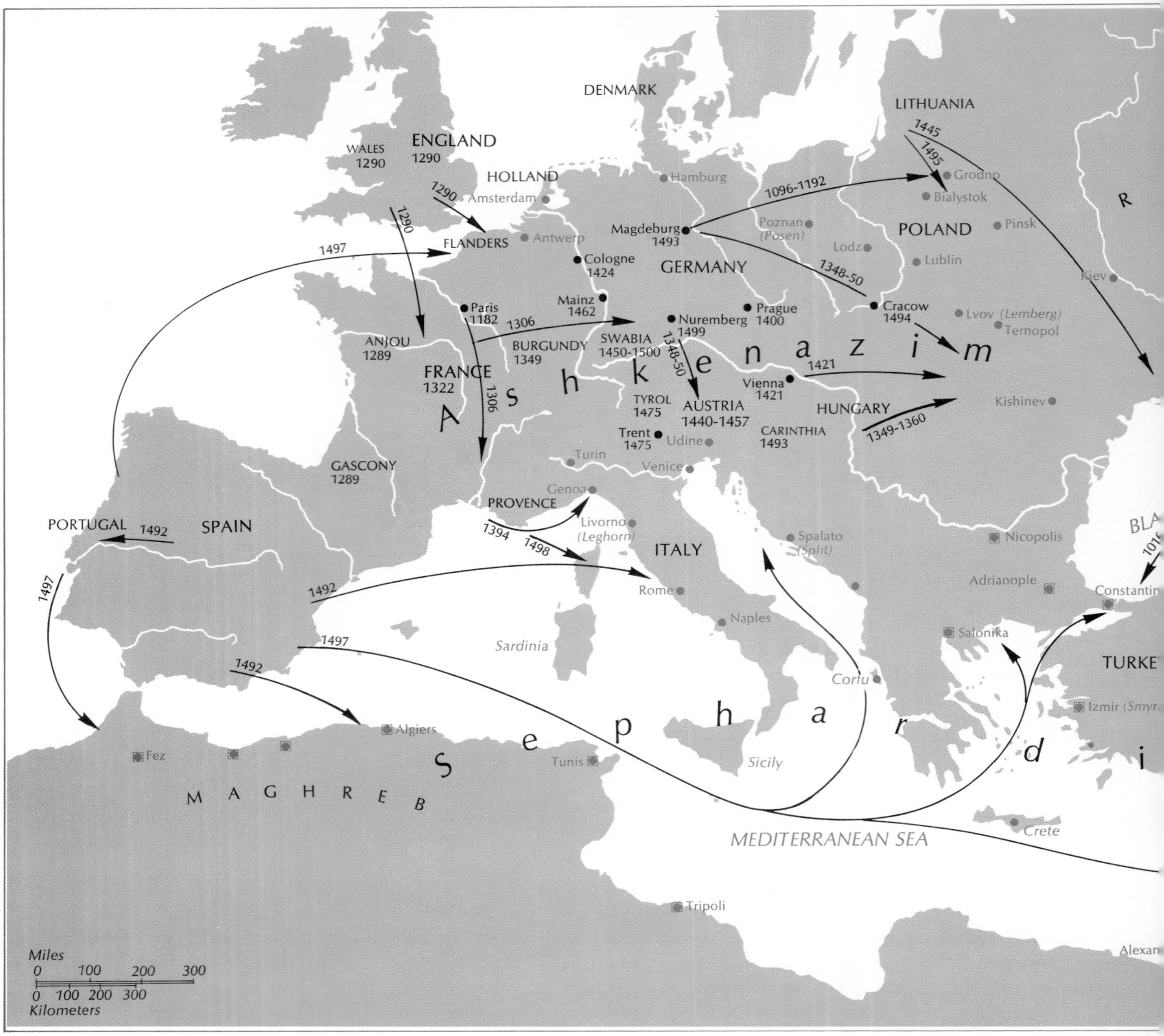

sinful to acknowledge the sovereignty of the Roman emperor, who was worshiped as god. Their slogan, "No Lord, but God," implied that to pay taxes to Caesar was a grave transgression of the Law.[11] To serve God is to refuse obedience to any mortal. The last holdouts of these extremist freedom-fighters was the fortress of Masada overlooking the Dead Sea.[12]

[11]Josephus, *Wars,* Book II, Chap. 8; *Antiquities,* Book XVIII, Chap. 1, §6.

[12]Josephus, *Wars,* Book VII, Chap. 9, §1.

HELLENISTIC JEWS. The two centers of the widely scattered Greek-speaking Jewish Diaspora were Alexandria in Egypt and Antioch in Syria. Although Hellenistic Judaism was essentially Pharisaic, it developed distinctive schools of thought. The works of Philo, a contemporary of Jesus, indicate that in their synagogues the allegorical method was pursued diligently.[13] Generally, they stressed the inner import of Scripture, and

[13]Philo, *Legum Allegoriae,* Vol. I.

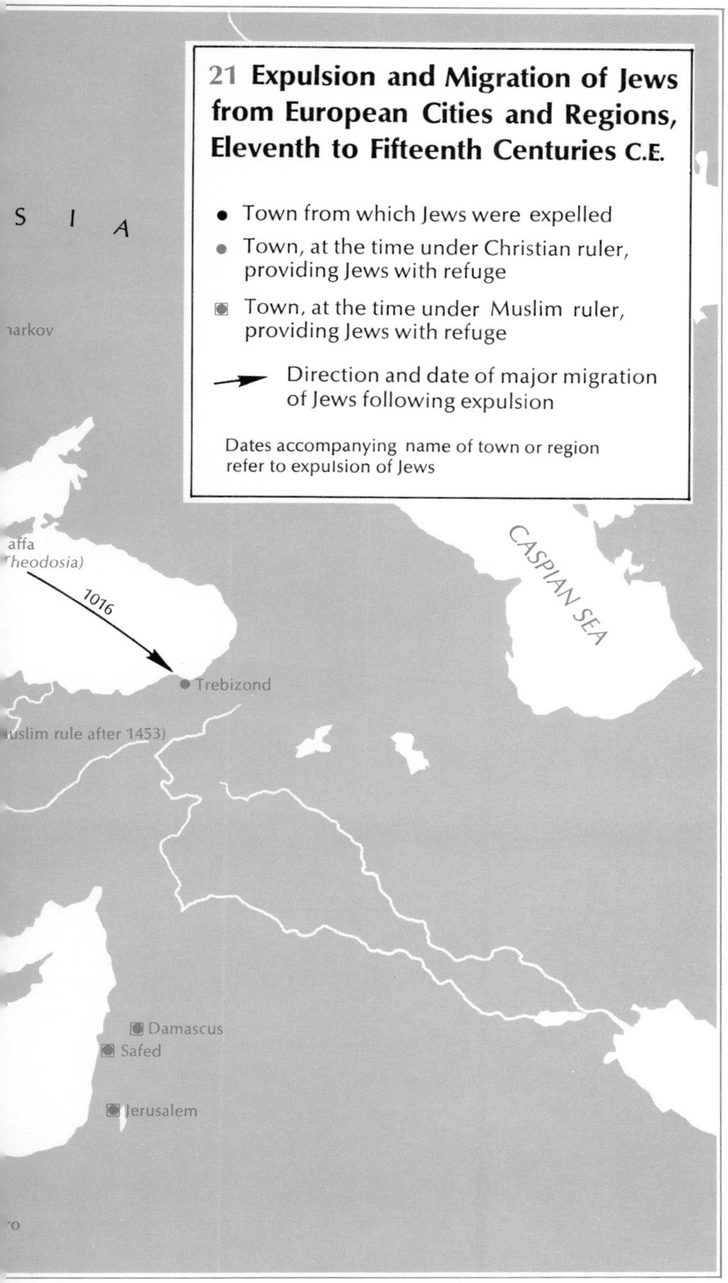

they emphasized the universal message of Judaism. Also, they employed the kind of rhetoric and metaphoric language that paved the way for the eventual removal of Christianity from the Jewish community.

JESUS AND THE APOSTOLIC COMMUNITY. The career of Jesus took place entirely within the Jewish community of Palestine, as it was then governed by the Roman procurator, Pontius Pilate, and the High Priest whose power derived from the imperial government. The teachings of Jesus belong to the broad spectrum of the then prevailing Pharisaic-Essenic thought, though in their unique and beautiful formulation the stamp of a striking personality is evident. In the tradition of the prophets, he rebuked the heads of the official schools for the failings that are inherent in a religious bureaucracy. He differed from those leaders in respect of certain ordinances, but such differences were not then sufficient to cause a schism. Decisive for subsequent developments was the claim made by him, or in his behalf, of his being the Messiah, "the Son of Man," a claim that was disallowed by the Pharisaic leaders in Jerusalem. To be sure, the High Priest, whose council decided to hand Jesus over to Pilate, was a Sadducee, whose prime concern was to nip in the bud a potentially disastrous messianic movement (John 11:47–53).

Generally, the Pharisees of the school of Hillel, then headed by Gamaliel, did not approve of the persecution of the Apostles, and they protested bitterly against the execution of James, "brother of Jesus," who headed the Christian community in Jerusalem.[14] But in the course of its own development, the Christian "way" diverged more and more from the teachings of the synagogue. The preaching of Paul and other Greek-speaking Jews appealed powerfully to "the fearers of the Lord," the semiconverts that thronged the synagogues in Syria, Asia Minor, and Greece (Map 20). The messianic Son of Man was now interpreted in Hellenistic terms as the Lord (*Kyrios*) and Son of God. The Great Revolt (65–70 C.E.), ending in the burning of the Temple, widened the breach still more, and the two communities anathematized one another in the beginning of the second century. By that time, the Hillelite Pharisees were the sole survivors of the holocaust, and a process of consolidation was set in motion, resulting in the editing of the rabbinic literature and the standardizing of the liturgy. The head of the Palestinian community was of the family of Hillel, a Patriarch; the head of the Babylonian center was an Exilarch; both claimed descent from King David.

Judaism in the Middle Ages

IN THE MUSLIM WORLD. Jews had lived in the Arabian Peninsula since the first dispersion, disseminating their monotheistic faith. Some powerful Arab tribes were converted to Judaism, particularly the Jewish King Dhu Nuwas after 516,[15] a generation or so before

[14] Josephus, *Antiquities of the Jews*, Book XX, Chap. 9, §1.
[15] Salo Baron, *A Social and Religious History of the Jews* (New York: Columbia U. P., 1952), Vol. III, pp. 60–69.

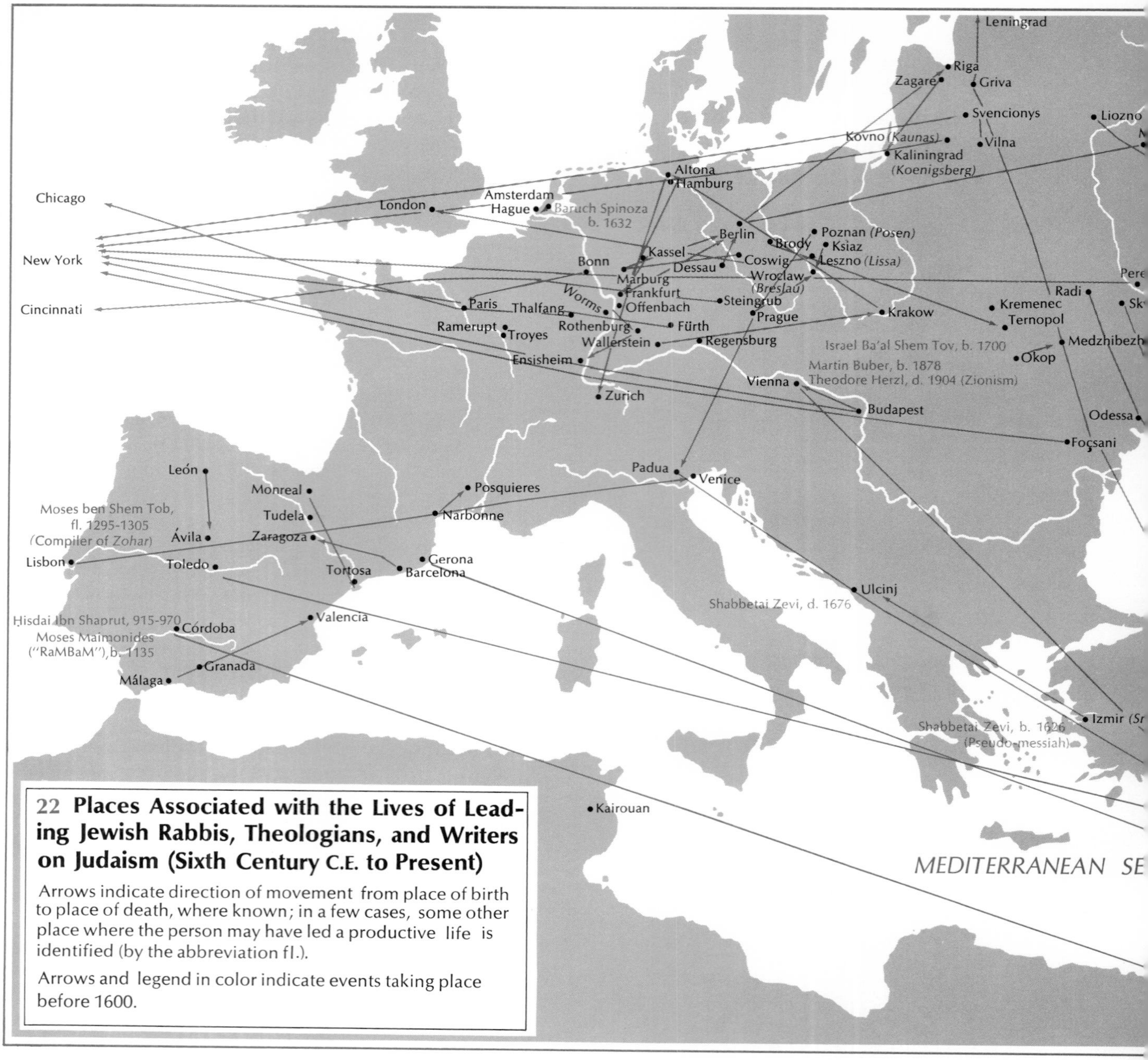

22 Places Associated with the Lives of Leading Jewish Rabbis, Theologians, and Writers on Judaism (Sixth Century C.E. to Present)

Arrows indicate direction of movement from place of birth to place of death, where known; in a few cases, some other place where the person may have led a productive life is identified (by the abbreviation fl.).

Arrows and legend in color indicate events taking place before 1600.

Acre	Moses Ḥayyim Luzzatto, d. 1747
Altona	Jonathan Eybeschutz, d. 1764 Solomon Ludwig Steinheim, b. 1789
Amsterdam	Baruch Spinoza, b. 1632
Avila	Moses ben Shem Tob, fl. 1295-1305 (Compiler of *Zohar*)
Baghdad	Seats of the *gaons*, heads of Talmudic academies, to 1089 C.E.
Barcelona	Ḥasdai Crescas, b. 1340
Berlin	Moses Mendelssohn, d. 1786 (Proponent of integration) Leopold Zunz, 1761-1802 Abraham Geiger, d. 1874 Hermann Cohen, d. 1918 Simon Dubnow, fl. 1922-1938 (Jewish cultural nationalism)
Bonn	Moses Hess, b. 1812 (Socialist-Zionist synthesis)
Brody	Nachman Krochmal, b. 1785
Budapest	Stephen S. Wise, b. 1874 Theodore Herzl, b. 1860
Cairo	Moses Maimonides ("RaMBaM") d. 1204 (Rationalist philosopher, codifier of Jewish law)
Chicago	Samuel Hirsch, d. 1889
Cincinnati	Isaac M. Wise, d. 1900 (American Reform movement)
Córdoba	Ḥisdai Ibn Shaprut, 915-970 Moses Maimonides ("RaMBaM"), b. 1135
Coswig	Hermann Cohen, b. 1842
Dessau	Moses Mendelssohn, b. 1729
Ensisheim	Meïr ben Baruch, d. 1293
Focşani	Solomon Schechter, b. 1847
Frankfurt	Abraham Geiger, b. 1810 (Reform movement) Samson Raphael Hirsch, d. 1888 Franz Rosenzweig, d. 1929
Fürth	Kaufmann Kohler, b. 1843
Gerona	Moses Naḥmanides ("RaMBaN"), b. 1194
Granada	Samuel ha-Nagid, 993-1056 Moses Ibn Ezra, 1070-1138
Griva	Abraham Kook, b. 1864
Hague	Baruch Spinoza, d. 1677
Hamburg	Samson Raphael Hirsch, b. 1808 (Neo-Orthodox movement)
Izmir (*Smyrna*)	Shabbetai Zevi, b. 1626 (Pseudo-messiah)
Jerusalem	Moses Naḥmanides, d. 1270 Isaac Luria, b. 1534 Abraham Kook, d. 1935 (Chief Rabbi of Palestine)

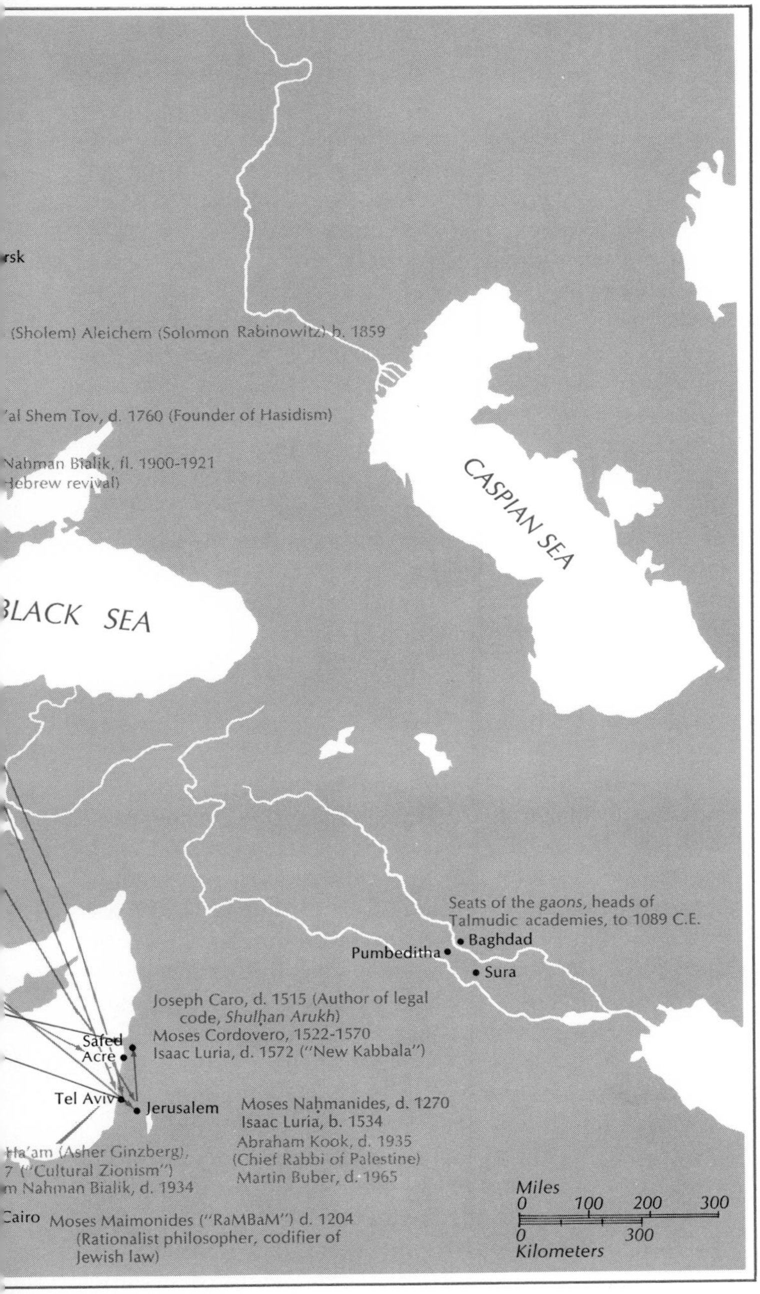

Jerusalem	Martin Buber, d. 1965
Kairouan	Nissim ben Jacob, 990-1062
Kaliningrad *(Koenigsberg)*	Israel Lipkin ("Salanter"), d. 1883
Kassel	Franz Rosenzweig, b. 1886
Kovno *(Kaunas)*	Louis Ginzberg, b. 1873
Krakow	Moses Isserles ("ReMa"), 1525-1572 (Ashkenazic gloss on *Shulḥan Arukh*) Yom Tov Lipmann Heller, d. 1654 Jonathan Eybeschutz, b. 1690
Kremenec	Isaac Baer Levinsohn 1788-1860 (Haskalah)
Ksiaz	Hermann Graetz, b. 1817
Kursk	Shneur Zalman, d. 1812
Leningrad *(St. Petersburg)*	Leon Gordon, d. 1892
León	Moses ben Shem Tob, b. 1250
Leszno *(Lissa)*	Leo Baeck, b. 1873
Liozno	Shneur Zalman, b. 1747 (Habad-Ḥasidism)
Lisbon	Isaac Abrabanel, b. 1437
London	Leo Baeck, d. 1956
Málaga	Solomon Ibn Gabirol, b. 1021
Marburg	Hermann Cohen, fl. 1876-1912
Medzhibezh	Israel Ba'al Shem Tov, d. 1760 (Founder of Ḥasidism)
Monreal	Joseph Albo, b. 1380
Mstislavl	Simon Dubnow, b. 1860
Narbonne	Abraham ben David ("RABaD III"), b. 1125
New York	Solomon Schechter, d. 1915 (Conservative Judaism) Shalom (Sholem) Aleichem (Solomon Rabinowitz), d. 1916 (Yiddish writer on *shtetl* life) Kaufmann Kohler, d. 1926 Stephen S. Wise, d. 1949 Louis Ginzberg, d. 1953 Mordecai Kaplan, fl. 1909- (Reconstructionist Judaism)
Odessa	Ḥayyim Nahman Bialik, fl. 1900-1921 (Poet of Hebrew revival)
Offenbach	Solomon Formstecher, 1808-1889
Okop	Israel Ba'al Shem Tov, b. 1700
Padua	Meïr ben Ephraim (Katzenellenbogen), d. 1565 Moses Ḥayyim Luzzato, b. 1707
Paris	Moses Hess, d. 1875
Pereyaslav	Shalom (Sholem) Aleichem (Solomon Rabinowitz) b. 1859
Posquieres	Abraham ben David, d. 1198 (Talmudic Academy)
Poznan *(Posen)*	Judah Loew ben Bezalel, b. 1515
Prague	Meïr ben Ephraim (Katzenellenbogen), b. 1473 Judah Loew ben Bezalel, d. 1609 Zacharias Frankel, b. 1801
Pumbeditha	[See: Baghdad]
Radi	Hayyim Nahman Bialik, b. 1873
Ramerupt	Jacob ben Meïr Tam, b. 1100
Regensburg	Judah ben Samuel he-Ḥasid, fl. 1180-1217
Riga	Simon Dubnow, d. 1941
Rothenburg	Meïr ben Baruch, fl. 1250-1290
Safed	Josepn Caro, d. 1515 (Author of legal code, *Shulḥan Arukh*) Moses Cordovero, 1522-1570 Isaac Luria, d. 1572 ("New Kabbala")
Skvira	Ahad Ha'am (Asher Ginzberg), b. 1856
Steingrub	Issac M. Wise, b. 1819
Sura	[See: Baghdad]
Svencionys	Mordecai Kaplan, b. 1881
Tel Aviv	Ahad Ha'am (Asher Ginzberg), d. 1927 ("Cultural Zionism") Ḥayyim Nahman Bialik, d. 1934
Ternopol	Nachman Krochmal, d. 1840
Thalfang	Samuel Hirsch, b. 1815 (Reform Judaism)
Toledo	Judah ha-Levi, 1086-1142 Abraham Ibn Daud ("RABaD"), 1110-1180 Joseph Caro, b. 1488
Tortosa	Joseph Albo, d. 1444
Troyes	Solomon ben Yizhak ("RaShI"), 1040-1105 (Bible commentator) Jacob ben Meïr Tam, d. 1171
Tudela	Abraham Ibn Ezra, 1090-1164
Ulcinj	Shabbetai Zevi, d. 1676
Valencia	Solomon Ibn Gabirol, d. 1057
Venice	Isaac Abrabanel, d. 1508
Vienna	Martin Buber, b. 1878 Theodore Herzl, d. 1904 (Zionism)
Vilna	Elijah ben Solomon ("The Gaon") 1720-1797 (Talmudic scholarly criticism; opponent of Ḥasidism) Leon Gordon, b. 1830 (Haskalah movement)
Wallerstein	Yom Tov Lipmann Heller, b. 1579
Worms	Meïr ben Baruch, b. 1215
Wroclaw *(Breslau)*	Zacharias Frankel, d. 1875 (Conservative movement) Hermann Graetz, fl. 1854-1891
Zagare	Israel Lipkin ("Salanter"), b. 1810
Zaragoza	Hasdai Crescas, d. 1410
Zurich	Solomon Ludwig Steinheim, d. 1866

the birth of Muhammad. Jews figured in the early history of Islam as citizens of the first Islamic state in Madinah, then as enemies, and later as *dhimmīs* or "protected community." They prospered mightily under the Umawi and 'Abāssī caliphates, with the religious center of Judaism being located in or near Baghdad, until 1038. With the establishment of the Umawi caliphate in Spain, Jewish culture flourished there (Map 22) and attained its Golden Age (tenth to thirteenth centuries). The Arab-Jewish symbiosis was one of the rare glories of the medieval world.

Jews engaged in all economic activities from agriculture to international trade, excelling in medicine, in the arts of navigation, and in the refining of metals. There arose among them poets and philosophers, mathematicians and scientists. Lively debates ensued concerning the validity of the rationalistic approach to theology, as represented by Maimonides, and the mystical philosophy, exemplified in the *Zohar.*

Although Muslim tolerance of Judaism differed at various times and in different places, the lot of Jews in the Islamic realm was generally better than in the Christian countries. Rare was the attempt to confine Jews to only one field of activity, as was done in the Christian West.

IN THE CHRISTIAN MEDIEVAL WORLD. The attitude of Christian authorities toward the Jews depended upon the predominance of one or another motif—the belief that the Jews were divinely appointed to serve as "witnesses of God" until such time as they would all be converted; the teaching that they were "accursed," doomed to degradation and punishment for "deicide"; the fact that Jews were needed to serve as commercial intermediaries between the Muslim and Christian worlds; the expertness of Jews in economic management and the skills needed for the building of cities; or the survival of Roman Law, which incorporated the seeds of a secular society.

During the Crusades, the Jews of Europe showed their strength of faith by preferring death in the tens of thousands to the abjuring of their faith. Still, in Spain, following a massive tide of pogroms, many Jews accepted the Christian faith in 1391 and in subsequent years. Most of them risked their lives day by day in order to retain a residual loyalty to Judaism. Thousands died in the dungeons of the Inquisition. Yet some of these secret Jews managed to retain their identity and faith for centuries. Nor was their zeal reduced by the cruel expulsion of loyal Jews from Spain in 1492, when upwards of thirty thousand families went into exile, although ten thousand families elected to accept conversion and remain. The majority of the Spanish exiles went to Portugal, where most of them were later compelled to undergo conversion. The Muslim world proved most hospitable to the Spanish refugees. Many fled to the New World, settling in Brazil and in the Caribbean islands. The Netherlands drew a steady stream of Marranos. The American Jewish community dates its origin from the immigration of refugees from Brazil and the West Indies in 1654.

On the European continent, Jewish emigration moved steadily eastward from the days of Charlemagne to the middle of the seventeenth century (Maps 21 and 22). After that time, reeling from the attacks of Russians and Ukrainians, Jews moved steadily to the West and the New World. Toward the end of the eighteenth century, the massive center of European Jewry was in the Pale of Settlement of the Russian Empire and in the contiguous areas of the neighboring Austrian and Prussian empires. By that time, only a small minority of Jews lived in Muslim lands.

Judaism in Modern Times

Jews participated in formulating the principles of a modern, secular state. On the continent of Europe, Spinoza was the great forerunner of this conception, and Moses Mendelssohn was its exponent in the generation before the French Revolution. The attitude toward Jews in the modern world varied generally in direct ratio to the strength of liberalism, as against the philosophies of the *ancien régime* or those of romanticism that extolled the irrationalism and aristocratic hierarchy of the Middle Ages. The rise of modern nationalism, especially of the blood-based type, produced a new kind of anti-Semitism, one based not on faith but on ethnic origin. Jews reacted to the challenge of modern nationalism in three ways: by accepting the nationhood of the people among whom they lived, by subscribing to a universalist philosophy that accorded only vestigial significance to ethnic groupings, or by absorbing the genius of modern nationalism into their own philosophy and reinterpreting their heritage accordingly.

The first policy was followed by the generation of the emancipation in France. The second policy was followed in Europe under the auspices of Western liberalism and, in the Russian Empire, under the aegis of socialism. In this way, the *Bund* was born, a party that attained great influence in Poland between the two world wars. The Reform movement in Germany and in the Anglo-American world attempted for several generations to divest Judaism of its ethnic encumbrances. The Zionist movement in all its variations represented the Jewish nationalist renaissance.

23 Jewish Emigration from Eastern and Central Europe, 1881-1939

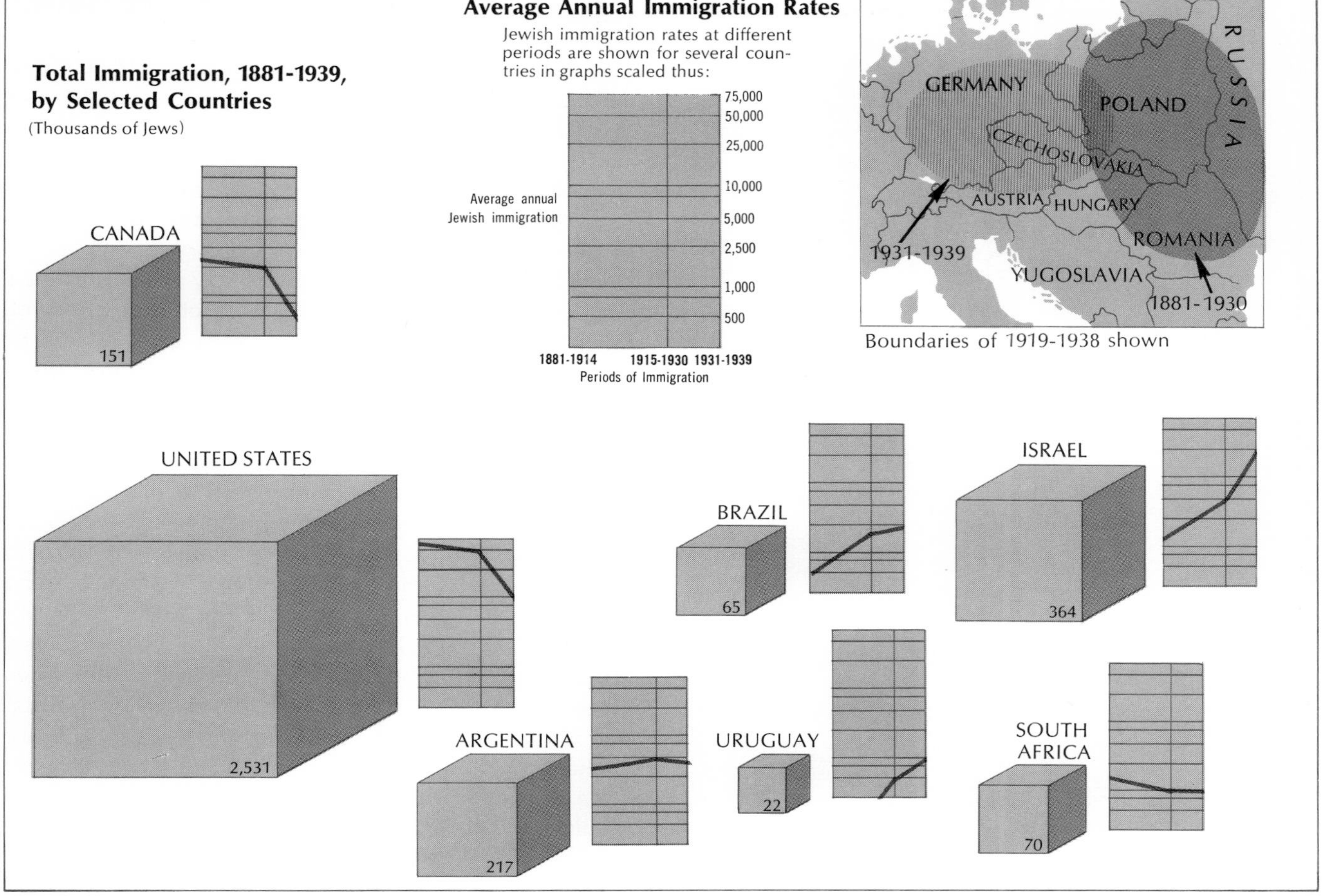

24 Change in Jewish Population 1939-1969

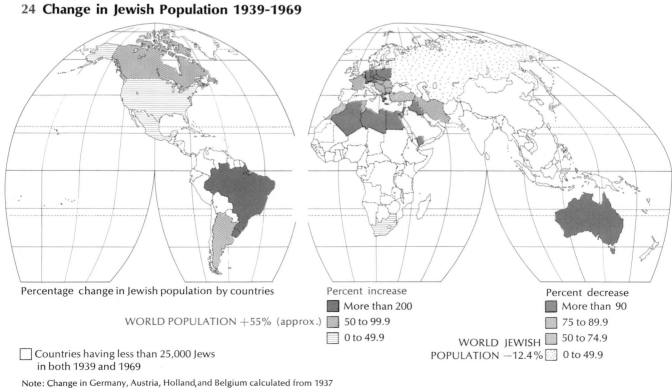

Percentage change in Jewish population by countries

WORLD POPULATION +55% (approx.)

Percent increase
- More than 200
- 50 to 99.9
- 0 to 49.9

Percent decrease
- More than 90
- 75 to 89.9
- 50 to 74.9
- 0 to 49.9

WORLD JEWISH POPULATION −12.4%

☐ Countries having less than 25,000 Jews in both 1939 and 1969

Note: Change in Germany, Austria, Holland, and Belgium calculated from 1937

25 Reduction of Jewish Communities in Eastern Europe 1933-1956

Jewish communities of less than 10,000 not shown

Jewish population of city	In 1933		In 1956
	●	10,000 to 50,000	•
	□	50,000 to 200,000	▪
	▲	more than 200,000	

Jewish communities in Poland and the western USSR were annihilated between 1939 and 1945; a few were partially reconstituted after the war by survivors who had escaped farther east in the Soviet Union.

26 Jewish Migration to Israel 1881-1970

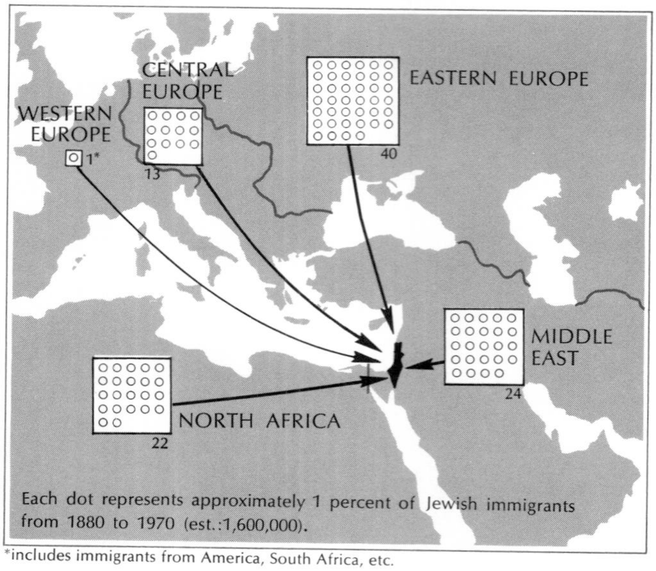

*includes immigrants from America, South Africa, etc.

ZIONISM. The primary roots of Zionism are religious. Throughout the medieval centuries, every upsurge of piety involved a migration to the Holy Land. So the Qaraites of eighth-century 'Irāq emigrated to the land of Israel. Later, the Qabbalists formed pietistic centers in Galilee, because in their belief religious experiences could be pure and genuine only in the Holy Land. Still later, messianic movements brought fresh settlers.

The Hassidim of eighteenth-century Poland, as well as their opponents, the *Mithnagdim* of the school of Elijah, Gaon of Vilna, sent hundreds of followers to Palestine. By the end of the nineteenth century, there were many circles of pietists in Jerusalem, Tiberias, and Safed, as well as in many agricultural colonies.

A second root of Zionism is the massive tide of Western nationalism and its concomitant eddies of xenophobic hatreds. In the modern world, Jewish history was viewed in a secular perspective, with a consequent transvaluation of the entire heritage of Judaism. The Conservative movement fostered the hope of Jewish rebirth in Palestine. Heinrich Graetz, the greatest Jewish historian, pointed his vast narrative in that direction. Dubnow's vision of the Jewish people as a spiritual nation that can be at home in every free society did not exclude a cultural center in the land of Israel. The rebirth of modern Hebrew literature and the growth of secularism helped to transmute the religious concern with the Holy Land as the home of the Divine Presence, *Shekinah,* into the secular ideal of a creative center for Jewish culture.

A third root of Zionism is the socialist ideal of a new cooperative society. European socialism came in two forms: utopian and "scientific," or Marxist. Many Russian Jews also felt the impact of Tolstoy's romantic ideal of creating a new man by scorning the comforts of an industrial civilization and returning to the simplicities of the life of a peasant. Zionist socialism combined the utopian, scientific, and religious motivations, evolving the great network of communes, or *Kibbutzim,* and the ideal of a *Halutz,* who is at once a dreamer and a worker, a practical farmer and an intellectual, an ascetic and a pragmatist, a Jewish loyalist and a forerunner of the universal society.

But the greatest impetus to the rapid building of the Jewish state was provided by a series of shocks that shattered the life of European Jewry (Maps 23 to 26). The Russian pogroms of 1880–1905, the Ukrainian massacres of 1917–1922, the Polish persecutions and pressures of 1922–1939, and, above all, the rise of Nazism in 1933 and its attempt to annihilate totally the Jews in its conquered territories from 1939 to 1945 produced social pressures that resulted in the presence of about

650,000 Jews within the borders of Palestine in May 1948, when the British mandate over its territory came to an end.

Thereafter a vast migration was launched from Europe with its teeming refugee camps and from the Arab world, where Jewish life became well-nigh intolerable on account of the war between Israel and the Arabs. The Jewish population in Israel today is derived about equally from European and Arab lands.

JUDAISM TODAY. The Jews of the world today are contained in three geographical areas: the Soviet world, particularly the USSR; the free world, centered around the USA; and the state of Israel (Maps 27 to 30).

In the Soviet world, the fires of Jewish loyalty were banked for more than half a century, but they were not extinguished. As a religion, Judaism was scorned along with all other religions—possibly more so. As a nationality, Judaism became suspect soon after the establishment of Israel, as loyalty to a state allied with the West. The so-called black years, 1949–1953, were particularly traumatic. Within Russia, there is hope for Jewish life only if the governing circles adopt a more tolerant attitude toward religion and pursue a more liberal policy generally. Considerable numbers of Russian Jews are likely to emigrate to Israel.

American Jewry is a broadly diversified community, divided along religious and cultural lines. The three

27 World Distribution of Jews c. 1970

Jews as a percentage of the population, by countries, 1970

☐ Less than 0.5 ☐ 0.5 to 0.99 ☐ 1.0 to 1.99 ☐ 2.0 to 2.99 ■ ISRAEL 86 percent
WORLD 0.7 percent

28 Jews in the United States

Jews as a percentage of the population, 1970

- ☐ Less than 0.5
- ☐ 0.5 to 0.99
- ☐ 1.0 to 2.99 U.S. 2.94 percent
- ☐ 3.0 to 6.0
- ■ NEW YORK 13.95 percent

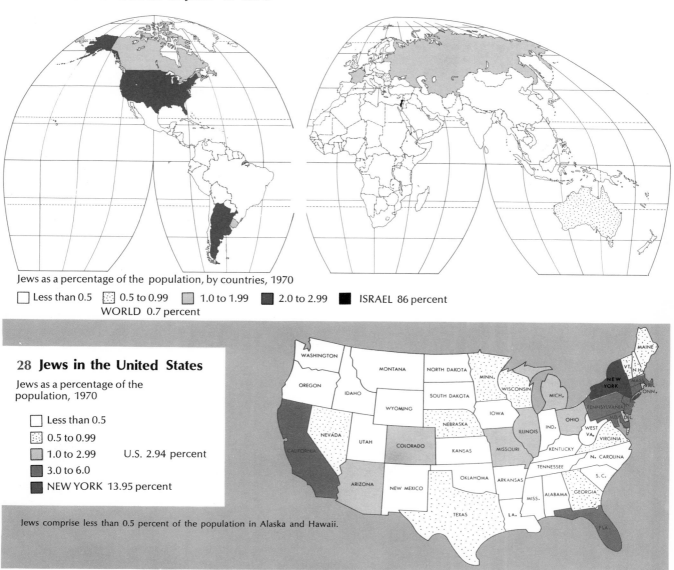

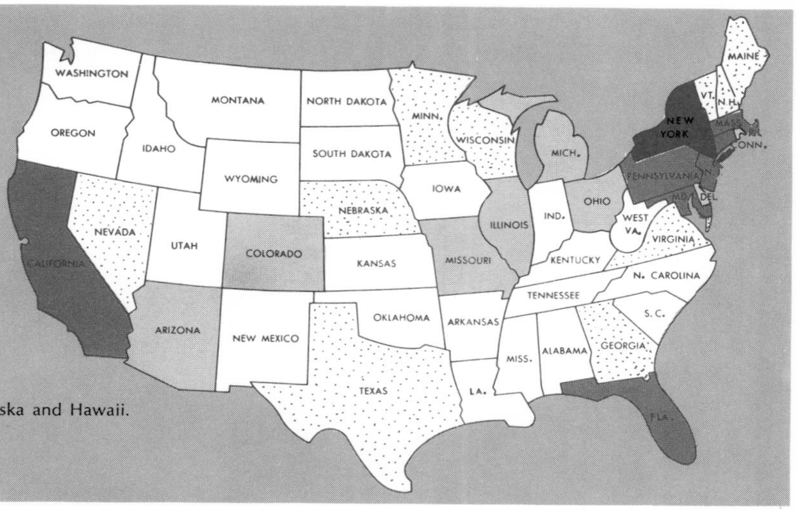

Jews comprise less than 0.5 percent of the population in Alaska and Hawaii.

29 Jewish Urban Communities (1956)

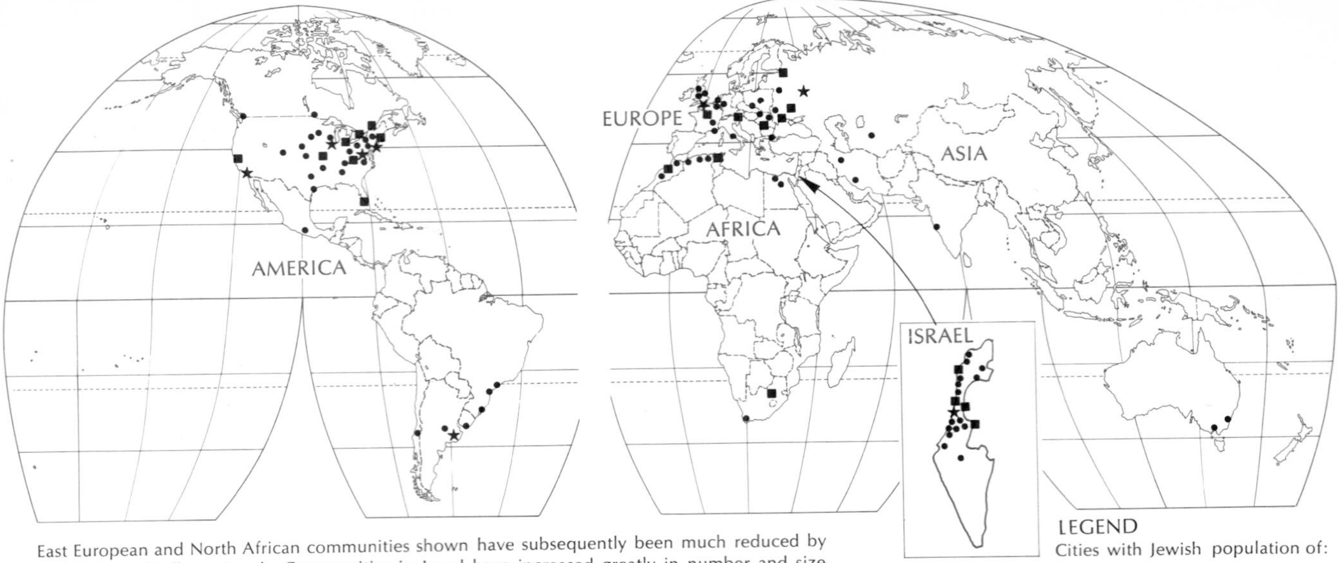

East European and North African communities shown have subsequently been much reduced by emigration, chiefly to Israel. Communities in Israel have increased greatly in number and size.

LEGEND
Cities with Jewish population of:
• 10,000 to 50,000
■ 50,000 to 200,000
★ more than 200,000

broad segments, Orthodoxy, Conservatism, and Reform, join forces in fund raising for local and national philanthropic and educational purposes. They also possess their own diverse central institutions and often take opposing stands on great public issues. In recent years, Jewish studies have been included in the academic programs of colleges and universities. The formation of Hebrew Union College, the Jewish Theological Seminary, Yeshiva University, Dropsie University, and Brandeis University and recently the establishment of the Reconstructionist Rabbinical College attest to the vitality of American Jewish life. The rapid breakdown of urban neighborhoods has stimulated the building of hundreds of new synagogues throughout the country. The whirlwinds of upheaval among the young have produced "Jewish radical" organizations, which combine Jewish loyalty with the search for a new style of life. Central organizations continue anxiously to feel the pulse of

30 World Jewish Population by Major Regions

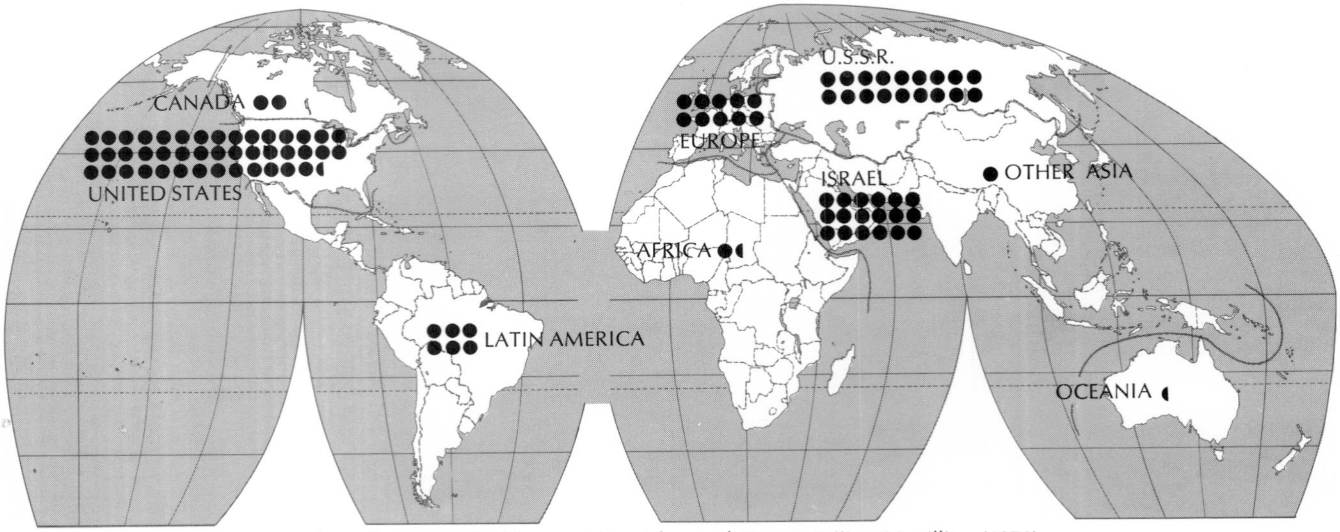

Each circle represents approximately 1 percent of the world Jewish population, totalling 14 million (1970).

Jewish life in America and in other lands, but the patient appears to have plenty of life in him.

Bibliography

AGUS, JACOB B. *The Meaning of Jewish History.* New York: Abelard Schuman, 1963.

BARON, SALO W. *A Social and Religious History of the Jews,* 16 vols. New York: Columbia U. P., 1952–1960.

BUBER, MARTIN. *Tales of the Hassidim,* 2 vols. New York: Schocken, 1947.

EFROS, ISRAEL. *Ancient Jewish Philosophy.* Detroit: Wayne State U. P., 1964.

Encyclopedia Judaica, 16 vols. New York: Macmillan, 1971.

Great Jewish Thinkers and Modern Jewish Thought, Vols. III and IV of the Great Books Series of the B'nai B'rith, ed., Simon Noveck. New York: B'nai B'rith, 1963.

GUTMANN, JULIUS. *Philosophies of Judaism,* tr., D. W. Silverman. New York: Holt, Rinehart and Winston, 1964.

HERTZBERG, ARTHUR. *The Zionist Idea.* New York: Meridian, 1960.

HESCHEL, ABRAHAM J. *God in Search of Man.* Philadelphia: Jewish Publication Society, 1956.

The Jewish Encyclopedia, 12 vols. New York: Funk and Wagnalls, 1901–1906.

KAUFMAN, YEHEZKEL. *The Religion of Israel,* tr., Moshe Greenberg. Chicago: U. of Chicago, 1960.

MAIMONIDES, MOSES. *The Guide of the Perplexed,* tr., Shlomo Pines. Chicago: U. of Chicago, 1963.

SCHOLEM, GERSHON. *Major Trends in Jewish Mysticism.* New York: Schocken Books, 1946.

WEIZMANN, CHAYIM. *Trial and Error.* New York: Harper, 1949.

ZEITLIN, SOLOMON. *The Rise and Fall of the Judean State,* 2 vols. Philadelphia: Jewish Publication Society, 1967.

PART THREE
UNIVERSAL RELIGIONS OF THE PRESENT

Theravāda Buddhism
Mahāyāna Buddhism (China)
Mahāyāna Buddhism (Japan)
Christianity
Islām

16

Theravāda Buddhism

G. P. Malalasekera

Genesis

Gautama, the Buddha

EARLY CAREER. *Buddhism* is the name given generally by Westerners to the religion founded by Gautama, known to his followers as the Buddha. Gautama was born in the sixth century B.C.E. (the accepted Theravāda date being 644 B.C.E.) in what is now Nepal (Map 31). It was then the kingdom of the Sākyas, a Kṣatriya (warrior) tribe whose capital was Kapilavastu. His father was Suddhadana, chief (*rajah*) of the kingdom, and his mother Mahā Māyā. He was born on the full-moon day of the month of Vaisakha (April–May) under a flowering *sāla*-tree in Lumbini Park, while Mahā Māyā was on her way from Kapilavastu to her parents' home in Devadaha.

The pious speak of many miracles that heralded the Buddha's advent into the world. On the day of his conception, Mahā Māyā dreamed that she had been taken to the Himalayas by the guardian gods of the world, bathed in scented water, and placed on a golden couch, whereupon a tusked white elephant, carrying a lotus, entered her through her right side. On the day of his birth, an immeasurable light filled the universe; the blind saw, the deaf heard, the dumb spoke. Fountains burst forth spontaneously, flowers rained from the sky, and music and perfume pervaded everywhere. The boy walked seven steps on lotuses immediately after his birth and declared himself lord of the world. Three centuries later, the Indian emperor Aṣoka erected in Lumbini a pillar to mark the spot of the Buddha's birth. It still stands there and is the center of Buddhist pilgrimage.

Five days after his birth, when the boy was presented to holy men and soothsayers, they saw on his person the marks of a superman and predicted that he would either be a world ruler or an "enlightened one," a Buddha. He was given the personal name of Siddhārtha, his family name being Gautama. Later, his contemporaries called him Śākyamuni (Sage of the Śākyans), and the Buddha generally referred to himself as the Tathāgata (One who has found the Truth or followed the Way of his predecessors, former Buddhas). For the Buddha did not claim to be a unique person. There have been many Buddhas in the past and there will be many more in the future, all preaching the same doctrine. A week after the child's birth, Mahā Māyā died and the boy was thereafter brought up by her sister, Suddhadana's second queen, Mahā Pajāpatī Gautamī, who proved to be a most devoted foster mother.

Young Siddhārtha was reared in the lap of luxury. Remembering the soothsayer's words, Suddhadana was determined that his son should be a world ruler and not a Buddha. The best teachers were engaged for his education, which consisted not only of knowledge of the

16-1 Sandstone Head of Standing Buddha at Saramath, India, 5th century C.E. (Courtesy of the National Museum, New Delhi.)

wisdom that great men could teach him but also proficiency in all the manly arts. It is said that the prince amazed his teachers by his rapid mastery of everything he was taught. But, even as a child, he was often seen sitting alone, wrapt in deep thought. Once, at a ploughing ceremony, to which he had accompanied his father, his nurses had left him alone under a tree and he was discovered seated cross-legged, in a trance. Years later, after his Enlightenment, he recalled this experience and what it had taught him.

Suddhadana did everything he could to prevent his son from becoming aware of the sorrows of life. Palaces were built for the various seasons of the year, furnished with the greatest luxury. He was surrounded with splendors and amusements of every kind. Strict precautions were taken to keep away from his sight the sick, the aged, and the infirm. No one was allowed to talk of such things as illness or death, misery or unhappiness of any sort. When the prince was sixteen years old, invitations were sent to all the eligible maidens of the land so that he could choose a wife from among them. Each maiden was to pass before the prince and receive from him a gift, the one he thought most beautiful getting a special one. The last in the line was Yasodharā (or Bimbā), but by then all the gifts were gone. "No gift for me?" she asked, and the prince, taking a string of jewels from his neck, fastened it round her waist, saying, "To the fairest of them all." Thus was his choice made, but before Yasodharā's father, Suppabuddha, consented, the prince had to show his prowess in open contest with his colleagues. This he did to the satisfaction and amazement of all concerned.

Theirs was a happy marriage, but their life was confined within the environs of their palaces. As time passed, the prince asked his father's permission to go into the world outside, and Suddhadana was too wise to refuse. He sent special messengers to the people, telling them of the prince's visit and asking them to ensure that everything he saw was good and beautiful; all unseemly sights were to be hidden away. But destiny would not be denied. Once given permission, the prince made several journeys in his chariot, accompanied by his loyal and wise charioteer, Channa, and, in spite of his father's precautions, he saw sights that moved him deeply—an old man bent with age, a sick man covered with ulcers, and a dead man being taken for burial. Talks with Channa assured him that these things were inextricably bound up with life. No one could escape them. Finally, he saw an ascetic whose features reflected his deep, inner peace.

These things filled Siddhārtha's sensitive mind with restlessness. He had every reason to be happy himself but the more he pondered, the more he became aware of the cruel realities of life and the more determined to find a way of escape from them. His quest for this was the role he was destined to play. Many, many millions of years ago, he had met the Buddha of a previous age, named Dipaṅkara, and then made a firm resolve that he, too, would one day become a Buddha, a teacher of gods and men. In pursuance of this vow, during countless lives thereafter, he had practiced the ten *pāramitā,* or perfections, needed for the attainment of that goal—generosity, morality, renunciation, wisdom, effort, forbearance, truthfulness, determination, loving kindness, and equanimity. During this long period of training, he was known as a *Bodhisatta,* a Buddha-to-be. And, now, this was his last life. As he kept

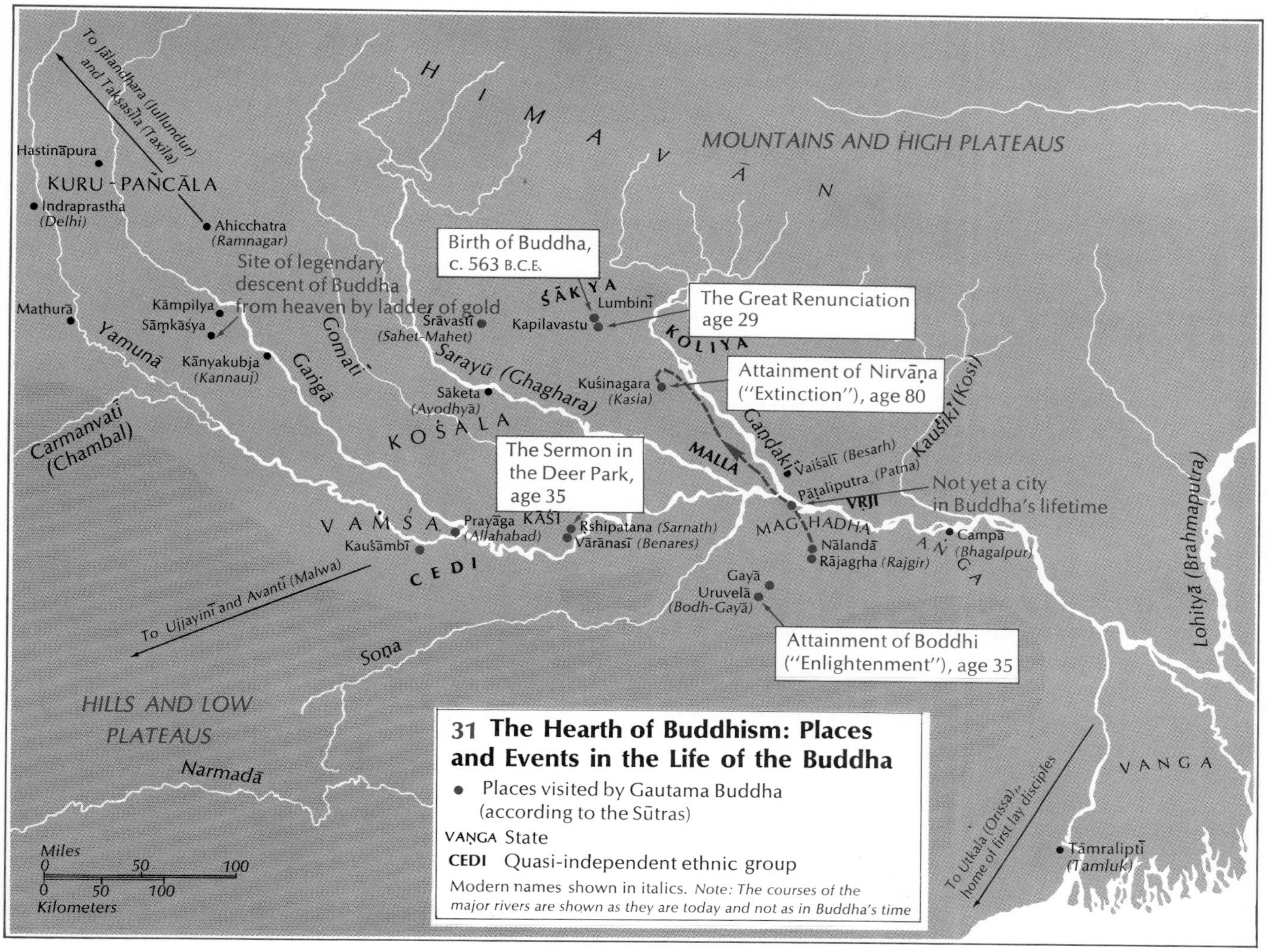

31 The Hearth of Buddhism: Places and Events in the Life of the Buddha

- • Places visited by Gautama Buddha (according to the Sūtras)

VAṄGA State
CEDI Quasi-independent ethnic group

Modern names shown in italics. *Note: The courses of the major rivers are shown as they are today and not as in Buddha's time*

pondering, the cumulative effect of his career as a *Bodhisatta* urged him on to make his final resolve. Then, in his twenty-ninth year, on the full-moon day of June–July, soon after the birth of his only child, Rāhula (meaning "bond"), he left home and family, determined never to return without succeeding in his quest for a Way that would bring happiness and freedom to all alike. Riding his favorite horse, Kanthaka, and accompanied only by Channa, he galloped away at night, unknown to anyone, till he had gone beyond the frontiers of his father's kingdom. Having given Channa his jewels and ornaments, he bade Channa return with the horse to Suddhadana and break the news to him. With a sweep of his sword he cut off his long tresses, which were a sign of nobility, and clad himself with but a single garment, the garb of an ascetic. This was his Great Renunciation, often represented in sculpture and painting. Seeing that his master would ride him no more, Kanthaka died on the spot, and Channa returned to Kapilavastu.

So began a long and tireless quest for the knowledge that would lead to a solution of the mystery of life. In those days, many people in India believed that happiness could be won only by purification through asceticism, and the more rigorous the asceticism, the more thorough the purification. Gautama himself took the same road and entered it with unparalleled determination. But before he took to extreme asceticism, he went to several famous teachers of religion who took personal pupils. Chief among them were Āḷāra Kālāma and Uddaka Rāmapūttā, who taught Gautama that mystic meditation was the way to emancipation. He learned all these teachers could tell him and zealously joined them in their religious experiences, but he realized that this was not what he sought.

Thereafter he went to other renowned men who believed that the road to emancipation was through the complete mortification of all emotions and the stifling of passions. Having decided to follow their precepts, he retired into a thick forest, near modern Buddha Gaya, and applied himself to the severest penances and self-tortures. He fasted till his stomach cleaved to his spine and his skin peeled off from his bones. The fame of his austerities brought five companions, who were later to become his first disciples. Extreme asceticism brought him to the point of complete physical collapse, and one night, while walking in deep meditation, he sank to the ground in sheer exhaustion and his companions left him for dead. He revived, however, and was convinced that austerity, however severe, would not lead him to insight and deliverance. He had already learned in his father's palace that a life of luxury was not the way either.

He now, therefore, again began to take food once a day, confining himself to strict abstinence from all sensuality. His erstwhile companions left him, disappointed. Having regained his strength and clarity of mind, he concluded that he should follow his own inspiration and discover his own method. He retired into a pleasant grove nearby, seeking Enlightenment from within by the complete development of his spiritual powers. And one day as he sat under a banyan tree in deep meditation, a cowherd's daughter, Sujātā, having made a vow that if she had a son she would offer food to the deity of that tree, came there, with her wish fulfilled, and seeing Gautama, gave him a bowl of milk rice. That was his only meal for forty-nine days thereafter. The previous night he had dreamed five great dreams and had awakened with the certainty that he would attain Enlightenment. Bathed and refreshed after his meal, he walked through the grove to a pipal tree nearby—to be known later as the Bodhi (Enlightenment) Tree—where a grass cutter gave him several handfuls of *kusa* grass, which he spread as a seat under the tree. And, there he sat, cross-legged and upright, saying, "Let my skin and bones shrivel and wither, my flesh and blood dry up; I will not rise without attaining supreme Enlightenment." This is called the Unbreakable Posture, *Vajrāsana.*

ENLIGHTENMENT. As he sat there into the night —it was another full moon, again in May, the month of Vaisakha—he went through his final and most strenuous struggle, the struggle against the passions and desires of the human heart, which he thought he had already conquered. But once more they arose within him—craving for existence and enjoyment, pride and prejudice, indolence, love of family life, power and wealth, all the delights of sensuous pleasure, gnawing doubt and delusion. In later ages, artists and poets represented this inward struggle in a magnificent allegory as a mighty battle between the solitary sage and Māra, the Tempter, Lord of the World of Passion. Māra offers Gautama the sovereignty of the whole world, which he rejects with scorn. Enraged, Māra summons his countless hosts, the destructive powers of Nature, to stop this mere mortal from wresting from Māra his dominion over human hearts, but Gautama is unmoved. Māra challenges Gautama's right to sit under the Bodhi Tree. What has he done to win that right? Gautama, seeing no other witness, touches the earth and calls upon the earth goddess to testify to his countless deeds of mercy and self-sacrifice. There is a mightly roar and the goddess appears in person to bear witness. Māra's monstrous elephant falls on its knees and his forces flee in panic. In a final, desperate attempt, Māra sends his fascinatingly beautiful daughters, Taṇhā, Ārati, and Rāga (Desire, Indolence, and Sensuality), but all in vain.

Boundless was the rejoicing of the ten thousand world systems at Gautama's victory. He had rent asunder the veil of illusion and ignorance; he had won supreme insight; he had become the Buddha, the Awakened One, the Supremely Enlightened One. With mind concentrated, with all defilements gone, with heart illumined, he saw in his mind's eye beings in the merciless whirl of *samsara,* repeated births and deaths, and the cause of their corruption leading to endless woe. He realized the Truth of Universal Suffering, the Truth of Craving being the cause of Sorrow, the Truth that there could be deliverance from suffering and sorrow, and the Truth of the Way leading to that deliverance. By reviewing his own experiences, he realized that it was only by avoiding the two extremes of self-indulgence and self-mortification and by following the Middle Path that lay between them that he had found the peace and happiness that he had sought so long. These were the discoveries he made as he sat under the Bodhi Tree. They came to be known as the Four Noble Truths and constitute the basis of the teaching that he bequeathed to the world. "Knowledge arose within me, and Eye arose within me, Illumination arose within me" was how he later described the event.

At dawn the next day, as he emerged from his meditation, he sang a poem of joy:

Many a house of Life has held me, seeking ever that which wrought
These prisons of the senses, sorrow-fraught. Sore was my strife.
But now, Thou builder of the prison, Thou, I know Thee.
Never shalt Thou build again these walls of pain, nor raise
The roof-tree of deceits, nor lay fresh rafters on the clay

Broken thy house is, and the ridge-pole split; delusion fashioned it.
Safe pass I hence, deliverance to attain.

The Buddha spent the next seven weeks near the Bodhi Tree, enjoying the bliss of his new-found peace. Then after some hesitation, he decided to preach his gospel in no uncertain terms: "Wide open are the doors of Immortality; let those that have faith put forth their effort." Thus was his resolve accomplished, made many aeons ago, to find the way of salvation and make it known to ailing humanity.

THE FIRST SERMON. Having decided to preach, he selected for his first sermon the Deer Park at Isipatana, now called Sarnath, near Benares. His human audience consisted of his old colleagues, the five ascetics who had left him when he gave up his austerities. It was a very practical sermon and went straight into the heart of the human problem. The Buddha declared that those who lead the religious life should avoid the two extremes of self-indulgence and self-mortification. Self-indulgence is low, vulgar, ignoble; self-mortification painful and crazy; both are equally profitless. There is a Middle Way, the good life. The good life is to be one's best in thought and word, in will and deed. It leads to insight and wisdom; its fruit is serenity, knowledge, enlightenment, and Nibbāna. The sermon contains an exposition of the Four Noble Truths already referred to. They are four irrefutable facts: the fact of suffering, the fact that this suffering is caused by craving for personal satisfaction, the fact that this suffering will cease when the craving is stilled, and lastly, the fact that this state can be reached by treading the Middle Way, the Noble Eightfold Path, consisting of right views, right aspirations, right speech, right conduct, right livelihood, right effort, right mindfulness, and right rapture. The sermon contains all the essentials of the Buddha's teaching and the elements of the Buddhist ideal. It is fundamentally a teaching of emancipation, and emancipation implies the existence of an evil from which men must be freed. Both facts are equally important and over and over again in the Buddha's discourses occurs the statement, "One thing do I teach and one only: suffering and the extinction of suffering."

It is significant that the first sermon, called the Turning of the Wheel of the Law, gives no account of such things as, for example, the creation of the world or of those who inhabit it. It promises no exemptions from pain or evil in return for prayer or ritual or sacrifice, no intervention by divine powers. The Buddha made no claim of being a savior able or willing to take upon himself the sins of mankind. The goal and reward of the higher life is not in any external state, but in the attainment of a peaceful and tranquil mind. Nibbāna is no sort of heaven, outside ourselves, but to be experienced here, in this world.

THE SANGHA. As the Buddha thus expounded his Doctrine, the *Dhamma,* one after another of his erstwhile

16-2 The Bodhi Tree at Buddha Gaya, India. Scene of the Buddha's Enlightenment. (Courtesy of the Press Information Office of the Government of India.)

16-3 Buddhist monks, Ceylon. (Courtesy of the Ceylon Tourist Board.)

colleagues were moved to understanding and asked to be ordained as monks by him. Thus came into being the third member of the Buddhist trinity, the Sangha ("the Order"). Other "conversions" followed in due course and more were ordained, with the formula "Come, O bhikkhus ['monks']." All who were thus ordained joined the Buddha in living together during the rainy season (*vassa,* "retreat") that followed, as was the custom of recluses in India.

By then, the number of monks had increased to sixty and the Buddha sent them forth in all directions, with the words, "Go ye forth for the good of the many, the welfare of the many, the happiness of the many, for the welfare and happiness of gods and men. Preach the Doctrine, glorious in the beginning, in the middle, and in the end. Let not two of you go in the same direction." So began the first Buddhist mission.

In the beginning of the Order thus founded there were very few rules, mainly the vows of celibacy, non-violence, and the absence of any personal property other than the barest minimum needed for existence: an alms bowl, two sets of robes, a needle, a rosary, a razor, and a filter (for removing little insects from the monk's drinking water). But as numbers increased, rules were made, always only as need for them arose, till in the end there were 227 such rules. The purpose of establishing this Order was to provide conditions in which individuals could follow the Middle Way free from egoistic limitations of family and property. The Sangha constituted a new society apart from the secular society, a society based on spiritual relations. As time went on the Sangha became institutionalized. Its procedures have always been democratic in principle. It continues to this day, the oldest unbroken institutional body in human history. It has never been antisocial. Some of its members, it is true, have retired into forests and caves for meditation and contemplation. The good monk strives to lead a life transcending egoism and bodily appetites. The vast majority of them live in the community, in monasteries, in the world, though not of the world. In return for the requisites given by the laity for their subsistence they provide various kinds of selfless service. Till very recently in Buddhist lands, the monasteries were schools, hospitals, dispensaries, and orphanages, and the monks were teachers, preachers, physicians, astrologers, guides, philosophers, and friends. Above all, they have been exemplars of the life that engages itself in the pursuit of Truth and the attainment of Insight. With recent social, economic, and political changes in these countries, some of the functions performed by monks have almost become obsolete and they are faced with the problem of how best they can adapt themselves to these changes without affecting their own fundamental character.

OTHER MISSIONS. Having sent forth his disciples, the Buddha himself went to Rajagaha, capital of Magadha, and preached the Dhamma to king Bimbisāra in fulfilment of a promise given to him earlier. Bimbisāra thus became the first royal patron of Buddhism and built for the Buddha a residence in the Bamboo Grove (Veluvana), which became one of the main centers of the new religion. Pasenadi, king of Kosala, was another such patron, together with his queen, Mallikā, a woman superior in intellect to her husband. There were other, prominent citizens, too, like the banker Anāthapiṇḍika, who bestowed on the Buddha the magnificent monastery, Jetavana, where the Buddha resided for twenty-five years. Among women patrons, the best known was Visākhā, a lady of forceful personality who converted her husband and his kinsfolk to Buddhism and lavished great gifts on the Order, including a storied building named after her.

THE ORDER OF NUNS. About a year after his Enlightenment, the Buddha visited his own kinsmen in Kapilavastu and won over the proud Śākyans not only by his persuasive preaching but also by the exhibition of his miraculous powers. During this visit he ordained his own son, Rāhula, then seven years old, and several of his cousins, young Śākyans, including Ānanda, who later became his constant companion and faithful attendant. In order to quell the pride of these Śākyans, their barber, Upāli, was ordained first and thus given seniority over them. A few years later the Buddha again visited Kapilavastu, having heard of his father's illness. Suddhadana died at the age of ninety-seven, and when his obsequies were over, his widowed queen, Mahā Pajāpatī Gautamī, and many other ladies of the court asked permission to join the Sangha. When the Buddha refused, they shaved their heads, put on the yellow garments of the monastic order, and stood weeping outside the Buddha's residence. Ānanda pleaded on their behalf, after securing the Buddha's acceptance of the fact that women were as capable as men of leading the good life and profiting thereby. The Buddha allowed their ordination after some hesitation, because he was aware of the problems involved, and laid down certain special rules to be observed by nuns. This was the beginning of the Order of *Bhikkhunis* ("nuns"), who later played an important role in the spread of Buddhism. No *Bhikkhunis* are now to be found in Theravāda lands, but the Order still flourishes in Mahāyāna countries. Later tradition attributes to the Buddha a remark that because of the ordination of women, the Doctrine, which would otherwise have lasted for a thousand years, would remain intact only for five centuries.

LATER YEARS. After his Enlightenment, at the age of thirty-five, the Buddha lived for forty-five years longer till he passed away by *Parnirvāṇa* (the complete cessation of phenomenal existence). During all this time he lived a life of ceaseless activity, going everywhere on foot, sleeping, it is said, only two hours at night. He would sometimes walk many miles to help a single person, maybe a poor farmer, an old woman, a slave in distress. Even as he lay dying, he insisted that an aged ascetic, who had come from afar, be brought to him for solace and comfort. He had a deep insight into suffering, which he considered the common and all-pervasive experience of mankind. When individuals sought him regarding their sorrows and perplexities, he would delve deep into the heart of the sufferer and prescribe specific remedies. A good example is that of Kisā Gautamī, a young widow whose three-year-old son had been stung to death by a snake while playing. Various people, out of sheer pity, were reluctant to tell her the sad truth, till someone referred her to the Buddha. The Buddha asked her to get a handful of mustard seed. "But, sister," he said, "it must come from a house where none have died." Frantic with grief, she rushed from house to house, but it was always the same story. Death had been everywhere and then insight dawned on her. She returned to the Buddha, consoled, joined the Order, and became an Arhant Theri, i.e. an enlightened elder.

16-4 Stone Head of the Buddha. Khmer art of the 12th century, Cambodia.

The Buddha moved amongst men and women as a friend and a brother. He gathered many followers, kings and commoners, brahmins and outcasts, noble ladies and harlots, and repentant sinners. He never claimed to be anything more than a man, though his humanity was a divine humanity. He was no superman, no incarnation of a god come down from heaven to be a savior. He insisted that all men were potential Buddhas. He was only a guide, a teacher of the Way. Spiritual emancipation was no divine gift of grace. Yet soon after his death, some of his followers deified him. It was not till several centuries later that they made images of him. Till then they worshiped him through symbols—the *stūpa,* the Bodhi Tree, the royal umbrella, and representations of his footprints. The Buddha set no limits to questions that people could ask of him and he was quick to recognize the infinite variety of men's dispositions. But he firmly refused to be involved with matters outside the purpose of his teaching—namely, suffering and deliverance from it.

The Buddha preached no dogmas; he asked his audiences to test the validity of his teachings by their own experience. In a famous discourse to the residents of Kālāma, who expressed their bewilderment because of conflicting views, he declared that men must not accept anything because it had authority behind it or because of tradition or the support of arguments. "Only when you are convinced that certain things when undertaken and performed conduce to loss and sorrow and others lead to profit and happiness, then only act according to your convictions," he declared. Such openness and flexibility in religious tradition is indeed rare.

The Buddha finally passed away, or as the book says, entered into *Parnirvāṇa,* in Kusinārā, in the royal path of the Mallas, the date, according to Theravāda tradition, being 544 B.C.E. "All component things decay and disappear; work out your salvation with diligence," were his last words. His body was cremated with great ceremony. The relics were divided into eight portions and were distributed among the rulers of eight clans who erected *stūpas* ("cairns") over them in their home towns. In course of time, many of these *stūpas* fell in ruins and the relics they enshrined found their way into many lands, till today almost every *stūpa* (dagoba, pagoda) in Buddhist countries claims to have at least one relic of the Buddha.

Flowering and Crystallization of Doctrine

The Buddhist Councils

Three months after the *Parnirvāṇa,* five hundred of his chief disciples (*arhants*) met in a cave near Rajagaha and at a Council (*Sangiti*) that lasted for three months agreed by common consensus upon what were to be considered the main teachings of the Buddha. The Buddha's injunction had been that after his death, his place as Teacher was to be taken not by any monk or group of monks but by Doctrine, the *Dhamma.* The teachings were accordingly collected together into what came to be called the three *Piṭakas* or Baskets (*Tipiṭaka*): the *Vinaya Piṭaka* (Basket of Discipline) contains the rules and regulations for monks and nuns; the *Sutta Piṭaka* (Basket of Discourses) consists of five collections (*Nikāyas*) of the teachings of the Master, collectively known as the *Dhamma,* and also some discourses of his disciples, both monks and nuns; and the third, the *Abhidhamma Piṭaka,* contains the more philosophical and psychological terms found in the Doctrine classified, analyzed, and expounded. These three Piṭakas form the canonical texts of the Theravāda (Doctrine of the Elders), the Buddhism now extant in Ceylon, Burma, Thailand, Cambodia, and Laos, and claims to be the original orthodox teaching of the Buddha. According to legend, the *Abhidhamma* was originally preached by Buddha to his mother, reborn in Thusita heaven. It was later transmitted to his disciples by his chief disciple Sāriputta. The *Tipiṭaka* is also known as the Pāli Canon, Pāli being the language in which the canonical texts have been handed down in Theravāda countries.

These texts were handed down almost wholly by word of mouth, till they were committed to writing in Aluvihāre, in Ceylon, in the first century B.C.E. There exists a great deal of exegetical literature on these texts, produced chiefly in Ceylon and Burma and mainly in Pāli, though many commentarial treatises have also been written in the languages of countries into which Buddhism later spread. The Council at Rajagaha, called the First Council, was followed by others, generally for the "purification" of the *Dhamma,* but sometimes also to settle disputes among the Sangha that threatened to create schisms. Thus, a century later, the Second Council met in Vesali, avowedly to discuss some minor rules of discipline, but it resulted in a large section of the Orders's breaking away from the main body. The Third Council was held in Aśoka's capital, Pāṭaliputta, under the emperor's patronage. It was after this Council that the great Buddhist missionary movements were initiated that propagated Buddhism beyond the seas. There are records of a fourth council, held probably in Kashmir under the auspices of Kanishka, at which the recital of various commentary treatises was the main item. The Ceylon Chronicles mention that after the introduction

16-5 Shwesandaw Pagoda, Prome, Burma. (Courtesy of the Archeological Department, Government of Burma.)

of Buddhism there, three councils were held: one in the second century B.C.E., the next in the first century B.C.E. (at which the canonical texts were committed to writing), and the third in the first century C.E. A Thai work, compiled by a Thai patriarch in 1789 C.E., speaks of nine councils: three in India, four in Ceylon, and two in Thailand. A great council, at which twenty-four hundred persons participated, was held in Mandalay, Burma, in 1871 C.E. under the patronage of King Min-don-min, after which the sacred texts were inscribed on 729 marble tablets. More recently, in 1954, was inaugurated another council, in Rangoon, under the auspices of the then prime minister, U Nu, in which monks from many lands took part, five hundred from Burma alone. It lasted for two years and ended in May 1956 with the celebration of the twenty-five hundredth anniversary of the Buddha's *Parnirvāṇa*. At the conclusion of the council was published a special edition of the Pāli Canon and its commentaries.

The Buddha's Teachings

The age in which the Buddha lived was one of great activity in many parts of the world, intellectual, social, political, religious, and spiritual. It was the age of Pythagoras, Heraclitus, and Lao Tzu, the age of the prophets and the triumph of democracy. In India itself it was a time of great ferment and change. There were many republics in the Buddha's day, many guilds of various sorts, and several schools like Taxila turning out large numbers of students. There was unlimited freedom of speech and discussion, and not only men but women, too, could express their views, unrestricted except by the courtesies of debate.

In the sphere of religion, the *Vedas* still held sway, and sacrifices, rituals, and ceremonies played an important part in people's lives. The Brahmins had almost complete control of religious observances, and they were the gods on earth who could make men happy not only in this world but also in the next. Side by side with these, there were various philosophers and teachers with their theories and speculations, their remedies to escape from the ills of existence. Some maintained that a life of pleasure was the best, for who knows what happens after death, if anything happens at all? Others said worldly enjoyment was deceptive because sense pleasures were ephemeral and could not, therefore, bring real happiness. They advocated austerity in various forms and degrees, some even recommending self-mortification. Yet others left family and home and lived in solitude, in meditative self-development, to solve the mysteries of life and seek answers to various questions about this life and the next. It was in such a world that the Buddha proclaimed his message, like a new theme. He declared that his Way was not the sole way but it was the best way; it was a narrow and straight way. Each person should investigate it for himself; there was nothing sacrosanct about it.

The Buddha wished to fulfill rather than to destroy the teachings of his contemporaries and his predecessors. He was a reformer rather than a revolutionary, and he made as much use as he could, therefore, of their beliefs and doctrines. Thus, for instance, he accepted without much demur the accounts of the universe prevalent in his day, though he formulated some of his own theories as well, but they were only incidental to his main teachings. There were other beliefs and practices, however, that he found necessary to reject.

One such was the belief in an almighty God (Brahmā, the Indians called him), the creator of the world, the disposer of all that has been, is, and is yet to be. It did not matter whether this God was a living being or an impersonal force. There can be no exception to the law of impermanence (*anicca*) that reigns in the universe. Having thus denied permanence to God (*Brahmā*), the Buddha denied also his domination over the creatures of the world. He also denied the claim of the Brahmins for supremacy and their social theory of caste, which depended on birth. The Buddha's declaration was that a man's worth was determined not by his birth but by his actions, his character.

THE DOCTRINE OF *KARMA*. Having disposed of Brahmā, the Buddha had to face the further question. If Brahmā did not rule the world, who or what was responsible for all that happened in it? Was it by mere chance that things happened? No, answered the Buddha, and proceeded to formulate the doctrine that came to be known as the law of *Kamma* (*Karma* in Sanskrit) and that forms one of the most fundamental of his teachings. As a well-known stanza states, "Those things that proceed from a cause, of these the Tathāgata has told the cause; And that which is their cessation, that, too, the Great Sage has declared."

The doctrine of *Karma* was not original with the Buddha, but he gave it a distinctly ethical interpretation. Briefly stated, it is the law of cause and effect. Everything that happens does so only by reason of some antecedent cause and, with the cessation of that cause, ceases to be. Otherwise stated, everything is the effect of some cause or causes and is itself the cause of some other effect. This law operates in every department of the universe and it is too intricate to follow in all its details. But as far as man is concerned, it is the law that governs his happiness and sorrow. It is a self-operating law; there is no law giver to put it into operation. Every act produces its own effect, experienced in this life or later, or in a succession of lives. The nature of the act, and therefore its resultant effect, depends on the quality of the will or volition (*cetanā*) behind it. As far as living beings are concerned, only volitional deeds are effective; hence the declaration by the Buddha of the supremacy of the mind. As a result of one's actions one may be born as a human being, a *deva* ("deity"), an animal, a *peta* ("wandering spirit"), or in one of the several *nirayas* ("places of woe"). But none of these existences is eternal. Within the operation of his own *Karma*, man has the power of choice. The Buddha laid great stress on the need for a man to be aware of what he does and what he leaves undone, and of the implications.

Though the present is the result of past actions, the

16-6 The Samadhi Buddha, Anuradhapura, Ceylon. (Courtesy of the Ceylon Tourist Board.)

Buddhist teaching of *Karma* is not one of fatalism or predestination. *Karma* is only one of five natural laws that explain physical and mental phenomena. Some of these laws are mechanistic. *Karma* is a continuous process and by our actions we can mold the future. The present is but momentary, but every fleeting present moment can be utilized as an opportunity for spiritual development or for the advancement of material well-being. The future is not fixed; there are many possible futures. The future is always being shaped but never finished. Thus man, by his own actions, becomes the creator of his own destiny, the master of his fate. The Buddha only points the Way; we must, if we so resolve, walk on it by our own effort, creating the Way for ourselves, for it is not a ready-made path. It needs great effort to reach the end of it and then we have no more need of the Way. To vary the metaphor, when we have crossed the ocean on a raft, the raft is thrown away.

REBIRTH AND NO-SOUL (*ANATTA*). The doctrine of Rebirth is the natural corollary to the Buddha's teaching of *Karma*. Both *Karma* and Rebirth had been taught by philosophers in India and elsewhere before the Buddha's day but the Buddha gave them new meaning and new significance. All other religions that speak of existence after death say that there is a survival of what is called an *Ātma* or soul This is defined as something that abides separate from the body, self-identical, unitary, a persisting entity, indestructible and divine. It is found in man from the moment of his birth to the moment of his death and continues thereafter in heaven or hell. It is separate for each individual, a spark from God or Brahmā and destined to return ultimately to its master. It is lord both of man's body and of his mind and its existence is to be accepted on faith.

The Buddha categorically denied all this; he declared that the belief in a permanent self or soul is the most pernicious of errors, the most deceitful of illusions. It is the root cause of all suffering, because such a belief breeds selfishness and egotism, producing craving for life and life's pleasures and thereby plunging beings into the ocean of *samsāra*, or continued existence. The Buddha arrived at this conclusion by a process of analyzing the two components of the human being, his body and his mind. That the body has nothing permanent in it is readily acceptable. A little thought will reveal that the mind is even less permanent. It is a complex of all sorts of factors—thoughts, feelings, consciousness, and subconscious elements—always changing, without any ego at the core. If the soul be divine, it should need no development. For life is a vast conglomeration of experiences, an ever-changing continuance of mental and physical events, a combination of mental and physical aggregates, working within the law of *Karma*. To call even the whole of our personality an *Ātma* or soul would be a fiction, an illusion, like calling a rainbow a reality, whereas it is only an illusion caused by rays of light and drops of water. Life is a process, a conditioning, with nowhere the least trace of anything permanent, like the figure of a whirling torch that creates the illusion of a perfect circle. The Buddha's teaching of No-soul or *Anatta* is not negative; it is a reality and, as such, positive.

If there is no soul what then is it that is reborn? The Buddha would say that the question is wrongly put. It should be: How and why does rebirth take place? The answer is that it is the unexhausted force of *Karma* at a person's death that produces rebirth. Death is merely an incident between one life and its successor. It is in order to explain the process of reincarnation that the Buddha promulgated his teaching of *Paṭicca-Samuppāda* or Dependent Origination. The classical formulation of this doctrine states that twelve "factors" condition each other in the sense that their origination and their cessation are linked together as though in a chain. Schematically expressed, the doctrine says, "This being present, that comes to be; this being absent, that ceases to exist." Thus, because of ignorance, karmic activities (deeds of body, speech, and mind) are performed, the aggregate of which produces the dying consciousness (*viññāna*). This, in turn, produces the rebirth-consciousness. In fact, the two are parts of a single, continuous stream of consciousness. The rebirth-consciousness produces name and form, i.e., the body and mind of the new life, its psychophysical organism. This, in turn, produces the six sense-fields (organs of sense), followed by contact, i.e., the impact of the senses producing feeling, craving, grasping, and coming-to-be (as a living being), followed by birth, old age, death, grief, sorrow, suffering, lamentation, despair, and the whole gamut of anguish. Thus is established the cycle of *samsāra*, or repeated existences.

THE PATH. The Way out of *samsāra* is the Noble Eightfold Path, the last of the Four Noble Truths, already briefly mentioned. It consists of Right View (knowledge of the Four Noble Truths), Right Aspiration (to renounce sensual pleasures and be free from malice, ill will, and desire to inflict pain), Right Speech (abstaining from every kind of wrong speech and adherence to truth), Right Action (conduct that is peaceful, honorable, pure, and benevolent), Right Livelihood (abstention from wrong and harmful occupations and living only by right methods), Right Effort (assiduous self-discipline, prevention of evil states of mind, and increasing and developing good states of mind), Right Mindfulness (com-

16-7 The Buddha calling the earth goddess to witness. Buddha Gaya, India, 5th century C.E., Pala Dynasty. (Courtesy of the Metropolitan Museum of Art, Rogers Fund, 1920.)

plete awareness of what one does, says, feels, and thinks, allowing nothing to happen heedlessly or mechanically), and Right Contemplation (leading to mental equipoise and tranquillity, and thence to ecstasy and rapture).

NIBBĀNA (Sanskrit, *Nirvāna*). The Buddha assures us that the follower of this Way succeeds in rooting out all attachments and greed and all hatred, malice, and evil, all tragic tensions and gnawing anxieties, all turbulent desires and passions that produce inner conflict, all the frustrations and disenchantments, the confused and complex motivations, both conscious and unconscious, that cause unhappiness and misery. Suffering has nothing mysterious about it; it is a solvable problem and here is the solution. Here is the Way out from suffering into happiness, to *Nibbāna,* and it is available to every human being.

The being who has reached *Nibbāna* is called an *Arhant,* a Perfect One, a Saint. There are four stages on the Way to *Nibbāna,* four degrees, as it were, of spiritual development. At each stage some of the fetters or obstacles that beset the wayfarer are destroyed till in the last stage, all the fetters have been shattered. *Nibbāna* implies nothing else but the pure condition of freedom from sorrow, based upon complete freedom from craving, through the highest appreciation of the truth about things as they really are. It is a condition that by itself is quite inexplicable, undefinable. As light prevails where there is no darkness, as rest prevails where there is no motion, so also *Nibbāna* is present where there is

16-8 Thuparama Dagoba, Anuradhapura, Ceylon. (Courtesy of the Ceylon Tourist Board.)

no sorrow or suffering. "How may *Nibbāna* be known," asks King Milinda of the *Arhant* Nagasena. "By deliverance from distress and danger, by peace, calm happiness, contentment and purity," is the answer. There is no place for *Nibbāna*, yet it exists, as fire exists though there is no place where it is stored. Unlike the *summum bonum* of most religions, *Nibbāna* is not a state to be reached only after death. It can be attained in this world, in this life. It is a positive state of bliss, of unbounded peace and joy, as testified in the numerous utterances of those who have attained it. *"Aho sukham, aho sukham,"* they exclaim: "Ah, what happiness, what bliss!" Their constant refrain is that of freedom won. The man who has attained *Nibbāna* clings to nothing, and nothing clings to him. In peace, profound and blest, he goes his way "like the clouds through the blue of heaven."

THE FINAL PASSING AWAY. When the *Arhant* dies, he is described as having entered *Parnirvāṇa*, the complete passing away, the final release, the utter waning-out and ending with no substratum or basis for rebirth.

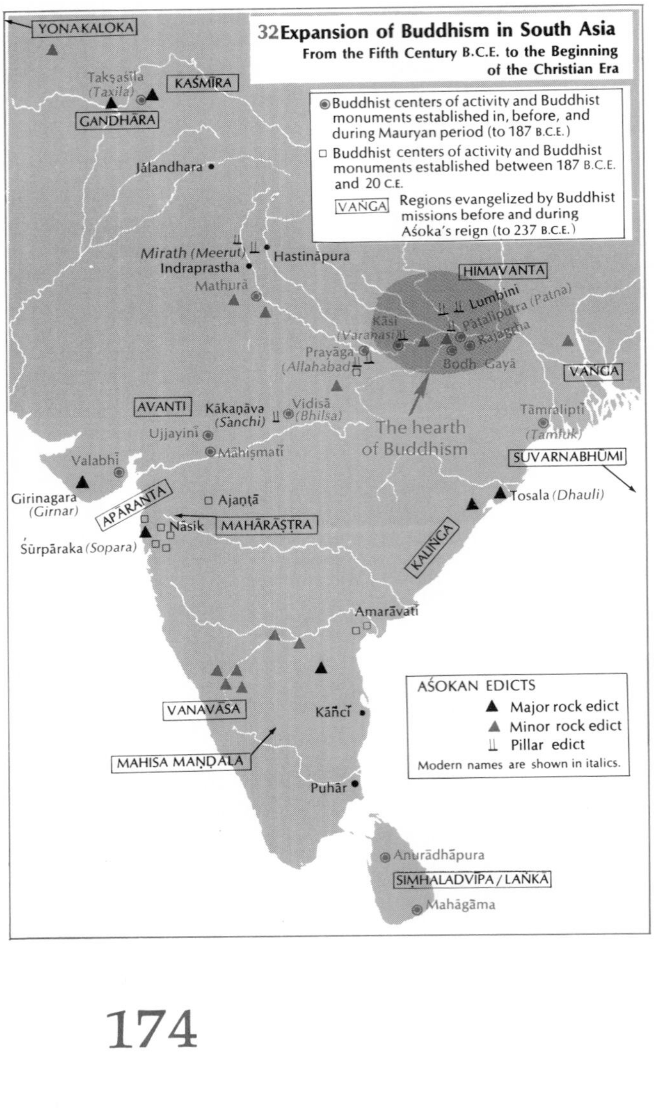

32 **Expansion of Buddhism in South Asia**
From the Fifth Century B.C.E. to the Beginning of the Christian Era

Of the being who has entered into *Parnirvāṇa* it cannot be said that he exists or does not exist; both propositions are equally false. One of the synonyms used by the Buddha for this stage is *amata*, which is the very antithesis of life as known to us. For life is inextricably bound up with death; we start dying the moment we are born. *Amata*, on the other hand, is a state in which there is no participation in any describable form of existence or, indeed, of nonexistence: "Nothing can be said of the Beyond-the-World in the speech of this Within-the-World, which will not be in some way false, misleading and incomplete."

Buddhism is the religion of Enlightenment. The texts often mention that its basis is compassion and its climax transcendental insight or gnosis (*paññā*). The whole teaching consists of the cultivation of three factors: ethics (*sīla*), contemplation (*samādhi*), and wisdom (*paññā*). Of these, ethics constitutes good conduct and needs no elucidation. *Samādhi* is the acquisition of mental tranquillity (*samātha*) by the complete absence of conflicts and tensions. This is acquired through *bhāvanā*, generally called meditation but involving much more than that. It is the very core of the Buddhist approach to life and comprises the development of all those faculties that broaden and deepen the mind, including such activities as the fine arts. It is well known that wherever Buddhism has spread, there has followed a florescence of painting, sculpture, architecture, literature (both prose and poetry), music, dancing, and drama. The great tolerance so characteristic of Buddhism is also part of this development. It is through contemplation that one gets a clear knowledge (*vipassana*) of the facts of existence and it is this that constitutes wisdom (*paññā*).

Historical Spread

Rise, Decline, and Revival of Buddhism in India

During the Buddha's lifetime his activities were confined to northern India and to a few small communities in the west of India, though there are legends that say that both the Buddha and some of his disciples visited several neighboring countries. During the next two centuries Buddhism spread into other parts of India, but it was not till the great emperor Aśoka embraced Buddhism (in the third century B.C.E.) that the religion had any real expansion (Map 32). His invasion of Kalinga in the eighth year of his reign was the turning point of his life. He repented of the loss of life he had caused and began to think of a religious conquest. He took various steps to encourage the people to observe the laws of piety and set up edicts carved on rocks and stone pillars for their guidance. His benefactions to Buddhism were immense; for instance, he is said to have erected eighty-four thousand *stūpas.*

Under his patronage was held the Third Buddhist Council, to determine the real nature of the Buddha's teaching. Thereafter he sent Buddhist missions to various countries: to the Yavanas (Iranian Greeks), to Gandhara, Kashmir, the Himalayan regions in the north, the western parts of India, and Suvarna-bhūmi, "the Land of Gold" (Malaya and Sumatra). Of these the mission to Ceylon, referred to earlier, was the most successful. His edicts also mention that he dispatched missionaries to far-off lands as well, to Syria, to Egypt, to Macedonia, to Epirus (in north Greece), and to Cyrenia in North Africa.

With the advent of the Sunga dynasty (ca. 185–80 B.C.E.), Buddhism lost official patronage, and its first king, Pushyamitra, is said to have persecuted the Buddhists. But by then Buddhism had won great popular support and made much progress. A large number of famous Buddhist establishments belong to this period, like the Bharhut *stūpa,* the Chaitya hall (chapel enclosing a *stūpa*) in the Karle cave, and the Sanchi *stūpa.* By this time, the cult of the worship of Buddha relics had also gained wide currency.

It was at this time that the Greeks (Yavanas) to the north of India adopted Buddhism with King Menander (Milinda) as a great champion of the faith. The Yavanas were generous donors to Buddhist establishments and also took part in missionary activities. They evolved a new style of Buddhist art, known as Gandhara or Indo-Greek art, which flourished chiefly in the Punjab and northwest India. It produced some of the finest specimens of Buddhist sculpture and it is generally believed that the first Buddha images originated in this area, as a result of Hellenic influence.

During the Kushan period that followed (ca. 50–ca. 320 C.E.) special mention should be made of King Kanishka, who ruled in Purushapura (Peshawar) in the second century. It is said that he consulted the Buddhist scriptures frequently and that a monk visited him daily to preach the *Dhamma.* He held a Buddhist council under the presidency of Vasumitra, with five hundred scholars participating. They produced commentaries on the *Tipiṭaka,* totaling 300,000 verses. Kanishka had the texts and commentaries inscribed on copper sheets, enclosed them in a stone receptacle, and erected a *stūpa* over them. This was also the period of the greatest development of Gandhara art, and monks from India carried Buddhism into central Asia and China. It also saw the emergence of a new form of Buddhism, the Mahāyāna. Many great scholars of Buddhism flourished at this time, e.g., Asvaghosa and Nagarjuna, and Mathura (Muttra) in the north and Amaravati in the southeast developed as important centers of Buddhist activity (Map 33).

Already on account of the rapid expansion of Buddhism and the absence of a coordinating organization, many Buddhist sects had sprung up in various parts of the country. At first, the origin of these sects was not due to any doctrinal differences but to geographical factors. But as time went on they developed their own traditions. Quite early, the Mahāsanghikas had formed into a separate group, with their center in Vesālī, and later they divided into eight different schools, each with a literature of its own. A century later, the Theravādina divided into two groups, the Sarvāstivādin and the Mūlasthaviravādin. The Sarvāstivādin flourished mostly in the north.

The Gupta period (ca. 320–ca. 620 C.E.), which succeeded the Kushan period, was a splendid time in the history of Indian culture. There was a great revival of Hinduism, and Buddhism too flourished, though there was some rivalry between the Brahmins and the Buddhists. The famous Chinese Buddhist pilgrim, Fa Hsien, visited India at the time of Chandragupta II (ca. 385–414 C.E.) and left a very interesting record of his travels, which included Ceylon as well.

It was in the Gupta period that Buddhist sculpture reached its climax, e.g., in Sarnath. So did painting attain its highest level, as in the Bagh caves, on the southern slopes of the Vindhya mountain, and in Ajanta, where the frescoes on the walls, ceilings, and pillars date all the way from before the Christian era to the seventh century C.E. The best of them belong to the second half of the fifth century and the beginning of the sixth. Ajanta also influenced painting in Ceylon, as seen in the famous Sigiriya frescoes. It was to the Guptas that the world-famed teaching institution of Nālandā owed its origin and development, as did the foundation of Valabhi. Harshavardhana was the last great royal patron of Buddhism, and he was a follower of the Mahāyāna. In eastern India most of the rulers of the Pāla dynasty were Buddhists, and they founded new monasteries, like those at Vikramaśīlā, Odantapurī and Somapurī, which kept alive the torch of Buddhist learning till the twelfth century.

But with the end of the Gupta period, Buddhism began to decline in India, partly because of its own internal dissensions, about which Hsiia-tsang has left accounts in his *Records,* but chiefly because of the opposition of the Hindus, championed by great figures like Śankara and Rāmanuja. Then came Islam, which gave Buddhism the *coup de grâce* and brought about its almost

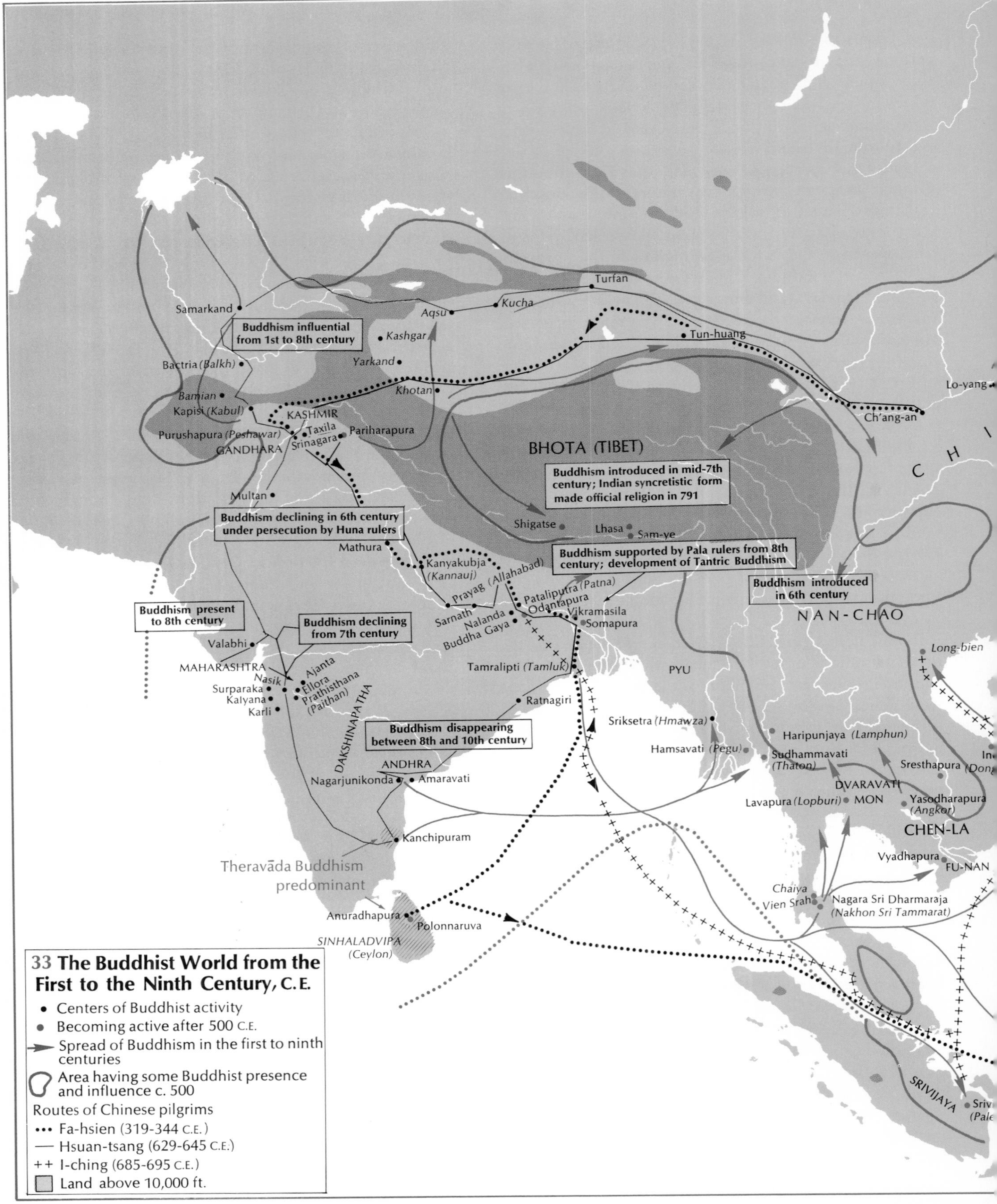
Turfan
Samarkand
Aqsu
Kucha
Buddhism influential from 1st to 8th century
Kashgar
Tun-huang
Bactria (Balkh)
Yarkand
Bamian
Khotan
Lo-yang
Kapisi (Kabul)
KASHMIR
Ch'ang-an
Purushapura (Peshawar)
Taxila
Pariharapura
GANDHARA
Srinagara
BHOTA (TIBET)
C H I
Buddhism introduced in mid-7th century; Indian syncretistic form made official religion in 791
Multan
Buddhism declining in 6th century under persecution by Huna rulers
Shigatse
Lhasa
Sam-ye
Mathura
Buddhism supported by Pala rulers from 8th century; development of Tantric Buddhism
Kanyakubja (Kannauj)
Prayag (Allahabad)
Buddhism introduced in 6th century
Pataliputra (Patna)
Odantapura
Buddhism present to 8th century
Sarnath
Nalanda
Vikramasila
NAN-CHAO
Buddhism declining from 7th century
Buddha Gaya
Somapura
Valabhi
Long-bien
MAHARASHTRA
Tamralipti (Tamluk)
PYU
Nasik
Ajanta
Ellora
Prathisthana (Paithan)
Surparaka
Kalyana
Karli
DAKSHINAPATHA
Ratnagiri
Sriksetra (Hmawza)
Haripunjaya (Lamphun)
Buddhism disappearing between 8th and 10th century
Hamsavati (Pegu)
Sudhammavati (Thaton)
Sresthapura (Dong...)
ANDHRA
DVARAVATI
Nagarjunikonda
Amaravati
Lavapura (Lopburi)
MON
Yasodharapura (Angkor)
CHEN-LA
Kanchipuram
Vyadhapura
Theravāda Buddhism predominant
FU-NAN
Chaiya
Vien Srah
Nagara Sri Dharmaraja (Nakhon Sri Tammarat)
Anuradhapura
Polonnaruva
SINHALADVIPA (Ceylon)
SRIVIJAYA
33 The Buddhist World from the First to the Ninth Century, C.E.
Centers of Buddhist activity
Becoming active after 500 C.E.
Spread of Buddhism in the first to ninth centuries
Area having some Buddhist presence and influence c. 500
Routes of Chinese pilgrims
••• Fa-hsien (319-344 C.E.)
— Hsuan-tsang (629-645 C.E.)
++ I-ching (685-695 C.E.)
Land above 10,000 ft.

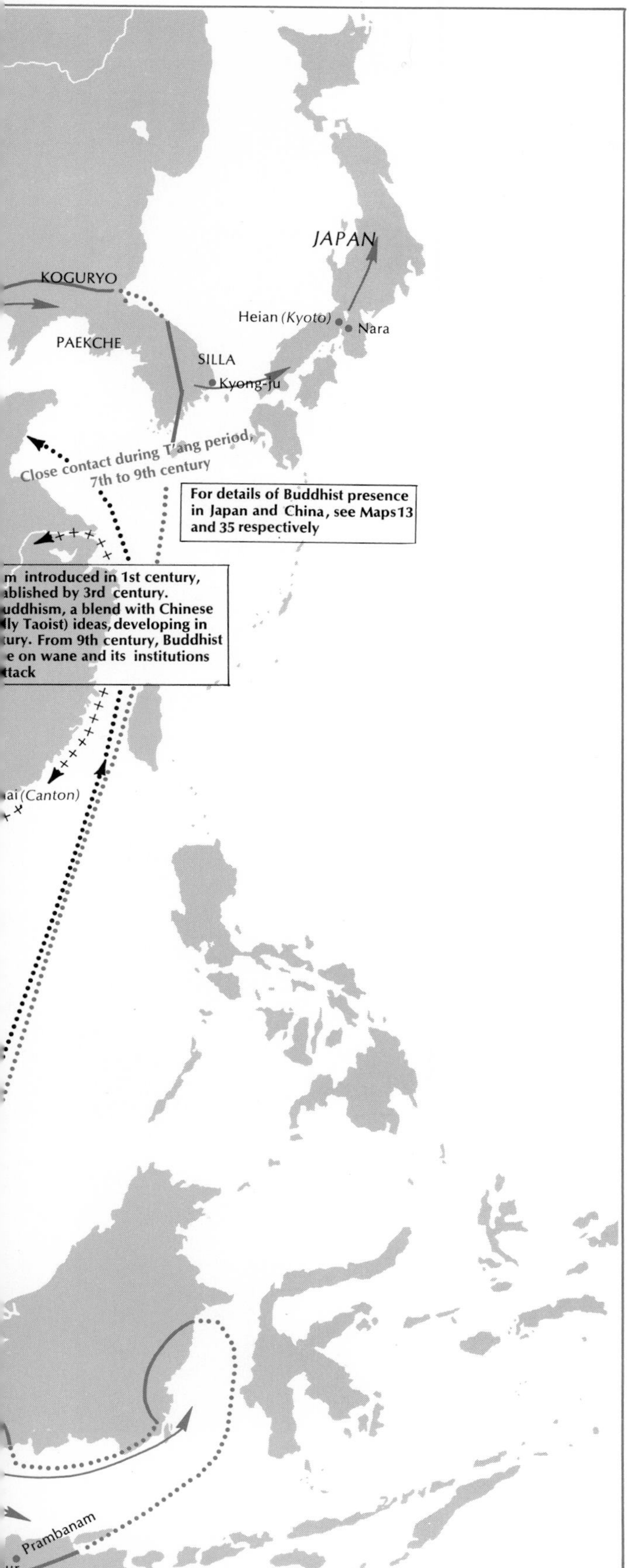

16-9 Bodhisattva from Polonnaruva, Ceylon. (Courtesy of the Archeological Department, Government of Ceylon.)

complete disappearance from the land of its birth. This state of affairs continued for several centuries.

Toward the end of the ninteenth century interest in Buddhism revived in India, partly as a result of the labors of Western scholars, who had begun to publish Buddhist texts and their translations and works of historical value for the benefit of their countrymen. Indian scholars were thereby inspired to make researches into their own culture, in which Buddhism had played so significant a part. Meanwhile, a movement was spearheaded by a Buddhist revivalist, the Anagārika Dharmapāla of Ceylon, to propagate Buddhism once more in the land of its birth, to restore Buddhist monuments that had fallen into ruin, and to get back for the Buddhists of the world their most hallowed shrine at Buddhagaya, the place of the Buddha's Enlightenment (Map 10). This holy place was occupied by Śaivite Hindus

16-10 The Buddhist Mahābodhi temple in Buddha Gaya, India, was built between 620 and 630 C.E. on the site of the original temple (erected by Aśoka) around Vajrāsana, the throne of the Buddha's Enlightenment. Story upon story of niches framing Buddha images form the decoration of the walls. (Courtesy of UNESCO/Cart.)

who, in an earlier generation, had desecrated the images of the Buddha. For this purpose Dharmapāla started the Mahā Bodhi Society and undauntedly carried on a vigorous campaign that won ultimate success.

After India obtained independence in 1948, there was a keen desire on the part of enlightened Indian leaders, chief of whom was India's first prime minister Jawaharlal Nehru, to do honor to India's greatest son, the Buddha. This awareness was evidenced when Buddhist symbols were enshrined in India's national flag and her state insignia. The Indian government started restoring many of the most sacred Buddhist monuments. In addition, members of the so-called "depressed" classes, who had suffered great disabilities from orthodox Hinduism, found in Buddhism a source of regeneration and under their leader, Ambedkar, embraced Buddhism in large numbers, so that there are now many millions of Buddhists in India (Map 11).

In Other Lands

CEYLON. Long before Buddhism declined and disappeared in India, it had spread out from the land of its birth and became a vital faith in many neighboring countries. The most notable was Ceylon, whose conversion in the third century B.C.E. by a mission sent by Aśoka has already been mentioned. Tissa, king of Ceylon at the time, erected various religious structures in his capital at Anurādhapura, including the Mahā Vihāra, where a branch of the Bodhi Tree from Gayā was planted. One of his successors, Duṭṭhagāminī, built the colossal Ruanveli Dāgoba, enshrining a large quantity of Buddha relics. Another, Vaṭṭagāmani Abhaya, built the Abhayagiri Vihāra, which later became the home of schismatic monks who preached a heresy known as the Vaitulyāvada. The Mahā Vihāra attained fame as a sect of learning to which scholars came from many lands, including the great commentator Buddhaghosa. It was in Ceylon that the Pāli *Tipiṭaka* was first committed to writing. In the ninth century the capital was moved to Polonnaruva and many religious structures were erected there, including colossal statues of the Buddha. King Parakkambāhu of the twelfth century brought about unity between the various groups of Buddhist monks. Ceylon was also the scene of great literary activity, and scholars from there were often invited to lands nearby.

In the sixteenth century, the capital again moved to Kandy because of foreign invasions, and there the most sacred sanctuary is the Daḷadā Maligāva, Temple of the Tooth. It contains a tooth relic of the Buddha brought to Ceylon in the fourth century.

There were several occasions in Ceylon's history when monks had to be invited from Burma and Thailand to restore the higher ordination of *bhikkhus.* In the recent past this has been the cause of divisions into so-called *nikāyas,* the largest being the Siyam Nikāya, which traces its higher ordination to monks from Siam.

The whole culture of Ceylon is deeply influenced by Buddhism, and in spite of many vicissitutes it is still the religion of the vast majority of the people. Having been dormant for nearly five centuries, Buddhism is now passing through a period of vigorous revival. There are several sects (*nikāyas*) among the monks. Their differences are not doctrinal but pertain to observances of the *Vinaya* or Discipline. In 1950, the Daḷadā Maligāva was the scene of the World Fellowship of Buddhists, which was the first attempt to bring together the Buddhists of all countries in the world. Twenty-nine countries sent delegates.

BURMA. Buddhism was first introduced into Burma probably in the fifth century C.E., though legends say that a mission was sent earlier by Aśoka. There is evidence that Theravada flourished in Burma in the fifth century C.E. in the kingdom of Sriksetra, with its capital near Prome. It was brought there by Indian missionaries from the eastern and the southern coasts of India. Theravada flourished also among the Mons and Talaings settled there and Hamsavati (Pegu) and Sudhammavati (Thaton) became important centers of religion before the eleventh century (Map 34). Earlier, the Mrammas had a powerful kingdom with Pagan as capital and gave their name (Mrammadesa) to the whole country. In 1044 Anawrahta (Aniruddha) became their king and embraced Theravada under Shin Arahan. He sent messengers to Manuha, king of Thaton, asking for a copy of the *Tipiṭaka* that had been brought earlier from Ceylon. When this was refused, he marched into Thaton, captured the king, and brought back to Pagan not only thirty sets of the *Tipiṭaka* but also all the monks and the relics found in Thaton. The whole country thereafter embraced Buddhism. Aniruddha erected numerous religious edifices and obtained from Ceylon, too, copies of the *Tipiṭaka.* Pagan remained a great center of Buddhism till it was destroyed by the Chinese army in 1287. The ruins of some five thousand dagobas and monasteries still can be seen there.

Burmese monks had been in the habit of visiting Ceylon as pilgrims and some of them also studied there. One such was called Chapaṭa, after the name of his village. He went to Ceylon and after completing his studies returned to Burma in 1180, accompanied by four Ceylonese monks. Together they established a new or-

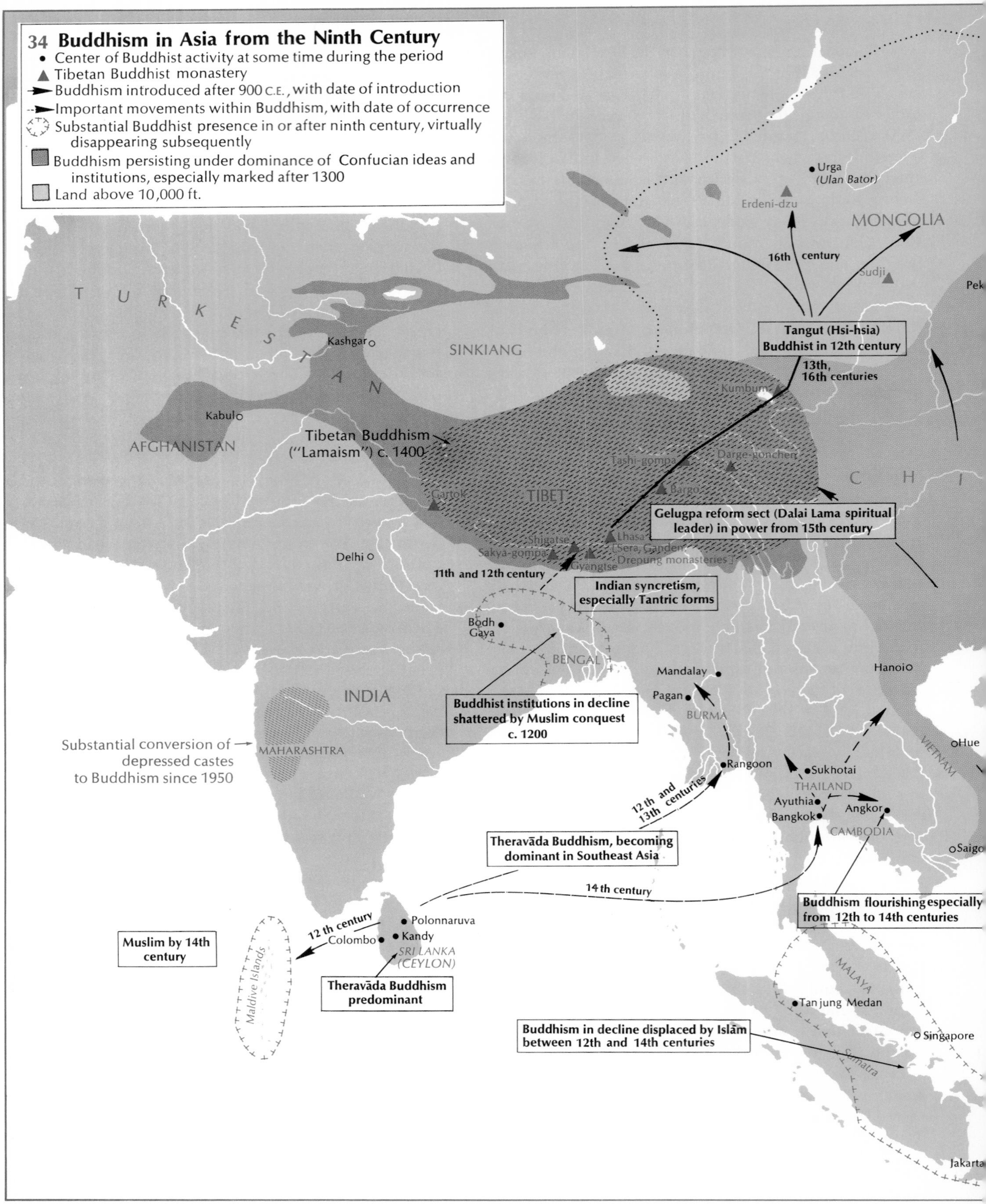

34 Buddhism in Asia from the Ninth Century
Center of Buddhist activity at some time during the period
Tibetan Buddhist monastery
Buddhism introduced after 900 C.E., with date of introduction
Important movements within Buddhism, with date of occurrence
Substantial Buddhist presence in or after ninth century, virtually disappearing subsequently
Buddhism persisting under dominance of Confucian ideas and institutions, especially marked after 1300
Land above 10,000 ft.
Urga (Ulan Bator)
Erdeni-dzu
MONGOLIA
16th century
Sudji
Pek
TURKESTAN
Kashgar
SINKIANG
Tangut (Hsi-hsia) Buddhist in 12th century
13th, 16th centuries
Kumbum
Kabul
AFGHANISTAN
Tibetan Buddhism ("Lamaism") c. 1400
Tashi-gompa
Darge-gonchen
Bargo
Gartok
TIBET
CHI
Gelugpa reform sect (Dalai Lama spiritual leader) in power from 15th century
Delhi
Shigatse
Lhasa
Sakya-gompa
[Sera, Ganden, Drepung monasteries]
Gyangtse
11th and 12th century
Indian syncretism, especially Tantric forms
Bodh Gaya
BENGAL
Mandalay
Hanoi
Pagan
INDIA
Buddhist institutions in decline shattered by Muslim conquest c. 1200
BURMA
Substantial conversion of depressed castes to Buddhism since 1950
MAHARASHTRA
VIETNAM
Hue
Rangoon
Sukhotai
THAILAND
12th and 13th centuries
Ayuthia
Bangkok
Angkor
CAMBODIA
Theravāda Buddhism, becoming dominant in Southeast Asia
Saigo
14th century
Buddhism flourishing especially from 12th to 14th centuries
12th century
Polonnaruva
Colombo
Kandy
SRI LANKA (CEYLON)
Muslim by 14th century
Maldive Islands
Theravāda Buddhism predominant
MALAYA
Tanjung Medan
Buddhism in decline displaced by Islām between 12th and 14th centuries
Singapore
Sumatra
Jakarta

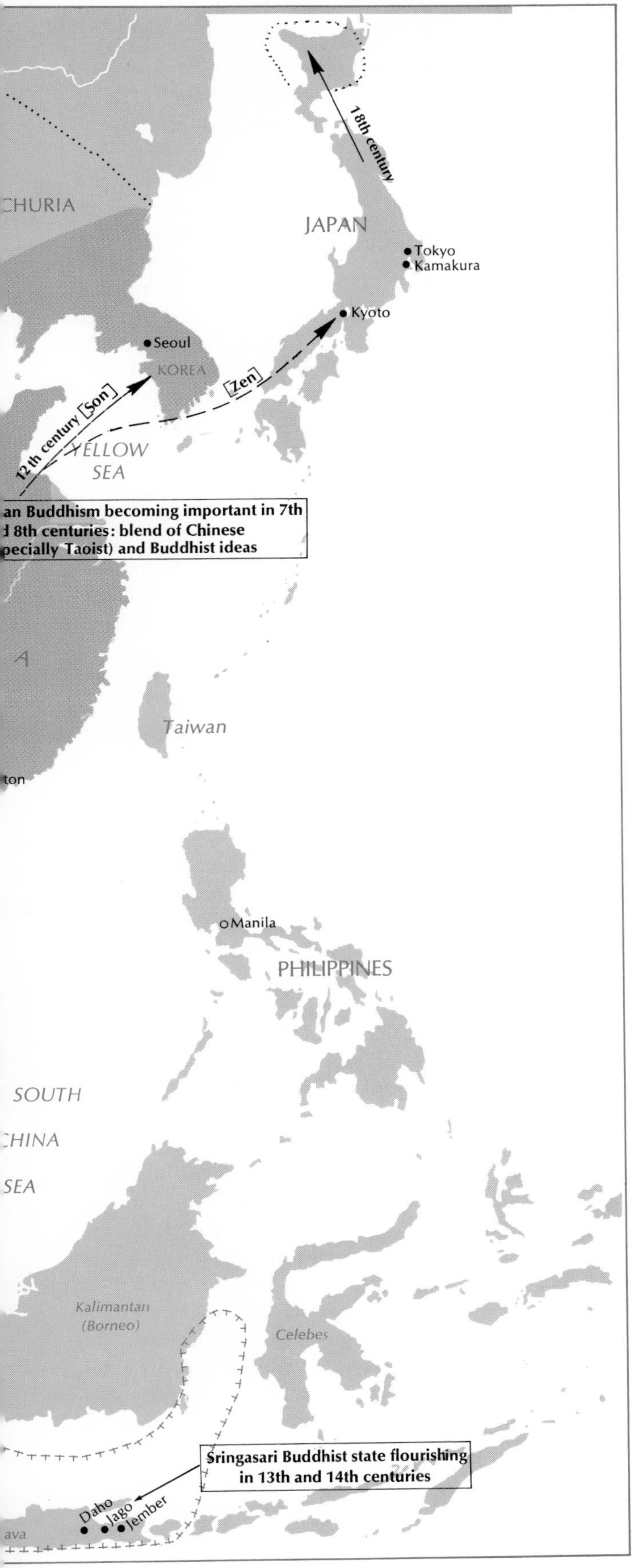

ganization of monks that came to be called the Sinhala Sangha. Burmese scholars produced a large number of literary works, chiefly commentaries on the *Abhidhamma* and works on Pāli grammar. When Pagan fell, Pegu became the capital and continued as the capital of the Mon kingdom till it was destroyed in 1535. King Dhammcati, who ruled there from 1472 to 1492, took great interest in promoting Buddhism and sent to Ceylon a number of Burmese monks who were given ordination in Kalyānī (near modern Colombo). When they returned, the king erected for them a *sīmā* ("consecrated hall") near Pegu, which was called the Kalyānī *sīmā*, and thereafter Burmese monks were ordained there. A long marble inscription gives details of this episode.

Near Pegu was a small fishing village called Dagon. It was so called from the Shwedagon Pagoda, which stood there, believed to contain the hair relics of the Buddha, brought by two merchants, Tapassu and Bhalluka. It thus became an important center of pilgrimage and was made into a town by successive Burmese kings. It was named Rangoon in 1755 and became the capital of Lower Burma and later the capital of the whole of Burma. Several Buddhist councils were held in Burma, which have already been mentioned, the last being in 1954–1956.

THAILAND. Evidence has been found that Buddhism was introduced into Thailand in the early centuries of the Christian era. After about the eighth or ninth century, both Thailand (Siam) and Laos formed part of Kambuja (Cambodia) and came under the influence of the Khmers, both politically and culturally. In all these regions Hinduism and Buddhism existed side by side.

In the middle of the thirteenth century, the Thais conquered both Siam and Laos and freed themselves from their Cambodian rulers. Under Thai kings, Buddhism and the Pāli language flourished everywhere in Siam and Laos. The Thai king, Sri Sūryavamsa Rāma, was not only a great patron of Buddhism but for some time a Buddhist monk. About 1361 he sent learned monks to Ceylon and invited an eminent prelate from that country to visit Siam. He propagated Buddhism and Pāli throughout the kingdom, including the territory now called Laos. From this period, Siam became a predominantly Buddhist country and Brahmanism gradually declined.

The introduction of Ceylonese Buddhism produced a body of Buddhist literature in Pāli of which the *Chāmadevi-vamsa* and the *Jinakālamālinī* are outstanding examples. Another Thai king, Rāma Khardeng (ca. 1275–1317), who ruled over central and southern Siam, had his capital in Sukhotai. Most of the monuments of

Sukhotai, like those of Mahā Tat and Sri Chum, are now in ruins but contain evidence of their ancient splendor. The style of architecture and sculpture developed at Sukhotai represents the ideal of Siamese art. Ceylonese monks had great influence in Sukhotai, especially those who came from the forest dwelling fraternity (*araññaka*).

After Sukhotai, the capital was Ayuthia. It was during this period that the great Wat Cūlāmaṇi ("temple") was built at Pisnulok and a shrine constructed for the footprints of the Buddha at Saraburi. Buddhist literature received a new stimulus. The ties with Ceylon became closer when the king of Ceylon, Kittisiri, sent three missions to Ayuthia, around 1750, to ordain Sinhalese monks there. Ayuthia was destroyed during the Burmese invasion of 1767, and a new dynasty, called the Chakri dynasty, established the new capital in Bangkok. It is the present ruling dynasty. Its first king, Rāma I, made a new and complete edition of the *Tipiṭaka* on palm leaves, now piously preserved in the royal palace. It was later printed. The king also issued several royal decrees to preserve the purity of the Sangha. His successors went further in associating Buddhism with the state, till Thailand became almost completely Buddhist. One of the most famous Buddha images, with which Thailand abounds, is the Pra Sihing, now in Bangkok, believed to have been originally brought from Ceylon. It is the holiest of all images in Thailand.

CAMBODIA. Present-day Cambodia is but a remnant of what was once a much larger kingdom, which included Cochin China, Laos, and southern Siam and which was formerly known as Funan. In about 540 C.E. the power of Funan was destroyed and the kingdom was occupied by the Khmers. In about 802, Angkor (from Sanskrit *Nagare*, "city") became the capital and from then on till the end of the thirteenth century was the classic period of Cambodian art, devoted both to Hinduism and to Buddhism. In the center of Angkor is the enormous Bayon temple, which probably originated as a Buddhist structure, with its seventy-two great sculptured human forms, thought to represent the *bodhisatva* Lokeśvara or Avalokiteśvara.

Archaeological finds indicate that from about the end of the fifth century C.E. Buddhism flourished in Cambodia, though it did not occupy its present position till later. The great emperor Yasovarman of the ninth century established a monastery for Buddhist monks. Jayavarman II (1181–ca. 1220) was a devout Buddhist and the records of his reign express beautifully the Buddhist view of life that prevailed in the country. He founded many magnificent religious institutions. The coming of Cambodia under the Thais in the thirteenth century completed its conversion to Buddhism. Even the Brahmanical gods in Angkor Vat were replaced by Buddhist images. Today there is hardly any trace of Brahmanical religion in the country except in some ceremonies.

LAOS, EUROPE, AND FURTHER. From Siam, the Thais spread to Laos. Several years after the fall of Ayuthiya, the capital, several small states united under the leadership of Fa Ngum and formed a kingdom. This "hero of Laos," was the son-in-law of Jayavarman Parameshvara of Cambodia and became a Buddhist through Jayavarman's influence. He established a Ceylonese Buddhist shrine in Luang Prabang and established Theravāda as the state religion, which it remains to the present day. A considerable Buddhist literature grew up in Laos of which the *Pannāsa Jātaka* (a collection of fifty *jātaka* tales in Pāli) is a classic example. There are many old monasteries and temples in Laos of the Ceylonese Theravāda school.

In Burma, Thailand, Cambodia, and Laos, Buddhism is now the state religion but not so in Ceylon. In Cambodia and Laos practically the whole population is Buddhist. In the first four countries, it is customary for all males to live the life of *bhikkhus*, at least during one rainy season (*vassa*), i.e., three months.

In course of time, Buddhism spread throughout Asia, but since it was the Mahāyāna that found its way into countries like China, Japan, Tibet and Korea, no mention is made of them in this chapter.

From about the ninteenth century, there has been an interest in Buddhism in the West, particularly in Europe. It was the Theosophists who, more than anyone else, first kindled this interest, though men like Schopenhauer had written about Buddhism even earlier. After 1900, a few Buddhist missionaries established missionary organizations in London, Paris, and Berlin, and later in Washington. These organizations are chiefly concerned with the Theravāda, though more recently much interest has been shown in the study of Zen Buddhism. The study of Theravāda was greatly stimulated by the work of the Pāli Text Society, which has published Pāli texts and their English translation. Many books on Buddhist topics in several European languages have also appeared in print. European Buddhists have appeared in the saffron robe of Theravāda monks from time to time, though they have been very few. There is reason to believe, however, that a Theravāda Sangha will come into being in Europe in the not-too-distant future.

There have been various conjectures about the total number of Buddhists in the world. No satisfactory statistics are available and figures have varied from 150 million to 500 million. It would be correct to say, however, that Buddhists are now to be found, in large or small groups, in most countries of the world except in

Africa, and their numbers keep on increasing (Maps 1 and 2).[1]

[1]Editor's Note: Theravāda Buddhism is a religion founded on the personal experience and teaching of Gautama, the Buddha. It has managed to preserve and adhere to these teachings as handed down by the traditions. The classical interpretation of that teaching is regarded as the flowering of its own genius. As we have just seen in the foregoing chapter, such flowering has taken place in the third century B.C.E. and has ever since remained the norm and standard of Theravāda worship, piety, and moral felicity. Obviously, to the Theravāda Buddhist the categories of "Decay" and "Reform" are inapplicable to his tradition. In his view, the Theravāda calls for no more than the emulation of the Buddha in accordance with the earliest record or flowering of his teaching. Conceivably, the categories of Decay and Reform can indeed apply to those Theravāda adherents—wherever there are such—who deviate in their daily worship and practice from the original teaching. But there is no movement in the Theravāda as yet that warrants either the name of "Decay" or that of "Reform."

However, should these categories be forced on the Theravāda Buddhist, and if, *per impossibile,* he is unfavorably disposed toward the Mahāyāna, it is likely that he would call its tradition an innovative departure from the pure teachings of the Buddha. In this case, he would permit himself to include the whole Mahāyāna tradition under the category of "Decay." "Reform" would then consist of all thoughts of and attempts—wherever such are in evidence—at purging the existent situation of the Mahāyāna from such innovations and re-establishing the faith in its original pristine purity.

Conversely, to the Mahāyāna Buddhist unfavorably disposed toward the Theravāda, the latter's long period of little or no change constitutes a kind of dormancy, if not "Decay," a state of ossification or insensitivity to the religious needs of the masses. In this view, the Mahāyāna is a flowering of Buddhism continuous with the classical flowering of the Pāli texts, and its late flowering is a "Reform" of both Theravāda and Mahāyāna "Decay."

This age, however, is one of ecumenism and interreligious understanding. Members and leaders of the great Buddha fellowship seek to develop amity as well as religious unity. Their inclination is to regard themselves all as followers of the Buddha—which they all truly are—and thus to see the Mahāyāna as another "flowering" of the Buddha's teaching on a par with the Theravāda "flowering." Under the new spirit, by "Decay" one can only mean the contemporary decline at the hands of scientism, secularism, and Communism since 1930, and by "Reform" whatever movements are currently germinating to counter the decay that has set in since 1930.

Bibliography

Anesaki, Masa haru. *Buddhist Art.* Boston: Houghton Mifflin, 1915.

Bode, M. H. *The Pali Literature of Burma.* London: Royal Asiatic Society, 1909.

Conze, E. *Buddhism, Its Essence and Development.* Oxford: Bruno Cassirer, 1960 [first pub. 1951].

——— et al. *Buddhist Texts Through the Ages.* Oxford: Bruno Cassirer, 1954.

Eliot, C. *Hinduism and Buddhism,* 3 vols. New York: Barnes and Noble, 1954.

Francis, H. T., and E. J. Thomas. *Jataka Tales.* Cambridge, England: The University Press, 1916.

Kashyap, Bhikkhu J. *The Abidhamma Philosophy.* Nalanda: Buddha-Vihara, 1954.

Malalasekera, G. P. *The Pali Literature of Ceylon.* London: Royal Asiatic Society, 1928.

Morgan, K. W. *The Path of the Buddha: Buddhism Interpreted by Buddhists.* New York: Ronald, 1956.

Murti, T. R. V. *The Central Philosophy of Buddhism: A Study of the Madhyamika System.* London: Allen & Unwin, 1955.

Nyanaponika, Thera. *The Heart of Buddhist Meditation.* Colombo: The Word Buddha Publishing Committee, 1954.

Thomas, E. J. *The Life of Buddha as Legend and History.* New York: Barnes & Noble, 1952.

———. *The History of Buddhist Thought.* New York: Barnes & Noble, 1959 [first pub. 1951].

Warren, H. C. *Buddhism in Translations.* Cambridge, Mass.: Harvard U. P., 1906.

17

Mahāyāna Buddhism (China)

C. Wei-hsun Fu

The importation of Indian Buddhism to China about two thousand years ago constitutes one of the most important chapters in the history of Chinese thought. In spite of its ideological confrontation with the indigenous traditions, especially Confucianism, Buddhism has not only contributed, after a long and hard course of assimilation and transformation, to the enrichment of Chinese philosophy and religion but has also established itself through the ingenious works of the Chinese Buddhists as a major system of Chinese thought and religious practice. Although China is not a Buddhist country in the proper sense of those words, Buddhism has at least achieved a status of virtual equality with Confucianism and Taoism as one of the Three Teachings (*san chiao*) in China. The Buddhist influence on Chinese culture is indeed far-reaching and many-sided, notably in the fields of philosophy, art, *belles lettres*, and popular religion. For instance, Neo-Confucian thought would not have developed without the challenge and stimulation of Buddhism with respect to metaphysical thinking, purification of the mind, meditative practice, and so on. Further, the early interaction of Buddhism with Taoist philosophy also paved a path toward the metaphysical synthesis of these two traditions, as well as toward a remarkable development of Chinese Mādhyamika, which extended Nāgārjuna's *śūnyavāda* ("doctrine of emptiness") to a new philosophic dimension. And, as far as the history of Mahāyāna Buddhism is concerned, it is unthinkable that this great philosophical religion would have reached its own culmination without the contributions made by the Chinese Buddhists. In fact, the unfinished task of Mahāyāna philosophy in India was accomplished by the Chinese Buddhists, resulting in, for example, the totalistic philosophy of the Hua-yen school, the Lotus phenomenology of the T'ien-t'ai school, and Ch'an (Zen) Buddhism, all these being typically characteristic of Chinese religious spirit. As to the Buddhist influence on popular religion, Pure Land Buddhism has, along with Taoist religion, always captured the religious hearts of common people who find no consolation for their souls in either rationalistic Confucianism or naturalistic Taoist philosophy. It was indeed due to the Buddhist introduction of such ideas as samsaric world-systems, karmic retribution, the Pure Land and the Hell, and so on to the earth-bound Chinese that they became more awakened to the religious meaning of the supernatural.

The Early Years of Buddhism in China

The exact date of the introduction of Buddhism in China is still a matter of conjecture among scholars on

17-1 Head of Buddha, North Wei Dynasty, c. 525. (Courtesy of the Philadelphia Museum of Art, photograph by A. J. Wyatt, staff photographer.)

Chinese Buddhism. It is quite probable that the Chinese became acquainted with this foreign religion as a result of their occupation of Turkestan toward the end of the second century B.C.E. We lack, however, a historical document about the coming of Buddhism before the history of the Northern Wei dynasty (386–534 C.E.). There has been an interesting story widely circulated among the Chinese Buddhists as the orthodox version of the beginning of Buddhism in China. It was said that Emperor Ming (reigned 58–75 C.E.) of the Later Han once dreamed of a golden statue of a man flying into the hall of the imperial palace. He was told by one of his ministers that this must be the foreign god named Buddha. Thereupon he sent an embassy to India in order to obtain the sacred texts. After several years the envoys returned to Loyang, then the Han capital, with two Indian masters, Kāśyapa Mātaṅga and Dharmaratna. They brought on a white horse many Buddhist works, and this was said to have occasioned the founding of the *Pai ma ssu* (White Horse Temple) in Loyang, the first Buddhist temple in China. But this may be no more than a pious legend invented by the Buddhists, for there exists no conclusive evidence showing that the *Pai ma ssu* did exist before 289 C.E. On the other hand, quite a number of scholars hold that as early as 2 B.C.E. a Chinese official received an oral transmission of the Buddha's teaching from a Scythian envoy, and they regard this as the earliest record of Buddhism in China. It seems safe to say at least that by the first century C.E. Buddhism had already stepped onto Chinese soil and that from about the middle of the second century onward, small Buddhist communities existed in the larger trading centers of north China (Map 35).

When Buddhism appeared in China, it was first mixed up with popular religious beliefs and practices of native origin. In order to make some headway among the Chinese at the time of the Confucian ascendancy, Indian Buddhism consorted with the growing religious Taoism, as this shared with (popular) Buddhism some superficial similarities in regard to sacrificial worship, meditative practice, respiratory exercises, rebirth or immortal life, and so on. This alliance with a native religion enabled Buddhism to avoid the Chinese prejudice against accepting the foreign tradition. An interesting apologetic writing entitled *Li huo lun* (the Disposition of Error), the authorship of which is attributed to Mou Jung, gives us a good example of how the Buddhists tried hard to avoid an ideological confrontation with the Confucian tradition, which dominated the religious life of the Chinese people during this period. In this apologia the author claimed that one could be both a good Chinese and a good Buddhist at the same time because there was no real conflict between the two ways of life and thinking. He manipulated both Buddhist and Confucian doctrines to remove obstacles confronting the early Chinese Buddhist church, such as the Confucian aversion to the shaving of the head and clerical celibacy, as well as the Confucian denial of samsaric world-systems and the nirvanic deliverance of all sentient beings.

But Mou's incoherent and confusing interpretations exposed clearly the early Chinese Buddhists' superficial understanding of Indian Buddhism without being able to delve into its philosophical depth. One important factor accounting for their lack of understanding is that there were then very few translated works available of Buddhist sutras, and therefore they simply had no access to the genuine ideas of Indian Buddhism.

From 148 C.E. onward, a number of foreign missionaries—Parthians, Kushans, and Sogdians, as well as a few Indian masters—came to China and engaged themselves with the Chinese followers in an immense translation activity. Because these missionaries had no sufficient command of Chinese, and very few Chinese Buddhists could understand Sanskrit or Pali, the difficulty was solved by the forming of a translation team, which consisted of the foreign master, a bilingual intermediary, and Chinese assistants, for such a cooperative enterprise. In this early effort of transmitting Buddhist ideas, there was always a heavy reliance upon the terms and concepts of indigenous traditions, particularly Taoist philosophy because of its startling resemblances to Buddhism in metaphysical thinking and way of life. In oral discourse, written translation, and exegesis, the Buddhists often used a device called *Ko-yi* ("matching concepts"), by means of which they tried to match a grouping of Buddhist ideas with a plausibly analogous grouping of indigenous ideas, e.g., the Buddhist *tathatā* (Thusness) with the Taoist *pên-wu* ("original nonbeing"), *śīla* ("morality") with the Confucian *hsiao-shun* ("filial obedience"), or *nirvāṇa* with the Taoist *wu-wei* ("nonaction"). Through such group undertakings the volume of translated works sharply increased. By the end of the

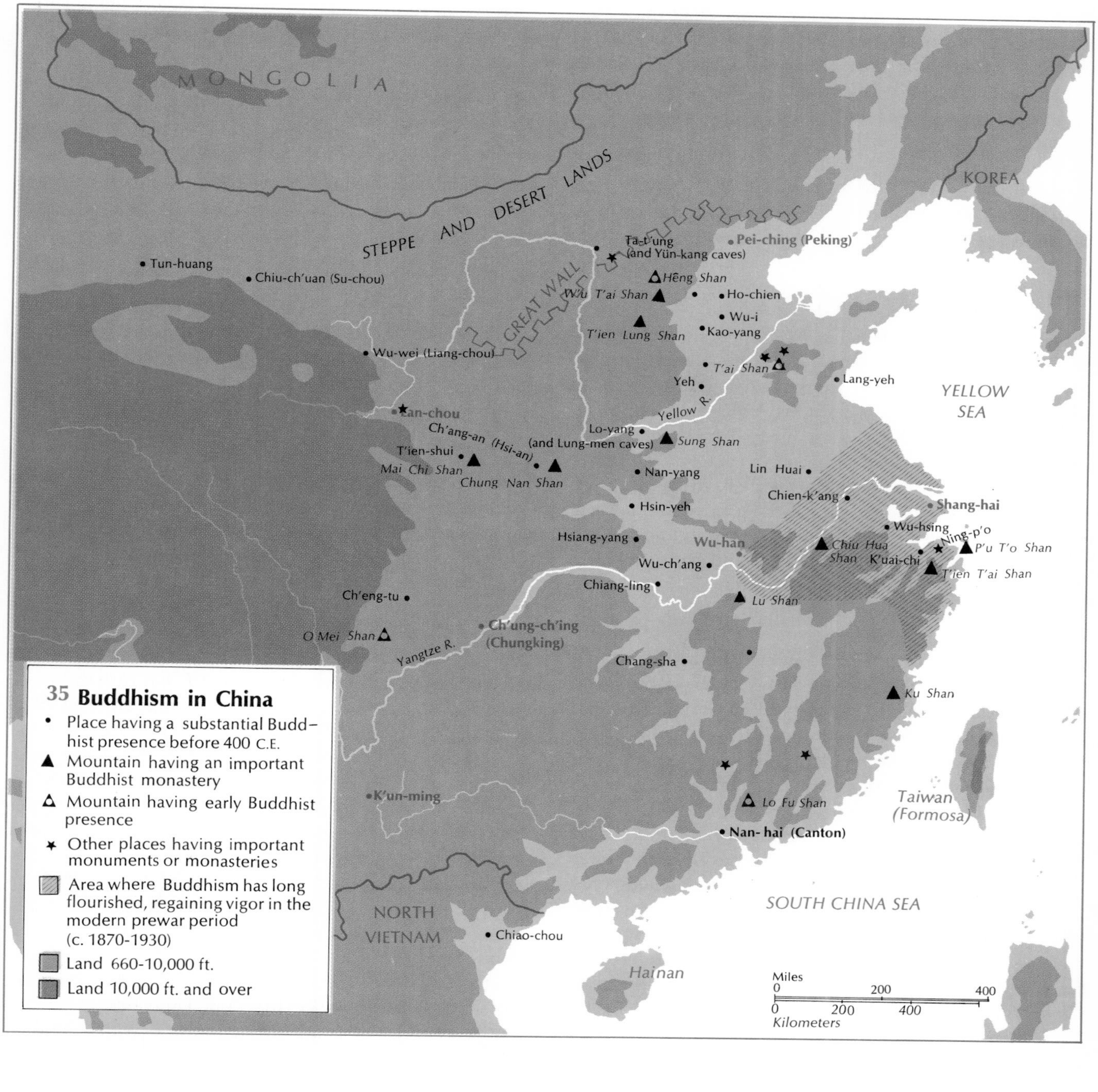

35 Buddhism in China

third century a good variety of both Hīnayāna and Mahāyāna sutras had been rendered into Chinese, including the *Prajñāpāramitā sūtras* (the wisdom literature), the Pure Land texts (the devotion literature), and the *vinayas* describing monastic rules and rules for the laity. The enormous increase and circulation of translated works during the period reflects an obvious fact that Buddhism had become more and more familiar and acceptable to the Chinese populace. According to the report made in the *Pien-chêng-lun* (the Clarification of Correct View), by about the year 300 Buddhist establishments in the two northern capitals of Loyang and Ch'angan alone numbered 180 and their clergy some 3,700. And there is ample evidence also that the Chinese began to undertake a Sinicization of Buddhist art by transforming the style of Indian stupas into that of Chinese pagodas, as well as by initiating the Chinese-styled sculptures and paintings of the buddhas and bodhisattvas.

From the downfall of the Later Han (220 C.E.) to the reunification of China under the first emperor of Sui (581), China was a country of political disunity and social instability. During the years 307–316, China suffered a mass invasion of the Huns, the Hsienpi, and other nomadic races that drove the indigenous population, the civilized Chinese, toward the south. Afterwards, north China, which comprised roughly the basin of the Yellow River, was occupied by the non-Chinese rulers, and south China was governed by a succession of weak and short-lived Chinese dynasties. The intellectual and religious climate during these three centuries provided a great opportunity for the growth and spread of Buddhism. First, the Confucian tradition had lost its supremacy after the fall of the Han and had gradually declined. The non-Chinese rulers in the north had little knowledge of and found no interest at all in the Confucian classics and ideas, whereas the southern Chinese embraced no more hope in Confucianism as a workable state ideology. Further, disgusted with the politicosocial turmoil, many intellectuals as well as ordinary people shifted their attention to something beyond mundane affairs for the solace of their troubled minds. Buddhism naturally seized upon this chance for its own advantage.

In south China Buddhism was closely associated with the Neo-Taoist movement, and both learned monks and Taoist philosophers were mutually engaged in metaphysical speculation and literary activities. The outcome was the flowering of Chinese Mādhyamika as well as the beginning of two philosophical schools, the Hua-yen and the T'ien-t'ai. Even after the Neo-Taoist movement faded away, the Buddhists still dominated the arena of Chinese philosophy and religion until the middle of the T'ang dynasty. The first important monk who contributed to the spread of Buddhism was Hui-yüan (334–416), whose early training was in Confucian classics and then in Taoist texts, but he finally converted to Buddhism and molded Taoist philosophy into the Buddhist system. He was also noted for his successful defense of the Buddhist clergy against the threat of government control or suppression. Another famous monk was Chih-tun (314–366), who was also versed in Neo-Taoism and related it to Buddhist doctrines. Meanwhile, he was credited with the introduction of a Mahāyāna idea into the old Chinese naturalistic notion of *Li* ("principle" or "reason"), so that the term came to mean "the absolute metaphysical principle" and reappeared in Neo-Confucian thought as the most important notion. The third monk worth noting was Chu Tao-shêng (365–434), whose writings made explicit the polarity of subitism (*tun*, or sudden awakening) and gradualism (*chien*) in Buddhism. This polarization became centuries later a matter of controversy between two competing schools of Ch'an and also served to characterize the two opposing wings of Neo-Confucianism. Among the southern rulers best known in promoting Buddhism was Emperor Wu of the Liang (ruled 502–549). In 517 he issued a decree that the temples of the Taoist religion, the strong rival of Buddhism, be destroyed and that the Taoist adepts return to the laity. He therefore won the Buddhist honorific *P'u-sa T'ien-tzu* (Bodhisattva Son of Heaven).

The outlook of Buddhism in the north was rather different. First, whereas the monastic community in south China generally enjoyed its independent status and claimed immunity against secular authority, it was in the north often controlled by the state and served as an instrument for state policy. Second, most eminent monks in the north were advisers to the rulers in political and military affairs. The Kuchan missionary Fo-t'u-têng succeeded in winning the favor of the northern rulers by his demonstration of magical power and prognostication, thus making Buddhist participation in state affairs still easier and more welcome. Because the north was more open to foreign missionaries arriving from central Asia, a great number of them came in after Fo-t'u-têng and established a center of translation with royal support. The famous Kumārajīva (334–413) arrived at Ch'angan in 401 and carried out his prodigious activities of translation with the assistance of a thousand monks. Many important Mahāyāna sutras and sastras (philosophical discourses) were beautifully rendered by him into Chinese, such as Nāgārjuna's *Mūla-madhyamaka Kārikās*, the *Vimalakīrtinirdeśa*, the *Saddharmapuṇḍarīka-sūtra* (the Lotus Scripture of Wonderful Law), the *Vajracchedikā-prajñāpāramitā-sūtra* (the Diamond Sutra), and the *Sukhāvatī-vyūha* (the Pure Land Scripture). All of these still stand as the orthodox works widely studied and recited by Sino-Japanese Buddhists today. Among those Chinese Buddhists participating in the immense work of translation, Tao-an (312–385), whose mentor was Fo-t'u-têng, was especially noted for a mature theory of translation he developed in order to remove any possible distortion of Buddhist ideas entangled in Neo-Taoist terminology.

Whereas the Chinese Buddhists in the south emphasized wisdom (*prajñā*) and learning, the Buddhists in the north promoted the living faith of the devotees. And in many respects the Buddhist faith in this region cut across class lines and helped unite a divided society consisting of both Chinese and non-Chinese. But the growing strength of the Buddhist faith and its organization inevitably caused the rulers some misgivings. Finally in 446, Emperor T'ai-wu of the Northern Wei carried out the first large-scale persecution of Buddhism in China by ordering the total destruction of all the Buddhist temples and properties and the execution of all monks. The emperor later regretted his action but was soon assassinated by his own minister. His successor Emperor Wên-ch'êng atoned for his grandfather's ruthless treatment of Buddhism by building sumptuous temples and monasteries, supporting such artistic works of piety as the cave temples of Yün-kang and making gifts of treasure and land to the Buddhist clergy. He also assigned T'an-yao to head the office of Chief of Monks and to carry out the gigantic project of creating the imposing array of caves and images of the buddhas and bodhisattvas out of the rocky walls at Yün-kang. The imperial court and the Buddhist community continued their joint efforts of rock sculpture at Lung-mên near Loyang during the years 495–530. Buddhist art reached its highest achievement in the grottoes of Yün-kang and Lung-mên.

During this period of disunity large numbers of Chinese Buddhists undertook the hazardous and long journey to India in order to visit the holy sites of Buddhism, study under renowned Indian masters, and above all, bring back the sacred scriptures to China. The most successful journey was made by Fa-hsien in 399–414, whose *Fo-kuo-chi* (Records of the Buddhist Country), along with *Ta-t'ang-hsi-yü-chi* (Records of the Western Journey in the Great T'ang Dynasty) written by another subsequent pilgrim Hsüan-tsang, became the most valuable documents concerning the religious situation of India at that time (Map 33).

After China was reunified under Emperor Wên of the Sui in 581, Buddhism was used as a state ideology to unite both the Chinese and the non-Chinese throughout the country. For this sake he took a symbolic action by enshrining the relics of the Buddha in various prefectural stupas; he also ordered that anyone who damaged or destroyed the Buddhist images be severely punished. His son Emperor Yang continued the Sui promotion of Buddhism and called himself a Buddhist disciple; he also strongly patronized two philosopher-monks Chih-yi (538–597), the founder of the T'ien-t'ai school, and Chi-tsang (549–623), the greatest systematizer of Chinese Mādhyamika.

17-2 Head of Buddha, possibly Sui (589–618) or early T'ang Dynasty (618–906). (Courtesy of the Philadelphia Museum of Art, photograph by A. J. Wyatt, staff photographer.)

The T'ang's overthrow of the Sui dynasty did not change the status of Buddhism but rather gave a greater opportunity for its development. Unlike the Han predecessors, the Sui and T'ang emperors relied heavily on an alien religion to augment the credenda and miranda of their power. Under the T'ang dynasty the development of Chinese Buddhism reached its apex and overshadowed both Confucian and Taoist traditions. Buddhism was the dominating vital force in the artistic and cultural life of the great T'ang capital Ch'angan. But most important of all, the philosophical doctrines of all (Mahāyāna) Buddhist sects were now developed into a complete system, resulting in the golden age of Mahāyāna Buddhism.

The Establishment of Sects or Schools

The division of Chinese Buddhism into discrete sects began in the fourth century. Based on the interpretation of Buddhist philosophy in Taoist and Neo-Taoist terms, "six houses and seven schools" were formed, including Tao-an's theory of original nonbeing, Fa-shên's theory of the originally nondifferentiated, and Chih Tao-lin's theory of matter-is-emptiness. These schools were led by individual thinkers and did not actually become contending denominations of religious practice. According to the traditional account, there existed in China ten major schools of Buddhism: three Hīnayāna schools (the Ch'êng-shih, the Chü-shê, and the Lü) and seven Mahāyāna schools. Hīnayāna Buddhism did not flourish because it did not suit the Chinese taste, whereas all Mahāyāna schools achieved crystallization during the Sui and T'ang dynasties.

The Chên-yen, which claimed to be the only esoteric school of Mahāyāna and used *mantras* (mystic words) and *maṇḍalas* (magical diagrams) for spiritual emancipation, exerted very little influence in China. The San-lun school is the Chinese representative of the Indian Mādhyamika school of Nāgārjuna and was introduced into China by Kumārajīva, who translated the three Indian works of the Middle Doctrine, two by Nāgārjuna and the third by his disciple Deva. These three treatises (*san lun*) were regarded as the basic texts in this school. The Middle Doctrine (Mādhyamika) of Nāgārjuna was elaborated by the early Chinese Buddhists and culminated in the systematic works of Chi-tsang. There are the three main aspects of his teaching: (1) the Middle Path of Nagarjunic Eightfold Negation, by means of which all one-sided perverse views are to be refuted; (2) the theory of "refutation of perverse views is itself revelation of the correct view," according to which the correct view maintained by the Mādhyamika is not a particular view in the positive sense but is no more than a thorough refutation of all perverse views so long as they exist; (3) the Middle Doctrine of twofold truth, according to which the distinction between transcendental truth (*paramārtha-satya*) and worldly truth (*saṁvṛti-satya*) is merely provisional and pedagogical (as skillful means) rather than real.

The above Chinese Mādyamika flourished in the period of disunity but declined after the rise of the Wei-shih (Vijñānavāda) or Fa-hsiang (Dharmalakṣaṇa) school, which corresponds to the Vijñānavāda or Yogācāra school of Indian Buddhism. Hsüan-tsang (596–664), the founder of this school, made a long journey to India in 629 for mastering the true teachings of (Mahāyāna) Buddhism. He returned, after seventeen years of pilgrimage, to Ch'angan and devoted the rest of his life to the monumental task of translating no less than seventy-five Buddhist texts, including Dharmapāla's *Vijñapti-mātra-tasiddhi* (Establishment of the Consciousness-Only System) and the *Mahāprajñāpāramitā-sūtra* (Great Scripture of Perfect Wisdom) in six hundred volumes. But the complete systematization of the idealistic doctrine was accomplished by his pupil K'uei-chi in the *Ch'êng-wei-shih-lun Shu-chi* (Philosophical Notes on Dharmapāla's *Vijñapti-mātra-tasiddhi*). This Mahāyāna idealism reduces all existence to one hundred *dharmas* ("factors of existence") in five divisions: Mind, Mental Functions, Form, Things Not Associated with Mind, and Noncreated Factors. But in the final analysis, everything is consciousness-only, which is divided into eight "parts." The external world is produced when *ālaya* ("store-consciousness"), which is in constant flux, is "perfumed" by "seeds" or effects of good and evil deeds. Once *ālaya* is purified completely, it will be transformed into the "perfect wisdom of the magnificent mirror" reflecting the ultimate reality *tathatā* (Thusness) or *Nirvāṇa*. This idealist school did not quite appeal to the practical mind of the Chinese and soon went into decline. It was once rejuvenated through the philosophical efforts of Ou-yang Ching-wu, Hsiung Shih-li, and others some fifty years ago but soon faded away.

From the philosophical point of view, the Hua-yen (Flower Garland) and the T'ien-t'ai (Lotus) are the most influential Mahāyāna schools in China. The name "Flower Garland" comes from the *Avataṁsaka-sūtra,* one of the most important Mahāyāna scriptures in India. But the school itself was first founded in China, nominally by Tu-shun (557–640) and systematically organized by Fa-tsang (643–712), the Great Master of Hsien-shou. Its main teaching consists in the "theory of the universal causation of the Realm of the Law," according to which all *dharmas* arise simultaneously and are in the state of Thusness. In its static aspect, Thusness is the Void (*śūnyatā*) or the noumenal realm of Principle (*Li*). In its dynamic aspect, it is the manifested or the phenomenal realm of Facts (*Shih*). It is due to the interrelatedness and interpenetration of these two realms of *Li* and *Shih* that the entire universe arises through reciprocal causation. Finally, this school emphasizes the entire universe of all Facts interwoven or identified in perfect harmony. This final reduction of the realm of *Li* to that of *Shih* reflects very strongly a Chinese transformation of the totalistic teaching of the *Avataṁsaka* scripture and had a deep influence on the basic ideas of two Ch'an schools Lin-chi and Ts'ao-tung, as well as on the formation of the Neo-Confucian metaphysics of *Li* and *Ch'i* ("material force").

The T'ien-t'ai school, which is distinctively of Chinese origin, may have been, philosophically speaking, more influential than the Hua-yen School. It uses the *Lotus Scripture of the Wonderful Law* as the basic text and is founded on the original interpretation given this text by Chih-yi (538–597), the Great Master of T'ien-t'ai (Heavenly Terrace), the mountain of Chê-chiang province where he taught Buddhist philosophy. In his work, *Mo-ho-chih-kuan* (Great Concentration and Insight), he expressed the view that the intellectual and contemplative approaches to Buddhism are but two wings of the same bird. This school, therefore, emphasizes both philosophical speculation and meditative practice. Chih-yi's main doctrine is that of the perfectly harmonious interpenetration of the three truths, namely (1) the emptiness or non-self-nature of all *dharmas* causally produced, (2) the provisional existence of all *dharmas,* and (3) the mean between emptiness and provisional existence of all *dharmas.* These three—emptiness, provisional existence, and the mean—are interwoven with one another: one is three and three is one. The Mean refers to the True State (*svalakṣaṇa*), Thusness, or the Absolute itself. Chih-yi further maintained that in every thought instant all the three thousand realms composing the world of provisional existence are immanently and simultaneously revealed. Hence his emphasis on concentration and insight embodied in such a thought instant. This philosophy of one-in-all and all-in-one is crystallized in the expression, "Every color or fragrance is none other than the Middle Path," a kind of totalistic view similar to that of the Hua-yen, and is reminiscent of Chuang Tzu's conception of "Tao is everywhere." Both schools teach that all sentient beings have the Buddha-nature and that there is therefore universal salvation for all. This doctrine, together with the synthetic and totalistic approach, is typically characteristic of Chinese thinking. Although the two schools gradually lost attraction because of their excessive speculation, their influence on Ch'an and other Mahāyāna schools, as well as on Chinese philosophy in general, has been indelibly strong.

But the most interesting and enduring school that reflects the practical, nonspeculative, and this-worldly mindedness of the Chinese is that of Ch'an or Meditation (*dhyāna*). Its unique style is fully expressed in the Ch'an jargon, "A special transmission (from mind to mind) outside the scriptures, non-reliance upon verbalism, a direct pointing to man's mind, and seeing into one's own Nature for the attainment of buddhahood." It was nominally founded by Bodhidharma, the first patriarch of Ch'an, who arrived in China in 420, but the initiation of the real Ch'an movement is attributed to Hui-nêng (d. 713), the sixth patriarch. Ch'an was divided into two competing sects after the fifth patriarch Hung-jên: the school of gradual enlightenment organized by Shên-hsiu (605?–706) and that of sudden enlightenment founded by Hui-nêng. Only the latter survived, for Hui-nêng's teaching of *Nirvāṇa* or *satori* here-and-now "in this very body" has been accepted as the orthodox doctrine of Ch'an. This orthodox sect was later divided into "five houses and seven branches," among which only two flourished and were imported to Japan for further development. The Lin-chi school, founded by Lin-chi Yi-hsüan (d. 867), prefers to use "shock therapy" of shouting and beating, as well as the *kung-an* (*kōan*) exercise of mind-sharpening question-and-answer between the Ch'an master and his disciples; whereas the Ts'ao-tung school, founded by Tung-shan Liang-chieh (807–869) and his pupil Ts'ao-shan Pên-chi (840–901), recommends the more moderate technique of *tsuo-ch'an* ("sitting in meditation") without any thought of acquisition or attainment, without any specific problem in mind. But in many cases the distinction in technique toward *satori* between the two schools is blurred, for their respective techniques are rather complementary to each other. In their theory that no discursive teaching is necessary for enlightenment, the Ch'an masters' concern is to identify the "original face" of the Buddha, whose enlightenment experience is ontologically efficacious in every "human" existence. Their simple, direct, and spontaneous approach toward enlightenment is a happy combination of Buddhist transcendentalism and Taoist naturalism. Ch'an has been so challenging and yet so attractive to other Buddhists as well as non-Buddhists that it not only has become a kind of universal practice in Mahāyāna Buddhism but has captured the minds of many wayward Neo-Confucianists, whose tradition is supposed to be diametrically opposed to Buddhism.

The Ching-t'u (Pure Land) school is the least philosophical but most popular in the Mahāyāna tradition, sometimes mixed up with Taoist religion to form a gospel of salvation for the masses. In contrast to all other Mahāyāna schools, which follow "the Holy Path" or "the Difficult Way" and insist on self-power emancipation from the cyclic wheel of life and death (*saṁsāra*),

the Path of Pure Land or the Easy Way advocates total reliance on superhuman power for the saving grace of the Buddha Amitābha. According to the Pure Land legend, when he was a bodhisattva named Dharmākara he took forty-eight vows, instrumental in his attainment of buddhahood. After he became a buddha, he was worshiped as a compassionate savior whose vows, particularly the eighteenth Original Vow, gave assurance to his believers of their direct rebirth in the Land of Bliss (*sukhāvatī*). Hence the simple invocation of Amitābha's name (*A-mi-t'o-fo* in Chinese) becomes the most common means for millions of Pure Land pietists to be released from the sufferings of the world. In Buddhist painting and sculpture it is a very popular theme to represent Amitābha sitting on a lotus throne in the Western Paradise, flanked by the bodhisattva Kuan-yin, the Goddess of Mercy.

The Pure Land doctrine originated in India. In China it was institutionalized as a Mahāyāna sect through the efforts of pioneers Hui-yüan and T'an-luan (476–542) and was firmly established and popularized through those of Tao-ch'o (d. 645) and his disciple Shan-tao (613–681). In Pure Land pietism we also find a number of Chinese transformations of Indian Buddhism. We have already alluded to the doctrine of universal salvation arising out of an ontologically determinative Buddha-nature in all men. This replaced the Indian doctrine, which denied salvation to the *icchantikas* (those unbelievers who have cut off their roots of goodness), and corresponded to the Mencian doctrine of the attainability of sagehood by all men, based on the idea of man's original, inborn goodness. Further, the Indian concept of supernatural rebirth in the Pure Land after death was transformed into that of existence of earthly living or continuation of human relations in the Pure Land, corresponding to the religious Taoist hope for everlasting life on earth or immortality in the "Isles of the Blessed." Thus, the main objective of the Pure Land faith in China is often the prolongation of human existence rather than its termination for the sake of supernatural deliverance from the ocean of human misery.

Despite all these transformations, Buddhism never really surrendered its Indian identity and became totally absorbed into the Chinese tradition. Still at variance with deep-rooted Chinese attitudes were Indian ideas and practices of monastic celibacy, vegetarianism, and above all, escape from mundane affairs for the sake of

17-3 Standing Kuan Yin, Goddess of Mercy, Sung Dynasty (12th century). (Courtesy of the Metropolitan Museum of Art, gift of Mrs. John D. Rockefeller, Jr., 1942.)

17-4 Buddha seated on lotus throne, Ming Dynasty, 1368–1644. (Courtesy of the Philadelphia Museum of Art, photograph by A. J. Wyatt, staff photographer.)

salvation. Indeed, there always existed an ideological conflict between Buddhism and the Confucian tradition. Beginning in the T'ang dynasty, Han Yü, Li Ao, and other Confucian scholars launched a severe attack on Buddhist life-denying escapism from productive human life and requested the imperial court to put a stop to the disastrous spread of Buddhism. In the Sung dynasty, the Ch'êng brothers, Chu Hsi and Lu Hsiang-shan, and other Neo-Confucianists, despite their debt to the Buddhist stimulus for the formation of Neo-Confucian thought, outspokenly accused the Buddhists of "selfishness," of renouncing human relationships and ethico-social obligations like filial piety. This Confucian critique continues to the present day.

Decline

From the late T'ang dynasty onward Buddhism lost its philosophical creativity and fell into steady decline. Neo-Confucianists wrested the intellectual initiative from the Buddhists under the Sung dynasty and restored the supremacy of the Confucian tradition in national life. Buddhist monasteries came to be regarded as a refuge for the disillusioned and underprivileged, as a place of service to the deceased and bereaved—a kind of situation similar to that of Taoist religion. Only Ch'an Buddhism was still an active cultural force in the Sung, but it also dwindled in later centuries. In the People's Republic of China today, the secularization of Buddhist temples, lands, and clergy that had proceeded the advent of Communism is pressed ever harder. It was reported that in 1930 Buddhist temples and shrines numbered 268,000 but were sharply reduced to less than 100 in 1954. The clergy numbered about 500,000 in 1931, but this number by 1954 had dropped to about 2,500. Although the Chinese Buddhist Association was organized in 1953, it seems unlikely that in the future Buddhism in China can prosper without some sort of modernization.

Bibliography

CHANG, GARMA C. C. *The Buddhist Teaching of Totality: The Philosophy of Hwa Yen Buddhism.* University Park: Pennsylvania State U. P., 1971.

CH'EN, KENNETH. *Buddhism in China: A Historical Survey.* Princeton: Princeton U. P., 1964. Also Princeton Paperbacks.

CONZE, EDWARD. *Buddhist Wisdom Books.* London: Allen & Unwin, 1958. Also Harper Torchbooks.

———. *Buddhist Thought in India.* London: Allen & Unwin, 1962. Also Ann Arbor Paperbacks.

DAYAL, HAR. *The Bodhisattva Doctrine in Buddhist Sanskrit Literature.* London: Kegan Paul, 1932.

HURVITZ, LEON. *Chih-I* (*538–597*): *An Introduction to the Life and Ideas of a Chinese Buddhist Monk, "Mélanges chinois et bouddhiques,"* Vol. XII. Bruges, Belgium, 1963.

INADA, KENNETH. *Nāgārjuna: A Translation of His Mulamadhyamakakārikā with an Introductory Essay.* Tokyo: The Hokuseido Press, 1970.

MURTI, T. R. V. *The Central Philosophy of Buddhism.* London: Allen & Unwin, 1955.

NARADA THERA. *The Buddha and His Teachings.* Colombo, Ceylon: Vijirarama, 1964.

NYANAMOLI, BHIKKHU (tr.). *The Path of Purification* (by Buddhaghosa). Colombo, Ceylon: A. Semage, 1964.

RAHULA, WALPOLA. *History of Buddhism in Ceylon.* Colombo, Ceylon: Gunasena, 1956.

———. *What the Buddha Taught.* New York: Grove, 1962.

SANGHARAKSHITA, BHIKSHU. *A Survey of Buddhism.* Bangalore, India: The Indian Institute of World Culture, 1957.

———. *The Three Jewels: An Introduction to Modern Buddhism.* London: Rider, 1967. Also Doubleday Anchor Books.

STCHERBATSKY, T. *The Central Conception of Buddhism.* London: Royal Asiatic Society, 1923. Reprint Motilal Banarsidass, Delhi, 1970.

SUZUKI, D. T. *Essays in Zen Buddhism* (Three Series). London: Rider, 1949–1953. Also Rider Paperbacks.

TAKAKUSU, JUNJIRO. *The Essentials of Buddhist Philosophy.* Honolulu: U. of Hawaii, 1947.

WELCH, HOLMES. *The Buddhist Revival in China.* Cambridge: Harvard U. P., 1968.

WELLS, KENNETH E. *Thai Buddhism, Its Rites and Activities.* Bangkok: Christain Bookstore, 1960.

ZÜRCHER, ERIK. *The Buddhist Conquest of China,* 2 vols. Leiden: Brill, 1959.

18

Mahāyāna Buddhism (Japan)

Joseph M. Kitagawa

Introduction and Growth of Buddhism in Japan

Whereas Buddhism in China sent its roots down into the subsoil of the family system, in Japan it found its anchorage in the "national structure" itself. The Buddhism that was initially introduced into the country in the seventh century from Korea was regarded as a talisman for the protection of the nation. The new religion was accepted by the Soga clan but was rejected by others, causing controversies that resembled remarkably the divisions caused by Buddhism's introduction into Tibet. In both of these countries, it was believed that the introduction of Buddhist statues had been an insult to the native deities, resulting in plagues and natural disasters. Only gradually were such feelings overcome. Whereas the Buddhism of the Soga clan was largely magical, under the influence of Prince Shōtoku, (573–621 C.E.), who became regent of the nation in 593, Buddhism recovered part of the religious depth that it had lost in its initial transmission to Japan. Shōtoku lectured on various sūtras that emphasized the ideals of the layman and the monarch and composed a Seventeen Article Constitution in which Buddhism was adroitly blended with Confucianism as the spiritual foundation of the state. In later times, he was widely regarded as the incarnation of the boddhisattva Avalokitesvara. During the Nara Period (710–794), Buddhism actually became the religion of the state. Emperor Shōmu actively propagated the faith, making Nara with its Great Buddha Statue (*Daibutsu*) the national cult center, and provincial temples made the system effective at the local level (Map 13). The fact that the *Kojiki* and *Nihongi* were produced at this time is clear indication of the inclusiveness of the early national ideology. The Kegon sect (the Japanese version of the Chinese Hua-Yen sect), with its emphasis on the Sun Buddha, Vairocana, and the doctrine of the interpenetration of all things, became the official ideology of the new Buddhist state. During the Nara period there were six different sects that were active. Except for Kegon and Hossō (a Yogacara school), these were primarily academic alternatives within Buddhism. During this period, the ideal of universal salvation, as taught in the *Lotus Sūtra,* and the role of the layman, expounded by the *Vimalakirti Sūtra,* were popularized in Japan. It soon became obvious, however, that monks were becoming too active in politics. During the reign of Shōmu's daughter, the monk Dōkyō tried to become emperor. Only the resistance of the aristocracy saved Japan from becoming a Buddhist theocracy on the order of Tibet. Because of this pressure from the monastic community, the court decided to move to Heian (Kyōto) in 794.

In 804 the monk Saichō (767–822) was sent to China

18-1 The great Buddha (Daibutsu) of Kamakura, Japan. Nearly fifty feet high, this bronze image of Amida Buddha was cast in 1252 under the direction of Ono Goroyomen. (Courtesy of the Japan National Tourist Organization.)

and returned to Japan later to preach the doctrines of T'ien-T'ai (Japanese Tendai). Whereas the Hossō sect had taught that there were some who could not be saved, Tendai stressed a gospel of universal salvation. The nationalistic overtones of Japanese Buddhism continued to be heard in the new schools of the Heian period. Tendai's monastic complex on Mt. Hiei, just outside Heian (modern Kyōto), was known as the "Chief Seat of the Buddhist Religion for Ensuring the Security of the Country." Shingon Buddhism, with its center at Mt. Kōya, was a form of Tantrism introduced into Japan by the monk Kūkai (774–835) in the early ninth century. Shingon (True Word) Buddhism emphasizes the unity of the believer with the Buddha as he performs various esoteric rites. The two mandalas (cosmoplans) called the "thunderbolt-element-circle" and the "womb-element-circle" are of primary importance in the worship of Shingon Buddhism. As we have seen, both Tendai and Shingon fostered a Buddhist-Shinto syncretism.

Even before the Kamakura period (1185–1333), a cult of Amitābha (the Japanese Amida) had begun to take root in Japan. The Pure Land sect (Jōdo-shū) was brought to Japan by Hōnen (1133–1212), and his follower Shinran (1173–1262) gave a new and radical twist to the teachings of the sect. Shinran, who married and lived "neither as a monk nor layman," began a movement that has been compared to the Lutheran Reformation. Rejecting the entire merit-karma way of thinking, Shinran taught that men could be saved by a single invocation of Amida. But even then, he believed, it was Amida who inspired the invocation. This marked what could be called the high point of Other-Power (i.e., dependence on Buddha's power to save, *tariki*) in the history of Buddhism. In the fifteenth century, Rennyo shaped Shinran's teachings and followers into a sect called True Pure Land (Jōdo-shin shū). This sect had its own armies and extensive temple lands. Today the Pure Land sects have more adherents than any other Buddhist groups in Japan.

In the thirteenth century, Japanese Buddhism produced its one "prophet," the monk Nichiren (1222–1282). This leader taught that salvation could be won by reciting the words *namu myō hō renge kyō* ("salutation to the Lotus Sūtra") and did not hesitate to attack other, contradictory doctrines. The fulfillment of his prediction of the Mongol attacks on Japan brought him fame throughout the country. Much of his nationalistic spirit lives on today in the Sōka-gakkai sect. It was also during the Kamakura period that Ch'an (Japanese Zen) began to be popular in Japan. The Lin-chi (Rinzai, in Japanese) school was introduced by the monk Eisai (1141–1215), who also wrote a tract called *Propagate Zen, Protect the Country.* In the thirteenth century, Dōgen (1200–1253) introduced the Ts'ao-tung school of Zen (Sōtō, in Japanese), with its emphasis on sitting in meditation (*zazen*). Zen soon became associated with the most important facets of medieval Japanese art and culture, giving to them its own unique spirit. Because it taught its followers a direct and unhesitating style of life, Zen became popular with Japan's military class.

During the chaos of the Ashikaga period (1333–1568), monks in most Buddhist monasteries took up arms to protect themselves and to extend their holdings. The soldier monks were called *sōhei.* An exception to this were the Zen sects, which were active even during this period developing and refining Japanese culture and aesthetics. It was during this period that Zen monks introduced Neo-Confucianism to Japan—a doctrine that would later turn upon its Buddhist patrons with a vengeance.

18-2 Golden Pavilion, Kyoto. (Courtesy of the Japan National Tourist Organization.)

18-3 Nanzenji Temple, Kyoto.

The Modern Period

Under the Tokugawa shōgunate (1603–1868), Buddhism became a kind of state religion, although being stripped of any autonomy it may have once enjoyed. Temples were now used for registering the populace—one way of preventing the spread of Christianity, a religion that the shōgunal government regarded as a political menace. This association with the Tokugawa regime made Buddhism quite unpopular at the beginning of the Meiji period (1868–1912), at least among the elite of the nation. At that time, in order to set up Shinto as the new state religion, it was necessary for the government to separate Shinto from Buddhism. Nevertheless, Buddhism continued to give its moral support to the nation. During the period of ultranationalism (ca. 1930–1945) Buddhist thinkers called for uniting the East in one great Buddhaland under the tutelage of Japan. After the war, Buddhist groups, new and old alike, began to emphasize Buddhism as a religion of peace and brotherhood. During the postwar period, the greatest visible activity among Buddhists has been among the "New Religions," such as Sōka-gakki and Risshō-kōseikai. These and other new sects display a high level of flexibility in adjusting to urban conditions and a remarkable talent for using the mass media. In general they are characterized by (1) a greater simplicity of belief than we find among the established, older religions, (2) rituals suited to the occasion, (3) a general tendency to stress an urban, salvational this-worldliness (instead of the rural, cosmogonic this-worldliness of the older religions), and (4) social forms that can absorb "grass-roots" people, people whose uprootedness has alienated them from traditional religion. With the disruption of village and family life caused by rapid urbanization, the New Religions often function as ersatz families.

Sōka-gakki (Value Creating Society) is a high-powered layman's movement that has grown up around the Nichiren Shōshū. This religion is based on the so-called threefold teaching of Nichiren: (1) *honmon no honzon:* the chief object of worship of the true teaching; (2) the Lotus Sūtra, and its ritual repetition as the chant, "namu myō hō renge kyō"; and (3) *honmon no kaidan:* the sanctuary of the true teaching, i.e., Sōka Gakkai's temple, Taisekiji, located at the foot of Mt. Fuji. This is the temple at which the Nichiren mandala is found. Sōka Gakkai, like most of the other New Religions, has placed strong emphasis on faith healing, saying, "Don't waste your money on medicine and doctors, join Sōka Gakkai!" The sect also has its own political party, the Kōmeitō (Clean Government Party), which has had remarkable success at the polls. Although its ideology is rather vague, Sōka Gakkai's politics tend toward nationalism and conservatism.

Risshō Kōseikai, the Society for Establishing Righteousness and Friendly Intercourse, is similar in many ways to Sōka Gakkai but lacks the belligerence of the latter. Founded in 1938, this sect emphasizes the *Lotus Sūtra* and the Eternal Buddha as the object of worship. While chanting the sacred title of the *Lotus Sūtra* is important, it is not regarded as sufficient for "salvation." Risshō Kōseikai shows its greater traditionalism (in contrast with Sōka Gakkai) by the emphasis it places on reverence for one's ancestors. In order to counter the public criticism it has suffered as a healing sect, Risshō Kōseikai has set up several hospitals.

There is a certain measure of cooperation among many of the New Religions in Japan today. Still, in spite of the phenomenal growth of the New Religions, the "established" sects continue to have an influence on the people that defies statistical measurement. Perhaps the most important item to bear in mind when one tries to chart the growth, flourishing, and decline of religions in Japan is the fundamental hospitality shown to all religions and the nonexclusive nature of most of the religions that have taken root in Japan (Maps 15 to 17).

Bibliography

ANEZAKI, MASAHARU. *History of Japanese Religion.* Rutland, Vt.: C. E. Tuttle, 1963 [first published 1930].

———. *Japanese Mythology* (in Vol. VIII of *The Mythology of all Races,* Ed., C. J. MacCulloch). Boston: Marshall Jones, 1928.

ASTON, W. G. *Shinto, the Way of the Gods.* New York: Longmans, 1905.

DE BARY, W. T., et al. *Sources of Japanese Tradition.* New York: Columbia, 1958.

DUMOULIN, HEINRICH. *A History of Zen Buddhism,* tr. Paul Peachey. New York: Pantheon Books, 1963.

ELIOT, SIR CHARLES. *Japanese Buddhism.* London: E. Arnold, 1935.

HOLTOM, D. C. *The National Faith of Japan: A Study in Modern Shinto.* New York: Paragon Book Reprint, 1965 [first pub. 1938].

KISHIMOTO, HIDEO (Ed.). *Japanese Religion in the Meiji Era,* tr. John F. Howes. Tokyo: Obunsha, 1956.

KITAGAWA, J. M. *Religion in Japanese History.* New York: Columbia, 1966.

MATSUMOTO, NOBUHIRO. *Essai sur la mythologie japonaise.* Paris: Paul Geuthner, 1928.

MURAOKA, TSUNETSUGU. *Studies in Shinto Thought.* Tokyo: Japanese National Commission for UNESCO, 1964.

NAKAMURA, HAJIME. *The Ways of Thinking of Eastern Peoples.* Tokyo: Print Bureau, Japanese Govt., 1960.

SASAKI, RUTH FULLER and ISSHŪ MIURA. *Zen Dust: The History of Koan and Koan Study in Rinzai (Lin-chi) Zen.* New York: Harcourt Brace Jovanovich, 1966–67.

SUZUKI, D. T. *Essays in Zen Buddhism.* London: Rider, 1958 [first pub. 1949–53].

THOMSON, HARRY. *The New Religions of Japan.* Rutland, Vt.: C. E. Tuttle, 1963.

VISSER, M. W. DE. *Ancient Buddhism in Japan.* Leiden: E. J. Brill, 1935.

19

Christianity

Gerard Sloyan

Genesis and Formation

Early Spread of Christianity, New Testament Period (Ca. 30–Ca. 130 A.D.)

The Gospel According to Matthew (ca. 80 A.D.) has two separate traditions about the spread of the *euaggelion* (literally, "good tidings") of Jesus Christ, one confining the "twelve apostles" to Jewish territory (10:5 ff.) and the other sending them, after Christ's resurrection, to the ends of the earth (28:19). The New Testament book The Acts of the Apostles, which is the continuation of The Gospel According to Luke, tells of the origins of the Christian movement. In this account it began in Jerusalem, spread to Samaria (the territory north of Palestinian Judaea), then to Phoenicia to the northwest, and south to Gaza and Egypt; afterward it went to the Syrian cities of Antioch and Damascus; then, through the efforts of various preachers of the Christian message (Barnabas, John, Mark, Silas, and Timothy, but chiefly Saul, called Paul), to Cyprus, the provinces of what is now Asia Minor (modern Turkey), modern Greece, Malta, and Rome (Map 36).

Reference is made in Acts to Apollos, a Jew of Alexandria in Egypt who had become a Christian, although where he had done so is not indicated (Acts 18:24), and to the fact that when Paul first came to Ephesus he found a number of Christians there (Acts 19:1). Paul wrote an extensive letter to the Christians at Rome, where he had never been (Romans 13:1) but where two kinsmen, Andronicus and Junias, who were Christians before him, resided (Romans 16:7). He arrived among the many he listed in Romans as known to him, in the status of a captive (Acts 28:15). Christians were also encountered by his party at Puteoli (Acts 28:14) near modern Naples.

Luke's book of Acts, like his Gospel, is not thought to be historical so much as a theologized account based on historical traditions of varying worth. His geographical data on Asia Minor accord well with what we know of the cities of that place and time.[1] He likewise appears dependable in details touching on the various public officials of the period, among them the proconsul of Achaia, Gallio (Acts 18:12), the governors of Judaea, Felix (Acts 23:26) and Festus (Acts 24:27; 25:1 ff.; 26:24), and King Agrippa II of Galilee and his sister Bernice (Acts 25:13; 25:25 ff.; 26:27 f.). Luke had a twofold purpose: to press the claim that Jerusalem was the place of origin of the Christian movement, rather than Galilee (the view favored by Matthew and Mark), and to advance the importance of Paul, with his mission to the Gentiles, over the apostles and elders of the Jerusalem

[1] William Mitchell Ramsay, *St. Paul, The Traveller and Roman Citizen* (London: Hodder, 1895), and *The Cities of St. Paul* (London: Hodder, 1907).

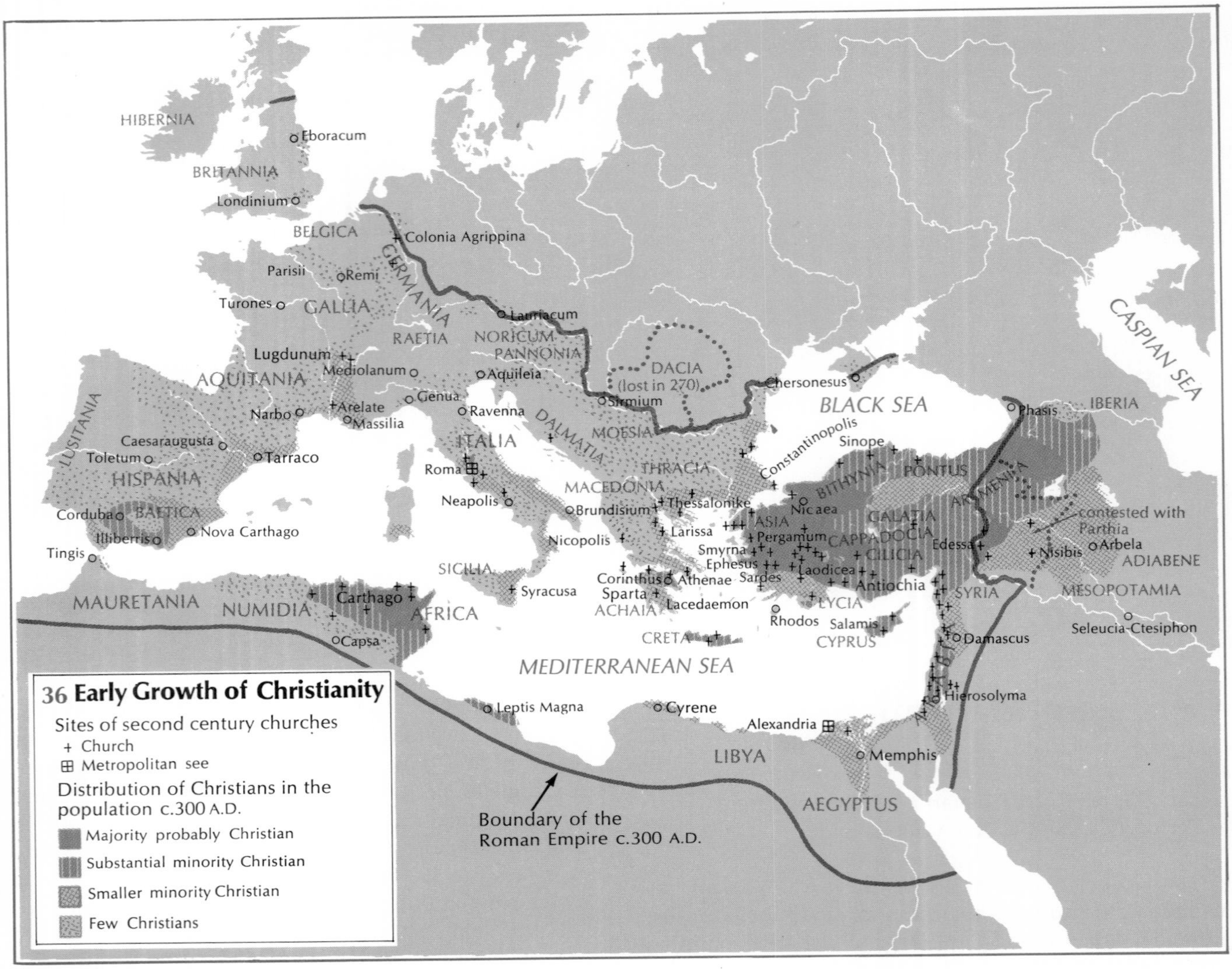

church (Acts 15:6), especially Peter and James. Yet Luke is above all a harmonizer, as witness the settlement between Jews and Gentiles he reports on in Acts 15, so little in accord with Paul's interpretation of the same events in Galatians 2. He describes the Christian situation as he knows it in the years 85–90, when the Jewish presence in the Church was receding and was already a minority in face of the large number of Gentiles and gentilized Jews who were coming to be the bulk of the Christian movement.

Christianity is called a "movement" consciously rather than a new religion because it came to birth from the womb of Judaism as a protest against the conception of the religion of Israel held by certain postexilic Jews, in particular those who were members of the Pharisee party. Jewish practice was anything but monolithic in the days of Jesus of Nazareth (d. ca. 30). Its chief groups were the predominant Pharisees ("the separated"), linguistic and ethnic purists, zealous for extralegal tradition, who traced themselves back to the Maccabean revolt of 167 B.C. and the subsequent Hasmonean dynasty; the Sadducees, a priestly aristocracy committed to the Law alone, not to later scriptures like the prophetic and sapiential books, above all not to the second-century book of Daniel, which taught the resurrection of the dead (12:2 f.); the Herodians, collaborators with the syncretistically oriented puppet dynasty that held power by sufferance from Rome; the Zealots, who were the extremist wing of those holding the Pharisee outlook and who wished to wrest power from the Romans by force; and the Essenes, who probably included the monastic community at Qumrân, not far from the shores of the Dead Sea, abstemious in all matters touching self-indulgence. The latter were desert dwellers in principle because of the debased character of city life and, in the case of the Qumrân group, despisers of the temple priesthood as well.

It is not easy to reconstruct a life of Jesus from the four Gospels, chiefly because their authors were more concerned with preaching his meaning for the faith communities of their times than to paint a historical picture of his words and deeds. Scholars differ importantly on the amount of historical tradition the four evangelists incorporated into their various accounts. From his sayings reckoned authentic by the greatest number of scholars, Jesus seems to have been a teacher in the Pharisee tradition (not the Sadducee, Essene, or Zealot) who had been a village carpenter, a man without formal rabbinic training. He represented Galilean Judaism, which sat lighter to the saddle than Judean Judaism when it came to observing the "traditions of the fathers" (i.e., the Pharisees of the previous 150 years). Rejection of his teaching by fellow Jews may have been partly on regional and cultural grounds, but his followers report them as exclusively ethical and religious. He is reported as not having cited the authority of other rabbis, thereby going against an important convention of his time. He acted as his own authority, teaching his hearers the meaning of Torah (the Law) in the spirit of Israel's prophets. He also seems to have claimed knowledge of the terms of the Last Age, a Jewish concept of the times, speaking of himself as having a key role in the working out of the plan of Israel's God, whom he referred to as "my Father."

The certitude of Jesus with reference to the future coming of God's rule or reign seems not to have included disclosure of when it would overtake men or in what form. He is described as having taught it as a matter of surprise and suddenness. That it would be coming on the world in its fullness soon is a conviction of several New Testament authors (among them Mark, Matthew, and Paul, with John an exception in that his eschatology is in the process of being realized as well as lying in the future). It is impossible to establish that it was the conviction of Jesus that the end of the age was imminent, though many scholars since J. Weiss and A. Schweitzer (late nineteenth and early twentieth centuries), taking the Gospels at face value, have maintained that it was.

In any case, according to the testimony of the Gospels Jesus was executed by Roman authority as guilty of sedition. The same sources implicate the religious leadership of his people and in particular the temple priesthood. He began to be preached by his followers—the only ones of whom we have any record—as risen from the dead and ascended to his Father, a concept that was in accord with the Pharisee hope but not the Sadducee. It differed from the Pharisee expectation in the important detail that this group supposed that all the just would rise together, not one individual as the "first fruits" of the remainder, as Jesus' followers began to preach concerning him.

The Christian community, like the solitaries of Qumrân, thought of itself not as a new religion but as the true Israel. It doubtless partook of the universalist Jewish hope of the times, which foresaw large numbers of "God fearers" among the Gentiles being aggregated to the Jewish people, whether by way of circumcision and observance of the whole Law or by a ritual cleansing that brought with it the necessity of keeping the seven "Noachian" precepts, some disciplinary, some ethical. The early followers of Jesus, all Jews or Jewish proselytes (cf. Acts 6:5; 10:2; 11:19 f.), were not sectarian in the sense that they made special ascetical demands or compelled segregation from others. There was no badge of membership such as abstention from particular foods or sex, no extra penitential practices. It was Pharisaic Judaism at odds with the temple priesthood and the practice of some Pharisee teachers, organized around the notion that God, in raising Jesus up from the dead, had fulfilled the promises contained in the Law, the prophets, and the psalms. Jesus by his exaltation at God's right hand had been designated "Lord" and "Messiah" (the latter afterward in Greek, "Christ"). He was a man in whom God dwelt intimately because, like the patriarchs and prophets of old, he possessed a large portion of God's spirit.

A verse in Luke's Gospel (23:2) contains the charge against Jesus that probably reflects best the reasons for his death: "We found this man subverting our nation, opposing the payment of taxes to Caesar, and claiming to be Messiah, a king." However the charge originated, it would constitute sufficient grounds for local imperial authority to dispatch him. Paul's reminder to the community at Corinth of the gospel he had preached while with them is important early testimony (ca. 50) that some among Christ's followers were proclaiming that they had experienced him as risen from the dead: "I handed on to you first of all what I myself received, that Christ died for our sins in accordance with the Scriptures; that he was buried and, in accordance with the Scriptures, rose on the third day; that he was seen by Cephas [Hellenized Aramaic form of the name that became Peter in Greek], then by the Twelve. After that he was seen by five hundred brothers at once, most of whom are still alive, although some have fallen asleep. Next he was seen by James: then by all the apostles. Last of all he was seen by me, as one born out of the normal course. . . . Indeed, I have worked harder than all the others not on my own but through the favor of

God. In any case, whether it be I or they, this is what we preach and this is what you believed" (I Corinthians 15:3–8; 10*c*–11).

This "gospel" Paul claims he did not receive from any man, nor was he schooled in it; rather, it came "from revelation by Jesus Christ" (Galatians 1:12). This probably is his way of denying dependence on anyone but "the Lord" for his faith or insights, but his gospel doubtless reflected the tradition that was abroad in the Hellenist-Jewish Christian circles of Damascus and Antioch, where Paul spent his early years as a believer in Jesus (see Galatians 1:17–21; 2:11; Acts 11:26). Luke tells of early difficulties between Hebraist and Hellenist Jews in the Jerusalem church that resulted in a scheme of poor relief for widows of the latter to be administered by seven men with Greek names of whom one—Nicolaus of Antioch—is described as a Gentile convert to Judaism (see Acts 6:1–5). The debates between one of the seven, Stephen, and Roman-freedmen Jews of Cyrene (i.e., the Roman province of Libya Cyreniaca), Alexandria, Cilicia, and Asia Minor resulted in his violent death (see Acts 6:8–7:58*a*) and the dispersion of others to Jewish communities in "Phoenicia, Cyprus, and Antioch" (Acts 11:19). Herod Agrippa I (41–44) beheaded James, the son of Zebedee (Acts 12:25). In 61 or 62, the high priest Ḥanan the Young put to death James the Just, leader of the Jerusalem church. He accomplished this between the governorships of Festus and Albinus, the latter of whom deposed him upon his arrival.[2] Peter and Paul are reported as having been put to death in Rome during Nero's reign, which ended in 68.[3]

The last clear indication in the New Testament of the geographic spread of the movement (first known as that of the "Christians" in Antioch, according to Acts 11:26) comes in the book of Revelation (ca. 95). There, letters are addressed to seven churches in the province of Asia by a certain John who says he writes from Patmos, which is off the coast of the province of Caria (Revelation 1:4; 9). The churches are those of Ephesus (2:1), Smyrna (2:8), Pergamum (2:12), Thyatira (2:18), Sardis (3:1), Philadelphia (3:7), and Laodicaea (3:14). The order is clockwise along a roughly circular Roman commercial road. One resident of Pergamum, Antipas, is spoken of as a martyr (2:12), presumably under Domitian. There is no mention of bishops.

Eusebius of Caesarea in his *History of the Church* (ca. 325) has a source that tells him that the Jerusalem Christians fled the city to Pella across the Jordan when Jewish Zealot resistance to Rome started the war in 66.[4] Again in 133–135 they were harassed as potential traitors during the war under Hadrian led by the Jewish patriot Bar Kochba. Eusebius, having listed fifteen Jewish bishops of Jerusalem up to 135,[5] names Mark as the first uncircumcised bishop of Aelia Capitolina—Jerusalem—from which rebuilt city the Romans ejected all Jews.[6]

[2] Flavius Josephus, *Antiquities of the Jews,* Book XX, Chap. 9, §1.
[3] See *Eusebius: The History of the Church from Christ to Constantine,* tr. G. A. Williamson (Baltimore: Penguin, 1965), Book II, Chap. 25.

Period Recorded by Extra-Biblical Literature to the Death of Irenaeus (Ca. 100–200)

Toward the end of the first century a solemn epistle in Greek, claiming to have been written "through the Holy Spirit,"[7] was sent from "the church of God at Rome to the church of God at Corinth" pleading for harmony and peace in the latter community. No author's name occurs within it, but Eusebius among others attributes it to Clement of Rome, whom he further identifies as the third bishop of that city after Peter.[8] For the Roman author of *I Clement, bishop* and *presbyter* seem to be interchangeable terms; furthermore, he makes no personal claim beyond that implied by the act of sending "envoys of trustworthiness and discretion" to be "witnesses between ourselves and you."[9] He cites as "noble figures of our own generation" and "most virtuous pillars of our church" Peter and Paul, saying that the latter "reached the farthest limits of the West."[10] Some are made to wonder by this if Paul's hope of setting out for Spain (Romans 15:24) was realized.

Hermas, Clement's older contemporary, writes in his *Shepherd* that one of two copies of a certain revelation is to be sent to Clement, who shall then "send it to the cities abroad, for that is his business."[11] The two indications together have led some to conclude that Clement was a kind of foreign secretary. He may have been the chief presbyter of his city but, if he was, it is a puzzle why Ignatius of Antioch in 107–109 did not single out his successor as such (Eusebius dates Clement's "bishopric" about 90–100), when he was naming the *episkopoi* of the other five churches he addressed.

The letters of Ignatius, Greek-speaking bishop of Antioch in Syria, were addressed from shipboard to the Asian churches of Ephesus, Magnesia-on-the-Maeander,

[4] *Ibid.,* Book III, Chap. 5.
[5] *Ibid.,* Book IV, Chap. 5.
[6] *Ibid.,* Book IV, Chap. 6.
[7] *Ibid.,* Chap. 63.
[8] *Ibid.,* Book III, Chap. 4, §15; Book V, Chap. 6.
[9] *Ibid.,* Chap. 63.
[10] *Ibid.,* Chap. 5.
[11] *The Shepherd of Hermas,* Vision II, §4.

Tralles, Rome, Philadelphia, and Smyrna and to the bishop of Smyrna, Polycarp. In captivity and headed for martyrdom, Ignatius refers to "those who have preceded me from Syria to Rome for the glory of God" (Romans 10). He says that "peace now reigns in the church at Antioch in Syria" (Philippians 10) despite the sending on after him of the deacon Philo and Rheus Agathopous, "who has renounced this earthly life" (Philippians 11). From Ignatius's letters it appears that Christianity was considered an offense but repression was not systematic.

Around 112 the governor of Bithynia on the Black Sea in Asia Minor, Pliny the Younger, reported to the emperor Trajan that Christians were to be found in town and countryside. They had evidently been executed for their profession of faith before this but Pliny wanted to know why and how he should proceed if they recanted. They gathered before dawn on a certain day of the week, he reported, sang hymns to a certain Chrestus as to a god, took an oath to abstain from crime rather than commit it, and reassembled to eat ordinary food. Pliny wrote that he had issued an edict forbidding secret societies and had tortured two deaconesses but had turned up nothing beyond "a depraved and extravagant superstition." What should he do? Should the Christian name itself be punished or only crimes attaching to it? Trajan answered that no hard and fast rule could be laid down except that no credence should be placed in the anonymous pamphlets Pliny had inquired about. Christians informed against who are found guilty of the charge are to be punished; yet Trajan sidesteps the main question about the nature of the charge. If Christians recant and "worship our gods," they are to be pardoned.

The island of Crete was evangelized by Titus according to the New Testament letter to him attributed to Paul (Titus 1:5–9). The same letter speaks of Nicopolis in Epirus on the west coast of Greece (north across the bay from Actium) as a place where Paul had "decided to spend the winter" (Titus 3:12). By the second century there is mention of churches at Develtum and Anchialo in Thrace, Larissa in Thessaly, Lacedaemon, and Cephalonia. The first information we have of a church at Byzantium is that a certain heretic named Theodotus went to Rome from there about 190.[12]

Marcion, the son of the bishop of Pontus on the Black Sea, came to Rome and was excommunicated there in 144, which means that there was a Pontic Christian community in the first quarter of the second century. Eusebius preserves certain traditions about the dispersion of the apostles that can scarcely be credited. Thus, Mark brought the gospel to Egypt,[13] Thomas to Parthia, and Andrew to Scythia north and east of the Caspian Sea.[14] Annianus is named as the first bishop in Egypt after Mark,[15] to be succeeded by Avilius after twenty-two years;[16] later came Celadion and Agrippinus.[17] We begin to have some certainty about Egypt with the accession of Demetrios as bishop in 180.[18] He was the man who entrusted the elementary instruction of adults to Origen when the latter lost his father in death at seventeen.

Paul wrote in his letter to the Romans that he had preached the gospel from Rome to Illyricum (15:19), the province north of Dalmatia on the Adriatic, which embraces modern northern Yugoslavia, Trieste, and Pola. Titus is spoken of as having preached in Dalmatia (II Timothy 4:11). Paul's expression of a desire to visit Spain (Acts 15:23) is echoed in *I Clement* 5,[19] which puts him "in the extremities of the West." The church council at Illiberi (Elvira) about 300 was presided over by the bishop of Acci (Guadix) east of Elvira in the province of what is now Cartagena. An early martyrology of the Spanish city of Adon mentions a mission from Rome in Peter's time to *Civitas Accitana.*

Paul may well have put in at Marseilles and Narbonne if he made the projected Spanish voyage, but of this we cannot be sure. The first dependable word we have on a church in Gaul is contained in the acts of the martyrs of Vienne and Lyons on the river Rhône during the reign of Marcus Aurelius, 161–180.[20] The date is 177. Pothinus, the bishop of the Greek-speaking colony of Asian immigrants, was a man of ninety who had known Polycarp of Smyrna (d. 156). His successor, Irenaeus, in his letter to Florinus told of having known Polycarp as a boy.[21] The gospel had probably been brought to Gaul in the reign of Hadrian, 117–138.

Commerce between Rome and Carthage was frequent. Although we may presume that there was an early Christian presence in the North African city, the first evidence for it is an inscription from the period of the African-born emperor Septimius Severus (193–211) in Hadrumetum, the Sousse of modern Tunisia. It occurs in a Christian catacombs in a sequence of tomb inscriptions that would put the spread of the gospel to Carthage about half a century earlier.

If the spread of Christianity in Greek-speaking (and later Latin) parts of the Empire seemed assured, its

[12] See Hippolytus, *Philosophoumena,* Book VII, Chap. 35.
[13] Eusebius, *History of the Church,* Book II, Chap. 16.

[14] *Ibid.,* Book III, Chap. 1.
[15] *Ibid.,* Book II, Chap. 24.
[16] *Ibid.,* Book III, Chap. 14.
[17] *Ibid.,* Book IV, Chap. 19.
[18] *Ibid.,* Book VI, Chap. 3.
[19] I Clement, Book V, Chap. 19.
[20] Eusebius, *History of the Church,* Book V, Chap. 1.
[21] *Ibid.,* Book V, Chap. 20.

progress in Palestine and eastward was by no means so certain. There are numerous indications in the New Testament that a spirit of Jewish ethnocentrism tended to confine it, if not to Jewish people, at least to those who would observe the Mosaic Law or the Noachian precepts (cf. Acts 6:13; 15:19 f.; 28 f.; 21:18–26; 28; Galatians 2:3–41). We know the form of Paul's argument in favor of the relaxation of observance better than we know the tradition of holding to it as represented by Peter. Peter seems to have feared the swallowing up of Jewish Christianity by the rising tide of a Jewish religious concern that had no place for Jesus.

Eusebius has preserved for us[22] from the fourth book of Hegesippus' *Memoirs* (ca. 180) an account of the stoning to death of James the Just (i.e., "the legal observant"), a kinsman of Jesus. James is reported as believing that Jesus was the Saviour and the Messiah, that mankind would rise in the flesh, and that One was coming who would be the just judge of all. At the same time, Hegesippus records resistance to James's teaching not only by "the Scribes and Pharisees" but also by members of "the seven sects" led by Thebuthis, Simon, Cleobius, Dositheus, Gorthaeus, and Masbotheus. These presumably Jewish-Christian groups begot another six named for persons identified later as leaders of gnostic Christian sects, Marcion among them. Hegesippus also identifies a half dozen Jewish groups hostile "to the tribe of Judah and to Christ."[23] Among these are the Essenes, the Galileans, and a sect that favored daily baptism.

Symeon the son of Clopas, another relative of Jesus, succeeded James as head of the Jerusalem community. The destruction of that city in 70 was evidently a hard blow for the small group of Jewish Christians. They continued to have faith in Jesus and to observe circumcision, the sabbath, and other Jewish feasts. They were held suspect by fellow Jews, however, and by the growing majority of Gentile Christians. They had to be gone from Jerusalem, like all Jews, by the decree of Hadrian in 135, which set up the new capital of Aelia there. Traces of the Jewish Christians are recorded in the *Gospel According to the Hebrews,* which Jerome translated into Latin but which we no longer have. The divergencies from the canonical Gospels mentioned by him are not great. The position of James is much magnified in it.

Jewish Christianity was still a force when the Samarian Gentile Justin wrote his *Dialogue with Trypho* around 160. The church members seem to have called themselves Ebionites ("the poor"). According to Irenaeus, some never accepted the tradition of Mary's virginity. Justin was sympathetic to their practice of the Law but Gentile Christians generally were put off by this fidelity, which they found incomprehensible.

From the time of Irenaeus onward (d. ca. 200), Jewish Christians were dealt with in the Gentile church as some kind of deviationist sect. Among the pieces of literature that appear to be Jewish works edited by Jewish-Christian hands are the *Testament of the Twelve Patriarchs* and the *Ascension of Isaiah;* Book V of the Sybilline Writings; "The Book of Parables" in *I Enoch; II Enoch;* and *IV Esdras.* Still other such compositions are the *Apocalypse of Peter,* the *Homilies of Clement,* the *Apocryphon of James,* and possibly the *Shepherd* of Hermas.

Christianity was established in Edessa, capital of the Syriac-speaking kingdom of Osroëne, in the second or possibly late first century. The most prominent member of this church to have embraced the Christian faith was the poet and astrologer Bardesanes, a close friend of King Abgar IX the Great (179–186), who likewise became a Christian. Bardesanes was thoroughly opposed to Marcion—the second-century matter-spirit dualist[24]—but was not entirely trusted for his doctrine in the church of Antioch, which lay 180 miles northwest of the Syrian capital Edessa. Around the year 200 the bishop of Edessa, Serapion, consecrated a certain Palut as its bishop. When the kingdom was incorporated into the Empire in 216, the Edessan church gave proof of its communion with Rome and Antioch, a matter which had been doubtful in the earlier Bardesanian period.

The Thaddeus to whom the evangelization of Edessa is credited, in a legend that Eusebius includes,[25] may be the Addai whom a sixth-century *Chronicle of Arbela* names as the evangelist of Adiabene in the late first century. This territory in eastern Mesopotamia across the Tigris from Osroëne had a first-century A.D. king, Izates, who with his mother, Helen, was a convert to Judaism. Their tombs are still to be seen in Jerusalem. There was a bishop in Arbela named Pekidha between 105 and 115. From 121, the bishops were Samson, Isaac, Abraham, Moses, and Abel. This is the region from which Tatian came, that pupil of Justin who later went on to Rome and became an Encratite, an ascetic preaching abstention from flesh meat and sex. Paradoxically, Jewish Christianity in its ideological offspring proved to be friendly to a variety of tendencies toward matter-spirit dualism, a development totally at odds with the Biblical spirit.

[22] *Ibid.,* Book II, Chap. 23.
[23] *Ibid.,* Book IV, Chap. 22.

[24] *Ibid.,* Book IV, Chap. 30.
[25] *Ibid.,* Book I, Chap. 13.

Formation of Doctrine; Gnostic Threat

The content of Christian faith during the first two hundred years is especially well testified to in the seven letters of Ignatius of Antioch to the churches of Asia Minor, in the *First Apology* of Justin (ca. 155), and in the treatise *Against Heresies* of Irenaeus, bishop of Lyons (ca. 190). It included belief that the Hebrew scriptures, inspired of God, prophesied that the expected Messiah was Jesus; belief in the innate goodness of matter rather than gnostic or docetic mistrust of it; and commitment to the morality of the later Biblical period except for a strict monogamy and a respect for celibate life not found in the Hebrew Scriptures. Doctrinally, Jesus was thought to be "the second after God" and the Holy Spirit the third, the former God's eternal Word in the flesh, the latter his continuing presence among men. God had created everything in heaven and on earth through Christ his Son in the power of the Spirit. A heavenly court of angels were his ministering spirits. They did his will in obedience, just as the devils of hell—Satan and his legions—resisted the divine command and tempted man to disobedience. Jesus had shed his blood on the cross as the price of man's redemption. Man had only to accept the gift in loving faith to receive a justification that would raise him up on the last day. Christ in glory would cause the resurrection of all who persevered in faith to the end. As Irenaeus put it, "But to the righteous and holy, and those who have kept his commandments and have remained in his love, some from the beginning of life and some since their repentance, he will by his grace give life incorrupt, and will clothe them with eternal glory."[26]

Undoubtedly the greatest threat to Christianity in the second and third centuries was the variety of gnostic systems that flourished in the Jewish and pagan worlds and came to have their being within Christian circles. Heterodox Judaism under Hellenist and Iranian influence was the matrix of these dualist mythologies, which held matter to have been created by a Demiurge who had been begotten by Sophia as an image of the supreme Father but had fallen from the pleroma of spirit. This pleroma was hierarchical and had as few as 30 eons and as many as 365 heavens, each formed with a group of angels. Constituents of the pleroma took their names from a variety of philosophical and Biblical terms: Sigē (Silence) and Ennoia (Thought), Nous (Mind) and Alētheia (Truth), Anthrōpos and Ecclēsia; from the supreme principle variously designated as Father, Bythos, and Supreme Monad, and from terms from the Johannine prologue (Logos and Zōē); and also from New Testament allusions like Christos and Stauros (Cross). The challenge to man was to acquire saving knowledge (*gnōsis*), which would free him from the grip of matter and send him safely on his celestial journey past the hazards of baleful powers high into the *plērōma*, the higher realm of spirit or light. It was the acquisition of *gnōsis* that comprised the main challenge. Vast catalogues of names and interrelationships had to be learned in dizzying patterns, but the chief knowledge to be acquired was that of the spiritual element within man that would free him from the entanglements of matter.

Irenaeus in his *Against Heresies* summarizes one such system, which he attributes to Valentinus: "There is an unnamable Dyad, of which one is called Ineffable and the other Silence. Then from this Dyad a second Dyad was produced, of which he calls one part Father and the other Truth. From the Tetrad were produced Logos and Zoe, Anthropos and Ecclesia, and this is the first Ogdoad [Octet]. From Logos and Zoe he says that ten powers were produced, as I said before, but from Anthropos and Ecclesia twelve, one of which, falling away and suffering a lack, brought about the rest of the business. He postulated two Boundaries, one between the depth and the rest of the Pleroma, dividing the begotten Aeons from the unbegotten Father, and the other separating their Mother from the Pleroma. Christ was not produced from the Aeons within the Pleroma, but was conceived by the Mother who was outside, according to her knowledge of better things, but with a kind of shadow."[27]

The chief philosophical influence on the Gnostics was that of Middle Platonism, which also operated on the Christian apologists (Justin, Diognetus, Theophilus of Antioch). Among the best known of these syncretist teachers were Valentinus, Cerinthus, Basilides, and Heracleon. The last two were familiar with Aristotelian categories as well, a tradition Christians tended to be wary of until the Arians employed it in the early fourth century. The Gnostics also made extensive use of Homer, especially as interpreted allegorically by the Neo-Pythagoreans, but their sources were not only pagan Greek but Oriental and Jewish as well, as Hegesippus makes clear. The myths of Jewish apocalyptic sects provided much of their material, with a strong dose of encratism (i.e., ascetic rigor) added.

If Marcion, Tatian, and Montanus the Phrygian prophet (fl. 156–175) developed systems inimical to

[26] Irenaeus, *Against Heresies,* Book I, Chap. 10.

[27] *Ibid.,* Book I, Chap. 11.

Christianity from within, its main adversary from without was Mani (d. ca. 277), a Babylonian of the Persian Sassani dynasty who claimed to be the revealer of a new religion. His radical dualism (Good and Evil, Light and Darkness) was an amalgam of Zoroastrian, Buddhist, Jewish, and gnostic Christian elements. Given freedom to teach by Shapur I after his accession (241), he was put to death by Zoroastrian priests under Bahram I after more than thirty years of activity. Mani left behind him an antimatter tradition that came to be known in Christian circles as Manicheism. It surfaced again over the centuries, in Spain as Priscillianism (fourth century), in the Balkans as the heresy of the Bogomils (tenth century), and in France as the teachings of the Cathari and Albigenses (both twelfth century). The tendency to reject sex and marriage and to proscribe alcohol and certain foods may be called profoundly anti-Christian, yet it seems to have developed from Syriac Christianity by way of the exaggeration of certain elements found therein.

If this Manichean spirit, so often attributed to Christianity as essential to it, flourished on the banks of the Euphrates, there is also the fact that in that region special buildings were first used for worship. Dura Europos has the earliest church building and baptistry we know of, from the Parthian period of the second century (and a decorated *mithraeum* and synagogue as well).

Beginnings of Theology; Persecutions

The late second century, as has been said, saw the writings of Irenaeus, who was not a theologian in the systematic sense but a pastor and teacher. The first two Christian writers to merit the title theologian are Tertullian (d. after 220), a Latin-speaking native of Carthage who as a young man was a lawyer in Rome, and in the Greek-speaking world Origen of Alexandria (d. 253–254). Each was extremely rigorous in his personal life, Tertullian to the point of leaving the Church and espousing Montanism. Origen's speculations took him outside what came to be the prevailing orthodoxy, teaching the subordination of the Spirit to the Son and the Son to the Father, an endless succession of worlds, and the ultimate blessedness of all creatures. Tertullian's biting sarcasm was directed first to persecutors and detractors of the Christian faith but later to laxists in the Church. These included those who permitted second marriage, who did not fast sufficiently, and who assumed that the "church of the bishops" can forgive, rather than "spiritual men," the apostles and prophets.

Clement of Alexandria (d. before 215) may be called the first Christian scholar. He was familiar with Holy Scripture and almost all of Christian literature up to his time. He cited several hundred pagan authors in his writings, many of these as he found them in previous collections of material. Clement saw the Christian philosophy anticipated in many ancient writings. He strove to show that the Christian *gnōsis* was superior to any other claim of knowledge and discussed at length the relation of religious to secular culture.

The deaths of Tertullian and Clement in the early third century make all the more remarkable the fact that the first record we have of Christianity in North Africa is the Acts of the Martyrs of Cillium in Byzacena (modern Qasrin in Tunisia) from the year 180. The missionaries may have come from Rome but just as likely from the eastern Mediterranean. There were both Latin- and Greek-speaking Christians in the North African provinces of Africa Proconsularis (northern Tunisia), Byzacena (southern Tunisia), Numidia (northwestern Tunisia), and Mauretania (Algeria, Morocco). The bishop of Carthage, Cyprian, who was martyred under the persecution of Valerian in 258, mentions churches in the Spanish cities of León, Astorga, Mérida, and Saragossa. A leader of the Spanish Church at the Council of Elvira (ca. 300) was Ossius or Hosius of Córdoba, who reappeared as Constantine's chief theological adviser at the Council of Nicaea in 325.

Decius (249–251) began to require sacrifice to the Roman gods by all his subjects because things were going badly in the Empire, among them the Gothic invasions, which began in 248. There was a great trade in *libelli* (certificates of having sacrificed) among members of the wealthier Christian class. The bishops of Rome, Antioch, and Jerusalem were martyred for their refusal to sacrifice. Cyprian at first fled Carthage but then came back to die; not, however, before he had challenged the Roman bishops Cornelius and Stephen on their policy of readmitting the lapsed, a stand that he ultimately came to adopt himself because of the large number of defectors.

The emperor Diocletian (284–305) ruled east of the Adriatic with Galerius as his assistant Caesar, and Maximian was the Augustus of the West assisted by Constantius, father of Constantine, as Caesar. Reverses in the Empire over the cost of the army, currency, taxation, and prices caused the emperors and their advisors to seek a scapegoat, which they found in Christianity. In 303 the Christian cathedral in Nicomedia near the imperial palace was sacked. Within a year all citizens were required to sacrifice to the imperial gods under pain of death.

The Constantinian Settlement; Council of Nicaea and Subsequent Catholic-Arian Struggle

Constantius died at York in 305 and was succeeded by his son, Constantine. Like his father, Constantine was a worshipper of *Sol Invictus* but he invoked the Christian God when he invaded Italy and attacked Maxentius at the Milvian Bridge near Rome in 312. There had been bitter persecution of the Christians in the East under Galerius (d. 311) and Maximin Daia, who came to be conquered by Licinius. The latter, in February 313, concurred with his Western counterpart Constantine in a policy of religious liberty for all (Edict of Milan). It has been estimated that at the time of this edict one eighth of the 50 million people of the empire were Christian. Harnack says that in some of the 120 provinces of the Empire half the population was Christian (Map 36).

Cyprian had held that a minister who abjured the Spirit by his cowardice had lost the right to transmit the gifts of the Spirit by his ministrations. This was not the Roman theology that came to prevail. It survived for long in Africa, however, in a nationalist colonial party known as that of the Donatists.

Constantine, newly and doubtfully Christian (he was baptized only toward the end of his life in 337), did not hesitate to constitute a council of bishops at Arles in 314 as a court of appeals for a contested Roman decision against the Donatists. He did something similar and much more influential in 325 in the city of Nicaea near Byzantium (later Constantinople). Desiring an unchallenged, official teaching for the Empire, he summoned a church council to hear charges that the presbyter of Alexandria, Arius, had been teaching that Jesus Christ, although "the first-born of all creatures" (cf.

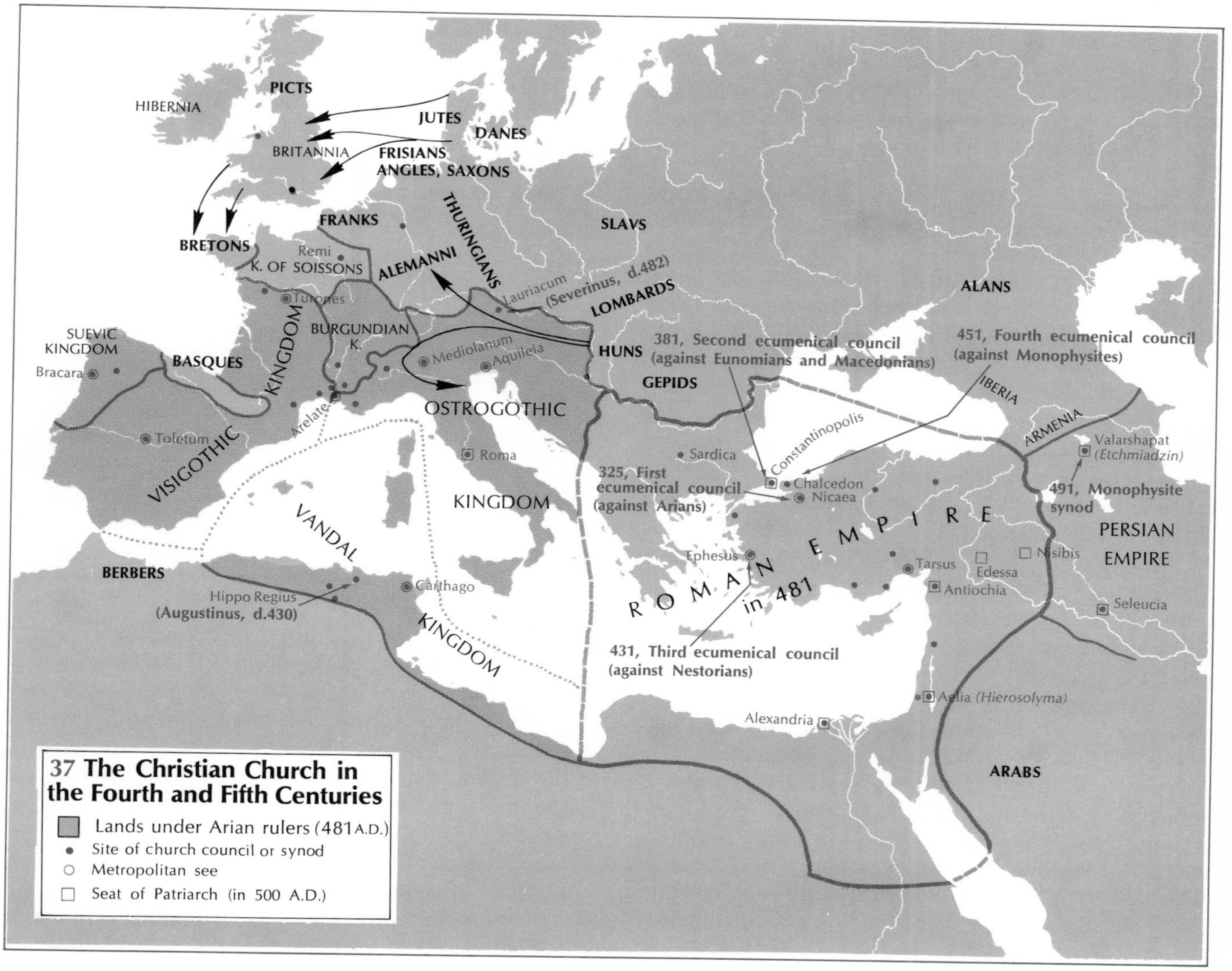

Colossians 1:15), was not one with the God and Father of all (Map 37). Even though Eusebius of Nicomedia, the court bishop who was later to baptize Constantine, defended Arius, the opposition party (which included Athanasius, the bishop of Alexandria) within the next three years prevailed over Arius. It adopted the creedal formula of Caesarea—whose bishop was the historian Eusebius so often cited above—which said that the Son was "of the Father's substance, God of God, light of light, true God of true God, of the same substance [*homoousios*] as the Father." Arius defended his teaching in person. The Council nonetheless condemned him explicitly. The emperor promulgated the creed as the law of the Empire.

We have the names of 220 bishops who attended. Only 5 were from the West, one being Hosius of Córdoba. Pope Sylvester did not attend but "sent priests to represent him." The bishops came from as far away as Scythia, Persia, and Mesopotamia. At the same council, an attempt was made to force celibacy on the clergy in their marriages, as had been legislated some years before at Elvira, but the attempt failed. Unmarried priests, however, were forbidden to marry after ordination. The computation of the date of Easter, a matter that had been much differed over, was set as the first Sunday after the first full moon of the spring equinox; this custom still prevails in the West.

The emperor (Constantius II, 337–361) had favored the Arian party and took its defeat with bad grace, convoking councils at Sardica, modern Sofia (342), Rimini, and Seleucia (both 359) to try to reverse the Nicaean settlement. In general, the two Eastern meetings favored the Arian position whereas Rimini reaffirmed the creed of Nicaea. The writings of Athanasius (d. 336) were influential in the fifty-year period that followed Nicaea. Numerous compromise formulas were devised (called erroneously "semi-Arian") describing the Son as "in all respects like the Father" or "of a nature like that of the Father." Arianism prevailed in the lifetime of Constantine's sons, Constantine II, Constantius II, and Constans. Julian (361–363) reverted to the Roman state religion, but succeeding emperors in East and West, notably Gratian (375–383), dealt paganism a set of serious blows. Pope Damasus (366–384) worked to consolidate the Catholic position. The Eastern emperor Theodosius called a council at Constantinople in 381—reckoned the second of the "ecumenical councils," although only Eastern bishops attended—at which those who denied the divinity of the Holy Spirit ("Pneumatomachi," "Macedonians," after Bishop Macedonius of Constantinople) were reprobated. The party of Sabellius or the modalists (Father, Son, and Spirit as three modes or forms assumed by the one God) received the same treatment. So did the teaching of Apollinaris of Laodicaea in Syria (d. ca. 390) that the Logos replaced Christ's human soul.

At the end of this council a baptismal creed recited at Constantia in Cyprus, of Jerusalem origin, was adopted. It said of the Holy Spirit that he was "Lord and Giver of life, who proceeds from the Father, who together with the Father is adored and glorified, and who spoke through the prophets." This so-called Nicaeno-Constantinopolitan Creed later had the phrase "*filioque*" ("and from the Son") added to it from Spanish usage, as will be seen below.

Influential writers of the period in the tradition that came to be reckoned orthodox were the brothers Basil of Caesarea (d. 379) and Gregory of Nyssa (d. 394) and their friend Gregory of Nazianzus (d. ca. 390). The latter served as bishop of Constantinople for a few days only, during its council. The three were called "the Cappadocian fathers." They had in common Nicaean faith, a deep interest in monasticism, and outstanding holiness. A Church father who was more a pastor than a theologian was Cyril, bishop of Jerusalem (d. 386), who composed twenty-four addresses to catechumens delivered in the Church of the Holy Sepulchre. He it was who worked numerous historical elements indicated by the *genius loci* into the baptismal liturgy of Easter eve.

Further Explicitation of Christological Doctrine

A summary of successive Church councils and the matter they dealt with may be helpful here. Understanding Nicaea and Constantinople to have been the first two general councils, the enumeration would be (3) Ephesus (431) against the teaching of Nestorius, Patriarch of Constantinople, that Mary gave birth to the man Jesus in whom God dwelt "as in a temple," and hence should not have the title *Theotokos* ("God-bearer"); against the teaching of the British (Irish?) monk Pelagius, with whom Augustine crossed swords around 412, that man can live without sin and can observe the commandments of God; (4) Chalcedon (451) against Eutyches and the Monophysites ("We declare that one and the same Christ . . . must be acknowledged in two natures without confusion, without change") and the Nestorians ("without division, without separation"); "the specific character of each nature is preserved and they are united in one person [*prosōpon*] and one hypostasis"; (5) II Constantinople (553), in which the emperor Justinian (527–565) contrived the condemnation of "Three Chapters" of anti-Nestorianism in the hope of restoring the Monophysites to Catholic unity, stressing the formula of Cyril of Alexandria, "one incarnate nature of the Word of God"; (6) III Constantinople (680–681) against the Monothelites, who held that in Christ there were "two volitions or wills and two natural operations," the human will being not opposed but obedient to "his divine and omnipotent will"; (7) II Nicaea (787) against those who opposed the veneration of images (Iconoclasts), a party that had been influential ever since the emperor Leo III, the Isaurian, had prohibited the veneration of icons in 730, possibly under Islamic and Jewish influence.

The more important Church fathers of the West in this period—those of the East except John Chrysostom (d. 407) having already been named—were Ambrose, bishop of Milan (d. 397), a pastoral figure; Jerome (d. 419 or 420), translator of the Bible from Hebrew and Greek into Latin in the "Vulgate" or popular version; and Augustine, bishop of Hippo (d. 430), the "doctor of grace" who gave shape to many Church doctrines in their Western expression.

Spread of Christianity Through Arian Influence

Wulfile (or Ulfila), a grandson of Christian Cappadocians who had been taken prisoner of war, was a bishop among the Germanic tribe of Goths north and south of the Danube, 341–383. The Arian bishop Eusebius of Constantinople had been his consecrator. He translated the Bible into the Gothic tongue, an important achievement. From Wulfila's time onward, all the Germanic tribes from the East that entered the Empire became Arian Christians, set against their Greek masters both politically and religiously (Map 37). John Chrysostom met with no success in persuading them to accept

19-1 St. Jerome in his cell, c. 1530 A.D. (Courtesy of the John G. Johnson Collection, Philadelphia.)

Nicaean orthodoxy. The Visigoths (West Goths) under Alaric sacked Rome in 410, then took southern Gaul and Spain in 419. Spain remained Arian until the late sixth century, when Recared the king, under the influence of Leander, bishop of Seville (d. 600), became a Catholic. Leander's brother Isidore, who succeeded him (600–636), is counted the last Church father of the West, a title accorded to John of Damascus (d. 749?) in the East.

The Ostrogoths (East Goths), who likewise were Arians, settled in Pannonia (modern Hungary) but moved on to Italy in 489, producing Theodoric the Great (ca. 455–526), the most renowned of all the Germanic kings. Theodoric in 493 conquered Odoacer, who had had himself proclaimed king of Italy in 476 upon the defeat of Romulus Augustus, the last emperor of the West. Theodoric consolidated his empire to include Italy, Sicily, Dalmatia, Pannonia, Noricum (Switzerland and the Tyrol), Rhaetia (Austria), and Provence, but it all fell into the hands of the Byzantines (552–553) after his death.

The Lombards, largely Arians, invaded Italy from Pannonia in 468. They took most of the peninsula except Ravenna, Rome, and some lands to the south, making Pavia their capital. They were gradually absorbed into an Italian and Catholic stream by 680. The Huns under Attila (d. 453) marched on Rome in 452, there to be persuaded by Pope Leo I (440–461) to desist from attacking the defenseless city. Genseric and his Vandals from Pannonia were similarly kept from destroying this city, which they had entered in 455. The Pope's convictions about the primatial nature of the see of Peter and Paul were very much to the fore in his conduct. The Vandals, who ruled in Africa from 428 to 533, were the most anti-Catholic of the invading tribes. Justinian, the Byzantine emperor (527–565), defeated them through his general Belisarius in 534, bringing to an end a century of persecution of the "homoousians" (Catholics) at their hands. Needless to say, the Arian tribes suffered equally at the hands of the Romans.

Expansion of Catholic Christianity in Europe, Nestorian and Monophysite Christianity in Asia and North Africa

The Burgundians were driven out of the Rhine Valley to Savoy along the Rhône, where, under the influence of Archbishop Avitus of Vienne, they left the Arian for the Catholic persuasion. They came under the rule of the Franks in 532, ultimately the most influential of all the Germanic tribes. The Franks proceeded from the Lower (i.e., northern) Rhine in a southwesterly direction around 450. Their young king Clovis (481–511) conquered the Romans in Gaul at Soissons in 486. Ten years later he became a Christian and a Catholic under the influence of his Burgundian wife Clotilda. Before his career of victory and political strategy was over, he had subjected the Alemanni, Burgundians, Thuringians, and Bavarians to Frankish rule.

Christianity reached England through the Roman colonists very early but it did not gain a firm hold until the sixth century. Angles, Saxons, and Jutes from the Continent swarmed over the island after 428, driving the Christian Britons to the west—modern Wales and Cornwall. Pope Gregory I sent Augustine and a band of Roman monks there in 598. By 601 he had established bishoprics at Canterbury and York. Pope Celestine I is reported to have sent a certain Palladius to be bishop to Ireland in 431. The effective apostle of that island, however, was Patrick (432?–461), a native Briton who, after monastic studies in Gaul, landed in the north and made Armagh his see. The whole island took on a monastic character after 520 under the influence of St. Finian of Clonard (Map 38). The chief foundations were at Bangor near Belfast (St. Comgall), Clonmacnois (St. Ciaran), and Clonfert (St. Brendan).

Scotland similarly was evangelized toward the end of the fourth century by a Briton named Ninian working in the north out of his monastery on Iona. Toward the end of the sixth century St. Columban carried the monastic rule of St. Fintan of Clonenagh to Luxeuil in France and Bobbio in Italy, whence it spread to some fifty other monasteries. It remained strong until Charlemagne proposed the less rigorous Rule of St. Benedict for all monasteries of his empire. Bodily severity became the Irish national tradition, along with the learning that marked the monastic schools. By the year 1200 early Irish monasticism had yielded to the Cistercian rule and that of the Canons Regular of St. Augustine.

Outside the Empire, Christianity spread from the eastern Syrians mentioned above (Edessa in Osroëne) to Sāsānī Mesopotamia. Shapur II, who ruled for seventy years (309–379) was a strong proponent of the Persian national religion, Mazdaism. He resisted Constantine's recommendation that Christianity be viewed favorably, as much for political as religious reasons. Shapur executed three successive bishops of Seleucia-Ctesiphon on the Tigris. Especially important was the school associated with the name of St. Ephraim (306–373), first at Nisibis, then back at Edessa. It stressed the prevailing Semitic culture of that region of the Empire rather than the imperial Greek or Latin. Shapur's successor, Yazdagird I (399–420), was tolerant of the Christians and received the overtures of bishop Maruthas. The latter organized the Persian church along the lines

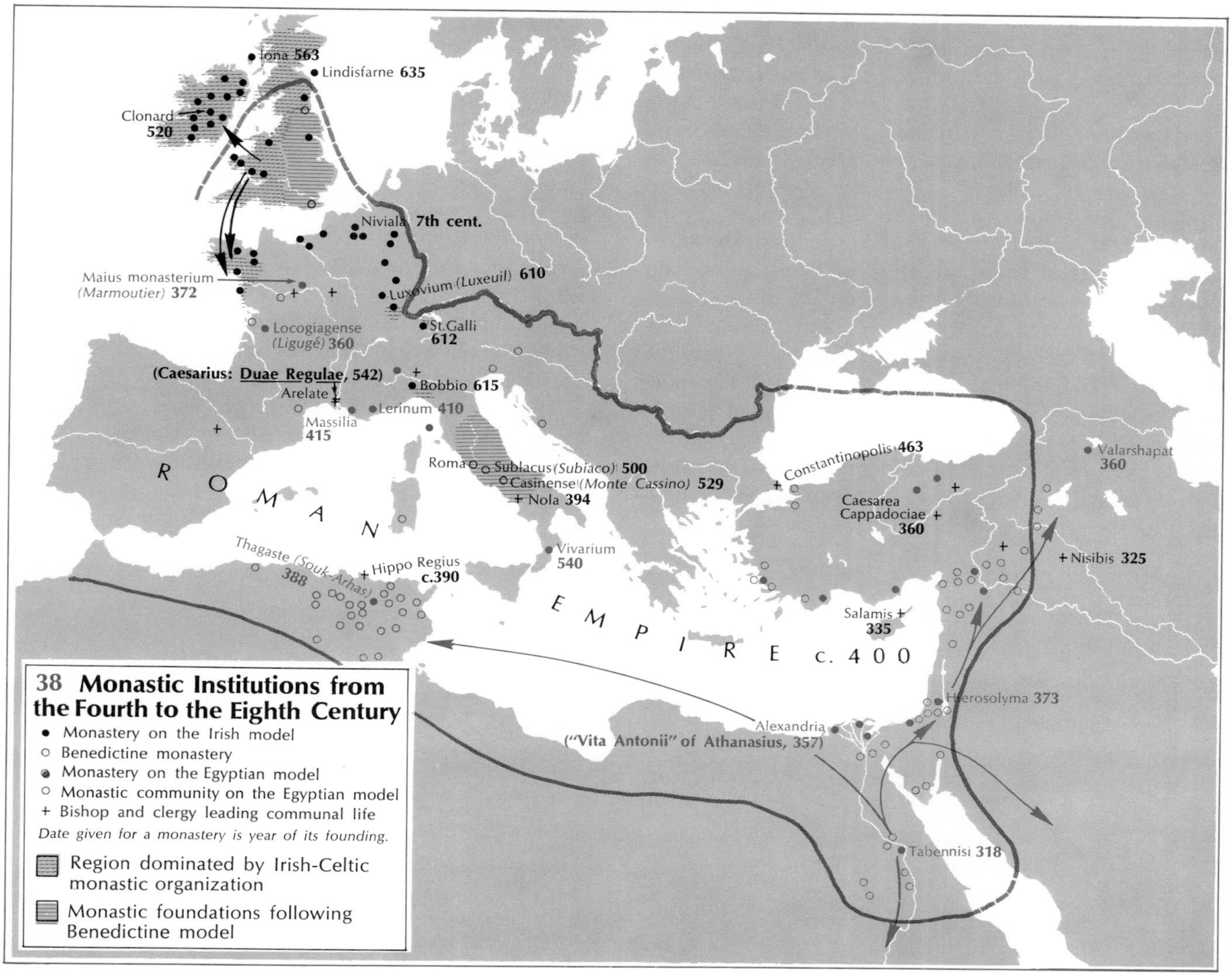

38 Monastic Institutions from the Fourth to the Eighth Century

of parish, diocese, and province; he also held a synod of bishops in 410 that adopted the teachings of Nicaea. By that date there were bishops on Bahrein in the Arabian Gulf and the region of Khurasan in northern Persia. Christian missionary effort, by this time Nestorian, brought the gospel to Kurdistan, the island of Socotra (sixth century), south India, and finally in the seventh century, China (Map 39).

The East Syrian see of Edessa was committed to the Nestorian or Antiochene school of Christology under the direction of Narsai (437–457), as contrasted with the Alexandrian theology that had prevailed at Ephesus and II Constantinople. Gradually, however, it came under the influence of the teaching of St. Cyril of Alexandria. Nisibis (Persian since 363) then became the capital of Nestorian thought under Narsai, who lived on until 502. This Nestorian Christology was only doubtfully heretical by a Nicaean norm, so nuanced was the formulation of the distinction of the two natures in the incarnate Word (in the tradition of Theodore of Mopsuestia rather than Cyril). The Catholics accused the Nestorians of believing in two persons in Christ and not two natures only, their formulation being that there was but one person in Christ. In the period after Chalcedon (451–600), that one person was widely assumed to be not human but divine. One thing certain was the opposition of Nestorianism to the Monophysite teaching that prevailed among the Arabs of the Syrian Desert and upper Mesopotamia. Bishop Barsumas of Nisibis (late fifth century) and the reformer Mar Aba (540–552) kept the Persian church in practical isolation from the territories west of it. The Christianity of this people was built on a twofold resistance to Monophysite and Mazdean influence.

The conversion of Armenia, which had long been a pawn between the empires of Rome and Persia, was the work of St. Gregory the Illuminator, who, between 280 and 290, brought Christianity from Cappadocia to King Tiridates and his realm. Bishops Nerses (d. 374) and Shanak (d. 439) consolidated the earlier gains. Early in the fifth century, Mesrob provided his people with an alphabet and subsequently the Bible, works of the Church fathers, and a liturgy in translation. The fifth-century efforts of King Yazdagird of Persia to convert the Armenians to Mazdaism were unsuccessful. An alphabet was devised for Azerbaijan in the Caucasus by the same Mesrob. Georgia, similarly, was given the Khutsuri alphabet for its language. In Georgia, the apostle was a nun whose name is not preserved (she is known as St. Nino and, in the *Roman Martyrology*, Christiana). By the holiness of her life and her preaching she is said to have influenced King Mirian to accept Christianity in 334.

Pharan in the southwest of the Sinai Peninsula became the episcopal see of a monk named Moses around 375. The conversion of some of the Saracens was brought about by his efforts and those of Queen Maria but nothing lasting eventuated either there, in Arabia, or among the Himyarites of Yemen in the southwest corner of that peninsula. The latter is mentioned in particular because of the embassy of Constantius to that people in the 350's. He sent an Arian convert named Theophilus the Indian, whose efforts were not successful. A community of Christians (like that of Jews) was to be found in the south Arabian city of Najran. A provincial king who had become a Jew, Dhu-Nawas, decimated the Christians in 573.

The conversion of Abyssinia took place out of Phoenician Tyre when two fourth-century Christians, shipwrecked off the Somali coast, made their way as slaves to the royal court at Axum. They became influential with the boy king Ezana, and one of them, Frumentius,

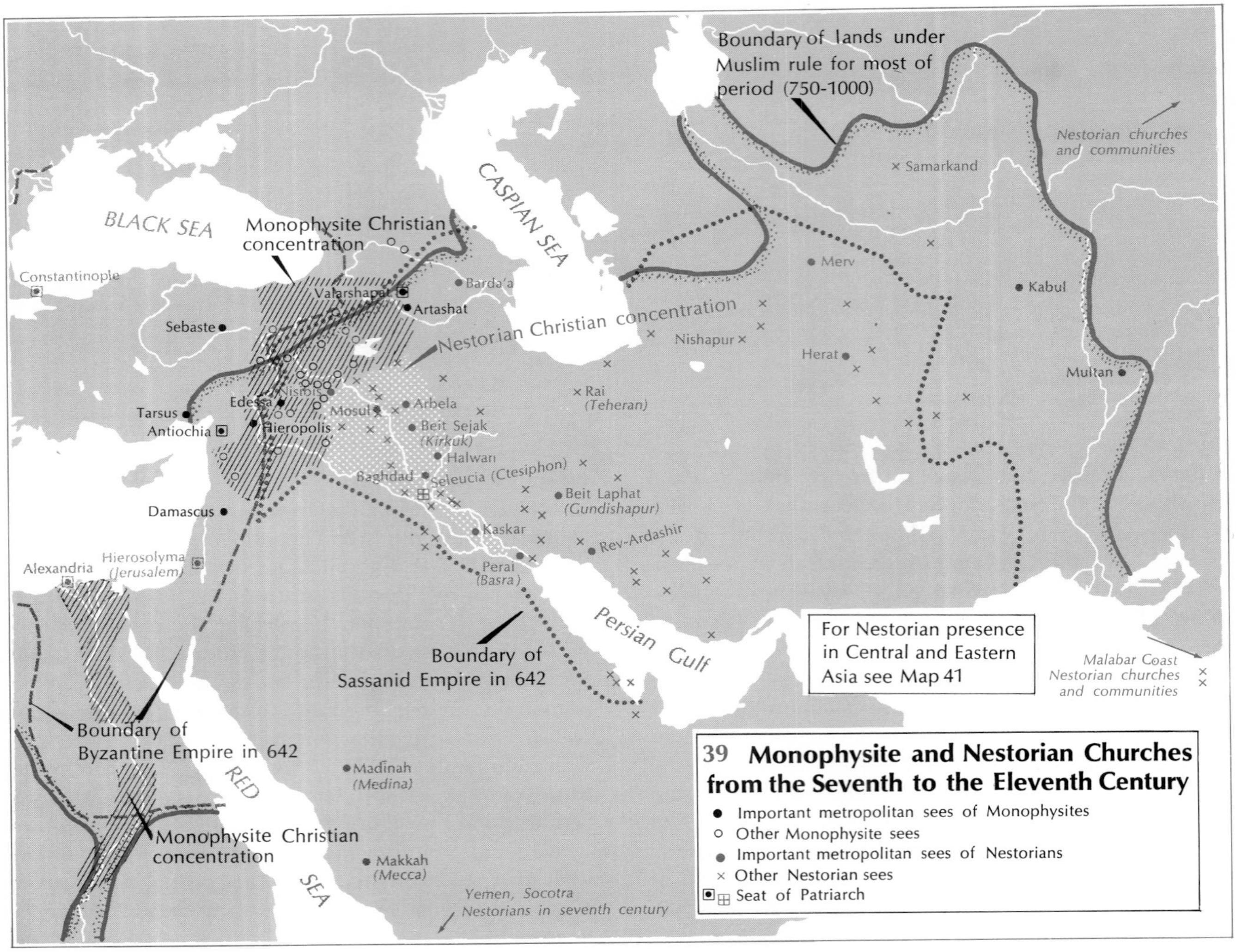

39 Monophysite and Nestorian Churches from the Seventh to the Eleventh Century

was named bishop by Athanasius of Alexandria some time between 325 and 350. This church, Nicaean from the start, shortly had its own version of the scriptures and a liturgy in the native Ge'ez tongue. In the sixth century nine missionary "saints" brought Monophysitism and monastic life. An Ethiopian king of that century, Kaleb Ella Asbeha, led an expedition to Yaman to retaliate for the massacre of Christians at Najrān. Most people of the region converted to Islām in 630.

The caliphates of Abū Bakr (632–634) and 'Umar (634–644), the first of which began only a decade after Muḥammad's flight from Makkah, brought an end to Christian dominance in the Middle East. The patriarchates were successively—Antioch (637), Jerusalem (638), and Alexandria (642)—brought under Muslim rule. The Egyptian Monophysite church rejoiced over its liberation from Byzantium, so bitter had been the Christological dispute between them. Armenia and Cyprus became Muslim under 'Uthmān I (644–656), Damascus under the Umawī dynasty (661–750), Carthage in 698, and the northwest coast of Africa over into Spain from the middle of the seventh century. Constantinople was besieged but not taken in 717–718. Christians and Jews were expelled from the Arabian Peninsula but, in general, Christians were not treated badly at Muslim hands. Positive political and economic sanctions in favor of Islam were among the factors that brought about a gradual religious change.

The political successes of Islam between 650 and 750, when it reached its zenith of expansion in western Mediterranean Europe, sent Greek and Syrian monks westward to Rome in numbers and assured the Greek character of the papal office. Muslim victories in North Africa, Syria, Palestine, and Spain served to bring Rome and Constantinople closer. Eleven out of seventeen popes in that period of one hundred years had a mainly Greek background, a distinct change from the Italian-dominated papacy of the century before. This meant that the two halves of the empire were held together by a religious tie. The emperor at Constantinople acknowledged the primacy of the Roman patriarchate and the pope, in turn, the Eastern emperor's authority. In 668 the Emperor Constans II was murdered in Sicily. This assassination brought to an end—though this could not have been known at the time—the political unity of the eastern Mediterranean, North Africa, and Italy under Byzantine rule. Five years before his death the emperor had visited Rome and been accepted as its lawful sovereign. This occurrence was not to be repeated for seven centuries, when an Eastern emperor came as a petitioner in the person of John V Palaeologus. That sovereign came to make his submission to the pope in 1365 in the vain hope of receiving help from the West against the Ottoman Turks. No pope visited Constantinople between 710 and 1967, when Paul VI made a visit to the patriarch Athenagoras.

The Division of Christian East and West

The Frankish Kingdom; Charlemagne

The newly converted nations of the West had no interest in a Greek papacy, Latin being their laboriously acquired second tongue. Conversely, such Latin-speaking popes as there were looked to the East for their culture, not to the barbarian West. But in 729, when the Byzantine emperor told Pope Gregory II not to display pictures of the martyrs and angels in his churches, the pope replied with spirit that as Peter's successor he had an obligation to the kingdoms of the West (England, Germany, and France), who honored Peter in his image "as if he were God himself on earth." In 753, when the empire was under increasing Lombard attack, Pope Stephen II—the first of a line of Latin popes that would last eight centuries—crossed the Alps to make some alliances that would strengthen claims of papal sovereignty. He made an agreement the next year with Pepin that divided political power in Italy between the pope and the Carolingian dynasty. The important difference was that although the emperor had been the pope's political superior King Pepin came to him as client; not yet as the emperor, however, until the pope should produce someone of his line for that purpose. The seizure of political power from the emperor by the pope had its practical outcome in 800, when, on Christmas Day, Leo III crowned Pepin's grandson Charlemagne emperor of the West.

This Frankish prince, illiterate though he was, took his defense of the churches in his domain, centered in Aachen, very seriously. After II Nicaea in 787 he and his advisers drew up a scorching attack on the decrees of that Greek-dominated council. This was a sort of warning to the pope, who had been represented there by legates. None of the Western churches had been represented because of the papal and Eastern supposition that in the realm of theology they had nothing to say. The pope affected to ignore this intervention because orthodoxy was a clerical preserve, but he could not successfully influence Charlemagne to drop to phrase "*filioque*" from the Nicaean Creed in masses cele-

40 The Ecclesiastical Organization of Europe c. 1050
(on the eve of the East-West division of Patriarch Michael Cerularius, 1054)
Iceland converted to Christianity c. 1000
Extension of influence of Church of Rome
Ecclesiastical organization gradually abandoned after 711, renewed after 1050
Northern limit of Muslim rule, c. 1050
Boundaries of Church Territories, c.1050
In communion with Church of Rome
In communion with Patriarch of Constantinople
In communion with Patriarch of Antioch
Overlapping jurisdiction of Rome and Constantinople in first half of eleventh century
See of Patriarch (all churches)
Church of Rome
Bishopric founded before 600
Archbishopric founded before 600
Status in 1050 established between 600 and 900
Status in 1050 established —or re-established following reconquest from Muslims— after 900 (with year of establishment)
Only the most important sees shown in Italy
Eastern Churches
See of Metropolitan; dates of establishment are unreliable and are not shown
Trondheim 1029
Bergen
1050
St. Andrews
Armagh
Dublin
995
York
Lincoln 1050
London
1050
Utrecht
1014
Aarhus 948
Lund 1048
948
965
1022
1048
948
918
Hamburg
Bremen
948
948
968
Gniezno 1000
Magdeburg 968
Köln
968
1028
967
968
Wroclaw 1000
Rouen
Paris
Reims
Mainz
Bamberg 1007
Prague 973
Krakow 1000
Tours
Sens
Bourges
Basel
Salzburg
Galitze
Kiev
Nov
1009
Gran 1000
1009
1009
1010
Kaločsa 1006
1030
1010
1009
1003
Bordeaux
Lyons
Vienne
Tarantaise
Milan
992
Aquileia
Grado
Lugo
915
Braga
León
980
1035
1022
1045
1045
Auch
Arles
Narbonne
Aix-en-Provence
Marseilles
Ravenna
Belgrade
1040
1000
1000
Split
Dristra
Lisbon
Toledo
Barcelona
Rome
1022
1022
1022
1034
Siponto 11th cent.
Bari 10th cent.
Benevento 969
Capua 966
Naples 990
Amalfi 987
Salerno 983
Acerenza 11th cent.
Brindisi
Otranto
11th cent.
Cagliari 11th cent.
Seville
Sta. Severina 10th cent.
Reggio
Palermo
Philippopolis
Adrianopolis
Thessalonike
Larissa
Smyrna
Patrai
Athenai
Rhodos
Gortyn

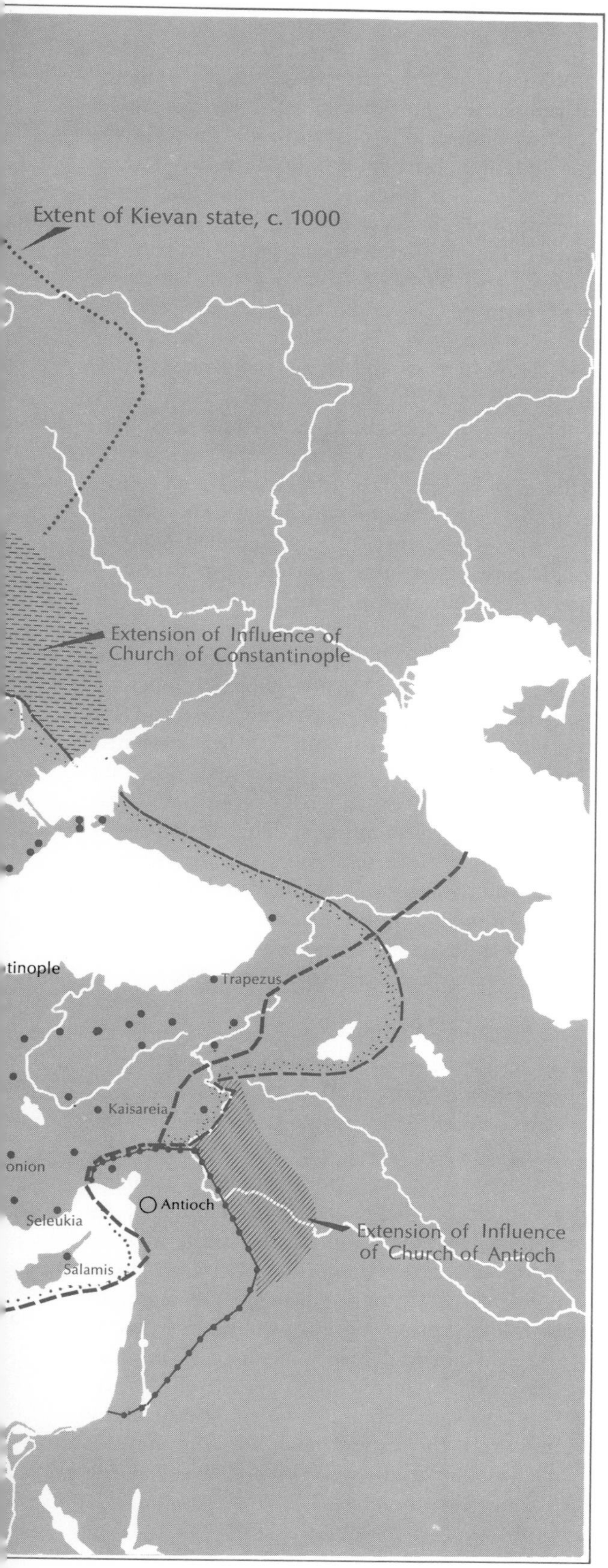

19-2 Byzantine church of *Santa Fosca* on the lagoons near Venice, 9th–11th century A.D.

brated at his court. The Roman rite, interestingly, did not include the Creed. When in 1030 the Emperor Henry II requested that it do so, there appeared on the scene the first claim of doctrinal difference between East and West. It came about almost imperceptibly and as a result of political pressure from the Western nations.

Claims of Doctrinal and Disciplinary Difference

The phrase *"filioque,"* which probably originated in Spain, declares that the Holy Spirit proceeds from the Father *and the Son,* whereas the traditional Eastern expression of the mystery would have been (had II Constantinople bothered to speak of it in 681, as it did not) "from the Father through the Son." Theologians of the East and West, both at the time and in subsequent councils attempting to achieve reunion, concluded that there was no real difference in the two formulations. (Pope Leo IX was defending it in 1050 under the figure of a fruit that could be said to come from the trunk of a tree, or from a branch, or from the trunk through the branch.) The offense of the West in Eastern eyes was that it had innovated through liturgical practice without consulting the East, through ordinary channels ending in conciliar settlement. Whatever the case, with this grievance from the side of Constantinople and Charlemagne's over the unilateral settlement, as he thought it, on images at II Nicaea, the latter council in 787 was the last to which both East and West were parties. It is reckoned the seventh of the ecumenical or churchwide councils. The Roman Church went on to convene eleven more before Trent, two of them restoring brief and fragile unity with the East (II Lyons, 1274, and Florence, 1438–1445) and three subsequent to the Reform (Trent, 1545–1563; I Vatican, 1869–1870; and II Vatican, 1962–1965).

The consolidation of Western political power from the eighth century through the eleventh (see Map 40) was marked by a thoroughgoing ignorance on the part of civil and Church rulers of how the East thought, and an even more abysmal ignorance of Islam. The practical result of this isolation was a division of Christendom marked by inertia on both sides. Pope Nicholas I (858–867) was able to assert his independence of the Frankish emperor Louis II and to rebuke the Eastern emperor for his deposition of Ignatius as patriarch of Constantinople. Louis had put a certain Photius in the see. The latter in 867 defied the pope for his introduction of Latin rites into the Church of Bulgaria and for teaching the theory of twofold procession (i.e., of the Spirit from the Father and the Son). In that same year a council at Constantinople declared the Roman Church heretical in certain matters and excommunicated Nicholas. Between 870 and 920 the quarrel between East and West continued unresolved.

19-3 *Oberzell,* early medieval church on the island of Reichenau (Germany), c. 900 A.D.

The Final Breach

This "Photian schism," as the West called it, led to an imperial request of the pope in 1024 for the independence of the Church of Constantinople in its own sphere. This led to a further and final confrontation between Pope Leo IX and Michael Cerularius, the patriarch of Constantinople, thirty years later. The latter two had a common enemy in the Normans, who held control in southern Italy and Sicily, an area that had been ecclesiastically Byzantine (i.e., under the patriarch of Constantinople) since the time of the Eastern emperor Leo III (714–741). The pope wanted to get his ecclesiastical power and the emperor his political power back from Norman control. The two could not come together, however, because of differences of church customs in the area. A letter of Bulgaria's leading churchman to the bishop of Apulia in 1052 worsened things. The pope's efforts to seek a settlement through a delegation to Constantinople two years later, written from captivity at the hands of the Normans, broke down altogether. His letter (September 1053) did not back down on papal policy or religious claims. He treated the emperor like a son who could bring peace but the patriarch Michael like a recalcitrant child. The patriarch answered by ordering the closing of all Latin churches in Constantinople, a move that the emperor could not arbitrate successfully. There followed in order Roman excommunication and Eastern anathema. The breach was rooted in political, cultural, and linguistic differences. Charges and countercharges of heresy were later developed, not well founded on either side. The separation was basically the falling out of brothers who had become estranged, laying their differences to resistance to divine truth.

The letter of Pope Leo IX was long (seventeen thousand words), aggrieved, and written in strong terms, such as "unexampled presumption and unbelievable affrontery." He said, "In prejudging the case of the highest See, the see on which no judgment may be passed by any man, you have received the anathema from all the Fathers of all the venerable Councils. As a hinge, remaining unmoved, opens and shuts a door, so Peter and his successors have an unfettered jurisdiction over the whole Church, since no one ought to interfere with their position, because the highest See is judged by none." The papal case was stated even more vigorously than this in terms like "temerity," "scurrility," and "synagogue of Satan," a wording that many have since regretted. But in fact such was the view of the terms of Christian unity held by the West at the time and for centuries to come.

Pope Gregory VII had dreamed as early as 1074 of

leading an army to liberate the Christians of the Middle East from the power of Islam. In 1095 Urban II activated the dream by offering indulgences—remissions of the temporal or purgatorial punishment due to sin—to all who would take part in a crusade. This exercise of papal power was contingent on sorrow for sin, God alone being the judge in such matters. In the enthusiasm of the hour, all such distinctions were lost sight of. It was taken for granted that Christ's promise to Peter of the keys of the kingdom (Matthew 16:19) included jurisdiction on immunity from all punishments short of hell fire. This use of papal power began as a spontaneous gesture that attempted to transfer the merits of the saintly to sinners in need. By the fourteenth century a massive edifice of pardons had been erected, chiefly the promise of full remission (a "plenary" indulgence) of sin and guilt on one's deathbed on condition of sorrow.

19-4 The Romanesque church of *St. Sermin,* Toulouse (France), 11th–12th century A.D.

The Crusades

The kingdoms of Aragon and Castile had taken Toledo from Muslim hands in 1085, the death date of the reformer pope Gregory VII. He had been the Benedictine monk Hildebrand, who was later to be venerated as a saint. Ten years later, in line with Gregory's zeal to be rid of evils like the purchase of church office and the conferring of bishoprics by princes, Pope Urban II at a reform council at Clermont (1095) brought the people to a fever pitch, inviting them to recover Jerusalem from the Muslims. Every kind of crude hanger-on took part in this spiritual adventure. European armies conquered Antioch in 1098 and Jerusalem a year later (see Map 58). Latin states were set up, to the great dismay of Byzantine Christians who had looked for help against Islam but not of this kind. Feuding between the two Christian parties led eventually to the sack of Constantinople by the Europeans in 1204 and the setting up of a Latin as the emperor of Byzantium. The Muslims, meanwhile, had capitalized on Christian differences and recaptured Edessa in 1144 (Ar al Ruha). A second crusade preached by St. Bernard of Clairvaux failed within the next five years to take either Edessa or Damascus. There was no ultimate recovery from this fiasco. With it, the reforming zeal of the age of Hildebrand seemed to be dissipated finally.

Intellectual and Monastic Growth

More authentic expressions of the Christian spirit than the Crusades were such intellectual products as the collection of decrees (*Decretum*) made by Gratian of the faculty of laws in the new university of Bologna; the four books of opinions (*Liber Sententiarum*) of Peter the Lombard, a theologian of Paris; the meditative treatises *Monologion* and *Proslogion,* and *Cur Deus Homo* of Anselm of Bec, an Italian monk who died as archbishop of Canterbury; and the treatises of Peter Abelard, a logician and theologian who wrote on dialectics and the mystery of the Trinity and made a compilation of the opinions of the Church fathers, *Sic et Non.* This twelfth-century activity had been spurred by the example of the rational spirit in Islam, which resulted in the availability of Aristotle's *Logic* and *Physics* through the commentaries of scholars like Ibn Sina (d. 1037) and Ibn Rushd (d. 1198).

In the realm of the spread of Christianity, the chief effort was monastic. The cluster of monasteries of Benedictine rule that had sprung from Cluny in Burgundy in 910 fell into decline after a *floruit* of about two hundred years. Their matching phenomena in Germany and Italy were the foundations stemming from Hirschau and Camaldoli. Spiritual succession in this line fell to the Cistercians, whose chief abbey (at Citeaux) was founded in 1098, and the Order of Prémontré or Norbertines, which came into existence in 1120. Both were deeply engaged in missionary activity in the Scandinavian countries, modern East Germany, Poland, and Bohemia. The effort was a Germanizing one at the start but later

Poland began to send its own missionaries to Prussia and Pomerania.

Papal Consolidation

The years 1050–1300 saw a development in the concept of the papacy from the spiritual primacy of the Roman bishopric to the more aggressive claims with which subsequent ages have become familiar. Cardinal Humbert of Silva Candida (d. 1061), adviser to Pope Leo IX (d. 1054), and Pope Gregory VII (d. 1085) are the important names here, along with the lawyer-popes Alexander III, Innocent III, Gregory IX, Innocent IV, and Boniface VIII. They erected the papal system of government into a formidable edifice through taking on cases for adjudication from all over Christendom, their clients being kings, nations, bishops, abbots, and nobles. The dispensation of justice and of benefits became the papal specialty.

A forged document known as the *Donation of Constantine* was influential in this development. In it the emperor supposedly gave to the Vicar of St. Peter preeminence over the sees of Antioch, Alexandria, Jerusalem, and Constantinople. He likewise transmitted the imperial insignia and gave him power of empire over Rome, all Italy, and the provinces of the West. The document was supposedly sealed by Constantine's having placed it on the body of St. Peter. The presence of those holy remains in Rome were, for a thousand years, the clearest title Peter's successors had to spiritual authority. Charlemagne's coronation as emperor by the pope was doubtless an attempt by the latter to show his supreme temporal lordship—a view in which Charlemagne did not concur. A donation in 962 by emperor Otto I to the popes, confirming them in their Italian posssessions, was the last such show of power for a while. Beginning with Leo IX (1049–1054), the popes of the next three centuries changed all that. The *Register* of letters of Gregory VII show him to have conceived his successorship to the "prince of the apostles" in terms of absolute monarchy. By the middle of the twelfth century, popes were using the title "Vicar of Christ," which formerly only kings and priests had used. They themselves had been content with the designation "Vicar of St. Peter."

As part of this heightened sense of papal power there came the multiplication of church councils called by the Roman bishop outside of Byzantine territory. IV Constantinople had been held in 869–870 to censure Photius. The West reckons this as the eighth ecumenical council though, understandably, the East does not. Within a span of less than a hundred years, four were held at the Lateran palace in Rome, all of them more or less constructive. They were as follows: (9) I Lateran (1123) against the investiture of bishops and abbots by way of simony or violence; (10) II Lateran (1139) against false claimants to the papacy and on points of discipline; (11) III Lateran (1179) which invoked the "secular arm" (i.e., the power of princes) against the Waldensians, who were trying to recapture the simplicity of the apostolic church, and the Albigenses, who tended toward Manicheism in their rigorously ascetic practices; (12) IV Lateran (1215), which reiterated the acts of III Lateran and strengthened the portions on excommunication and the confiscation of the land of heretics; (13) I Lyons (1245), a series of complaints of Pope Innocent IV against the pretensions of the emperor Frederick II. The IV Lateran Council also defined, against the Albigenses, Cathari, and other heretics, that "by divine power bread and wine are transubstantiated into the Body and Blood

19-5 St. Francis, by Fra Angelico. (Courtesy of the John G. Johnson Collection, Philadelphia.)

of Christ." This term for the *conversio* (*metastoichēsis*) of elements, *transubstantiation,* was first introduced by Hildebert of Tours (d. 1133).

Spread of Christianity Through the Mendicant Friars

This was an age of academic achievement. The monks of an earlier period had given way to the friars, itinerant preachers who lived by begging. Among the best known of these groups are the Franciscans and the Dominicans, named for their respective Italian and Spanish founders, St. Francis (d. 1226) and St. Dominic (d. 1221). The ideal of poverty was paramount with Francis, whereas concern with the literacy of his "little brothers" was minimal. Dominic had an ideal of learning from the start. For him poverty was but a means to the apostolic life. Gradually the adherents of both gravitated toward the newly founded universities. There they produced numerous scholars and mystics, of whom the best known among the Order of Preachers (Dominicans) were Albertus Magnus, Thomas Aquinas, Henry Suso, and Meister Eckhart, and the outstanding Friars Minor (Franciscans) Bonaventure, Duns Scotus, William of Ockham, and Roger Bacon. At the peak of their medieval development there were an estimated twenty-eight thousand Franciscans and twelve thousand Dominicans.

The friars were no less interested in mission activity than in preaching and study in Europe. A Franciscan general chapter of 1219 sent Berard of Carbio and his companions to Morocco to preach the Christian faith. As was to be expected they met with resistance from the Muslim population. Only in Spain and in the Latin crusaders' states was sustained preaching activity possible. Beheading was the fate of the Morocco mission, as also of a similar one to Tunis a year later. The Dominicans were the chief Christian evangelists in Tunis, where they were more realistically instructed by Pope Honorius III to care for the needs of resident Christians among the merchant, mercenary, and captive classes. St. Francis journeyed to the Holy Land in 1219 with a missionary end in view, but his foundation of friaries there was sparse. Scattered Franciscan and Dominican houses are

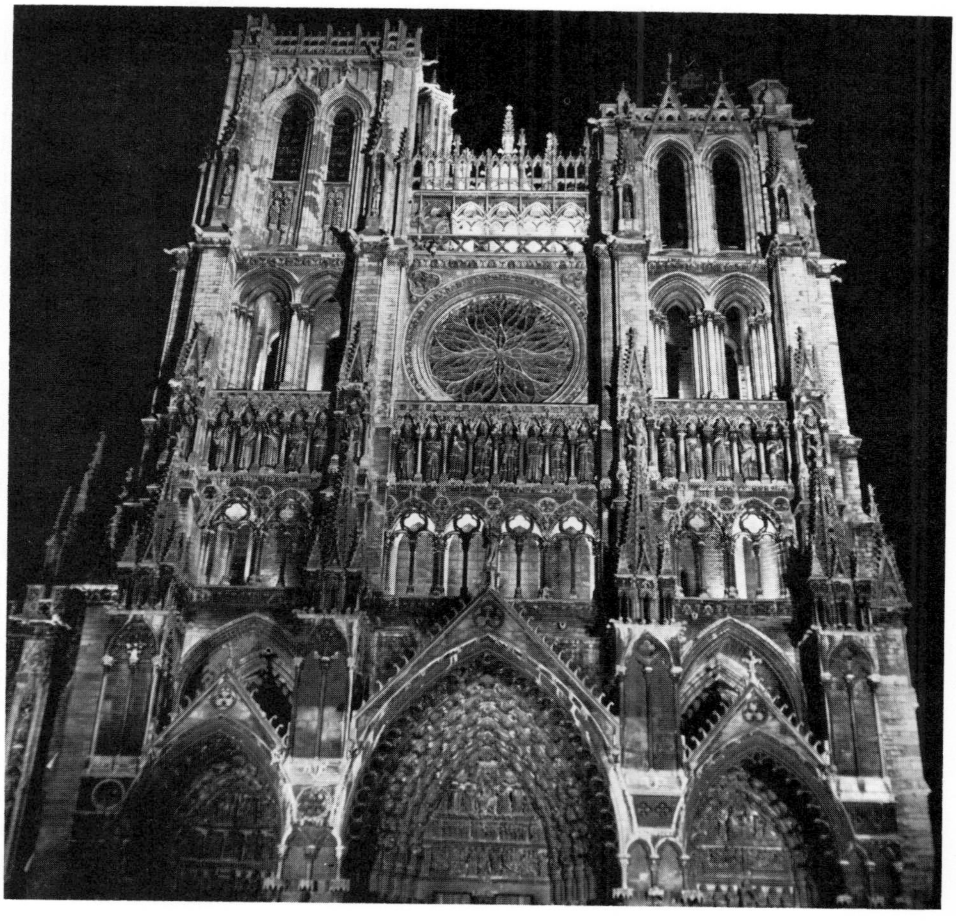

19-6 *Amiens Cathedral* by night.

19-7 *Vezelay,* Burgundy, interior of the abbey.

recorded. Pope Innocent IV was in correspondence with certain Muslim princes in 1245. William of Tripoli and Ricoldus of Monte Croce, both of whom knew Arabic, reached the crusaders' states and Baghdad respectively toward the end of the thirteenth century but without making converts in any numbers. Each tried seriously to comprehend Islam, something that cannot be said of many who came after them. With the fall of Acre in 1291 the crusaders' states collapsed and missionary efforts came to an end. St. Raymond of Peñafort, O.P. (d. 1275), and Blessed Raymond Lúll, possibly O.F.M. (d. 1316), set up schools of Arabic language and culture for a missionary purpose. Peñafort is credited with urging Aquinas to write his *Summa Contra Gentes* as a handbook for Christian missionaries in theological dialogue with Muslims.

Friar Philip, the Dominican provincial superior of the Holy Land, reported that in 1236 the Jacobite (Monophysite) patriarch of Antioch, Ignatius II, along with a number of his clergy, and the Egyptian Jacobite bishop and a Syrian Nestorian prelate had come into communion with the West. Perhaps they were motivated by the need they experienced for help against the Mongols. Pope Gregory IX immediately communicated with these Eastern Christians and also corresponded with the rulers in Georgia, where Franciscans and Dominicans were to be found. Further diplomatic moves toward the Christian East were made in the pontificate of Innocent IV when, about 1245, embassies were sent to Orthodox prelates in Armenia, Antioch, and Jerusalem. It seems clear that cooperation against Islam was the motivating force of these overtures.

More religiously oriented were the journeys of two Franciscans, William of Ruisbroek to Karakoram (1253–1255) and John of Monte Corvino (d. ca. 1330), to the court of great Khan Mangu at Khanbalik (Peking) in the papacy of Nicholas IV (1288–1292) (Map 41). During the early years of Nicholas's reign, the vicar of the Nestorian catholicos of Persia, Mar Jaballah III, came to Rome. He was sent back with letters to several resident Latin Christians and a profession of faith for the catholicos. Early in the fourteenth century Ricoldus de Monte Croce and other Dominicans reached the Persian area. The eastward expansion of Christianity grew through the spread of Italian merchant colonies and the friars' attempts to serve their religious needs. A Latin missionary diocese was set up in Khanbalik in 1307 by Clement V, with John of Monte Corvino as its bishop. John XXII created a separate province to the south in 1318, naming a Dominican the archbishop of Sultaniyyah in Persia. The chief recipients of these ministrations were the scattered Oriental Christians, Nestorians, Alans, and Armenians who had penetrated the Chinese cities. Monte Corvino reported some six thousand converts, however. Auxiliary sees to Peking were set up, including one at Zaitun on the coast. The Franciscans in the fourteenth century established vicariates in the Mongol Khanate of the Kipchak (modern Tadzhikistan); in the Middle East at Trebizond, Tabriz, and Constantinople; and in Cathay (eastern Turkestan and China).

Both mendicant orders were active in Persia and Armenia, achieving there a measure of Christian unity rather than the conversion of non-Christians. John of Monte Corvino reported a hundred or so Indian converts on his way to China. Jordan Catalani, a Dominican, won over a few more on the west coast in 1320 and 1329. There was a Latin church at Quilon in 1342. The Mongol dynasty was replaced by the Mings in 1363, a fact that made a large difference. Also of influence on missionary expansion were the adverse effect of the Black Death (1348–1349), the Hundred Years' War (from 1337), and the Great Western Schism (1378–1417).

A sixth-century Byzantine writer, Cosmas Indicopleustes, knew of missions "among the Bactrians, Huns, Indians, Armenians, Medians, and Elamites" as well as having heard of the St. Thomas Christians of India and communities in Ceylon. A monument at Hsian-Fu indicates that Nestorians had reached China in the seventh century. Slavic peoples were evangelized by both Latins and Byzantines in the eighth to tenth centuries, culmi-

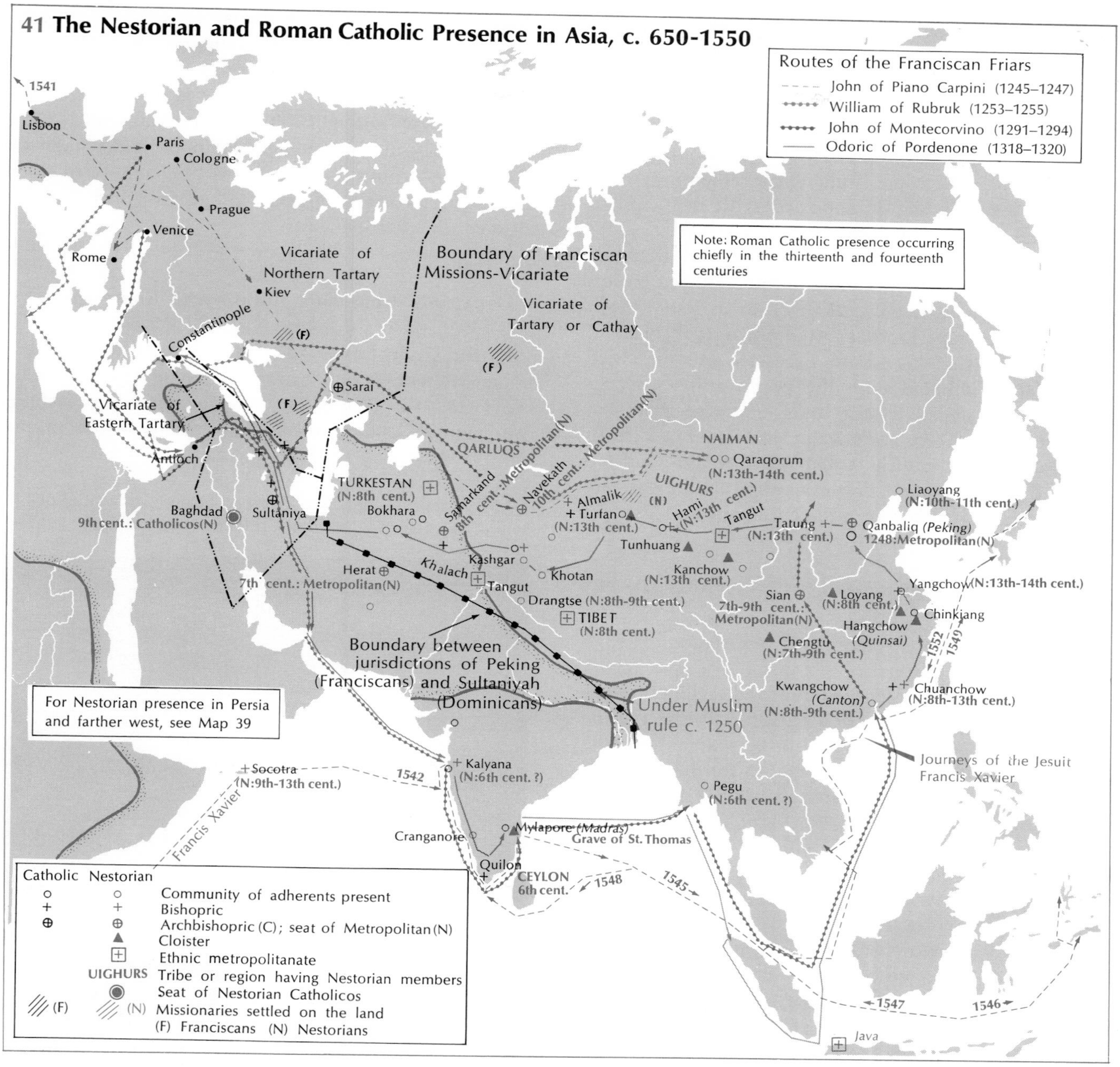

41 The Nestorian and Roman Catholic Presence in Asia, c. 650-1550

Routes of the Franciscan Friars
- - - - John of Piano Carpini (1245–1247)
····· William of Rubruk (1253–1255)
•••••• John of Montecorvino (1291–1294)
———— Odoric of Pordenone (1318–1320)

Note: Roman Catholic presence occurring chiefly in the thirteenth and fourteenth centuries

For Nestorian presence in Persia and farther west, see Map 39

Catholic	Nestorian	
o	o	Community of adherents present
+	+	Bishopric
⊕	⊕	Archbishopric (C); seat of Metropolitan (N)
▲		Cloister
⊞		Ethnic metropolitanate
UIGHURS		Tribe or region having Nestorian members
	⦿	Seat of Nestorian Catholicos
⧄ (F)	⧄ (N)	Missionaries settled on the land
		(F) Franciscans (N) Nestorians

nating in the baptism by the latter of St. Vladimir of Kiev (ca. 988). The Russian Church, jurisdictionally dependent on Byzantium until 1589, reached out to the Ugro-Finnish northeast, especially when the Mongols captured Kiev in 1240 and the capital was moved to Novgorod. The fourteenth century saw the monastic efforts at evangelization of St. Sergei of Radonej at Murmansk and Solovkij, and Stephen of Perm (responsible for the conversion of the Chuyashes and Lapps). The Mongols had become Muslims before their fall in

conquest by the Ming dynasty in 1368. The fall of Constantinople at Muslim hands in 1453 gave Russia a great sense of its importance as a Christian bastion, with Moscow as the "Third Rome." The taking of Kazan on the Volga in 1552, a Muslim Tatar stronghold, meant the Russification of that area. Thirty years later the conquest of Siberia began and within another six decades cossacks had reached the Pacific.

All of this political expansion brought Christianity in some form in its wake. The Treaty of Nerchinsk (1689) allowed a Russian Orthodox presence in Peking. In the eighteenth century, out of Siberia, missions were established at Kamchatka, among the Yakut, Buryat, and Chukchi tribes, and in the Aleutians and Alaska (the latter two from the Valamo monastery). Kazan became the center of intense missionary activity in 1854. The metropolitan of Moscow, Innokentij Veniaminov, was responsible for a strong Orthodox presence in Japan and Korea in the nineteenth century.

Returning to the West, between 1305 and 1378 the papal court was located at Avignon in southern France by popes faced with political disorder in Italy. Much of the mission expansion reported above took place in the earlier years of this period. Excessive administrative centralization coupled with the pomp and luxury of court life succeeded in alienating many segments of Catholic Europe from the Roman See. The Fraticelli in Italy, John Wyclif and the Lollards in England, and Jan Hus and the Bohemian Brethren were among the late fourteenth- and early fifteenth-century protest groups.

Schism in the West

Gregory XI paid a visit to Rome from Avignon in 1378 and died there. A Roman mob installed Urban VI by acclamation, and the French-dominated Avignon cardinals named Clement VII. For almost forty years Europe witnessed the scandal of two sets of claimants to the papal office and from 1410 to 1415 a third—the work of a Council of Pisa that deposed both of the others. The Council of Constance (1414–1418), reckoned as the sixteenth ecumencial council, achieved the resignations of Gregory XII of the Roman line and John XXIII of the brief Pisa line (two of the incumbents) but not that of Avignon's long-term Benedict XIII (1304–1423), who was isolated into powerlessness. Martin V was elected pope by the conclave and immediately nullified the claim of Constance (1415) that a council was superior to the pope. By such a display of personal strength was the disedifying schism ended.

Renaissance and Reform

The Renaissance papacy was marked by incumbents who were a strange mixture of political intelligence, cultural leadership, and moral laxity. The best known of these was Alexander VI, Rodrigo Borgia (1492–1503), the greatest statesman; Julius II, Giuliano della Rovere (1503–1513); and the most ill-starred, Leo X, Giovanni de' Medici (1513–1521). The eighteenth ecumenical council, V Lateran, took place during much of the latter's pontificate. Whereas the council was dedicated to reform, he was not. His Dutch successor, Adrian VI (1522–1523)—the last non-Italian pope and a man of austere life—could do little in his brief tenure to stem the abuses or the magnificence against which the reformers directed their attack.

Departures from Communion with Rome

Martin Luther, an Augustinian canon of Wittenberg's university with its one faculty of theology, took a public stand (1517) against abuses attaching to the preaching campaign of the Dominicans in Germany, which prom-

19-8 Martin Luther, workshop of Lucas Cranach. (Courtesy of the John G. Johnson Collection, Philadelphia.)

ised papal indulgences to contributors to the dome of St. Peter's. He provided a theological rationale when summoned the next year by a papal legate and would not back down. By 1520 he was excommunicated. Thereafter, on the basis of his study of the writings of St. Paul, he developed his doctrines of justification by faith alone and the common priesthood of the faithful, which made priestly ministrations (other than preaching) needless. Luther was prophetic, exuberant, and profound in his religious insights, even when they took an antirational turn.

In 1518 a secular priest named Huldreich Zwingli

42 The Church of Rome and the Protestant Reformation

(1484–1531), who claimed he had held his views before he heard of Luther but who was surely influenced by him, began a reform movement in Switzerland. Zwingli was more intellectually and less religiously inclined than Luther. An iconoclast in worship forms, he was so rigorously committed to the scriptural principle that he permitted almost nothing that the Bible did not specifically allow. The two reformers came together at Marburg in 1529 along with Bucer, Melanchthon, and Oecolampadius. They achieved a general agreement that broke down only when it came to the Eucharist. Luther held for a real presence of Christ's body and blood in the bread and wine by his word recorded in scripture. Zwingli could only grant Christ's spiritual presence in the faithful on the occasion of the meal. As a result of these Marburg conversations, the Lutheran estrangement from the Swiss reformers continued deep.

John Calvin was a French Catholic layman trained in law and theology at Orléans and Paris who gained employment teaching scripture in Geneva while on a chance visit to that haven of reformers. In 1536 he published a Latin handbook of theology, *Institutes of the Christian Religion.* Calvin had a tidy mind and set himself to organizing the polity and ministry of a Church no longer under papal control (Map 42). He took the primitive church as described in Acts for a model, attempting to organize Geneva along these lines. He never quite succeeded but he did get the church consistory to regulate manners and morals in the spirit of his own inflexibility. This was the keenest intellect of the Reformation.

The radicals of the Reformation departed from certain traditional understandings of the early Church, to which the above three adhered, and held to a New Testament literalism. Chief among them were the Anabaptists, who denounced infant baptism and any traffic with civil authority (the use of force, going to law, taking oaths); Jacob Hutter (d. 1536) and his *Bruderhof* of common life in Moravia; and Menno Simons (d. 1561), the chief Anabaptist figure of Holland. Meantime in England the ideas of the reformers were meeting with stern resistance from Catholic King Henry VIII. His unhappiness with the papacy for not annulling his marriage to let him seek a male heir brought about a change, however, making him declare himself supreme in all matters touching on the Church in England. The continental reformers had been antimonastic on a theological principle that reprobated "works" (celibacy, fasting, life by rule). Henry was simply rapacious, needing Church and abbatial lands for revenue to finance his wars with France. The net effect was the same in England as in Europe, a spoliation of the monasteries and a turning out of their occupants to secular pursuits or refuge in France and Italy.

The chief faith-statement of the Lutheran persuasion was the Confession of Augsburg in 1530 ("Men cannot be justified in the sight of God by their own strength, merits or works but are justified freely on account of Christ through faith. . . . God imputes this faith for righteousness in his own sight" [Romans 3 and 4]). The bishops of Queen Elizabeth's reign in England promulgated Thirty-Nine Articles of faith in 1571, which taught the classical doctrines of Reformed Protestantism in a matrix of the old religion. The Westminster Confession of 1643, the classic English-language statement of Presbyterian faith, contains these articles characteristic of Calvin's thought: "X. *Of Effectual Calling.* All those whom God hath predestinated unto life—and those only—He is pleased, in His appointed and accepted time, effectually to call by His Word and Spirit . . . not from anything foreseen in man, who is altogether passive therein."

Catholic Reform; Eastern Reinvigoration

The Catholic answer to the challenge of the reformers was a long overdue council held at Trent in northern Italy, 1545–1563. Considered the nineteenth ecumenical council by Rome, it met in three sessions of three to six years each and affirmed the reliance of that Church on Scripture and subsequent tradition, on the effective power of the sacraments received in faith, and on man's freedom to sin even after he is justified. The Council called justification a work of God which man must be disposed to by a motion of his own will.

In the East during the Middle Ages the chief Orthodox theologian had been Gregory Palamas (ca. 1296–1359), a monk of St. Sabas Monastery on Mt. Athos. He was archbishop of Thessalonica from 1350 onward, spending several of these early years as a captive of the Turks. He is identified as a hesychast (from *hesychia,* "meditative contemplation") because of his defense of the life of his monks against the Calabrian monk Barlaam. He employed Plato and Aristotle and, possibly, Islamic views of God as the foundation of his theology, which included a distinction between God's nature and his operation. He also taught that the saints, both here and hereafter, experienced God's "energy" (i.e., activity) rather than his essence. Gregory viewed the Holy Spirit who sanctifies the saint as the uncreated grace present to him to render him God-like.

Eastern patriarchates other than those that preceded the first seven councils (Constantinople, Alexandria, Antioch, and Jerusalem) had been founded in Bulgaria (917) and Serbia (1346), afterward in Russia (1589), and Rumania (1925). Self-governing churches of the East at present include the catholicate of Georgia and the churches of Cyprus (formed in 431), Sinai (1575; one hundred members in modern times), Greece (1830), Poland (1924), Albania (1937), and Czechoslovakia (1951). Still other autonomous churches associated with various patriarchates are to be found in Finland, Estonia, Latvia, Hungary, China, Japan, and Macedonia; also three Russian churches outside Russia and those of the Ukrainians and the Ruthenians abroad. The Greek Church in North and South America is under the Patriarch of Constantinople. This listing does not include the Nestorian (e.g., Armenian) or Monophysite (e.g., Coptic) Churches, which II Constantinople (553) declared unorthodox.

More than six hundred bishoprics were under the "Ecumenical Patriarch" of Constantinople in the eleventh century (Map 40). By the mid fifteenth century (1453) he was politically subservient to Muslim caliphs. Today he has about 1.5 million Christians under his jurisdiction and resides in Phanar, a section of Istanbul.

Pan-Orthodox synods have been called in modern times, but with only moderate success: at Istanbul in 1923, at Moscow in 1948, and in 1961 in Rhodes. The prevailing polity in the East is one of autonomous churches.

Spread of Christianity Through Jesuit Missionary Effort

In post-Trent Europe, the chief agents of the expansion of Roman Christianity were the Jesuits. This religious order of clerks regular (i.e., neither monks, friars, nor secular clergy) was formed as the *Compañia de Jesús* at Paris in 1534 by Iñigo de Loyola, a Basque nobleman, who took the name of the Church father Ignatius. In 1540 the company was papally approved. They had initially taken vows of poverty, chastity, and service in the Holy Land, but when this proved impractical they offered themselves to the apostolic service of the pope (1538). The religious society was not formed for any professed counter-Reformation purpose. Nonetheless, when few heeded the challenge to carry out Trent's reforms besides Carlo Borromeo, cardinal archbishop of Milan, Cardinal Hosius of Poland, and Philip Neri in Rome, the Jesuits stepped into the breach. Their chief work turned out to be education, with missionary expansion in second place. Among the better-known figures in the restoration of a much-threatened Catholic life in Europe were Peter Canisius, a Dutchman who worked in German-speaking lands; Robert Bellarmine, an Italian polemicist and theologian; and the Spanish Francisco Suarez, the best theological thinker produced by the Society. Months after the order's founding a fellow Basque of Ignatius, Francis Xavier (d. 1552) was dispatched with three others to the East. At Ignatius's death in 1556 his followers were found in Africa, Asia, and the New World. Two hundred years later, nine out of ten were at work in colonies of Spain and Portugal in Asia and the Americas (Map 43).

A group of Jesuits went to Ethiopia in Ignatius's lifetime. They were later found in Morocco and Egypt and in Portuguese settlements on the west coast of Africa and Madagascar, where they tried to protect the Africans from the depredations of slave traders. Much more extensive efforts were made in India, China, Japan, and the Philippines, where they followed the course of empire, but also in Persia, Tibet, Ceylon, Malaya, Siam, Indochina, and the East Indies.

Roberto de Nobili began experiments in cultural accommodation among the Brahmins of Madurai beginning in 1606. His dream of "incarnating" the church in Indian culture was swept away with the papal suppression of the Jesuits in Europe (1773). Another attempt at adaptation was that of Matteo Ricci in China. In 1585 he and some Jesuit companions set up at Chaoking the first Christian congregation in China since the medieval Franciscan missions. He reached the imperial court at Peking in 1601 and there was given a subsidy for researches into his academic specialties, mathematics and astronomy. Ricci accommodated himself in dress and manners, first to Buddhist thought and practice, then in scholar's robes to the Confucian way of life. He devised a Christian liturgy in Chinese, used Chinese terms for the divinity, and suggested that converts to Christianity continue their ancient practice of honoring ancestors. This led to the famous "Chinese rites controversy" in Roman circles, where protracted resistance to foreign cultures and to the Jesuits alike led to an adverse settlement by the papacy in 1742. Catholic mission activity has had a Western cultural cast in all parts of the globe ever since.

Catholics reached three hundred thousand in Japan between Xavier's arrival there toward the end of his life and 1614. Political changes in the next thirty-five years brought persecution (111 Jesuit martyrs) and an effective closing of Japan to Christianity over the next two centuries. The Philippines became largely Christian under Spanish control from the late sixteenth century onward.

In North and South America, Jesuits and Fransciscans were the chief public instructors in New Spain (Peru, Mexico, and a much-extended Paraguay). By the mid eighteenth century there were but a hundred Jesuits in French-dominated lands and less than twenty in English-dominated lands. The Catholicizing of eastern Canada and of certain Indian tribes in what came to be

44 Distribution of Protestant Denominations in the English Colonies c.1750

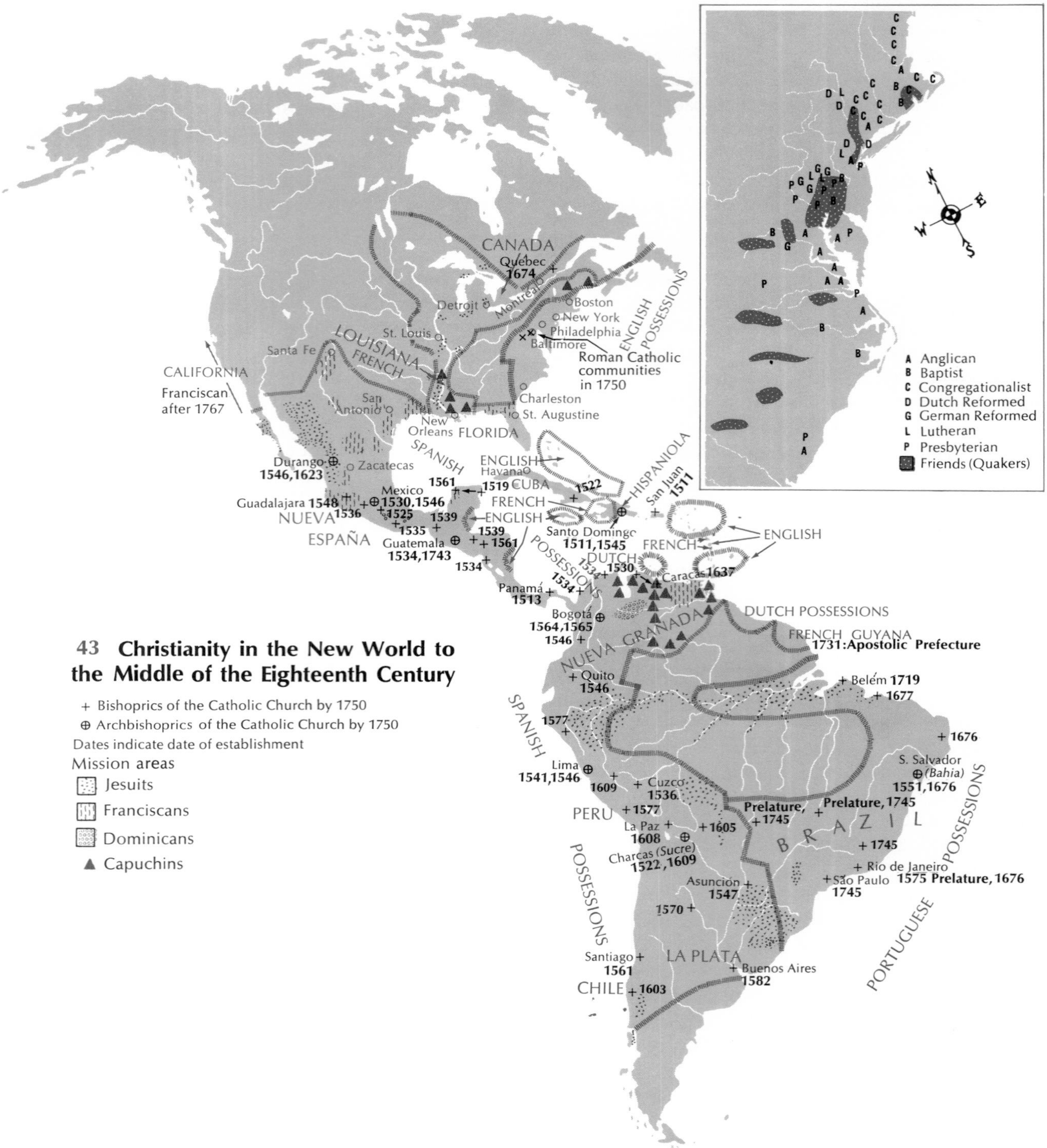

43 Christianity in the New World to the Middle of the Eighteenth Century

+ Bishoprics of the Catholic Church by 1750

⊕ Archbishoprics of the Catholic Church by 1750

Dates indicate date of establishment

Mission areas

- Jesuits
- Franciscans
- Dominicans
- ▲ Capuchins

the Louisiana Purchase followed French colonization and was much broader than just a Jesuit venture.

It would be a mistake to view the centuries that followed the Council of Trent (1545–1563) in terms of Jesuit activity only. Pope (from 1712 onward, St.) Pius V was important in the work of consolidating the reform legislation enacted by that Council. This Dominican friar, Michael Ghislieri, was ascetic in private life and intransigent on public questions. During his papacy (1565–1572), he attempted with a reformer's zeal to reverse the numerous excesses of his humanist predecessors. He attacked the venality of the Curia, his entrenched bureaucratic council; insisted on the innovation of special dress for the secular clergy; and saw to the reform of liturgical books such as the missal and the breviary (a canonical book of prayers for specified hours). Pius V was severe with the French Protestants, known as Huguenots; showed signs of favor to the repressive Spanish Duke of Alva in the Netherlands; and excommunicated Queen Elizabeth I of England (1558–1603). The bull of 1570 by which he did so, *Regnans in excelsis,* created a crisis of conscience in Catholic subjects, who were thereby called upon to view their queen as treasonous, and effectually destroyed the possibility of a religious settlement on that divided island.

An ill-fated insurrection of Catholic partisans of Queen Mary of Scotland, encouraged by the promise of Spanish help, occurred in 1569. The pope's failure to consult King Philip II of Spain about the excommunication served to alienate that sovereign. The practical effect of the bull was a succession of penal laws against Catholics in England from 1571 onward. No Catholic bishop was consecrated until 1623 and many persons went to death or exile.

Influential as the excommunication was for subsequent Christian history, it was matched in its effects by activity in another sphere. In 1566 a Calvinist synod in Antwerp declared that armed resistance to the Netherlands' Spanish ruler, Philip II, was permissible. Two years later William of Orange, the Silent, took the lead in the anti-Spanish movement. He became a Calvinist formally only in 1573. In 1579 the country was divided into a Calvinist north and a Catholic south (much later to become the countries of Holland and Belgium). The north was recognized by Spain in 1609 and became fully independent in 1648. This tiny commercial nation was to become as influential in the spread of its version of Christianity as England was in its and France and Spain in theirs.

French repression of reformers of Lutheran sentiment had been preceded by various murderous actions against the Waldensians (*Vaudois,* after Valdes, a twelfth-century merchant of Lyons) in Provence in 1545 and 1555–1559. The term *Huguenot,* of obscure origin (possibly from *Eidgenossen,* "conspirators"; or after one of their leaders, Hugues Besançon; or *huguenaux,* from a tower in Tours named for the legendary King Hugon), was applied to those reformers increasingly under the influence of their fellow countryman Calvin, from the time of the first appearance of his *Institutes* (1536). The movement came into the open with a national synod in 1559, the last year of the reign of King Henry II. Bitter wars of religion followed, sometimes numbered at seven, with the St. Bartholomew's Day Massacre (of Protestants, in 1572) as the high point. The rise to power of the Huguenot prince Henry of Navarre in 1584 (Henry IV, 1589–1610) led to the liberating Edict of Nantes in 1598, despite his having become a Catholic in 1593. It was a compendium of previous edicts of toleration of Protestants and was noteworthy in the history of freedom of conscience in that it proposed a state in which Catholics and Protestants lived side by side. Actually, it could be characterized as a state within a state, because Catholicism remained the established religion of France. Protestants, however, were granted their own schools, cemeteries, royal revenues, law courts, and designated places of worship. The Catholics, for their part, were allowed freedom to celebrate the Mass in Protestant towns. This legal settlement remained in nominal effect until its revocation under Louis XIV in 1685, despite serious breaches resulting from the political policies of the prime ministers Richelieu and Mazarin. Some 200,000 to 300,000 Huguenots left France when this final protection of law was removed. Many went to England, but some went to New Rochelle in the colony of New York (after La Rochelle, one of two last "places of surety" for Huguenots, following the Peace of Montpelier in 1622). In 1787, the Edict of Toleration restored partial religious and civil rights to the Protestants. Full equality with the Catholics came only with the *Code Napoléon* (1804).

Mary Stuart, Queen of Scots from infancy until her imprisonment by her cousin Elizabeth (1542–1567), was a Catholic who became a claimant to the English throne upon her youthful marriage to Francis II of France (1559). Her father had been James V, king of Scotland, son of James IV and nephew of Henry VIII through his sister Margaret. Queen Elizabeth was not in favor of a Catholic and pro-French Scotland and so supported a band of Scottish lords sympathetic to the religious reform. In 1557 these chieftains had declared themselves by solemn covenant "Lords of the Congregation" to defend the Word of God. John Knox had spent the year 1555–1556 in Scotland after enduring long exile under

19-9 The Cathedral of *Salisbury*, England.

Mary Tudor, during which year he brought the lords into political unity and wrote *The First Blast from the Trumpet Against the Monstrous Regiment of Women.* Directed at petticoat and papist rule by Mary, it succeeded in alienating Elizabeth on the brink of her accession, when Scotland could have used some help from England. Knox came back from Geneva in 1559, preaching against Mary before she came to the Scottish throne (July 10). A year short of four days later, a Treaty of Edinburgh between France and Scotland turned over to the Lords of the Congregation the government of Scotland in the name of the king and queen of France. Francis II died four months later at age sixteen, leaving a queen only slightly his senior to attempt the restoration of the old religion in Scotland. In her foreign alliances she proved no match for the reform party, and the Parliament in stages repudiated the authority of the pope, abolished the mass, and accepted a confession of faith drafted by John Knox. A disastrous second marriage to Lord Darnley and subsequent bad counsel from the unscrupulous Lord Bothwell preceded her abdication in 1567. She spent the next twenty years in prison before being beheaded by Elizabeth, during all of which time the Calvinist settlement made strides in everything but a polity of local presbyteries. The Reformation was established *against* the crown in Mary's short reign of eight years in Scotland. That of England was established *by* the crown. Hence, it was with a sense of personal victory by the common folk over royalty that the Scots came together with England under a common throne in 1603 (James VI of Scotland as James I of England; d. 1625).

It is evident from the above account how potent the force of arms was in religious change. Royal power was not the sole component, however. There was genuine religious conviction in the hearts of the people fostered by preaching and counterpreaching. At the same time, class structure and social change were never far below the surface in these new and conflicting loyalties. There was much blood shed in every land. This bloodshed was recorded in works like John Foxe's *Book of Martyrs* (later known as *Acts and Monuments*), an account written in Basel in 1556–1559 that told of deaths in the reign of Mary Tudor (1553–1558). It was modeled, in turn, on Jean Crespin's *Book of Huguenot Martyrs.* Cardinal William Allen, founder of the English College at the new university of Douai (1568), wrote a similar history of the English mission. A total of 438 priests was sent back to the homeland by 1603, 123 of them to be executed and some 60 lay-men or -women for harboring them.

The Puritan movement in the Church of England derived its name from the supposed rigidity of its adherents and their purity in religious observance. Strict reformers of morals in this age were not confined to any party or country. The theater, dancing, and other seasonal revels were early targets of this spirit. The whole tone of Europe, Protestant and Catholic, was a reforming one. The Calvinists did not have a corner on moral rigor. What marked them off from Catholic "puritans" like Loyola or Anglican ones like William Laud and Jeremy Taylor was the attempt to engage the power of the state in enforcing these standards. In no European country did the various Calvinist consistories achieve the measure of political power they would have wished. Laud, Archbishop of Canterbury (1633–1645), was bitterly opposed to Calvinist incursions into the English Church by the group popularly known as Puritans. Under Stuart King Charles I he opposed them from the standpoint of orthodoxy, i.e., Catholic but not Roman Restoration. He was accused of Arminian sympathies (after Jacob Arminius, d. 1609) for his refusal to accept strict Calvinist predestinationism. His strictures drove some members of the Church of England into nonconformity and subsequent exile to Holland and North America.

The English Baptists originally baptized by pouring water like their Anglican and Catholic counterparts, but gradually under continental influence they came to baptize by immersion. They were marked by a simplicity of dress and manner, an antiritualist spirit, and a fierce independence from civil and ecclesiastical governments, all hallmarks of the radical reformation or Anabaptist conviction.

Archbishop Laud's insistence on episcopal polity and the use of *The Book of Common Prayer,* which had been the work of Thomas Cranmer (1549–1552), drove many into separatism. The Westminster Assembly (1643–1649) of the Calvinist-dominated House of Commons framed the Westminster Confession to replace the Thirty-Nine Articles of Religion (i.e., Anglican faith, 1563) and a longer and shorter catechism. All became normative for Presbyterian faith in Scotland but never in England. Another important development of the Cavalier return to power was the strength of the Society of Friends ("Quakers") founded by George Fox (1624–1691). Deriving his ideas in part from the German mysticism of men like Caspar Schwenkfeld (1490–1561) and Jakob Boehme, John Tauler, and Henry Suso, Fox stressed personal divine illumination ("the inner light"), simple speech and dress, and total pacifism. A colony of his followers was founded at Philadelphia by William Penn in 1682, bringing with them in 1683 Mennonite weavers from the German town of Crefeld to Germantown, near Philadelphia.

The voyages of Columbus to the New World under the patronage of the Spanish sovereigns Ferdinand and Isabella resulted in the promulgation of a bull (1493) by Pope Alexander VI giving the Spanish control over the Americas. It instructed them to bring the Catholic faith to *"los Indios,"* as Columbus designated the inhabitants of the Caribbean islands. As early as his second voyage of that same year, this mariner with a sense of mission had brought with him a Benedictine monk, Bernardo Buíl. A "line of demarcation" had been drawn by the pope in the aforementioned bull 100 leagues west of the Azores and the Cape Verde Islands. Everything east of it was declared Portuguese territory, everything west Spanish. In 1494 the Treaty of Tordesillas between those two nations moved the line 270 leagues farther west. This brought Brazil into the Portuguese sphere. The voyages of Duarte Pacheco Pereira for Portugal (1498) and Amerigo Vespucci, first for Spain (1499–1500) and then for Portugal (1501–1502), led to the plundering of Central and South America by the *conquistadores* in the first half of the sixteenth century. Evangelization and civilization were taken to be one in that era, with results such as schools, printing presses, and progress in the arts. As early as 1511 a bishopric had been established in San Domingo; Mexico, the capital city of that country, had a university by 1544. Missionaries, chiefly Franciscans, Dominicans, and Augustinians, accompanied the rapacious soldiery. Among the latter, some of the most unscrupulous (like Cortés in Mexico) were nonetheless marked by a crusading zeal. Cortés's slaughter of the Aztecs at Cholula (1519) and Pizarro's of the Incas at Cajamarca in Peru (1532) are infamous.

The Indians found a champion in the Dominican friar Bartholomew de las Casas (1494–1566), whose father had sailed as a seaman with Columbus. The first priest ordained in the New World (1510), he crossed the ocean fourteen times in his persistent efforts to secure justice for the Indians. He incurred the wrath of commercial interests but finally won the backing of Spain's primatial bishop, the humanist scholar Cardinal Ximenes (1495–1517). Emperor Charles V decreed in 1542 that Spanish and Indian were equal before the law. Unfortunately, equal efforts were not exerted in behalf of the African slaves who were regularly being transported to the colonies; the emancipation of slaves in all parts of Brazil did not come about until 1888. De las Casas wrote a treatise to establish that good example and peaceful preaching were the only acceptable means of conversion in a religion that made claims like those of Christianity. The work was not published until 1941. His traditional theological opponent was a certain Sepulveda, who maintained that the soldiers were merely protecting the missionaries and making the preaching of the gospel possible. The first theoretical treatment of the problems of evangelizing indigenous peoples was the work of a Jesuit who had served the Indians in Peru, Joseph Acosta. He wrote *On the Preaching of the Gospel Among the Savages,* a work that went into all the thornier problems, such as mass baptism (a papal bull of 1537 had declared the Indians capable of receiving this sacrament), the role of the military, and the feasibility of a native clergy. Mexico got its first Indian priest in 1679, Chile in 1794.

The New World; Worldwide Mission Expansion

English-speaking North America became Christian largely through the efforts of the dissenting Protestant groups that sought refuge there (Map 44). The best known are the Congregationalists of Calvinist persuasion (Plymouth Colony, Massachusetts Bay Colony, Connecticut), the Baptists (Rhode Island), the Friends (Pennsylvania), and the Moravians, Mennonites, and other German Pietist groups (largely Pennsylvania but also North Carolina). The Church of England was strong in Virginia, Georgia, and the Carolinas, and the Dutch Reformed Church followed the colonizing efforts in New York and East Jersey. Followers of John Wesley were strong in the Middle Atlantic States down to Georgia beginning in the late eighteenth century. The Methodist Episcopal Church, incorporated in Baltimore in 1784, was the first independent, national church organization in North America.

Protestant missions did not depart from the normal pattern of following colonial expansion (chiefly British and Dutch) until the turn of the nineteenth century. The Church of England had organized the Society for Promoting Christian Knowledge (1699) and the Society for the Propagation of the Gospel in Foreign Parts (1701). Beginning in 1706 German Pietists under the auspices of the King of Denmark had missions in India. Some eighteenth-century mission efforts by Count Zinzendorf brought Moravian teachers to the West Indies, India, Ceylon, Russia, Central America, Greenland, Labrador, the Gold Coast and South Africa and among the Indians of North America. In 1792 the Baptist Missionary Society was founded in England and William Carey was posted to India to translate the Bible into the languages of that country (out of a college in Serampore) and into Chinese (Map 45). The evangelically oriented (i.e., Non-

45 Nineteenth - Century Catholic and Protestant Missions in the Old World

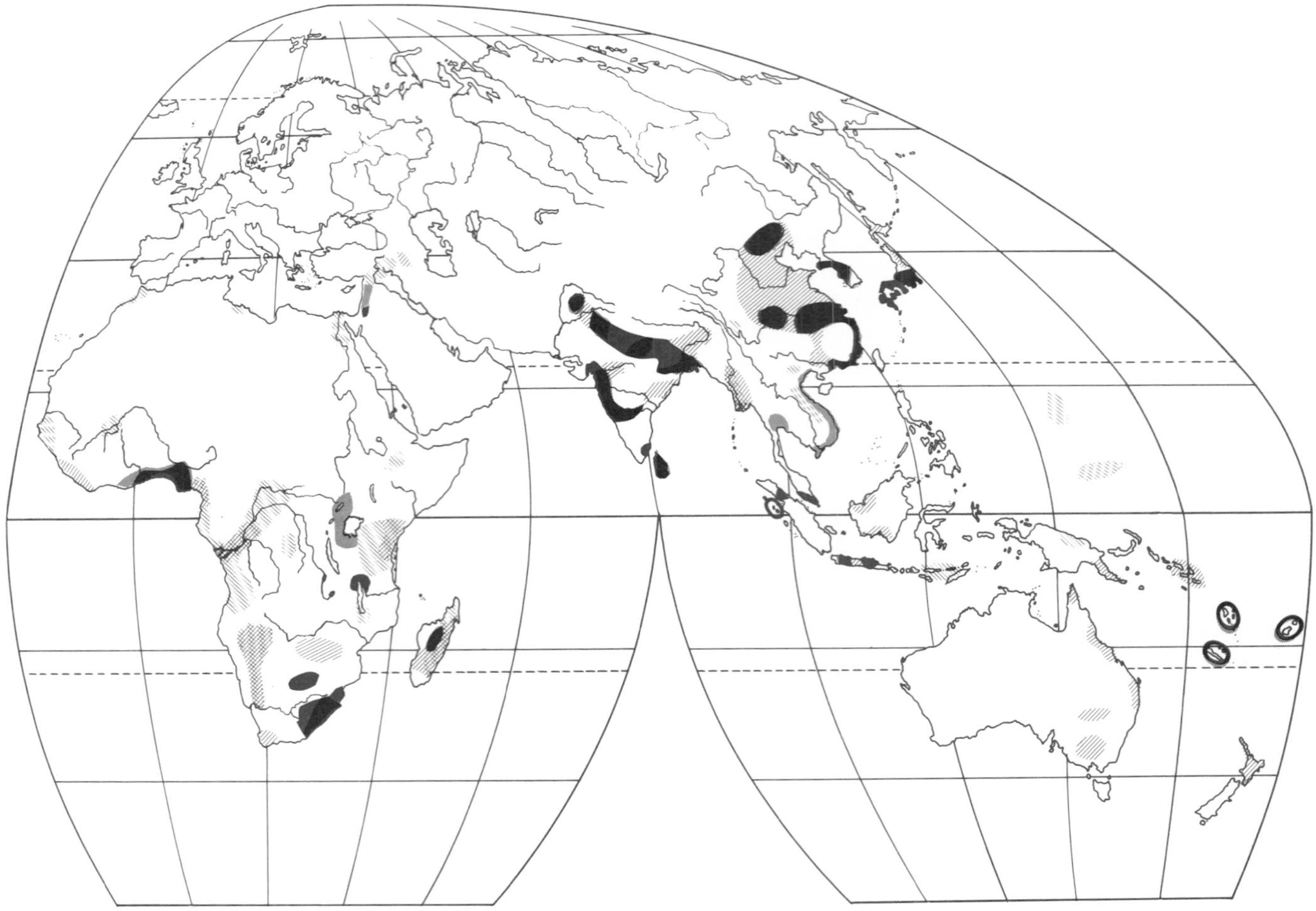

	Predominantly Catholic missions	Predominantly Protestant missions	Both active
Intense activity			
Moderate activity			
Little or no activity			

conformist) London Missionary Society was founded in 1795 and the Church Missionary Society in 1799. The British and Foreign Bible Society came along in 1804, the American Bible Society in 1816. Other foundations that were to be influential were the Netherlands (1797) and Basel (1822) Missionary Societies. The Student Volunteer Movement for Foreign Missions (1886) had as an original member John R. Mott (1855–1865), who served as a link to the World Council of Churches (1948) through his chairmanship of the World Missionary Conference held in Edinburgh (1910) and the International Missionary Council (1921). The latter embraced the overwhelming majority of the Protestants of the world, as does the WCC, which incorporated into itself the IMC as its Commission on World Mission and Evangelism.

The Roman Church had suffered serious setbacks in the periods of the French enlightenment and Revolution, not to speak of the Napoleonic wars. The mid nineteenth century brought further tremors in Germany and France, and the gradual unification of Italy (1849–1870) was achieved largely at the expense of the Papal States. Pius IX, pope from 1846 to 1878, sought compensation for this political loss by strengthening the internal working of his Church and its spiritual influence. In 1854 he promulgated the long-held Catholic belief in the sinlessness of Mary from her mother's womb as the "dogma of the Immaculate Conception." This autonomous doctrinal declaration paved the way for a formal statement of the pope's incapacity to err when speaking from the papal chair (*ex cathedra*) in matters touching faith or morals (the "dogma of papal infallibility"), which was proclaimed July 18, 1870, at the ten-month-long I Vatican Council, reckoned the twentieth ecumenical council by the Roman Church. Its agenda contained carefully prepared inquiries into the major faith questions of the age, but Pius terminated it after one session, once he had got the truncated declaration of Church authority he sought.

In German Protestant circles throughout the nineteenth century giant strides were made in critical-historical scholarship on the books of the Bible and auxiliary disciplines (archaeology, paleography, Egyptology, and Assyriology). At first these told against the Protestant principle of the Bible as the sole rule of faith because the supposed verbal inspiration that was thought to protect it from the vagaries of ordinary literature was seen not to have had this effect. Rationalist teachers like S. H. Reimarus, L. Feuerbach, and D. F. Strauss were followed by men of more traditional belief, such as F. Schleiermacher, F. C. Baur, S. Kierkegaard, A. Ritschl, and M. Kahler. All of the latter, in a variety of ways, asserted a principle of faith that depended neither on the inerrancy of the sacred books nor on those matters that could be held with certainty about the historical Jesus.

The twentieth century in Christian scholarship built on the nineteenth, with the researches of H. Gunkel (Old Testament), J. Wellhausen (Old Testament and New Testament), A. Schweitzer (New Testament), A. Loisy (New Testament), M.-J. Lagrange (Old Testament and New Testament), and above all R. Bultmann (New Testament). Loisy and Lagrange were Catholic scholars, the rest Protestant. The discovery of the implications of modern scholarship for faith were largely resisted in the Catholic Church by Pope Pius X, who acted against an immanentist and subjectivist tendency. These he lumped together with the conclusions of solid research under the name of *Modernism,* formally condemning it (1905 and 1910). This action set theological progress in that Church back seriously—whatever benefits it may have had for orthodoxy—until after World War II (1945). Pope Pius XII (1939–1958), besides his diplomatic efforts in World War II, distinguished himself by producing a number of important encyclical letters on the Church (1941), the Bible (1943), and liturgical worship (1948).

The pent-up need for a council of the Roman Church, which had not had one since 1870, was met by Pope John XXIII with the convening of II Vatican (1962–1965), the twenty-first ecumenical council. This was announced as a pastoral council, but it proved to be a vindication of the theologians who had been declared suspect by an encyclical letter of Pius XII in 1950 (*Humani generis*). Its sixteen published documents attended to such diverse matters as relations with Eastern Christians, Jews, Muslims, members of other non-Christian religious traditions, and unbelievers. There were also decrees on internal questions, such as the nature of the Church, Scripture and nonscriptural tradition, and missionary activity. The document on the Church and the modern world (*Lumen gentium*) is the one likeliest to be of lasting significance. It omitted attention to the question of contraception (birth control) at the express direction of Pope Paul VI (1963–). This practice had been explicitly forbidden by papal teaching in an encyclical letter of Pius XI (1930). Pope Paul addressed himself to the question in 1968 (*Humanae vitae*) by prohibiting the practice absolutely, a teaching that has not met with widespread acceptance from clergy and laity around the globe.

The recent internal reform activity of the Roman Church has acted as the catalyst of similar efforts among the Protestant and Orthodox groups. Ecumenical, understood as interfaith, activity has reached new dimen-

46 Distribution of Christianity c.1970

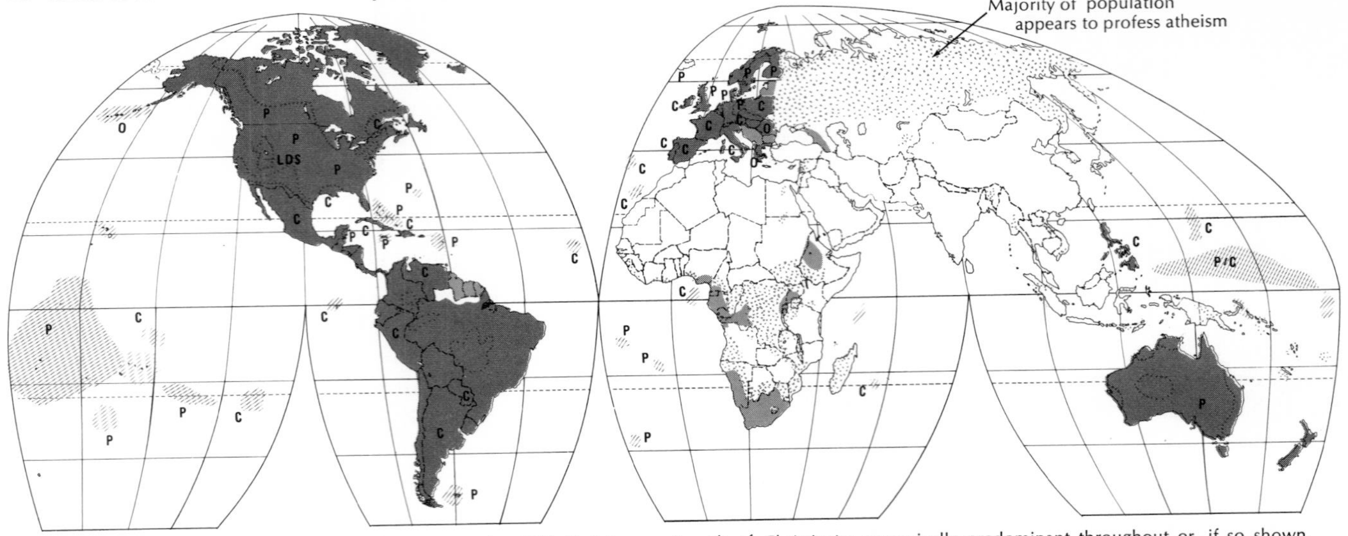

Countries and territories with population more than 90% Christian
Christians in a majority elsewhere
Christians in a substantial minority

Branch of Christianity numerically predominant throughout or, if so shown, in part of predominantly Christian country:
C Roman Catholic – **LDS** Church of Latter Day Saints (Mormons) – **O** Orthodox (Greek, Bulgarian, Russian, etc.) – **P** Protestant

47 World Christian Population by Major Regions c. 1970

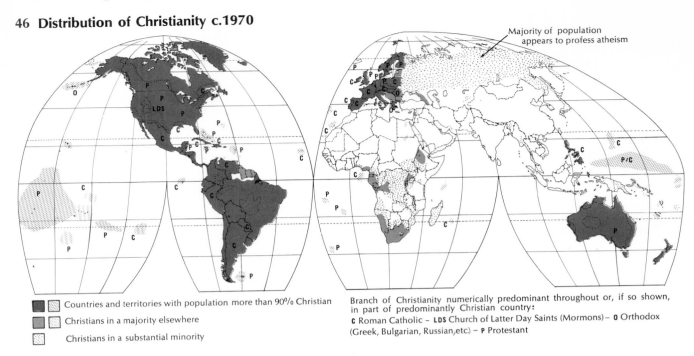

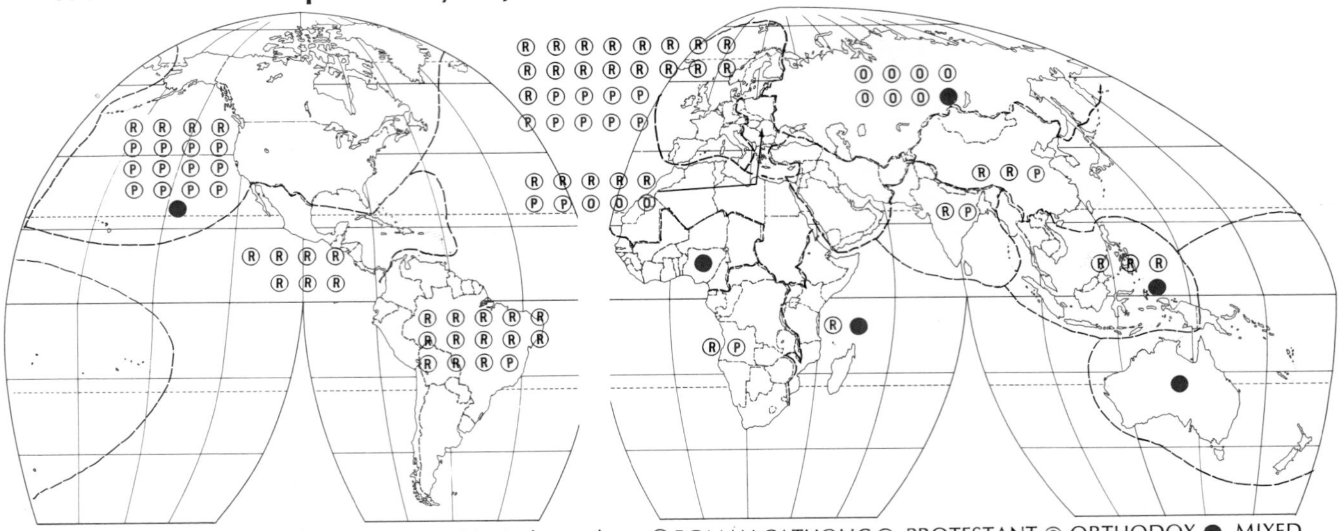

Division among the major Christian communities is shown thus: Ⓡ ROMAN CATHOLIC Ⓟ PROTESTANT Ⓞ ORTHODOX ● MIXED
Each circle represents approximately 1 percent of the world Christian population, totalling 1.2 billion. Number of circles is less than 100 because of rounding

sions as all the Christian bodies face together the challenges of Marxism and the increased secularization of the Western society in which they have been dominant. A very recent phenomenon in all the Christian communions has been the vigorous Pentecostal and Fundamentalist (i.e., biblically literalist) response to modern challenges. It remains to be seen what the effects of this individual and largely nonsocial stance will be.

Meanwhile, the Third World clamors to be taken seriously in all the Christian Churches and in the Muslim world. On the Christian response in that sector, the survival of that faith tradition seems to depend.[28]

[28] For the geographic distribution of Christianity in the world and in the United States today, see Maps 46, 47, and 48.

48 Christian Denominations in the Conterminous United States

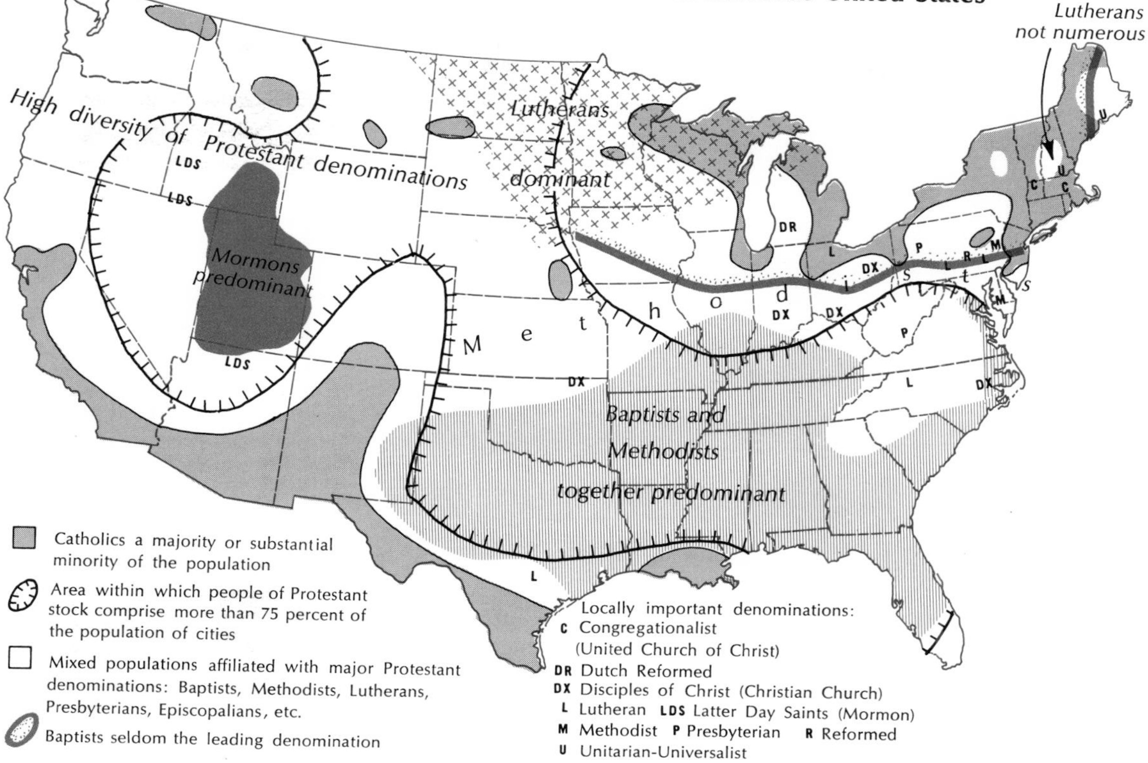

Bibliography

AHLSTROM, SYDNEY E. *A Religious History of the American People.* New Haven: Yale U.P., 1972.

BARRETT, C. K. *The New Testament Background: Selected Documents.* London: S.P.C.K., 1957.

BETTENSON, HENRY. *Documents of the Christian Church,* 2d ed. London: Oxford U.P., 1963.

BULGAKOV, S. *The Eastern Orthodox Church.* London: Centenary, 1935.

CALLINIKOS, CONSTANTINE. *A Brief Sketch of Greek Church History,* tr., Katherine Noatzio. London: Faith, 1931.

CHADWICK, OWEN (Ed.). *The Pelican History of the Church,* 6 vols. Baltimore: Penguin, 1961–1970.

DANIÉLOU, JEAN, and HENRI MARROU. *The Christian Centuries,* Vol. I, "The First Six Hundred Years." London: Darton, Longman and Todd, 1964.

DENZINGER, H., and A. SCHÖNMETZER. *Enchiridion Symbolorum,* 32d ed. Barcelona: Herder, 1963.

Eusebius: The History of the Church from Christ to Constantine, tr., G. A. Williamson. Baltimore: Penguin, 1965.

HARNACK, ADOLF. *The Mission and Expansion of Christianity in the First Three Centuries.* New York: Harper Torchbooks, 1962.

KELLY, J. N. D. *Early Christian Doctrines.* New York: Harper, 1958.

KIDD, B. J. *Documents Illustrative of the Continental Reformation.* Oxford: Clarendon, 1911.

———. *Documents Illustrative of the History of the Church,* 3 vols. London: S.P.C.K., 1923–1941.

LATOURETTE, KENNETH SCOTT. *A History of the Expansion of Christianity,* 7 vols. New York: Harper, 1937–1945.

———. *Christianity in a Revolutionary Age,* 5 vols. New York: Harper, 1958–1962.

MERRIMAN, R. B. *The Rise of the Spanish Empire,* 4 vols. New York: Macmillan, 1918–1934.

NEILL, STEPHEN. *Anglicanism,* 2d ed. Baltimore: Penguin, 1960.

——— (Ed.). *Twentieth Century Christianity.* New York: Doubleday Dolphin, 1963.

——— and Ruth Rouse. *History of the Ecumenical Movement, 1517–1948.* London: S.P.C.K., 1954.

WARE, TIMOTHY. *The Orthodox Church.* Baltimore: Penguin, 1963.

Zernov, Nicholas. *The Church of Eastern Christians.* New York: Macmillan, 1946.

Also see pertinent articles from F. L. Cross, *Dictionary of the Christian Church* (Oxford: Clarendon Press, 1957); J. Höfer and K. Rahner (eds), *Lexikon für Theologie und Kirche,* 10 vols. (Freiburg: Herder, 1957–1965); M. R. P. McGuire (senior ed.), *New Catholic Encyclopedia,* 15 vols. (New York: McGraw-Hill, 1967); and *Religion in Geschichte und Gegenwart,* 6 vols., 3d ed. (Tübingen: J. C. B. Mohr [Paul Siebeck], 1959).

20

Islām

Isma'īl R. al Fārūqī

Genesis and Formation

Origins

Questioned about its own historical origins, Islām answers that its predecessor was *ḥanīfiyyah* (tradition of the *ḥanīfs*), with which it even identified itself (Qur'ān, 10:105; 2:135). The fact that numerous teachings and precepts of Islām have parallels in the Jewish and/or Christian traditions supports neither the claim of inter-religious borrowing nor that of development within Judaism or Christianity. Both these religions were known in Arabia, but they were not regarded as native, and their adherents were treated as aliens. Not so the *ḥanīfs*, who, tradition tells us, were thoroughbred Arabs and members of their tribes in good standing. Neither Jewish nor Christian in faith, they rejected association with any of the cults prevalent in pre-Islāmic Arabia, could enter Makkah, rove at will within the Ḥaram (sacred sanctuary), and commanded the greatest respect and trust everywhere. It is also certain that these *ḥanīfs* towered above the usual tribal solidarities and differences without renouncing or being denied by the tribal loyalties, that they professed adherence to the faith of Abraham, Noah, and the early prophets of the "Semitic" peoples, and that they were monotheists. It was common knowledge that to them belonged the expertise in religion, in the legends of early "Semitic" history as well as in Judaism and Christianity. Moreover, Arabia knew them as highly oriented and ethically motivated universalists, and their very name acquired in Arabic usage the meaning of moral uprightness and rectitude, of religious purity. The quest for the historical origins of Islām is therefore a quest about the *ḥanīfs* and their religion.

Besides the Arabic meaning already indicated, *ḥanīf* in its Aramaic/Syriac version of *hanepai* means "deviant" or "rejected"; and the obvious referent, that from which the *ḥanīfs* deviated and were rejected, were the catholic establishments of their parent faiths: Roman (imperial) Christianity and Rabbinic Judaism. This is true of the Christian era. In former centuries, the term may have referred to men at variance with the Ezraic ethnocentric crystallization of Hebrew religion; with the Davidic temple, sacrificial religion of Judea; or with the Phoenician-Canaanite cult, into which ancient Mesopotamian religion had degenerated. Such deviants however could not have found refuge in Arabia, much less be incorporated into the fabric of its tribal society, unless there already were in Arabia native Arabs who sympathized because they shared in a common fund of religious ideas and vocabulary. The *hanepai* would then be accepted as "cousins" rejoining and enriching their more ancient roots. This leads to a redefinition of *ḥanīfiyyah* as the ancient "Semitic" tradition of religious ideas interpreted by and preserved in Arabia as its own indigenous tradi-

20-1 The Ka'bah at Makkah at the time of pilgrimage. In the center stands the cubicle housing the Black Stone. It is draped with a cloth covering of black embroidered with gold. (Courtesy of Anīs Aḥmad).

tion. The legends of Mesopotamia, the accounts of the patriarchs, the revelations of the prophets, the birth of Jesus and the *dénouement* of his life and career—all these must have had an Arabian version in which the *ḥanīf* crystallized his vision and read his identity. For it was no news to the unbelieving Makkans when the Qur'ān reported to them that Abraham was their ancestor and the founder of their city and *Ḥaram.* Otherwise, some record of their contention of its claims would have survived, for men and tribes do not take lightly new claims about the identity of their ancestors or about the origins of their religious shrine and city. The parallelisms between Islām and the Judeo-Christian tradition find their ground in the common treasury of ideas in which all the "Semitic" peoples share. Reversing the uncritical claim that Islām is a development of Judaism and Christianity, we may hold that Judaism and Christianity are themselves development of a "Semitic" religious tradition; or better, that they are moments in a developing "Semitic" consciousness of which the Sumerian, Babylonian, Noahic, Abrahamic, and Mosaic religions are the earlier crystallizations, the Rabbinic and Pauline some of the later, and the Islāmic the latest. The answer to the question, "What did Islām take from *ḥanīfiyyah?*" is simple: everything *ḥanīfiyyah* had to offer! The Prophet's personal consciousness, which served as matrix of revelation, was nourished and disciplined by the *ḥanīfī* tradition and thus readied for a recrystallization of the "Semitic" vision that was to come in Islām. Just as the Dead Sea Scrolls have shed considerable light on one main deviant from Rabbinic Judaism and the Gnostic writings have done a similar job for Roman Christianity, the *ḥanīfiyyah* tradition has done the same for Islām. The connection of the Jewish and Christian deviants to the *ḥanīfiyyah,* and of the latter to Islām, is certain, though little research has been done to chronologize and substantiate it.

Besides this ideological fountain of Islām, there is one other historical source: Makkah. Makkah was the cultural matrix of revelation just as Muḥammad's consciousness was the personal matrix. At the close of the sixth century, the city had achieved a position of eminence and sophistication on all fronts. *Economically,* the city was at the center of a trade complex that extended to Madagascar, the Philippines, and Constantinople and whose routes all met in it. Caravans as large as thirty thousand camels bringing the exports of Africa and Asia to Makkah and carrying their goods to Egypt, Persia, and Byzantium were common sights. The maritime trade on the Red Sea, which the Romans had previously built, had declined with the influence of Rome as the overland route to the ports of the eastern Mediterranean prospered. *Socially,* tribalism had by then reached in Makkah its highest point of development. Jurhum, the oldest tribe to settle in Makkah in legendary prehistory, had lost its hegemony over the city to the tribe of Khuzā'ah, probably as a result of the general dislocation following the rise of the kingdom of Ḥimyar in South Arabia *circa* 115 C.E. The Jurhumis made a triumphant comeback under Quṣayy *circa* 400 C.E. It was Quṣayy who made his tribe—to be known henceforth by the name of his sixth ancestor, Quraysh—the dominant power in Makkah as well as in Arabia. It was the prototype of all tribes. Its many clans fought fiercely with one another but united and acted as one man in face of a common enemy. Tribal loyalty was never greater, and it generated an ethos in which genealogical purity, courage, honor, hospitality, and eloquence measure the degree of esteem, whether on the personal or the collective level. The tribe was the ultimate source of all rights, all privileges, and all duties, and the clan the immediate guarantor of these among the members themselves. In turn, the clan consisted of "houses," in which the *pater familias,* as scion of the tribal stock, exercised limitless power over wife, offspring, and property.

Politically, Makkah was the nerve center of a very elaborate system of intertribal alliances and agreements that guaranteed the safety of the trade routes and the general interests of all. It was the depot of the southbound and the northbound, the east- and the westbound men and goods. Any violation by any clan or by any tribe convulsed the whole Peninsula with unrest to everybody's detriment. Precisely such was Ḥarb al Fijār (the Immoral War, 582–586 C.E.), which was sparked by al Barrād's (Kinānah tribe) assassination of ʻUrwah (Hawāzin tribe), who was preferred by King Nuʻman of Ḥīrah to guide his caravan across Kinānah territory and the territory of their allies, the Quraysh (Map 49). For four years, the countryside knew no secu-

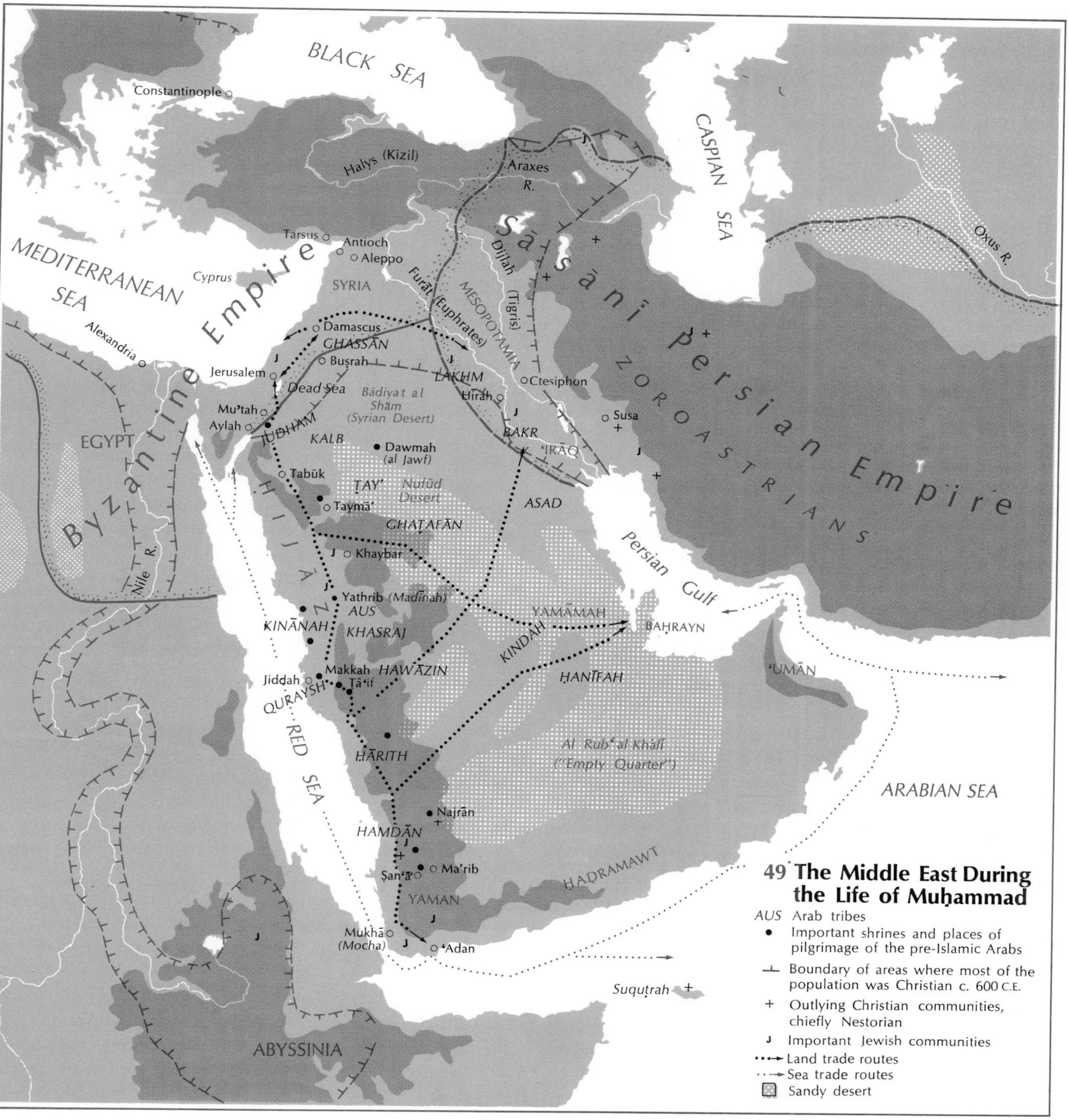

49 The Middle East During the Life of Muḥammad

rity until a general peace, Ḥilf al Fuḍūl (the Virtuous Treaty), was signed by all parties and their affiliates. The political system provided for four holy months during which no hostility of any kind was tolerated and all routes were absolutely safe for caravans and pilgrims. Beyond these months, safety was a function of the most delicate balance of power between the various tribes and clans.

Religiously, Makkah contained the Ḥaram (sanctuary), at the center of which stood the Kaʻbah, the house that Abraham and Ismaʻīl built for worship of the One God and that subsequently came to hold over three hundred sacred statues, stones, or other objects representing all or most of the tribal gods of Arabia. One religious sentiment whose object of veneration was the Kaʻbah united all the Arabs under the leadership of the Quraysh tribe which held the keys of the temple and performed the sacred duties of *sidānah* ("priestly care"), *siqāyah,* and *rifādah* ("hospitality to the pilgrims"), as well as the properly political and governmental functions belonging to Makkah. The temple was hence both the religious and the political center of all Arabia. And it was for this reason that imperial Christian Abyssinia, once it gained a foothold in Yaman in 525 C.E. following the persecution and massacre of the Christians of Najrān in October 523 C.E. by the Jewish government of Yaman, had to launch a campaign to sack Makkah and destroy the Kaʻbah in 570–571. This took place in the "Year of the Elephant," the birth year of the Prophet, but the campaign failed, and Makkan religion and dominion superseded Abyssinia in the south.

Makkan religion had no eschatology, no life after death, no judgment, and neither paradise nor hell. Man's life terminated at death except for one's progeny, for the memory of his great deeds, and for the eloquent poetry with which he described those deeds. Essentially utilitarian and hedonist, the Arab spent all the wealth his trade or meagre agriculture provided on the pleasures of the hour. God he certainly recognized as the ultimate being, but devoid of relevance. The gods and goddesses of the Kaʻbah (above all, Lāt, Manāt, ʻUzzā, and Hubal) were his intercessors. To them he resorted for blessing his new infant and his prospective trade or battle. They were the object of his gratitude for every good he enjoyed, and their priests helped him by divination to settle the problematic issues of daily life. Once a year he honored the Kaʻbah as his religious focus through a pilgrimage whose rites included circumambulation and the sacrifice of cattle.

Culturally, the Makkans achieved the highest level of refinement and sophistication in the art of the word. They had neither architecture nor painting nor sculpture. The desert landscape helped them develop the strongest imagination, as the unconcern for writing helped them develop the most prodigious memories. Poetry never played a deeper or more significant role in the life of any people. It was not only the national obsession and concern but the national archive, the voice of conscience, and the collective ego. The first and archetypal Arab was Yaʻrub ("he who eloquizes"), and the very name "Arab" connotes poeticalness. The Arabic language and poetry and the music to which the verses of poetry were recited all obeyed the same laws of symmetry and repetition and realized identical patterns. No part was unique and any group of parts constituted in their sequence a momentum that can by nature never be brought to conclusion. It was natural that the word would be the locus of any epiphany, for to the Arabs it was man's highest and noblest achievement. The Prophet himself is reported to have once observed, "The eloquent word is indeed powerful and moving," thus echoing the Mesopotamian attribution of metaphysical efficacy to the word of God.

Muḥammad

Born an orphan in 570–571 C.E., the year in which Makkah was miraculously saved from impending destruction by the Abyssinians, Muḥammad grew in the shadow of his grandfather, leader of Makkah. After the latter's death, Muḥammad was cared for by his uncle. He was first a herdsman, then a tradesman in the employ of Khadījah, a widow whom he eventually married. He was a happy husband for a quarter of a century and the father of six children from this marriage.

Muḥammad had an impeccable character. His contemporaries knew him as sincere, honest, and truthful beyond compare (Qur'ān, 64:4). They called him *"al Amīn"* ("the faithful"). Tradition has preserved a number of anecdotes from this early period of his life, and these tell eloquently of intuitive brilliance, profound wisdom, and religious determination in the process of maturing. He was often found in pensive mood, and he would every now and then withdraw to a solitary retreat, a cave outside the city (Ghār Ḥirā') to satisfy his longing for meditation.

When he was about forty-two years old, on a night in Ramaḍān, the month of fasting and moral stocktaking, Muḥammad had a vision. As he meditated in his cave retreat, an angel seized and compelled him to recite the first verses of the Qur'ān to be revealed: "Read! In the name of your Lord who created man of a clot! For your Lord-Creator, is the more generous! He taught by the pen. He taught man that which he did not know" (96:1–6). Returning home in panic, he confided to his devoted wife his suspicion that he had become possessed or struck by a terrible sickness. Khadījah went to her cousin and family friend, Waraqah ibn Nawfal, a notable *ḥanīf,* for advice. Waraqah was struck with awe and joy that God had chosen to address yet one more message to man through Muḥammad. After her fears had been dissipated, she returned in joy to congratulate her husband and beg him to stand firm. Even this zealous confidence did not remove Muḥammad's doubt, which lasted for several months and took several apparitions of the angel and Qur'ānic revelations to eradicate. It was after the revelation of *sūrah* 93, reassuring that God had not forsaken him, that Muḥammad felt certain of and in his mission. Henceforth, his whole life was moved by one spring—fulfillment of the divine command.

The message was simple and straightforward. The gods and goddesses of Arabian religion were only names, and the previous revelations of the prophets had been so tampered with and interpreted through alien categories as to become hardly recognizable (2:75; 4:45; 5:44). There is no God but God, the eternal, living, omniscient, and omnipotent God, the transcendent God (112:1–4). Nothing, absolutely, is like unto Him (42:11). Everything is profane; only God is holy. This world and all it supports that He has created and continues to sustain is not in vain. It is man's to master, to use, and to enjoy and was created by God to be the theater wherein the drama of human life may be played. Man, the crown and *raison d'être* of creation, is higher than the angels because he is endowed with moral freedom and responsibility, the condition of ethical value which is the highest and dominant portion of the divine will or pattern. Man enjoys cosmic dignity for only he is capable of the ethical, as distinguished from the utilitarian, actualization of the divine will in creation. That is all there is to the creation of man. On entering the world, man is ethically a *tabula rasa.* What gets written thereon is his own doing. God has equipped him with faculties that, if properly developed and used, can yield the requisite knowledge of truth, goodness, and beauty. Moreover, He has gratuitously given man that knowledge in revelation. The present revelation is the last, for it shall be immune against corruption by tampering or interpretation; and it is valid for all times and places because it is only a conceptualization of axiological principles. The translation of these first principles into laws or prescriptions for conduct is man's prerogative and hence always renewable because it cannot escape the relativities of space and time.

As to his destiny, man is the author. He can only fulfill or not fulfill the purpose of creation, and both are his decision and his doing. It is not enough to wish fulfillment; man must fulfill *in actuo* and bring about, as result of his own deed, the real transformation of space-time. On a scale of absolute justice, where no person shall bear any except his own burden, man will be judged on the Final Day, receiving the reward or punishment he has earned. In this judgment, every imbalance on earth in the relationship of virtue to happiness will be redressed and settled.

This is the lesson Muḥammad taught. He and those whom he converted were set aflame by the vision, while his opponents were incensed and enraged. The emergent community was subjected to vilification, boycott, and persecution. As it grew, so did the temper and gravity of the attacks. Even his protector-uncle asked Muḥammad to reconsider, but the Prophet answered, "If they put the sun in my right hand and the moon in my left that I relinquish this cause, I shall never accept." After their delegate made a final try to bring Muḥammad to reason with promises of kingship, untold wealth, and free medical service to cure him of his "madness"—and returned from the conference converted to Islām!—the opponents plotted in their despair to put an end to the malaise by assassination.

Having sensed the imminent danger, Muḥammad emigrated on July 16, 622 C.E. to Yathrib (henceforth called "Madīnah al Nabiy," or briefly, al Madīnah), where he had already sent most of his followers and with whose leading tribes, the Aws and Khazraj, he had already entered into a bond of mutual security that supplanted the former security arrangement with the clan of Hāshim in Makkah (Map 50).

The Prophet's first work in Madīnah was the promulgation of a constitution and the launching of the Islāmic polity on its universal mission. The Muslim community is only one of the nuclei of the Islāmic polity, the others being the Jewish community, the Christian community, and, by extension, all other non-Muslim communities that choose to enter into a bond of peace with the Islāmic state. The nucleus communities as well as the polity as a whole constitute an open society whose membership is the birthright of any man anywhere, regardless of rank, race, or faith. Each community is to govern the life of its members in accordance with its own faith, and the polity stands always obliged to enable every community to uphold and honor its own religious tradition. The only condition is that of peace, of loyalty to the polity, whose *raison d'être* is the safeguarding of that peace, that is, of a world order in which ideas are free to move and truth is enabled to convince whomsoever it may. Because Islām holds the unity of God equivalent to and convertible with the unity of truth, it could afford to abide by man's responsible decision for the truth. The remaining years of Muḥam-

50 Central Arabia at the Time of Muḥammad
Showing the location of events in the Prophet's life

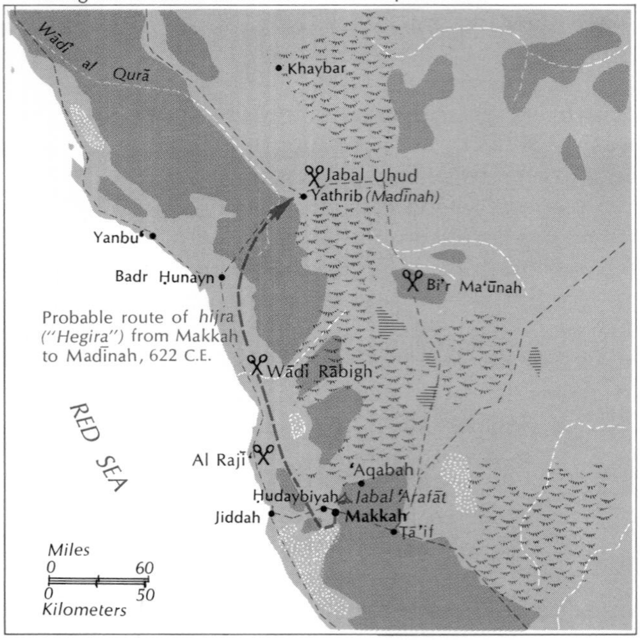

Site of battle between Madinan followers of Muḥammad and Makkan forces
Caravan routes
Mountains and hills — Sand — Salt flat — Lava bed *(harrat)*

mad's life, as well as the energies of his companions, were directed to persuade all men through sound teaching and to terminate, with force if necessary, any opposition to ideas by violence. To this purpose, they hurled themselves onto the stage and took history by the horns.

The Prophet continued to receive revelations as he concerned himself with remolding the lives of the converts into the Islāmic pattern. He taught and preached on every occasion, and he sent his best men to convey the message to the Jews in and around Madīnah and to the Arabs in the vicinity and beyond. He joined the *muhājirūn* (Makkan emigrants) and the *anṣār* (Madīnan helpers) together in bonds of fraternal cooperation and mutual assistance. He institutionalized the *adhān* (call to prayer from the minaret). The prayers were institutionalized earlier on the occasion of the Prophet's *Isrā'* (nocturnal journey to al Aqṣā sanctuary in Jerusalem) and *mi'rāj* (17:1) (his ascension thence to heaven in 621 C.E.). He established the institutions of *zakāt* (annual wealth-sharing) and fasting (during the month of Ramaḍān from dawn to sunset) and elaborated the law as he adjudicated disputes and approved or condemned events around him. He conferred with a Christian delegation from Najrān in the south, converted some, and granted the others status under the constitution. He did what he could to stop the Makkan enemies who were bent upon destroying him and his cause. He harassed their caravans in order to make up for some of the *muhājirūn's* properties, which had been confiscated by the Makkans, and to pressure them to desist from their aggression. He was met on the plain of Badr by a mobilized army determined to achieve what the *Hijrah* or emigration of the Prophet had foiled. The result of the encounter (2 A.H.) was a complete defeat of the superior Makkans by a small band of companions, each one of whom was an exemplar of Islāmic commitment and sacrifice. Two years later, on the slopes of Mt. Uḥud, the Makkans came close to their objective and inflicted heavy losses on the Muslims but missed making their

20-2 The Mosque of the Prophet at Madīnah, on the site of the first mosque of Islām, which was built by the Prophet. It is here that the Prophet is buried.

20-3 Qubbat al Ṣakhrah al Musharrafah (The Dome of the Rock), Al Quds (Jerusalem), built by Caliph ʻAbd al-Malik in 691 C.E. This monument is built over the rock which is revered by Jews, Christians, and Muslims. The latter venerate the Rock as the spot whence Muḥammad ascended to heaven on his nocturnal journey from Makkah (Qur' ān, 17:1) and because of its association with Abraham and Jesus whom they honor as prophets of God.

victory in the field conclusive. They returned again later that year after mobilizing most of the non-Muslims of West Arabia and laid siege to Madīnah. The Muslims fortified their city overnight and dug a ditch in front of the vulnerable portion to prevent a cavalry assault from that side. After a futile siege of a fortnight's duration, a terrible desert storm made havoc with the Makkan camp and they withdrew in panic and disorder. When pilgrimage time arrived and, according to Makkan tradition, hunting or fighting were religiously proscribed, the Muslims came to Makkah to perform the rite. They were prevented but were promised that they might perform the rite the following year without molestation, provided that they enter into a pact of peace and nonaggression. This pact was named ʻAhd al Ḥudaybiyah (628 C.E./6 A.H.) after the place where the Muslims had camped. The following year the Muslims returned to perform the pilgrimage, the Prophet establishing the ritual in all detail, transvaluing its old polytheistic meanings, and infusing it with the values of Islām. After two years of peace, allies of Makkah attacked, killed, and refused to make amends to allies of the Muslims. The Makkans stood by their defiant allies in violation of the Ḥudaybiyah treaty. The Muslims therefore mobilized and entered Makkah without battle on January 10, 630 C.E./8 A.H. Instead of revenge, Muḥammad honored the Makkans, forgave them, presented Islām to them, and welcomed many of them who decided to give up polytheism for Islām's pure transcendence and absolute unity of the Godhead. With his own hands, the Prophet broke down the statues and other idols of the Kaʻbah and reconsecrated the house that Abraham built for worship of the One and only God.

The allies of Makkah saw otherwise. Led by the numerous and strong clans of the Hawāzin tribe, a number of other tribes (including Thaqīf, Nasr, and Jusham) assembled southeast of Makkah and resolved to march to battle. They were met and defeated at Ḥunayn by the Muslims, whose ranks were now reinforced with the fresh Makkan converts. Again Muḥammad forgave his opponents and invited them to enter the new faith, which they did in large numbers. Thaqīf tribe took refuge in the city of Ṭā'if, to which the Muslims laid a siege of two months, after which the city opened its gates and its people joined the ranks of Islām. This year is known as ʻĀm al Wufūd or Year of Delegations, in reference to the numerous delegations sent to lands within and outside Arabia to invite their peoples to join Islām, as well as delegations received by the Prophet from such lands to pledge conversion of their peoples to the faith.

News of all these victories and changes in the political face of Arabia—for to join the Islāmic religion meant political, social, economic, and military unification with the Islāmic state as well—could not have failed to reach the great empires to the north, whose frontier puppet states included a number of Arab tribes directly concerned with the Arabian scene. Moreover, the Jews played a special role in bringing about direct confrontation between the Muslims and Byzantium.

From the first year after the Hijrah, the Jews of Madīnah became restive, despite the fact that the new constitution granted them more than they could possibly hope for as a minority. Relations began to deteriorate with the conversion to Islām of ʻAbdullah ibn Salām, one of their most distinguished leaders, which they sought to compensate by fomenting trouble between the two native Madīnah tribes with whom they were affiliated. When this plot did not work, the Banū Qaynuqāʻ branch openly blasphemed God and His Prophet and brought about their own banishment to the north. After Badr and Uḥud, the Banū al Naḍīr branch plotted again, this time with the Makkans and other anti-Muslim tribes, and succeeded in bringing about the Makkan siege of Madīnah, 4 A.H. While the Muslims were under siege, the Banū Qurayẓah branch withdrew from the city's defense lines to their own fortified homes and signaled to the Makkans to enter the city from their side. Had this offer come before the storm that destroyed the enemy camp, it would certainly have brought about Makkan victory. After the Makkans and their allies withdrew, the Muslims dealt with the Jews as traitors to the state and banished the majority of them to the north.

It was this new formation of tribal politics in the north that contributed largely to the Muslim-Byzantine confrontation. The banished Jews sought new allies and found them in Byzantium. Khaybar, with its older and newer Jews banished from Madīnah, had already attracted a warning Muslim raid in 628 C.E./6 A.H. for their plotting with Byzantium. When Muḥammad sent fifteen unarmed missionaries to Dhāt al Ṭalḥ, they were put to the sword by the area's Byzantine governor. The Muslims responded with an army under four generals, which was defeated, and three of its leaders were killed. Muḥammad turned his attention to Makkah, and as soon as the southern front was Islāmized and consolidated, a greater army than ever was dispatched to the north, headed by the nineteen-year-old son of a killed leader of the previous campaign. At Dawmat al Jandal, this army scored only a minor and inconclusive victory, but it was the beginning of a series of battles in which the two powers became necessarily engaged.

Political and military events, however, were not the Prophet's major concern. His eye was always on the minds and consciences of the people. To convince them, to purify them, to have them rededicate their lives, to energize their consciences with new values—these concerns occupied him constantly and dragged him unwillingly into military confrontation. Before the Hijrah, he once traveled to Ṭā'if to teach Islām but was pelted with stones and insults. In 625 C.E./3 A.H. he sent six of his best men to the tribe of Hudhayl for the same purpose and at their own request—but they were betrayed by the Hudhayl. In the unmatched encounter, the six Muslims fought for their lives against overwhelming odds. Three perished and the other three were delivered for a price to their Makkan enemies, who crucified them. Later on in the same year, the same tragedy was repeated—this time with forty of his companions whom the Prophet sent to teach Islām to Banū ʻĀmir and Ḥarrah tribesmen. Only one survived to tell the tale of betrayal and horror. Muḥammad could simply not resist any invitation to teach Islām, and everything in him impelled him to risk all in its cause. In 628 C.E./6 A.H. he accepted the humiliating terms of the Hudaybiyah treaty against his people's advice and the rebellion of some. He knew he needed the peace to talk sense to the large unbelieving majority, and time proved him right. The two years of peace had more than trebled the number of Muslims. In 629 C.E./7 A.H. he sent delegations to the archbishop of Egypt, the Negus of Abyssinia, Byzantine Emperor Heraclius, and Persian Emperor Chosroes, calling them to Islām and offering them peace and friendship and surety for their thrones and empires. As we have seen, after his most serious military victories he forgave and declared an amnesty, that his enemies might enter Islām in dignity and honor. He died with a contented conscience, having fulfilled his mission, conveyed the Qur'ān, exemplified righteousness, and launched the political state of Islām on its brilliant career. Indeed, this conscience of his could suffer itself to be the carrier of the verse, "Today I [God] have completed to you [the Muslims] your religion, granted you My total blessing, and accepted religion itself as 'Islām'!" (5:4). And Muḥammad could add, as he did, "Every man is to man a brother. 'The noblest of men is only the most righteous'" (49:13). He was buried the next day in Madīnah, within the mosque he himself had built, on June 9, 632 C.E./10 A.H.

The New Old Religion

ISLĀM AND MAKKAN RELIGION. Ideologically, Islām was a continuation of the ancient Mesopotamian tradition and a recrystallization of Judaism and Christianity. From the Mesopotamian tradition it reaffirmed the following principles: that reality is dual—transcendent, divine, and creatorly on one hand, and phenomenal, profane, and creaturely on the other; that the divine is relevant to the profane and that this relevance is the law of nature and the moral law; that with man's causal efficacy, creation is malleable and capable of realizing the divine will or pattern, of fulfilling the relevance of the creator for the creature; that man's *raison d'être* is service of the divine through such realization; and finally, that his fate will be blest or unblest depending on his fulfillment or otherwise of divine command. To buttress its ethic, Islām also recrystallized the legends of Adam, Noah, Abraham, and the patriarchs, as well as the traditions of ancient history to charge them with Islām's own ethical lessons. Each chronicle was recast in more than one mold to the purpose of teaching the new ethos. In cult and liturgy, Islām accepted the sacredness of Makkah and of its temple and reestablished pilgrimage, thus anchoring the new faith in the Makkan understanding of the ancient "Semitic" tradition. But it rejected Arab associationism (i.e., setting up deities to share the power with God), destroyed the idols of the Ka'bah, abolished priesthood and sacrament, and rededicated the temple to the One and only God (Map 51). Islām ruled out all intercession or mediation with the divine and opened wide the gates of immediate communion with God to all creatures. On this base, it

51 Makkah (Mecca)

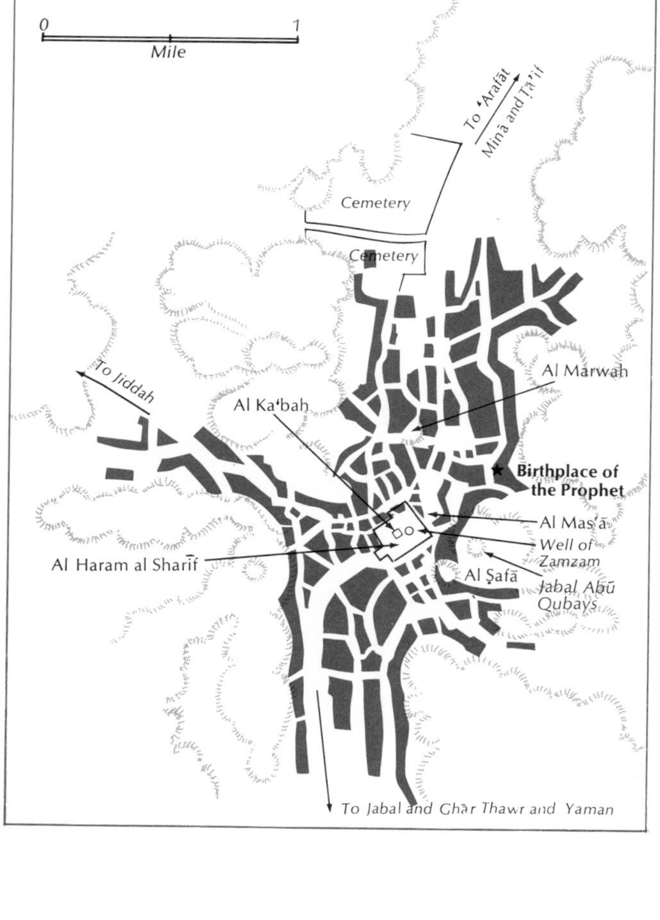

founded a new and absolute egalitarianism of all men. It adopted the Arabian institutions of the holy months and Ramaḍān, the month of fasting. Above all, aware of the tremendous threat that translation from language to language poses for the religion intended to cross cultural and ethnic frontiers and envelop mankind, Islām assigned elect status to Arabic and all the cultural categories innate therein. The Arabic word, in the highest aesthetic forms of the literary tradition of Arabia, became the carrier of the divine and inseparable therefrom. Islām reemphasized the Jewish and Christian ideas of personal immortality, of resurrection of the body, of the Day of Judgment and of eternal reward in paradise and punishment in hell. But it founded the new institutions of five prayers a day (*ṣalāt*), of enforcible wealth-sharing (*zakāt*), and of universal appropriation and daily reading of the scripture.

On the front of personal ethics, Islām rejected Arabian hedonism and its foundation, that is, the vanity and purposelessness of existence. Rather than the "muddling through" for which the Makkans were notorious, Islām gave its adherents a new sense of personal dignity, of vocation as God's vicegerents on earth, as higher than the angels, endowed with the cosmic duty of realizing the divine pattern, and of global responsibility for man's history. Islām taught the Muslim *taqwā*, or the fear of God, and thereby made the voice of conscience efficacious in determining personal conduct. It taught him a new ethic of contentment, honest work and truthfulness and a respect for the elder and the next of kin combined with legal responsibility for their welfare. It disciplined his individualist *joie de vivre* and taught him that the best marriage is a monogamous one without closing the door in the face of those whose personal circumstances prescribed otherwise. It reemphasized the traditional Arab values of honor, bravery, hospitality, and chivalry but divested them of their old tribalist association. Against excess, even in value, it taught a golden mean.

On the front of social ethics, Islām rejected the tribe as the limit of security and social cohesion, Makkan inequality and class distinctions, and the limitless power of the *pater familias* over his wives, children, and slaves. It upheld a universal *pax Islāmica* based on the equal rights of all persons and races and expanded the tribalist cohesiveness to include the universal community. Woman acquired full legal personality, and the female slave rose to the status of the free wife upon conception of her first child. The male slave of a recalcitrant master unmoved by the voice of conscience to manumit him was empowered to ransom himself upon refund of the price originally paid for him. The life of society was no more dependent upon intertribal treaties or a strategic balance of powers but upon public law, both within the Muslim community and the Islāmic state and without. It was the greatest innovation in international relations not only to found them on law but to recognize not only the states as subjects thereof but the individuals as well. Islām gave the state, as it did the person, a new sense of mission and a new dignity. It emphasized the power of government to rule—the more the better—and demanded obedience and advice from the citizens as long as all are subject to the public as well as to the moral law. Islām protected the citizen, Muslim and non-Muslim, the latter by granting him the freedom to govern his life by his own Jewish or Christian law as exercised by his peers, and the former by making heretication virtually impossible, there being no ecclesiastic *magisterium* to pronounce on Islāmicity except the consensus of the *ummah* across the generations. Islām sought and made a society in which ideas could travel and contend without hindrance and in which the best argument could and did win—in short, an *Academia grosser Stils,* or school on large scale.

On the front of culture, the foregoing religious foundation created a literate, culture-seeking community with a splendid obsession for book owning and reading and for calligraphy. The Qur'ān became the first best seller before the age of printing. The myths of land and tribe, of the numinous in man and nature, of the starry heavens or unfathomable self and any romantic attachment to them—all fell under the ruthless blows of Islām's rationalism, universalism, and separation of the creator from the creature. For the first time in man's history, creation became totally and absolutely profane, providing natural science with its first and essential principle.

ISLĀM AND THE WORLD RELIGIONS. Islām's regard for Judaism and Christianity was always one of self-identification with them as predecessor religions founded incontestably upon revelations from God to His prophets. But this self-identification was never uncritical of that which, in Judaism and Christianity, had gone astray from the straight path of divine will. The Qur'ān repeatedly declares the Hebrew prophets, including Jesus, as prophets of God and defines the Muslim as the person who believes in all the prophets and does not distinguish among them. All the revelations they brought from God, whether as to credibility or to essential content (3:84) are holy, divine, and worthy. The Qur'ān gives its own representation of the history—and revelation—content of these prophets. It presents them as moments in a continuing divine revelation whose essence is one and the same, namely, that God is, that He is one, and that man is to serve and obey Him by fulfilling the divine command, which is the *summum bonum* (16:36). The representation that emerges is obviously different from that which Jews and Christians today recognize as canonical. Islām's view is, however, corroborated by the fact that rather than a factual history of the founders, all that we have is, whether in the case of the Hebrew prophets or of Jesus, simply a representation by later adherents that, for a variety of reasons, only happened to become normative. Without a doubt, there were other representations by other adherents who called themselves Jews and/or Christians, some of which have survived but mostly in descriptions by their enemies. Such other adherents of Judaism and Christianity may well have been the *hanepai* aforementioned. It is not therefore farfetched to claim that in identifying itself with Judaism and Christianity, Islām did so on a base from which it criticized the other representations as human aberrations.

Islām recognizes that the Hebrews were elected by God in that He made of them prophets to convey His messages, that this election is through and through moral, and that they have long fallen off from it by failing to live up to the religious and moral standards revealed. The Jews are not unique in having been at times impious, unjust, or uncharitable. On this level all men are alike. However, they are uniquely blameworthy on three other counts compromising the absolute transcendence of God and the consequent absolute quality of all men *vis-à-vis* Him. The first of these is that of ascribing children to God, as the angels, or demi-gods, are described in Genesis 6:2,4, where the term *bene ha Elohim* is predicated of beings who enter into sexual relations with the "daughters of men". It is equally that of predicating to God fatherhood of the king, as in Psalms 2:7; 89:26; II Samuel 7:14; I Chronicles 17:13; etc., or fatherhood of the people Israel, as in Isaiah 9:6; 63:14–16; Jeremiah 3:19; 31:9; Hoseah 1:10; etc. That the fatherly relation is convertible to sonship is evident from the foregoing passages as well as Exodus 4:22f and Psalms 89:26f. The second charge is that of mistaking their election to messenger for God as divine favoritism, as in Deuteronomy 9:5–6, etc., which is the base of the Biblical doctrine of election and promise, of Jewish ethnocentrism through the ages. The third is that of failing to preserve the revealed words of God and calling "word of God" that which redactors and editors had reworked. Certainly this is not to question the integrity of the Biblical text *since,* but *before,* canonization. The Septuagint, (Codex Vaticanus, with Genesis 1–46 missing, fourth Century), the earliest, most complete text of the Bible we have, is an intricately woven fabric of writings and traditions of many periods, generations, authors, and schools. Biblical criticism has corroborated the Qur'anic view that the Torah as we know it today does not come from the sole hand of Moses, but that many hands have contributed to it. However, the Qur'ān lays no absolute or universally valid charge. Its critiques are always directed to "some Jews," to "those Jews who . . ." Indeed it takes care to remind its readers that some of "the People of the Scripture," as Christians and Jews are called, are believers in good standing with God, that they have no reason to be sorry, and that great reward awaits them in the hereafter (3:113–114; 5:69).

As to Christianity, Islām has been even more friendly and tolerant. Besides reassuring them as it did the Jews that its critique is directed only to the excessivists among them, it openly teaches friendship to them as they are pious and humble and spend their nights in prayer and worship (5:85). Islām affirms not only the prophethood of Jesus but also his virgin birth. However, it regards him as human through and through and pours its wrath on his deifiers, whose work produced trinitarian theology. Further, Islām has no sympathy for the Christian soteriological principles of vicarious guilt and suffering. Nothing counts for man or against him except what he himself has earned personally, and no salvation will be his unless he has transcended himself to the outside world and produced the necessary works. Islām categorically denies the crucifixion and accounts for Jesus' encounter with his executioners in the manner of the Gnostic Christians (i.e., through Jesus' disappearance from the scene), but for different reasons (4:156). Whereas the Gnostics held that Jesus could not suffer death because he was wholly spirit, the Qur'ān asserts that he could not have died by crucifixion because such a shameful debacle of the prophet is tantamount to frustration of the almighty God who sent him.

Islām's views of Judaism and Christianity were not foreign to many Jews and Christians in Arabia, Egypt, and other areas of the Near East and North Africa. Despite the fact that the Roman Church had imposed itself on the whole Roman world by the time Muḥammad began to preach, the old views must have continued and the Near Easterners' subscription to the Roman creed must have been only skin-deep. It took only one or two generations for most Christians of these lands to convert to Islām. Although the Muslim might call this a miracle, the historian will see it as due to the fact that Islām's call recrystallized older and indigenous principles that the Christian recognized and reappropriated as his own.

Finally, Islām did not relate itself at all to the religion of Persia except to condemn its Manichaean forms. This negative attitude was due to the fact that Ḥanīfism, Judaism, and Christianity had all benefited from Persian religious thought long before Islām. Eschatology, Day of Judgment, paradise and hell, personal resurrection, angelogy and demonology had all become *Ḥanīfī,* Jewish, and Christian. As Islām identified itself with these traditions, it naturally incorporated the Persian elements as *Ḥanīfī,* Jewish, or Christian, not as Persian. On the other hand the Persian representation of the deity as fire together with all the cultic paraphernalia of the fire temple Islām condemned as idolatry. For centuries the Persians had been suffering from an iniquitous caste system, legalized incest, and social immobility for both the affluent and the miserable. The brotherhood, equality, universalism, and the ethical purity that Islām brought to family life must have been irresistible. Here too, as in Syria and Egypt, people joined the ranks of Islām *en masse,* and it was only a generation before the majority had converted to the "new old faith."

The Conquests and Spread of Islām

CONQUESTS. At the death of Muḥammad in 632 C.E./11 A.H., all but a few distant pockets of Arabia had joined Islām. In a number of cases, however, Islāmicity was skin-deep. When Muḥammad passed away, the superficially Islāmized tribes thought the time opportune for breaking away. They did—some on the ideational level by following new prophet-pretenders, and most on the practical level by refusing to hand the *zakāt* collection to the polity headquarters in Madīnah. The territories of Yaman, Yamāmah, and ʿUmān and the tribes of Ṭay', Asad, and Ghaṭafān fell in the latter category; and the territories of Baḥrayn and Ḥaḍramawt and the tribes of Banū Ḥanīfah, and Banū Tamīm in the former. All were crushed in military campaigns conducted by Khālid ibn al Walīd in the first year of Abū Bakr's caliphate, 632–634 C.E./11–13 A.H. When the first caliph died a year later, the whole of Arabia stood united and poised to carry out its mission to other lands.

There was no need to wait for a new *casus belli,* for operations in the northwest had never completely stopped. The Prophet died while a new army was being mobilized to be sent north to undo earlier defeats, and his first successor saw the army off—but the campaign was again inconclusive. Skirmishes, war preparations, and threats took place continuously, though as the Prophet had done earlier, Abū Bakr had to turn his attention to the home front first. Once this was united and consolidated, Abū Bakr mobilized five armies and sent them out, four in the direction of Byzantium and one in that of Persia. The first two under the commands of Yazīd ibn Abū Sufyān and Shuraḥbīl ibn Ḥasanah marched together on the Tabūk-Maʿān road; the third under ʿAmr ibn al ʿĀṣ took the coastal route via Aylah (modern 'Aqabah); the fourth under Abū 'Ubaydah al Jarrāḥ took the pilgrim route of Madīnah-Damascus; and the fifth under Khālid ibn al Walīd took the desert road to south 'Irāq. The last was to achieve the first victory in the summer of 633 C.E./12 A.H., with the conquest of 'Ayn al Tamr, northwest of Kūfah. The fall saw the first two armies making battle against Sergius's army at Wādī 'Arabah, at which the Byzantine force withdrew and was met again and annihilated at Dathīn, midway between Wādī 'Arabah and Ghazzah. It was then that Heraclius marched from his capital at al Ruhā (Edessa) and took personal command of operations. 'Umar ibn al Khaṭṭāb, who succeeded Abū Bakr on his death, ordered the fifth army to join the Muslims in the west. Khālid managed to reach Syria in the short span of eighteen days—an impossible feat by any standard—gave fierce battle to the Byzantines at Marj Rāhīṭ on Easter Day 634, and veered south to Buṣra. It was there that the Byzantines were given their first serious defeat, caught as they were between the five pincers of the Muslim armies. While the first army took Ajnadayn in the fall of 634 and al Fiḥl (Pella) in January 635, the other four pursued the enemy and gave him another battle (February 635) at Marj al Suffār, which decided the fate of Damascus, though it took several more months for that city to surrender. The fate of all Syria was decided at the Battle of Yarmūk on August 6, 636, when having regrouped their forces, the two contestants battled to the bitter end. Most of the natives welcomed the Muslims as kin-liberators from Byzantine politics, economic exploitation, church persecution, and social tyranny. Jerusalem refused to surrender to anyone but the caliph, who journeyed thither in person in 635 C.E./15 A.H. to receive the keys and pledge the assurance of the Islāmic state for the safety of Christianity and its shrines, practices, and traditions. Caesarea, Sergius's capital, being supplied by the navy, surrendered in October 640 C.E./19 A.H. Syria was then divided into four parallel sections stretching from the Mediterranean to the inland desert—Ḥims, Dimashq (Damascus), al Urdunn (Jordan), and Filasṭīn (Palestine). Al Jābiyah, near Damascus, became a central military base.

Further east, the local forces left behind by Khālid ibn al Walīd when he was ordered to Syria, were reinforced by eastern Arabian tribesmen under the generalship of al Muthannā ibn Ḥārithah. His first encounter with the Persians was the Battle of al Jisr (the bridge) near al Ḥīrah, where the Muslims suffered defeat. After regrouping, al Muthannā was victorious over Mihrān, his counterpart at al Buwayb in October 635 C.E./14 A.H. Neither battle was conclusive. The Syrian campaign over, 'Umar ordered Sa'd ibn Abū Waqqās to take charge of a portion of the Muslim army in Syria and proceed to the eastern front with Persia. The two hosts met at Qādisiyyah, where Sa'd inflicted defeat upon Rustum (June 637 C.E./16 A.H.), pressed on to al Madā'in (Ctesiphon), and occupied it. Baṣrah and Kūfah were founded as military bases from which to conduct further operations. In December of the same year, the battle of Jālulā' put an end to the new regime of Yazdagird III, though the new king himself lasted until December 652 C.E./33 A.H., when he was killed by one of his own generals at Marw as the Muslims pressed on further east. His intermediate capital, Nihāwand (Ecbatana), was overrun in the Battle of Nihāwand, December 641 C.E./20 A.H. Another Muslim army now advanced from Syria by the northern route under Iyād ibn Ghamm. This year saw the conquest of the remaining portions of the Persian Empire, Mawṣil (Mosul), Khūzistān (Elam), and Pars. Iṣṭakhr (Persepolis) was fortified and was not occupied by 'Abdullah ibn 'Āmir until 649, after which he pressed on to Khurāsān. In the meantime, Mukrān, Balūchistān, and parts of Armenia were conquered.

Pacification of Syria and the quick reestablishment of law and order with a cooperating population released further troops for deployment in another theater. From the winter of 639 C.E./18 A.H., a strong force under 'Amr ibn al 'Aṣ moved in the direction of Egypt and, within a few months, conquered al 'Arīsh, al Farāma (Pelusium), Bilbays, and 'Ayn Shams and stood in front of Babilyūn (Babylon), the capital of Egypt, south of the Delta. In the following year, as al Zubayr ibn al 'Awwām joined 'Amr's army with another reinforcement from Madīnah, Babilyūn and Naqyūs (Old Nikiu) were conquered. Fusṭāṭ (Old Cairo) was founded as military base and capital, and a treaty was negotiated with Cyrus, Archibishop of Alexandria, recognizing his independence from Byzantium. Without delay, 'Amr reopened the canal linking the Nile to the Red Sea, which remained in use till the Suez Canal was opened in 1869. When in 645 C.E./24 A.H. Emperor Constans sent a marine army under Manuel and reoccupied Alexandria, 'Amr moved to drive the Byzantines out. The job took only a few months to accomplish and 'Abdullah ibn Abū Sarḥ was charged with developing a navy to operate from this newly acquired port. In less than three years, the Muslim fleet of Alexandria was strong enough to conquer Cyprus and add it to the empire. With another naval force based at 'Akkā (Acre) and built by Mu'āwiyah (then governor of Syria), the two fleets cooperated in establishing Muslim power in Cyprus, conquering Arwād (Aradus, an island west of Tarsus), attacking Rhodes, and ending Byzantine naval supremacy in the Mediterranean with the Battle of Dhāt al Sawārī, fought near Phoenix off the Lycian coast in 655 C.E./34

20-4 Mosque of Aḥmad ibn Ṭūlūn, al Qāhirah (Cairo), 876–879 C.E. The minaret at the far left is copied from the famous minaret of the Sāmarra Grand Mosque.

20-5 Dome of Gur Emir, the mausoleum of Tīmūr, Samarqand, U.S.S.R., 1404 C.E. The dome is covered with bright blue tiles, the drum and lower part of the building with ornamental brick work making calligraphic designs in Arabic Kūfī script.

A.H. Indeed, even Sicily underwent its first Muslim attack as early as 652 C.E./31 A.H.

On land, 'Amr ibn al 'Āṣ continued his advance westward. Barqah (Pentapolis) fell in 643. So did Lawātah and the Berber region of Tripoli. In a joint operation by land and sea, 'Abdullah ibn Abū Sarḥ conquered Ifrīqiyah and its capital, ancient Qarṭājannah (Carthage), in the west. Southward, on the Nile, he concluded a peace treaty with the Nubian capital, Dongola, giving free access to Muslim missionaries and officially recognizing the new converts.

No sooner had the Umawīs established themselves in power and brought the eastern provinces under full control than they launched a series of campaigns that brought Islām to China in the northeast, to India in the south, and to Western Europe in the west. The years 663–671 C.E./42–52 A.H. saw the completion of the conquest of Khurāsān province. This was necessary before any further advance could be made. Thereafter, with the arrival of al Ḥajjāj upon the troubled scene of the east, which was slow to recognize the Umawi caliphate, 'Abd al Raḥmān ibn al Ash'ath hastened at the head of an army toward Kābul and the Afghānistān region. He subdued them in 699. Qutaybah ibn Muslim was dispatched in 704 C.E./85 A.H. to rule Khurāsān from the capital, Marw, and to bring Islām to the neighboring countries. Lower Ṭukhāristān and its capital, Balkh (705); Bukhārā (706); the rest of Sughd, including Khwārizm (modern Khiva) and Samarqand (710); Farghānah and Jaxartes provinces (713); Kashghar and Chinese Turkestān (715); and, after a rebellion by the Khazars, al Shāsh and Ṭashqand (751)—all were brought under the dominion of Islām (Map 52).

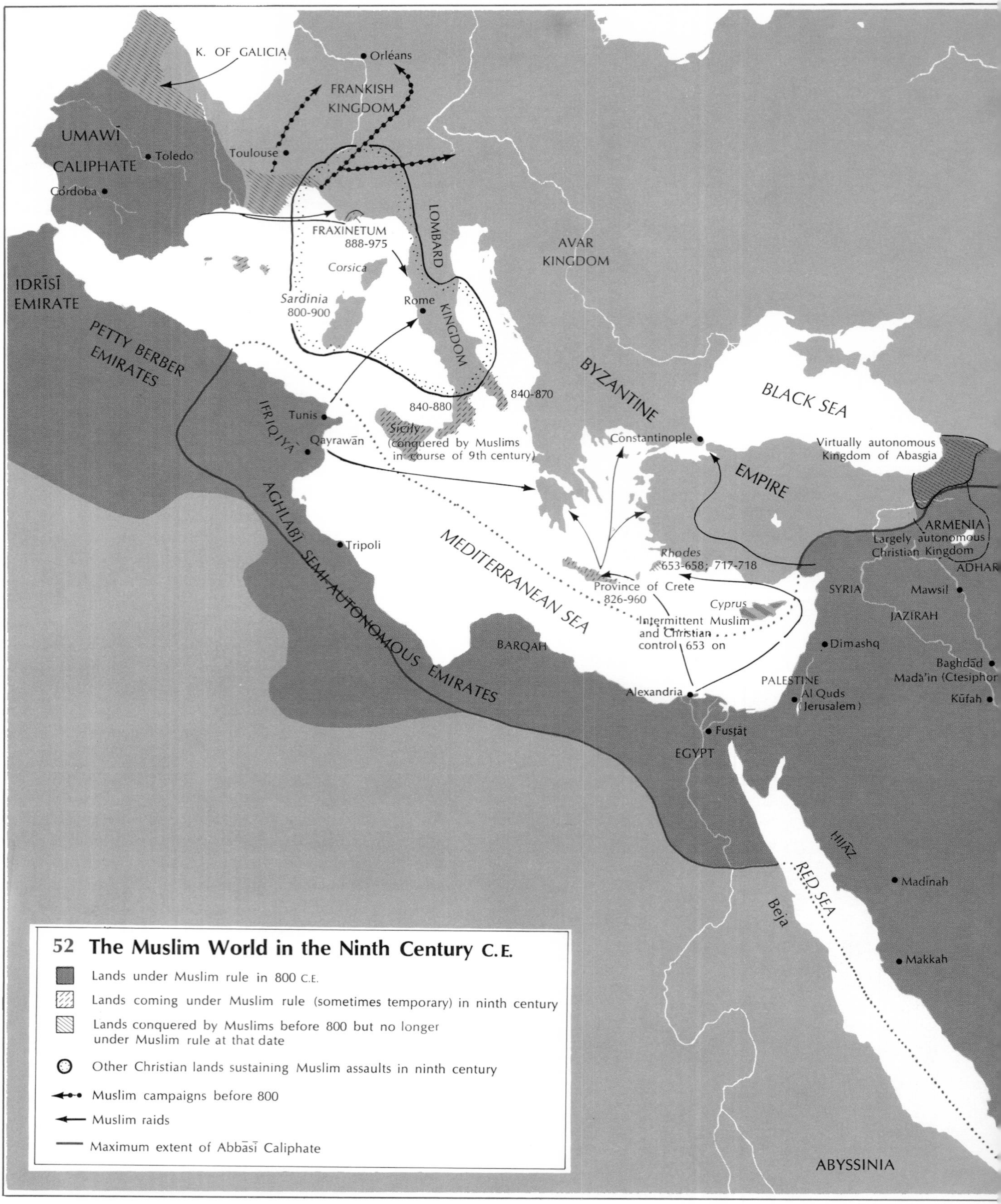

52 The Muslim World in the Ninth Century C.E.

- Lands under Muslim rule in 800 C.E.
- Lands coming under Muslim rule (sometimes temporary) in ninth century
- Lands conquered by Muslims before 800 but no longer under Muslim rule at that date
- Other Christian lands sustaining Muslim assaults in ninth century
- Muslim campaigns before 800
- Muslim raids
- Maximum extent of Abbāsī Caliphate

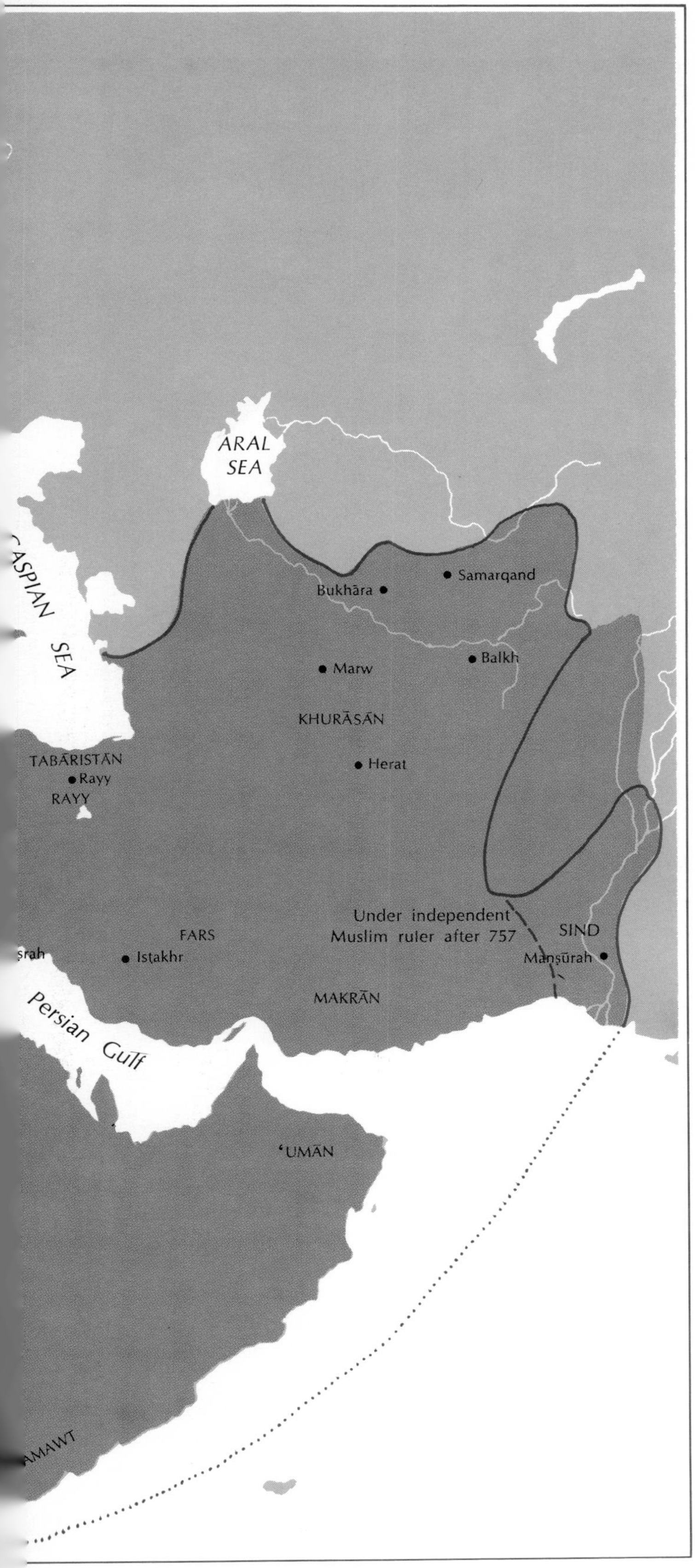

To the southeast, Muḥammad ibn Qāsim was sent in 710 C.E./93 A.H. to save Muslims captured by Sindhi pirates when their ships went aground near Daybul, and engagement with Hindu forces was inevitable. Ibn Qāsim conquered Daybul al Nirūn (modern Hyderabad), Sind, and, pressing north after the enemy, added the whole of Sind and parts of the Punjāb including Multān in 713 C.E./96 A.H.

The front with Byzantium stabilized and a number of frontier defense fortifications were built in earnest at Malaṭiyyah (Melitene), Ṭarsūs, Adhanah, al Massīsah (Mopsuestia), and Mar'ash (Germanicia) called *al 'Awāṣim* or the fortresses. A number of second-line fortifications called *al thūghūr* ("the openings") were raised from Awlās on the Mediterranean, past Ṭarsus, to Sumaysat (Samosata) on the Euphrates. However, Justinian II was dealt defeat at Sebastopolis in Cilicia in 692 C.E./72 A.H. Al Ṭuwānah (Tyana) in Cappadocia was wrested from him in 707, and Sardis and Pergamos in 715. The chain of military action and reaction even brought about an inconclusive thirteen-month siege of Constantinople, 716–717 C.E./97–98 A.H.

'Uqbah ibn Nāfi', the Umawi governor of Ifrīqyah, founded al Qayrawān in 670 C.E./49 A.H. as military base to provide security and capital whence to direct the Islāmic mission into the western part of North Africa. He completed the march until stopped by the shore waves of the Atlantic. It fell to his successor, Mūsā ibn Nuṣayr, to extend the Islāmic empire beyond the water, onto the European continent.

In July, 710 C.E./91 A.H., General Ṭarīf was sent with a small force on a reconnaissance mission and landed in Ṭarīfa, named after him. Julian, Count of Ceuta, supplied the ships. When in the following year Ṭāriq ibn Ziyād arrived with fresh reinforcements, Julian again supplied the ships, and the troops were assisted by Bishop Offas, brother of Witiza, whose throne King Roderick had usurped. Ṭāriq (whence the name "Jabal Ṭāriq," which was hispanicized into "Gibraltar") inflicted a crushing defeat on Roderick on the shore of the Barbate River. The whole plain to Toledo then lay open to him. The cities fell one after another after little or no siege and little or no fighting. Only Ecija suffered a fierce battle before it opened its gates. Mūsā ibn Nuṣayr followed with more troops within a year. Medina Sidonia, Carmona, Seville, and Merida fell in 713 C.E./93 A.H. Saragossa and Toledo followed in the same year. By 717 C.E./98 A.H. only the Pyrenees stood between the Muslims and France, and they were crossed in the same year. Septimania and 'Arbūnah (Narbonne) fell in 720, and the Muslim force pressed in the direction of Toulouse, seat of Duke Endes of Aquitaine. In 724 C.E./106 A.H., 'Ambisah al Kalbī, new governor of

20-6 The double-storied arcades of the Umawī Mosque in Qurṭubah (Cordova), Spain. Founded by ʻAbd al-Raḥman I in the eighth century, the mosque was enlarged several times in the subsequent three centuries. (Courtesy of the Spanish National Tourist Office.)

Andalus, crossed the Pyrenees with another force and added Carcassonne and Nîmes to his possessions. Two years later his successor added Septimania up to the Rhone, the Albigeois, Rouergue, Gevandan, Le Velay, and Rodez, then marched into the Dauphiné, Lyonnais, and Burgundy, occupying Mâcon, Chalon-sur-Saône, Beaune, and Autun. By 732 the Muslims had taken Toulouse and the whole of Aquitaine and had vanquished its duke. Bordeaux and Tours were taken, and the Muslims stood at Poitiers, having occupied all the territory south and southeast of that city. Met by Charles Martel, their advance was stopped, and they had to withdraw further south to consolidate their lines.

In 734, the Muslims crossed the Rhone and captured Arles, St. Rémy, and Avignon, fortified the Languedoc, and reoccupied Lyons and Burgundy. For a hundred years, they remained entrenched in southeast France. As the pressure mounted on them from the north, the Muslims chose to push their frontiers east and northeastward toward Switzerland and only to harass the enemy to the north by such daring attacks as their naval raid on the island of Oye on the Brittany coast in 827

C.E./211 A.H. The year 831 was to witness another Muslim naval attack against Marseilles, as well as an advance by ships up the Rhone estuary.

It was in 889 C.E./275 A.H. that a small number of Muslims sailed up the Gulf of St. Tropez, founded a colony at Fraxinetum, and launched a Muslim presence in Switzerland that was to last two whole centuries. From there they fanned out quickly and brought most of western Switzerland under their dominion. They crossed the defiles of the Dauphiné, Mont Cenis, and the valley of Susa and settled themselves in the Alpine passes. The attack on Piedmont had to await the arrival of new troops under 'Abdul Raḥman in 920 C.E./319 A.H. In less than a decade the territories west of Liguris had been taken. Valais, Grisons, Geneva, Fréjus, Toulon, Great St. Bernard (then known as Mt. Jupiter), and the Aosta Valley were taken in 939–942 C.E./224–227 A.H. The country of the Grisons came next, and its abbeys of Disentis and Coire (Chur) were taken. The Muslims reached the lake of Geneva and marched toward the Jura Mountains, taking Neuchâtel and St. Gall around 956. In Piedmont, they built fortresses at Fressinet and Fenestrelle to defend their possessions against the Huns. The first Hun attack came in 952 with the Battle of the Orbe. Although Muslim presence reached its apex in this decade, their military situation henceforth began to deteriorate. For a century it followed the declining fortunes of the Umawī caliphate in Spain, and it came to nought under persistent blows from different directions. The Huns and the Hungarians from the north and northeast were menacing. Hugh, the Count of Provence who was carving for himself a new kingdom, appealed to his brother, the emperor of Constantinople, to attack the Muslim ports with "Greek fire." Guillaume, Count of Dauphiné, was responding to the wave of resentment that stirred the Christian population at the Muslims' capture of Mayeul and their building a fortress there. Finally, the Spanish mainland, the last source of manpower for the Muslim colonies in France and Switzerland, erupted with rebellions and was then divided into a number of petty emirates pulling apart from one another and engaging in internecine struggles. The final chapter came to a close after 1050, when the Normans hastened the Muslim defeat and withdrawal from south France as well as south Italy, Corsica, Sardinia, and Sicily.

The front with Byzantium maintained its calm during the first half of the eighth century. In 782 C.E./165 A.H. Hārūn al Rashīd, sent an expeditionary force to Constantinople, where it imposed a treaty (ninety thousand dinars annually) on Irene, the queen regent. Later, Nicephorus II (802–811) repudiated the treaty unilaterally. Harūn invaded, captured Hiragla and Tuwanat, and forced Nicephorus to sign a more humiliating treaty. Ani, capital of Armenia, fell to Muslim hands in 1064, and the fate of the Caucasus was decided in 1071 after Muslims won the decisive battle of Manzikart north of Lake Van and took Romanus Diogenes, the Byzantine emperor, prisoner. That date also marks the beginning of Turkish settlement in the Asia Minor plateau, where Iznik (Nicaea) was made provincial capital in 1077.

SPREAD OF ISLĀM. In the Qur'ān, God commanded His Prophet, "Call all men unto your Lord with wisdom and arguments yet more sound, with comely, wise exhortation; argue with them always with better arguments. Proclaim that the truth has come from your Lord. Whoever wills, will believe; whoever does not, let him persist in disbelief. . . . No coercion in religion. Truth and right guidance are now clearly distinct from error and misguidance. . . . Remind and warn. That is your commission. You have no imperial authority over any man. . . . Had God willed it, all men on earth would have been believers. But He did not! Would you then compel men to believe?" (Qur'ān, 16:125; 18:29; 2:257; 88:21–26; 10:99) Muḥammad made these principles the bases of his preaching and mission, and the Muslims followed his example.

In Arabia, Muḥammad never lost a chance to preach and to argue out the new religion. More than once he exposed himself to insult and stone throwing for preaching. He was tricked into sending out his best companions to preach Islām, only to fall into captivity, indeed death traps, at the hands of their unbelieving hosts. The drive to preach, to call, to argue, and to enlighten pressed him to overlook danger. Even God chided him, as many Qur'ānic verses show, for taking the matter to extremes (5:44; 3:176; 6:33). Singlehanded, He overcame the unanimous opposition of his followers to his acceptance of a humiliating armistice with Makkah to the end of preaching Islām in peace. In his moment of military triumph, he never lost sight of his preaching mission, but restoring the dignity of the vanquished with praise and safeguarding of their autonomy, he would invite them to join the new faith. His strategy never failed to pay off: at his death, the whole of Arabia was converted, for the most part by Muḥammad's personal preaching. There were non-Muslim pockets left: the Christians of Yaman and the Jews of northwest Arabia. The former had argued the faith with the Prophet, were not convinced, and were sent back by him with gifts and honors under the protection of his own guards. Not convinced by logic, they were later convinced by Islām's successes under 'Umar. The Jews continued their plotting with Byzantium and were caught in the military operations of that empire.

20-7 Two mosques of Cairo: At left, the mosque-mausoleum-madrasah complex of Sulṭān Ḥasan, 1354–62 C.E.; at right, Rifāʿī Mosque, built by King Ḥusayn Kāmil in 1920.

As to the Arab tribes of the petty buffer states between Byzantium and the Arabian Peninsula, the religious appeal of Islām, combined with the feeling of Arabness embodied in the language and the consciousness of which it is the vehicle and expression, carried them over to Islām. The expanding military line was equally, but for entirely different reasons, identical with the religious. Outside of Arabia, where Arabness of tongue and consciousness was only a meager deposit of earlier generations, conversion was mostly due to the religious appeal of Islām. Certainly, the hatred that heretication and persecution at the hand of the Roman Church produced in the native Christians of the Near East, their politicoeconomic exploitation by the Byzantine Empire, and the attraction of a new victorious society and civilization—all contributed to conversion. But *appeal* implies that it takes time to make a point. Hence apart from the rush of conversion at the initial entry of the Muslim armies into these lands, the majority of the people everywhere kept their old religions for generations afterward.

The first people to convert *en masse* were the Egyptians. They were Christians who separated themselves from the Roman Church at Chalcedon in 541 C.E. on the issue of the dual nature of Christ. Their monophysite creed had led to persecution by the Melkite Royal Church of Alexandria, which enforced the monothelite compromise of Emperor Heraclius and stood on his support. Under the governorship of ʿAmr (641–663), Egypt paid 14 million dinars in yearly poll-tax revenue levied on adult, lay, and capable non-Muslim males. Under Muʿāwiyah (661–680) that same revenue fell to 4 million.

Nubia's Christianization was newer than Egypt's (first century C.E.), for it took place in the sixth century, but it preserved its religion down to the twelfth century. The first mosque to rise in Soba, capital of Christian Nubia, was built in the tenth century. In the fourteenth century, conversion went hand in hand with the intermarriage of Arabs of the Juhaynah tribe with the natives. According to Ibn Baṭūṭah, the king of the chief city (Dongola) embraced Islām and ruled over a largely Christian population. The Nubians finally yielded to the appeal of Islām in large numbers as their neighbors to the south embraced it and the Muslims of the north continued to send missionaries who gave evidence of their candidness by identifying themselves with the natives through intermarriage.

Abyssinia and the lands south of Nubia were for the

20-8 Jāmiʿ Mosque, Nairobi, Kenya, twentieth century.

most part Christian, and so was the western shore of the Red Sea. In the tenth century Abū 'Abdullah Muḥammad, himself a native convert, attracted as many as a quarter million and contested the authority of the king of Amhara. The Muslims were subjected to persecution under King Saifa Ar'ad (1342–1370). Aḥmad Gran, son of a Christian priest, mobilized the Muslim petty kingdom of Adal against Abyssinia. Many Christian chiefs converted to Islām, along with their troops and followers, in the second quarter of the sixteenth century. The entry of the Portuguese onto the scene helped Christian Abyssinia politically and militarily, but it accelerated the conversion to Islām of the Horn of Africa, the east, north, and northeast of Abyssinia itself, and the shore of the Red Sea (Map 53).

West of Egypt, Africa was for the most part Christian. The Vandals had devastated the land, massacred its inhabitants, and pillaged its cities, as Synesius of Cyrene has told us, long before the advent of Islām. Tripoli's Thorismund (496–524) was a pagan. Following Belisarius's victories in 534 and the restoration of Africa to the Roman Empire, the Synod of Carthage counted 217 bishops. Justinian's persecutions ruined the country a second time. Three hundred years after Arab conquest there were still 40 bishoprics, and in 1053 Pope Leo IX lamented that the membership was only five. The slowness of the decay of the North African churches is evidence that the Muslims were in no hurry and that they allowed the process of personal persuasion ample time to produce conversion. By 1246, the bishop of Morocco was the only ordained leader left. The last remnants—people who lived in the isolation of impenetrable mountains, and beyond, on the slopes leading to the desert—were converted by Ṣūfīs expelled from Spain following the fall of Granada in 1492.

Further South, mass conversions did not take place until the first two decades of the eleventh century, when Yaḥyā ibn Ibrahīm, a Ṣanhāja chieftain, sought and found on his return from pilgrimage the missionary and learned man of his choice in the person of 'Abdullah ibn Yasin. Together, they established themselves on an island in the Senegal River, where they built a *ribāṭ*, that is, a devotional retreat which is at the same time a mosque, a fortress, and a school for the instruction of the natives in Islām. The thousands they converted, instructed in Islām, and drilled in the *ribāṭ* were called *Murabiṭūn*. These were enjoined to return, each to his fellow tribesmen, in order to call them to Islām. Yaḥyā ibn Ibrahīm later raised an army of them and gradually built an empire that covered the whole of North Africa—west of Tunis—and Spain. The political and military successes provided further appeal to prospective members. The clans of Lamtuna and Jadala, both of the Sanhāja tribe, were the first to bring Islām to the Senegal and Niger river basins. The second Murābiṭ ruler, Yūsuf ibn Tashfīn, founded Morocco and its capital, Marrakush, in 1062.

The kingdom of Ghana received from the Murābiṭūn its first Muslim dynasty in 1076. The kingdom of Songhay received its first Muslim king in 1079. Jannah and Timbuktu, the two great caravan cities, were founded by Muslims in 1100. Kunburn, whose pagan chief had converted to Islām, soon became another radiating center for Islāmic influence. Having conquered the kingdoms of Ghana and Mali, the Mandingo tribesmen carried Islām to the Hausa people. In this they built over earlier foundations laid by Arab Muslims from Egypt, Kordofan, and the Lake Chad region. In fact, Kanem was already an Islāmic kingdom, extending from Chad to Egypt and the Sudan and enjoying considerable power and prestige. Darfur got its first Muslim king in the fourteenth century in the person of a Tunjar (Arab) tribesman who served the local king well, brought prosperity and security to the land with his wise government, married the king's daughter, and proselytized the people.

20-9 Courtyard (ṣaḥn) of Qarawiyyīn Mosque, first built in 859 C.E., enlarged in 956 C.E., and rebuilt by Yūsuf ibn Tashfīn in 1082 C.E., in Fās, Morocco.

53 Muslim Rule and Influence from the Second Half of the Thirteenth Century C.E.

- Under Muslim rule c. 1250–1300 C.E.
- Areas continuing under Muslim rule to the present time with a majority or large minority of non-Muslims c. 1250–1300 C.E.
- M Substantial Muslim communities (c. 1250 C.E.) in areas never under Muslim rule
- Previously under a century or more of Muslim rule but no longer so by 1250 C.E.
- Coming under Muslim rule after 1300 C.E. (Number refers to century of acquisition)
- Acquired and lost by Muslim rulers after 1300 C.E. (Numbers refer to centuries of acquisition and loss)
- Under Muslim rule in thirteenth century and subsequently not (Number refers to century of loss)
- Spread of Muslim power and influence in Africa (Number refers to century of occurrence)

Note: Changes of short duration are not indicated.

In the eighteenth century, the Fulbe tribe produced the great reformer and missionary ʿUthmān Danfodio. On his pilgrimage he met the Wahhābīs of Arabia (see the section entitled "Wahhābiyyah" at the end of this chapter), studied their doctrine and returned aflame with new religious enthusiasm to reform his countrymen and spread Islām. Danfodio united all the Muslim groups of the region in one powerful organization, raised the banner of revolt against the pagan Hausa kingdom of Gober in 1802, and subjugated all the Hausa states in

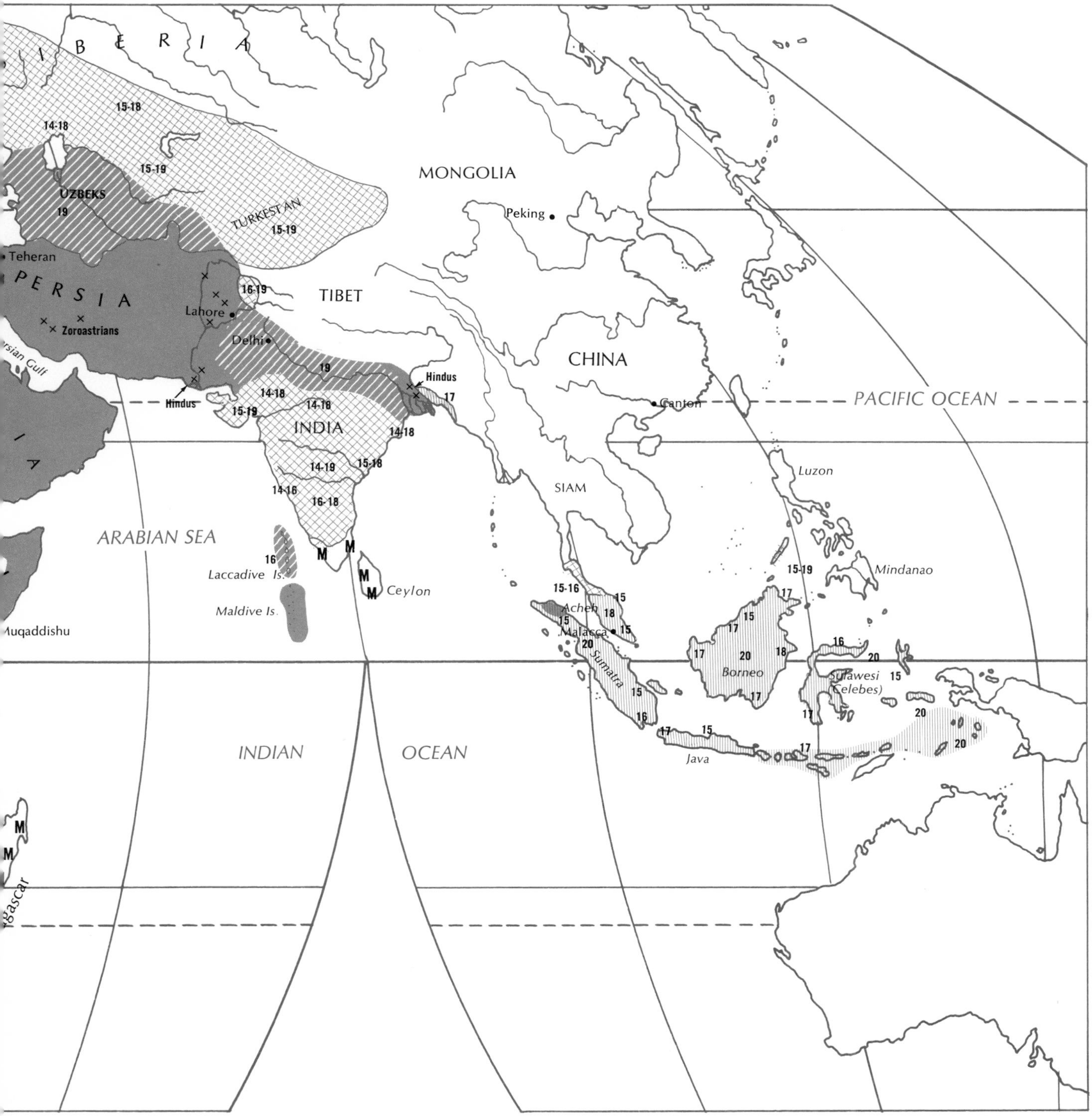

the process. His power cut into pagan tribes in the equatorial forest, reaching and transcending the regions of Adamawa in Ibo country in the southeast and Ilorin in Yoruba country in the southwest.

Muḥammad 'Uthmān Amīr Ghānī was another Muslim committed to missionary travel. He started out from Makkah in 1835 for the Dongola and Kordofan territories, where he converted thousands of people and contracted many marriages with their daughters to cement the brotherhood of Islām. After his death in 1853,

54 Travels of Ibn Baṭuṭa (1325-1354 C.E.)

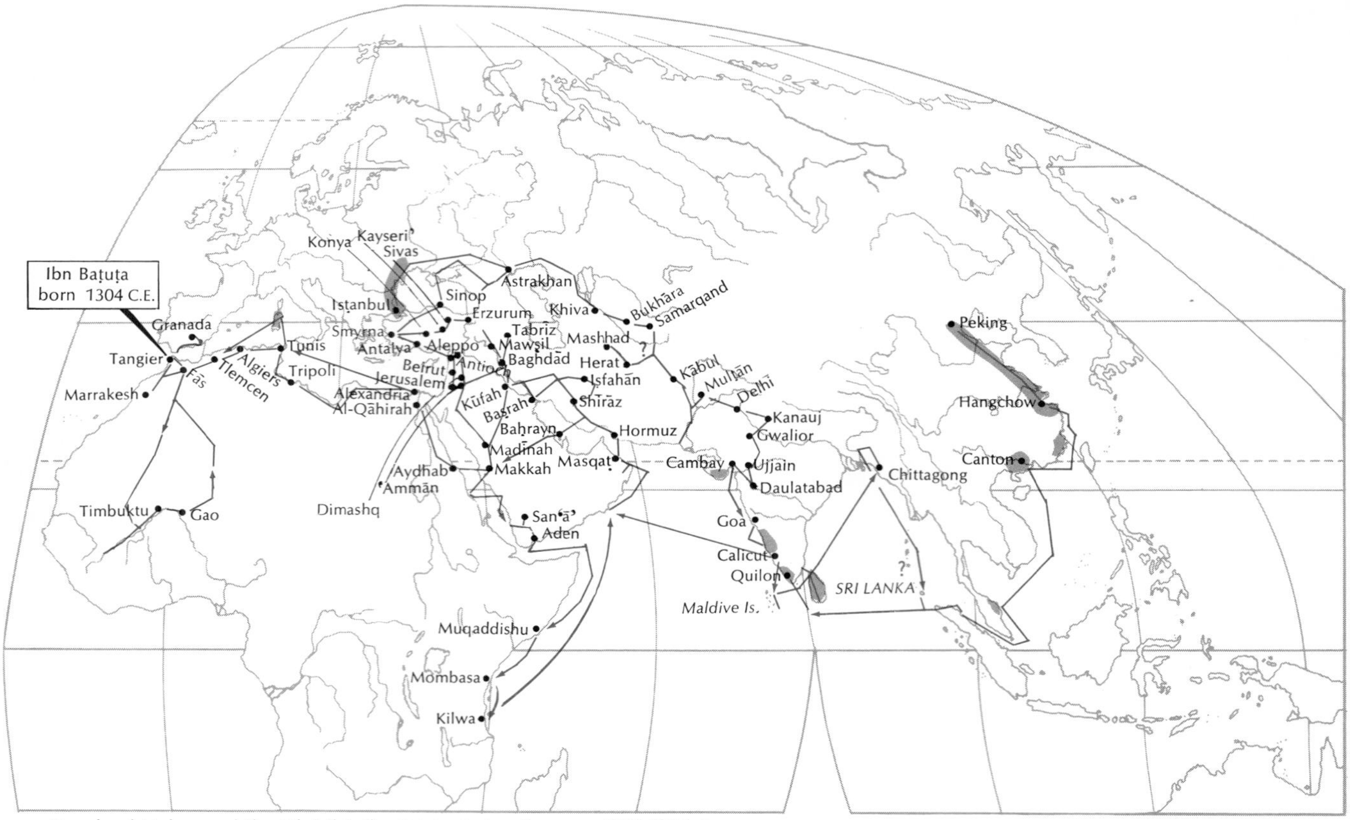

→ Travels of Muḥammad ibn-'Abdallah ibn Baṭuṭa during the years 1325–1354 C.E.

■ Lands visited by Ibn Baṭuṭa that were not then under Muslim rulers

his scions from these marriages continued his work under the name "Mirghaniyyah."

The Qādiriyyah brotherhood (see the section entitled Ṣūfism in this chapter) made its first center in Walata and later in Timbuktu. It established centers of learning and mission in Kanka, Timbo (Futah-Jallon), and Musardu in Mandingo country. Its men acted from these centers as scribes, jurists, doctors, and teachers, as well as diligent missionaries.

The Tijaniyyah brotherhood accounted for many converts in the Upper Niger and Senegal. It was launched by al Hajj 'Uthmān (1797–1865) after his pilgrimage to Makkah, where his zeal for the faith was awakened. The upper basin of the Niger witnessed another zealous caller to Islām, Imām Aḥmadu Ṣamūdu, known also as Samori. He taught Islām to the natives who dwelt between the sea and Wasulu. He conquered the city of Fulindiyyah in 1876 and from it sent out his followers calling the tribesmen to Islām. He died a prisoner of the French colonial government in 1900.

The first Muslims of East Africa south of Bab al Mandib were the Zaydī Shī'ahs (see in the following pages the section entitled "Zaydī School"), who were running away from persecution during the ninth and tenth centuries. The first city they built was Muqaddishu. A little later, 'Alī, son of Sulṭān Ḥasan of Shīrāz, came with his following and, being a Sunnī, decided in favor of another site further south. He founded the city of Kiloa. Further immigrants from Arabia founded other cities on the coast and developed a lively trade between the African hinterland and the Arab world while continuing to call the Africans to Islām.[1]

Flowering

It is of crucial importance to keep in mind that there is no history of the Islāmic faith because Islām was whole and complete at birth. The essence of Muḥammad's religious consciousness has remained identically

[1] For additional cartographic treatment of the extent and duration of Muslim rule, see Maps 54 and 55.

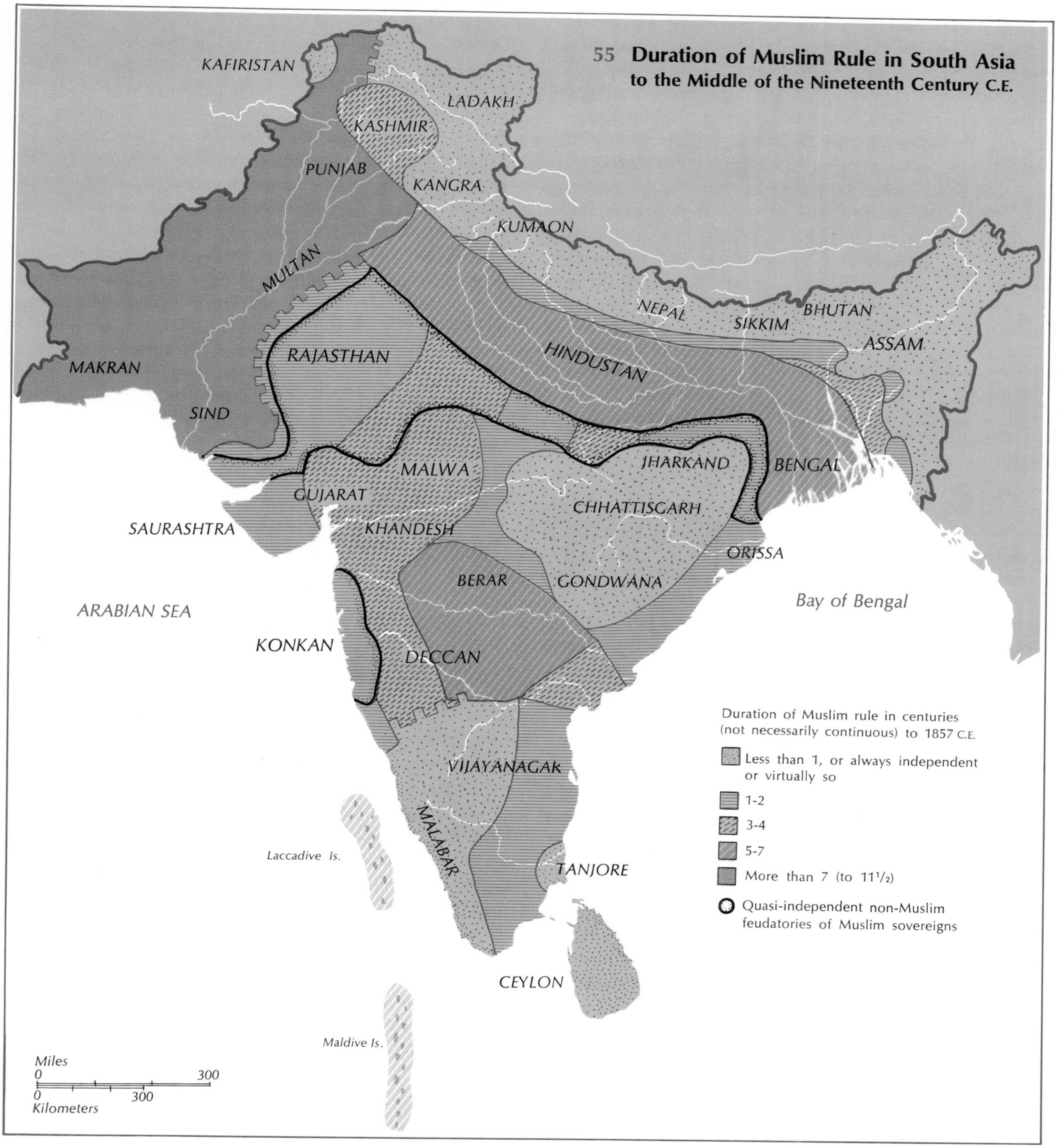

that of all his followers across the generations. The one sense in which Islām may be said to have had a history is when it is taken to refer to the Muslims' efforts at understanding and realizing the religious and moral commandments of God. Such history is not the history of Islām but of Muslimness, of the adherents' responses to the call of the Divine. Such is the history of their *legomena* and *dromena*. In the sense of *fiqh*, or prescriptive law, the Sharī'ah by which the Muslim means the totality of Islām's prescriptions—religious, moral, political, economic, etc.—is the work of men. It is divine only derivatively, insofar as it is a practical embodiment of first principles that are Qur'ānic, revealed, and divine. Equally, theology, with its creedal statement, definition, arguments and counter-arguments, elaborations and exegeses, has evolved. Like the Sharī'ah, it is divine only derivatively, the eternal element in it—wherever such is in evidence—being only that of which it is the conceptualized, systematized expression. By the "flowering of Islām" is meant, therefore, the flowering of its *fiqh* ("law") and *kalām* ("theology"), not of itself as religion.

Sharī'ah (Fiqh)

Possessed by the consciousness of God as lord and judge and by the vision of His will as the ultimate imperative of human action, the Muslim hurled himself onto the stage of history. In Madīnah the work was done by the Prophet; outside, by his followers. In both cases the work was one of translating the religious principles and ethical ideals of Islām into concrete directives for action. As the Prophet was pressed to furnish answers to his followers' questions, so were the savants of the community pressed for answers to the new problems Muslims were meeting as rulers and judges, farmers and traders, soldiers and craftsmen. The savants fell upon the Qur'ān and the example of Muḥammad as sources and began the process of translation into terms applicable to the concrete situations at hand. The Qur'ānic verses were subjected to the widest possible interpretations and analysis with a view to drawing therefrom legal precepts (*istinbāṭ al aḥkām*). The sacredness of its *verba* and the fixity of its text enabled it to play the role of an anchor base to which the exegete and jurist had to and could return no matter how extended their extrapolations. In this process, jurists and exegetes presented to Muslim consciousness a plethora of Qur'ānic meanings. On the other hand, the jurists had searched the biography of Muḥammad for the same purpose. But because that biography had no fixed text and its traditions mixed up the normative with the nonnormative annals of the Prophet's life, it had first to establish the veracity of its components. The factual had thus to contend with its opposite. In the process, the traditions multiplied and the jurists insisted on *al sunnah al ṣaḥīḥah* (the verified *sunnah*) as those traditions that internal (i.e., textual and contentual) and external (i.e., pertinent to history and transmission) criticism alone established as true so that it could serve as base for law elaboration.

Some of this translation of the Qur'ān and the verified *sunnah* ("traditions") of Muḥammad took place in Madīnah. As it was capital of the empire during the Rāshidūn caliphate (632–659), a number of problems were referred to it from the provinces for solution, and the solutions became legal precedents. The prestige the Rāshidūn caliphs enjoyed and the proximity to the Prophet of the first generation Muslims added to the weight of these precedents. Some juristic activity continued after the center of gravity had shifted first to Damascus (after 659) and then to Kūfah and Baghdād (after 750), though in the main the essential rudiments of law were developed with this legal experience of Madīnah as basis. Madīnah's legacy did not become a school of law until other schools in the provinces had succeeded in establishing themselves.

THE MĀLIKĪ SCHOOL. Mālik ibn Anas, founder of the school known by his name, lived in Madīnah and died there in 795 C.E./179 A.H. (Maps 56 and 57). When Caliph Hārūn al Rashīd, the greatest man of the age, wrote asking Mālik to come to Baghdād so that the caliph's sons might learn from him, Mālik answered, "Knowledge does not travel but is travelled to!" Of his many works, only *Al Muwaṭṭa'* survives, giving us a summa of laws, legal precepts, and seventeen hundred juridical traditions of the Prophet. Naturally, his school tends toward simplistic consistency, limiting the sources of law to the Qur'ān, the verified *sunnah*, and the *ijmā'* ("consensus") of the Prophet's companions. Even within each of these categories he assigned top priority to the text, then to its common sense meaning, and finally to the meaning that requires analysis or elaboration. The Mālikī school remained in force in Makkah, Madīnah, and the whole of Ḥijāz (western Arabia, excluding Yaman) until the Wahhābīs imposed Ḥanbalī law when they conquered the territory between 1921 and 1925. As tribes from central and west Arabia moved first to Egypt and then fanned south to the Sudan and North Africa, they carried Mālikī law with them to these areas, where it still predominates. The North Africans extended the dominion of Mālikī law to all the territories of West Africa. Islāmic Spain had known no other school of law during its seven centuries of history.

ḤANAFĪ SCHOOL. The founder of the Ḥanafī school was al Nu'mān ibn Thābit, born in Kūfah in 80 A.H. to a fresh convert to Islām from Kābul. He was known by the title name of Abū Ḥanīfah. He studied under the greatest masters of Ḥadīth and jurisprudence, who welcomed him to their company on account of his superior intellect and dedication to the juristic discipline. Twice in his life he was invited, then asked, and

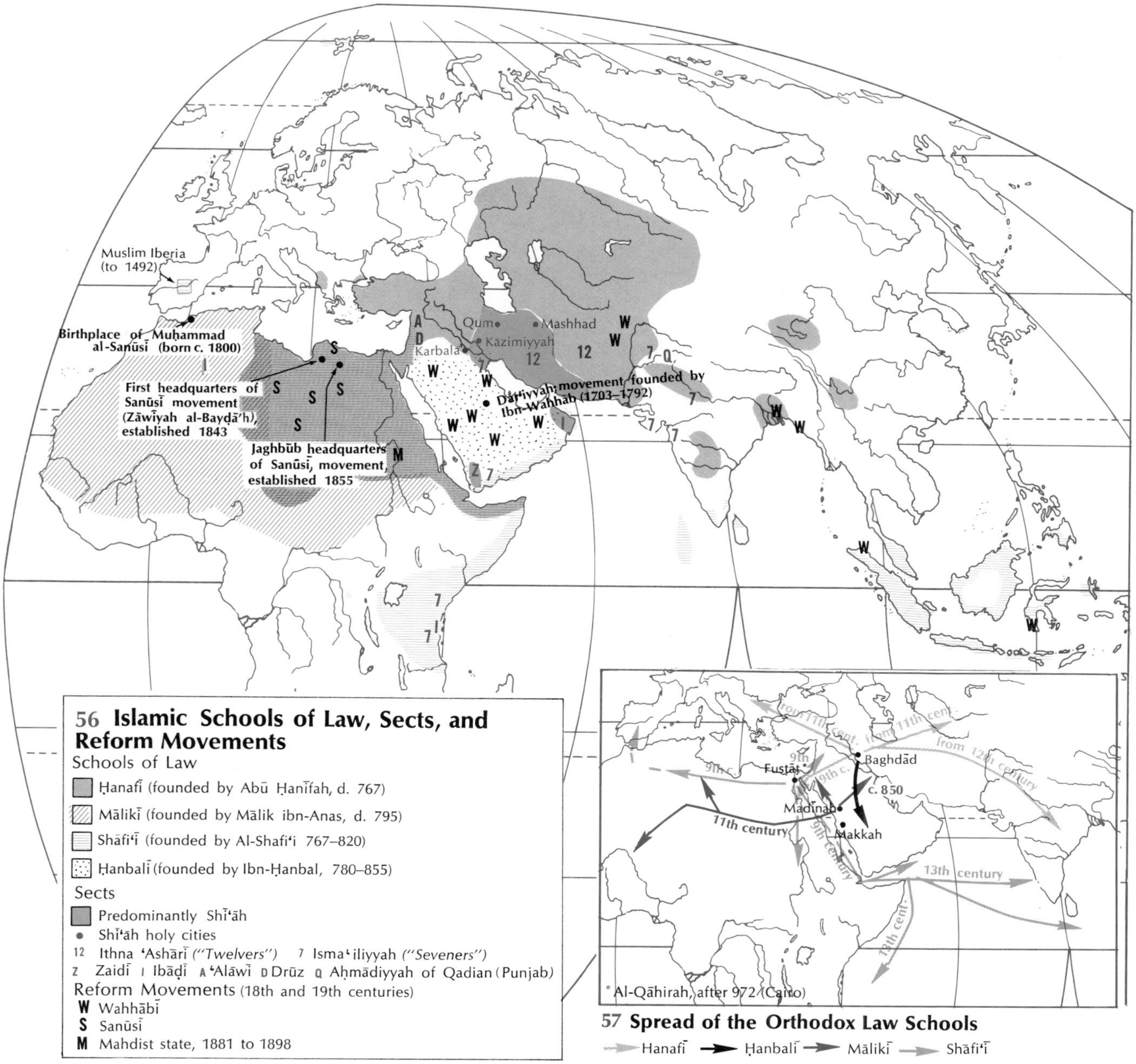

56 Islamic Schools of Law, Sects, and Reform Movements

57 Spread of the Orthodox Law Schools

finally punished for refusing to assume the position of supreme justice, first by the Umawīs and second by their mortal enemies, the 'Abbāsīs. His freedom to speak authoritatively on all matters without the slightest suspicion of *parti pris* was thus preserved.

What prompted Abū Ḥanīfah to develop the methodology he did was, above all, the infinite variety of problems that life in 'Irāq, Persia, and the Eastern lands presented and their radical difference from those that the Prophet's companions faced in Madīnah. The very novelty of the problems precluded the application of old Madīnah solutions, and the new solutions could not be simple extensions of the old verdicts. Moreover, the genius of Abū Ḥanīfah saw that because Islām was destined to be the religion of all men at all times and places, its law must have a method whereby the Islāmic view could be translated into creatively new prescriptive legislations whenever and wherever the need arose. This necessitated the establishment for jurisprudence of principles of lawmaking that, though they have been known to previous generations, were not recognized as integral to the lawmaker's or jurist's equipment.

20-10 Ṭāhir Mosque, the state mosque of the Sultanate of Kedah, one of the states of Malaysia, twentieth century.

According to Abū Ḥanīfah, the sources of Islāmic law are the Qur'ān, the *sunnah* (precedents of the Prophet), *Ijmā'* ("consensus"), *Qiyās* ("analogical deduction"), and *Istiḥsān* ("creative juristic preference"). He acknowledged the prior authority of the first two sources in agreement with all other jurists. *Qiyās* did not present a problem because the content deduced is "logically" contained in the premises and is hence not really new. The principle is then extensional rather than creative. As for *Ijmā'*, he argued that it is perfectly legitimate to choose among the companions those whose consensus one wishes to take into account. This was novel, as most other jurists regarded the companions as constituting in their majority a solid unity of Islāmic opinion. Through the fifth source of Islāmic law, i.e., *Istiḥsān,* Abū Ḥanīfah pressed his case for creativity. To accept *Istiḥsān* as a "source of law," his opponents argued, is to open wide the gates of change and innovation. Rightly so, Abū Hanīfah would answer, for nothing less would solve the new problems the Muslims face while saving justice, equity, and progress.

Abū Ḥanīfah wrote no books, but he lectured to and discussed juristic problems with a number of brilliant followers who took it upon themselves to commit to writing and to implement (for many of them were jurists and judges) the master's views. His teachings quickly became an established tradition. Adherents of the Ḥanafī school constitute the greatest majority of Muslims. It was the official school of the Ottoman Empire and of most regions under 'Abbāsī rule. Today it is the school officially followed in 'Irāq, Syria, Palestine, Jordan, Egypt, Libya, Afghanistan, and Pakistan. Though not official, it is the school to which belong Muslims of Turkey, Albania, and the USSR and the majority of Indian and Lebanese Muslims.

SHĀFI'Ī SCHOOL. This school was founded by Muḥammad ibn Idrīs al Shāfi'ī, born in Ghazzah the very year Abū Ḥanīfah died, namely, 768 C.E./150 A.H. He grew up in Makkah and lived most of his life in Egypt. He traveled much in search of knowledge and befriended the followers of Abū Ḥanīfah. His voracious appetite for knowledge left no book which he did not study nor learned man with whom he did not familiarize himself.

Attracted to the jurisprudential discipline at a very early stage, he realized that the greatest need of the age was for a proper science of jurisprudence to guide the Muslim community in its search for ways and means of realizing Islām's values. So far, the great jurists like Abū Ḥanīfah and Mālik ibn Anas, and their followers, had dominated current legal opinion, but there was no systematic treatment of the bases on which the laws stood or of the methods by which laws were derived. Al Shāfi'ī rose up to the task, and his *Risālah,* a critical analysis of jurisprudential principles in Islām, was the first work the Muslims produced in the discipline.

Another current issue that impelled al Shāfi'ī to lay down the principles of Islāmic jurisprudence once and for all was the differing roles assigned to the *sunnah* of the Prophet by the jurists. The *sunnah,* when critically verified and established through the canons of textual, ideational, and transmissional criticism, must enjoy a priority equal to that of the Qur'ān itself. Where it agrees with the Qur'ān, the Sunnah is granted this status without difficulty. Where it does not, it is innovative; but who are we to deny the Prophet such prerogative when we accept the very Qur'ān itself on his authority? The Muslims' answer that in such cases they would fall upon *Ijmā'* to sift the acceptable from the inacceptable is wrong, al Shāfi'ī argued, because there is little on which a really universal consensus could be proved. That is why Abū Ḥanīfah and his school demanded consensus to support the validity of the *sunnah,* their purpose being to shortcut the process and elevate *Istiḥsān* to the level of source of law. That is also why Mālik ibn Anas and his school demanded that the *sunnah* in question be supported by the actual practice of Madīnah, their purpose being to restrict innovation as much as possible. For his part, al Shāfi'ī declared even the *ḥadīth* reported by one reporter only is valid and hence canonical if the reporter is personally honest, knowledgeable, and trustworthy and if the report is attributed to the Prophet. *Istiḥsān* he totally rejected, and he allowed limited usage of *Qiyās* by tightening the rules of deduction and of *Ijmā'* by requiring it to be universal.

Al Shāfi'ī's school has spread in Egypt, the Sudan, and the south Arabian littoral, whence it was exported to some parts of East Africa and to Southeast Asia. It is in Malaysia and Indonesia that it enjoyed universal acceptance. Up until the Wahhābīs turned it to the Ḥanbalī School, central Arabia (including Ḥijāz) followed al Shāfi'ī.

THE ḤANBALĪ SCHOOL. Unlike the first three schools of *fiqh,* the Ḥanbalī school originated and continued to be associated with theological and political movements and thus shared the fortunes of these movements. The founder, Aḥmad ibn Ḥanbal, was born in Baghdād in 780 C.E./164 A.H. and grew up in the capital at its highest moments of glory. He followed al Shāfi'ī's jurisprudential methodology and applied himself to *ḥadīth* collection and criticism and *ḥadīth*-based legal analysis. When in 813 C.E./198 A.H. al Ma'mūn acceded to the caliphate and made the Mu'tazilī dictum of the createdness of the Qur'ān integral to the state religion, Ibn Ḥanbal took leadership of the opposition, asserting eternal status to the Holy Book. He was whipped in public and imprisoned for twenty years until the accession of al Mutawakkil in 847 C.E./231 A.H. He became a symbol of the masses' opposition to their rulers, and his steadfastness in face of torture won him admiration and devotion among the people. The majority of the people in 'Irāq followed the Ḥanbalī school throughout the ninth to eleventh centuries and converted to the Ḥanafī school under influence of the Saljūq Turks.

20-11 Part of Al Masjid al Jāmi' (Central Mosque) in Iṣfahān, Iran, built by Malik Shāh, 1072–92. This is the greatest monument of Saljug Turk architecture.

The issue behind the question of the createdness or eternity of the Qur'ān was how far a Muslim might go in creative, innovative interpretation of the Islāmic way of life. Those who argued for createdness, namely, the Mu'tazilah, had gone a long way in free interpretation guided by reason, new knowledge, and the commonwealth. Only thin partitions separated them from the Shī'ah, where heavily allegorical interpretations were the rule and where political and religious subversion was defended as the command of an infallible *imām* whose knowledge was secret and innate. Moreover, the age was one of ideological instability. Certainly, Islām was ascendant and supreme, but the polyglot masses of peoples of the empire were still relatively new in their Arabized—if old in their Islāmized—status, and Hindu, Buddhist, Christian, Jewish, Hellenic, Gnostic, and other traditions were rubbing shoulders in most people's minds. Whereas the created status of the Qur'ān would have encouraged free interpretation of the text it deemed historically conditioned, the eternal status theory furnished limits beyond which free interpretation could not go. By holding every letter and word eternal, it gave its Arabic meaning the capacity to play anchor to every understanding and removed this anchor from the vicissitudes of space and time. The Ḥanbalī school is therefore essentially conservative, placing *qiyās* and *ijtihād* last on the list of sources of Islāmic law, resorted to only in the rare case of the total silence of all other sources. This school subjected the diversionary or *mursal ḥadīths* invoked by many liberal interpreters to the strictest test of compliance or harmony with the Qur'ān and thus repudiated all that was constructed upon them. More important still, the Ḥanbalī school buttressed and helped to preserve pristine Arab Islām by anchoring it to the Arabic Qur'ān. Ibn Ḥanbal's spirit of resistance encouraged his followers to oppose any encroachment upon Arab Islām in the name of Islām. It was within the Ḥanbalī remnants in Syria that the greatest reformer, Ibn Taymiyah (1263–1328 C.E./661–728 A.H.) was born and in its school reared and educated. Today it is the only law permitted in Su'ūdī Arabia.

ZAYDĪ SCHOOL. This school of jurisprudence refers itself to, though it was not founded by, Zayd ibn 'Alī Zayn al 'Ābidīn, third grandson of the Prophet, who died in 739 C.E./121 A.H. The adherents of this school regard Zayd as worthier than his brother Muḥammad al Bāqir to succeed his father in the *Imāmate* ("leadership") of the Shī'ah. The concern of this school is more political than jurisprudential. The latter is a situational consequence of their political isolation, once they took over power in Yaman and practically locked themselves up in its mountains for a millennium and a century. Yaman is today the only place where this school has followers, but they have converted the whole population of the country.

As for law, the Zaydīs follow most of the principles of the Sunnī schools (the four aforementioned schools) and differ from them not in jurisprudence but in law. Their better-known differences from Sunnī law revolve around the legitimacy of obviating actual ablution of the feet when not soiled by going out or being bare, of animals killed for food by non-Muslims, and of marriage to Christian and Jewish wives. They also took issue with their fellow Shī'ah against temporary marriages.

IMĀMIYYAH SCHOOL. The Imāmiyyah school constitutes the bulk of the Shī'ah fellowship and has been the official school of Iran since the Ṣafawī takeover in the sixteenth century. A fair percentage of the population of 'Irāq and a much smaller percentage of west Pakistanis and Indians belong to this school. Like the Zaydīs, the concern of the Imāmīs is mainly political, not jurisprudential. On the latter level, their differences are no more serious than those that separate the four Sunnī schools from one another.

The school follows the Shī'ah majority, or Twelvers (see the section in this chapter entitled "Theology and Sects"), in matters affecting their communal existence and the Shafi'ī school in matters affecting personal-status law. Like the Zaydīs, they have their own canonical collections of *ḥadīths,* which are less rigorous than the *Ṣaḥīḥs* recognized by the Sunnīs. *Qiyās,* as a source of law, does not appeal to them, but the Ḥanafī principle of creative interpretation (the Shī'ah call it by the general name of *ijtihād*) does. Because their theology grants to their *imāms* ("leaders") unlimited authority, ascribing it to the charisma they inherited directly from the Prophet, the *imām* for them is himself a living source of law almost as much as the Prophet had been.

The real founder of Imāmī law was Muḥammad ibn al Ḥasan al Qummī (d. 903 C.E./290 A.H.). It is in matters of personal status that Imāmī law differs from all Sunnī schools. Like the Zaydī, the Imāmī school accepts temporary marriage, restricts divorce by requiring two witnesses to be bodily present when it is pronounced, and prohibits intermarriage with Christians and Jews.

Interschool ecumenism has had a long history. Even the most ardent Ḥanafīs—for example, the Ottomans who fought a war to the knife with the Shī'ah of Iran—had recognized that justice and equity had claims prior to loyalty to school. For generations, Imāmī law had been taught in al Azhar and other Muslim law colleges with a view to putting at the disposal of the future judge all the options possible to achieve a higher justice. In the modern age, the six aforementioned schools are fast

20-12 Courtyard of Madrasah al 'Aṭṭārīn, built by Abū Sa'īd 'Uthmān in Fās, Morocco, 1322 C.E.

losing their old importance, which was once defended by force of arms. In the current remolding of Islāmic law it is unlikely that the old distinctions will have much effect. However, though these may not survive the present century, the new crystallizations of Islāmic law might generate new schools, human beings and their problems being always variegated and different.

Theology and Sects

The definitiveness, the finality of the Qur'ānic revelation and the absolute integrity of its text demanded and enabled the Muslim to devote all his mental energies to the practical task of rekneading the world into the likeness of the divine pattern. Because of this paramountly practical bent of mind, demanding a total concern with the world and history, Muslim genius poured itself into law and jurisprudence rather than theology. Moreover, Islāmic theology originated not in questions of pure speculation but with problems arising out of Muslim efforts to Islāmize the world. The problems themselves, as well as their earliest solutions, betray their practical origin and concern. These are the relation of grave sin to *īmān* (religious conviction and commitment); freedom and determinism; and the nature of the divine attributes. The first was the result of the rebellion against 'Alī ibn Abū Ṭālib, the fourth caliph, by a group of his followers, and their subsequent secession from his camp. Known by the name of al Khawārij (the exiters, or seceders), they held that the Muslim who commits a grave sin has lost his *īmān* and is to be counted among the enemies of Islām. By this belief they sought to rationalize their rebellion against 'Alī's willingness to arbitrate his differences with the Umawīs, his political antagonists, for the Khawārij could at no cost reconcile themselves to negotiation with their Muslim enemies. By declaring such enemies non-Muslims at war with Islām, they gave themselves the ideological protection needed. The overwhelming majority of Muslims rejected this position and declared that regardless of his moral state, the grave sinner is still a Muslim and that only apostasy, the assertion of a faith contrary to Islām or the denial of God and of His unity, can cause the Muslim to lose his status as a member of the community. The greater portion of this majority were hence called Murji'ah, i.e., holding only God entitled to judge on the Day of Judgment. The remaining minority were the Mu'tazilah, who assigned to the grave sinner a standing in between faith and nonfaith.

Led by 'Abdullah al Rāsibī, the Khawārij grouped to give battle to 'Alī at the Nahrawān Canal in 659 C.E./37 A.H. and were defeated. A disgruntled Khārijī, 'Abd al Raḥman ibn Muljam, assassinated 'Alī two years later at Kūfah. The Umawīs put the Khawārij to flight, and they took refuge in the unreachable heights of 'Umān, whence they raided and occupied portions of the gulf provinces, including Fars (Persepolis), Kirmān, and other cities. In 698 C.E./79 A.H., 'Irāq's governor, al Ḥajjāj, sent two of his ablest generals, al Muhallab ibn Abū Sufrah and Sufyān al Kalbī, with the charge of ridding the empire of the Khawārij once and for all. By 788 C.E./81 A.H. the Umawī armies had kicked them out of the cities and provinces they occupied. Subsequently, a number of them emigrated to the East African coast and founded a community in Zanzibar. Others established themselves in North Africa when those lands were under Fāṭimī (Shī'ah) dominion and survive to the present day in microcommunities in Jarba Island (Tunisia), Jabal Nafūsah (Libya), and Mzāb and Wargla (Algeria). Apart from the Khawārij and the little history they account for, no Muslims have sought to sit in judgment on the Islāmicity or otherwise of their fellow Muslims except under the provisions of the law of apostasy. The defeat of the Khawārij meant the rejection of their *īmān* doctrine.

The second theological problem to confront the Muslim mind was that of freedom and determinism. Jahm ibn Ṣafwān had pushed the Murji'ah principle to its ultimate conclusion ("Once a Muslim, always a Muslim") and combined it with a thoroughgoing determinism that denies man any responsibility for his deeds. This view, known as Jabriyyah, never became a movement and remained a mere school of thought. Jahm himself was involved in an uprising against the Umawīs in Transoxania and was put to death when it failed in 746 C.E./128 A.H.

The opposite view was called Qadariyyah. It held man morally capable and free. Its genesis is ascribed to Ma'bad al Juhanī and his pupil, Ghaylān ibn Marwān, both of Kūfah. But the man who founded a school on this principle and developed it systematically was Wāṣil ibn 'Aṭā of Baṣrah (699–749 C.E./80–131 A.H.). In his hands, moral freedom and responsibility were made the groundwork of a total view of life, and their implications for the nature of God were fully worked out. The school is known under the name of Mu'tazilah. It flourished at a time when Islām needed men to fight its intellectual battles against Christianity and Manichaeanism. The movement achieved political power with the accession of al Ma'mūn and his appointment of the Mu'tazilī Aḥmad ibn Abū Du'ād as supreme justice. The movement prospered and branches grew in all cities, but it came to sudden death under al Mutawakkil in 856 C.E./241 A.H.

The Mu'tazilah ideas, however, lingered on in the teachings of many brilliant theologians. In modified versions the same ideas were integrated into the Shī'ah. The latest and perhaps the most comprehensive and systematic exposition of these ideas come in the works of al Qadi 'Abd al Jabbār (932–1024 C.E./320–415 A.H.), the chief justice of Rayy under the Buwayhīs. The core of Mu'tazilah doctrine has consisted of five principles: the absolute unity and transcendence of God, the moral freedom and responsibility of man, the reality of God's judgment of man, the intermediate position of the grave sinner between faith and nonfaith, and the ethical imperative enjoining the good and preventing evil.

The third problem to confront the Muslim mind was the status of the divine attributes. Three positions were taken in harmony with the views already held on the other two problems. The first view understood the attributes literally and thus was taken by the Mushabbihah, or anthropomorphists. The allegorist view, which tended to dilute the attributes' impact upon consciousness, understood them figuratively and was taken by the Mu'aṭṭilah or allegorists. Finally, the intuitive view took the mean course between anthropomorphism and allegorical dilution. Against the latter it asserted the literal veracity of every attribute, and against the former it called for an intuitive understanding of the meaning intended. This was the view of the Ṣifātiyyah, or attributists. They were the majority.

The views of the majority in all of these matters were synthesized by Abū al Ḥasan al Ash'arī (873–935 C.E./259–323 A.H.). The main body of the community later accepted his synthesis as a truer crystallization of the Islāmic view. The community was assisted in this self-identification by Niẓām-al Mulk, the Saljūq vizier under Malikshāh (1072–1092 C.E./464–484 A.H.) who founded and endowed many a college named "Niẓāmiyyah," where al Ash'arī's synthesis was taught to the masses of students.

Following the debacle of 'Alī in his struggle with Mu'āwiyah, it was natural that his followers found common cause with the malcontents of the empire. These were Christians, Jews, nationalist Persians resentful of Arab success, or adherents of various religious denominations of Persian religion. Thus anti-Arab, anti-Islām, anti-empire, and anti-new-order forces found in the Umawī dynasty a common enemy. The buildup grew in direct proportion to the empire's expansion. In time, these forces toppled the Umawīs from power. In 747 C.E./129 A.H., Abū Muslim launched the revolution at Marw. It took two and a half years before the fire of rebellion reached Ḥarrān, where the last of the Umawīs had moved his capital. Abū al 'Abbās was declared caliph in Kūfah in 749 C.E./131 A.H.

Up till then there was nothing religious distinguishing either the Shī'ah (literally, "party") of 'Alī or their sympathizers and allies from other Muslims. Theirs was totally a political cause. This political cause was special, however, in that it aimed at restoring power to the Prophet's family, from whom it was said to have been usurped by the Umawīs.

And it was restored. The new caliph was of the Hāshim clan and the house of the Prophet, indeed a great-grandnephew of Muḥammad on his father's side. But no sooner had he achieved power than he turned against his own supporters and, singling out the Shī'ah, subjected them to persecution. His son, al Manṣūr (754–755 C.E./136–159 A.H.), was even more opposed to the Shī'ah. For the wave that brought both to power could not countenance any deviation from or threat to the dominion of the pristine Arab understanding of Islām. Except for the brief interlude of Mu'tazilah power under al Ma'mun, al Mu'taṣim, and al Wāthiq (813–847 C.E./197–232 A.H.), all the 'Abbāsī caliphs observed the same line.

Shorn of all hope for success and power, the Shī'ah went underground—not politically, for they were incapable even of underground political activity, but ideologically. With the triumph of Islām and of Arabism, the flowering of Islāmic civilization and culture, and the spread of Arabic, all the other malcontents went underground, laden with despair. It was in this catacomb atmosphere that Shī'ism began to transform itself from something political into something religious.

The political partisanship for 'Alī as legitimate aspirant to the caliphate became eschatological messianism, or the expectation of the coming of a savior who would reestablish justice in an unjust world. Because of the futility of the hope, the *imām* (literally, "leader"; hence the name *imāmiyyah* for the majority of the Shī'ah) would do his work beyond time. Their Islām prevented the Shī'ah from assigning divine status to the *imām*. Hence, they granted him infallibility, as his wisdom was biologically inherited from the Prophet through his daughter, Fāṭimah. Further, they granted to the last known descendant of 'Alī and Fāṭimah, or the last one they acknowledged as legitimate, the power to return at the end of time or at some future date. This implied either that he would not die or that he had the power of self-resurrection. Again, their Islām kept them from following a line threatening to divine transcendence, and they therefore declared that the last *imām* "disappeared" (*ghaybah*) rather than died.

Decay

Ṣūfism

GENESIS. Ṣūfism (Taṣawwuf) is the name of a movement that dominated the whole Muslim world for a millennium. The term derives from *ṣūf*, i.e., "wool" and refers to the blue woolen garment worn by the Ṣūfīs or adherents. The earliest use of the term in literature occurred in the early ninth century C.E./first half of the third century A.H., and later Ṣūfīs claimed the name was as old as Islām. Use of the woolen garment is probably earlier, for it must have taken a generation before the appellative could have acquired the ideational content evident in its earliest usage. Four streams of thought contributed to its formation. First was the general asceticism and rigorous self-mastery and discipline that desert living bred in its native sons. In the more sensitive persons this asceticism could blossom into an ethical freedom from the world and its attachments, the more to dedicate themselves to the public cause. Indeed, the enthusiasm that the vision of Islām generated in the Prophet's contemporaries was partly a transvaluation of this already-existent attitude. Desert asceticism, recast in the mould of Islām, spoke through Abū Dharr al Ghifārī, a Companion, who chastized the Umawīs for the sumptuousness their court displayed.

Second was Arab poetical genius, which Islām fired, equipped with a new vocabulary and new ideas and challenged titillatingly with the literary sublime—the Qur'ān—whose phrases, similes, figures of speech, cadences, and aphorisms had taken all Arabs by storm and carried them off to heights of absolute beauty. The innate talent and the force of the Islāmic spirit combined to produce poetry of love and praise of God and of His Prophet. Arab Muslims delighted themselves with such poetry, and the more sensitive cultivated the recitation of this poetry as catharsis, experiencing it as genuinely purging, uplifting, purifying, and conducive to the highest spiritual state. Rābi'ah al 'Adawiyyah (b. 714 C.E./95 A.H.) in Baṣrah catered more to this need than anyone else, as she expressed love of God in the most exquisite poetry.

Third was the Gnostic stream of thought, prevalent in Egypt and the Fertile Crescent, to which the Muslims have become heir and which many converts from Christianity and Judaism brought into the Islāmic stream with them as cultural traits or modes of thinking. It was Dhū al Nūn al Miṣrī (d. 860 C.E./245 A.H.) who first introduced the Gnostic categories into Islāmic thought and interpreted the Islāmic religious experience in Gnostic terms. Though known before him, the categories of gnosis, emanation, and illumination, the ennead of *logoi* or intellects, and so on entered the Islāmic stream through his effort, assisted by his contemporary in Baghdād, al Ḥārith ibn Asad al Muḥāsibī (d. 857 C.E./242 A.H.).

Fourth was the Indian (mainly Buddhist) stream of thought, which preceded Islām in vast areas of south, southeast, and central Asia. It expressed itself in open estrangement from the world and its affairs and in contemplation, the chanting of litanies, repeated prayers and invocations, and, at times, open self-mortification. Abū Yazīd Ṭīfūr al Bisṭāmī (d. 874 C.E./260 A.H.) was the first Muslim to make of it a system and to popularize the use of the terms *fanā'* ("self-annihilation toward the world") and *baqā'* ("survival in God"). It was also at this time that the life story of Ibrahīm ibn al Adham (d. 776 A.H./159 C.E.) acquired wide circulation, told, as it were, in a garb that recalls the life story of Gautama, the Buddha.

All these streams nourished a growing awareness among Muslims that the road to felicity lay in less involvement in the affairs of this world. The political fortunes of the community had for a long time fallen into the hands of godless leaders who could by no stretch of the imagination represent the political interest of Islām. The great social ethic of self-giving for the cause of God held by the fathers had then become a hunt for personal advantage, or self-assertion, and created tyranny. Instead of more and better involvement, the mood of the time, generated by a failure of nerve, pulled the Muslim masses away with disgust. This in turn aggravated the malaise and pushed the Muslim world further toward passivity, decay, and general deterioration. Hence the appeal of Bisṭāmī's new emphasis.

FLOWERING. It was the special merit of al Junayd al Baghdādī (d. 910 C.E./298 A.H.) to pull together all these streams and to recast them in an integral, thoroughly Islāmized and mighty stream of thinking. Indeed, he utilized Qur'ānic categories and terms, the better to integrate these ideas into Islāmic culture. After him the intellectual blossoming of Ṣūfī doctrine (theology, philosophy, and ethics) and literature registered the highest levels of creativity. It was as if the original genius, or spiritual energy, which had poured itself first into political and military conduct, then into building the most perfect system of law of humanistic and natural science, had now turned toward mysticism. Al Sarrāj (d. 1021 C.E./412 A.H.), al 'Aṭṭār (d. 1230 C.E./626 A.H.), al Ḥallāj (d. 922 C.E./309 A.H.), al Ḥujwīrī (d. ca. 1074 C.E./467 A.H.), al Qushayrī (d. 1072 C.E./463 A.H.), ibn al Rūmī (d. 1273 C.E./642 A.H.), al Ghazālī (d. 1111 C.E./504 A.H.), and ibn al 'Arabī (d. 1232 C.E./630 A.H.) are some of the greatest mystical thinkers that ever lived. Whether in the depth of the human psyche and personality or at the height of spirituality and speculative thought, these men provided the spiritual nourishment of whole ages. Fraternities sprang up and covered the whole territory, and people flocked to them to learn the shortcut path to spiritual bliss and salvation that Ṣūfism furnished. In turn, these fraternities spread in specialized directions among people of similar needs or professions, and their "guilds" came to lay complete hold on economic life throughout the Middle Ages.

The Ṣūfī fraternity was a hierarchy headed by the Shaykh, or elder, to whom unquestionable obedience was due by all. At the bottom stood the *murīd,* or applicant-candidate, willing but unqualified for initiation into the Ṣūfī truths, which, relying heavily on allegorical interpretation of most Qur'ānic and other Islāmic vocabulary, leaned ever more closely toward esotericism. In between were a number of stages, or *maqāmāt,* that the initiate ascended as he grew wiser, older, and more experienced. Coexisting, but not necessarily corresponding to these stages, were the states (*aḥwāl*) into which the Ṣūfī could induce himself, beginning with the renunciation of physical property and other attachments and then progressing through giving up worldly desires, contentment, fear of God, feeling of the divine presence, and finally arriving at *gnosis* (or *Kashf*) and *ittiḥād* (or union with God).

The Ṣūfīs fought victorious battles against those advocates of externalism or legalism who held that any observance of the law, however mechanical, leads to salvation; against the philosophers, who in the interest of safeguarding divine transcendence emptied the godhead of its normativeness, providence, compassion and turned the living, commanding God into an inert principle of metaphysics; and against the recalcitrant will, whether of Muslims or non-Muslims, to bend itself in front of the ubiquitous divine presence. With their exemplary humility, sincerity, devotion, and realization of the professed values in their own persons, the Ṣūfīs were an irresistible force wherever they went. They succeeded in converting to Islām countless millions of people. Moreover, they produced classics of literature in every Islāmic language, especially in Arabic and Persian.

DECAY. Whether in idea or practice, Ṣūfism contained within itself the germs that were later to grow into the strongest forces of stagnation and decay. Unfortunately, Ṣūfī ranks became infested with charlatans who took advantage of the people's credulity of their desire to alleviate their personal burdens, of their concern for their fate in the hereafter. The earliest Ṣūfī treatises were already full of clarifications and warnings designed to repudiate the fake. First, allegorical interpretation could, by definition, have no rules and had to depend on the intuitive good sense of the interpreter. When common sense is absent, interpretation can run wild. And it did, degenerating into esotericism. Second, concern for spiritual welfare—which is the first care of the religion of Islām—can be pursued with excessive emphasis placed on it, at the cost of this world. Islām never meant to deny or even deprecate this world. As far as social ethics are concerned, world denial can lead to disastrous consequences, beginning with withdrawal from public life, then insulation, and finally cynical unconcern, thus enabling the weakest tyrant to get by, literally, with murder. Third, the emphasis on the spiritual leans toward understanding natural events in terms of spiritual causation, which when invoked readily may well hinder empirical investigation, opening the gates wide to alchemy, astrology, and numerology (rather than chemistry, astronomy, and mathematics). Fourth, "pantheism," "unity of being," and "union with divinity" are theories that tend to gloss over distinctions of good and evil; evil is just as much an "actuality" as good, and if man is in one aspect divine and in another human, it is likely that the two will get mixed up when his personal welfare is at stake. Some Ṣūfī Shaykhs arrogated to themselves the title *Quṭb,* or "pole around which the world revolves," and others declared, to the consternation of their fellow Muslims, not only that they could perform little miracles called *Karāmāt* but that in his state of *ittiḥād* the Ṣūfī is God. Al Ḥallāj was crucified for his statement, "I am the Truth; there is nothing within my coat except He." Others, in order to induce

20-13 The Pearl Mosque was built in 1659 by the Mughal Emperor Aurangzeb. Part of the palace complex at Delhi, this mosque takes its name from the fact that it is made of white marble. (Courtesy of UNESCO/Cart.)

quickly the mystical trance, allowed a little wine, plenty of music and chanting and whirling (hence "the whirling dervishes"), and pursued their object, even neglecting the duties of the Sharī'ah. It was a slick argument that convinced them that if they pursued and achieved the *ḥaqīqat* (Divinity as Truth), what use can they have for the Sharī'ah (the law)?

It was the great al Ghazzālī who fought Ṣūfism's greatest battle. He waged a two-pronged war against the philosophers and the 'Ulamā', who were the guardians of the Sharī'ah. He silenced the former and converted the latter. True, he purged Ṣūfism of most of its aberrations and made it respectable—indeed honorable. But soon after his death, the wild energies of Ṣūfism broke loose again, the 'Ulamā' resistance and guardianship having become too weak to hold them.

The same century in which al Ghazzālī died saw the total fragmentation of the Muslim world and dissolution of the caliphate's power and prestige only fifty years before the Tatar storm then looming on the horizon. And then this storm descended upon the dazed people with unknown fury. There had never been a holocaust as fierce and devastating as that unleashed by Genghis Khan and Hulagu.

This tragic conclusion did not alter the course of Ṣūfism. On the contrary, it gave it a new ally, namely, conservatism. Faced with the threat of extinction, Muslim leaders ordered the gates of creativity and innovation in legal matters locked and counseled literal observance of the precepts of Islām, and blind obedience. Decay thus developed for itself a system and became an ideology endowed with working institutions.

The Crusades

When Pope Urban II delivered his famous call to arms against the Muslims in Clermont, France, at the end of 1095, the Muslim world was divided against itself. The bigger divisions were the Fāṭimī caliphate of Egypt, which dominated the Mediterranean shoreline from Tripoli (Libya) to Tripoli (Lebanon) and possessed a strong fleet; and the more eastern regions dominated by the Turkish military. Whereas the Fāṭimīs were united and centralized, the Turks were splintered into so many groups that almost every city in Asia Minor, Syria, Lebanon, Palestine, and 'Irāq had an autonomous self-declared sovereign Turkish ruler. The strongest of these groups were those of the Saljūq Turks of Asia Minor and the Atabegs of Syria-'Irāq.

The former had been expanding at the cost of Byzantium for decades. But when they came to the outskirts of Constantinople and threatened to occupy the remaining enclave, Alexius Commenus was forced to appeal to the pope for help. Besides this provocation, which provided Christendom with a justification for war against Islām, it must be remembered that the Crusades had causes that ran deep into history. Though the Christians had scored two victories over the Muslims by checking and repulsing their advance into France and Sicily, their resentment of previous defeats suffered in Byzantium, North Africa, and Spain was very strong. Moreover, Pope Urban II thought of war as a possibility for reuniting the Eastern Church with Rome, severed from 1009 and confirmed in its separation in 1054. Both the papacy and Byzantium hated and feared another common enemy just as strongly as they did the Muslims. This enemy was the Christian Normans, who had been showing the papacy their power and expanding their dominion at the papacy's expense for decades. As pilgrims and escorts of pilgrims, the Normans gave equal reason for distrust to the Byzantines, whose land they pillaged and crossed as a sovereign army. Indeed they even imposed and levied taxes of their own on the helpless population wherever they marched. It was thought that a crusade would help direct these marauders to other lands.

The Christian pilgrim from western Europe paid a tremendous toll in expense, insecurity, suffering, and often death. He was subject to rapacious Venetians if he traveled by sea; to savage Huns and Bulgars, pagan Magyars, and many other untold risks of the road, if he traveled by land to Constantinople. Whether in self-defense or deliberately, the pilgrims and their Norman escorts acted like aggressors upon the properties and lives of the people whose territories they traversed. They regarded the Byzantine Christians as enemies and heretics, and they marched through Byzantium as though it were enemy territory. Certainly, political division in Muslim lands contributed to the deterioration of public security and increased the pilgrim's risks. But the pilgrim's risks in the lands of Islām were only one consideration. Taken as a whole, all these reasons were preparing Christian Europe psychically for a crusade to keep open the pilgrimage route through war.

Besides these causes, there were some economic ones and others having to do with domestic politics. In the eleventh century, Europe was a feudal continent whose lords ruled like tyrants over helpless and ignorant people. The lords sought more wealth and they had heard that the Orient, which included Byzantium with its jewel city, Constantinople, was rich. Serfs, convicts, pariahs, and other dross sought freedom from their miseries through a holy war. Peter the Hermit had preached to them that pilgrimage and a holy crusade would efface any sin, any history. Noblemen and princes, denied their inheritances through the practice of primogeniture, sought adventure as well as riches.

The First Crusade (1097–1147)

Answering the call of Urban II, 150,000 Normans and Franks marched to Constantinople in 1097. On the way thither, they began their "holy work" by killing Jews—the "infidels" of Europe—wherever they found them, ransacked their synagogues, and extorted funds from them to pay for the costs of the Crusade. Their first encounter with the Muslims was at Eskishehir (Dorylaeum) in the same year. Their victory ended the Muslims' presence in the western half of Asia Minor. The Crusaders then split into three branches (Map 58). Baldwin of Boulogne went through Armenia, captured Ruhā (Edessa) in 1098, and founded the first Christian Latin state there. Tancred of Sicily went through Cilicia and captured Ṭarsūs. Bohemond proceeded directly to Antioch, occupied it, and founded there the second Latin state. While Bohemond sat on his newfound throne, his general, Raymond of Toulouse, captured Ma'arrat al Nu'mān, and the fortress of Ḥuṣn al Akrād dominating the Orontes passage to the Mediterranean. In the process, he put to the sword over 100,000 Muslims who surrendered to him (January 13, 1099) and committed their city to the flames. The march south continued. Ramlah fell in June 1099, and the siege of the thousand-man Egyptian garrison of Jerusalem began. At first, the Crusaders walked barefoot around the walls and blew their horns in the expectation that the walls would come

58 Crusader Attacks and Muslim Response in the Twelfth and Thirteenth Centuries C.E.

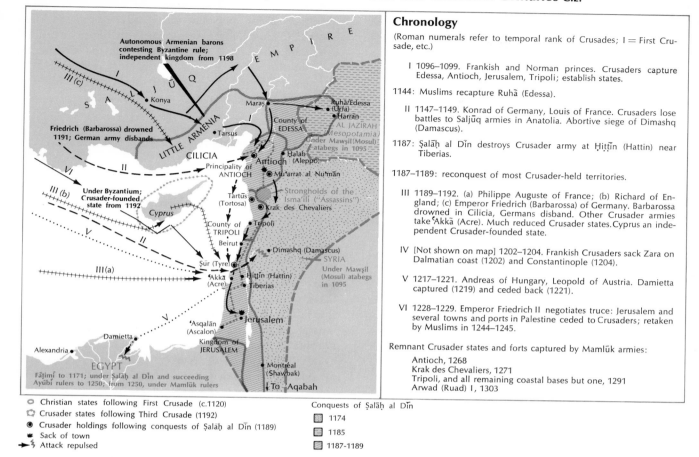

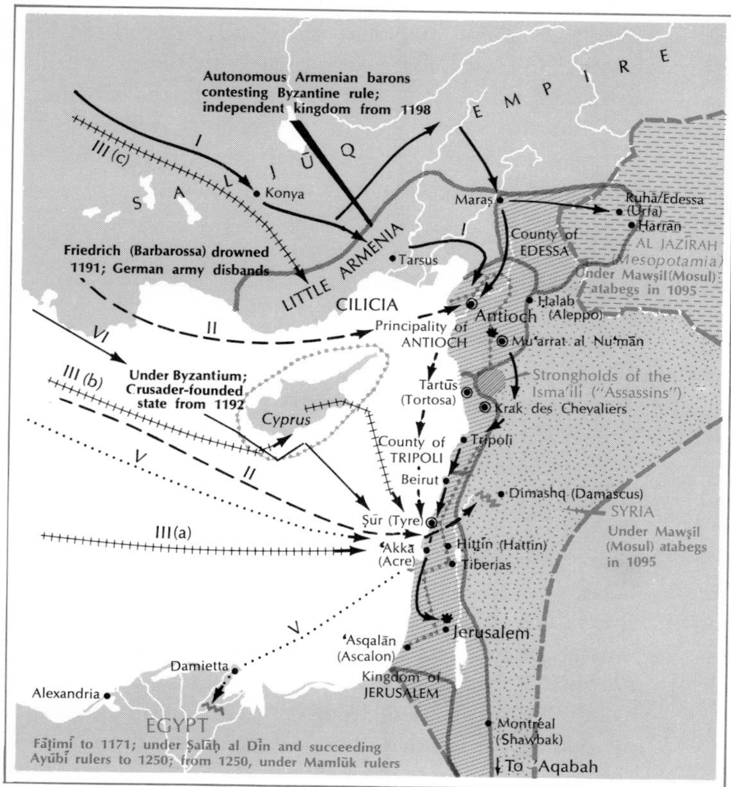

Chronology

(Roman numerals refer to temporal rank of Crusades; I = First Crusade, etc.)

I 1096–1099. Frankish and Norman princes. Crusaders capture Edessa, Antioch, Jerusalem, Tripoli; establish states.

1144: Muslims recapture Ruhā (Edessa).

II 1147–1149. Konrad of Germany, Louis of France. Crusaders lose battles to Saljūq armies in Anatolia. Abortive siege of Dimashq (Damascus).

1187: Ṣalāḥ al Dīn destroys Crusader army at Ḥiṭṭīn (Hattin) near Tiberias.

1187–1189: reconquest of most Crusader-held territories.

III 1189–1192. (a) Philippe Auguste of France; (b) Richard of England; (c) Emperor Friedrich (Barbarossa) of Germany. Barbarossa drowned in Cilicia, Germans disband. Other Crusader armies take 'Akkā (Acre). Much reduced Crusader states. Cyprus an independent Crusader-founded state.

IV [Not shown on map] 1202–1204. Frankish Crusaders sack Zara on Dalmatian coast (1202) and Constantinople (1204).

V 1217–1221. Andreas of Hungary, Leopold of Austria. Damietta captured (1219) and ceded back (1221).

VI 1228–1229. Emperor Friedrich II negotiates truce: Jerusalem and several towns and ports in Palestine ceded to Crusaders; retaken by Muslims in 1244–1245.

Remnant Crusader states and forts captured by Mamlūk armies:

Antioch, 1268
Krak des Chevaliers, 1271
Tripoli, and all remaining coastal bases but one, 1291
Arwad (Ruad) I, 1303

- Christian states following First Crusade (c.1120)
- Crusader states following Third Crusade (1192)
- Crusader holdings following conquests of Ṣalāḥ al Dīn (1189)
- Sack of town
- Attack repulsed

Conquests of Ṣalāḥ al Dīn
- 1174
- 1185
- 1187-1189

tumbling down. When this failed, they prepared for battle, and a month later (July 15, 1099) they stormed the walls; herded thousands of men, women, and children into al Aqṣā Mosque, where some of them had already sought refuge; and slaughtered them wantonly. Upon the fall of Jerusalem and its environs, Baldwin ceded the first Latin kingdom to his brother Godfrey and journeyed from Ruhā to Bethlehem, where he was crowned "King of Bethlehem" on Christmas Day, 1100.

The new kingdom spread from 'Aqabah on the Red Sea to Beirūt. Later it was to include 'Akkā (Acre) (1124), 'Asqalān (Ascalon) (1153), and Caesarea (1101). A desert road through Wādī 'Arabah, passing by Shawbak (Montréal), was built, but the Crusaders never went beyond the Jordan River. They directed their attention to the coastline, and even there many Muslim pockets remained. Raymond of Toulouse took his army to the road again and captured Bint Jubayl (Byblos) in 1104. He besieged Tripoli and stormed it on July 12, 1109. The Crusaders brought with them the only administrative system they knew—feudalism. Thus the districts of Ruhā, Tripoli, and Antioch became fiefs of the kingdom of Jerusalem.

The first serious Muslim reaction came from the hands of 'Imād al Dīn Zangī (1127–1262), Atabeg ruler of Mawṣil, who had carved a kingdom for himself out of Ḥalab, Ḥarrān, and northern 'Irāq. He gave battle to the Crusaders, recaptured Ruhā in 1144, and carried off Joscelin II in chains. The fall of the crusader king reverberated through Europe, and the Franks' cry for help brought about the Second Crusade.

The Second Crusade (1147–1149)

In the meantime, Zangī's son, Nūr al Dīn, a more illustrious ruler than his father, added Dimashq, the rest of the principality of Ruhā, and all of Tripoli to his realm. Both Bohemond III and Raymond II of Tripoli were brought to Ḥalab, the capital, in chains. In front of this surge of Muslim energy, the Second Crusade achieved little. Led by Conrad III of Germany and Louis

VII of France, its army consisted of French and German knights, Templars and Hospitallers, and foot troops furnished by the kingdom of Jerusalem. It all came to no more than a four-day siege of Dimashq. The crusaders withdrew to their coastline fortresses before Nūr al Dīn could arrive on the scene to give them battle. However, the Muslim scene was to witness still more mobilization. Ṣalāḥ al Dīn was appointed vizier in 1169 under the last Fāṭimī caliph of Egypt, al ʿĀḍid (1160–1171). He began by turning the country into the fold of Sunnī Islām and bringing it under the ʿAbbāsī caliphate of Baghdād. He united it to Syria, including Jordan, while his brother united Ḥijāz and Yaman to the growing kingdom. Al Maghrib (North Africa), Nūbia, and northern ʿIrāq were also added. Thus the Muslims were poised to meet the Crusaders. On July 1, 1187, Ṣalāḥ al Dīn advanced to Tiberias and captured it. The Crusaders rallied on the plateau of Ḥiṭṭīn a few miles to the west. Two days later, they received a crushing defeat. On October 2, 1187, Ṣalāḥ al Dīn liberated Jerusalem, rededicated al Aqṣā Mosque, and drove the Crusaders back to their coastline positions. The news of the fall of Jerusalem brought about the Third Crusade.

The Third Crusade (1189–1192)

The Third Crusade was the biggest of the Crusades. It included Frederick Barbarossa, emperor of Germany; Richard the Lion-Hearted, king of England; and Philippe Auguste, king of France; and their respective armies. Frederick took the land route and drowned in the river Salaf (Calycadmus) in Cilicia. His death caused his followers to forsake the cause, abandon their colleagues, and return home.

Richard first seized Cyprus and then concentrated all forces against ʿAkkā, which he took in 1191, after a siege and battles that lasted for two years. It was this siege that provided the theater for the greatest deeds of heroism and chivalry of the Middle Ages and that poets, artists, and chroniclers immortalized in their *chansons de geste.* An armistice followed, during which Ṣalāḥ al Dīn and Richard exchanged gifts. Ṣalāḥ's personal physician treated sick Richard, and Richard gave his sister in marriage to Ṣalāḥ's brother, that the couple might receive from both leaders the kingdom of Jerusalem as a wedding present. It was arranged that the coast would be Frankish domain, the hinterland Muslim.

Dynastic troubles among Ṣalāḥ's heirs weakened the Muslim camp. The Crusaders took advantage of Muslim division and reoccupied most of the towns Ṣalāḥ al Dīn had wrested from them, including Jerusalem (1229). The victory was temporary, however. For the Crusaders suffered from the same disease of dynastic disputes. Knights seeking personal glory, adventurers seeking booty, and Hospitallers competing with Templars pulled Christian unity apart. Moreover, while the Crusaders were at the mercy of the extortionist Venetian and Genoese mariners who supplied them, Europe lost interest and sent neither men nor supplies.

The Other Crusades

The Fourth Crusade (1192–1194)[2] was fought at Tibnīn south of Beirūt, bringing defeat to the Crusaders. The Fifth Crusade (1202–1204)[3] never went beyond Constantinople, where the crusaders vented their enmity against the city, its people, and its churches, including Hagia Sophia. The Crusaders returned home with their mules loaded with chalices, gems, gold, and silver from the altars of Christian Constantinople. The Sixth Crusade (1217–1221)[4] was diverted to Egypt on the advice of Genoese and Venetian traders anxious to master the Red Sea trade route. The Crusaders occupied Dumyāṭ (Damietta) (1219) and marched on to al Qāhirah (Cairo). As the Nile rose, the Egyptians opened all dikes and flooded the country. Cut off from their sources of supply, the Crusaders were beaten. King Louis of France, the commanding general, was taken captive, and another Crusade ended in failure. The last two debacles taught the papacy a lesson but had little effect on Frederick II, king of Germany, who launched a Crusade of his own.[5] The papacy seized the opportunity of Frederick's absence to attack parts of his own kingdom in Europe. When the news reached him, he abandoned Palestine and returned home.

The Effects of the Crusades

The balance sheet of results and consequences of the Crusades is heavily weighed on the side of the tragic. From the Muslim side, they were wild surges that had no valid justification and that brought about nothing but

[2] This is not counted as a separate crusade in the Western historiographical convention. What are called the Fifth and Sixth Crusades in this text are known in that convention as the Fourth and Fifth, respectively. The latter convention is followed in Map 58.
[3] The Fourth Crusade in Western historiography.
[4] The Fifth Crusade in Western historiography.
[5] The Sixth Crusade (1228–1229) in Western historiography.

bloodshed and grief. Christianity, its churches, and its holy sites were guaranteed by Caliph ʿUmar in 635 and were never threatened. Certainly under some regime, governor, or another, some Christians stood at a disadvantage or were abused. But the overall policy of the Islāmic state, as well as the overall record of that state, remained true to ʿUmar's commitment. The Crusaders did not add to the civilization of the Muslims, for they were far less civilized and less cultivated. Muslim learning, craftsmanship, arts, and culture flowed from East to West. The Crusaders returned to Europe loaded not only with the material products of the Muslim world, with which every church and every nobleman's home was adorned, but with the ideas that later helped to bring about the Renaissance.

Modern Movements

If in the context of religion studies *modern times* means the breakdown of long-held conservatism, the introduction of liberal thought, and the reform of old institutions the better to fit the spirit of a worldwide modern age, then Islām's "modern times" began in the thirteenth century with Taqiyy al Dīn Aḥmad ibn Taymiyah (d. 1328 C.E./727 A.H.). For later thinkers have not yet introduced a single reform idea that this towering genius of the late Middle Ages had not thought of and elaborated. Though Ibn Taymiyah was not successful in realizing his ideas of reform and the Middle Ages finally engulfed him, his ideas were seeds that lay buried for three and a half centuries, came back to life with tremendous vigor in the eighteenth century, and then engulfed the whole Muslim world. The germination took place in the center of the Arabian Peninsula, in the midst of the desert, where no foreign foot had ever trodden, no foreign influence had ever been felt. It is therefore false to assume that Islāmic modern history began with the Napoleonic invasion of Egypt, that Islāmic reform or modernism began with the advent of Western influence. On the other hand, there should be no doubt that when Western influence did come, it hastened the work of reform by aggravating the problems of the Muslim world.

The inner decay of Islāmic society showed itself forcefully in the fall of Baghdād and all of the eastern provinces to the Tatars, who advanced on Syria and marched through its southern regions unchecked. Ibn Taymiyah, a Syrian commoner born in Ḥarrān, rose to the challenge. He not only succeeded in raising an army in Egypt with which he checked the Tatar advance at ʿAyn Jālūt (1260 C.E./656 A.H.), and thus saved Egypt, but found the time to write what amounts to a whole library to diagnose the disease and prescribe the cure. His mind scanned the whole spectrum of Islāmic thought, penetratingly analyzed its components, showed where it went wrong, and sought to redress and reorient it toward self-fulfillment. The road he saw opening before him was the normative practice and understanding of the earliest Muslim generations. These, he contended, are fit for all times and places. Just as the Muslims' abandonment of them led to their decay and weakness, a return to the pure fount of Islām would bring to them strength, creativity, and felicity. Since Ibn Taymiyah, all Islāmic modernism has been "conservative" in the sense of seeking to re-create an earlier state of affairs; but it has been dynamic and creative because that past contains the divine will, which for the Muslim is the Qur'ān and which is forever new and energizing. Ibn Taymiyah demolished the epistemology and hermeneutic of the Ṣūfīs, the Bāṭinīs, and the Shīʿah, accusing them all of cultivating esotericism, of betraying reason and common sense. He argued that if the revealed words of the Qur'ān and the prophet's legacy of traditions are taken to mean anything other than what they say (i.e., if they are subject to allegorical interpretation as these schools advocated), then Islāmic meanings and values will be dislocated, undermined, and eventually supplanted by something non-Islāmic. The original meanings of Holy Writ are established by the lexicography and usage of the early generations, who used its terms and who left us a legacy of their works to study and follow. In them Muslim understanding has its secure anchoring. From the time the Ṣūfīs popularized allegorical interpretation, the religions and moral categories of the Muslims began to slide; they lost their criticality, their intellectual and spiritual virility. Astronomy began to give way to astrology, mathematics to numerology, chemistry to alchemy, and knowledge to ignorance. That is particularly true of the Muslims' abandonment of the inductive method elaborated and used by the jurists for the deductive method freshly learned from Aristotle. Muslim thinkers applied the former to law as well as to natural science and did well. But when their methodology became an endless analysis of definitions according to *a priori* categories, their thinking became sterile. The Ṣūfīs, on the other hand, chose a Gnostic methodology wherein human effort avails nothing, comparative dialectic is vain, and no new evidence can shake what has been given by "illumination" or *gnosis*. Both avenues weakened Muslim intellectuality until it could move no more.

In personal ethics, the one method developed vacuitous legalism devoid of spirit and moving appeal, and the other, a dilution of the moral imperative (the Sharī'ah), developed a personal relativism permitting and justifying indulgence. On the social level, the Ṣūfī preoccupation with personal spiritual welfare cultivated individualism, but the Ṣūfī brotherhood with its hierarchy, at the head of which stood the unquestioned elder-chief, and its perpetual practice of *dhikr* (repeated litanies and prayers) pulled the individual away from home and family, from the community and state. The home and family were left to fend for themselves; the community and state were left to rapacious army generals and corrupt viziers. The foundations of both institutions floundered. Those of the family gave way to vice and those of the state to inefficiency and tyranny on the home front and weakness and division abroad.

Ṣūfīsm destroyed the Muslim's faith in himself, in his world, and in his destiny by directly attacking world affirmation and preaching renunciation. Gradually, the Muslim lost his activism, his involvement in the processes of history, and his consciousness of responsibility for his own existence and that of his fellow man. Ṣūfīsm cultivated saint worship and taught that the saints enjoyed the power to influence the judgment of God, thus helping to increase moral complacency. Its exaggeration of the immediacy and nearness of God through the imagery of lover and beloved increased the threat of anthropomorphism, and its pantheist doctrine brought the unrefined follower closer to idolatry. Above all, it weakened his sense of religious identity by teaching an ineffable mystical experience open to all without distinction, reachable through many avenues besides the Islāmic path of the Sharī'ah, and resulting in no necessary visible observances or effects.

Ibn Taymiyah did not only criticize and condemn. He elaborated an inductive logic for jurisprudence and the natural sciences. He repudiated *ijtihād* ("creative interpretation") as a source of law because the Ṣūfīs used it to justify their innovative allegorical interpretations, just as he denounced their recourse to *Ijmā'* ("consensus") for the same reason. In order to put an end to their non-Islāmic vagaries, Ibn Taymiyah redefined *Ijmā'* as the consensus of the Prophet's companions (i.e., of the first generation of Muslims) and tied *ijtihād* down to an inductive logic in which no *a priori* categories are assumed and no deduction from them constitutes valid knowledge. He redefined the social imperatives of Islām, giving the duty of participation in the political process first place among the duties of religion. In order to enable all Muslims to fulfill this societal requirement and thus to exercise the political rights conferred upon them by their membership in the Ummah, Ibn Taymiyah repudiated the necessity of a single caliphate for all. As long as the Muslim world was already fragmented, he thought reconstruction had better start on the local level.

20-14 An illumination of the first sūrah of the Qur'an, entitled "Al Fātiḥah ("The Opener"). The seven āyāt (verses) of this short sūrah are written in the cloud banks of the central medallion and preceded by the initial invocation: "In the name of God, the Merciful, the Compassionate." This sūrah is recited by Muslims in every prayer ritual. It fills a role in Islām comparable to that of the Lord's Prayer in Christianity.

Ibn Taymiyah condemned the innovations introduced by the Ṣūfīs along with their motives and justifications. In Qur'ānic spirit, he denounced saint worship, insisting that intercession belongs to God alone, and to the Prophet only by divine concession. Equally, he reinterpreted the Islāmic notions of God and man, refuting the Ṣūfī understanding of divine power as nihilating human freedom and responsibility. Criticizing the determinists al Ash'arī and al Ghazzālī (and their followers, whether Ṣūfī or non-Ṣūfī), he sought to harmonize man's creatureliness with his freedom and responsibility.

Wahhābiyyah

Inspired by the revolutionary ideas of Ibn Taymiyah, which he had studied well, Muḥammad ibn 'Abd al Wahhāb (1703–1792 C.E./1115–1206 A.H.), a native of Dar'iyyah in central Arabia, began to teach them to his fellows in 1729 (Map 57). Soon he converted Prince Su'ūd, the ruling governor of the district, and with the prince's help the teaching became overnight a rampaging movement. Village by village and tribe by tribe, the whole of central Arabia responded to the call of reform with great enthusiasm. Ibn 'Abd al Wahhāb touched a sensitive cord, and laying the blame for all decay at the door of Ṣūfīsm, people readily rose to this intellectually simple and vigorous call for return to the activism, affirmation, and pietism of the earliest fathers. In pursuit of this ideal, the Wahhābīs destroyed the shrines and mausoleums of all saints, dissolved the brotherhoods, enforced Ḥanbalī law throughout the land, and generated a new surge of Islāmic pietism. They attacked Ṣūfīsm on all sides and on the social side they created an alternative to the Ṣūfī brotherhood (whose purpose is devotional), a new fraternity whose purpose is economic and military. They founded a number of collective settlements, the first of their kind in modern history, called *Ikhwān* or brethren, where the members had joint ownership of the means of production, namely, land and water supply, and enjoyed a collective setup for consumer purchases, product sales, representation at government administrative offices, and defense. Shortsightedly, however, recruitment for and organization of these settlements were on tribal lines, relying primarily on tribal loyalties. Thus, when these loyalties shifted, the collectives fell apart.

The Wahhābiyyah movement was fated to run against the ailing Ottoman Empire, where Ṣūfī brotherhoods had become long-established vested interests. The Wahhābīs gave battle in the Ḥijāz as well as in 'Irāq, capturing Karbalā' in 1802 and Makkah in 1803. For the Ottomans this was an insurrection that could only weaken the Empire in its confrontation with an aggressive, colonialist West and they mobilized the public to put the movement down. Ambitious Muḥammad 'Alī, governor of Egypt, saw an opportunity to enhance his power and prestige and to extort autonomy for his rule in Egypt by performing the hatchet-man role for the Ottomans. He organized an expeditionary force and launched two campaigns, the second of which carried the Egyptians into Dar'iyyah (1813 and 1818 C.E.), where the ruling prince was captured and exiled to Cairo.

Defeat notwithstanding, the movement captured the minds of Muslims with its relentless logic of Islāmic purity, common-sense monotheism, piety, activism, freedom with responsibility, return to the Qur'ān, and loyalty to the earliest fathers, the Prophet's companions. A remnant of Wahhābī power survived in a pocket of central Arabia, which made a spectacular comeback when the Ottoman Empire's last crisis occurred during World War I. The heirs of the House of Su'ūd sprang from the same base, Dar'iyyah, to seize most of Arabia and establish the Su'ūdī kingdom.

Though Wahhābī military power did not reach beyond the Arabian Peninsula, the religious power of their ideas stirred up the four corners of the Muslim world. Wahhābī ideas were disseminated among the pilgrims who came to Makkah. Their ideas could not help but reach

20-15 Sulṭān Aḥmad Mosque, Istanbul, Turkey. Also known as "the Blue Mosque" because of the color of its beautifully tiled interior, this mosque was built between 1609 and 1616. (Courtesy of Dr. Guthrie Birkhead.)

the pilgrims in Makkah, even before Makkah itself fell into their hands in 1803 C.E./1218 A.H., for no pilgrim could have resisted the debate of significant religious-political events taking place in the hinterland lying beyond Makkah. Whether openly, therefore, when the Wahhābīs were in power, or under the immunity pilgrims enjoyed during their pilgrimage before a Wahhābī victory or after a Wahhābī defeat, the message reached new ears. Sayyid Aḥmad Barelī in the west and Sharī'at Allah in the east carried the message and its enthusiasm to the Indian subcontinent, already prepared by an earlier reformer, Shāh Waliyyullah (1703–1762), whose ideas were very similar to those of ibn 'Abd al Wahhāb. Muḥammad ibn 'Alī al Sanūsī (d. 1859 C.E./1275 A.H.) in the north, 'Uthmān dan Fodio in the west, and Muḥammad Aḥmad al Mahdī in the east spread the reform across Muslim Africa.

Sanūsiyyah

The Sanūsiyyah movement tried to take advantage of the good of both Ṣūfīsm and Wahhābīsm and succeeded. From the Ṣufīs, it took its organization, terminology, and pietistic enthusiasm. It called its apprentices *murīds*, its elders *shuyūkh* (plural of *shaykh*), and its centers *zawāyā* (plural of *zāwiyah*). The main religious activity in the life of the *zāwiyah* was *dhikr*. But here the analogy stops. None of the vagaries or even speculations of Ṣūfī thought were tolerated. Sanūsī thinking kept itself close to the Sharī'ah and traditional theological thinking. It was not intellectually innovative because it diagnosed the malaise as a discrepancy between the will and a mind already possessing the Islāmic truth. The Muslim was, in its view, recalcitrant, not erring. Error and misguidance the Sanūsīs saw in Ṣūfī speculative

59 Distribution of Muslims c. 1970

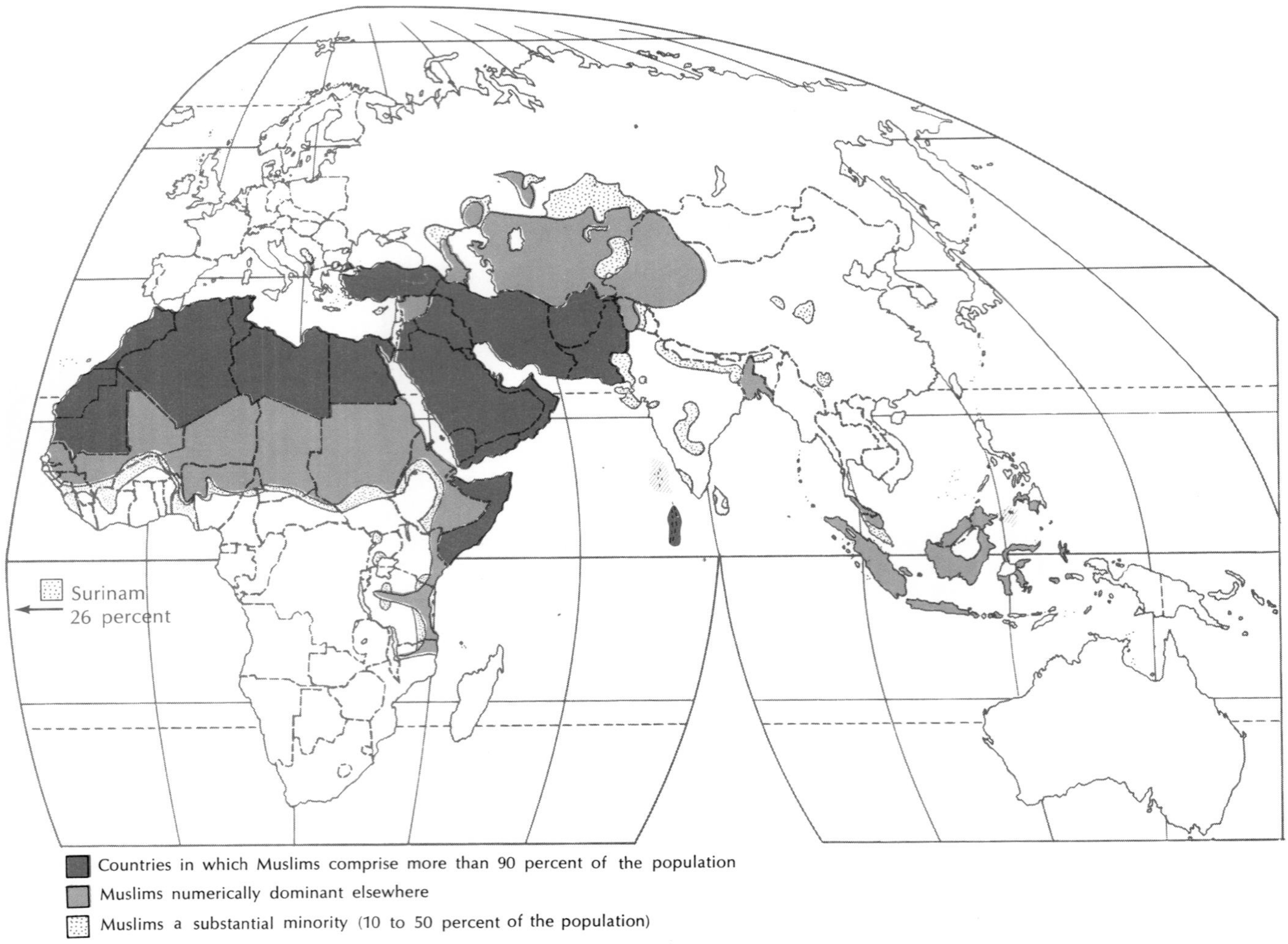

60 World Population of Muslims by Major Regions

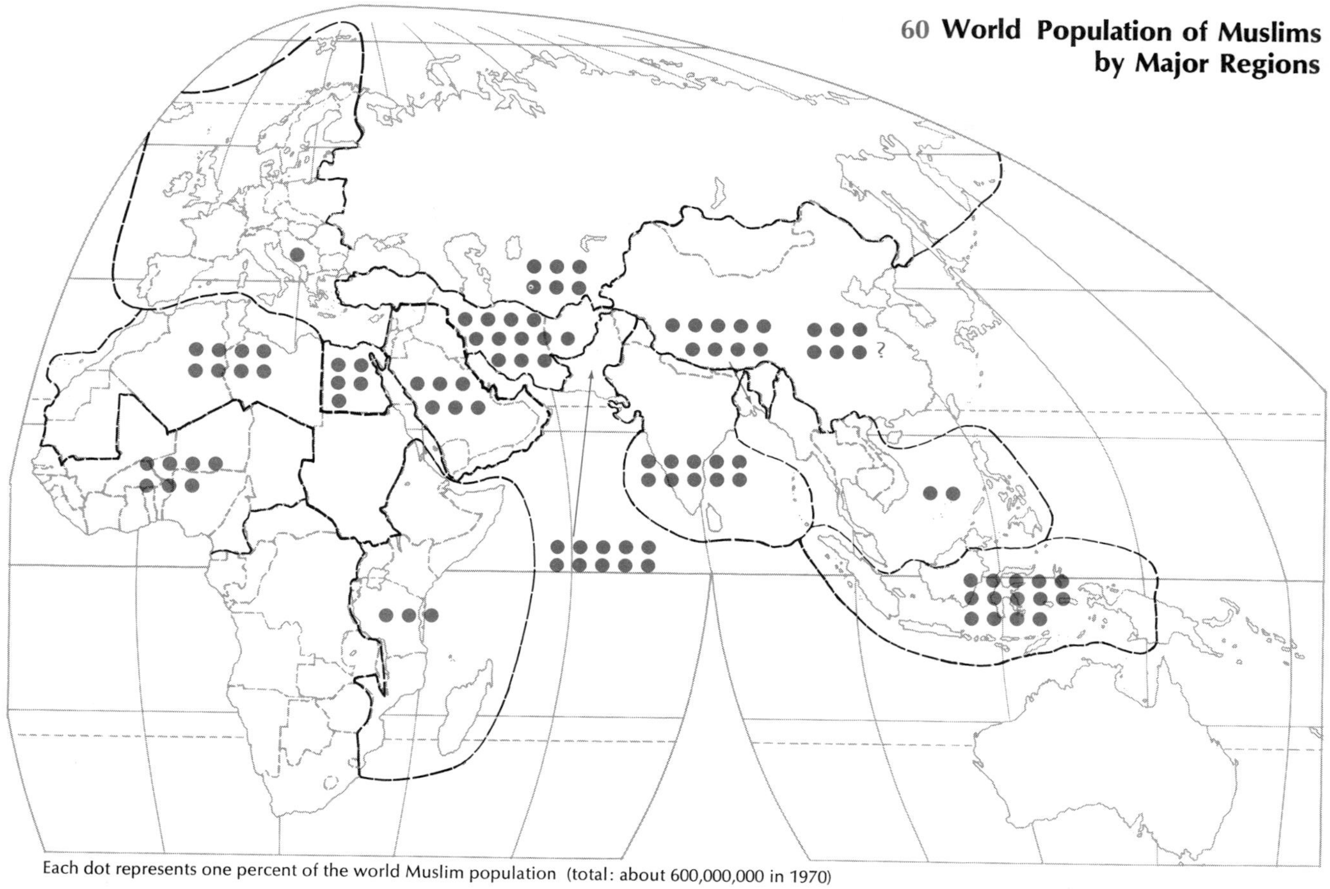

Each dot represents one percent of the world Muslim population (total: about 600,000,000 in 1970)

thought, and they avoided them. All their energies were hence poured on the activist pursuit of economic, political, and military regeneration. Begun in Algeria, the building up of *zawāyā* or community centers for the movement spread in all directions. French military expansion, however, gradually pushed the Sanūsīs out of Algeria into Tunisia and later out of Tunisia into Libya. Eventually, the capital of the movement became Jaghbūb in south Cyrenaica, the headquarters of a network of several hundred *zawāyā* supporting a large army of mounted soldiers, reaching deep into Chad, the Niger, and operating clandestinely as centers of resistance throughout the western territories already fallen to the French.

Jaghbūb was in all respects the model. The center was the mosque, where not only the devotions but all councils were held. Radiating from it were the farms and houses reclaimed and built by all but held individually by the members and their families. The water system depended upon wells dug and managed by the collective according to a strict timetable and exact measurements. Purchases and product distribution, as well as armament production, were in the hands of central planners appointed by the movement. The central mosque was also an institute of learning where missionaries and future leaders were trained not only in the art of calling men to the new religious movement but also in the military arts, as well as in agriculture and livestock improvement.

Both the Wahhābiyyah and the Sanūsiyyah constitute the models of modernist movements throughout the Muslim world. The former inspired the military confrontation of the Muslims against Britain in India, culminating in the wars of 1859; against the Spaniards in the Philippines; and against the Dutch in the Indonesian basin. It sparked the Farā'idī (ritualists—so-called because of their strict observance of Islāmic rituals) revolt in Bengal, the Tobacco revolt in Persia, and continuous upheaval and unrest in Egypt and 'Irāq. The Sanūsiyyah, on the other hand, inspired the Tījāniyyah, Mahdiyyah, and Mīrghaniyyah movements, in which political-military resistance was secondary to the moral and spiritual revivification of the individual through Sūfī practices. All movements were however knocked out by the military might of the colonial powers advancing on the

61 Muslims in South Asia

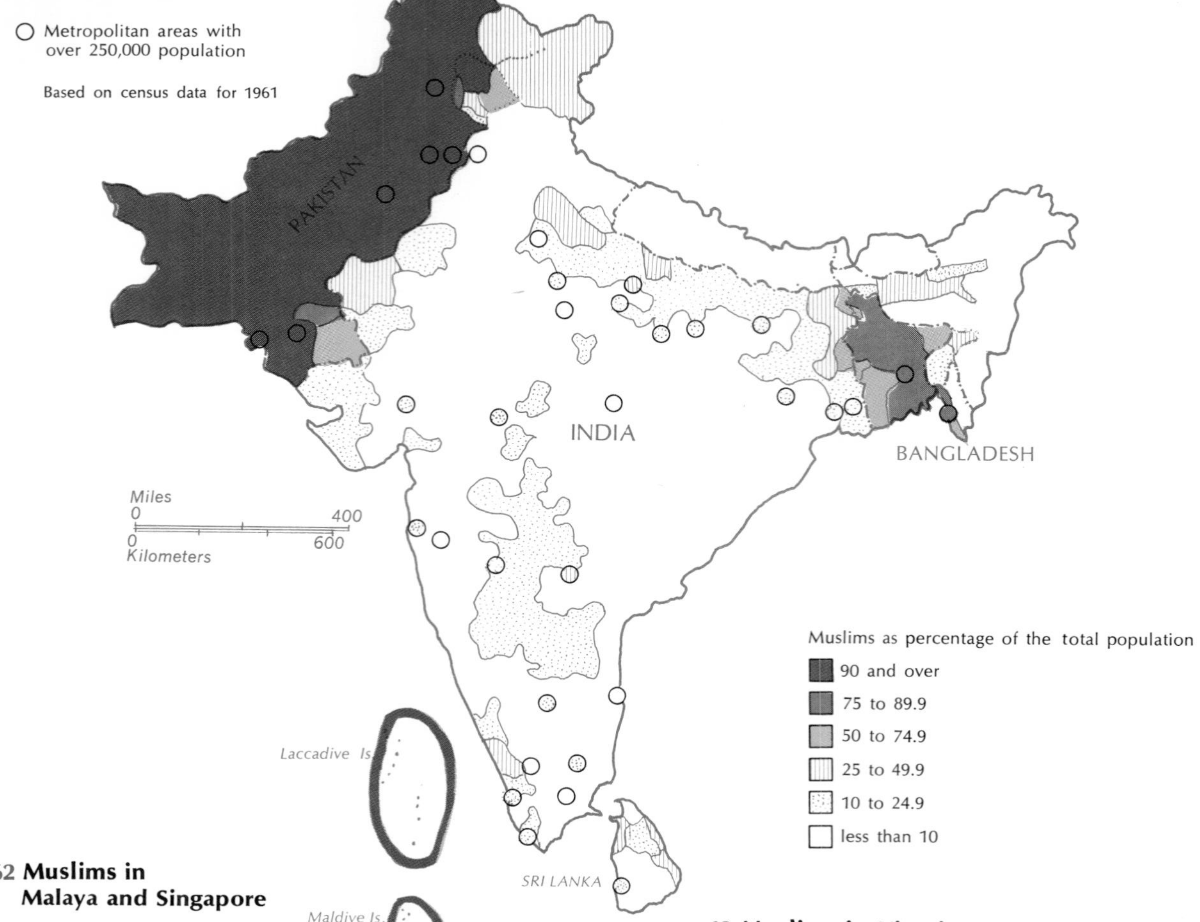

62 Muslims in Malaya and Singapore

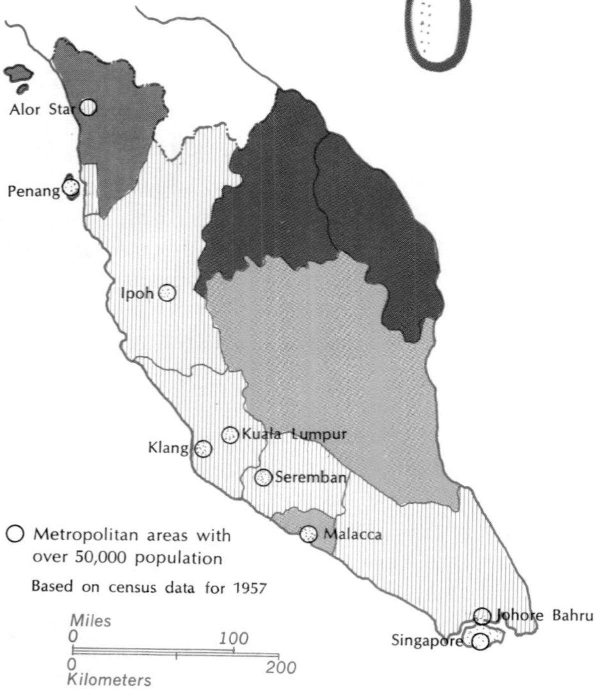

63 Muslims in Nigeria

Based on census data for 1952

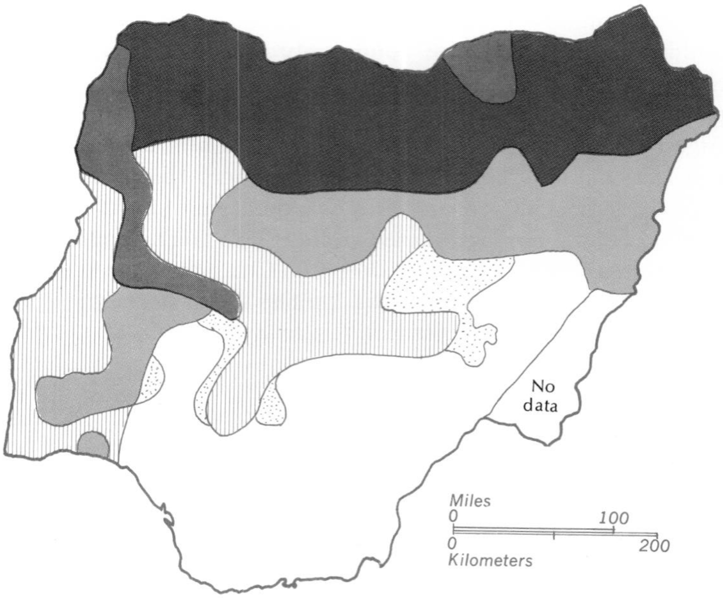

64 Islām, Culture, and the State

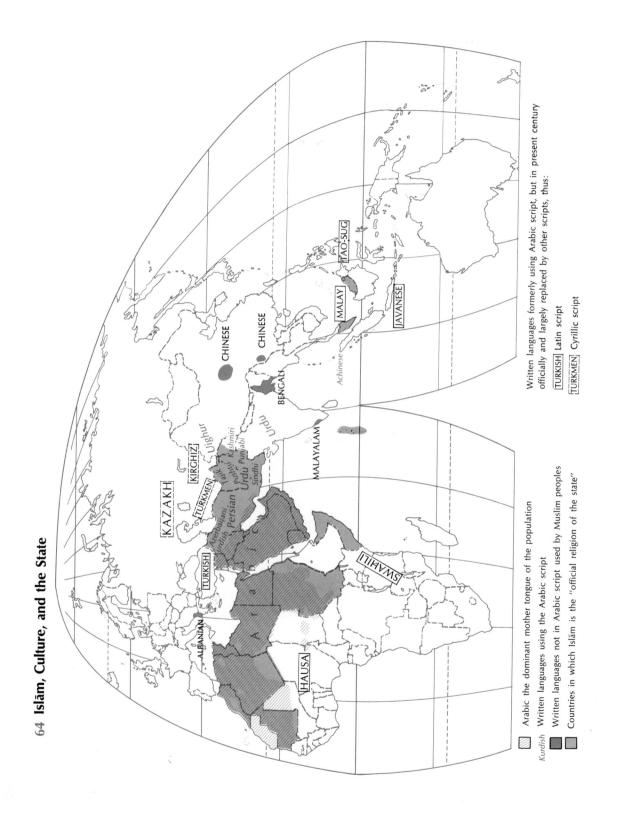

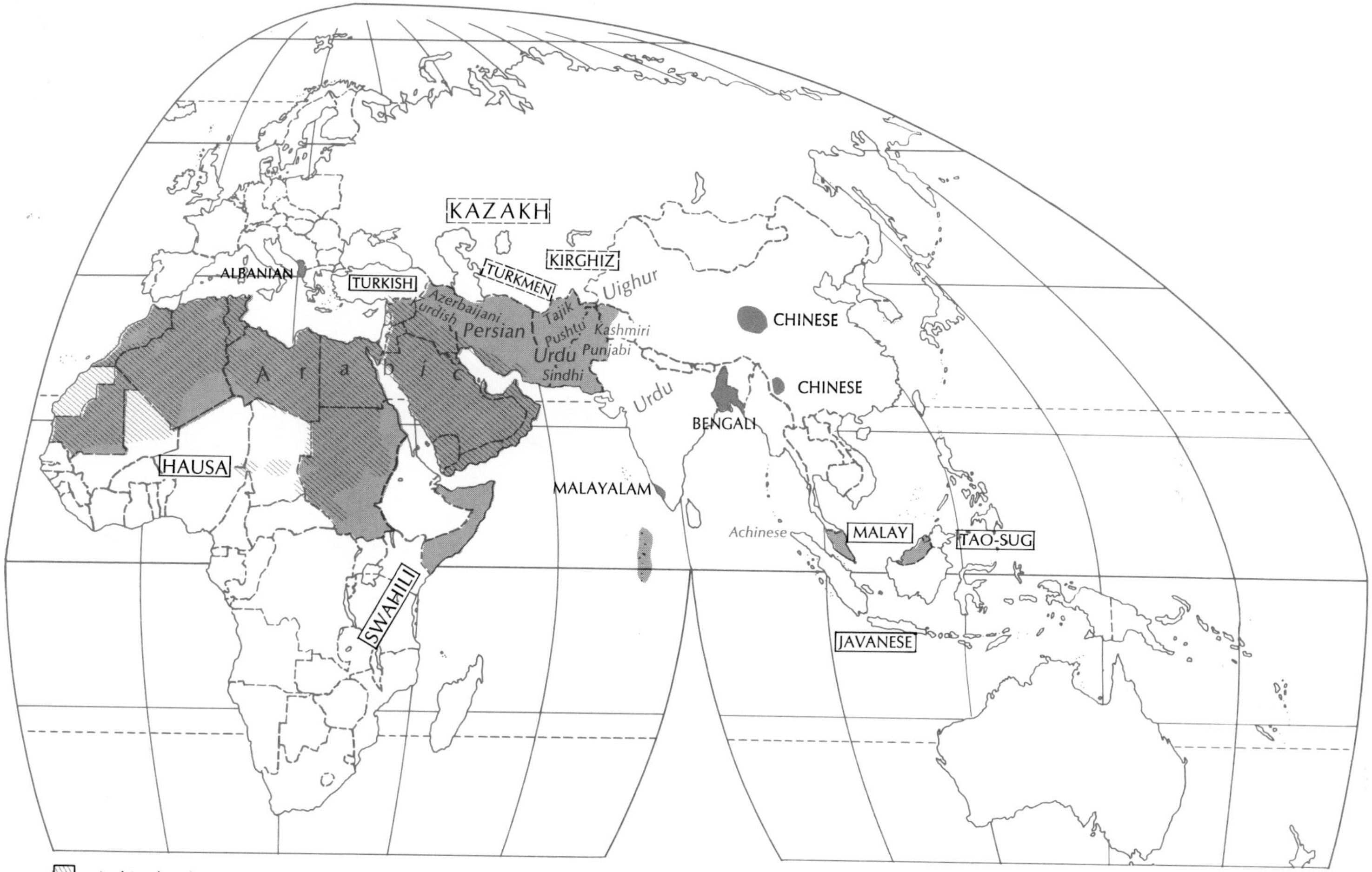

(hatched)	Arabic the dominant mother tongue of the population
Kurdish	Written languages using the Arabic script
(dark)	Written languages not in Arabic script used by Muslim peoples
(grey)	Countries in which Islām is the "official religion of the state"

Written languages formerly using Arabic script, but in present century officially and largely replaced by other scripts, thus:

TURKISH Latin script

TURKMEN Cyrillic script

65 Pilgrim Traffic to Makkah (Mecca)

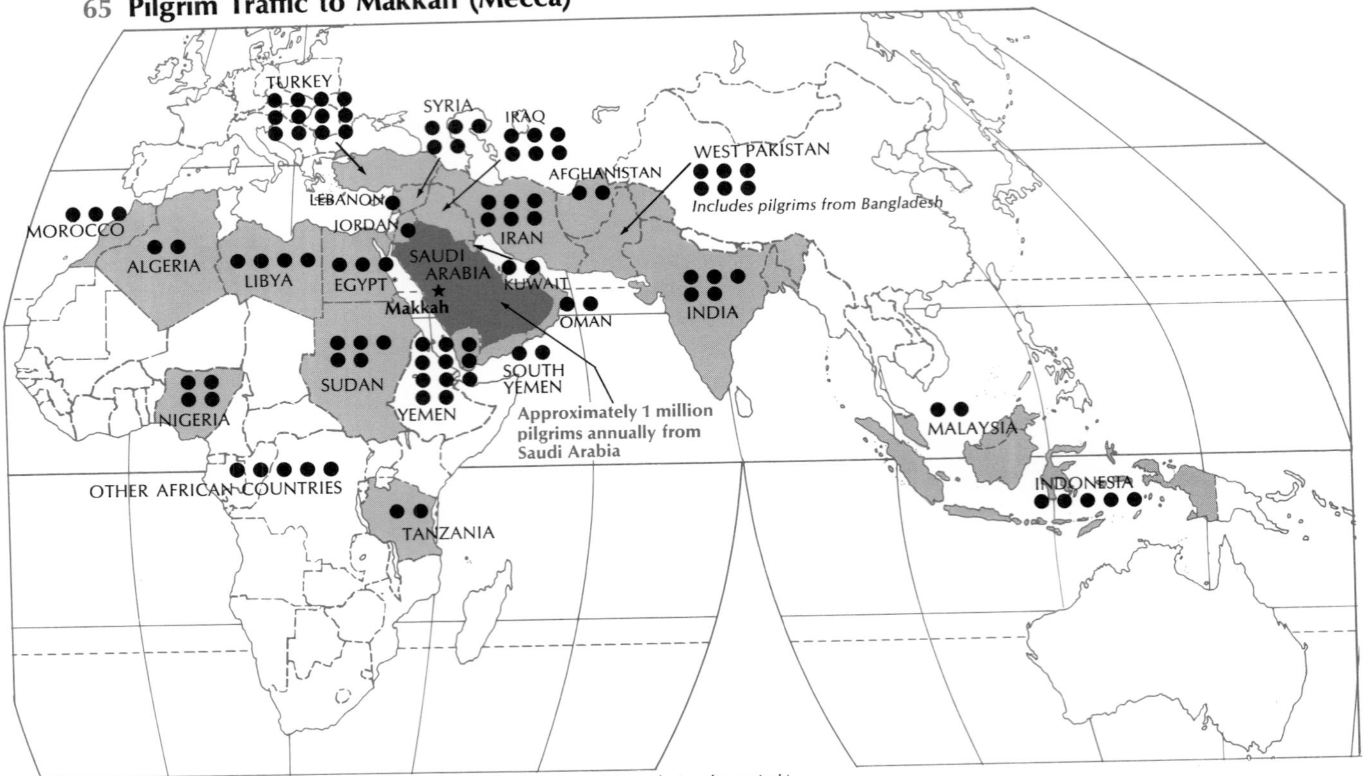

* (Note: The relatively small number from Egypt is a result of political conditions during the period.)

● = One percent of total annual foreign pilgrim traffic (total: about 350,000) to Makkah in the late 1960's, by country of origin.

Muslim world. Only these Muslim movements' military activities, however, were stopped; and even so, only for a limited interval.

Present Fluidity

The advent of colonial administration set off a chain of reactions. On one hand, guerrilla resistance, demonstrations, strikes, and political disturbances punctuated the geography and history of most colonial regimes. On the other, new schools designed to give the Muslims mastery of Western science and technology were built. Aligarh Muslim University in India, built with British encouragement by Sir Sayyid Aḥmad Khān (1817–1900), and the Institut d'Egypte in Cairo, built by the French, and the American University of Beirut—all have contributed, for different motives, to Muslim modernization. World War II provided the occasion for another Muslim attempt at getting rid of the colonial presence in the lands of Islām. Most Muslim countries achieved independence soon after the end of hostilities.

Independence, however, did not bring the Muslims into successful competition on the world scene with the Western world; nor did it achieve the internal reforms in education, social reorganization, public administration, and *ummah* reconstruction.[6] Moreover, the neocolonial West invented new strategies and techniques to divert Muslim energies from the needed reforms and thus rendered ineffective any opposition to continuing their old exploitation. These and like debacles, which were in evidence in some Muslim countries even before political independence, have left the modern Muslim conscience disenchanted with all past attempts at reform. A process of radicalization has been set in motion that has produced in the last few decades movements of secular nationalism in the various Muslim countries, as well as the totalist Islāmism of the Ikhwān al Muslimūn (Muslim Brethren). The two views were so radicalized that they divided—and still do divide—the Muslim world masses between them. The 1952 Egyptian revolution sought to combine the aspirations of both, as it was inspired by both. The impossibility of the attempt became painfully evident in 1967, with military defeat and collapse. The same disillusionment seized the

[6]For a cartographic presentation of Islām in the world today, see Maps 59 to 65.

Muslims of the Indo-Pakistan subcontinent in 1970 at the dismemberment of Pakistan. In the meantime, Muslim masses press ever forward toward radicalization. On this road, the ideal of the Prophet's career and the genuine felicity of his companions on all fronts of life continue to move and to inspire the contemporary Muslim, for they constitute the ultimate norm of radical reconstruction of self and society.

Bibliography

'Affīfī, A. *The Mystical Philosophy of Muḥyī al Dīn Ibn al 'Arabī.* Cambridge: Cambridge U. Press, 1939.

'Alī, 'Allāmah 'Abdullah Yūsuf. *The Message of Islam.* Lahore: Ashraf. n.d.

Ameer 'Alī, Sayid. *The Spirit of Islam.* London: Christophers, 1922.

Arberry, A. J. *The Doctrine of the Ṣūfīs.* Cambridge: The University Press, 1933.

———. *Introduction to the History of Ṣūfism.* London: Longmans, Green & Co., 1943.

———. *Ṣūfism.* London: Allen and Unwin, 1950.

Arnold, Thomas. *The Preaching of Islam.* Lahore: Ashraf, 1956.

Arsalān, Amīr Shakīb, *Our Decline and Its Causes,* tr., M. A. Shakoor. Lahore: Ashraf, 1952.

Brockelmann, C. *Geschichte der arabischen Literatur.* München/Berlin: R. Oldenbourg, 1937–1942.

Daniel, N. *Islam and the West.* Edinburgh: The University Press, 1960.

Enan, M. A. *Decisive Moments in the History of Islam.* Lahore: Ashraf, 1949.

Fyzee, A. A. A. *Outlines of Muḥammadan Law.* London/New York/Bombay: Oxford University Press, 1955.

Hamidullah, M. *Le Prophète de l'Islam,* 2 vols. Paris: J. Vrin, 1955.

———. *Introduction to Islam.* Paris: 1959.

———. *The Muslim Conduct of State.* Lahore: Ashraf, 1945.

Hell, Joseph. *The Arab Civilization,* tr., S. Khuda Bakhsh. Cambridge: W. Heffer and Sons, 1926.

Hitti, P. K. *History of the Arabs.* London: Macmillan Co., 1937.

The Holy Qur'ān, tr., 'Allamah 'Abdullah Yūsuf 'Alī. Washington, D.C.: American International Printing Co., 1946.

Ibn Hisham. *The Life of Muhammad,* tr., A. Guillaume. London/New York/Toronto: Oxford U. P., 1955.

Iqbāl, M. *Six Lectures on the Reconstruction of Religious Thought in Islam.* Lahore: M. Ashraf, 1932.

Irving, T. B. *Falcon of Spain.* Lahore: Ashraf, 1962.

Al Khatīb Al Tibrīzi, Muhammad ibn 'Abd Allah. *Mishkat al Maṣābiḥ—Al Ḥadīth.* tr., James Robson. Lahore: Ashraf, 1960–65.

Muhājir, A. M. R. *Lessons from the Stories of the Qur'ān.* Lahore: Ashraf, 1965.

Al Qushayrī, Muslim ibn al Hajjāj, *Ṣaḥīḥ Muslim,* tr., M. 'Abdul Ḥamīd Ṣiddīqī. Lahore: Ashraf, n.d.

Nicholson, R. A. *The Mystics of Islam.* London: G. Bell, 1914.

———. *Studies in Islamic Mysticism.* Cambridge: The University Press, 1921.

Padwick, C. E. *Muslim Devotions.* London: S.P.C.K., 1961.

Pickthall, M. M. *Cultural Side of Islam (Islamic Culture).* Madras: Universal Publishers, 1959.

Sarwar, Ḥāfiẓ Ghulām. *Philosophy of the Qur'ān.* Lahore: Ashraf, 1955.

Schimmel, A. *Gabriel's Wing: A Study into the Religious Ideas of Sir Muḥammad Iqbāl.* Leiden: E. J. Brill, 1963.

Sharīf, M. Rayḥān. *Islamic Social Framework.* Lahore: Ashraf, 1963.

Shaykh, M. Sa'īd. *Studies in Muslim Philosophy.* Lahore: Ashraf, n.d.

Shushtery, A. M. A. *Outlines of Islamic Culture.* Bangalore City: Bangalore Press, 1938.

Smith, W. C. *Modern Islam in India.* London: V. Gollancz, Ltd., 1946.

———. *Islam in Modern History.* Princeton: Princeton U. Press, 1957.

Watt, W. Montgomery. *Free Will and Predestination in Early Islam.* London: Luzac, 1948.

———. *Muhammad at Mecca.* Oxford: The Clarendon Press, 1953.

———. *Muhammad at Medina.* Oxford: The Clarendon Press, 1956.

APPENDIX
CHRONOLOGIES

B.C.E.	EGYPT	SYRIA-PALESTINE
7000		Prepottery Neolithic Culture (Jericho) 7000–5000
6000		
5500	Fayyūmī Culture	
5000		Pottery Neolithic (Jericho and Other Villages in Palestine, Syria) 5000–4000
4500	Tasian and Badarian Cultures	
4000		Chalcolithic Cultures 4000–3300 Migration from Arabian Peninsula Akkadian Settlement Ghassulian
3500	Mesopotamian Stimulation I–II Dynasties: Unification and Founding of Dual Monarchy. 3100–2700 Narmer (Menes)	Early Bronze Age or Proto-Urban 3300–2300
3000	Old Kingdom. The Pyramid Age 2700–2200	

A
Religions of the Past

ASIA MINOR	MESOPOTAMIA	PERSIA
	Prepottery Neolithic (Jarmo) 7000–5000	
City-States Catal Huyuk		
Hacilar		
	Neolithic Ḥassūna 4500 Ḥalaf 4300	
	'Ubayd, Warqa, Jamdat Naṣr 4000–3000	Pre-Archaemenid 4000–2000 Early settlements at Sialk, Susa, Tepe Hisar, Tepe Giyan, etc.
Troy	Migration from Arabian Peninsula Akkadian Settlement	
Alaca Kuyuk	Sumerian City-States 2800–2360	

B.C.E.	EGYPT	SYRIA-PALESTINE
	III Dynasty 2700–2650 Djoser, Builder of the Step Pyramid IV Dynasty 2650–2500 Snefru 2650 Khufu (Cheops) 2600 Khaf-Re 2560 Men-kau-Re 2525	Migration from Arabian Peninsula Amurru (Amorite) Settlement
2500	V Dynasty 2500–2350 Ne-user-Re 2425 Pyramid Texts 2350–2175 VI Dynasty 2350–2200 Pepi I 2325 Pepi II 2275–2185 Intermediate Period 2200–2050 VII–XI Dynasties: Rise of Provincial Pharaohs and Decentralization. Coffin Texts VII–VIII Dynasties 2180–2155 IX–X Dynasties 2155–2050 Meri-ka-Re 2100 XI Dynasty 2135–2000	Middle Bronze Age 2300–1500
2000	Middle Kingdom 2050–1800 XII Dynasty 1990–1780	
1900		
1800	Intermediate Period II XIII–XVII Dynasties 1800–1550 Hyksos Rule 1730–1570	Patriarch Abraham and Sons
1700	Khayan 1620	Hebrews in Egypt 1650–1280
1600	Kamose 1580 New Kingdom (Empire) XVIII–XX Dynasties 1570–1090 XVIII Dynasty 1570–1305 Expulsion of Hyksos 1570 Ah-mose I 1570–1546	
1550	Amen-hotep I 1545–1525 Thut-mose I 1525–1495	

ASIA MINOR	MESOPOTAMIA	PERSIA
	Amorite Migration from the Arabian Peninsula Akkadian Empire 2360–2180	
Beycesultan	Quti invasion 2180 Quti Rule 2180–2080? Ur III Dynasty 2112–2004 Transfer from Pastoral to Agricultural Economy before 2000	
	Four Amorite Dynasties: *Assyria* 1950 Cappadocian Colonies *Mari* *Isin* 2017–1735 *Larsa* 2025–1763	Elamite Kingdom 2000–640
	Babylon I 1894–1595 Lipit-Ishtar c. 1865	
Hittite Old Kingdom 1740–1460	Hammurabi 1792–1750 Warad-sin 1770–1759	
Labarnas 1680–1650 Hattusilis I 1650–1620 Mursilis I 1620–1590	Bim-sin 1758–1698 "Mari Age" 1750–1697	Kassite Invasion of Babylon from Persia c. 1680
	Shamsi-adad I 1748–1717 Zimri-lim 1730–1700 Kassite Dynasty 1730–1161	
nvasion of Mesopotamia, Defeat of Babylon 1535	Hittite Invasion (Mursilis I) 1535	

B.C.E.	EGYPT	SYRIA-PALESTINE
1500	Thut-mose II 1495–1590 Thut-mose III 1490–1436 Queen Hat-shepsut 1486–1468	Late Bronze Age 1500–1200 Migrations from Arabian Peninsula 1500–1200
1450	Amen-hotep II 1439–1406 Thut-mose IV 1406–1398	Aramean Settlement in Damascus, Phoenicia, Jordan Valley
1400	The Amarna Period: Amen-hotep III 1398–1361 Amen-hotep IV (Akh-en-Aton) 1369–1353 Smenkh-ka-Re 1355–1352 Tut-ankh-Aton 1352–1344	
1350	Eye 1344–1342 Har-em-hab 1342–1303 XIX Dynasty 1305–1200 Ramses I 1303–1302 Seti I 1302–1290	Mitanni
1300	Ramses II 1290–1224 Exodus of Hebrews 1280	Hittite Invasion by Muwattalis 1300 Exodus and Amphictyony with Midian, Horeb, and Other N.W. Arabian Tribes. Migration to the Jordan Valley 1280–1150
1250	Mer-ne-Ptah 1224–1214	Invasions by Sea Peoples
1200	XX Dynasty. Weakness, Anarchy. Sea Peoples Defeated. 1200–1090 Set-nakht 1197–1195 Ramses III 1195–1164 Ramses IV–XI 1164–1090 End of the Empire	Southern Highlands Ruled by "Judges" 1200–1020 Philistines Settle on Coast of Palestine 1160?
1150	Post-Empire XXI–XXVI Dynasties 1150–525	Deborah 1125
1100	XXI Dynasty (Thanite) 1090–935	Gideon
1050		Fall of Shiloh 1030? Samuel Saul 1020–1000 — Arameans
1000		David 1000–961 — Rezon, King of Damascus

ASIA MINOR	MESOPOTAMIA	PERSIA
Hittite Empire 1460–1190?	Migration from Arabian Peninsula	
	Rise of Assyria	
Suppiluliumas 1380–1340 Defeated Mitannians in North Syria	Assur-uballit I 1354–1318	
Muwatallis 1306–1282	Invasions of Mitanni c. 1325	
Invasion of Palestine Hattusilis III 1275–1250	Adad-nirari I 1297–1266 Shalmaneser I 1265–1235	
	Tukulti-ninurta I 1234–1197	
Defeat by Sea Peoples Hittite Empire Ends Hittites into Syria in Conjunction with Sea Peoples Migrations Phrygians 1200–7th cent.	Assyrian Weakness	
	Tiglath-pileser 1118–1078	
	Assyrian Revival	

B.C.E.	EGYPT	SYRIA-PALESTINE	
950	XXII Dynasty 945–725 Sheshonk I 945–914	Solomon 961–922 Schism 922 *Judah* 922–587 Rehoboam 922–915 Abijah 915–913 Asa 913–873	 *Israel* 922–721 Jeroboam I 922–901 Nadab 901–900
900	Expeditionary Force to Palestine (Judah) →		Baasha 900–877 Elah 877–876 Zimri 876 Omri 876–869
875		Jehoshaphat 873–849	Ahab 869–850 Prophet Elijah
850		Jehoram 849–842 Ahaziah 842 Athaliah 842–837 Joash 837–800	Ahaziah 850–849 ← Jehoram (Prophet Elisha) 849–842 Jehu 842–815
825			Jehoahaz 815–801 Jehoash 801–786
800		Amaziah 800–783 Uzziah 783–742 Prophet Azariah	Jeroboam II 786–746 ←
775	XXIII Dynasty 759–715		Prophet Amos
750		Jotham Co-regent c. 750 Jothan 742–735 Prophet Isaiah Prophet Micah Ahaz 735–715	Prophet Hosea Zechariah 746–745 Shallum 745 Menahem 745–738 Pekahiah 738–737 ← Pekah 737–732 Hoshea 732–724 ←
725	XXIV Dynasty 725–709 XXV Dynasty (Ethiopian) 716–663 Shabako 710–696	Hezekiah 715–687 701– Assyrian Invasion 701–688	Fall of Samaria 722 to Assyria

ASIA MINOR	MESOPOTAMIA	PERSIA
	Assur-dan II 934–912	
	Adad-nirari II 912–890	
	Assur-nasir-pal II 883–859	
	Shahmaneser III 859–824 Conquest of Syria (Battle of Qarqar) 853	
	Shamsi-adad V 824–811	
	Adad-nirari III 811–783 Invasion of Syria	
	Tiglath-pileser III 745–727	
	Assyrian Invasion of Syria 737	
		Medean Empire 728–550
	Shalmaneser V 727–722	
	Sargon II 722–705 Assyrian Invasion of Syria, Palestine	
	Sennacherib 705–681	

B.C.E.	EGYPT	SYRIA-PALESTINE
700	Tirhakah 685–664	Manasseh 687–642
675	Assyrian Invasion (Sack of Thebes) 663 XXVI Dynasty 663–525 Psammeticus I 663–609	Assyrians Pass Through to Invade Egypt 663
650		Amon 642–640 Josiah 640–609 Prophet Jeremiah
625	Neco II 609–593	Prophet Zephaniah Prophet Nahum Jehoahaz 609 Jehoiakim 609–598
600	Psammaticus II 593–588 Apries (Hophra) 588–569	Prophet Habakkuk Jehoiachin 598–597 Zedekiah 597–587 Prophet Ezekiel Fall of Jerusalem 587 to Chaldean forces, Exile
575	Ah-mose (Amasis) 569–525 Chaldean Invasion Under Nebuchadnezzar 568	Migrations from the Arabian Peninsula Nabatean Settlement
550		Prophet Isaiah II Cyrus's Edict of Return 538 Zerubbabel
525	Persian Invasion Under Cambyses Persian Rule 525–460	Temple Rebuilt 520–515 Prophets Haggai, Zechariah

ASIA MINOR	MESOPOTAMIA	PERSIA
	Esarhaddon 681–669	
Lydians 7th cent.–546	Assurbanipal 669–633? Assyrian Invasion of Egypt 663	
	Assur-etil-ilani 633–629? Sin-shar-ishkun 629?–612 Neo-Babylonian Empire	
	Nabopolassar 626–605 Invaded Assyria → Fall Nineveh 612 →	Cyaxares 625–585 Invaded Assyria
	Nebuchadnezzar 605–562	
	Invasions of Palestine 597, 587	Astyages 585–550
	Invasion of Egypt 568 Amel-marduk 562–560 Neriglissar 560–556 Nabonidus 556–539	←
Lydians Defeated by Cyrus 546 Persians 546–331	Persian Invasion of Chaldea 539 Conquest of Babylon by Cyrus	Achaemenid Empire 550–330 Cyrus 550–530 Cambyses 530–522 Invaded Syria-Palestine, Egypt, Asia Minor
←	Persian Rule	Darius I Hystaspes 522–486

B.C.E.	EGYPT	SYRIA-PALESTINE
500		Settlement of Nabateans in S.E. Palestine c. 500 Prophet Obadiah
475	Rebellion of Inaros 460–454	Prophet Malachi
450		Nehemiah Governor under Persians 445–428? Ezra
425	Egypt Regains Independence 401 XXVII–XXX Dynasties 401–342	Bagoas Governor
400		
375	←	
350	Second Persian Invasion 342 Greek Invasion 332	Greek Invasion 333 Seleucids and Ptolemies Rule 315–200 ← from Greece
325	Ptolemy Rule 323–146 Ptolemy I Logi 323–285 → Conquest of Palestine 315	Battle of Ipsus 301
300	Ptolemy II Philadelphus 285–246	
275		
250	Ptolemy III Energetes 246–221	
225	Ptolemy IV Philopator 221–203 Ptolemy V Epiphanes 203–181	
200	Ptolemy VI Philometor 181–146	Seleucid Conquest 200–198 Seleucid Rule 200–167
175		Maccabean Rebellion 166–160 Jonathan 160–143

ASIA MINOR	MESOPOTAMIA	PERSIA
		Battle of Marathon 490 Xerxes I 486–465 Battles of Thermopylae, Salamis 480
		Artaxerxes I 465–424
		Xerxes II 423 Darius II 423–404 Artaxerxes II 404–358
		Artaxerxes III 358–338
Greek Invasion 334	Macedonian Invasion 331	Arses 337–336 Darius III 335–331 Macedonian Invasion 330 Alexander and Macedonians Rule 330–323
Seleucids 311–100	Seleucids	Seleucids and Parthians 312 B.C.E.–224 C.E. Seleucus I 312–281
Ptolemaic Incursions		
Kingdom of Pergamum Under Attalids		Parthian Dynasty Founded in Khurāsān 250–174
		Struggle with Seleucids
Kingdom of Pergamum in Western Asia Minor Seleucid Power Waning		Mithridates I 174–127 Defeated Babylon

B.C.E.	EGYPT	SYRIA-PALESTINE
150		Simon Maccabeus High Priest and Prince at Jerusalem 143–135 Jewish Independence John Hyrcanus High Priest and Prince 135–105 Antiochus Destroys Jerusalem Walls 133
125	Ptolemy IX c. 117 Alexander I and Cleopatra II 107–	Walls Rebuilt by Hyrcanus Aristobulus 105–104 Alexander Jannaeus 104–78
100	Ptolemy XIII 81– (Auletes)	Six Years' Struggle with Pharisees 88–82
75	Ptolemy XIII Recognized as Consul by Caesar 59	Aristolus II 69–63 Rome: Pompey Conquers Jerusalem 63 Hyrcanus II High Priest and Ethnarch 63–40
50	Pompey Defeated and Killed 48 Library of Alexandria Burned 47 Ptolemy XIII Killed 46 Cleopatra III Reigns with Ptolemy XV Ptolemy XV Killed 45 Octavius Defeats Anthony and Cleopatra 31 Egypt a Roman Province 30	Caesar Appoints Antipater to Rule Judea 47 Herod the Great 40–4 Captures Jerusalem 37
25		Completes Rebuilding of Temple 18
0		

ASIA MINOR	MESOPOTAMIA	PERSIA
Roman Influence	Seleucids Roman Influence	Mithridates I Defeats Seleucids 129
		Mithridates II 124–91 Height of Parthian Power
		Rise of Roman Influence 91–
Roman Conquest 67		
	Parthia Roman Influence	Parthia Roman Influence

B

Religions of the Present

Hinduism

B.C.E. 4000–2500	Indus Valley Civilization
4000–1200	Vedic Period
1200–900	Later *Vedas, Brāhmaṇas,* earlier *Upaniṣads, Āraṇyakas,* and *Mahābhārata.*
900–600	Later *Upaniṣads,* Kapil's *Sāṁkhya Sūtras,* Gautam's *Nyāya Sūtras,* and Kaṇāda's *Vaiśeṣikha-Sūtras.*
600–500	Yāska's *Nirukta,* rise of Ājīvika nihilism, Cārvāk materialism, and the challenge of Mahāvīra and the Buddha.
500–300	Vālmīki's *Rāmāyana, Manu's Law-Book,* Vyāsa's *Gītā,* Vātsyāyana's *Kāmasūtra,* Kauṭilya's *Arthaśāstra,* Baudhayana's *Gṛhasūtra,* and Bādarāyana's *Brahmasūtra.*
300 B.C.E.–200 C.E.	Rise of the Bhāgavata (Nārāyaṇīya, Sātwata, Pañcarātra, Vāsudeva, and so on) and Pāśupata *Bhakti* sects; anthologies of Tamil religious poetry begin.
200 B.C.E.	Jaimini's *Mīmāmsā-sūtras,* composition of *Dharma-Śāstras,* Kātyāyana's treatise on grammar, and Patanjalis *Mahābhāṣya.*
100 B.C.E.–100 C.E.	Śabara Swāmi's *bhāṣya* on Jaimimi's *Sūtra,* composition of *Caraka Saṁhitā,* Akṣapāda's *Nyāya-sūtra;* beginning of the Gāndhāra art, overseas expansion of Hinduism.
300–400	Umāswāmi's (Jaina) *Tattvārthādhigama,* Vātsyāyana's *Bhāṣya* on the *Nyāya-sūtra,* Bharata's treatises on Hindu dance and drama (Bharata-nātyam); Purāṇas take present form.
500	Vaśiṣṭha's Yoga-Vāśiṣṭha; Hindu *Nātya-Śāstra* at its height; rise of Hindu and Buddhist Tantricism.
600	Flourishing of Tamil *Bhakti* movement (Ārvārs *Vaiṣṅavas,* and Nāyanār Śaiva saints).

700	Nālāriya-Divya-Prabandham (Tamil Vaiṣṇava poem) composed, flourishing of Buddhist and *Sākta* Tantricism. Beginning of Vedānta-darśana; Udyotkara and his Nyāya-treatise (*Nyāya-Vārtika*) flourishes.
700–800	Gauḍapāda and his *Māndūkya-Kārikā;* Śankarāchārya and his Bhāsya on the *Barahma-sūtra;* flourishing of the *Advaita-Vedānta.*
800–900	Vācaspati Mishra's *Bhāmatī,* Jayanta's *Nyāya marnjarī,* Haribhadra's (Jaina) *Ṣaṭdarśana-Samuccaya,* Guṇabhadra's *Ātmānuśāsana.*
800–900	*Bhāgavat Purāṇa;* Sundarmūrti (Śaiva Nāyanār of south India); Vāmana and Ānandavardhana (Hindu writers on rhetorics and aesthetics).
800–900	Rise of Hindu orthodoxy: Kumārila's *Ślokavārtika;* Prabhhākara's *Bṛhatī;* Pārthasārathī Mishra's *Vidhiviveka, Tantra-ratna;* Somananda's *Śivadṛṣṭi;* beginning of mediaeval Hindu temples, decline of Buddhism.
1000	Abhinavagupta, the great Kashmiri writer on theology and aesthetics; Nemichandra, his great Jaina text *Dravyasaṅgraha;* Naṁbi Andār's *Tirumurai.*
1000	Utpala's *Pratyabhijñā sūtra.*
1017–1137	Rāmāmuja and the rise of Viśiṣṭhādvaita school of Vedānta (Ramamuja's *Śrībhāṣya, Vedāntāsāra,* and so on), Sekkirar's *Periapurāṇam* (Śaiva text).
1199–1278	Madhva and the rise of the Dvaita School of Vedānta; Madhva's works: *Ṛg-bhāṣya, Karmanirṇaya, Gītābhāṣya, Mahābhārata-tàtparyya-nirṇaya.*
1197–1276	Nimbārkāchārya and the rise of the Bhedābheda School of Vedānta; Nimbārkacharya's works: *Madhvamukha-mardana, Vedānta tattva-bodha, Daśaślokī,* and so on.
1190–1200	Shri Harṣa, the Vedāntic dialectician, and his *Khandana-Khanda-Khādyann;* Gangeśa Bhatta, the Nyāya logician and his *Tattva-Chintāmaṇi.*
1200	Hemachandra, the great Jaina grammarian; Jaideva, the great poet of Rādhā-Kṛṣṇa cult.
1300–1400	Lallā (poetess of Kashmir) Meykaṇḍer's *Śivajñānbodham.*
1400–1500	Visnuswāmim, Vallabhāchāryya, Viṭṭhalswāmin, and the flourishing of the Kṛṣṇa-bhakti movement; important works: *Kṛṣṇa-bhāsya, Subodhinī, Anubhāṣya.*
1485–1533	Chaitanya, the flourishing of the emotional, erotic Kṛṣṇa-bhakti movement, and the Acintyabhedābheda school of Vedānta.
1500–1550	Madhusūdana Saraswatī's *Advaitasiddhi;* Appaya Dikṣita's *Advaita-nirṇaya,* and the rise of Advaitic metaphysics.
1500–1700	The Great Six-Gowswāmins of Vṛndāvana, and systematization of the Vaiṣṇava theology, and aesthetics; important works: *Digdarśanī; Haribhaktivilāsa; Govindavirudāwalī, Bhāgavat Sandarbha,* and *Bhaktirasāmṛtasindhu.*
1500–1600	Kabirdas, his *Sākhīs,* and flourishing of the Nirguṇa-bhakti movement, the Nātha sects, Nāmadeva, Guru Nānak (founder of Sikhism).
1600	Tulasidas, his Ramacharitamānas, and flourishing of the Saguṇa Rāma-bhakti movement.
1500–1600	Mirabai, the Vaiṣṇava poetess; Śankaradeva, Vaiṣṇava poet of Asama; Sūradāsa, the great blind poet of the Kṛṣṇa-bhakti school; Saint Tukarama of Maharastra.
1600–1700	Shrinivas, Krishnadas Kavirāja, Baladeva, Rāmaprasāda, Rādhāballabhadāsa, Kṛshnadāsa, and so on—all of the post-Chaitanya erotic-mysticism of the Bengal-Vaiṣṇavism.
1824–1883	Swami Dayananda Saraswati (founder of Ārya-Samāja).

1836–1886	Shri Paramahamsa Ramkrishna (Vaisṇava saint).
1847–1933	Mrs. Annie Besant (Theosophist).
1861–1941	Rabindranatha Tagore.
1863–1902	Swami Vivekananda (Hindu reformer).
1872–1950	Aurobindo Goṣa (Yogi and nationalist).
1869–1948	Mohanadas Karmachanda Gāndhi (Yogi and politician).
1856–1920	Balgangadhar Tilak (Hindu dharma and Indian politics).
1895	Birth of Āchārya Vinobābhāve (a saint-socialist).

Jainism

B.C.E. 8th century	Pārśva.
477	Nirvāṇa of Mahāvīra.
end of 4th cent.	Bhadrabāhu dies; Council of Pāṭaliputra.
4th–3rd cent.	Oldest texts.
mid 3rd cent.	Nirgranthas and Ājīvikas mentioned in the inscriptions of Aśoka, grandson of Chandragupta Maurya.
3rd–2nd cent.	Aśoka's grandson Samprati promotes the spread of Jainism in the Telugu and Tamil countries.
2nd cent.	Mathurā inscriptions.
mid 2nd cent.	Inscription of king Khāravela of Kaliṅga (Orissa).
56	Favored by the Jainas as Year 1 of the Vikrama era.
C.E. 1st cent.	Earliest scholastic works in Prakrit.
1st–2nd cent.	Division of the Digambaras and the Śvetāmbaras (schism in 80 or 83).
2nd–3rd cent.	Kundakunda and Umāsvāti, Digambara and Śvetāmbara dogmatists.
up to 7th cent.	Prakrit scholasticism of the Śvetāmbaras flourishes. Gradual spread of Jainism to western India.
503	Council of Valabhī (980 or 993 after Mahāvīra).
about 527	Defeat of Mihirakula, the persecutor of the Jainas and others.
7th–9th cent.	Digambara scholasticism flourishes in the Deccan and in South India.
815–877	Rāstrakūta King Amoghavasa I, patron and poet.
10th–11th cent.	King Muñja of Mālava (974–995) and king Bhoja of Dhārā (1010–1055) in central India.
about 980	Image of Bāhubali at the Digambara center of Śravana-Belgola in Mysore.
late 10th cent.	Beginning of the decline in the south.

1032	Completion of the oldest temple at Dilwara (Delvāḍā) in Abu in Rajputana.
1088–1163	Śvetāmbara polyhistor Hemacandra at the court of King Kumārapāla (1144–1173) of Gujarat.
mid 12th cent.	Abhayadeva and Malayagir, Śvetāmbara scholiasts.
1177	Oldest temple at Girnar in Kathiawar.
end of 12th cent.	Muslim conquests. Some Jains convert to Islam.
about 1300	Merutuṅga's Bhaktāmarastotra, famous Śvetāmbara hymn.
1453 or 1474	Lunkājī Mohta (Lonka Shah, Lumpāka), Śvetāmbara reformer.
16th cent., latter half	Renovation of Śatruñjaya, the Śvetāmbara temple town near Pālitānā in Kathiawar.
16th cent., end	Hīravijaya and other Śvetāmbaras at the court of Emperor Akbar (1556–1605).
1624–1688	Yaśovijaya, prolific Śvetāmbara author.
1654	The Sthānakavāsi or Ḍhuṇḍiyā, a Śvetāmbara reform movement led by Lavajī.
about 1760	The Terāpanth of Bhīkhanjī Svāmin (1727–1804) founded.
1837–1897	Vijāyānanda Sūri (Ātmārāmjī).
1868–1922	Vijayendharma Sūri.
1881	Vijayendra Sūri born.
1893	All-India Digambara Conference.
1903	The *Jain Gazette* (succeeded by the *Voice of Ahimsa,* 1951).
1906	First All-India Sthānakavāsī Jain Conference.
1910	All-India Jain Association.
1913–1925	The Abhidhānarajendra, a Śvetāmbara encyclopedia by Vijayarājendra (1827–1907).
1949	Jain World Mission founded.

Sikhism

1469 C.E.	Guru Nanak's birth.
1539	Nanak crystallizes his position, combining elements from both Islam and Hinduism. Nanak's death.
1552	Angad, first successor to Nanak, dies. Amar Das separates Sikhs from Udasis.
1581	Arjun becomes leader; makes Amritsar holy city; compiles the *Adi Granth.*
1606	Sikh missionary activity. Har Gobind becomes guru and arms the Sikh people for military action. Total separation of Sikhs from Hindus.
1645	Death of Har Gobind; self-sacrifice of his disciples on his pyre.

1695 Gobind Singh teaches military combat of Islam; founds the Khālsā, Pahul. Doctrine of the unshorn locks, devotion to arms, title of *"singh."*

1701 Gobind Singh composes *Vichitr Natak.*

1708 Death of Gobind Singh in South India, where he took refuge.

1752 Sikhs defeated by Aḥmad Shāh Abdālī.

1755 Taymūr expels Sikhs from Amritsar.

1761 Muslim victory over Marathas at Panipat.

1764 Sikhs become masters of Lahore. Sikhs form political system, *Gurumattas* ("assemblies"), and achieve independence.

1707–1774 Sikh ascendancy in Punjab, Kashmir, Multan.

1783 Sikhs defeated at Meerut.

1802 Sikh leader Ranjit Singh forms alliance with British.

1804 Sikhs fight with British against Hindus and Muslims.

1823 Sikhs march against Peshawar and reduce it to submission.

1832 Ranjit Singh yields to British economic and political ascendancy.

1839 Death of Ranjit Singh.

1845 Worsening of Sikh-British relations.

1846 Battles with the British and final defeat of Sikhs. Establishment of British hegemony in all fields in northwest India.

China

B.C.E. ca. 2000 to ca. 1520	Hsia kingdom (legendary?)	
ca. 1520 to ca. 1030	Shang (Yin) kingdom	
ca. 1030 to 722	Chou dynasty (Feudal Age)	Early Chou period
722 to 480		Spring and Autumn period
480 to 221	Birth of Confucius 551 B.C.E.	Warring States period. Birth of Mencius 371 B.C.E. Chuang Tzu (ca. 369–ca. 286 B.C.E.)
221 to 206	First Unification	Ch'in dynasty
202 to C.E. 9	Han dynasty	Former Han
9 to 23		Hsin interregnum. Importation of Indian Buddhism by 1st century C.E.
25 to 220		Later Han. Origin of Taoist religion (143 C.E.)
220 to 265		Three Kingdoms period

First Partition	Shu (Han)	221 to 264
	Wei	220 to 265
	Wu	222 to 280

265 to 317	Second Unification	Chin dynasty: Western
317 to 420		Eastern. Kumārajīva's arrival in Ch'angan (401 C.E.)
420 to 479		(Liu) Sung dynasty. 1st persecution of Buddhism (446 C.E.)
	Second Partition	Northern and Southern dynasties (Six Dynasties)
479 to 502		Ch'i dynasty
502 to 557		Liang dynasty
557 to 587		Ch'en dynasty
386 to 535		Northern (Thopa) Wei dynasty
535 to 554		Western (Thopa) Wei dynasty
534 to 543		Eastern (Thopa) Wei dynasty
550 to 577		Northern Ch'i dynasty
557 to 581		Northern Chou (Hsienpi) dynasty
581 to 618	Third Unification	Sui dynasty
618 to 907		T'ang dynasty. Hsüan-tsang's Western Journey to India (629–645 C.E.)
907 to 960	Third Partition	Wu Tai (Five Dynasty period): Later Liang Later T'ang (Turkic), Later Chin (Turkic) Later Han (Turkic and Later Chou)
907 to 1125		Liao (Chhitan Tartar) dynasty. 4th persecution of Buddhism (955 C.E.)
1144 to 1211		West Liao dynasty (Qarā-Khiṭāi)
990 to 1227		Hsi Hsia (Tangut Tibetan) state
960 to 1126	Fourth Unification	Northern Sung dynasty
1127 to 1279		Southern Sung dynasty. Chu Hsi's Neo-Confucian synthesis (1130–1200 C.E.)
1115 to 1234		Chin (Jurchen Tartar) dynasty
1260 to 1368		Yuan (Mongol) dynasty
1368 to 1644		Ming dynasty. Wang Yang-ming (1473–1529 C.E.)
1644 to 1911		Ch'ing (Manchu) dynasty
1912		Republic of China
1949		People's Republic of China Maoist purge of the Three Teachings since 1949

Japan

Jomon Period (5th or 4th millenium to ca. 250 B.C.E.)

Yayoi Period (c. 250 B.C.E. to 250 C.E.): blending of Melanesian, Austro-Asian, Austronesian, and northeast Asian cultures. Wet-rice cultivation and metals introduced.

538 to 552 Introduction of Buddhism.

593 Prince Shōtoku becomes regent.

594 Buddhism proclaimed the state religion.

604 Seventeen-Article Constitution.

666 Hossō school introduced in Japan.

701 First Confucian festival celebrated in Japan.

710 Capital established at Nara.

712 *Kojiki* completed.

713 *Fudoki* (topographical records with legendary materials) commenced.

720 *Nihonshoki* (*Nihongi*) completed.

745 Gyōgi appointed archbishop.

752 Dedication of Great Buddha Statue at Tōdai-ji, Nara.

794 Heian-kyō (Kyōto) becomes capital.

797 *Shoku-Nihongi* (Chronicle of Japan, Continued) completed.

805 Saichō founds Tendai school.

806 Kūkai founds Shingon school.

909 Shōbō, systematizer of Mountain Priesthood (*Shugen-do*), dies.

927 *Engishiki* (court rituals and prayers of the Engi period) compiled.

972 Death of Kūya, popularizer of devotion to Amida.

1175 Hōnen founds Pure Land sect.

1215 Death of Eisai, transmitter of Rinzai Zen.

1224 Shinran (1173–1262) founds True Pure Land Buddhism.

1227 Dōgen (1200–1253) transmits Sōtō Zen to Japan.

1253 Nichiren (1222–1282) founds the Nichiren sect.

1338–1573 Muromachi or Ashikaga period.

1339 Publication of *Records of the Legitimate Succession of the Divine Sovereigns* by Kitabatake Chikafusa.

1549 St. Francis Xavier arrives in Japan.

1603 Tokugawa Period begins: influence of Confucianism. Buddhism becomes instrument of government policy.

1622 The "Great Kirishitan Martyrdom" of Nagasaki.

1744 Ishida Baigan, founder of the Shingaku movement, dies.

1798 Motoori Norinaga (1730–1801) completes his *Commentary on the Kojiki,* a landmark in the Shinto renaissance.

1868 Meiji restoration. Capital moved to Tokyo.

1868–1871 The persecution of Buddhism.

1871 Shinto brought under government control.

1872 National priesthood established.

1899 Department of Education forbids teaching of religion in public schools.

1939 Religious Bodies Law gives Department of Education complete control of all religious sects.

1945 Disestablishment of State Shinto; Growth of New Religions.

Zoroastrianism

B.C.E. 837	Parsua and Amadai mentioned in cuneiform inscriptions, beginning with Shalmaneser III chronicles.
824–812	Campaigns into Persia under Assyrian monarchs Shamsu–Adad IV.
810–745	More campaigns into Persia under Adad-Nirari III and Tiglath-Pileser III.
722	Upon fall of the northern kingdom of Israel, Israeli aristocracy transplanted to Media.
708	Empire of the Medes founded by Deioces.
655	Phraortes.
633	Cyaxares. Invasion by the Scythians. Unrest among the Persian tribes.
628	Birth of Zoroaster in Chorasmia.
615	End of Scythian invasion.
585	Peace between Medes and Lydians.
558	Cyrus succeeds his father Kambujiya as king of Anshan.
553	Cyrus rebels against Astyages.
551	Death of Zoroaster.
550	Defeat of Astyages and fall of Ecbatana to Cyrus.
546	Cyrus assumes kingship over all Persia and attacks the Greeks. Spread of Zoroastrianism.
538	Fall of Babylon. Cyrus crowned King of Babylon.
528	Cambyses.
525	Conquest of Egypt.
521	Darius I.
508	First Athenian embassy.
465	Xerxes assassinated. Artaxerxes I.
455	Revolt in Egypt.
424	Xerxes II.
404	Artaxerxes II.
380	Campaign in Cyprus.
358	Artaxerxes III.
345	Persian reconquest of Egypt.
335	Darius III in Persia. Alexander in Greece.
327	Alexander in India.
323	Death of Alexander.

322–224 C.E.	The Parthian Arsacids.
312	The Seleucids.
250	Arsaces founds the Parthian Dynasty.
123	Peace with Hadrian.
199	Pillage of Ctesiphon under Septimius.
205	Birth of Mani in Ecbatana (Hamadan) in a Parthian royal family.
224–651	The Sāsāni Empire.
224	Revolt of Ardashir I against Tiridates, Priest-King of Persepolis.
226	Ardashir I enters Ctesiphon in triumph.
241	Sabur I (Sapor). *Avesta* collected and canonized. Zoroastrianism becomes official state religion without excluding other religions. Mani assumes role as prophet within Zoroastrianism and begins to preach reform.
242	Sabur I converts to Manichaeanism and the new reformed religion spreads.
252	Sabur I reconverts to Zoroastrianism and Mani flees into exile in India.
272	Hormuz I.
273	Bahram I. Mani returns from India to resume call to reform.
274	Bahram I converts to Manichaeanism.
275	Bahram I reconverts to Zoroastrianism and condemns Mani to death.
276	Mani executed at Gundaysabur.
421	Peace with the Romans.
488	Kobad.
497	Jamasp. Kobad.
570	Invasion of Yaman.
579	Hormazd IV.
590	Chosroes (Khusraw) II.
614	Capture of Jerusalem by the Persians.
624	The Romans recover Asia Minor and Armenia.
625	The Romans recover Jerusalem.
630	Delegation of Muslims visits Chosroes II and invites him to Islām.
632	Yazdigird III.
635	Battle of Qādisiyyah. Fall of Ctesiphon (Madā'in) to Muslim hands.
642	Battle of Nahāwand, last stand of Persian forces against Muslim forces.
651	Murder of Yazdigird III by his generals and end of Persian Empire.

Theravāda Buddhism

The chronology of Buddhism, as of Hinduism, has never been exact because of traditional Indian aversion to historiography. Although scholars disagree among themselves on the interpretation of the historical evidence (internal criticism and scant archaeological data), the various schools and sects of Buddhism construct their own chronologies. Following is a chronology of Buddhism according to the Theravāda tradition compiled by the editor from *2500 Years of Buddhism*, ed. P. V. Bapat. Delhi: Ministry of Information, 1956.

536 B.C.E.	Birth of the Buddha.
529	The Buddha abandons all and retires into the forest. Mahavira dies. (477 according to the Jains).
519	The Buddha's sermon at Benares.
476	Death of the Buddha.
473	First Congress of Buddha's followers.
363	Second Congress of Buddha's followers at Vaisali.
274	Launching of Buddhist missions. Asoka ascends to the throne of India.
253	Mahendra's Buddhist mission to Ceylon.
236	Aśoka dies. Beginning of Mahāyāna Buddhist tradition.
160	Preparation of Prajñā pāramitā.
80	Preparation of the *Mahāyāna Sutra:* Lotus of the Good Law. Buddhism begins its decline in India.
78–100 C.E.	Kanishka's struggle to save Buddhism in northern India.
160	Nāgārjuna.
220	First Buddhist missions in Vietnam.
372–290	First Buddhist missions in China and Korea.
399–414	Fa Hsien journey to India.
310	Buddha's tooth relic brought to Ceylon (Kandy) from India.
420–452	Foundation of Nalanda by Kumara-Gupta. First Buddhist missions to Burma, Java, Sumatra.
430	Buddhaghosha and Fa Hsien visit Ceylon (402 C.E. in Burmese sources).
552	First Buddhist missions in Japan. Crisis of Buddhism in Cambodia at the hands of Hinduism.
572	Shotoku Taishi promotes Buddhism in Japan.
610	Buddhism proclaimed state religion in Japan.
650	First Buddhist Temple in Tibet.
720	First Buddhist Missions to Siam.

749	First monastery in Tibet: Padina-sambhava.
c.800	Buddhism elbows out Hinduism in Kashmir. Mahāyāna grows in Cambodia. Islām supplants Buddhism in central Asia and Sind.
1065	Indian invasions of Ceylon and weakness of Buddhist orders.
1320	Decline of Mahāyāna and growth of Hinayana in Cambodia.
1340	Buddhism envelops Laos.
1360	Buddhism proclaimed state religion in Siam. Ordination in Ceylon of Burmese Bhikkhus.
1480	Hinduism replaces Buddhism in Java; Islām replaces Buddhism in Sumatra.
1656	Dutch replace Portuguese in Ceylon.
1750	Thai delegation of Bikkhus ordained at Kandy by Saranam Kara.
1753	Siamese sect started in Ceylon.
1796	British replace Dutch.
1801–1810	Amarapura and Ramanya sects in Ceylon started.
1848–1871	Mandalay Council corrects the text of the Tipiṭaka.
1880	Revival of Buddhism.
1956	2500th anniversary of the Buddha's enlightenment.

Christianity

29 or 30 A.D.	Death of Jesus of Nazareth and preaching by his followers of his resurrection from the dead.
Ca. 37	Paul's flight from Damascus, driven from the city by the ethnarch of King Aretas IV of Nabatea.
Between 41 and 44	Herod Agrippa I executes James the son of Zebedee.
Ca. 44	Peter leaves Jerusalem for coastal cities of Palestine, as first recorded "missionary" of the Twelve.
45–46 or 47–48	Evangelization of South Galatia (Acts 13-14).
49	Paul in Galatia and Macedonia.
50	Paul arrives at Corinth.
51	Paul in Athens.
54	Paul arrives in Ephesus.
56	Paul arrives in Jerusalem.
61–63	Paul imprisoned in Rome.
Ca. 110	Martyrdom of Ignatius of Antioch in Rome.
110–135	Polycarp to the Philippians.

Ca. 140	Ariston of Pella composes what is probably the first literary apology for Christianity in its struggle with Judaism.
Ca. 140	Death of Papias, bishop of Hierapolis.
140–145	Valentinus writes *Gospel of Truth* (Gnostic).
Ca. 150	Latin becomes common language of Christian communities in the West.
Ca. 150	Justin writes his *Apology.*
177	Martyrdoms of Lyons and Vienna.
180	*Passio Martyrum,* oldest Latin Christian document that can be dated with certainty; North Africa.
Ca. 200	Tertullian's *De Praescriptione Haereticorum* shows that Apostolic communities are older than the heresies.
232	Origen founds adult catechetical school at Caesarea in Palestine.
235	Death of Hippolytus, author of *Apostolic Tradition.*
325	First Council of Nicaea (I ecumenical council); Arianism condemned.
Ca. 325	Eusebius, bishop of Caesarea in Palestine, writes his documented *History of the Church.*
330	Macarius of Egypt retires to desert.
335	Church of Holy Sepulchre built in Jerusalem by Constantine.
336	Death of Arius.
345	Death of Aphraates, earliest Syrian Church father ("the Persian sage").
346	Death of Pachomius, the hermit.
361–363	Unsuccessful attempt of Emperor Julian ("the Apostate") to restore Roman state religion.
373	St. Ephraem, Syrian hymn writer ("Lyre of the Holy Spirit") and Church father, dies.
381	First Council of Constantinople (II). Creed of Nicaea reaffirmed; Macedonianism (denying divinity of the Holy Spirit) and Apollinarianism (affirming that the *Logos* took the place of the human soul in Christ) condemned.
Ca. 390	Death of Apollinaris of Laodicea, friend of Athanasius and opponent of Arianism; influential in the history of Christology.
400	Death of St. Martin, bishop of Tours.
404	Jerome translates Rule of Pachomius.
420	Death of Jerome, translator of Bible from Hebrew and Greek into Latin (*"versio Vulgata"*), ca. 385–406.
428	Death of Theodore of Mopsuestia.
431	Council of Ephesus (III). Nestorianism (affirming total separation of two natures and persons in Christ) and Pelagianism (teaching man's capacity for good and evil at birth apart from God's grace) condemned. Mary declared "God-bearer" and not merely "Christ-bearer."
430–435	Death of John Cassian, promoter of spread of monasticism in the West.
451	Council of Chalcedon (IV). Christological faith affirmed, following the *Tomus* ("Book") of Pope Leo I, against Apollinarianism and Nestorianism, but in particular Eutychianism (which taught a single nature, human and divine, after the incarnation). Condemnation of Dioscorus, Bishop of Alexandria and separation of the Coptic Church.

486 Sabas of Cappadocia founds Monastery of Mar Saba in the Valley of the Kidron, Judaea.

Ca. 547 Death of Benedict of Nursia, patriarch of Western monasticism.

553 Second council of Constantinople (V). Condemned the Christological writings of Theodore of Mopsuestia, Theodoret of Cyrus, and Ibas of Edessa as Nestorian or semi-Nestorian.

597 Ethelbert baptized at Kent.

604 Death of Pope Gregory I, who laid foundations of medieval papacy that was to govern the Western world after the 6th century.

649 Death of John Climacus, hermit, at Mt. Sinai.

680–681 Third Council of Constantinople (VI and last acknowledged as ecumenical by Anglican communion). Condemned monothelitism and monergism (teaching one will and operation in Christ, not two).

787 Second Council of Nicaea (VII and last ecumenical council acknowledged as ecumenical by the Eastern Orthodox churches). Defended the legitimacy of images of Christ and Mary and the other saints against the iconoclast party.

813 Emperor Leo V revives iconoclasm, the struggle against sacred images.

869–870 Fourth Council of Constantinople (VIII, as acknowledged by the Church of Rome). Declared Photius, patriarch of Constantinople, whom the emperor had put in the place of the deposed Ignatius, to be in heresy and schism.

1053 Following Photian schism of 1024, worsening and breach of relations between the Church of Rome and the Church of Constantinople. Reciprocal charges and condemnation.

1085 Death of Lanfranc of Pavia, teacher at Bec, Archbishop of Canterbury.

1096 Crusade of Peter the Hermit.

1099 (July 29) Death of Pope Urban before knowing that Crusaders had taken Jerusalem.

1123 First Lateran Council (IX). On the investiture of prelates by royalty.

1141 Death of Hugh, most famous of canons of St. Victor in Paris.

1139 Second Lateran Council (X). Against false claimants to the papacy and on points of discipline.

1142 Death of Peter Abelard, logician and religious thinker.

1153 Death of St. Bernard of Clairvaux, "second founder" of Order of Citeaux ("Cistercians").

1160–1164 Death of Peter the Lombard, author of *Libri IV Sententiarum,* most widely used medieval textbook in theology.

1176 Carthusian order established.

1179 Third Lateran Council (XI). Against followers of Peter Waldo ("Waldensians") and Albigenses, the former poor men of evangelical life and the latter spirit-matter dualists denying legitimacy of sex and marriage.

1214 Pope Innocent III accepts the vassalage of John ("Lackland"), King of England.

1215 Fourth Lateran Council (XII). Similar condemnations as in Third Lateran; legislated annual reception of the Eucharist during the Easter season.

1215–1218 Meeting of St. Francis and St. Dominic.

1221 Death of St. Dominic.

1245	First Council of Lyons (XIII). Against claims of Frederick II.
1274	Second Council of Lyons (XIV). Reunion with Greek Church sought.
1274	Death of St. Thomas Aquinas.
1292–1294	Death of Roger Bacon, Franciscan scholar and scientist.
1300	Boniface VIII declares first jubilee year of pilgrimage to celebrate the centennial of Christ's birth; awards pilgrims plenary indulgence of temporal punishment due to sin.
1311–1312	Council of Vienne (XV). Abolition of Knights Templars; condemnation of various heresies.
1315	Brethren and Sisters of the Free Spirit appear in Swabia, Switzerland, the Netherlands, and Italy.
1384	Death of John Wyclif, Oxford professor, reformer, translator of Bible, preacher.
1414–1418	Council of Constance (XVI). Condemnation of Wyclif and Hus.
1420–1431	Hussite Crusade, proclaimed by Sigismund.
1438–1445	Council of Florence (XVII). Renewed attempt at reunion with the Greek Church.
1512–1517	Fifth Lateran Council (XVIII). Reform of the Church.
1517	Luther's *Ninety-five Theses* posted at Wittenberg and Telzel's *Counter Theses.*
1517	Death of Cardinal Ximenes, humanist reformer, framer of *Complutensian Polyglot Bible.*
1521–1522	(May to March) Luther detained in Wartburg Castle.
1523	Zwingli defends his *Sixty-seven Articles* in public debate in Zurich.
1525	(May–June) Luther's conflict with peasants in revolt.
1526	Capuchins, as renewed form of the Franciscans, established by Matteo di Bascio.
1535	Aristrian edicts issued against Anabaptists.
1539	Henry VIII's *Six Articles of Religion.*
1541	Francis Xavier (1506–1552) sails for India.
1545–1563	Council of Trent (XIX). Moves at counter-Reformation through teaching on canon of the Bible, grace, free will, justification, the sacraments; reform of liturgical books; institution of seminaries.
1547	Calvinistic Ordinances for the Supervision of the Churches effective in Geneva.
1549	Xavier reaches Japan.
1551	Death of Martin Bucer, reformer.
1552	Death of Xavier.
1559	English Act of Uniformity.
1562	Catholics procure January edict to deprive the Huguenots of their places of worship.
1585	Jesuits expelled from England.
1593	Martyrdom of John Greenwood and Henry Barrow for organizing separatist (i.e., from Church of England) meetings in London.

1594 Death of Giovanni da Palestrina, whose *Missa Papal Marcelli* in 1565 set a pattern that was officially adopted as the "true form" of ecclesiastical music.

1600 Death of Richard Hooker, Anglican divine.

1604 Geneva Bible. Theodore Beza publishes his popular edition of the Greek Testament, with Latin version.

1623 Bishop Josaphat Kunsevitch, Ukrainian in communion with Rome, murdered in a popular uprising (later canonized).

1647 Westminster Shorter Catechism.

1648 "Cambridge Platform" reaffirming the congregational principle in New England Puritanism.

1649 Society for the Propagation of the Gospel in New England.

1655 Revised manual of Russian Church services issued and approved by a Church council.

1655 Massacre of Waldenses, Piedmont.

1689 Toleration Act, William and Mary, in England.

1690 Death of John Eliot, American missionary, who translated the Bible into Mohican.

1699 Society for Promoting Christian Knowledge founded.

1701 Society for the Propagation of the Gospel in Foreign Parts founded.

1705 First German Pietist missionary goes out to Tranquebar.

1705 Danish-Halle Mission founded.

1732 Moravian Missions, first mission attempts of this church, to St. Thomas and Greenland.

1738 John Wesley's Aldersgate Experience.

1739–1741, 1744–1748 George Whitfield preaches in America.

1754 Death of Christian Wolff, rationalistic theologian.

1759 Jesuits expelled from Portugal.

1760 Death of Count Nicholas von Zinzendorf, German Pietist.

1767 Jesuits expelled from Spain and France.

1768 Death of Herman S. Reimarus, father of literary criticism of New Testament.

1773 Jesuits dissolved by papacy.

1774 First Unitarian Church, London.

1784 Coke ordained a bishop by John Wesley.

1790 (November 27) Decree requiring clerical oath in France.

1792 Particular Baptist Society for the Propagation of the Gospel founded.

1795 London Missionary Society founded.

1798 Netherlands Missionary Society founded.

1798 Death of Christian Friedrich Schwarz, most noted of 18th-century missionaries from Halle.

1799 Religious Tract Society founded.

1799 Church Missionary Society (Anglican) founded.

1804 British and Foreign Bible Society founded.

1809 Entire Bible translated into Bengali by William Carey (d. 1834), Baptist.

1810 American Board of Commissioners for Foreign Missions founded.

1817 United Evangelical Church, Germany.

1817–1818 Wesleyan Methodist Missionary Society.

1817 United Foreign Mission Society founded.

1826 United Foreign Missionary Society merges with American Board.

1831 Belgian Constitution guarantees freedom of religion.

1831 Death of Hegel.

1833 Declaration of Faith of the Congregational Union of England and Wales.

1834 Death of Schleiermacher.

1834 Adoniram Judson, Baptist, translates entire Bible into Burmese.

1842 Death of William Ellery Channing, U.S. leader of Unitarians.

1844 YMCA founded by Sir George Williams.

1845 John Henry Newman joins Roman Catholic Church.

1846 Evangelical Alliance founded.

1854 Pope Pius IX teaches the Immaculate (i.e., sinless) Conception of Mary by her mother in virtue of foreseen merits of her Son.

1869–70 First Vatican Council (XX). Decrees on the nature of faith and papal infallibility when teaching emanates "from the chair," i.e., is of set purpose, meant to take its force from the papal office.

1855 Death of Soren Kierkegaard.

1859 Charles Darwin's *Origin of Species.*

1863 Ernest Renan's *Life of Jesus.*

1867 Evangelical Alliance, American Branch, founded.

Ca. 1870 Birth of "social gospel."

1871 Papal States lost to Italian nationalists.

1872–1875 Bismarck's *Kulturkampf* in Germany, anti-Catholic laws.

1889 Christian Social Union founded, England.

1889 Death of Albert Ritschl.

1890 Death of John Henry, Cardinal, Newman.

1894 World's YWCA founded.

1895 World Student Christian Federation founded.

1895 Bible Conference at Niagara Falls, which set up the five "fundamentals" of American Protestantism.

1902 Leo XIII establishes a Biblical Commission to control Biblical dissidents.

1910 World Missionary Conference.

1910 Death of Mary Baker Eddy, founder of Christian Science.

1910 World Missionary Conference, Edinburgh.

1912 Death of William Booth, founder of the Salvation Army.

1918 Death of Walter Rauschenbusch, American social moralist.

1921 International Missionary Council organized.

1923 Death of Ernest Troeltsch, religious social theorist.

1925 Scopes trial, Dayton, Tennessee, over Darwin's theory of evolution.

1925 Life and Work Conference, Stockholm.

1927 Faith and Order Conference, Lausanne.

1931 *Non abbiamo bisogno*—Pope Pius XI denounces Mussolini for breaking his treaty and for curtailing "Catholic Action" in Italy.

1937 *Mit brennender Sorge*—Pope Pius XI denounces Nazism as a way of life alien to Catholicism.

1937 Faith and Order, Edinburgh.

1937 Life and Work, Oxford.

1938 Provisional Committee, World Council of Churches, Utrecht.

1944 Evangelical Alliance, American branch, dissolved.

1945 (October 19) Stuttgart Declaration by surviving leaders of Confessing Church.

1951 World Evangelical Fellowship established.

1955 Death of John R. Mott, architect of the modern ecumenical movement.

1960 Baptist World Alliance on Religious Liberty.

1962–1965 Second Vatican Council (XXI). Pastoral and liturgical reforms, including new rites for all the sacraments and the use of living languages in the liturgy.

Islām

570 Year of the Elephant, Birth of the Prophet in Makkah.

595 Marriage of Muḥammad to Khadījah.

610 First revelation of verses from the Qur'ān. Conversion of Khadījah, Abū Bakr, and 'Alī.

614 First migration of Muslims to Abyssinia.

615 Conversion of 'Umar.

617 Death of Khadījah.

621 Isrā' and Mi'rāj. Muḥammad's night journey to Jerusalem. First 'Aqabah covenant. Conversion of some people of Yathrib.

622 Second 'Aqabah covenant. Emigration of the Prophet to Yathrib, henceforth called *Madīnah al Nabiyy* ("City of the Prophet"). The Covenant of Madīnah: constitution of the first Islāmic state.

624 Battle of Badr, first Muslim military victory.

625 Battle of Uḥud, first Muslim military defeat.

626 Battle of the Ditch, ending with withdrawal of Makkan forces and exposure of Jewish traitors within Madīnah.

628 Ḥudaybiyah Pact with Makkah.

630 Conquest of Makkah.

632 Farewell pilgrimage. Death of the Prophet.

632–659 The Rāshidūn Caliphs:
632–634 Abū Bakr, First Caliph
634–644 'Umar, Second Caliph
644–656 'Uthmān, Third Caliph
656–659 'Alī, Fourth Caliph

632–634 Arabia unites itself.

634–635 Conquest of Jordan, Palestine, Syria, Lebanon, Persia.

641–643 Conquest of Egypt, Libya, Carthage, Nubia.

645 Building of Muslim fleet at Egyptian and Syrian bases.

652 Conquest of northeast Persia. Death of Abū Dharr al Ghifārī, first ascetic in Islām.

657 Al Rāsibī secedes from 'Alī's camp and founds al Khawārij.

659 'Alī defeats the Khawārij at Nahrawān.

661 'Alī assassinated by the Khārijī, Ibn Muljam.

670 Conquest of Algeria and Morocco.

698–699 Khawārīj practically destroyed.

c. 700 Ibn Ibāḍ founds Ibāḍiyyah sect.

705–715 Conquest of Central Asia, Sind, Spain.

716–717 Unsuccessful siege of Constantinople.

724 Muslims begin conquest of France.

728 Death of al Ḥasan al Basṛī, ascetic teacher.

730	Zaydiyyah sect established in Yaman by Zayd.
732	Muslim advance checked at Poitiers.
734	Muslims conquest of western Switzerland.
747–750	'Abbāsī revolution and Umawī downfall.
776	Abū Hāshim al Kūfī, first Muslim ascetic to wear ṣūf ("wool") and be called a Ṣūfī.
801	Rābi'ah al 'Adawiyyah, poetess and mystic.
827	Muslim attack on Oye and Brittany.
830	Founding of Bayt al Ḥikmah in Baghdād by al Ma'mūn.
838	Al Ḥārith ibn Asad al Muḥāsibī, author of the first complete treatise on Ṣūfīsm.
849	Mālikī jurisprudence promulgated in Spain and North Africa.
861	Dhū al Nūn al Miṣrī, integrator of Gnosticism with Ṣūfīsm, dies.
874	Al Qaddāḥ institutes Shī'ah leadership first at Baṣrah and then at Salamiyyah. Nuṣayriyyah sect founded by Muḥammad ibn Nuṣayr.
875	Abū Yazīd al Bisṭāmī, integrator of Indian mysticism with Ṣūfīsm, dies.
909	Fāṭimī rule founded in North Africa by 'Ubayd Allah al Mahdī.
910	Junayd al Baghdādī, first Ṣūfī interpretor of the Qur'ān, dies.
910–958	Fāṭimīs take most of northwest Africa and begin drive eastward.
922	Manṣur al Ḥallāj, first vagrant Ṣūfī to be executed.
935–939	Attack and conquest of Geneva.
969	Fāṭimīs take over Egypt, found al Qāhirah (Cairo) as capital, and march on Syria.
972	Founding of al Azhar University at al Qāhirah.
975	Fāṭimīs take over Yaman.
1021–1035	Fāṭimīs lose North Africa.
1043	Fāṭimīs lose all empire but Egypt.
1071	Normans seize Sicily.
1077–1166	'Abd al Qādir al Jīlī (al Jīlānī), founder of first Ṣūfī brotherhood.
1111	Abū Ḥāmid al Ghazālī, reconciler of Ṣūfīsm with Islāmic orthodoxy, dies.
1175	Aḥmad al Rifā'ī, founder of the Rifā'iyyah Ṣūfī brotherhood, dies.
1258	'Alī al Shādhilī, founder of the Shādhiliyyah Ṣūfī brotherhood, dies.
1273	Jalāl al Dīn al Rūmī, founder of the Mawlawiyyah Ṣūfī brotherhood, dies.
1276	Aḥmad al Badawī, founder of the Badawiyyah Ṣūfī brotherhood, dies.
1500	Foundation of the Bektāshī Ṣūfī brotherhood.

Modern Islām

1703 Birth of two greatest reformers of modern times: Muḥammad ibn 'Abd al Wahhāb at 'Uyaynah (Arabia) and Shāh Waliyyullah at Delhi.

1728 Return to Dar'iyyah (Arabia) of Muḥammad ibn 'Abd al Wahhāb from a tour of Muslim countries and his launching of anti-Ṣūfī revivalist reform.

1729 Accord of Ibn 'Abd al Wahhāb with Muhammad ibn Su'ūd, Amīr of Dar'iyyah, to found the Wahhābiyyah movement.

1730–31 Spread of Wahhābī doctrines in Najd, Kuwait, Ḥijāz, especially among pilgrims.

1732 Pilgrimage of Shāh Waliyyullah of Delhi to Makkah, and his dream that God wanted him to lead a reform movement and regenerate the *ummah.*

1736 Foundation of the Ikhwān, first collective settlements, in East and Central Arabia, on the basis of revitalized Islam and cooperative agriculture.

1750 The Dutch gain foothold in Java.

1760 Shāh Waliyyullah of Delhi (1703–1762) advises Najīb al Dawlah, Moghul Premier of India, to invite Prince Aḥmad Shāh Abdālī of Afghanistan to join in the war against the Hindu Marathas.

1761 Aḥmad Shāh Abdālī's victory over the Marathas at Panipat (India).

1774 'Uthmān dan Fodio's preaching tour in Kebbi, West Africa.

1784 English occupy Penang Island (Malaysia).

1785 Muslim revolt against Chinese Emperor led by Shi San, a Muslim.

1786 'Uthmān dan Fodio begins 5-year mission in West Africa.

1786–91 Thai invasion of Muslim Patani Kingdom on their southern frontier.

1788 First life of the Prophet published in Chinese.

1796 'Abd al Qādir, almami of Futa Toro, attacks Kajor, West Africa. Khasonke chief embraces Islām.

1802 Wahhābīs capture Karbalā' ('Irāq), Shī'ah pilgrimage center.

1803 Declaration of war by Shā 'Abd al 'Azīz of Delhi against Britain. Wahhābīs capture Makkah and Madīnah. Wahhābiyyah movement reaches Indonesia and most other Muslim countries through pilgrims returning from Makkah.

1804 Hijrah of dan Fodio from Degel to Gudu, West Africa.

1809 Foundation of Sokoto which led to the conversion of the Hausa tribes to Islām.

1810 Jihād (holy war) of Shaykh Ḥamad in Masina, West Africa.

1813 Egyptian army, acting as proxy for the Ottoman Empire, suppresses the Wahhābiyyah in the Ḥijāz but fails to defeat it. Wahhābī resurgence and destruction of Egyptian army.

1818 Egyptian second military expedition to Arabia. Defeat of the Wahhābīs and occupation of their capital, Dar'iyyah. Exile of 'Abdullah, son of Muḥammad ibn 'Abd al Wahhāb (1752–1827) to Egypt.

1821–30 Revolt led by Jehangir Khan in Sinkiang. Sayyid Muḥammad bin ʻAlī al Sanūsī (1787–1859) performs pilgrimage and decides to reside in Makkah and Madīnah for study under Wahhābī ʻulamāʼ and for meditation. Wahhābī influence sparks Jihād to establish Islāmic state in Malaya, Java.

1822 Muslim-Sikh battles under Shāh Ismaʻīl and Sayyid Aḥmad Shahīd, both of whom had been taught by the son of Shāh Waliyyullah. First Arabic printing press at Būlāq, Cairo.

1824–25 Anglo-Dutch Treaty dividing Malay Archipelago between Dutch and English. Al Ghazzālī's *Iḥyāʼ ʻUlūm ad Dīn* translated into Malay.

1827–31 Establishment of the Caliphate of Peshawar, first claim to the caliphate outside the Ottoman Empire in modern times.

1830 Confrontation of al Sanūsī with al Ḥanīsh, Shaykh of al Azhar, and repulsion of Sanūsī as innovator. French invasion of Algeria.

1831–37 Al Sanūsī's second visit to Makkah. Establishment of first Sanūsī *zāwiyah* at Abū Qubays near Makkah.

1833 Reestablishment of Wahhābī power in Darʻiyyah and Najd.

1835 Establishment of military and medical academies in Egypt and of the school of languages with Rifāʻah Rāfiʻ al Ṭahṭāwī as first director.

1843 Founding by al Sanūsī of the mother *zāwiyah* at al Bayḍāʼ (Libya), and launching of the Sanūsiyyah Movement.

1850–63 Reform Movement led by Khayr al Dīn Pāsha in Tunisia. Reforms in the Zaytūnah Mosque University. Promulgation of Western-inspired codes of law by Ottoman Empire (commercial, 1850; penal, 1858; commercial procedure, 1861; and maritime commerce, 1863). Niẓāmiyyah courts established throughout Empire to administer these laws leaving Sharʻiyyah courts with matters of personal status.

1853 Al Ḥājj ʻUmar's proselytizing expeditions in West Africa, spreading the Tījānī allegiance among Muslims as well as Islām among non-Muslims.

1855–80 Revolt in Yunnan (China) led by Muḥammad Sulaymān.

1856 Sanūsiyyah headquarters moved to Jaghbūb where new Islāmic university is founded.

1857 Last armed struggle for freedom from the British in the Indian subcontinent.

1862 Sulṭān Jamāl al Aḥlām ascends Sulu throne and negotiates protectorate status for Sulu under Spain.

1869 Acheh (Sumatra) vainly seeks help from Ottoman Empire against Dutch.

1872 Opening of Dār al ʻUlūm, Cairo. Sinkiang liberated under leadership of Yaʻqub Khan and recognized by Russia, Turkey, and Great Britain.

1873 Dutch attack Acheh and capture the Sulṭān. Resistance continues.

1874 Foundation of Aligarh Muslim University (India) by Sayyid Aḥmad Khan (1817–1900).

1875–1902 Sanūsiyyah reaches peak of political and religious expansion under the leadership of Sīdī Muḥammad al Sanūsī (1846–1902), the founder's son. Capital moved to Kufra (1895). *Zāwiyahs* prospering throughout Muslim World.

1877 General Tso occupies Sinkiang after death of Yaʻqūb Khan.

1881 Battle of Aba (Sūdān) between Ottoman and al Mahdī's armies. Al Mahdī's victory and launching of his movement across the Sūdān.

1882–83 Decisive victories by al Mahdī in the Sūdān.

1884 Muḥammad ʻAbduh and Jamāl al Dīn al Afghānī publish *Al ʻUrwah al Wuthqā,* magazine for Pan-Islamic reform and unity. Later, ʻAbduh publishes *Al Manār.*

1885 Khartoum falls to Mahdīs. Gordon killed. Islāmic state proclaimed and war against Ṣūfism and the *madhāhib* (schools of law). Al Mahdī is succeeded by his son ʻAbd Allah.

1887–89 Decline of religious zeal in the Sūdān. Mahdī's way becomes a *madhhab* with its own religious institutions.

1888 M. Ghulām Aḥmad's "revelation" commanding him to initiate Aḥmadiyyah movement (India).

1891 M. Ghulām Aḥmad's second "revelation" telling him that he is the reincarnation of Jesus Christ.

1896–1903 British occupy Ilorin, Sokoto, and Kano, West Africa.

1898–99 Mahdist forces defeated at Keweri by Egyptians. Khalīfah ʻAbdullah killed in Fashoda, Sūdān.

1900 "Aḥmadiyyah Sect" adopts its name.

1901 French invasion of Morocco.

1902 Aḥmadiyyah begins publication of *The Review of Religions.* Promulgation of "The Sūdān Sharīʻah Law Courts Ordinance" which set up high, provincial, and district courts to administer the *Sharīʻah* according to the Ḥanafī school (as in Egypt).

1905 Rashīd Riḍā becomes editor of *Al Manār* and uses it as platform for the Salafiyyah Movement.

1906 Muslim League Party founded in India.

1906–09 France and England occupy Kawar, Bilma, ain Galacca (Borku), Wadai, and kill Muḥammad al Banānī, Sanūsī leader. Lodges of the order destroyed and Sanūsī men interned (north, central, and west Africa).

1910 *Sharīʻah* Courts Organization Regulations enacted in Egypt.

1911 Religious freedom to Chinese Muslims. First Chinese Muslim journal published.

1911–17 Anti-Dutch uprising in East Indonesia, Sumatra, and Kalimantan.

1912 Muḥammadiyyah, first modern Islāmic educational organization in Southeast Asia, founded by Diporegoro in Jogjakarta.

1915 Sīdī Muḥammad Idrīs succeeds as leader of the Sanūsiyyah Movement.

1920 The Sāliḥiyyah Ṣūfī Brotherhood spreads in Eastern Sūdān. Khilāfat movement in India in support of the Ottoman Caliphate.

1921–24 Wahhābīs seize Ḥā'il (Arabia) and Makkah from Ottoman puppets and form the kingdom of Suʻūdī Arabia under Wahhābī ideology.

1922 Italy invades Libya; S. M. Idrīs exiled, but resistance continues.

1924 Abolition of the Caliphate by Republican Turkey.

1925 Chinese Muslim college established in Tsinan, Shantung Province. Publication and proscription of ʻAlī ʻAbd al Rāziq's *Al Islām wa Uṣūl al Ḥukm,* first plea for a secular state.

1926 World Islāmic Congress assembles in Cairo, and later in Makkah, to discuss abolition of the Ottoman Caliphate. Publication of Ṭaha Ḥusayn's *Fī al Shiʻr al Jāhili,* questioning Islamic sources.

1926–27 "Purification of Islām Society" founded at Fās by ʻAlāl al Fāsī and a similar association at Rabāṭ by Balafrej. Fusion of the two under "The Moroccan League for Islāmic Reform and Progress."

1927–28 Foundation of the Association of Muslim Youth and of al Ikhwān al Muslimun by Ḥasan al Bannā (1906–1949) in Egypt.

1928 ʻUmar Mukhtār assumes Sanūsiyyah leadership in Cyrenaica.

1929 Society of Algerian ʻUlamā' founded; its weekly organ, *Al Baṣā'ir,* begins publication.

1930 Idea of Pakistan suggested by Muḥammad Iqbāl.

1930–31 Italy closes all Sanūsī *zāwiyahs,* banishes their elders and executes ʻUmar Mukhtār. Reorganization of the Sharīʻah Courts and their procedures in Egypt.

1933 Muslim Chinese revolt against national government; establishment of East Turkistan Republic under leadership of Sayfuddin of Sinkiang. Al Ikhwān branches spread throughout Near East and North Africa. Publication of *Majallat al Ikhwān al Muslimīn.*

1936 Al Bannā enters the political field by addressing an open letter to King Fārūq and the heads of Muslim states asking for Islāmic reform.

1940 The "Pakistan" Resolution.

1941 Jamāʻat-i-Islāmī Movement founded by Sayyid Abū al Aʻlā Maudūdī.

1944 Signing of the "Covenant of the League of Arab States."

1945 Indonesia achieves independence.

1946 Libya's United National Front welcomes return of Sanūsī rule. Abolition of family *waqf* in Egypt.

1947 Founding of Pakistan as sovereign Islāmic state. Aḥmadiyyah headquarters moved from India to Pakistan.

1948 National Congress led by Muḥammad Riḍā al Sanūsī proclaims new constitution for Libya. General Malay uprising against British colonialism. Palestine War. Egyptian Government orders dissolution of the Ikhwān.

1949 Assassination of al Bannā.

1950 Ma Hu-Shan leads revolt against Communist indoctrination of Muslim children.

1951 Fusion of all Moroccan associations into "The Moroccan National Front," and of all Algerian associations into "The Algerian Front for the Defense of Liberty."

1951–52 ʻUthmān, Chinese Muslim leader, executed by Communist China. Kansu Province resists Communist seizure of *waqf* land belonging to religious trusts.

1952 Revolution of Free Officers in Egypt led by Muḥammad Najīb.

1953 Persecution of Aḥmadiyyah followers breaks out in Pakistan.

1954–55 Unification of the Niẓāmiyyah and Shariʻah courts in Egypt, Tunisia.

1955 Founding of the Muslim College of Malaya.

1955–56 Return of Muḥammad V to independent Morocco. Independence of Tunisia.

1956 First constitution of Pakistan. End of British occupation of Egypt and Sūdān. Sūdān becomes Islāmic republic.

1957 Malaysia achieves independence under Islām as state religion.

1959–60 National Pan-Somali Movement formed in Muqaddishu. U.N. General Assembly terminates Somalia's trusteeship and grants independence.

1961	Muslim Family Laws Ordinance, Pakistan, reforming marriage divorce and inheritance laws.
1962	ʿAbd al Nāṣir proclaims the "National Charter" in Egypt. Second constitution of Pakistan. Algeria achieves independence.
1964	Bourguiba's edict against fasting in Ramaḍān. Jamāʿat-i-Islāmī declared unlawful.
1965	Sayyid Quṭb, leading Ikhwān thinker, executed in Egypt.
1966	Nigeria gains independence and forms federal republic.
1967	Muslim independence movement in Thailand and Thai colonial settlement in Muslim region.
1971	India invades East Pakistan. Bangladesh established as independent secular state.

Subject Index

Ā

Ācāryas, 84–88
  Śaṅkara, 84
  Prākṛt, 85–86
African religions, *see* Traditional religions in Africa
After-life, *see* Eschatology
Amerindian religions, 51–58
  institutionalization of "spirit power," 51
  initiation, 52
  apotheosis of cult objects, 52
  recourse to psychotropic plants, 53*f*
  cosmology, 57
  the "trickster" functions, 57
Ancestor worship
  in traditional African religions, 63, 67
  in Chinese religions, 112
Animals
  in Ancient Egyptian religion, 21, 25
  sacrificial
    in Canaan-Phoenicia, 30
    in Greek religion, 41
    in Shamanism, 46, 48, 57
    in traditional African religions, 67
Animism
  in traditional African religions, 62–64
  in Chinese religions, 110
Apocalyptic, 146–147
Arabic literature, 6
  in pre-Islāmic times, 240
  the Qur'ān as, 246
Art
  as literary aesthetics of the Semites, 6
  Egyptian stylization in, 21
  visual in Egypt, 25
  as dance in Amerindian religions, 52–53
  in traditional African religions, 66–67
  in Vedic Hinduism, 76
  in Śastras, 83
  in Ācāryas, 87
  in Bhakti, 89*f*
  and Japanese religion, 131
  Buddhist in China, 188–189
  literary in pre-Islāmic Arabia, 240
  Islām's sanctification of the literary of the Qur'ān, 245
Ārya-Samāj, 95
Asceticism
  in Shamanism, 46–48
  in Amerindian religions, 52
  in Hinduism, 78, 80, 83–84, 95
  in Jainism, 97–103
  in the Buddha's teachings and career, 162–164, 170
  and "The Path," 172–174
  and Chinese piety, 186
  in Mahāyāna Buddhism, 192
  in Christianity, 207
  in Christian Ireland, 212
  in Western Europe, 219*f*
  in Islām, 267–269
  see also Ethics
Avesta, 136
  Zand of Mani, 136

B

Bhagavad Gītā, 70, 84
Biblical Criticism, 233
  in Islām, 246–247
Brahmanas, 76–77, 79
Brahmo-Samāj, 95
Buddhism, 83
  Chinese, 109
  source of in China, 115
  relation of to Taoism, 121
  persecution of by Taoists, 123*f*
  decline of in China, 123–124
  mixture of with Shinto, 130
  see also Theravāda Buddhism and Mahāyāna Buddhism

C

Canaan-Phoenicia, 29–32
  gods of, 29–30
  temples, 30

Canaan-Phoenicia (*cont.*)
clergy, 30
sacrifice and funerary rites, 30–31
relation to Ḥanīfiyyah, 237
see also Syria, Greater
Caste, Old Hindu, 70*f*
Vedic, 73, 78
in modern Hinduism, 95
in Jainism, 102–103
Iranian system, 133–134
relation of Brahmins to Buddhism, 170
Islām's combat of Zoroastrian, 247
Christianity, 201–236
relation to Greco-Roman religions, 35, 43
relation to traditional religions in Africa, 62
location in Africa, 61–62
genesis of, 201*f*
relation to Judaism and Jewish sects, 202–203
monastic orders, 202–222
Jesus' career, 203–204
early community, 203–205
Roman persecutions of, 208*f*
the Nicene Creed, 210
spread of in Europe, Asia, and Africa, 211–215
East and West Roman Empires and, 215
birth of Western, 215
final breach of Orthodox and Catholic, 218–219
missions to Asia, Africa, 223–224
Lutheran Reformation, 224*f*
Calvinism and radical reformers, 226
Jesuits and their mission, 227
spread in the Americas and Asia, 228
Catholic-Protestant persecutions in Europe, 229–230
and Marxism, 233–234
not an origin of Islām, 237
Christian community in the Islāmic state, 241
Islām as recrystallization of, 244, 246–247
Classics
of China, 111, 116
of the Changes, 116*f*, 120
Confucianism
genesis, 109–113
Analects of Confucius, 111*f*
flowering of with Mencius, 113–114
reform, 115
decay, 188
Cosmology
Mesopotamian, 10*f*
Ancient Egyptian, 15–17, 22*f*, 24*f*
Hindu, 80*f*
Jain, 98*f*
Confucian, 114*f*
neo-Confucian, 116*f*
Taoist, 117*f*
neo-Taoist, 120*f*
Japanese, 128
early Iranian, 133
Zoroastrian, 134–135
Manichaean, 136
Councils
Buddhist, 168–170, 175
first Mahāyāna, 175, 179, 181
Church at Elvira, 205
Arles, 209
Nicaea, 209–210
Seleucia, 210
Constantinople (second ecumenical), 210
Ephesus, 210
Chalcedon, 210
II Constantinople, III Constantinople, 210–211
II Nicaea, 211, 215, 218
II Lyons, Florence, Trent, I and II Vatican, 218
Crusades, 270–273
in Christian history, 219
Cult
Mesopotamian, 5*f*, 8–9, 10–11
Egyptian, 21–22, 24–26, 27
in Canaan-Phoenicia, 30–31
Greco-Roman, 41*f*
Shamanist, 46–48
Amerindian, 51*f*
in traditional African religions, 62*f*, 65–67
in Vedic Hinduism, 76*f*
Bhakti, 89*f*
Jain, 100
Confucian, 114
Taoist, 122–123
Shinto, 130–131
Zoroastrian, 135
early Hebrew, 139–141
Pharisaic, 146
Theravāda Buddhist, 179
Christian, 203, 205, 211, 226
Islāmic, 245

Death
Mesopotamian view of, 8, 13, 15
in Ancient Egyptian religion, 24–26, 28
concern for in Canaan-Phoenicia, 31
in traditional religions of Africa, 64–65
in Hinduism, 75*f*
Jain view of, 99–100
Buddhist view of, 162, 170, 172, 174
Demons, Demonology
in Hinduism, 75
in Confucianism and Taoism, 112
in Zoroastrianism and Manichaeanism, 133, 134*f*, 136
Doctrine of the Mean in Chinese religions, 114, 116
Donation of Constantine, 220

Egypt
Ancient, 15–28
contrast of religion with Mesopotamian religion, 15–17
cosmic order, 16–17
political order, 18, 21
polytheism, 21
creation of man in, 21–22
meaning of life in, 22*f*
ethics in, 23–24
notion of afterlife, 24–25
decay of religion, 26*f*
skepticism and cynicism in, 27–28
Eschatology
Mesopotamian, 8*f*
Egyptian, 24*f*
in the religion of Canaan-Phoenicia, 31
Greco-Roman, 41*f*
in Amerindian religions, 57
in traditional African religions, 65*f*
Vedic Hindu, 75–76
Jain, 98–99
Zoroastrian, 135–136
absence of in Judaism, 139
Pharisaic, 146
Jesus' of the Last Age, 203
in pre-Islāmic Makkan religion, 240
Islāmic, 241, 245
Ethics
Mesopotamian, 8*f*, 11*f*, 13*f*
Ancient Egyptian, 15*f*, 18*f*, 21*f*
Ancient Egyptian as science of nature, 23–25, 26–28
Greco-Roman, 36*f*, 41–43
Shamanistic, 45*f*, 48
in Amerindian religions, 51*f*, 53*f*
in traditional African religions, 63, 65–67
Hindu Vedic, 75–76
Hindu Smrti, 78

Śastra, 82*f*
in the Bhagavad Gītā, 84
in Ācāryas, 84–88
in Bhakti Hinduism, 89*f*
Jain, 99–101
Confucian, 110*f*
Mencian, 113*f*
neo-Confucian, 114*f*
Taoist, 118*f*
neo-Taoist, 120
early Iranian, 133
Zoroastrian, 135
Manichaean, 136
Mazdakian, 136–137
in early Judaism, 140–141
Pharisaic, 146
Essene, 147
Buddhistic, 162*f*
Buddhist monk discipline, 165–167
in the Buddha's teachings, 170–172
of the Buddhist Path, 172–174
in Mahāyāna Buddhism, 190–193
of Jesus, 203
of Jewish proselytes, 203
Christian, 205
Christian of universalism, 206
marriage in Christian, 207, 210
combat against Manichaean, 208
Calvin's and that of the radical reformers, 226
place of will in Christian and the doctrine of justification, 226
pre-Islāmic Arabian, 240
of Islām, 241
Islāmic of egalitarianism, 244–245
Islām's personal and social, 245–246
Ethnocentrism
Jewish, 142, 206, 237
European and the Jews, 152

Fire-worship
in Hinduism, 74
Zoroastrian and Islām, 247
Fo-kuo-chi (Records of the Buddhist Country), 189

Gnosticism
and Christianity, 207*f*
and the Islāmic view of Christianity, 247
God, gods
in Mesopotamian religion, 5*f*, 7*f*, 9–10
in ancient Egyptian religion, 16*f*, 21*f*, 24*f*
in Canaanite-Phoenician religion, 29–30
in Greater Syria, 33–34
in ancient Greek and Roman religion, 40*f*
in Amerindian religions, 52*f*
in traditional African religions, 62*f*
in early Hinduism, 73
in Vedic Hinduism, 74–75
in the Upanishads, 77
in the Śastras, 83
in Bhakti, 88*f*
in Jainism, 99
in Sikhism, 105*f*
in Confucianism and Taoism, 109, 112
in neo-Confucianism, 114*f*
in Taoism, 117*f*
in the religions of Japan, 127*f*
Iranian theories of, 133–135
in early Judaism, 139, 140
in Pharisaic thought, 146
in Buddha's teaching, 170
in the teachings of Jesus, 203
in pre-Islāmic Makkan religion, 240–241
Islāmic unization of (tawḥīd), 241, 245
Great Learning, 114
Greece, Ancient, 35–44
relation of to Western culture, 35
records of, 35–36
pre-Olympian religion of, 36–40
Olympian myths, 40*f*
theory of man, 41
relation to Roman religion, 41
decay, 42*f*
mystery cults, 43
relation to Christianity, Judaism, philosophy, and Zoroastrianism, 43
relation to Asian Shamanism, 48

Ḥanīf, Ḥanīfiyyah, 237*f*
al Ḥaram al Sharīf (The Holy Sanctuary of Makkah), 240
Heaven (Paradise)
in Confucianism, 112
in Zoroastrianism, 135
Buddhist Nibbana as, 165, 169, 173–174
in Mahāyāna Buddhism, 190–193
in Islām, 245
Heresy
in Christian doctrine, 220, 224, 229
absence of in Islām, 246
Hinduism, 69–96
sources and texts, 69–73
relation to Sanskrit and Tamil, 70–71
relation to Hittites and Persians, 73
the Vedas, 74–76
Brāhmaṇas, 76–77
Upaniṣads, 77–78
Smṛti, 78–82
Śastras, 83–84
Bhagavad Gītā, 84
Ācāryas, 84–88
Bhakti, 88–94
modern reform, 94–96
Jainism and Buddhism as reform of, 97*n*
Huai Nan Tzu, 119–120

Immortality
in Ancient Egyptian religion, 24–25
in traditional religions of Africa, 64
in Jainism, 99
in Chinese religion, 112
in Taoism, 122–123
in Zoroastrianism, 135
in the religion of the Essenes, 147
in Buddha's teaching, 172
in Mahāyāna Buddhism, 186
in Christianity, 203
in Islām, 245
Indian American, *see* Amerindian
International law, Islām's innovation in, 246
Islām, 237–281
relation to Mesopotamian religion, 3*f*
location in Africa, 61–62
relation to Sikhism, 105–106
origins of, 237*f*
relation to Judaism and Christianity, 237*f*
to Ḥanīfiyyah, 238
to Makkah, 238*f*, 244
Muḥammad's career, 240–244
relations with Byzantium, 244
with Judaism, 244
redefinition of the holy and profane, 246
and the world religions, 246–247
spread in Arabia, 247, 253
in Byzantium, 247
in the Fertile Crescent, 248
in Persia, 248
in Armenia and the Caucasus, 248

Islam (*cont.*)
in Africa, 249, 255–258
in Central Asia, 249
in India and Europe, 251–253
in Egypt, Nubia, and Abyssinia, 254–255
flowering of thought and culture, 258*f*
sects, 265*f*
mysticism and decay, 267–269
modern movements, 273–279
present fluidity, 280–281

Jainism, 97–103
relation to Hinduism, 97*n*, 102–103
to Buddhism, 98
to Muslim India, 102
genesis of, 97*f*
flowering of, 98*f*
schism, decay, and revival, 101*f*
Judaism, 139–157
relation to Greco-Roman religions, 43
to Zoroastrianism, 137
genesis of the faith, 139*f*
relation to Canaan-Phoenicia, 139–140
the Second Commonwealth, 141–144
sects, 144–149
relation to Jesus and apostolic community, 148
relations with the Muslim world, 149–152
with medieval Christendom, 152
and modernism, 152–153
and Zionism, 154*f*
Jewish community in the Islāmic state, 241
Islām as recrystallization of, 244, 246–247

Kojiki, 127

Law
revelation as promulgation of the law, 9
ancient Near Eastern law as content of divine will, 10–11
of Lipit-Ishtar, 10
of Hammurabi, 10
as revelation in Greater Syria, 34
in Judaism, 139, 144
the Sadducees and the law, 146
Jewish law and early Christianity, 202–203, 206
obedience to law as essence of religious experience in Islām, 258–259
divinity and humanity of in Islām, 259–260
flowering of Islām as flowering of its law, 260
sources of Sharī'ah, 260
the main schools of and jurisprudence, 260–264
inter-school ecumenism and modern times, 264–265
Li-Chi, 114
Li-huo lun (The Disposition of Error), 186

Magic
Mesopotamian, 8*f*, 12*f*
Ancient Egyptian, 21, 24–25
in Greco-Roman religions, 41*f*, 43*f*, 48
Shamanistic, 48
Amerindian, 51*f*, 53*f*, 57
in traditional African religions, 63*f*, 65*f*, 67
in Taoism, 121–122
divination and in Japan, 130–131
in Japanese Mahāyāna Buddhism, 195
Mahābhārata, 83; *see also* Smṛti (Epics)
Mahāyāna Buddhism (China), 185–194
genesis and Fa Hsien pilgrimage, 175, 184
early history of, 185–190
relation to Taoism, 186
to Confucianism, 188
to the Chinese state, 188
persecution of, 189
sects and schools in, 190–193
decline of, 193
Mahāyāna Buddhism (Japan), 195–199
genesis, 195
Pure Land Buddhism, 196
Zen, 197
and modernism, 198–199
relation of to Shintō and Christianity, 198
Manichaeanism
and Zoroastrianism, 136
and Christianity, 208
influence of on Christian asceticism (Albigenses), 220
and Islām, 247
Mantras, 93–94
Mazdakism, 136
Mencius, Book of, 113; *see also* Confucianism
Mesopotamia, 3–14
flowering of Semitic consciousness, 3–4
transcendence of gods, 5–6
monotheism, 7
polytheism as associationism, 8
notion of human destiny, 8
meaning of revelation in, 9–10
cosmic order as creation, 10
social order as matrix of cosmic order and civilization, 11–12
cultural supremacy of, 12
decay, 12*f*
contrast with Ancient Egypt, 15–16
Messianism
as culmination of Zoroastrian eschatology, 135
as product of Jewish exile in Babylon, 140–141
as fulfillment of the Jewish hope for salvation (Christianity), 207
as consequence of Shī'ah defeatism and despair, 266–267
as product of Ṣūfī decay, 268
Mīmāmsās, *see* Śastras
Minorities, Islām and religious, 246
Mission
Jewish in the diaspora in antiquity, 144
of Gautama, the Buddha, 165–166
Buddhist spread in India, 174–179
Buddhist foreign, 175
Fa Hsien's, 175
modern Theravāda Buddhist, 179–183
early Christian activities, 201*f*
Christian in Europe, 211–212
in Asia-Africa, 212–215
by mendicant friars, 221–223
Christian to Muslim lands, 221–222
to Central Asia and the Far East, 222–224
Jesuit, 227*f*
Christian in the Americas, 227*f*, 231*f*
modern Christian to India and China and South East Asia, 227–229
Muḥammad's in Arabia and beyond, 242–244

of the essence of Islām, 253
Islāmic activities in Western Asia, the Nile Valley and Abyssinia, 254–255
in North Africa and Spain, 255
in the Western Sūdān, 255–257
Modernism
and traditional religions in Africa, 67
and Hinduism, 94*f*
and Sikhism, 106–108
and Confucianism, 117
and Taoism, 124
and Shintō, 131
and Zoroastrianism, 137
and Judaism, 152*f*
and Buddhism in South and South East Asia, 172–183
and Theravāda Buddhism in India, 177
and Theravāda Buddhism as state religion in Ceylon, Burma, Thailand, Cambodia, and Laos, 182*f*
and Mahāyāna Buddhism in China, 193
and Japan, 198–199
and Christianity, 233–234
and Islām: the contemporary movements, 273–281
Monasticism, 210, 219
monastic orders, 221
Monotheism, *see* God
Mystery Cults
in Ancient Greece and Rome, 43*f*
Mysticism
in traditional African religions, 65
Hindu, 88, 95
Sikh, 105
Taoist, 118–119
Buddhist, 164
Islāmic (Ṣūfism), 267–269
see also Pantheism

N

Near East, Ancient, 1–44
as cradle of civilization, 3
as a unity and integral theater, 3–7
emigrations from Arabia as source of Near Eastern civilizations, 5–6
linguistic unity of, 5–6
geographic, ethnic, and religious unity of, 7
theogony, 7–8
anthropogony, 8–10
cosmogony, 10–12
decay of, 12–13
Egypt as other pole of, 15
Egypt as contrasting in religion and culture to those of the Semitic Near East, 16–28
Canaan-Phoenicia and Greater Syria as extensions of the Semitic Near East, 29*f*, and as a decaying form of religion and culture, 33–34
Nihongi, 127
Nuns, Buddhist order of, 167
Christian order of, 214
Nyāya, *see* Śastras

P

Pantheism
Ancient Egyptian religion as exemplar of, 16*f*
as Egyptian monophysitism, 17–20
Hindu, 77*f*, 84*f*
Taoist, 120
see also Mysticism
Pharisees, 146
Philosophy
and Greco-Roman religions, 43
Vedic Hindu, 69
Upaniṣadic Hindu, 77–78
Śastra Hindu, 82–88
and Chinese religions, 109–110
Christian in the Middle Ages, 221
in the Enlightenment and modern periods, 232–233
Islāmic, 265*f*
Pien-chêng-lun (Clarification of Correct View), 188
Pilgrimage
in traditional African religions, 66
in Hinduism, 72–73, 81, 91
in Sikhism, 106
in pre-Islāmic times, 240
the Islāmic institution of as the fifth pillar, 243, 245
Prayer, *see* Cult, ethics
Predeterminism
Essene, 147
Calvinist, 230
Ṣūfī, 267–268
Priesthood
in Mesopotamian religion, 9*f*
in Ancient Egypt, 18*f*, 21*f*, 22*f*
in Canaan-Phoenicia, 30
in Ancient Greece and Rome, 41*f*, 43*f*
in Shamanism, 45*f*, 47*f*, 52*f*, 57
in Amerindian religions, 51, 57
in traditional African religions, 63*f*, 65*f*
in early Hinduism, 70–71
in Jainism, 98, 100
in Taoism, 123–124
in Shintō, 131
early Iranian, 133
Zoroastrian caste, 134–135
Manichaean, 136
in early Judaism, 139
Jewish in the various sects, 144–148
Buddha's Sangha, 165
Buddhist in Theravāda South and Southeast Asia, 178–184
Chinese Buddhist, 188–189
Jewish and the trial of Jesus, 203
first Christian, 204, 208
Christian and marriage, 210
pre-Islāmic Makkan, 240
absence of in Islām, 245
Purāṇas, 83; *see also* Smṛti

Q

Qur'ān, The Holy
and the Ancient Near East, 6
the revelation of the Prophet Muḥammad, 240*f*
as apogee of Arabic literary development, 240
as the last and final revelation, 241
as the first best seller, 246
criticisms of Jewish and Christian scriptures, 246–247
as first source of Islāmic law, 260

R

Rāmāyana, *see* Smṛti
Records of The Legitimate Succession of The Divine Sovereigns, 130
Reform, *see* Modernism
Revelation
in Mesopotamian religion, 9–10
in Ancient Egyptian religion, 15–17, 23–24
Greco-Roman theory of, 40*f*
in traditional religions of Africa, 63*f*
and St. Paul, 203–204
of the Qur'ān to Muḥammad, 238
Islām's preservation of the text of, 240, 244
Islām's criticism of Jewish and Christian, 241, 246–247
Rome, Ancient, *see* Greece

S

Sacrament
in Hinduism, 78–79
in Jainism, 101
in Zoroastrianism, 133
in Christianity, 203, 226
Sacred Writings, *see* Revelation
Sacrifice
in Canaan-Phoenicia, 30*f*
in Greco-Roman religion, 36*f*, 43*f*
in traditional African religions, 63
in early Hinduism, 73
in the Bhagavad Gītā, 84
in Bhakti Hinduism, 90*f*
in Chinese religions, 112
in the religion of the Hebrews, 144
among the Samaritans, 144
Sadducees, 146
Essenes, 147
in Chinese Mahāyāna Buddhism, 186
Christian objection to sacrifice to Roman gods, 208
in pre-Islāmic Makkan religion, 240
Sadducees, Jewish sect, 146
relation to Jesus and Christianity, 146, 202–203
Samaritans, Jewish sect, 144–146
Sāmkhya, *see* Śastras
Śastras, 82–86
Sāmkhya, 82
Yoga, 83
Vaiśeṣika and Nyāya, 83
Mīmāmsās, 83
Sects, Jewish, 144–149
Samaritans, 144
Sadducees, Pharisees, and Apocalyptic, 146–147
Essenes and Zealots, 147–148
Hellenistic Jews, 148
Buddhist sects in Japan, 195–197
Sōka Gakkai and Risshō Kōseikai, 198–199
relation of Jewish to Christianity, 202–203, 206
Jewish Christians, 206
Docetists, Ebionites, 208
Donatists, 209
Arians, 210
Macedonianists, 210
Sabellianists, 210
Nestorians and Pelagians, 210, 213
Monophysites, monothelites, and iconoclasts, 211
filioque, 217*f*
Photian schism, 218
birth of Protestantism, 229–230
Quakers, 231
in Islāmic history, 265–267
Secularism
and Chinese religions, 115
Confucianism and Marxist, 117
Taoism and Marxist, 124
in Japan, 131
Judaism and, 152
and Mahāyāna Buddhism in China, 193
Islām's absolute separation of the sacred from the profane and secularization of empirical reality, 244
Semitic Consciousness
flowering of, 3–4
decay of in Mesopotamia, 13–14
contrast with Ancient Egyptian consciousness, 15–16
and in greater Syria, 33–34
Islām as crystallization of, 237–238
Shamanism, 45–58
nature of, 45
the Shaman, 45–47
confrontation with Buddhism, Christianity, and Islām under Genghis Khan, 47–48
relation of to hunting, 48
to Zoroastrianism and Ancient Greece, 48
as base of all Amerindian religions, 51
practices and beliefs of in Chinese religions, 112, 123
early Japanese, 127*f*, 130
Sharī'ah
origin of, 260
juristic schools: Mālikī, 260; Ḥanafī, 260–262; Shāfi'ī, 262–263; Ḥanbalī, 263–264; Zaydī, 264; Imāmī, 264–265
see also Law
Shintō, 127–132
genesis, 127*f*
mixture with Confucianism and Buddhism, 130
and the imperial state of Japan, 131
Sikhism
genesis and development, 105*f*
relation to Islām, 105
history of the Sikh community, 106
relation to Hinduism, 106–107
crisis and reform, 106–107
Slavery, Islām's struggle against, 245
Smṛti, 78–82
Vedāngas, 78–79
epics, 79–80
Purāṇas, 80–81
Society
Mesopotamian, 8, 11–12
contrasting Mesopotamian and Egyptian societies, 15–17
Egyptian society as nature, 18*f*
in traditional African religions, 64–65
clan and blood relation as central to African, 64
ethical standards of African, 65–66
Hindu Vedic, 76
Bhakti, 88*f*
Taoist, 118*f*
early Japanese, 127
Iranian, 133
Hebrew, 140–141
anti-social nature of Mahāyāna Buddhism in China, 193
pre-Islāmic Makkan, 239–240
Islām's combat of tribalism and formation of around the bond of faith, 245
Islāmic as the universal brotherhood under the moral law, 245–246
Soteriology
Zoroastrian, 135, 137
Jewish, 140–141
in Mahāyāna Buddhism (Pure Land), 191, 196
Christian, 206
absence of in Islām, 240, 245
State
Religion and the state in Mesopotamia, 10–12, 14–16
in Egypt, 15*f*, 18*f*, 26*f*
in Ancient Greece and Rome, 41*f*
in Sikhism, 106, 108
in Confucianism and the religious thought of Mencius, 113–114
cult in China, 115
Taoist theory of, 118–119, 121
Taoism as religion and persecution of other religions, 123
unity of religion and under Shintō in Japan, 130–131
of Zoroastrianism and in Iran, 134
Judaism and the European, 152*f*
Judaism and the Zionist state of Israel, 154*f*
pre-Islāmic state of Makkah, 241
the Islāmic, 241
Islāmic innovation in constitutional and international law, 245–246
Ṣūfī, Ṣūfism (Taṣawwuf)
relation to Hinduism, 88
and to Sikhism, 105
genesis of in Muslim World, 267
flowering of in literature, pietism, and missions, 268
decay of and aberration to

individualism, alchemy, and immanentism, 268–269
al Ghazzālī's reconstruction of, 269
Sūtras
Jain, 98
see also Smṛti
Syria, Greater, 33–34
as integral part of the Arab theatre, 33
relation to Mesopotamia and the Arabian Peninsula, 33
relation to Hebrew religion, 34

Tantras, 90*f*
Taoism, 109–115
origins, 117
Lao Tzu, 117
Liu-An, 119
Chuang Tzu, 119
Neo-Taoism, 120*f*
relation to Buddhism, 121, 186
Chang-lu, 121–122
confrontation with Buddhism, 123
division into ninety sects and decline, 123*f*, 188
Tao-te-ching, 117–118
Temple(s), Shrines
the Zigurrat in Mesopotamia, 11
the function of in Ancient Egypt, 24–25
in Canaan-Phoenicia, 30
in Ancient Greece and Rome, 35–36, 38–40
in traditional African religions, 66
in Hinduism, 91
in Jainism, 100–101
in Sikhism, 107–108
in Chinese religions, 109
in Shintō, 131
in Zoroastrianism, 134
history and importance of the first Jewish, 144
of the second Jewish, 146
among the Essenes, 147
in Mahāyāna Buddhism in China, 186, 188–189
in pre-Islāmic Makkah, 240
purification of the Ka'bah by the Prophet Muḥammad, 243
Theology, *see* God
Theravāda Buddhism
Gautama's career, 161*f*, 165
the Buddha's mission and Sangha, 165–168
spread of in India, 174–179
in foreign lands, 175
confrontation of with Islām in India, 175–177
and modernism, 177–179
modern development of in Ceylon and Burma, 179
in Thailand, Cambodia, and Laos, 181–182
as world movement, 182–183
in China, 190
Torah, 139, 144
Jesus and the Torah, 203
Traditional religions in Africa, 61–68
sources, 61
location in Africa, 61
relations with world religions, 62, 67
God in, 62
spirits in, 63*f*
man, 64
after-life, 64*f*
magic and witchcraft, 65
religious meanings, 65*f*
pilgrimage, 66
sacred objects, 67
future of, 67
Transmigration, in the Upaniṣads, 78
in the Sastras, 83
in Bhakti, 90*f*
in Jainism, 101
in Sikhism, 105
in the Buddha's teachings, 172
Ts'an-t'ung-ch'i, 122

Upaniṣads, 77–78
Upavedas, *see* Smṛti

Vaiśeṣika, *see* Śastras
Vedāngas, *see* Smṛti
Vedas, 71; 73–76; 170

Yoga, see Śastras

Zealots, 147–148; Jesus and, 202
Zionism, 154*f*
Zoroastrianism
relation to Shamanism, 48
to Greco-Roman religions, 43
relation to Vedic Hinduism, 133
early history of, 133
theology of, 134
ethics of, 135
decay and reform of, 136
relation to Manichaeanism, 136
to Mazdakism, 136–137
contributions of to Judaism and Christianity, 137
and Islām, 247

Index of Proper Names

Aachen, 215
Aba, Mar, 213
'Abbāsī(s), 261, 262
  Caliphate, 152
'Abd al Jabbār, al Qāḍī, 266
'Abd al Raḥman, ibn al Ash'ath, 249
  ibn Muljam, 265
'Abd al Raḥman III, Caliph of Cordoba, 253
'Abdullah al Rāsibī, 265
'Abdullah ibn Abū Sarḥ, 248, 249
'Abdullah ibn 'Āmir, 248
'Abdullah ibn Salām, 244
'Abdullah ibn Yasin, 255
'Abdullah Yūsuf 'Alī, 281
Abel, 206
Abélard, Peter, 219
Abgar IX, King, 206
Abhaya Vattagāmani, 179
Abhayagiri Vihāra, 179
Abraham, 5, 34, 139, 140, 142, 206, 237, 240, 243, 245
Abrahams, W., 67
Abu, 34
Abū al 'Abbās, 266
Abū 'Abdullah Muḥammad, 255
Abū Bakr al Ṣiddīq, 215, 247, 248
Abū Dharr al Ghifārī, 267
Abū Ḥanīfah, 260, 261, 262, 263
Abū al Ḥasan al Ash'arī, 266
Abū Muslim al Khurāsānī, 266
Abū 'Ubaydah al Jarrāḥ, 248
Abū Yazīd Tīfūr al Bisṭāmī, 267
Abyssinia(n), 26, 240, 244, 254, 255
Acci (Guadix), 205
Achaea, 40 (Achaia), 201
Acosta, Joseph, 231
Acre, *see* 'Akka
Acropolis, 35
Actium, 205
Adal Kingdom, 255
Adam, 245
Adamana, 257
Addai, 206
Adhanah, 251
Adiabene, 206
al 'Āḍid, 272
Aditi, 74, 75
Ādityas, 74
Adon, 205
Adrian VI, 224
Adriatic Sea, 205, 208
Aegean Sea, 36
Aegina, 35
Aelia, 206
Aelia Capitolina, 204
Afghanistan, 70, 249, 262
'Afīfī, A., 281
Africa, 4, 45, 48, 61–68, 183, 209, 212, 215, 227, 237, 355
  East, 105, 258, 263
  Horn of, 255
  Muslim, 276
  North, 35, 41, 62, 175, 208, 212, 215, 247, 251, 255, 260, 265, 270
  Proconsularis, 208
  West, 63, 260
Agathocles, 31
Agathopous, Rheus, 205
Agni, 74, 75
Agora, 35
Agra, 88
Agrippa I, Herod, 41, 204
Agrippa II, 201
Agrippinus, 205
Agus, Jacob B., 139, 157
Ahlstrom, Sydney E., 235
Aḥmad Barelī, Sayyid, 276
Aḥmad ibn Abū Du'ād, 266
Aḥmad ibn Ḥanbal, 263, 264
Aḥmad Khān, Sayyid, 280
Ahriman, 134, 135
Ahura Mazda, 134, 135
  Mazdaism, 214
Ajantā, 175
Ajnadayn, 248
Akalaṅka, 101
Akāli(s), 107
  Party, 107, 108
Akbar, 102
Akhu, 34
'Akkā, 222, 248, 271, 272
Akkad(ians), 5, 10, 11, 12

Akkadian (language), 7
Alans, 222
Alaric, 212
Alaska, 51, 224
Albania, 227, 262
Albertus Magnus, 221
Albigenses, 208, 220
Albigeois, 252
Albinus, 204
Albright, F. W., 5, 31, 33, 34
Alemanni, 212
Aleutians, 224
Alexander the Great, 33, 144
Alexander III, 220
Alexander VI, 224, 231
Alexandria, 148, 201, 204, 208–210, 213, 215, 220, 226, 248
Algeria, 208, 277
'Alī ibn Abū Ṭālib, 265, 266, 267
'Alī, ibn Sulṭān Ḥasan of Shīrāz, 258
Aliganj, 103
Aligarh Muslim University, 208
Allen, William, 230
Alps, 215
Altaic Peoples, 128
Aluvihare, 169
Alva, Duke of, 229
Ālvars, 69
'Ām al Wufūd, 243
Amarāvatī, 175
Amaterasu, 127, 128, 130
Amaunet, 17
Amazonia, 53, 56
Ambedkar, 179
'Ambisah al Kalbī, 251
Ambrose, 211
Ameer Ali, Sayyid, 281
America(ns), 42, 51, 52, 57, 127, 227, 231
  Central, 231, 232
  Latin, 62
  Meso-, 52
  North, 52, 53, 62, 230, 232
  South, 51–53, 62, 231
American Bible Society, 233
American Indians, Amerindians, 51, 52, 56, 57
American University of Beirut, 280
Amhara, 255
Amharic (language), 5
Amida, 196
Amitabha, 192, 196
Ammon, 26
'Ammu, 34
Amoghavarṣa, King, 101
Amorites, 12, 34
Amos, 141
'Amr ibn al 'Āṣ, 247–249, 254
Amritsar, 106
Amun, 17
Amurru, 11
An, Liu, 119
Anabaptists, 226
Anagarika Dharmapāla, 177
Ānanda, 167
Anat, 29
Anath-Bethel, 30
Anathapidika, 167
Anatolia, 4, 33
Anavadya, 97
Anawrahta, 179
Anchialo, 205
Āṅḍāl, 88
Andalus, 252
Āndhra, 87–89, 101
Andrew, 205
Andronicus, 201
Anesaki, Masa Haru, 183, 199
Angad, 106
Angkor, 182
Angles, 212
Ani, 253
Aniruddha, 179
Annianus, 205
Anselm of Bec, 219
Anshar, 7
Antigone, 41
Antioch, 148, 201, 204–208, 215, 219, 220, 222, 226, 270–271
Antipas, 204
Antwerp, 229
Anu, 10, 11, 137
Anuradhapura, 179
Ao, Li, 116, 193
Aosta Valley, 253
Apas, 74
Apastamba, 79
Aphrodite, 40
Apollinaris, 210
Apollo, 36, 41, 201
Apostate, *see* Julian
Appar, 85
Appenine Peninsula, 36
Apulia, 218
'Aqabah, 248, 271
al Aqṣā (Mosque and Sanctuary), 242, 271, 272
Aquinas, Thomas, 221, 222
Aquitaine, 252
Arab, 5, 7, 8, 213, 240, 242, 254
  World, 155, 258
Arabia(n) Desert, (n)Peninsula, 3, 5, 12, 26, 33, 137, 149, 214, 215, 237–240, 243, 245, 247, 253–254, 256, 258, 260, 263, 273, 275
  Su'ūdī, 264, 275
  West (Ḥijāz), 243
Arabian Gulf, 213
Arabic (language), 5, 245
Ar'ad, Saifa, 255
Aragon, 219
Arameans, 12
Āratī, 164
Arbela, 206
Arberry, A. J., 281
'Arbūnah, 251
Archer, J. C., 108
Arctic, 45
Ardashir, 136
Ardhamāgadhi, 98
Ardhanārī, 85
al 'Aṭṭār, Farīd al Dīn, 268
Attila, 212
Atum, 17, 18, 25, 26
Augsburg, 226
Augustine, 21, 136, 210, 211, 212
Augustinians, 231
Augustus, 36, 43, 208
Augustus, Romulus, 212
Aurelius, Marcus, 205
Aurobindo, 70, 95
Austria, Rhaetia, 212
Austro-Asians, 127
Autun, 252
Avalokitesvara, 182, 195
Avignon, 224, 252
Avilius, 205
Avitus of Vienne, 212
Awadhī, 80
Awlās, 251
Aws, 241
Axum, 214
Aylah, 247
'Ayn Jālūt, 273
'Ayn Shams, 248
Ayuthia, 182
al Azhar, 264
Azores, 231
Aztec, 56, 231

Baal, 29–31, 34, 41
  Hammon, 30
Baalbeck, 36
Baalu, 30
Bāb al Mandib, 258
Babilyūn, 248
Babylon, 12, 33 (ia), 142
Bacchus, 43
Bacon, Roger, 221
Bactrians, 222

Badarayana, 84
Badarī, 70
Badarīnāth, 73
Badr, Battle of, 242, 244
Baeta, C. G., 67
Bagh, 175
Baghdād, 152, 222, 260, 263, 267, 272, 273
Bahādur, Tegh, 106
Bahrām I, 136, 208
Baḥrayn, 213, 247
Bai, Maira, 88
Bailey, Cyril, 44
Balagangadhara, 95
Baldwin of Boulogne, 270, 271
Bālī, 94
Balit, 34
Balkans, 208
Balkh, 249
Baltimore, 232
Baluchistan, 248
Banaras (Benares), 89, 98, 165
Bāṅdā, 106
Banerjee, Indubhusan, 108
Bangkok, 182
Bangor, 212
Banū 'Āmir, 244
Banū Ḥanīfah, 247
Banū al Naḍīr, 244
Banū Qaynuqā', 244
Banū Qurayẓah, 244
Banū Tamīm, 247
Baptists, 230, 231
Baptist Missionary Society, 232
Barbarossa, Frederick, 272
Barbate (river), 251
Bardesanes, 206
Barlaam, 226
Barnabas, 201
Baron, Salo, 149, 157
Barqah (Pentapolis), 249
Barrett, C. K., 235
Barsumas, 213
Bartholomew de las Casas, 231
Bartholomew, St.('s) Day, 229
Baruch, 147
Basarh, 97
Basava, 87
Basel, 230
Basel Missionary Society, 233
Basham, A. L., 103
Basil, 210
Basilides, 207
Baṣrah, 248, 266, 267
Bassae, 35
Baur, F. C., 233
Bavarians, 212
Bayon, 182
Beaume, 252
Beirut, 271, 272
Belfast, 212
Belgium, 229
Belisarius, 212, 255
Bellarmine, Robert, 227
Benares, *see* Banaras
Benedict VIII, 224
Benedict, Ruth, 57
Benedict, Saint, 212
Bengal, 87, 88, 98
Berard of Carbio, 221
Bering Strait, 46
Beringia, 51
Berlin, 182
Bernard of Clairvaux, 219
Bernard, Great St., 253
Bernarde, B., 67
Bernice, 201
Besançon, Hugues, 229
Besant, Annie, 95
Bethel, 30
Bethlehem, 271
Bettensen, Henry, 235
Bhadrabāhu, 101
Bhallūka, 181
Bhārata, 73, 80
Bhāratavarṣa, 73, 99
Bharhut, 175
Bhartṛhari, 85
Bhāskara, Laugakshi, 96
Bihār, 97, 98, 100
Bilbays, 248
Bimba, 162
Bimbā, 162
Bimbisāra, 167
Bint Jubayl (byblos), 271
Blackfoot, 52
Black Sea, 205
Blavatsky, Madam, 95
Bleek, D. F., 67
Boas, Franz, 49, 51, 57
Bobbio, 212
Bodde, Derk, 124
Bode, M. H., 183
Bodhidharma, 191
Boehme, Jakob, 231
Bogomils, 208
Bogoraz, Waldemar, 48
Bohanan, L., 68
Bohemia, 219
Bohemond, 270
Bohemond III, 271
Bologna, 219
Bonaventure, 221
Boniface VIII, 220
Bordeaux, 252
Borromeo, Carlo, 227
Bosatsu, Gyogi, 131
Bothwell, Lord, 230
Bottero, J., 31
Brahmā, 85
  Brahman, 17, 76, 77, 78, 84, 85, 89, 91, 95
Brahmaṇ-aspati, 74, 75
Brahmāvarta, 70
Brandeis University, 156
Brazil, 56, 152, 231
Breasted, A. C., 27
Brethren, the Bohemian, 224
Bṛhaspati, 74
Britain, 4, 107, 277
British Empire, 107
British Foreign Bible Society, 233
Britons, 212
Brittany, 252
Brockelmann, Carl, 281
Bronze Age, 29, 30
Buber, Martin, 157
Bucer, 226
Buddha, Gautama, 69, 79, 83, 97, 98, 123, 161, 163, 165–172, 179, 182, 191, 192, 196, 198, 267
Buddha, Lochana, 131
Buddhagayā, 164, 177
Buddhaghoṣa, 179
Buil, Bernardo, 231
Buisson, R. du Mesnil, 31
Bukhārā, 249
Bulgakov, S., 235
Bulgaria, 218, 226
  Bulgars, 270
Bullock, C., 68
Bultmann, R., 233
Burgundy, Burgundians, 212, 219, 252
Burke, T. C., 103
Burma, 94, 169–170, 179, 181–182
Burrows, Millar, 147
Buryat, 45–48, 224
Buṣrā, 248
Buwayb, 248
Buwayhīs, 266
Byblos, *see* Bint Jubayl
Byzacena, 208
Byzantine, 212, 222, 248, 270
  Empire, 254
Byzantium, 205, 209, 215, 219, 223, 238, 244, 247, 248, 251, 253, 254, 270

Caesar, 43, 203
Caesarea, 204, 210, 248, 271
Cagnolo, C., 68

Cain and Abel (legend), 5
Cairo, 280
see also al Qahirah
Caitanya, 88
Cajamarca, 231
California, 53
Callinikos, Constantine, 235
Calvin, John, 226, 229
Calvinists, 230
Calycadmus River, see Salaf
Camaldoli, 219
Cambodia, 94, 169, 182
Canaan(ites), 12, 29–32, 34
-Phoenicia, 29
Canada, 56, 105, 227
Cāṇakya, 82
Canarese, 102
Caṅdīdās, 88
Canisius, Peter, 227
Canopus, 43
Canterbury, 212, 219, 230
Cape Verde Islands, 231
Capitoline Trinity of Sbeitla, 36
Cappadocia(ns), 211, 214, 251
Capua, 36
Caquot, A., 32
Carcassonne, 252
Carey, William, 232
Cari, 204
Caribbean, 52, 56, 152, 231
Carmona, 251
Carolina, North, 232
South, 53
Carothers, J. C., 68
Carthage, 30, 31, 205, 208, 215; (-inians), 31
Caskel, W., 31
Caspian Sea, 205
Castile, 219
Castor, 41
Catalina, Jordan, 222
Cathari, 208, 220
Cathay, 222
Caucasus, 214, 253
Celadion, 205
Celestine I, 212
Cephalonia, 205
Cephas, 203
Cerinthus, 207
Cerularius, Michael, 218
Cerveteri, 35
Ceuta, 251
Ceylon, 94, 169, 170, 175, 177, 179, 181, 182, 222, 227, 232
Ceylon Chronicles, 169
Chad, 61, 255, 277
Lake, 255
Chadwick, Owen, 235
Chaitya Hall, 175
Chakri, 182
Chalcedon, 210, 213
Chalon-sur-Saône, 252
Ch'an (zen), 185, 191, 197
Chan, Wing-tsit, 124
Chandāvarkar, G. A., 96
Chandragupta II, 175
Chang, 124
Chang, Carsun, 124
Ch'ang-Ch'un, Ch'iu, 124
Chang, Chung-Yuan, 124
Chang Church, 122
Chang, Gama, 193
Ch'angan, 188, 190
Channa, 163
Chao, 114
Chaoking, 227
Chaos, 17
Chapata, 179
Charina, 162
Charlemagne, 152, 212, 215, 217, 220
Charles I, 230
Charles V, 231
Charles, L. H., 147
Chatterjee, Satischandra, 96
Chê-Chiang, 191
Chê-Wang, 123
Ch'en, Kenneth, 193
Chen, Tai, 117
Chên-Yen, 190
Ch'êng, 114, 193
Chêng-ch'ang, Chang, 124
Ch'eng-Chu, 116
Ch'êng-shih, 190
Cheyenne, 52
Ch'i, 114
Chi-hsia, 114
Chi-tsang, 189, 190
Chicago Parliament of Religions, 95
Ch'ien-chih, K'ou, 123
Chih-tun, 188
Chih-yi, 189, 191
Chikafuse, Kitabatake, 130
Chile, 231
Ch'in Dynasty, 115
China, Chinese, 47, 83, 109, 117, 121, 123, 127, 128, 136, 137, 175, 182, 185, 194, 195, 213, 222, 227, 232, 249
Chinese Buddhist Association, 193
Ch'ing Dynasty, 117
Ching-Wu, 190
Cholula, 231
Chorasmia, see Khawārizm
Chosroes, 244
Chou, 112, 116, 118, 123
Chou Dynasty, 118
Chou, Tun-yi, 116
Chrestus, 205
Christmas Day, 271
Chrysostom, John, 211
Chu, 114
Chu, Ch'eng, 114
Chu-she, 190
Chu, Yang, 113
Ch'ufu, 111
Chukchi, 46, 47, 224
Chum, Sri, 182
Chung-shu, Tung, 115
Ch'ung, Wang, 115
Church of Alexandria, 254
Church of England, 230
Church Missionary Society, 233
Chuyashes, 223
Cidambaram, 93
Cilicia, 204, 251, 270, 272
Cillium, 208
Cistercians, 219
Citeaux, 219
Clement V, 222
Clement VII, 224
Clement of Alexandria, 208
Clement of Rome, 204
Cleobius, 206
Clermont (France), 219, 270
Clonenagh, 212
Clonfert, 212
Clonmacnois, 212
Clopas, 206
Clotilda, 212
Clovis, 212
Cluny, 219
Cochin China, 182
Coire, 253
Colombo, 181
Columban, St., 212
Columbus, 231
Commenus, Alexius, 270
Confucius, 110, 112, 113, 115, 118, 120
Congregationalists, 231
Connecticut, 231
Conrad III of Germany, 271
Constance, 224
Constans II, 215
Constantia, 210
Constantine, 208, 209, 210, 212, 220
Constantine II, 210
Constantinople, 209, 210, 215, 217, 218, 219, 220, 222, 223, 226, 238, 253, 270, 272
see also Istanbul
Constantius, 208, 209, 210, 214
Constantius II, 210
Conze, Edward, 183, 193

Cook, S. A., 32
Copt, Coptic Church, 227
Cordoba, 208, 210
Corinth, 203, 204
Cornelius, 208
Cornwall, 212
Corsica, 253
Cortes, 231
Cosmos, 11
Coyote, 57
Cranmer, Thomas, 231
Crefeld, 231
Crespin, Jean, 230
Crete, 35, 40, 41, 205
Cross, F. L., 236
Crusades, 152
Ctesiphon, 212, 248
Cūlamaṇi, 182
Cumont, Franz, 44
Cunningham, J. D., 108
Cyprian, 208, 209
Cyprus, 201, 204, 210, 227, 248, 272
Cyrenaica, 277
Cyrene, 204
Cyrenia, 175
Cyril, 210, 213
Cyrus, 133, 135, 141, 248
Czechoslovakia, 227

Dādū, 89
Daedalus, 41
Dagan, 29
Dagon, 181
Dahood, M. J., 31
Daia, Maximin, 209
Dalada Maligava, 179
Dales, G. F., 71
Dalmatia, 205, 212
Damascus, Dimashq, 5, 201, 204, 215, 219, 248, 260, 271, 272
Damasus, Pope, 210
Damietta, *see* Dumyāṭ
Dammann, E., 68
Danfodio, 'Uthmān, 256
Daniel, Book of, 202
Daniel, N., 281
Danielou, Jean, 235
Danquah, J. B., 68
Danube, 211
Dārfūr, 225
Dar'iyyah, 275
Darnley, Lord, 230
Dās, Amar, 106
Dās, Rām, 106
Dasas, 71
Dāsgupta, Surendranāth, 96
Dasvus, 71
Dathīn, 248
Dattātreya, 85
Dauphiné, 252, 253
David, King, 143, 149
Dawmat al Jandal, 244
Day of Judgment, 146, 265
Dayal, Har, 194
Daybul, 251
Dea Coelestis, 41
Dead Sea, 148, 202
  Scrolls, 238
De Bary, W. T., 199
Decius, 208
Deer Park, 165
Delhi, 105, 106
Delos, 36
Delphi, 36, 41, 43
Delta, 248
  see also Nile
Delwara, 100
Demeter, 43
Demetrios, 205
Demiurge, 207
Denmark, 232
Denzinger, H., 235
Deschamps, H., 68
Des Places, E., 44
Deutero-Isaiah, 141
Deva, 75, 91, 190
Devadāha, 161
Devanandā, 101
Develtum, 205
Devī, 78, 81, 82, 84, 85, 90
Dhammcati, 181
Dharmakara, 192
Dharmapāla, 179
Dharmaratna, 186
Dhāt al Ṭalḥ, 244
Dhorme, Edouard, 13
Dhū al Nūn al Miṣrī, 267
Dhū Nuwās, 214
Dhū al Sawārī, 248
Dido, 41
Didyma, 36, 41, 43
Digambarahs, 101, 103
Dimashq, *see* Damascus
Diocletian, 208
Diodorus, 31
Diogenes, Romanus, 253
Diognetus, 207
Dionysus, 43
Dipankara, 162
Disentis, 253
Dodds, E. R., 49
Dogen, 197
Dokyo, 195
Dominic, St., 221
Dominicans, 221, 224, 231
Dominitian, 204
Dongola, 249, 254, 257
Doric Temple, 35
Dorylaeum, *see* Eskishehir
Dositheus, 206
Douai, 230
Dougga, 35
Dravida, Dravidians, 71, 101
Dropsie University, 156
Dubnow, 154
Duchesne-Guillemin, Jacques, 137
Duke Endes of Aquitaine, 251
Dumoulin, Heinrich, 199
Dumuzi, 4
Dumyāṭ, 272
Dura-Europos, 36, 208
Durkheim, Emile, 51, 57
Durrānī, Aḥmad Shāh, 106
Durya, 90
Dussaud, R., 32
Dutch, 279
Dutch Reformed Church, 232
Dutt, Manmatha Nāth, 96
Duṭṭhagāminī, 179

Easter Day, 248
Eastern Church, 270
Ebionites, 206
Ecbatana, 136
  see also Nihāwand
Ecija, 251
Eckhart, Meister, 221
Edessa, al Ruhā, 206, 212, 213, 219, 248
Edict of Milan, 209
Efros, Israel, 157
Egypt(ians), 3, 5, 15, 28, 33–34, 43, 62, 139, 141, 148, 175, 201, 205, 227, 238, 244, 247–248, 254–255, 260, 262–263, 267, 270, 272–273, 275, 277
Eisai, 197
Eissfeldt, O., 32
El, 29, 30, 31, 34
Elam, Elamites, 11, 222, 248
Eleusis, 43
Eliade, Mircaea, 48, 68, 96
Elijah, 154
Eliot, Sir Charles, 183, 199
Elizabeth I, 226, 229
Elohim, 34; bene ha, 246
Elvira, 208, 210
  see also Illiberi

Enan, M. A., 281
England, 105, 212, 215, 224, 226, 229, 231
English, 106, 107
Enkimdu, 4
Enlil, 8, 10, 11, 12, 15
Enoch, 147
Ephesus, 201, 204, 210
Ephraim, St., 212
Epidaurus, 41
Epiphanes, Antiochus, 146
Epirus, 175, 205
Episcopal Church, 232
Erman, Adolph, 28
Esarhaddon, 30
Eshmun, 30, 34
Eskimo, 47
Eskishehir, 270
Essenes, 147, 202, 203, 206
Esther, 141, 142
Estonia, 227
Ethiopia, 16, 61, 62, 142, 227
Ethiopic (language), 5
Euphrates, 15, 208, 251
see also Tigris-Euphrates valley
Eurasia, 45
Euripides, 42
Europe(ans), 35, 45, 70, 75, 127, 152, 182, 212, 215, 219, 221, 224, 226–227, 230, 270–273
Western, 249, 270
Eusebius of Constantinople, 211
Eusebius of Saesarea, 204, 205, 206, 210
Eutyches, 210
Evans, E., 68
Ezana, 214
Ezekiel, 141, 146
Ezra, 144, 147

Fa-hsing, 190
Fa-hsien, 189
Fa-shen, 190
Fa-tsang, 190
Fabre, P., 44
Farā'iḍī, 377
al Farāma (Pelusium), 248
Farghānah, 249
Fars (Persepolis), 265
al Fārūqī, Isma'īl R., 3, 15, 33, 133, 237
Fatḥpur Sikrī, 102
Fāṭimah, 267
Fāṭimīs, 270
Fei, Han, 115
Felix, 201
Fenestrelle, 253
Ferdinand, 231
Fertile Crescent, 3, 4, 7, 12, 26, 27, 267
Festugière, A. J., 44
Festus, 201, 206
Feuerbach, L., 233
Field, Dorothy, 108
al Fiḥl (Pella), 248
al Fijār, Battle of, 239
Filasṭīn (Palestine), 248
see also Holy Land
Findeisen, H., 48
Finian of Clonard, 212
Finland, 227
Fintan, St. of Clonenagh, 212
Florence, 218
Florinus, 205
Fo-t'u-teng, 158, 189
Fortunatus, 36
Forum, 36
Fox, George, 231
Foxe, John, 230
France, 48, 212, 215, 226, 229–230, 233, 251, 253, 270
Francis II, 229, 230
Francis, H. T., 183
Francis, St., 221
Franciscans, 221, 227, 231
Frankfort, Henri, 9, 18, 21, 24, 28
Franks, 212, 270
Fraticelli, 224
Fraxinetum, 253
Frederick II, 220, 272
Frejus, 253
French, 4, 280
Revolution, 152
Fressinet, St., 253
Friends, 231
Frumentius, 214
Fu, C. Wei-hsun, 109, 185
Fu-chih, Wang, 117
Fu, Wang, 123
Fulbe, 256
Fulindiyyah, 258
Funan, 182
Fung, Yu-Lan, 124
Fusṭāṭ, 248
Fyzee, A. A. A., 281

Gadādhara, 83
Galerius, 208, 209
Galilee, Galileans, 154, 201, 206
Gall, St., 253
Gallio, 201
Gamaliel, Rabban, 146, 149
Gaṇapati, 90
Gāndhāra, 175
Gāndhi, Mahātmā, 70, 80, 95
Gaṇeśa, 82, 84, 90, 91
Gaṅgeśa, 83
Gaon of Vilna, 1
Gaster, T. H., 32
Gauḍapāda, 85
Gaul, 205, 212
see also France
Gautama, *see* Buddha
Gautamī, Kīsā, 167
Gautamī, Mahā Pajāpati, 161, 16
Gayā, 179
Gaza (Ghazzah), 201, 248, 262
Geb, 17
Ge'ez, 215
Genitrix, Venus, 43
Geneva, 226, 230, 253
Genghiz Khan, 48, 124, 269
Genseric, 212
Georgia, 214, 222, 227, 232
Germantown, 231
Germany, East, 219
Gevandan, 252
Gevirtz, Stanley, 29
Gezer, 30
Ghana, 255
Ghassān, 5
Ghaṭafān, 247
Ghaylān ibn Marwān, 266
al Ghazālī, Abū Ḥāmid, 268, 269, 274
Ghislieri, Michael, 229
Ghurye, G. S., 96
Gibraltar, 251
Giles, H. A., 124
Gilgamesh, 12
Ginsburg, H. L., 32
Gion, 130
Girschman, R., 137
Go-Daigo, Emperor, 130
Gober, 256
Godfrey, 271
Gold Coast, 232
Gordon, C. H., 38
Gorthaeus, 206
Goshtasp, *see* Vishtaspa
Goths, 211
Graetz, Heinrich, 154
Graham, A. C., 124
Gran, Aḥmad, 255
Granada, 255
Grant, Frederick C., 44
Grant, M., 44
Gratian, 210, 219
Gray, J., 32

Gray, R. F., 68
Greece, Greeks, 4, 36, 40, 41–43, 45, 48, 133, 149, 175, 201, 205, 227
Greek (language), 70, 203
Greenland, 232
Gregory I, 212
Gregory II, 215
Gregory VII, 218–220
Gregory IX, 220, 222
Gregory XII, 224
Gregory of Nazianzus, 210
Gregory of Nyssa, 210
Gregory, St., 214
Gressmann, H., 44
Grisons, 253
Guadix, *see* Acci
Guatemala, 56
Guillaume, 253
Gujarat, 87, 100, 101, 103
Gulf of St. Thropez, 253
Gundaysabur, 136
Gunkel, H., 233
Gupta, 175
Gurmukhī, 105, 107
Guthrie, W. K. C., 44
Gutmann, Julius, 157

Hadfield, P., 68
Ḥaḍramawt, 247
Hadrian, 36, 41, 43, 204–205
Hadrumetum, 205
Hagia Sophia, 272
Hai-Ch'an, Liu, 124
al Hajjāj, 249, 265
Ḥalab, 271
al Ḥallāj, 268
Hallo, William W., 13
Haman, 141
Ḥamīdullah, Muḥammad, 281
Hammurabi, 10, 11, 12, 34
Haṁsavatī, 179
Han, 120, 186, 188–189
  Later, 122
Ḥanafī School of Law, 260, 262, 264
Hanan, 204
Ḥanbalī School, 263–264
Hanchung, 122
Hanuman, 91
Hao, Ch'eng, 116, 119
Hao, Ts'ui, 123
Haoma (Soma), 133
Harappā, 71
Harden, D., 32
Hargobind, 106
Hari-Viṣṇu, 87
Harihara, 85
al Ḥārith ibn Asad al Muḥāsibī, 267
Harnak, Adolph, 209, 235
Ḥarrah, 244
Ḥarrān, 266, 271, 273
Harrison, Jane Ellen, 44
Harshavardhana, 175
Hārūn al Rashīd, 253, 260
Hāshim, Banū (Clan), 266
Hassidim, 154
Hatshepsut, 21
Hauhet, 17
Hausa, 255, 256
Hawāzin (tribe), 239, 243
Hayley, T., 68
Hazor, 30
Hebrew, 5, 10, 18, 139, 140, 246
  Bible, 5, 6
  Patriarchs, 5
Hebrew Union College, 156
Hegesippus, 296, 207
Heian, 195, 196
  Later, 130
Heidel, Alexander, 13
Helen, 206
Heliopolis, 17
Hell, Joseph, 281
Heng, Chang, 122
Henry II, 217, 229
Henry IV, 229
Henry VIII, 226, 229
Henry of Navarre, 229
Hephaistos, 35, 41
Hera, 41
  Temple, 35
Heracleon, 207
Heraclitus, 170
Heraclius, 244, 248, 254
Hermas, 204, 206
Herod, Herodians, 43, 202
Herodotus, 133
Hertzberg, Arthur, 157
Heschel, Abraham, 157
Ḥijāz, 3, 5, 260, 263, 272, 275
Hildebrand, 219
Ḥilf al Fuḍūl, 240
Himalayas, 73, 161
Ḥims, 248
Ḥimyarites, 214
Hindi (language), 88
Hippo, 211
Ḥirā', Ghār, 240
Hiragla, 253
Ḥīrah, 248
Hirano, 130
Hiraṇyagarbha, 74
Hiravijaya, 102
Hirschau, 219
Hitti, P. K., 281
Ḥiṭṭīn, 272
Hittites, 4, 12, 13, 33, 73
Hofer, J., 236
Holland, 226, 229, 230
  see also Netherlands
Holton, D. C., 199
Holy Land, 142, 154, 221, 222, 227
  see also Filasṭīn (Palestine)
Homa, *see* Haoma
Homer, 42, 43, 207
Honen, 196
Honorius III, 221
Horeb, 34
Hormuz, 136
Horus, 25
Hosea, 141
Hosius, 208
Hosius of Cordoba, 210
Hosius of Poland, 227
Hospitallers, 272
Hosso, 195, 196
Hotar (Zoatar), 73
Hsi, Chu, 114, 116, 193
Hsian-Fu, 222
Hsiang-Kuo, 120, 121
Hsiang-shan, Lu, 116, 193
Hsien-shon, 190
Hsienpi, 188
Hsiu, Hsiang, 120
Hsuan-tsang, 189, 190
Hu, 17, 21
Hua-yen, 185, 190, 191, 195
Huai-nan, 119
Huart, Clément, 137
Hubal, 240
Ḥudaybiyah, 243, 244
  'Ahd al (treaty), 243
Hudhayl, 244
Hugh, Count of Provence, 253
Hugon, 229
Huguenots, 229
Hui-neng, 191
Hui-yuan, 188, 192
Huitzilopochtli, 52
al Hujwīrī, 268
Hulagu, 269
Hultkrantz, Ake, 57
Humbert of Silva Candida, 220
Ḥunayn, 243
Hung, Ko, 123
Hungary, Hungarians, 212, 227, 253
Huns, 136, 188, 212, 222, 253, 270
Hurrians, 12
Hurvitz, Leon, 194
Hus, John, 224
Ḥuṣn al Akrād, 270
Hutter, Jacob, 226

Ḥyderabād, 251
Hyksos, 26, 27
Hyrkanos, John, 146

Ibn 'Abd al Wahhāb, 276
Ibn al 'Arabī, 268
Ibn Baṭūṭah, 254
Ibn Ḥanbal, *see* Aḥmad ibn Ḥanbal
Ibn Hishām, 281
Ibn Rushd, 219
Ibn Sīnā, 219
Ibn Taymiyah, Taqiyyuddīn Aḥmad, 264, 273, 274, 275
Ibo, 257
Ibrahīm ibn al Adham, 267
Idowu, E. B., 68
Ifrīqyah (Tunisia), 249, 251
Ignatius, 204, 205, 207, 218, 227
Ignatius II, 222
al Ikhwān al Muslimūn (the Muslim Brethren), 280
Illiberi (Elvira), 205
Illyricum, 205
Ilorin, 257
'Imad al Din Zangi, 271
Imāmīs, 264
Imāmiyyah School, 264
Inada, Kenneth, 194
Inari, 130
Inca, 51, 231
India(ns), 17, 71, 73, 80–81, 84–85, 89, 91, 94–95, 99, 136, 142, 166, 170, 174–175, 177, 185–186, 189–190, 192, 213, 222, 227, 231, 232, 249, 262, 264, 277, 280
Indicopleustes, Cosmas, 222
Indies, East, 227
  West, 62, 152, 232
Indochina, 227
Indo-Europeans, 4, 12, 56, 75
Indonesia(ns), 94, 263, 277
Indra, 73, 74, 75
Indrabhūti, Gautama, 98
Indus, 70, 71, 106
Innocent III, 220
Innocent IV, 220, 222
Institut d'Egypte, 286
International Missionary Council, 233
Iona, 212
Iqbāl, Muḥammad, 281
Iran(ians), 47, 133–137, 264
'Irāq, 154, 248, 261–265, 270–272, 275, 277
Ireland, 212
Irenaus, 204–207
Irene, 253
Iron Age, 29
Irving, T. B., 281
Isaac, 139, 140, 206
Isabella, 231
Isaiah, 141, 142
Ise, 130
Isidore, 212
Isin, 12
Isis, 17, 36, 43
Isma 'īl, the Prophet, 240
Ispatana, 165
Israel, 141, 154, 155, 203
Istanbul, 227, 275
  see also Constantinople
Italy, 209, 212, 215, 219, 220, 224, 226, 233, 253
Iwashimizu, 130
Iyād ibn Ghamm, 248
Izanami, 127
Iznik, 253
  see also Nicaea

Jabal Nafūsah (Libya), 265
Jaballaḥ, Mar III, 222
al Jābiyah, 248
Jabriyyah, 265
Jackson, Abraham V., 137
Jacob, 139, 140
Jadala, 255
Jaghbūb, 277
Jahm ibn Ṣafwān, 265
Jaiminī, 84
Jain, Champat Rai, 103
Jainī, Jagmandarlal, 103
Jalulā', 248
Jamālī, 97
Jambūdvīpa, 73, 98
Jambūsvāmin, 98
James, son of Zebedee, "the Just," 202, 204, 206
James I, 230
James IV, 229
James V, 229
James VI of Scotland, 230
James, brother of Jesus, 149
Jannah, 255
Japan(ese), 127–132, 182, 195–199, 224, 227
Jarba Island (Tunisia), 265
Jaxartes, 249
Jayadeva, 89
Jeremiah, 141, 142
Jerome, 206, 211
Jersey, East, 232
Jerusalem, 43, 142, 146, 149, 154, 201, 204, 206, 208, 210, 215, 219, 220, 222, 226, 242, 248, 270, 271, 272
Jesuits, 227
Jesus, 146, 149, 201ff
Jetavana, 167
Jethro, 34
Jewish Theological Seminary, 156
Jews, 43, 203, 233, 242, 244, 139ff
Jimmu, Emperor, 128
Jina, 69
al Jisr, Battle of, 248
Jnanadeva, 87
Jñānasambanda, 85
Job, 13, 43
John, 201, 203, 204
John XXII, 222
John XXIII, 224, 233
John of Damascus, 212
John of Monte Corvino, 222
Jordan, 262, 271, 272
Josephus, Flavius, 144, 147, 148, 149
Joshua, 144
Josiah, 141
Judaea, 144, 201, 232
Judah, 206
Juhaynah, 254
Julian, 210, 251
Julian, the Apostate, 43
Julius II, 224
Jumnā, 20
Junayd al Baghdadi, 268
Jung, Mou, 186
Junias, 201
Juno, 41
Jupiter, 41
Jura Mountains, 253
Jurhumis, 238
Jusham, 243
Justin, 206
Justinian, 212, 255
Justinian II, 251
Jutes, 212

Ka'bah, 240, 245
Kabīr, 69, 88, 89
Kābūl, 70, 249, 260
Kahler, M., 233
Kailāśa, 70, 73
Kāka, 7
Kaladi, 84

Kālāma, 168
Kālāma, Ālāra, 163
Kālidāsá, 82
Kaliṅga, 174
Kaltenmark, Max, 124
Kalyān, 87
Kalyānī, 181
Kāmākhyā, 73
Kamakura Period, 196, 197
Kamban, 80, 88
Kambuja, 181
Kamehatka, 224
Kanada, 83
Kāñchi, 95
Kañcīpura, 85
Kandy, 179
Kanei, 85
Kanem, 255
Kanishka, 169, 175
Kanka, 258
Kanra, 56
Kanṭhaka, 163
Kanyākumāri, 73
Kapelrud, A. S., 32
Kapila, 82
Kapilavastu, 161, 163, 167
Karakoram, 222
Karbalā', 275
Karle, 175
Karṇa, 80
Karṇāṭaka, 87
Kashgar, 249
Kashmir, 70, 88, 90, 106, 169, 175
Kashyap, Bhikkhu, 183
Kassites, 12, 13, 73
Kastha, 101
Kasuga, 130
Kaśyapa, 83
Kāthiāwār, 73, 103
Kaufman, Yehezkel, 157
Kauket, 17
Kauṭilya, 82
Kazan, 223, 224
Kegon, 195
Kelly, J. N. D., 235
Kenya, 61
Kenyatta, Jomo, 68
Kerala, 84
Keret, 30
Kerma, 26
Khadījah, 240, 241
Khajurāho, 100
Khālid ibn al Walīd, 247, 248
Khalu, 34
Khan Mangu, 222
Khanbalik (Peking), 222
Kharatra, 103
Khardeng, Rama, 181
Khāsis, 71
al Khaṭīb al Tibrīzī, Muḥammad ibn 'Abdullah, 281
al Khawārij, 265
Khawārizm (Chorasmia), 133, 136, 249
Khaybar, 244
Khazars, 249
Khazraj, 241
Khiva, 249
Khmers, 182
Khmum, 21, 22
Khurāsan, 136, 213, 248, 249
Khutsuri, 214
Khuzā'ah, 238
Khuzistan, 248
Kidd, B. J., 235
Kierkegaard, Soren, 233
Kiev, 223
Kiloa, 258
Kindah, 5
Kiowa, 52
Kiptchak, 222
Kirmān, 265
Kishimoto, Hideo, 199
Kitagawa, Joseph M., 127, 195, 199
Kitano, 130
Kittisiri, 182
Knoz, John, 229, 230
Kobad, King, 136, 137
Kochba, Bar, 204
Kofan, 56
Kofun, *see* Tumulu
Kohli, Sunder Singh, 108
Kols, *see* Mundas
Komo, 130
Kordofān, 257
Korea, 182, 195, 224
Kosala, 167
Krader, Lawrence, 45, 48
Kramer, Samuel N., 6
Krishan, Har, 106
Kronos, 41
Kṛṣṇa, 74, 76, 80, 89, 91
Kṣetrasya Pati, 74
Kuan-yin, 192
K'uei-chi, 190
Kūfah, 248, 260, 265, 266
Kuk, 17
Kukai, 196
Kumāra, 82, 84, 88, 90, 91
Kumārajīva, 188, 190
Kumārila, 84
Kunburn, 25
Kundakunda, 101
Kurdistan, 213
Kushān, 175, 186
Kusinaro, 168
Kyoto, 130, 195, 196
Kyushu, 128

La Barre, Weston, 48, 51
Labrador, 232
Lacedaemon, 205
Lacquer Garden, 119
Laeuchli, Samuel, 35
Lagrange, M. I., 32, 233
Lakhm, 5
Lakṣmaṇa, 80
Laksmi, 74, 88, 90, 91
Lalitā, 90
Lalla, 88
Lamtuna, 255
Langdon, S., 13
Languedoc, 252
Laodicaea, 204, 210
Laos, 94, 169, 181, 182
Lapps, 223
Largemont, R., 32
Larissa, 205
Larsa, 12
Lāt, 240
Lateran Palace, 220
Latin (language), 70
Latins, 222
Latourette, Kenneth S., 235
Latvia, 227
Lau, D. L., 124
Laud, William, 230, 231
Lawatah, 249
Leander, 212
Lebanon, 29, 33, 270
Legbo, 57
Legge, James, 124
Leo I, 212
Leo III, the Isaurian, 211, 215, 218
Leo IX, 217, 218, 220, 255
Leon, 208
Levenson, J. R., 124
Lewis, I. M., 48
Liang, 188
Liang-Chieh, Tung-shon, 191
Liber Pater, 43
Libya, 262, 277
Libya Cyreniaca, 204
Lienhardt, G., 68
Liguris, 253
Lin, Yu-tang, 124
Lin-chi, 191
Ling, Chang or Taoling, Chang, 121, 123, 124
Lipit-Ishtar, 10

Loisy, A., 233
Lokeśvara, 182
Lollards, 224
Lombards, 212
Lommel, Andreas, 48, 49
London, 36, 182
London Missionary Society, 233
Louis II, 218
Louis VII of France, 271, 272
Louis XIV, 18, 229
Low, D. A., 68
Lowie, Robert H., 57
Loyang, 186, 188, 189
de Loyola, Inigo, 227, 230
Lu, 113, 114, 117, 190
Lu, Chang, 122
Luang Prabang, 182
Lucinius, 209
Ludlul bel Nemeqi, 13
Luke, 201, 202, 203, 204
Lull, Raymond, 222
Lumbinī Park, 161
Lung-men, 189
Luther, Martin, 224, 225, 226
Luxeuil, 212
Lyon, 205, 207, 218, 220, 229, 252
Lyonnais, 252

Ma'ān, 247
Ma'arrat al Nu'mān, 270
Maat, 21, 23, 36
Ma'bad al Juhanī, 266
Macauliffe, M., 108
Maccabee, Judah, 146
Macdonnel, A. A., 96
Macedonia, Macedonians, 175, 210, 227
Macedonius, Bishop, 210
Macon, 252
Madagascar, 61, 227, 238
Madā'in, 248
Madhya Pradesh, 100
Madīnah, al Nabiyy (Yathrib), 105, 152, 241, 243, 244, 247, 248, 260, 261, 263
Madras, 88
Madurai, 85, 227
Magadha, 167
al Maghrib (North Africa), 272
Magna Mater, 41, 43
Magnesia (the Maeander), 204
Magyars, 270
Mahā Bodhi Society, 179
Mahā Vihāra, 179
Mahādevan, T. M., 96
Mahārāṣtra, 87, 95
Maharṣi, Ramana, 95
Mahāsaṅghikas, 175
Mahāvīra, 97, 98, 99, 100, 101
Mahdiyyah, 277
Mahendravikrama, 85
Maimonides, Moses, 152, 157
Maison Carrée of Nîmes, 36
Makkah, Makkans, 34, 105, 215, 237, 238, 239, 240, 242, 243, 244, 245, 253, 257, 258, 260, 262
Mal, Arjun, 106
Malachi, 142
Malage, 30
Malalasekera, G. P., 183
Malaṭiyyah, 251
Malaya, Malaysia, 94, 175, 227, 263
Mali, 61, 255
Mālik ibn Anas, 260, 262, 263
Mālikī School, 260
Malikshāh, 266
Mallas, 168
Mallika, 167
Malta, 201
al Ma'mūn, 263, 266
Manabus, 57
Manas, 75
Manāt, 240
Mandalay, 170
Mandingo, 255, 258
Mandir, Jal, 100
Mani, 136, 137, 205
Manicheism, 270
Manikkavacakar, 85
Manu, 70, 79
Manuel, 248
Manuha, 179
Manzikart, 253
Māra, 164
Mar'ash, 251
Marburg, 226
Marcion, 205, 206, 207
Marduk, 7, 8, 10, 11, 12
Margaret, 229
Mari, 5, 12
Maria, 214
Ma'rib, Dam of, 5
Marj Rahīṭ, 248
Marj al Suffār, 248
Mark, 201, 203, 205
Marrakush, 255
Marranos, 152
Mars, 41
Marseilles, 31, 205, 253
Martel, Charles, 252
Martin V, 224
Maruthas, Bishop, 212
Maruts, 74
Marw, 248, 249, 266
Marxism, 234
Mary, 206, 210, 233
Mary of Scotland, 229
Masada, 148
Masao, Oka, 127
Masbotheus, 206
Massachusetts, 231
Massisah, 251
Mātaṅga, Kaśyapa, 186
Mātariśvan, 75
Mathurā, Muttra, 101, 175
Matsumoto, Nabuhiro, 199
Matsuo, 130
Matthew, 201, 203, 219
Mauretania, 208
Maurya, 82
Mawṣil, 248, 271
Maxentius, 209
Maximian, 208
Māyā, 56
Maha, 101
Mayeul, 253
Mazarin, 229
Mazatec, 53, 56
Mazdak, 136, 137
Mbiti, John S., 61, 68
McGuire, M. R. P., 236
McLeod, W. H., 108
Medea, Medes, Medians, 36, 41, 42, 133, 222
Medina Sidonia, 251
Mediterranean, 16, 26, 27, 29, 208, 215, 248, 251, 270
Mehta, Narasiṁha, 87
Meiji, Emperors, 131
Melanchton, 226
Melanesia(ns), 127, 128
Melkite, Royal Church, 254
Memphis, 17
Menander, *see* Milinda
Mencius, 113, 114, 115
Mendelssohn, Moses, 152
Mennonites, 232
Merida, 208, 251
Merriman, R. B., 235
Meru, 98
Mesopotamia(ns), 3–13, 15, 16, 18, 22, 23, 26, 33, 34, 134, 206, 210, 212, 213
Mesrob, 214
Mexico, 52, 56, 227, 231
Meyerowitz, E. L., 68
Micah, 141
Micronesians, 128
Middle Ages, 12, 152, 226, 272, 273

Middle East, 91, 219, 222
Middle Kingdom (Egypt), 20, 27
Midian, 34
de Midici, Giovanni, 224
Mihrān, 248
Milan, 227
  Edict of, 209
Milinda, 174, 175
Milkom, 34
Milqart, 30, 34
Milvian Ridge, 209
Min-don-min, King, 170
Minerva, 41
Ming, 117, 124, 186
  Dynasty, 117, 222, 223
Mirghaniyyah, 258, 277
Mirian, 214
Mirura, Isshu, 199
Mitannis, 73
Mithilo, 87, 88
Mithnagdim, 154
Mithra (Mitra), 36, 43, 73, 74, 75, 91, 135
Mleccha, 70, 71
Moan, 5
Moghuls, 106
Mohenjo-Daro, 71
Mohr, J. C., 236
Mon Kingdom, 181
Mongol, 12, 124, 197, 222, 223
Monophysite, 227
Mons, 179
Montanus, 207
Montezuma, 51
Montpelier, 229
Montréal, 271
Moore, C. A., 125
Moravia, Moravians, 226, 236
Morgan, Kenneth, 96, 183
Morocco, 208, 221, 227, 255
Moscati, Sabatino, 6, 12, 32
Moscow, 223, 224, 227
Moses, 34, 139, 141, 202, 206, 214
Mot, 29, 34
Mott, John R., 233
Moulton, J. H., 137
Mount Abu, 100
Mount Athos, 226
Mount Cenis, 253
Mount Gerizim, 144
Mount Hiei, 196
Mount Jupiter, 253
Mount Koyo, 196
Mount Lunghu, 124
Mount Manadara, 98
Mount P'eng Lai, 121
Mount Uḥud, 242
Mrammadesa, 179
Mrammas, 179
Mu'āwiyah, 248, 254, 266
Muhājir, A. R., 281
Muhallab ibn Ḥajjāj, 265
Muḥammad, 152, 215, 238, 240, 241, 243, 244, 247, 253, 258, 260, 266
Muḥammad Aḥmad al Mahdī, 276
Muḥammad 'Alī, 275
Muḥammad al Bāqir, 264
Muḥammad ibn 'Abd al Wahhāb, 275
Muḥammad ibn 'Alī al Sanūsī, 276
Muḥammad ibn al Ḥasan al Qummī, 264
Muḥammad ibn Idrīs al Shāfi'ī, 262
Muḥammad ibn Qāsim, 251
Mukrān, 248
Mula, 101
Mulṭān, 251
Mundas (Kols), 71
Muqaddishū, 258
Muraoka, Tsunetsugu, 199
Murji'ah, 265
Murmansk, 223
Murray, Gilbert, 44
Murti, T. R. V., 183, 194
Mūsā ibn Nuṣayr, 251
Musardu, 258
Mushabbihah, 266
al Mu'taṣim, 266
al Mutawakkil, 263, 266
Mu'tazilah, 264, 265, 266
Muthannā ibn Ḥārithah, 248
Muttra, 175
Mycene, 40, 41
Mysore, 89, 101, 103
Mzāb, 265

Nāblus, 146
Nadel, S. F., 68
Nādir Shāh, 106
Nāḍis, 74
Nāgārjuna, 175, 188, 190
Nāgasena, 174
Nahrawān Canal, 265
Najrān, 214, 215, 240, 242
Nakamura, Hajime, 199
Nālandā, 175
Nāmadeva, 87
Nānak, 69, 88, 105, 106
Nānāvati, Rajendra, 97
Naples, 201
Nāqyūs (old Nikiu), 248
Nara Period, 105
Nārada, Thera, 194
Narang, Gokul Chand, 108
Nārāyaṇa, 70, 74
Narbonne, 205
Narsai, 213
Nasatyau, 73
Nasr Tribe, 243
Nathamuni, 88
Naunet, 17
Nayarars, 69
Nazareth, 202
Near East(erners), 3, 5, 7, 12, 45, 247, 354
  Ancient, 1, 3–13, 15–27, 29–31
Needham, J., 125
Negeb, 5
Nehemiah, 144
Nehru, Jawaharlal, 179
Neill, Stephen, 235
Neo-Confucianists, 120
Neo-Pythagoreans, 207
Neo-Taoist, 121
Nepal, 94
Nephtys, 17
Nerchinsk, 223
Neri, Philip, 227
Nero, 204
Nerses, 214
Nestorius, Nestorians, 210, 222, 227
Netherlands, 152, 229, 233
  see also Holland
Neuchatel, 253
New Rochelle, 229
New York, 229, 232
Ngum, Fa, 182
Nicaea, 208, 209, 210, 213, 218
  see also Iznik
Nicephorus II, 253
Nichiren, 197
Nicholas I, 218
Nicholson, R. A., 281
Nicolaus, 204
Nicomedia, 208, 210
Nicopolis, 205
Niger, 255, 258, 277
Nigeria, 61
Nihāwand (Ecbatana), 248
  Battle of, 248
Nikhilananda, Swami, 96
Nile, Delta, 3, 4, 16, 17, 18, 21, 26, 248, 272
Nilsson, M. P., 44
Nimes, 252
Ninian, 212
Nino, St., 214
Nisibis, 212, 213
Niẓām al Mulk, 266

Niẓamiyyah, 266
Noah, 237, 245
de Nobili, Robert, 227
Noricum, 212
Normans, 218, 258, 270
North Star, 26
Nu, U, 170
Nubia, Nubians, 254, 272
Nu'mān of Ḥīrah, 239
Nu'mān ibn Thābit, 260
Numidia, 208
Nun, 16, 17
Nur al Din, 271, 272
Nut, 17
Nuwās, Dhū, King, 149
Nyānaponika, Thera, 183
Nyaramoli, Bhikku, 194
Nyāya, 83

Obelisks, 30
Oceania, 45, 48
Odantapuri, 175
Odoacer, 212
Oedampadius, 226
Oedipus, 41, 42
Offas, 251
Olcott, Colonel, 95
Oldenburg, U., 32
Old Testament, 5, 34
Olmstead, A. T., 137
Olympus, 41
Oppenheim, A. Leo, 13
Orbe, Battle of the, 253
Order of Premontre or Norbertines, 219
Orestes, 42
Orient, 270
Origen, 205, 208
Orinoco, 56
Orissa, 101
Orleans, 226
Orontes, 270
Orpheus, 48
Orvieto, 35
Osfia, 36
Osiris, 17, 18, 25, 26
Osroene, 206, 212
Ossius, 208
Ostia, 36
Ostrogoths, 212
Otto I, 220
Ottoman, Empire, 215, 262, 264, 275
Ou-Yang, 190
Oye, 252

Padan Aram, 5
Padwisk, C. E., 281
Paestum, 35
Pagan, 181
Pajjusana, 101
Pakistan(is), 262, 264, 281
  West, 105
Pala, 175
Palamas, Gregory, 226
Palatine Hill, 41
Paleologus, John, 215
Paleo-Siberians, 56
Palestine, 29, 33, 149, 154, 155, 206, 215, 262, 270, 272
  see also Filasṭīn
Pali, 109, 187
Pali Texts Society, 182
Palitana, 100
Palladius, 212
Pallas, 41
Pallava, 71, 85
Palut, 206
Pankaruru, 56
Pannonia, 212
Pantheon, 36
Pao-chen, Hsiao, 124
Paraguay, 227
Parakkambāhu, 179
Parameshvara, Jayavarman, 182
Paris, 182, 226
Parjanya, 74
Park, Willard Z., 57
Parrinder, E. G., 68
Parsons, E. C., 57
Pārśvanātha, 97
Parthenon, 35
Parthia, Parthians, 186, 205
  Parthian Period, 208
Pārvatī, 91
Paropuri, 98, 100
Pasargad tribe, 133, 136
Pasenadi, 167
Pātalīputra, 82
Pātalīputta, 169
Patañjali, 83
Pathans, 106
Pati, 90
Patmos, 204
Patnā, 101
Patrakesarin, 102
Patrick, 212
Paul, 201, 202, 203, 204, 205, 206, 225
Paul VI, 215, 233
Pavia, 212
Pegu, 181
Pekidha, 206
Peking, 224, 227
  see also Khanbalik
Pelagius, 210
Pella, 204
  see also al Fihl
Pelepponesus, 35
Pen-chi, Ts'oo-shan, 191
Peninsula, *see* Arabia
Penn, William, 231
Pennsylvania, 231, 232
Pentapolis, *see* Barqah
Pentateuch, 43
Pepin, 215
Pereira, Duarie Pacheco, 231
Pergamon, 36, 41
Pergamos, 25
Pergamum, 204
Pericles, 35
Persepolis, *see* Fars
Persia(ns), 7, 43, 73, 210, 213, 214, 222, 227, 238, 247, 248, 277
  see also Iran
Persian Empire, 141, 142, 248, 261
Persian (language), 70
Peru, 56, 229, 231
Peshawar, 175
Peter, the Hermit, 270
Peter, the Lombard, 219
Peter, St., 220, 225
Peyote, 53
Phanar, 227
Pharan, 214
Pharaoh, 18, 20, 21, 23, 25, 27
Pharisees, 146, 149, 202, 203
Philadelphia, 204, 205, 231
Philip II, 229
Philippe-Auguste, 272
Philippines, 227, 238, 277
Philistines, 12, 33
Philo, 73, 139, 148, 205
Phoenicia, 30, 201, 204
  see also Canaan
Phoenix, 248
Pi, Wang, 120
Pickthall, M. M., 281
Piedmont, 253
Pilate, Pontius, 149
Pin, Chang, 123
Pisa, 224
Pisnulok, 182
Pius, Antoninus, 36
Pius V, 229
Pius IX, 233
Pius X, 233
Pius XI, 233
Pius XII, 233
Pizarro, 231
Plato, 42, 43, 226

Pliny the Younger, 205
Plymouth, 231
Po-yang, Wei, 122
Pois, 248
Poitiers, 252
Pola, 205
Poland, 152, 154, 219, 220, 227
Pollux, 41
Polonnaruva, 179
Polycarp, 205
Pomerania, 220
Pompei, 36
Pontus, 205
Pope, M. H., 32
Portugal, Portuguese, 152, 227, 231, 255
Poseidon, 41
Pothinus, 205
Pra Sihing, 182
Prabhācandra, 102
Prajā-pati, 74, 75, 78
Prakṛit, 45
Priene, 43
Priscillianism, 208
Pritchard, James, 4, 10, 12, 68
Prome, 179
Prometheus, 41, 42
Provence, 212, 229
Prussia, 220
Ptah, 17, 18
Ptah-Hotep, 24
Pueblo, 51, 57
Punjāb, 88, 95, 106, 108, 175, 251
Punjābī (language), 105
Purandaradās, 87
Puritans, 230
Puruṣa, 75, 76
Purushapura (peshawar), 175
Pusan, 74
Pushyamitra, 175
Puteoli, 20
Pyrenees, 251, 252
Pythagoras, 170

Qabbalists, 154
Qadariyyah, 266
Qādiriyyah, 258
Qādisiyyah, 248
al Qāhirah, 272
see also Cairo
Qaraites, 154
Qarṭājannah (Carthage), 249
Qasrīn, 208
Qayrawān, 251
Quilon, 222
Quirinus, 41
Qur'ān, 6
Quraysh, 238, 239, 240
Qusayy, 238
al Qushayrī, Abū al Qāsim, 268
al Qushayrī, Muslim ibn al Ḥajjāj, 281
Qutaybah ibn Muslim, 249

Rābi'ah al 'Adawiyyah, 267
Rādhā, 89
Rādhākrishnan, S., 95, 96
Radin, Paul, 57
Radloff, W., 48
Rāga, 164
Rāghavan, Veṅkataraman, 69, 73
Rahner, Karl, 236
Rahula, Walpola, 163, 167, 194
Rai, Gobind, 106
Rai, Har, 106
Rājagaha, 167, 168, 169
Rājasthan, 87, 88
Rākṣasas, 75
Rām, Rājā, 95
Rāma, 80, 95
Rāma I, 182
Rāma, Sri Sūryavaṁśa, 181
Ramaḍān, 240, 245
Rāmadās, 87
Rāmadās of Bhadrācalam, 88
Rāmakrishna, 70, 95
Rāmaliṅgasvāmī, 88
Ramana, 70
Rāmānanda, 89
Rāmānuja, 88, 89, 175
Rāmapūttā, Uddaka, 163
Rameśvaram, 73
Ramlah, 270
Rangoon, 170, 181
Rāshidun Caliphate, 260
Rashnu, 135
Rasmussen, Knud, 49
Rau, T. A. Gopinatha, 96
Raven, 57
Ravenna, 212
Raymond II, 271
Raymond, St. of Penafort, 222
Raymond of Toulouse, 270
Rayy, 266
Re, 26
Recared, 212
Reconstructionist Rabbinical College, 156
Red Sea, 20, 238, 248, 255, 271, 272
Reichard, Gladys, A., 57
Reimarus, S. H., 233
Rekhmire, 18
Remy, St., 252
Rennyo, 196
Renaissance, 273
Renou, Louis, 96
Rhine, 212
Rhode, Erwin, 49
Rhode Island, 231
Rhone, 205, 212, 251, 253
Ricci, Matteo, 227
Richard I, the Lion Hearted, 272
Richelieu, 229
Ricoldus of Monte Croce, 222
Rimimi, 210
Rissho-Kosekai, 198, 199
Ritsch, A., 233
Roderick, 251
Roman Church, 233, 247, 254
Rome, Romans, Roman Empire, 1, 4, 12, 35, 36, 41, 43, 136, 137, 144, 146, 201, 204, 205, 206, 208, 209, 212, 214, 215, 220, 222, 224, 226, 227, 238, 255, 270
Rosenthal, F., 32
Rouergue, 252
Rovere, Giuliano della, 224
Roy, Mohan, 95
Ruanveli, 179
Rūdra, 74
Rūdra-Śiva, 74
Ruhā, 248, 270, 271
Rumania, 226
al Rumi, Jalaluddin, 268
Russia(ns), 152, 223, 233
Rustum, 248
Ruthenians, 227

Saba's Monastery, 226
Sabellius, 210
Sabratha, 36
Sābūr, 136
Sa'd ibn Abū Waqqās, 248
Sadducees, 202, 203
Safed, 154
Sahara, 16, 45
Sai Baba or Shirdi, 95
Saicho, 195
Śakala, 74
Śakti, 81, 90, 91
Śākyamuni, 161
Śākyas, 161
Salaf River (Calycadmus), 272

Ṣalāḥ al Dīn al Ayyūbī, 272
Saljūq Turks, 263, 270
Samantabhadra, 101
Samaria, Samaritans, 144, 201
Samarqand, 249
Saṁgha, 100, 102
see also Saṅgha
Samori, 258
Samprati, 101
Samson, 206
Samudu, Aḥmadu, 258
San Domingo, 231
Sanchi, 175
Saṅgha, 181
Sangharakshita, Bhikshu, 194
Ṣanhāja, 255
Śaṅkara, 69, 84, 85, 95, 175
Śaṅkaradeva of Assam, 88
Sanskrit, 45, 71, 90, 170, 187
Sanūsīs, 277
Sanūsiyyah, 276
Saphon, 30
Saraburi, 182
Saracens, 214
Saragossa, 208, 251
Sāranāth, 175
Sarasvati, Svāmi Dayānanda, 90, 95
Sarayu, 70
Sardes, 36
Sardica, 210
Sardinia, 253
Sardis, 204, 251
Sarma, D. S., 96
Sārnāth, 165
al Sarrāj (Ṣūfī thinker), 268
Sarwār, Ḥāfiẓ Ghulām, 281
Sasaki, Ruth Fuller, 199
Sāsānī Dynasty, 134, 136, 208
Satan, 207, 218
Saturn, 41
Saul, 201
Savitar, 74
Savoy, 212
Saxons, 212
Scandinavia, 219
Schimmel, A., 281
Schleiermacher, F., 233
Schliemann, 35
Scholem, Gershon, 157
Schonmetzer, A., 235
Schopenhauer, A., 182
Schubring, Walther, 10
Schweitzer, A., 203, 233
Schwenkfeld, Caspar, 231
Scotland, 212, 229, 230, 231
Scotus, Duns, 221
Scythia, 205, 210
Sebastopolis, 251
Seele, Keith C., 28
Segesta, 35
Seleucia, 210, 212
Selimunte, 35
Semites, 33
Senegal, 61, 255, 258
Sepoy Mutiny, 107
Septimania, 251, 252
Sepulveda, 231
Serampore, 232
Serapion, 206
Seth, 17
Severus, Septimius, 205
Seville, 212, 251
al Shāfi'ī, 263
School, 262, 264
Shāh Waliyyullah, 276
Shahristānī, 'Abdul Karīm, 137
Shalem, 34
Shamanism, 45–49
Shamash, 10
Shan-tao, 192
Shanak, 214
Shang, 112
Shantung, 111
Shāpūr I, 208
Shāpūr II, 212
Sharī'at Allah, 276
Sharīf, M. Rayḥān, 281
Shash, 249
Shatrunjaya Hills, 100
Shawbak, 271
Shaykh, M. Sa'īd, 281
Shen-hsiu, 191
Shī'ah, 264, 265, 266, 267
Shih-li, Hsiung, 117, 190
Shingon Buddhism, 196
Shinran, 196
Shinto, 127–132
Shirdi, 95
Shirokogoroff, S. M., 49
Shiromoni Gurdwara Prabandhak Committee, 108
Shirwān, Anū, 137
Shomu, 195
Shotoku, 195
Shu, 17
Shudagon Pagoda, 181
Shulmanu, 30
Shuraḥbīl ibn Ḥasanah, 247
Shustery, A. M. A., 281
Siam, 181, 182, 227
Siberia, 45, 51, 57, 223, 224
see also Paleosiberians
Sibero-America, 57
Sicily, 35, 212, 215, 249, 253, 270
Siddhārtha, 97, 161, 162
Sidon, 30
Ṣifātiyyah, 266
Sigiriya, 175
Silas, 201
Simon, 146, 206
Simons, Menno, 226
Sinai, 26, 34, 214
Sind, 106, 251
Singh, Dalip, 106
Singh, Gobind, 105, 106
Singh, Khushwant, 105, 108
Singh, Rangit, 106
Singh, Sabha, 107
Singh, Sher, 108
Singh, Trilochan, 108
Sinhala, 181
Sisyphus, 41
Sita, 80
Śiva, 70, 71, 74, 78, 81, 85, 87, 90, 91, 93
Sivāji, 87
Siyam Nikaya, 179
Slotkin, J. S., 57
Sloyan, Gerard, 201
Smith, E. W., 68
Smith, W. C., 281
Smith, W. R., 32
Smyrna, 205
Soba, 254
Society of Friends (Quakers), 231
Society for Promoting Christian Knowledge, 232
Society for the Propagation of the Gospel in Foreign Parts, 232
Socotra, 213
Socrates, 23, 42
Sofia, 210
Soga, 195
Sogdians, 186
Soissons, 212
Soka-gakkai, 189, 197, 199
Solomon, 141, 143, 147
Solovkij, 223
Soma (Homa, Haoma), 73, 74, 76
Somalia, 61
Somanāth, 73
Somapuri, 175
Songhay, 225
Sopher, David E., viii, xi
Sophia, 207
Sorrento, 35
Sousse, 205
South Africa, 232
South Pacific, 128
Spain, New, 227
Spain, 48, 121, 152, 204, 205, 208, 212, 215, 217, 227, 229, 231, 253, 255, 260, 270, 277

Spier, Leslie, 57
Śrāddha, 74
Śrī, 74, 90
Śrīkṣetra, 179
Sriperumbudur, 88
Śrīraṅgam, 89
Ssu, Li, 115
Ssu-ma, Ch'ien, 117
Ssu, Tzu, 113, 114
Stambha, 76
Stcherbatsky, T., 194
Steindorff, George, 28
Stephen, 204, 208
Stephen of Perm, 223
Stephen II, Pope, 215
Stonehenge, 35
Stuart, Mary, 229, 230
Student Volunteer Movement for Foreign Missions, 233
Suarez, Francisco, 227
Subartu, 11
Sūdān, 61, 62, 255, 260, 263
Sudarśana, 91
Śuddodana, 161, 163, 167
Sudhammavati, 179
Sudharman, 98
Suez Canal, 248
Sufyān al Kalbī, 265
Sughd, 249
Suhastin, 101
Sui, 188, 190
Sujātā, 164
Sukhotai, 181, 182
Sulṭāniyyah, 222
Sumatra, 175
Sumaysaṭ, 251
Sumer, Sumerians, 5, 10
Sundaramūrti, 85
Sung, 117, 119, 193
  Dynasty, 116
Sunga Dynasty, 175
Sunion, 36
Sunnī School, 264
Sunnīs, 264
Suparṇa, 75
Suppabuddha, 162
Sūradāsa, 88
Sūrya, 73, 74, 76, 78, 84, 91
Suse, 253
Suso, Henry, 221, 231
Su'ūd, Amir, 275
  Āl (House of), 275
Su'ūdī Arabia (Saudi Arabia), *see* Arabia
Sutlej, 70
Suvarṇa-bhūmi, 175
Suzuki, D. T., 194, 199
Śvetāmbara, 101, 103
Switzerland, 212, 226, 252, 253
Sylvester, 210
Symeon, 206
Synesius of Cyrene, 255
Synod of Carthage, 255
Syria (Greater Syria), 3, 4, 29, 33, 34, 148, 149, 175, 204, 205, 210, 215, 247, 248, 262, 264, 270, 272, 273
Syrian Desert, 5, 213

Tabrīz, 222
Tabūk, 247
Tadjikistan, 222
Tagore, Rabindranāth, 95
Taqiyyuddin Aḥmad ibn Taymiyah, 273
T'ai-wu, 189
Ṭā'if, 243, 244
Taisekiji, 198
Taiwan, 124
Takakusu, Junjiro, 194
Takamimusubi, 128
Talaings, 179
Tamil, 71, 80, 85, 87, 102
Tamil Nad, 85, 88, 90
Tamilnadu, 88
T'an-luan, 192
T'an-yao, 189
Tang, 116, 123, 188, 189, 190, 193
Tanhā, 164
Tanit, Face of Baal, 30
Tannit, 41
Tanūkh, 5
Tao-an, 189, 190
Tao-ch'o, 192
Tao-lin, Chih, 190
Tao-sheng, Chu, 188
Taoling, Chang, 122
Tapa, 102
Tapassu, 181
Ṭarīf, General, 251
Ṭarīfa, 251
Ṭāriq ibn Ziyād, 251
Ṭāriq Mountains, 251
Tarquinia, 35
Tarragonna, 43
Tarsus, 248, 251, 270
Ṭashqand, 249
Tat, Mahā, 182
Tatar, 269, 273
Tatian, 206, 207
Tauler, John, 231
Tax, Sol, 57
Taxila, 170
Tay, 247
Taylor, Jeremy, 230
Taymanavar, 88
Tayy, 5
Te-jen, Liu, 124
Tefnut, 17
Teicher, Morton L., 57
Templars, 272
Tendai, 196
Terah, 34
Tertullian, 208
Teutonic (language), 70
Texas, 52, 56
Thailand, 94, 169, 170, 179, 181, 182
Thais, 181, 182
Thaqīf, 243
Thaton, 179
Thebes, 26, 41
Thebuthis, 206
Theodore of Mopsuestia, 213
Theodoric the Great, 212
Theodosius, 210
Theodotus, 205
Theophilus, 207
Theophilus the Indian, 214
Theseus, 41
Thessalonica, 226
Thessaly, 205
Thomas, the apostle, 205
Thomas, E. J., 183
Thompson, Stith, 57
Thomson, L. G., 125
Thorismund, 255
Thrace, 205
Thraosh, 135
Thuringians, 212
Thyatira, 204
Ti, Ching, 120
Ti'amat, 7, 10
Tiberias, 154, 272
Tiberm, 36
Tibet, 106, 136, 182, 195, 227
Tibnin, 272
T'ien-t'ai, 185, 189, 190, 191, 196
Tigris, 15, 206, 212
Tigris-Euphrates Valley, 3
Tījāniyyah, 258, 277
Tilak, 95
Timbo (Futah-Jallon), 258
Timbuktu, 255, 258
Timothy, 201
Tiridates, 44
Tīrthaṅkaras, 97, 99, 100
Tirupati, 89
Tiruvannamalai, 95
Tissa, 179
Titus, 205
Tivoli, 36, 43

Tokugawa, 198
Toledo, 219, 251, 257
Tolstoy, 154
Torah, 43, 146
Tordesillas, Treaty, 231
Toulon, 253
Toulouse, 251, 252
Tours, 229, 252
Trajan, 205
Trans-Jordan, 29, 33
Transoxania, 265
Trebizond, 222
Tratles, 205
Trent, 218, 226, 229
Trieste, 205
Tripoli (Lebanon), 270
Tripoli (Libya), 249, 255, 270, 271
Trisala, 97, 101
Troy, 41
Tsai, Chang, 116
Tsang, Hiouen, 175
Ts'ao, Ts'ao, 122
Ts'ao, Tung, 191, 197
Tsou, 113
Tsung, Hsuan, 123
Tsung, Kao, 123
Tsung, ming shih, 124
Tsung, Wu, 123
Tsung, yen Chang, 124
Tu-hsiu, Chen, 117
Tu-shun, 190
Tudor, Mary, 230
Tukharam, 87
Tulasi, Tulasidas, 80, 88, 89
Tumulus (Kotun) period, 178
Tun-yi, Chou, 116
Tungus, 45, 47
Tungusis, 128
Tūnis, Tūnisia, 205, 208, 221, 255, 277
see also Ifrīqyah
Tunjar, 255
Tuny, 115
Turkestān, 186, 222
Chinese, 249
Turkey, Turks, 4, 201, 226, 262, 270
al Tuwānah (Tyana), 253, 281
Tuwelvers, 264
Tyagaraja, 88
Tyre, 30, 31, 214
Tyrol, 212
Tzu, Chuang, 112, 119, 121, 191
Tzu, Chung, 120
Ṭzu, Hsun, 114, 115
Ṭzu, Huai Nan, 119, 120
Tzu, Lao, 117, 118, 119, 121, 123, 170
Tzu, Mo, 113

Ucchista, 76
Udayana, 83
Uddyotakara, 83
Ugarit, 29, 30, 31
Uḥud, 294
Ukemochi, 127
Ukrainians, 152, 227
Ulfila, *see* Wulfile
'Umān (Oman), 247, 265
'Umar ibn al Khaṭṭāb, 216, 248, 253, 273
Umāsvāti, 101
Umawī, 152, 249, 261, 265, 266, 267
United States of America (USA), 86, 105, 155
USSR, 155, 262
see also Russia
Upper Volta, 61
'Uqbā ibn Nāfi', 251
Ur, 5, 12
Uranus, 41
Urban II, 219, 270
Urban VI, 224
Urdunn (Jordan), 248
'Urwah, 239
Usas, 74
'Uthmān I, 215
'Uthmān dan Fodio, 276
'Uthmān, al Ḥājj, 258
'Uthmān, Muḥammad Amīr Ghānī, 257
Uttar Pradesh, 98, 103
Utu, 10, 'Uzza, 240

Vairocana, 195
Vaisākha, 161
Vaiśālī, 97
Vaiśeṣika, 83
Vaitulyavāda, 179
Vāk, 74
Valabhi, 101, 175
Valais, 253
Valamo, 224
Valentinus, 207
Valerian, 208
Vālmīki, 79, 80
Van (Lake), 253
Van Dijk, J. J. A., 13
Van Setters, John, 28
Vandals, 212, 255
Varsva, 98
Varuṇa, 73, 75
Vaśiṣṭha, 69
Vāstoṣpati, 74
Vatican, Vatican Council, 218, 233
Vātsyāyana, 82, 83
Veith, Ilza, 125
Le Veley, 252
Veluvana, 167
Venetians, 270
Veniaminov, Innokentij, 224
Vesali, 169, 175
Vespucci, Amerigo, 231
Vestal Temple, 36
Vidyānanda, 101
Vidyāpati, 88
Vidyārṇava, Śrīśa Chandra, 96
Vienne, 36, 295
Vietnam, 94
Vijāyanagara, 73
Vijñānavāda, 190
Vimarṣa, 90
Vindhya, 175
Virginia, 53, 232
Viśākha, 167
Vishtaspa (Goshtasp), 136
Visigoths, 212
Viṣṇu, 74, 75, 78, 81, 82, 84, 85, 87, 88, 90, 91, 93
Visser, M. W., 199
Viśvakarman, 74
Viśvāmitra, 69
Viśvavat, 74
Vivekānanda, Swāmī, 70, 95, 96
Vladimir, St., 223
Volga, 223
Vṛtra, 75
Vulcan, 41
Vyāsa, 79, 80, 84

Wādī 'Arabah, 248, 271
Wahhābīs, 256, 260, 263, 275
Walāta, 258
Waldensians, 220, 229
Wales, 212
Waley, Arthur, 125
Wang, 114, 117
Waraqah ibn Nawfal, 241
Ware, Timothy, 235
Wargla, 265
Warren, H. C., 183
Washington, 182
Wāṣil ibn 'Aṭā', 266
Wasulu, 258
al Wāthiq, 266
Watson, Burton, 125
Watt, W. Montgomery, 281
Wei, 122, 123

Northern, 123, 186, 189
Wei-chin, 120
Wei-shih, 190
Weiss, J., 203
Weizmann, C., 157
Welch, Holmes, 125, 194
Wellhausen, J., 233
Wells, Kenneth E., 194
Wen, 120, 189
Wen-Amon, 30
Wen-ch'eng, 189
Wesley, John, 232
West, 94, 117, 124, 136
Westminster, 226, 231
Wilhelm, Hellmut, 125
Wilhelm, Richard, 125
William of Ockham, 221
William of Orange, 229
William of Ruisbroek, 222
William of Tripoli, 222
Williams, R., 103
Wilson, John, 17, 27, 28
Wissler, Clark, 57
Witiza, 251
Wittenberg, 224
Wooley, C. Leonard, 13
World Council of Churches (WCC), 233
World Missionary Conference in Edinburgh, 233
World War I, 275
World War II, 280
Wright, Arthur, 125
Wu, Emperor, 123, 188
Wu, John, 125
Wulfile, 211
Wyclif, John, 224

Xavier, Francis, 227
Ximenes, Cardinal, 231

Yahweh, 43
Yaḥyā ibn Ibrahīm, 255
Yajña (Yasna), 73
Yājñavalkya, 79
Yakut, 45, 224
Yama, 76
Yamāmah, 247
Yaman, 3, 5, 214, 215, 240, 247, 253, 260, 264, 272
Yamato, 128
Yamm, 29, 34
Yamuna, 88
Yang, C. K., 125
Yang, Emperor, 189
Yang-ming, Wang, 117
Yangtse River, 127
Yapaniya, 101
Yarmūk, Battle of, 248
Yasna, *see* Yajña
Yaśodā, 97
Yaśodhara, 162
Yathrib, 241
see also Madinah
Yavanas, 175
Yayoi Period, 128
Yazdagird III, 248
Yazdagird I, 212, 214
Yazīd ibn Abū Sufyān, 247
Year of the Elephant, 240
Yellow River, 188
Yellow Turbans Rebellion, 122
Yen, Tsou, 121
Yeshiva University, 156
Yi, Ch'eng, 116
Yin-hsi, 118
Yi-hsuan, Lin-chi, 191
Yōgācāra, 190
York, 209, 212
Yoruba, 257
Yuan-chien, Shao, 124
Yuan-sung, Wei, 123
Yudhiṣṭhira, 80
Yugoslavia, 205
Yu, Han, 116, 193
Yu-Ian, Fung, 115
Yu-Lan, Fung, 117
Yung, Shao, 116
Yun-kang, 189
Yusuf ibn Tashfin, 255
Yu-wei, K'ang, 117

Zaddok, 146
Zaehner, R. C., 137
Zaitun, 222
Zanzibar, 265
Zarādusht, Zarathustra, *see* Zoroaster
Zayd ibn 'Alī, 264
Zaydī School, 258, 264
Zaydī Shī'ah, 258, 264
Zayn al 'Ābidīn, 264
Zealot, 147, 202, 203
Zebedee, 204
Zeitlin, Solomon, 157
Zen, *see* Ch'an
Zernov, Nicholas, 236
Zeus, 41, 43
Zizendorf, 232
Zoatar, *see* Hotar
Zoroaster, Zoroastrianism, 75, 80, 133–136, 137
Zubayr ibn al 'Awwām, 248
Zurcher, Erik, 194
Zurwān-i-Akinarak, 134
Zwingli, H., 225, 226